A Treasury of
YIDDISH STORIES

A Treasury of
YIDDISH STORIES

Edited by

IRVING HOWE & ELIEZER GREENBERG

With drawings by Ben Shahn

New York

THE VIKING PRESS

1954

Published in October 1954

Published on the same day in the Dominion of Canada
By The Macmillan Company of Canada Limited

Library of Congress catalog card number: 54-9599

PRINTED IN THE U.S.A. BY THE VAIL-BALLOU PRESS, INC.

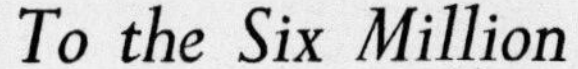

To the Six Million

Table of Contents

Part Three
JEWISH CHILDREN

Part Four
BREAKUP

Part Five
NEW WORLDS

Part Six
FOLK TALES

Introduction

"... I would tell you, ladies and gentlemen, how much better you understand Yiddish than you suppose."—Franz Kafka.

In the eight or nine hundred years since the birth of the Yiddish language there has accumulated not only a rich heritage of oral folk literature but also a body of written materials: improvised prayers, religious commentaries, didactic tracts, autobiographical narratives, travel records, simplified Bible stories for women, and, in some instances, literary or quasi-literary works. But Yiddish literature—in the sense of a sequence of imaginative writings composed by individual artists who possess some awareness of their identity and role as artists—is hardly more than a hundred and fifty years old. Historically the position of this literature resembles that of underdeveloped countries which, beset by industrialism, try to compress into a few feverish decades the experience that for other nations has taken centuries. The decay of the religious community, the Enlightenment, the rise of individualism, the turn to bohemianism, the challenge of radical ideologies, the burden of alienation, the new appetite for cultural affirmation—all this, and more, which comprises the history of the modern intellect and is so sharply refracted in modern writing, has been pressed into the brief life of Yiddish literature.

It is a literature virtually unknown to Americans. The reasons for this neglect are many: translations that are often inadequate, because done by devoted non-literary people, or are twisted into sentimentality, because done by translators whose attitude toward Yiddish is one of familiar condescension; a body of criticism in English that has seldom risen above the level of special pleading; and a curious resistance, if not indeed a snobbish parochialism, among American literary people. There is, of course, another and more serious reason: the cultural distance between East European Jewry and Western society is much larger than the distance, say, between American and French culture. The reader who is to find pleasure in Yiddish literature needs a minimum of special information but a good deal of imaginative curiosity: he must be willing to enter an unfamiliar world and to adjust himself to literary modes and expectations that differ from those of his own culture. But any literate person—even if he has never heard of the *shtetl* (the little town in which most East European Jews lived and which is the frequent setting for the stories in this anthology)—will be able to enjoy *A Treasury of Yiddish Stories.*

We have tried to organize the book in a simple way. The Introduction provides some historical and critical background; the Authors' Notes include a few items of biographical information and very brief comments on the individual stories; and finally there is a glossary of those Yiddish words—they have been kept to a minimum—which it seemed impossible or profitless to translate and which have therefore been transliterated.

A Treasury of Yiddish Stories is, of course, far from being an exhaustive selection of Yiddish prose. Anyone familiar with Yiddish writing will be able to list names of distinguished or worthy authors who have not been included. Nor will it be difficult to see that even among those who are represented a number of writers appear in an inadequate or partial way. Some authors could not be included because we did not wish to have certain themes repeated too frequently; some, because we discovered that a story which reads well in Yiddish may limp in translation; some, because their references were so special that they could be understood only by readers deeply rooted in Yiddish culture; and some—we simply ran out of space. But our primary interest has not been to introduce individual authors; it has been to present a rounded sampling of Yiddish prose fiction.

We have no desire to make extravagant claims: Yiddish literature can boast no Shakespeares, no Dantes, no Tolstois. But neither can many other widely translated literatures. Each literature, whether it is of the first or second rank, has its distinctive ethos, its special aroma; and Yiddish literature, within its brief and tragic history, has brought forth a number of remarkable figures and has been characterized by attitudes we should look to with admiration, perhaps even yearning.

I: THE WORLD OF THE EAST EUROPEAN JEWS

For several hundred years there existed in Europe—mainly in Russia, Poland, Rumania, and Galicia—a culture probably without parallel in Western history. Bound together by the firmest spiritual ties, by a common if fluid language, and by a sense of destiny that often meant a sharing of martyrdom, the Jews of Eastern Europe were a kind of nation, yet without nationhood; a people, yet persistently denied the dignity of being people. Theirs was both a community and a society: internally a community, a spiritual kingdom; and externally a society in peril, a society on the margin. The result was an experience highly unified, singular, and contiguous. Though the forces of disintegration that afflicted the West were destined to penetrate the ghetto as well, they came later and had far less impact. The world of the East European Jews showed severe signs of internal stagnation, but its recent destruction came not from within but from without.

The central trait of this culture was its orientation toward other-worldly values—but this may be too simple a way of putting it. For the world of the East European Jews, at least in its most serious and "ideal" manifestations, did not accept the Western distinction between worldly and other-worldly, between that which is due to Caesar and that which is due to God. Kierkegaard's dictum that "between God and man there is an infinite, yawning, qualitative difference" might have won their approval as a description of the quality of being, but not as a statement of moral obligation. To be sure, the East European Jews had to abide by the distinction between worldly and other-worldly in order to survive, but they refused to recognize it as just or necessary or inevitable. In their celebration of the Sabbath and in the sharp line they drew between the Sabbath and the rest of the week, they tacitly recognized that they had to live, however unwillingly, by the ways of the world; but this was the price of exile and dispersion. Ideally, the worldly and other-worldly should be one—and one on earth—penetrating each other to the point of becoming indistinguishable. The Sabbath, goes a Jewish legend, is a foretaste of the world to come, the world in which every day will be a Sabbath. Every Jew would have immediately recognized the symbolic power, the profound gesture of *justice* in the refusal of a rabbi in Peretz's drama *Die Goldene Kait* (*The Golden Chain*) to accept "the week," those six worldly days that lie beneath the glory of the Sabbath.

Saying this, we recognize the danger of romanticizing the Jewish world, of assuming that it was all of one piece and forgetting that much of it was ignorant, provincial, superstitious, and sometimes even corrupt, as a good deal of Yiddish writing bears witness. Yet one must understand the human impulse, the profoundly tragic emotion, that has led many writers to romanticize the *shtetl.* Given the pressures from without and a slow stagnation within, this world was bound to contain large portions of the ignorant, the provincial, and even the corrupt; and, indeed, one of the immediate motive forces behind the appearance of the new Yiddish literature in the nineteenth century, especially behind the work of its founding father, Mendele, was the desire to stir the blood of a society that had gone sluggish, to cleanse a people that had suffered too long from the effects of isolation, poverty, and violence. Once the foundations of this society began to crumble, an impulse arose among the Yiddish writers—most notably in the later stories of Peretz—to romanticize the very world that Mendele had so bitterly attacked. And once this world had been destroyed in the gas chambers, the romantic impulse became irresistible; it acquired a new and almost holy authenticity; for how could the Yiddish writers separate the sanctification of their martyrs from the celebration of the world that had given rise to them?

Nonetheless, the description we have suggested of worldliness and other-worldliness among the East European Jews need not depend on any romantic emotion. For the fact that the bourgeois revolution had not yet triumphed in Eastern Europe, and had barely brushed against its Jewish enclave, meant that the Jews continued to think and act primarily in non-economic, non-commercial terms. The struggle for livelihood, continuous and seldom successful, necessarily occupied much time, but it was never regarded as the reason for existence. Life was seen in terms of ends, not functions.

Scholarship—not as "pure" activity, not as a form of intellectual release, but as the pathway to God—was extraordinarily honored among the Jews. One's prestige, authority, and position depended to a considerable extent on one's learning. Those who were learned sat at the eastern wall of the synagogue, near the Holy Ark in which the Torah lay. Women often became breadwinners so that their husbands could devote themselves to study, while householders thought it their duty, indeed, a privilege, to support precocious sons-in-law who studied the Holy Word. In an elegiac memoir of the East European Jews, Abraham Heschel has given a somewhat idealized yet not irrelevant picture of the role of learning:

> A blazing passion permeated all intellectual activities. It is an untold, perhaps incommunicable story of how mind and heart could merge into one. Immersed in complicated legal discussions, they could at the same time feel the anguish of the Divine Presence that abides in exile. In endeavoring to unravel some perplexity raised by a seventeenth-century commentary on a commentary on the Talmud, they were able in the same breath to throb with sympathy for Israel and all afflicted people. Study was a technique for sublimating feeling into thought, for transposing dreams into syllogisms, for expressing grief in difficult theoretical formulations, and joy by finding a solution to a difficult passage in Maimonides. Tension of the soul found an outlet in contriving clever, almost insolvable, riddles. In inventing new logical devices to explain the Word of God, they thrilled with yearning after the Holy. To contrive an answer to gnawing doubts was the highest joy. Indeed, there was a whole world of subdued gaiety and sober frolic in the playful subtleties of their *pilpul* [dialectic].
>
> Their conscious aim, of course, was not to indulge in self-expression—they were far from being intent upon exploiting the Torah—but humbly to partake of spiritual beauty. Carried away by the mellow, melting chant of Talmud-reading, one's mind soared high in the pure realm of thought, away from this world of facts and worries, away from the boundaries of the here and now, to a region where the Divine Presence listens to what Jews create in the study of His Word. . . .

There was another side, of course. Scholarship often degenerated into abysmal scholasticism. Intellect could be reduced to a barren exercise in distinctions that had long ago lost their living reality. Manual labor was frequently regarded as a mark of social disgrace, a badge of coarseness and ignorance. Among the more orthodox or fanatical, modern thought met furious resistance: how could the works of man measure against the Word of God? Secular books were sometimes smuggled into the yeshivas and read on the sly by students, who hid them behind Talmudic tomes, eagerly examining the forbidden contents as they chanted the Talmudic singsong, half in precaution and half in mockery. Some rabbis, to be sure, were ready to receive the new learning of the West, but by and large the *shtetl* felt that any large infiltration of Western thought would be its undoing; and it was right.

Traditional though this society was and colored throughout by religious emotion, it was not a theocracy: the rabbis, for all their power, were not its undisputed rulers. Rather, it was dominated by a caste of the learned in uneasy alliance with, and eventual dependence on, the somewhat wealthier merchants. In their formal value system, the Jews gave absolute precedence to the learned, but, as in any other formal system, this precedence was sometimes honored more in the breach—or the reminiscence—than the observance. The closer this world came to modern life and the more it was drawn into the orbit of history, the more did wealth challenge and usurp the position of learning. There was never, it is true, a formal dispossession of learning by wealth; but, often enough, between learning and wealth there existed a subterranean rivalry that at times broke into the open. What preserved a certain degree of social fluidity was that learning, at least potentially, was open to everyone and not the exclusive property of any group or caste.

Socially this world had not yet split into sharply defined classes. Though some Jews settled in the larger cities, such as Warsaw and Lodz, where they hardened into a proletariat and middle class, most of them continued to live in the *shtetl.* One could hardly speak of rival classes in the *shtetl,* since few Jews owned any massive means of production and fewer still sold their labor power. Only if the pressures of the external world had suddenly been removed would the suppressed economic conflicts within the *shtetl* have reached full expression. As it was, the *shtetl* nestled in the crevices of a backward agricultural economy, where Jews, seldom allowed to own land, lived by trading, artisanship, and their wits. There were, however, rigid castes, based partly on economic position and partly on religious status—that is, learning. Those who romanticize the *shtetl* seldom remember, or remember to report, that it was customary for the artisans to be shunted off into separate synagogues and that within the synagogue itself the social hierarchy was precisely reflected by the seating arrangement. The *shtetl* did not, strictly speaking, have social classes, but it was still far from being a democratic community. Similarly, the concept of *yichus,* which pertains to family status and pride, helped split the *shtetl* into rigid castes. *Yichus,* it is true, did not refer primarily to—but neither did it ignore—wealth; a Jew who suddenly became wealthy would make it his business to "buy" himself *yichus,* generally through the marriage of himself or his children, and would not always find this an easy thing to do. Squeezed together by the pressures of the external world, the Jews still found ways of demarcating themselves into prestige groups.

Because the *shtetl* lived in constant expectation of external attack—

and not merely expectation: it was periodically subjected to pogroms —all the internal tendencies that made for disintegration were kept in check. The outer world, the world of the gentiles and the worldlings, meant hostility, sacrilege, brute force. It meant the threat of the fist against the Word.

This condition of permanent precariousness gave the East European Jews a conscious sense of being at a distance from history, from history as such and history as a conception of the Western world. Living in an almost timeless proximity with the mythical past and the redeeming future, with Abraham's sacrifice of his beloved son to a still more beloved God and the certain appearance of a cleansing Messiah—for heaven was *real,* not a useful myth, and each day that passed brought one nearer to redemption—the Jews could not help feeling that history was a little ridiculous: a trifling, though often a troublesome trifling, of the frivolous gentile era. The more painful the blows of the outer world, the more secure became the belief in the Messiah—up to the point, that is, where the Jews began to lose the binding force of traditional belief. At the same time the Jews were able to gain an insight into that moral weakness of Western culture which has only recently become common knowledge: they enjoyed, as it were, a perspective from the social rear. Behind their sense of being at a distance from contemporary history lay both a conscious value system and an immediate feeling of deprivation: they were cut off from the world at an all too visible point, the limits of their social grasp were pathetically clear. Later, when the *shtetl* began to crumble under alien pressures, the sense of history, suddenly rising to acute consciousness, became almost an obsession: or, more accurately, the modern idea of time as the very stuff of life, which can never be held or held back, was absorbed into a faith that had always been addressed to eternity, so that certain of the political movements among East European Jews—notably Zionism and Socialism—received nutriment from the very faith they had begun to displace.

While this world existed—be it historical miracle or historical sport —it was remarkably coherent in its view of itself. Yiddish literature repeatedly turns to the theme that the material poverty of this world is dreadful, yet seldom rests with social description or complaint; it insists that hunger—a subject, said Sholom Aleichem, on which his characters were experts—could always be transcended by a people secure in its destiny. And so too could the blows of the outer world. In the writings of Peretz and Sholem Asch, the idea, deeply embedded in Jewish psychology, that the spirit of endurance cannot be broken by external attack received repeated expression. Some of Peretz's later stories turned the lives of his heroes and heroines into a continuous chain of miracles—but miracles, it must be added, that he had come to see primarily as metaphors.

The world of the East European Jews was a world in which God was a living force, a Presence, something more than a name or a desire. He did not rule from on high; He was not a God of magnificence, not an aesthetic God. The Jews had no beautiful churches: they had ramshackle wooden synagogues. They rejected—or, more accurately, were oblivious to—the view that beauty is "its own excuse for being." Beauty was a quality rather than a form, content rather than arrangement. The Jews would have been deeply puzzled by the idea that the aesthetic and the moral are distinct realms, for they saw beauty above all in behavior. One spoke not of a beautiful thing but of a beautiful deed or event. Only later did Jewish intellectuals discover that even in the usual Western terms there was an innocent beauty in Jewish liturgical music, the carving of the Holy Arks, the embroidery of prayer shawls, the calligraphy and ornamentation of the Holy Scripts. But where they saw these things as objects or qualities to be isolated for aesthetic inspection—and this is true even in the paintings of Marc Chagall—their ancestors had seen them as integral elements in the cultivation of God's Word.

For it was the word that counted most. Yiddish culture was oriented toward speech: its God was a God who spoke. And He was a plebeian —or if you wish, a folk—God, perhaps immanent but hardly transcendent. Toward Him the Jews could feel a peculiar sense of intimacy: and, indeed, they had suffered enough in His behalf. In prayer His name could not be spoken; yet in or out of prayer He could always be spoken to. Because the East European Jew felt so close to God he could complain to Him freely, and complain about Him too. Thus Rabbi Levi-Yitzchok of Berditchev, a leader of the Hasidic movement, wrote a chant that is an indictment, though a loving indictment, of God:

> Good morning to You, Lord of the Universe!
> I, Levi-Yitzchok, son of Sarah of Berditchev,
> Have come with a claim against You
> On behalf of Your people Israel.
> What do You have against Your people Israel?
> Why do You afflict Your people Israel?
>
> . . .

And I, Levi-Yitzchok, son of Sarah of Berditchev, say,
I shall not stir from here.
From this spot I shall not stir,
There must be an end to this,
The exile must come to an end!
Magnified and sanctified be His Name!

The intimacy between God and man was not really mystical. Although there was a mystical strand in the Jewish tradition, centered in the esoteric books of the Cabala, the mystical experience as a direct and private encounter with God's Presence was not central to the Jewish world. The relationship to God was social, intimate, critical; and at times seemed to follow, like a series of rationalistic deductions, from the premise of the Chosen People. Rilke, the great German poet, also speaks to God, but he speaks from an agonized distance: the God to whom he turns is closer to the conventional image of the Old Testament God—stern, merciless, august—than is the God to whom the Yiddish writers spoke, a God who had been humanized and taught the uses of mercy. Similarly, the despair with which Kafka knocks on the door of the Lord makes one doubt whether he expected the door to be opened, whereas the intimacy and at times almost critical impatience with which Yiddish folk writers of the Hasidic period appealed to the Lord leave no doubt that they believed He would respond.

One of Sholom Aleichem's characters, speaking about the misery of the Jews, remarks, "Apparently if He wants it that way, that's the way it ought to be. Can't you see? If it should have been different it would have been. And yet what would have been wrong to have it different?" But the very Jews who could ask such terrible questions—questions, one may suppose, that gave God some sleepless nights—also realized that there were grounds for complaint against themselves; they knew they had caused Him more than a little trouble. As the Yiddish proverb has it: "If God were living on earth, people would break His windows."

Together with a living God there went a holy language, Hebrew, known by the educated, yearned for and admired by the ignorant. The events of Jewish life were divided into two endless days, the Biblical yesterday and the exile of today. History was regarded less as a vertical movement through time than as a horizontal simultaneity; Jewish history was not seen in terms of the scientific assumptions of most modern historians but as an emanation of a pure idea: the idea of the Chosen People. In a sense, history did not exist; there was only the endless expectation until the Messiah came. And in such a world Hebrew would clearly have an honored place, as the language of the Book, the language of Abraham, Jacob, and Moses: a language not unaffected by the passage of time but meant, ultimately, to stake out a defiance of time.

Near and beneath Hebrew flowed another language, Yiddish. Untended, elbowed away from the places of honor, it nonetheless grew freely and richly. Based originally on a mixture of Middle-High German dialects, it soon acquired an international scope, borrowing freely from almost every Indo-European language. The interplay of the language of piety, Hebrew, with the language of the street and the home, Yiddish, made for remarkable literary effects. Yiddish itself was a language of great plasticity, neither set nor formalized, always in rapid process of growth and dissolution; it was a language intimately reflecting the travail of wandering, exile, dispersion; a language drenched with idiom, and thereby a resourceful term in a dialectic of tension of which the thesis was Hebrew and the synthesis a blend of speech so persistently complex and ironic—really a kind of "underground" speech—as to qualify severely the very values it was dedicated to defend.

The moral and psychological burdens which this world took upon itself were at least as great as the burdens of hatred that fell upon it from the outside. A frequent, often pathetic theme in Yiddish literature deals with the internal struggle of the young yeshiva student, in whom the postures and emotions of faith seem almost ineradicable, so deeply has he been steeped in the sense of the Jewish past, but who finds the atmosphere of the yeshiva stifling and yearns for fresh air, for the sun, for playfulness, for spontaneity. Nature is not a frequent presence in Yiddish writing; it hardly could be in a culture so desperately besieged and so thoroughly committed to the exploration of moral order; but when it does appear it is often used self-consciously—most of all by Mendele—as a counterpose to that deadening of human energies which long years of study may entail.

In some important respects, however, the Jews did make their peace with natural impulse. The view that sexual activity is impure or at least suspect, which if not native to Christianity has certainly been its frequent accompaniment, was seldom found among them. The distrust of the human body, the self-immolating depreciation of sex, which form so important a part of the Western tradition, were but faintly present in the world of East European Jewry. Paul's remark that it is better to marry than to burn would have seemed strange, if not downright impious, to the East European Jews, who believed that marriage and procreation, far from being a lesser evil, were a positive good. Because the urge for perpetuation came to be regarded as a holy obligation—in so precarious a society it had to be—the idea of sexual activity as a form of play and pleasure marvelous in itself was absent from the Jewish world, at least in its earlier period. But this was still very far from the puritan notion that the human body is suspect. Similarly the idea of a programmatic withdrawal from community life—the idea of asceticism—played a minor role in Jewish life, partly because a society of deprivation is not likely to be tempted by the luxury of self-deprivation. On the other hand, the concept of romantic love, which some writers have related to the Christian distrust of the body, appears only during the twilight of the *shtetl,* when the values of the West have begun to eat away its foundations. Traditionally, marriages were arranged by families, with the wealth and social rank of the groom counting for more than personal feelings. In Sholom Aleichem's writing, and still more so in the work of the Yiddish writers who follow him, romantic love as a spring of behavior quickly comes to signify the break-up of traditional forms and values.

At the peak of its development the *shtetl* was a highly formalized society. It had to be. Living in the shadow of lawless disorder, the *shtetl* felt a need to mold its life into a pattern of lawful order. Within its narrow and cramping boundaries it had to discover its own satisfactions: it lived, so to speak, by the ritual of expectation. The 613 *mitzvos* or commandments a pious Jew must obey; the precise way in which a chicken is to be slaughtered; the singsong chant with which the Talmud is to be studied; the kinds of food to serve on Friday evening and at the close of the Sabbath; the way in which shoes should be put on each morning; the shattering of a glass by the groom during the marriage ceremony—these were the outward signs, the ritual tokens, of the need for inner discipline and order. They were the expression of the Jewish ethos as well as the penalty the Jews paid for having to live by a pattern of stylized rigidity.

No other living gesture of the Jewish world symbolizes this internal unity so thoroughly as the rituals connected with food. Food became a link between the holy and profane, the community and the person, husband and wife, mother and children. Precisely because of its scarcity, it was a means of expressing love and releasing anger. The happiest holidays of the year meant special foods, the holiest a denial of food. For this was a world in which everything was highly patterned—everything, at least, that could be brought within the area of its control. The sense of collectivity had to dominate and suppress the stirrings of individuality, for the community was the manifestation of God's Covenant with Israel, as the family was the living core of the community.

Besieged from without and declining within, the world of the East European Jews clung to its ways, and to nothing more fiercely than the myth of the Chosen People, the full irony of which it was the first to recognize, above all in the network of humor it threw up against the alien world. Under the pressure of secular thought this myth gave way, but only to another claim to a unique destiny. If God didn't choose us, went the Yiddish proverb, then the world chose us. How bitter was the irony of this remark no one could know until the world of the East European Jews came to its end in the ashes of Maidenek and Auschwitz—at the time and place, that is, when Western civilization collapsed.

II: SOME RELIGIOUS AND INTELLECTUAL CURRENTS

Yiddish literature was shaped, and buffeted, by four major religious and intellectual currents: the Haskalah, or Enlightenment; Hasidism, or a movement of religious revival; Zionism; and Socialism. Since the latter two are more familiar, it may be convenient to glance at them first, though it should be mentioned that during the formative period of Yiddish literature—the so-called "classical" period during which its three major figures, Mendele, Peretz, and Sholom Aleichem, began to write—neither Zionism nor Jewish Socialism had even come into existence as organized groups. By this time both the Haskalah and Hasidism had become exhausted as movements within the Jewish world, yet the echoes of their original power were still more significant than the new voices that were preparing to speak, with Zionist or Socialist accents, in Warsaw and Lodz.

By its very nature Zionism could neither accept nor rebel against the *shtetl* world: its deepest desire was rather to leave the *shtetl* behind, to break away from everything it stood for. Zionism in Eastern Europe had little contact as yet with the masses of Jews, either in the cities or the towns; for its program still seemed abstract, perhaps attractive as an ideal but not very significant with regard to the immediate social problems and intellectual struggles. Because it desired a return to the homeland where Hebrew would be the national tongue, Zionism looked with some disfavor, if not yet hostility, upon Yiddish, the language of exile; and this attitude brought it into sharp clash with those young Jewish intellectuals who proclaimed themselves Yiddishists, partisans of Yiddish as the language of the folk experience and the folk martyrdom, or who looked forward to an era of universal human brotherhood in which there would no longer be any need for a special solution to the Jewish problem.

To be sure, the idea of an "in-gathering of the exiles," which Zionism expressed in national-political terms, had an obvious and, with time, a powerful appeal for Jews throughout the world; but it could have only a slight immediate impact on Yiddish culture at the turn of the century, for Zionism lived by a vision of a future in which the basis of everything that was distinctive in the culture of the East European Jews would be radically changed. In the end, of course, the impact of Zionism upon Jewish life and Yiddish literature would prove incalculable, but during the years when the earlier Yiddish writers were setting the main patterns of the literature, the Zionist idea only occasionally shaped the manner in which they portrayed East European Jewish life.

By contrast, Jewish Socialism exerted a considerably greater influence upon the early Yiddish writers, for it seemed to offer a more immediate and easier solution to the problems of the Jewish masses. The Bund, as the Jewish Socialist organization was called, gave the younger Yiddish writers a perspective on their immediate experience: it suggested a way of looking back on their own past. The idea that the *shtetl,* no less than the whole Jewish community, could be seen in terms of the Marxist analysis of society—and how neatly the Marxist ideal blended with the Prophetic conception of redeeming the world!—was clearly a bold innovation for writers who had, many of them, only yesterday been students at the yeshiva. A large number of stories, novels, and poems about the *shtetl* were actually composed by young writers who had fled to large cities like Warsaw, then the center of Yiddish culture, in search of an intellectual breadth and a literary companionship that the *shtetl* could not even begin to provide. There are other reasons why the atmosphere of Jewish Socialism proved congenial to many of the younger Yiddish writers in the years between 1900 and World War I: the Bund, as part of its secular emphasis, exalted Yiddish, the language of the masses, and denied Hebrew, the language of the rabbis; it offered Yiddish writers a milieu in which for the first time they could discuss the works of Western writers and could brush against the manners and tones of cosmopolitanism; and it raised the possibility of finding a new audience in the Jewish working class.

Zionism and Socialism, in varying degrees, affected Yiddish literature after its main characteristics were determined, but the Haskalah and Hasidism, being more indigenous to the religious life of the Jews, were earlier, profounder, and more deeply formative influences. Both the Haskalah and Hasidism arose in a world where traditional religious forms had become stiff and crusted; where rabbinism often exercised a tyranny of opinion, ruthlessly proscribing expressions of modern thought; where scholarship, having often degenerated into casuistry, had lost its traditional power; where superstition (the cult of the *dybbuk,* the belief in transmigration of souls, and so on) had assaulted the dignity of belief; and where the false Messianism of the seventeenth and eighteenth centuries (Sabbatai Zevi, Jacob Frank) had left a heritage of moral dismay. Meanwhile, the Enlightenment beckoned from the West. The experience of Solomon Maimon, who grew up in Poland during the late eighteenth century and wandered to Germany, there to become a prototype of the Westernized Jewish intellectual, is inscribed in his magnificent *Autobiography* as both record and warning. From Maimon it was only a step to Heine, who said, half in earnest and half in jest: *"Das Judentum ist keine Religion: es ist ein Unglück."* It was to combat these moods of demoralization, these incipient feelings of separation from traditional sources of belief, that both the Haskalah and Hasidism, each in its vastly different way, appeared.

Hasidism, one of the most spectacular religious revivals in modern history, arose in the eighteenth century, mainly in Poland and the Ukraine. Hasidism—the word means "pietism"—was a movement of religious enthusiasm and ecstasy, centering on the wise men, or *zadikim,* who set patterns of behavior for their followers and were said to help them reach closer to the Divine. Coming at a time when East European Jews were starved for spiritual nourishment, Hasidism quickly swept across Poland and the Ukraine; at the peak of its power it claimed the support of nearly half the Jewish masses. Only among the Jews of Lithuania, traditionally hard-bitten in their orthodoxy and rationalism, did Hasidism fail to make much headway. So violent were the struggles that during the latter part of the eighteenth century the Jewish leaders in Lithuania actively persecuted Hasidic preachers, even turning some over to the Russian authorities as dangerous elements and strictly forbidding intermarriage with, or burial rites for, the heretics.

The leading historian of European Jewish life, S. M. Dubnow, who is violently anti-Hasidic, has tried to explain—and thereby perhaps minimize—Hasidism as part of a recurrent phenomenon in Jewish religious life. "There has been apparent from time immemorial," he writes, "a struggle for supremacy between two principles in Judaism: the formalism of dogmatic ritual and the direct religious sentiment. The discipline of the Law was in continual conflict with mystical meditation, which gave considerable latitude to individual inclination in the domain of religion. Such was the nature of the struggle between Pharisaism and Essenism in ancient times, between Talmudism and the Cabala in the Middle Ages, and between rabbinism and mystic-Messianic movements from the sixteenth to the eighteenth centuries."

All this may well be true, yet it hardly accounts for the sudden explosion of fervor with which so many East European Jews greeted Hasidism; nor does Dubnow's suggestion that its popularity in the Ukraine was related to the low cultural and economic level of that region quite exhaust the problem. The truth is that Hasidism, whatever one may think of it, obviously satisfied some deep and long untended appetites among East European Jewry. To a religion that had come to subsist too much on dry bread it added the refreshment of a little wine.

The founder of Hasidism, the Baal Shem Tov, was a healer of the sick and a miracle worker; a genuinely good man, simple, pious, wise. Preaching a kind of romanticist ethic [1]—had he lived a century later in New England, he would have called himself a Transcendentalist—he proclaimed the divinity of all men: "Every Jew is an organ of the *Shekhinah,* or Divine Presence." Disciples came to him from all over Eastern Europe and then wandered off to spread the word to every

[1] The similarities between Hasidic attitudes and those of various romantic writers who were appearing in the West simultaneously or only a few decades later is a subject, full of fascinating possibilities, that has yet to be explored. The Danish critic Frederik Schyberg has been one of the few to notice these similarities. In his excellent book on Whitman he writes: "We find traces of neo-Platonism, Persian Sufism, and Jewish Hasidism in Whitman, all colored with the common pantheistic characteristics; in them individuality is lost in the All like a drop in the sea. Hasidism, which arose in protest against orthodox Judaism, is strongly stamped by the cabalistic, but 'Asceticism is sinful' is one of its chief tenets, and in Rabbi Baal Shem, its founder, we have a Polish Jewish Rumi, or Whitmanesque figure. His remarkable preference for ordinary, elemental people, for artisans and cab-drivers, is one of the points of resemblance, but even more important is the notorious Hasidic cult of friendship for which the rabbi recruited young men from their homes and their work to follow him on 'the great highway' in the same peremptory fashion that Whitman used in 'Song of Myself' and 'Song of the Open Road.'"

corner of the Jewish world. Soon there was hardly a Jewish community in Poland or the Ukraine that lacked a "court" with its *zadik* and disciples.

Hasidism sought wisdom, not knowledge; insight, not system; experience, not doctrine. The core of its teaching was the concept of joy, of a life given over to religious fervor and ecstasy. "The Hasidic movement," writes Martin Buber, the religious philosopher who spent years collecting its legends and stories, "did not weaken the hope in a Messiah, but it kindled both its simple and intellectual followers to joy in the world as it is, in life as it is, in every hour of life in this world, as that hour is. Without dulling the prick of conscience or deadening the sense of chasm between the ideal pattern of the individual limned by his Creator and what he actually is, Hasidism shows men the way to God who dwells with them 'in the midst of uncleanness.' . . . Without lessening the strong obligations imposed by the Torah, the movement suffused all the traditional commandments with joy-bringing significance, and even set aside the walls separating the sacred and the profane, by teaching them that every profane act can be rendered sacred by the manner in which it is performed."

The characteristic expression of the Hasidic ethos came through in Yiddish tales about the sayings of the Hasidic fathers, cryptic remarks, aphorisms embedded in paradox—a remarkable mixture of visionary wisdom and credulous superstition. Hasidism was important not for its theological doctrine but for its emotional refreshment, and even when it dipped into religious metaphysics it did so mainly to restore intimacy between man and God, what Martin Buber has called the I-Thou relationship. To Jews who had been sated with "Thou shalt not" it offered the possibility of release, an emotion of soaring and togetherness in *this* world; for Jews who were groaning under the weight of poverty and misery the *zadik* was a charismatic figure to whom one could turn for solace and advice, his court a place to which one could come for companionship and forgetfulness.

Hasidism brought together the idea of closeness to God with the traditional Jewish emphasis on community. Gershom Scholem, the historian of Jewish mysticism, declares that the true originality of Hasidic thought was that "as mystic moralists the Hasidim found a way to social organization. . . . He who has attained the highest degree of spiritual solitude, who is capable of being alone with God, is the true center of the community, because he has reached the stage at which true communion becomes possible. To live among ordinary men and yet to be alone with God, to speak profane language and yet draw the strength to live from the source of existence"—this was the goal of Hasidism.

That the Lord might be served in rapture, Hasidism favored dancing and sometimes drinking; it stimulated exercise in communal ecstasy; it looked upon love-making, with one's wife, as a blessing. "Song," said Reb Nachman of Bratzlav, one of the purest among the Hasidic sages, "is the very heart of the world." And not the words but the *nigun,* the melody, was the essence of the song—though by *nigun* they meant not merely the melody but the tone, the inner feeling, the spiritual line. (In one of Peretz's stories, "Between Two Mountains," followers of two Hasidic sects dispute over the *nigunim* of their masters, and it soon becomes clear that far more than the mere melodies—nothing less, in fact, than the very moral essence—of their songs is at stake.) Nor did Hasidism deny the value of prayer and study: it merely insisted that joy was the spur to prayer and joy the end of study. Hasidism was a radical repudiation of the long tradition of Jewish woe—indeed, in its programmatic insistence on joy there was something almost ruthless and insensitive, as I. J. Singer suggests in his subtle story "Repentance." But its great strength was that it broke away from that terrible duality of body and spirit, material and ideal, the tree and the ghost, which has made so much of religion a method of organized torment.

Hasidism declined for many reasons, not the least of which was the dubious institution of the *zadikim.* Buber has tried very hard to provide a rationale for these tyrant-sages: "Through the *zadik* all the senses of the Hasid are perfected, not through conscious directing, but through bodily nearness. The fact that the Hasid looks at the *zadik* perfects his sense of sight; his listening to him, his sense of hearing. Not the teachings of the *zadik* but his existence constitutes his effectiveness. . . ." Perhaps. But the finale of Hasidism was squalid, a degeneration into warring cliques, each of which proclaimed the unparalleled saintliness of its leader, and many of which sank into rank corruption. As S. M. Dubnow has written with some asperity: "The profitable vocation of *zadik* was made hereditary. There was a multiplication of *zadik* dynasties contesting for supremacy. The 'cult of the righteous,' as defined by the Baal Shem Tov, degenerated into a system of exploitation of the credulous."

The Haskalah first arose in Germany during the middle of the eighteenth century. Except for a thin layer of the wealthy, who had been granted special privileges by the petty German states and had often tried to consolidate these privileges by converting to Christianity, the situation of the German Jews was pitiable. Living in economic misery almost as acute as that of the East European Jews and under legal disabilities that were sometimes even worse, the German Jews lacked that strong communal life which in Poland and Russia offered some compensation, at least, for hunger and oppression. Pressed into humiliating ghettos in the manner of the Middle Ages, poorly educated in both religious and secular subjects, the German Jews retained only a weak tie with traditional Jewish values yet had nothing with which to replace them. Germany itself, however, was undergoing a certain spiritual renovation. Largely because of the influx of ideas and moods from the French Enlightenment, intellectual life in Germany was opening up and a mild liberalization was taking place. Now was the time, felt the Haskalah leaders, for the Jews to break through, or glide past, the ghetto walls and take their place in the modern world—if only, that is, they could be raised to the intellectual level that might make this possible. The Haskalah leaders, who at first came mainly from the merchant class and the intelligentsia, worked to include secular subjects in Jewish education, in order to lessen the role of the Talmud; they tried to scrape the accumulated barnacles of superstition and dead ritual off the body of the faith and to find ways of reconciling the core of traditional Judaism with modern thought in philosophy, science, and education. Moses Mendelssohn, the outstanding figure of the Haskalah, translated the Pentateuch into German so that his fellow Jews would find it easier to study the Bible.

The Haskalah has sometimes been described as a forerunner of "assimilation"—a loaded word in Jewish discourse that suggests the Jews surrender their identity and lose themselves in the non-Jewish world. But this characterization is not entirely fair, for the Haskalah was basically an effort to salvage a declining faith and really desired that Judaism preserve itself by confronting, and where necessary absorbing, the best of the Enlightenment. Rationalist in temper, the Haskalah recognized that a rigid orthodoxy would be the least effective way of coping with secular modernism; like analogous reform movements within Christianity, it tried to take the sting out of secular criticism by meeting it halfway, though hardly more than halfway.

As the Haskalah drifted eastward, it underwent gradual modifications. In Germany it was oriented toward a partial entry into the outer, gentile world; in Russia and Poland its main emphasis was on the intellectual revival of the Jewish world itself. In Germany the Haskalah often meant a stepping stone to secular culture; in Poland and Russia, where the rabbinate was powerful and unyielding, it involved the very real danger of ostracism. In Germany the Haskalah favored the replacement of Yiddish by German as the language of daily life, with Hebrew left safely intact as the language of prayer; but in Eastern Europe the Haskalah intellectuals found that if they were to reach the Jewish masses they would have to employ Yiddish, the very language they had identified with provincial meanness and obscurantism. They turned to Yiddish grudgingly, as a tactic, but soon the best writers among them came to love its pithiness and freshness. Much Yiddish writing in the first half of the nineteenth century was didactic in intention, a curious mixture of the homiletic and the imaginative, political polemic and primitive genre drawing, all meant to further the Haskalah program for ventilating Jewish life with restrained drafts from the West. But with the appearance of Mendele, the first major Yiddish writer of the modern era, and even in the work of several immediate predecessors, the Haskalah influence gradually became transformed from an explicit moralism into a moral perspective that shaped but did not consume the work of art.

From the conflict between the Haskalah and Hasidism, often very fierce and bitter, there arose an intellectual self-consciousness and an eagerness for self-scrutiny that made possible the growth of a formal literature. The Haskalah was the property of an intellectual aristocracy; Hasidism was unashamedly plebeian. The Haskalah desired to elevate Hebrew; Hasidism turned lovingly to Yiddish. The Haskalah desired to face the modern world, Hasidism to turn a religious back on the modern world. Yet both were efforts to preserve the integrity of a people, though, as it happened, neither was allowed to live out its span. Soon Zionism and Socialism came to attract the best young minds; and then came the century of Maidenek and Auschwitz.

III: THE LANGUAGE AND THE EARLY LITERATURE

The picture we have sketched of the *shtetl* and its intellectual life is not, of course, meant to be faithful to any given moment of history; it is a composite, a synthetic version, of the Jewish experience in Eastern Europe during the past two or two and a half centuries. But Yiddish as a language extends far deeper into the past, and modern Yiddish literature, for all its youthfulness, has its sources not merely in the immediate life of the Jews but also in the historical encounters and traditions of a language that can be traced back to the close of the Middle Ages.

For the Jews, Hebrew has always been *loshon hakodesh,* the sacred tongue. But at least since the time of the Second Temple, Hebrew has had to compete—or at best coexist—with a variety of languages and dialects, which drove it out of the market place, if not the House of Prayer. During the period of the Second Temple, Aramaic was the daily language of the Jews. After the fall of the Temple the Jews who remained in Palestine began to adopt Greek as their mundane tongue. Many Jews in the Near East and North Africa have spoken Arabic for centuries. More recently the Sephardic, or Spanish, Jews have used Ladino in daily speech, while the Ashkenazic, or Eastern, Jews have used Yiddish. This bilingualism has not always made for peace in the Jewish world, since the rabbis and orthodox scholars repeatedly resisted the penetration of the vernacular, which they took to signify, and with some reason, the threat of the profane.[2] But since Jewish life has itself been so persistently torn between the urge to the sacred and the pressure of the profane, bilingualism has been almost inevitable—indeed, an indispensable means for regulating the tension between sacred and profane.

Yiddish first began to develop in the Rhine region between the tenth and twelfth centuries. Gradually the Jews adapted the German of that time and place to their own needs, developing over the centuries a language that, despite numerous detractors within and without the Jewish world, is a distinct linguistic entity. At the beginning this language consisted mainly of German words transliterated into Hebrew characters; then the original German underwent changes in pronunciation and in meaning and syntax. Meanwhile, Hebrew was there, a resource from which to draw, a treasury of sanctified memories and associations.

Since the Jews were usually confined to narrow areas for large portions of their lives, a new vocabulary reflecting their special experience was inevitable. And since the Jews of Europe, whatever their status in one or another country, always tried to maintain some relations with one another, foreign words from both West and East, from the Romance and the Slavic groups, were gradually introduced. After the large-scale

[2] Nor did this resistance diminish over the centuries. As late as the second half of the eighteenth century, a Talmudic commentary was banned, and in some cases even burned, in Eastern Europe because it contained a Yiddish appendix. (See Israel Tsinberg's *Die Geschichte fun Literatur bei Yiden.*)

Jewish migration eastward, to Poland and Russia, there followed a major infusion of Slavic elements into the language, so that to this day Slavic ranks only behind Hebrew and German as a source or component of Yiddish.

By the end of the thirteenth century Yiddish was well on the way to being a language in its own right, still dependent on the languages from which it stemmed yet clearly distinct from them. In the eyes of the Jewish community, to be sure, Yiddish did not yet enjoy—and only during the last century can it be said ever to have enjoyed—a full equality with Hebrew; it served rather as an auxiliary to Hebrew, a crutch with which to make one's way across the treacherous Diaspora. But it was extraordinarily virile and stubborn, and its survival over the centuries reflects the miracle of Jewish survival itself. Always eclectic, endlessly assimilative yet never allowing its identity to be destroyed, Yiddish continued to draw from almost every European and Near Eastern language; after the mass migration of Jews to America in the late nineteenth and early twentieth centuries, it gained new and rich reinforcements from English.

Whatever the tensions—and they have never been quite dissolved—Yiddish and Hebrew were intimately linked. The comparison sometimes made between Jewish bilingualism and the bilingualism of European countries where Latin served as the language of the church is not really very useful. For Latin *did* become a dead language, relegated mainly to priests and scholars, while even at the lowest points of Jewish experience, when ignorance and poverty blighted the ghetto, Hebrew was known and used by considerable numbers of Jews. One reason for this may be that the idea of a professional priesthood never acquired the hold among the Jews of the Diaspora that it did in Christian Europe; the Jewish community was never ready to accept the idea that religious discourse is a proper area for specialization; every Jew, it was assumed, would know some Hebrew, and until the present century most did have at least a smattering of the holy tongue.

Nor was Hebrew ever replaced in the way Latin was. Under alien and temporal pressures Hebrew was pushed out of "the week" and back into the Sabbath, but this in no way decreased the veneration the Jews felt toward it: on the contrary, the language was thereby raised to a still more honored position.[3] Very probably, this was the only way Hebrew

[3] In Peretz's "Devotion without End" the hero is punished for his overbearing pride. The worst punishment that Peretz can conceive for him is that, at one stroke, he forget all the Hebrew he knows.

could be preserved through centuries of dispersion. But preserved it was, and when Yiddish came, it was not a replacement but an addition.

Like the language itself, the early literature in Yiddish can be traced to three major sources: traditional pietistic writings in Hebrew; the secular writings and folk materials of the surrounding gentile cultures; and the experience of exile, dispersion, and persecution.

The very earliest Yiddish literature of which we have some small traces is an oral and manuscript literature. During the twelfth and thirteenth centuries there grew up among the medieval Jews a bardic literature, derived from the German *Spielmann* literature. Such popular German romances as the *Hildebrand Lied* and *Dietrich von Bern* were adapted into Yiddish and recited or sung by Jewish troubadors. Gradually, subtly, these epics, romances, and stories were given a somewhat Jewish flavor. References to Christian myth and ceremony were excised; physical violence and struggle were underplayed; the value system of chivalry was subjected to humane modulations; and at times seemingly incongruous elements of tragic feeling, barely present in the original materials, were introduced in the Yiddish adaptations.

The Jewish troubadors and scribes had resources in their own culture as well.[4] A few Yiddish lyrics have survived from this early period; they express, with homely earnestness, the quality of Jewish religious life and the burden of sustaining it in exile. Such poems, together with translations of and glosses on Biblical passages, were sometimes collected in manuscript anthologies by wealthy Jewish women. Though of limited literary interest, these writings, which waver in theme between predictable piety and glimpses of folk life, represent the first efforts to use Yiddish as a literary vehicle.

Perhaps the first sustained work in Yiddish that has distinct literary merit is the *Shmuel Buch* (*Samuel Book*), which appeared in the mid-sixteenth century, though its unknown author wrote at least a hundred years earlier. An epic poem of some grandeur, it elaborates the Biblical stories of King David, celebrating feats of Jewish heroism in a manner that makes David into a blend of ancient monarch and medieval knight.

[4] Historians of Yiddish literature disagree on the extent to which early Yiddish culture was dependent on the surrounding European cultures or drew from traditional Hebrew sources. Israel Tsinberg, previously cited, advanced the theory that even the anonymous composers of epics and romances drew heavily from Hebrew literature, while Max Erik, a somewhat more sociological critic, places the greatest emphasis on German sources. (See the latter's *Die Geschichte fun der Yiddisher Literatur fun die Aeltste Zeiten bis Haskale-Tekufa.*)

This shuttling between borrowed and indigenous materials is characteristic of Yiddish writing in the early period: it seems to reflect a lingering uncertainty as to the possibilities of the language, an unformulated question as to its capacity for independent life when flanked by Hebrew and the languages of Europe. After the invention of printing, however, the use of Yiddish increased tremendously, both in adaptations of stories and poems from adjacent cultures and as a means of religious instruction and folk expression.

It was to the Jewish woman that most of these early printed works were directed. For her there was no loss of dignity in reading simplified Biblical commentaries in Yiddish; no slur upon her religious status in reciting the Psalms in Yiddish translations somewhat less grand than the Hebrew original or in mulling through the immensely popular *Tsenna Urenna,* a late sixteenth-century compendium of Biblical paraphrases in Yiddish prose and verse, homely exegesis, wise comments from contemporary sages, all woven into one text; it was not even an aspersion on the Jewish woman if she read something as frivolous as the Yiddish recasting of the King Arthur stories that appeared in the sixteenth century.

In the numerous collections of women's prayers, or *Tehinot,* which began to appear toward the end of the sixteenth century, the Jewish woman found her deepest and most authentic expression. These prayers, at first translated from the Hebrew, are very different from the formal and impersonal—that is, communal—prayers of the synagogue. They are prayers to be murmured at home, as the Jewish woman lights her candles on the Sabbath Eve and indulges herself in a moment of communion with her God. Personal outpourings of emotion, these prayers are intimate, direct, unyielding—requests for family health and prosperity, elaborate expressions of woe, complaints to a God seen not as a distant mover but as an immediate protector. Though they sometimes spill over into sentimentality, the *Tehinot* are rich in pathos and charming in their innocence, an impressive mode of folk expression.

The distinction we have tentatively suggested between borrowed and indigenous materials—between, say, the Yiddish version of the King Arthur stories and the *Tehinot*—is strongly insisted upon by many Yiddish critics who wish to establish a clear line of Jewish tradition in the literature. Thus Samuel Niger, the leading contemporary Yiddish critic, makes a crucial distinction between two widely read Yiddish works of the sixteenth century. One of these is the *Bova Buch,* by a gifted writer named Elijah Bochur. A verse narrative in *ottava rima,* it consists of a free version of an Italian romance, itself an adaptation of the English tale of Bevys of Hampton. The other is the famous *Maase Buch* (*Story Book*), a collection of more than two hundred and fifty tales drawn mainly from Talmudic sources but also including some European folk material. Both these immensely popular books went through numerous editions and were no doubt read by much the same audience. Niger insists, however, that such translated romances as the *Bova Buch* "are alien to the Jewish life-rhythm, the Jewish cultural tradition. . . . They created readers or listeners for Yiddish; they did not create a Yiddish literature. They were greatly loved by Jewish women and the Jewish folk; but not every book that is popular is a folk book. . . . The alien *Bova Buch* was popular, but the homely *Maase Buch* was a folk book." [5] In any case, these two works mark the high point of Yiddish writing during the High Renaissance.

In the seventeenth and eighteenth centuries there was a stream of Yiddish books, but not many of them would tempt modern literary tastes. Works of ethical reflection multiplied; a certain amount of crudely satirical verse and prose appeared; the folk song continued to be one of the more vital elements in oral Yiddish literature. But by common agreement the one Yiddish work of this interim period that can still be read with unqualified pleasure is the memoirs of Glueckel of Hameln, written in the late seventeenth and early eighteenth centuries. Marvelously rich in genre pictures, full of the most telling details of Jewish family life, these memoirs are a masterpiece of narrative and descriptive composition.

In the middle of the eighteenth century, with the rise of Hasidism, and during the early years of the nineteenth century, with the penetration of the Haskalah into Eastern Europe, there began an imposing renaissance of the Yiddish literary imagination.

Hasidism helped prepare the way for modern Yiddish literature by validating the language, by raising it to a plane of esteem as the companion of Hebrew. Its use of Yiddish was entirely spontaneous and natural, in sharp contrast to those Jewish intellectuals who a few decades later made gingerly decisions to turn from Hebrew and German to Yiddish. Hasidic leaders like Rabbi Nachman of Bratzlav were genuinely inspired poet-sages whose allegories and parables raised the tradition of Yiddish storytelling to a new level of moral and literary value. As a result, in the violent battles that took place during the mid-nineteenth century as to whether Yiddish was a worthy vehicle for

[5] Samuel Niger, *Die Tsveisprachikeit fon Unzer Literatur.*

Jewish expression or merely a corrupted "jargon," the power of the Hasidic tradition, by then diminished but still considerable, was entirely on the side of Yiddish. But the unique contribution of Hasidism to Yiddish literature was not merely that it lent prestige to the language or gave the Yiddish writers a reservoir of folk stories; it was rather that the stories and their meanings still seemed fresh and new, so that when Peretz turned to the Hasidic tales he could feel the peculiar excitement that comes from drawing upon folk material already secure in the tradition yet still quick with the breath and passion of life.

The Hasidic tales were told orally by the masters and copied by their disciples; the Haskalah literature of the early nineteenth century was the work of men who began consciously to think of themselves as writers. In fact, it may be said that the major contribution of the Haskalah to Yiddish literature was not ideological at all, but simply the *idea* of writing—that is, the idea that a secular career as a writer was worthy of a mature Jewish intelligence. Half moralists and half artists, the early Haskalah writers now seem largely to have been defined, and limited, by their didacticism and their dependence on a provincial audience; a few of them, however, like Solomon Ettinger in his realistic comedy *Serkele,* and Isaac Meier Dick in his hundreds of "enlightened" stories, stood clearly on the threshold of modern Yiddish literature.

However, it was not merely the work of their predecessors that acted upon Mendele, Sholom Aleichem, and Peretz, the "classical" trio of Yiddish prose. It was also the folk experience, the folk imagination, which in the late nineteenth century was still alert and vivid. Yiddish literature is distinctive for its closeness to folk sources: it borrows heavily from folk sayings, folk wisdom, and, above all, folk humor. The literature itself, written by self-conscious artists, cannot properly be said to be a folk literature, but much of its special charm and intimacy comes from the fact that its moment of "classicism" in the late nineteenth century occurred when the folk materials were still alive to the literary imagination, yet the idea of craft and composition, in the literal meanings of those words, had begun to fascinate writers. A meeting of the traditional and the modern, Yiddish literature draws simultaneously from the Hasidic wonder tales and the grotesque fictions of Gogol; from the comic legends about Hershel Ostropolier, a kind of Jewish Till Eulenspiegel, and the fiction of Chekhov; from folk stories about the Rothschilds and the world-view of Cervantes.

A word should be said here about Jewish folk humor, surely one of the most remarkable products of East European life. That a people at the very bottom of the social scale, upon whom the heaviest weights of history descended, should nonetheless have expressed so much of its ethos through a complicated network of jokes, witticisms, satiric stories, symbolic shrugs and gestures—this may be explained, if it can be explained at all, by the fact that humor was its first and only line of defense, though in a sense an impregnable defense. Only if they took the myth of the Chosen People with the utmost seriousness, yet simultaneously mocked their pretensions to being anything but the most wretched people on earth, could the Jews survive.

Even more fundamentally, remarks the American critic Clement Greenberg, "the Jewish joke came to remind [the East European Jew] that his self-absorption, as expressed in a millennial culture that, for all its modifications according to time and place, still attempted to perpetuate itself as if in a timeless and placeless vacuum, was foolhardy. (My son has just lost his wife, who left him with three small children; his house has burned down, and his business gone bankrupt—but he writes a Hebrew that's a pleasure to read.) The Jewish joke criticized the Jew's habit of explaining away or forgetting the literal facts in order to make life more endurable. . . . When religion began to lose its capacity, even among the devout, to impose dignity and trust on daily life, the Jew was driven back on his sense of humor. . . . Invoked to correct a disequilibrium caused by religious preoccupations and by the need to preserve self-esteem, [the Jewish sense of humor] learned to argue with God and dispute with Him, ironically, those final questions around which generations of sages had spun their reverent dialectic."

Jewish humor is seldom carefree and only occasionally gay. Unlike American humor, Jewish humor is overwhelmingly social: its great themes are precisely those events which make the Jewish experience so tragic. At times Jewish humor provides a means of indirect social aggression, and at other times it releases the sharpest, most mordant self-criticism. For example, the excessive intellectuality of the Talmudic mind is mocked—though not that alone—in a group of folk stories about the "Wise Men of Chelm," who find the most intricate ways of doing the most stupid things. Or consider the following folk tale:

> You tell a joke to a peasant and he laughs three times—when you tell it, when you explain it, and when he understands it.
>
> A landowner laughs only twice—when he hears the joke and when you explain it. For he never understands it.

An army officer laughs once—when you tell the joke. He never lets you explain it, and that he is unable to understand it goes without saying.

But when you start telling a joke to another Jew, he interrupts you. "Go on! That's an old one!" And he proceeds to show you how much better he can tell it himself.

This little story is rich in social commentary, reflecting the relationships between the East European Jews and the classes of Czarist Russia, as well as some basic attitudes of the Jews themselves. Nearest to them was the peasant, with whom it was possible, at times, to trade and live peaceably. True, you had to explain things to him three times, but if you took the trouble he understood. The landowner, envied by the landless Jews, can never understand: he lives apart, in another social region. Still more so does the army officer, who represents not merely the terrifying power of Czarism but also the whole detested idea of the military. After these increasingly sharp thrusts against the alien world, the joke turns, as it should, inward, and delivers the sharpest criticism against the impatience and intellectual overconfidence of the Jews themselves.

Another folk story reminds the listener that in the old days Jewish boys used to be snatched off the streets and sent to the army. If they weren't married they'd be taken at any age. "So Jews being Jews, they found a way out." Children were married at the ages of six and seven, and husbands could be seen playing marbles in short pants.

Once [continues the story] a Jew, seeing such a child, asked him why he wasn't at school. The little boy answered, "I don't go to school any more. I was married yesterday." So the Jew asked again, "If you got married yesterday and are now the head of a family, why aren't you wearing long pants?" The child answered, "Yesterday I got married, so I wore the pants; today my little brother is getting married, so he's wearing the pants."

This is hardly a light-hearted joke, but what strikes one as so marvelous is that the underlying misery of the life it reflects is never made explicit: since folk humor is an *internal* humor, the misery is taken entirely for granted and is then discarded or, if you wish, transcended. (One finds the same wry mockery of their own sufferings in the Jewish proverb: "If a poor man eats chicken, one of them is sick.") It is from such homely materials that the best and most indigenous Yiddish writings come, at once an expression and a defiance of fate.

IV: CONTOURS OF A LITERATURE

Modern Yiddish literature focuses upon the *shtetl* during its last tremor of self-awareness, the historical moment when it is still coherent and self-contained but already under fierce assault from the outer world. Between language and milieu there is a curious, ambivalent relationship: the one seems to batten on the other. Yiddish reaches its climax of expressive power as the world it portrays begins to come apart.

The Yiddish of Mendele and Sholom Aleichem is a remarkably fluid and intimate language. Perhaps because it is a language forged in opposition to the most powerful groups within the Jewish community, perhaps because it is the voice of the folk rising organically from the life of the folk, Yiddish is breezy in tone, richly idiomatic in flavor, free in its literary possibilities. This very freedom, of course, is also a severe burden: many a Yiddish writer suffers from the absence of inherited modes and forms.

When the first major Yiddish writers appeared toward the end of the nineteenth century, the language did not impose upon them any stylized patterns of expression—which allowed them verbal spontaneity and improvisation but also forced them to create, as it were, the very standards of usage from which they were already deviating. At its peak, however, Yiddish was neither a folk voice nor a sophisticated "literary" language. It was open at both sides, still responsive to the voice of the folk yet beginning to model itself on literary patterns of the West. The most valuable writing in Yiddish appears at the moment when the two opposing forces, the folk voice and the self-consciously literary, achieve an exquisite, if almost always precarious, balance. To strike an extreme comparison which is not meant to suggest an equation of value between the two literatures: Yiddish found itself for a moment in the position of creative youthfulness that English enjoyed during the Elizabethan Age.

It is almost inevitable that in speaking of Yiddish literature one should refer to an inner dialectic, a tension of counterposed elements: the traditional past and the immediate experience, the religious structure and the secular infiltration, the folk voice and the modern literary accent. But even Yiddish literature itself can be seen and, by its most important critics, has been seen as part of a similar dialectic. The pioneering Yiddish critic Baal Machshoves, and in our own time Samuel Niger, repeatedly employ the formula, "two languages and one literature." Such a view of the relationship between Yiddish and Hebrew is partly motivated, no doubt, by a desire to preserve the historic continuity of the Jewish tradition, and partly by the fact that any empirical study of the formation of Yiddish literature must constantly take into account the Hebrew base and the Hebrew component. "Bilingualism," writes Niger, "became among us an accepted fact, a tradition. . . ." The essence of the Jewish experience, he continues, was reflected in this "partnership between Hebrew and Yiddish," a partnership that is indissoluble no matter who would wish to dissolve it. And when he turns to the late nineteenth century Niger finds a great deal of evidence to support his theory. Mendele, the first major Yiddish writer, began by composing in Hebrew and only later, in 1863, did he turn to Yiddish. During the last decade of his life Mendele translated back into Hebrew the works he had written in Yiddish—with the result that his position as a pioneer in modern Yiddish literature is matched by an equivalent position in modern Hebrew literature. Among recent writers there are numerous examples of a similar bilingualism: the great Hebrew poet Chaim Bialik wrote Yiddish verse; the distinguished Hebrew poet Zalman Schneour has written stories and novels in Yiddish. Nor are these to be taken merely as instances of creative virtuosity. The cultural kinship between the two literatures is so profound that almost any well-educated serious writer in the one literature must be affected by and concerned with the other. Ultimately both literatures draw from and give expression to the same ethos.

But not entirely the same ethos. The theory of "two languages and one literature" is indispensable to an understanding of Yiddish literature; it helps to clarify, for example, how the presence of Hebrew in the background enables Yiddish literature to avoid the painful fate of those literatures of small countries which either become stalled in provinciality or fall into a slavish imitation of the latest vogue from Paris. Yet a too rigorous application of the theory might soon blur those elements and modes that are unique to the Yiddish. For there *is* something qualitatively unique to the whole cultural aura of Yiddish, something in its characteristic gestures and tones that is summoned by the word *Yiddishkeit*. One way of making this point, perhaps, is to note that Yiddish literature releases a profound yearning for a return not to the supremacy of Hebrew but to those conditions of life that would make possible the supremacy of Hebrew—that is, a yearning for the end of the dispersion and a reintegration of Jewish life. But during most of the span of Yiddish literature this is a hope impossible to realize; and it is the recognition of its impossibility that gives rise to that distinctive Yiddish note which cannot and should not be assimilated into Hebrew, or any other, culture.

Somewhat along the same lines, the Yiddish critic B. Rivkin has advanced the theory that Yiddish literature, more through necessity than choice, came to serve as a substitute for a "would-be territory," thereby taking over the functions of a nation that did not yet exist. This meant that many of the communal needs which for other peoples were met by the nation had somehow to be satisfied by Yiddish literature. In the historical interim during which the hold of religion had begun to decline and the idea of nationality had not yet reached its full power, Yiddish literature became a central means of collective expression for the East European Jews, fulfilling some of the functions of both religion and the idea of nationality. In the absence of a free and coherent national life it had to provide the materials for a sense of national identity; and even as, in honesty, it reported the realities of the *shtetl* and the Pale, it had also to nurture and exalt their collective aspirations. From many points of view, of course, this was an impossible task for any literature, let alone one as frail and youthful as the Yiddish; yet something of the moral seriousness—though little of the metaphysical boldness—that we admire in the nineteenth-century Russian novel is also to be found in Yiddish literature precisely because the Yiddish writers thought of their work in supra-literary terms. One could not say of Yiddish literature, as the critic Chernyshevsky has said of the Russian, that it "constitutes the sum total of our intellectual life"; but one can say that the Yiddish writers came before their audience, as did the Russian writers of the nineteenth century, with an instinctive conviction that their purpose was something other than merely to entertain and amuse. The achievements of Russian literature are obviously greater than those of the Yiddish, but both share the assumption that the one subject truly worthy of a serious writer is the problem of collective destiny, the fate of a people.

Among the East European Jews the taste for imaginative literature did not come easily or quickly. They had to struggle for it, and struggle, most of all, against themselves. "It was natural," writes B. Rivkin, "for Jews to ask, 'Why literature?' After all, literature was a late development among Jews. The world around them had a well-established literature with its own forms. But here was a people living in an unnatural environment, without its own territorial and governmental organs, without its own self-sustaining social and economic structure. . . . The pioneer of Yiddish literature was, therefore, confronted with the difficult, almost impossible task of justifying literature to the people, and with the not much easier task of creating something equivalent to a natural environment. The first task was fulfilled by Mendele, the second by Sholom Aleichem." [6]

Literature had to be *justified,* it had to be assigned a moral sanction—which is not to say that the Yiddish pioneers, either the writers or the critics, meant that it had to be moralistic. But what, they seemed to be asking themselves, is the distinct use and end of Yiddish literature? How does it take its place in the larger Jewish tradition? The answer they implicitly gave was that Yiddish literature should focus upon one particular experience, the life of dispersion; that it should release, as only imaginative writing can, the deepest impulses of that life and thereby provide a means of both consecrating and transcending the *shtetl.* Yiddish literature, like any other, has always had its schools, groups, and cliques, but there is hardly a Yiddish writer of any significance whose work is not imbued with this fundamental urge to portray Jewish life with the most uncompromising realism and yet to transcend the terms of the portrayal. How could it be otherwise? Simply to survive, simply to face the next morning, Yiddish literature had to cling to the theme of historical idealism. Beyond hope and despair lies the desperate *idea* of hope, and this is what sustained Yiddish writing.

A literature that, even as it is still reeling from the pain of birth, must assume the formidable task of preserving the national sense of identity and adapting it to the unfamiliar modes of the modern world—such a literature will inevitably turn to language as the only available unifying principle. In another time and under different circumstances language might simply be seen as the familiar, accepted vehicle of cultural realization; but here it becomes, so to speak, the very substance and issue of culture, the living repository of the past and future. The effort to create a Yiddish literature meant the effort to affirm a linguistic patriotism: both are expressions of the urge to national dignity, which became so passionate in the Jewish world of the late nineteenth and early twentieth centuries.

At that time there sprang up the literary and linguistic movement called Yiddishism. Peretz was one of its major spokesmen and Dr. Chaim Zhitlovsky its most ardent defender. How astonishing it now seems—a movement designed to "defend" a language spoken by millions of people, the very people to whom the writers addressed themselves with such assurance and warmth; a movement that felt obliged to

[6] B. Rivkin, *Die Grunt-Tendentsen fun Yiddisher Literatur in America.*

justify the existence of a flourishing culture at a time when it needed not apologetics but air, space, and time.

Yet, from another point of view, the Yiddishist movement is entirely understandable. The Yiddish writer felt only too keenly his problem of being part of a national-religious tradition that went back into the depths of history, while he wrote in a language that had barely been touched by modern literary forms and within a culture that had barely acknowledged the idea of non-religious expression. As a result he could not help being self-conscious in his relation to the language; he could not help proclaiming its virtues while cursing its limitations. A writer in French or English, whether conservative or radical in matters of style and diction, took his language for granted: it was *there*; he did not think to question its historical stability or expressive capacities. But for the Yiddish writer of a half-century ago things were very different. Writing for an audience hardly prepared to apply sophisticated standards but only too ready to scrutinize his every word and thought, he had to find everything out for himself. He had to discover, if he could, why Yiddish seemed to lend itself so naturally to intimate speech and to resist so stubbornly more formal address; why it collaborated with the lyric poet so willingly and with the epic so grudgingly; why it took to the picaresque narrative of a Cervantes but not to the psychological webbing of a Henry James; why it frequently reached the loving empathy of a Turgenev but so seldom the metaphysical rhetoric of a Melville. Just as the Yiddish writer had the task of reweaving the fabric of national consciousness, so he had to improvise, to conquer and create, his own language.

Most of the time, this meant an utterly loving, fiercely defensive attitude toward Yiddish. But sometimes it led to the kind of comparison the early Yiddish poet Simon Frug made between the language and the assorted scraps of bread in a beggar's sack—or to his even more bitter remark that Yiddish was a patchwork so curious that it would prevent the Jews from entering heaven: the angel at the gate wouldn't understand it. In his long poem "Monish," Peretz wrote with a blend of affection, irony, and exasperation:

Differently my song would ring
If for gentiles I would sing,
Not in Yiddish, in "Jargon,"
That has no proper sound or tone.
It has no words for sex-appeal
And for such things as lovers feel.

Yiddish has but quips and flashes,
Words that fall on us like lashes,
Words that stab like poisoned spears,
And laughter that is full of fears,
And there is a touch of gall,
Of bitterness about it all.

(*Translation by Joseph Leftwich*)

Once Yiddish literature is seen as the not quite prepared inheritor of national-cultural tasks, it becomes easier to speculate on those of its qualities that often puzzle readers who have not known it from birth.

The fascination with individual character, with the endlessly minute exposure of motives and manners, which pervades twentieth-century Western literature, is only occasionally present, and that during the more recent decades, in Yiddish fiction. The reader of this book may well be struck by a good many representative figures: the student tortured by a conflict between belief and secular desire; the Jewish householder trembling on the edge of poverty yet proud in his independence; the Jewish child wavering between gaiety and sadness; the ignoramus or sainted fool who proves holier than the men ordained to holiness. Such figures stay in the mind, they have the endurance of archetypes, but they are not, in any sense familiar to most Western readers, "individualized" characters; and if the stock notions of criticism are applied, these stories will be difficult to make out.

In reading Yiddish fiction one seldom has the desire to remember more about the characters than their stark, generalized traits. Anyone reading Lamed Shapiro's "Smoke" is likely to remember the Jewish merchant who is at the center of the story; but who will care to know that his name is Menasha? For even so modern a writer as Shapiro, who breaks from many of the traditions of "classical" Yiddish literature, still sees his characters more in their aspect of typicality than as uniquely demarcated individuals.

Not even Sholom Aleichem's Tevye the Dairyman, one of the great figures of modern literature, can be said to be thoroughly individualized; he is seen in the round, in his social relations, in his accustomed gestures, in his inimitable speech, and above all in his typical situations; but not in his inner reflections, not in those moments of exposed consciousness or dream life when he has no defense against the observing eye. For, in the nature of things, a character in Yiddish literature must always have a defense. It is hardly an accident that Tevye tells his stories *to* Sholom Aleichem; he consciously organizes, he provides comment, he lends perspective—and so dominant a speaker is not a convenient choice, at least in literature, for a display of depth psychology. The Yiddish story is sometimes a monologue, more often a dialogue, very seldom a plunge into private rumination. The major Yiddish writers, at least those who began publishing before World War I, are largely untouched by that passion for fret-work psychology which makes modern writing a thing of marvelous refinement but also tends to dissolve behavior into a stream of perceptual notation.

In this respect Sholom Aleichem and Peretz are more like Kafka than any of the three are like most modern writers. The Yiddish masters are largely unconcerned with the psychology of individual difference; Kafka consciously puts it aside. Whether Kafka was greatly influenced by the Yiddish tradition remains an unsettled question, though the similarities between his stories and some of the Hasidic tales are remarkable. But he is akin to the Yiddish writers in that he deals not with psychological arithmetic, the numbers of individual configuration, but with the algebra of situation and emotion. That is why you cannot find in Kafka, as you cannot find in Peretz, those delicately modeled and infinitely subtle character studies we associate with James and Proust. What matters most to the Yiddish writers is the context, the contour, the choreography of social behavior: in short, collective destiny. And even when an occasional writer—like Jonah Rosenfeld in his harrowing story "Competitors"—deliberately employs modern psychological insights, he takes hold of them in their generalized form, he does not try to embody them in private deviations.

This point holds more strongly for the Yiddish story than the Yiddish novel, if only because the story as a genre cannot achieve the detailed scrutiny of character that is possible to the novel. But that can hardly be the whole explanation; something else, something related to the inner qualities of Yiddish culture, must also be involved.

A culture that has gained inner security or has even begun to decline a little, a culture that has bitten eagerly into the apple of power and success, is likely to indulge itself in the luxury of individual self-examination. Introspection, spiritual testing, self-doubt—these familiar elements of Western life are tied to that sense of estrangement and aloneness, that sense of the self as an insupportable burden, which everyone in an industrial civilization seems to feel to one extent or another. In the literature that appears at such a time the probing of individual differences and nuances in behavior will be far advanced.

Suppose, however, that you are living in a society that, whatever its weaknesses and faults, is still coherent internally but is constantly threatened from without. Such a society, particularly when its ethos rests upon the assumption that God has granted it a unique destiny, will inevitably aspire toward cultural expressions of a collective type. In this society the individual will not be disdained but neither will he be exalted; he will be seen rather as the agent and embodiment of the community, who must be prevented, if he shows any such inclinations, from tumbling into the pits of Western egotism. It follows that in the literature of such a society the central concern will be not with individual specification but with the unifying patterns of conduct.

Just as the appetite for "individualized" characterization, so chronic among modern readers, cannot be satisfied by Yiddish literature, so will those critics who think of prose fiction mainly in terms of an interplay of social manners be somewhat perplexed by Yiddish literature. The gradations of social manners revealed in a Jane Austen novel depend upon the existence of an ordered world that has had time to settle, ripen, and develop freely; a world that has become sufficiently relaxed to allow its tendencies toward diversification of manners to reach their bloom. But this could never be the case with the world of the East European Jews. Even their pathetic little snobberies, even the cruel vanities of their caste system, were enacted within a sharply compressed area. There wasn't the social space—nor even, by the way, the geographical space—that would make possible a full display of contrasting manners within such a world. In a few later Yiddish writers like Lamed Shapiro one does find the idea of manners as index to morality and belief, particularly in his story "Eating Days"; but this remains the exception rather than becomes the rule.

Moreover, the social differences among the East European Jews, considerable as these soon became, were never so deep as the social differences between themselves and the outer world. To be a Jew was the determining condition of one's life, far more so than one's wealth or poverty, learning or ignorance. The wealthy Jew of the *shtetl* was far better off than the poor one, but they lived within a few houses of each other, often on the same muddy street, and they trembled equally before the drunken or inflamed peasant. Even in the cities the social range between Jew and non-Jew was almost always greater than the range between wealthy and poor Jew. Clearly, this was not a climate in which fine discriminations of manners could flourish.

But a more fundamental fact needs to be stressed. The notion that a man's appearance reflects, in some mysteriously strategic way, the qualities of his soul—a notion that pervades American writing and in the work of such writers as John O'Hara has become an obsession—never took deep hold in Yiddish literature. Nor in the Russian either. Tolstoi believed that a man's destiny is not a function of his social role; Dostoevski believed that the elder Karamazov, wretched buffoon that he was, could rise to salvation; and the Yiddish writers also knew that in essential human experiences not the play of manners but the direct, fearful encounter of moral assumptions was fundamental. The approach to prose fiction in terms of social manners is clearly valuable, but there are kinds of literature with which it cannot cope. A Jewish belief has it that the world is sustained by thirty-six secret and entirely inconspicuous saints; in Peretz's story "Devotion without End," one of these secret thirty-six suddenly appears, an artisan who has gone unhonored and unnoticed. What can a study of social manners tell us about a saint whose saintliness derives from a secret covenant?

A similar hypothesis may help explain why Yiddish literature, particularly the prose, is so poor in formal experimentation. (By contrast, recent Yiddish poetry has been sensitive to modernist techniques in Western poetry—often with striking results.) A literature so heavily weighted with national tasks is not likely to know the freedom—the possibility for play, in both senses of the word—that is needed for literary experiment. Most of the innovations of twentieth-century literature result from a feeling among major writers that various inherited styles, manners, or genres have become "exhausted"—exactly what "exhausted" means here we shall not try to say—and that radical shifts in literary strategy are necessary if imaginative writing is not to stagnate. At least until recently, the Yiddish writers have found themselves in quite another situation. Among them there was not time enough for a style or genre to become "exhausted"; they were still at the stage of trying to press urgent materials and themes into whatever style or genre seemed to be at hand. The literary curve that ends with avant-garde writing had just begun for them. Nothing could yet seem used up, few things had even been tried; the problem was rather that their material was frequently too immediate to be pacified into the forms they could usefully control.

Yiddish writing is preoccupied, above all, with themes; life is still beating urgently at the doors of art. "The writer was struggling with his themes," begins a story by David Pinski, a Yiddish writer who spent a lifetime struggling with his themes; and this opening sentence might well be the epigraph of all Yiddish literature. For the Yiddish writers did not work in a culture sufficiently at ease to encourage the kind of art that abandons any effort directly to reflect or reform the world in which it appears. The sense of aesthetic distance, the aristocratic savoring of isolation, which make for an intense concern with formal literary problems, were not available to the Yiddish writer. From birth, so to speak, he was an "engaged" writer: in that sense he was indeed chosen. Art for art's sake, whether as a serious commitment or a shallow slogan, finds little nourishment in the soil of Yiddish literature, even though an occasional attempt is made to transplant it there. But then, how could any theory of pure aestheticism take hold in a culture beset by the primary questions of existence and survival?

If the unique circumstances of Yiddish literature imposed certain disabilities and burdens, the advantages gained from its position of historical precariousness now seem far greater. For whatever its limitations of scope and form, Yiddish literature is endowed with a moral poise, a security of values that is very rare in any age.

We live in a time when the literature most likely to be valued by serious people is intense, recalcitrant, and extreme; when the novel is periodically combed for images of catastrophe; and the possibilities of life seem available only through ultimates, prophecies, and final judgments. Formally we accord Dostoevski and Tolstoi equal honor, but in our hearts we feel closer to Dostoevski; his seems the true voice of crisis, and we know ourselves to be creatures of crisis. None of this is said by way of depreciation, for we too join in this response and believe it to be necessary or at least inevitable to our time.

Yet it would be good if we could also celebrate another kind of literature: the kind that does not confront at every moment the harsh finalities of experience, or strip each act to its bare motive, or flood us with anguish over the irrevocability of death. In such writers as Turgenev, Chekhov, Silone, and Sholom Aleichem there is a readiness—never purchased at the price of complacence—to value those milder virtues which can cause only impatience in many modern minds. These writers—let us call them the writers of sweetness—do not assume evil to be the last word about man, and they seem to add: Even if it is the last word, there are others to be declared before we reach it. They do not condescend to the ordinary, or scorn the domestic affections, or suppose heroism to be incompatible with humbleness.

Sweetness is a quality our age suspects. Not many of us are sweet or care to be; and those few who are seem almost ashamed of their gift. "Sweetness and light" now seems a phrase of faint ridicule, calling to mind a genteel academicism. But when Matthew Arnold used the phrase—and we might remember that Jonathan Swift used it before him—he was hardly seeking a warrant for complacence; he knew that the quality of sweetness need not exclude the most stringent realism.

Everything we know about Yiddish literature strengthens our confidence in these remarks. Here is a literature that explored poverty as few others have, that studied the misery of this life as intensely as the French have studied the politics of sex. But while we do not wish to suggest that Yiddish literature has been without its voices of desperation and violence—anyone who reads the stories of Jonah Rosenfeld, Zalman Schneour, and even, in part, Peretz will find plenty of both—we are repeatedly struck by the tone of love, that final register of moral poise, with which such masters as Sholom Aleichem and Peretz faced the grimmest facts about Jewish life.

Why should this be so? Not, we would suggest, because of any special virtues in Jewish life or character; not even because of the distinctive religious cast of the *shtetl.* When Mendele wrote his tribute to the compressibility of the Jewish stomach, and Sholom Aleichem had his Tevye declare, "I was, with God's help, a poor man," these writers were expressing an ethos that reflects a unique historical condition. The East European Jews could be as greedy as anyone else, and as unscrupulous in their pursuit of a livelihood; but they were cut off from the world at an all too visible point; they knew that the fleshpots, tempting as they might be, were not for them. Who in the *shtetl* world was not finally a *luftmensch,* a trader who dealt in air, exchanging nothing for nothing and living off the profits? This precarious position made the ironic shrug a symbolic national gesture; it made the feeling of fraternity with the poor a foundation for Peretz's earlier realistic stories and Sholom Aleichem's marvelous flights into surrealism.

Because of its own limitations, the world of the East European Jews made impossible the power-hunger, the pretensions to aristocracy, the whole mirage of false values that have blighted Western intellectual life. *The virtue of powerlessness, the power of helplessness, the company of the dispossessed, the sanctity of the insulted and the injured*—these, finally, are the great themes of Yiddish literature.

Nor does the sentiment of humaneness have anything in common with the populist rhetoric and sentimentality we have come to know in American literature; no one could have been more caustic than Mendele and Peretz in their attacks on their own world. What it signified was that, in the end, the best Yiddish writers knew to whom their sympathies were pledged, and never doubted for a moment that they stood as perhaps the last spokesmen of a tradition the outer world would not tolerate. They wrote from a firm sense of identification, an identification that was simultaneously inheritance and choice; and this was the source of their moral security.

None of this has anything to do with *shtetl*-nostalgia. Nor is it uniquely Jewish: the sense of fraternity with the poor is as fine in Silone as in Sholom Aleichem. It is only that the Jews—with God's help—have had more occasion than most peoples to look into the matter.

Before he died Sholom Aleichem wrote: "Bury me among the poor, that my grave may shine on theirs and their graves on mine." He did not speak for himself alone.

A culture that has been able to resist the temptations of worldly power—or has been blocked at the threshold of those temptations—will naturally favor an image of heroism very different from the one we know in Western literature. Few Yiddish novels or stories contain heroes who satisfy the Aristotelian formula. The rhythm of *hybris* and the climb from *hybris* into humility is not really organic to Yiddish literature, though conspicuous examples of it can, of course, be found. Most Yiddish writers, especially those in the generation of Sholom Aleichem and Peretz, place a far greater stress upon the theme of anti-heroism.[7] Rejecting the whole ethos of historical aggrandizement

[7] Perhaps this throws some light on two problems with regard to Yiddish literature, one technical and the other historical.

A good many Yiddish stories deliberately avoid the traditional ending of a dramatic climax. Why? Surely the Chekhov influence cannot be the only reason. Might there not be a connection between this narrative strategy and the theme of anti-heroism—with the absence of climax a kind of rhythmic equivalent to the refusal of heroism?

The prevalence of this theme may also help explain why Zionists have been tempted to look with impatience upon Yiddish literature. In the nature of their effort, the Zionists desired to retrieve—or improvise—an image of Jewish heroism; and in doing so they could not help finding large portions of Yiddish literature an impediment. The fact that Yiddish literature had to assume the burden of sustaining a national sense of identity did not thereby make it amenable to the needs of a national ideology. Having for so long been exposed to the condition of powerlessness, Yiddish culture could not quickly accustom itself to the climate of power.

as it has come to us from the Greek drama and been colored by the era of Christian expansion, the Yiddish writers express through the theme of anti-heroism their admiration for those who do not exert their social will but live and endure in silence, as well as their contempt for what the outer world takes to be greatness but which they often feel is no more than an appetite for blood. Sholom Aleichem's Tevye the Dairyman is the embodiment of the anti-heroic Jewish hero whose sheer power of survival and comment makes the gesture of traditional heroism seem rather absurd. Peretz too is fascinated by the problem of heroism, but, being more "modern" than Sholom Aleichem, he ends with a more ambivalent feeling. In a number of his stories the victim is seen as the sanctified agent of moral purity, but in his later work Peretz turns upon this theme with a bitter impatience, as if to say that Jewish heroism has degenerated into weak passivity.

Among the writers of the generation that follows Sholom Aleichem and Peretz there is a deliberate effort to revive the tradition of Jewish heroism (see the dramatic little story by Sholem Asch called "Sanctification of the Name"). These writers, particularly Asch and Joseph Opatoshu, reject the pacific tenor of "classical" Yiddish writing; they seek to inspire their readers with a militant, almost warlike readiness to struggle in behalf of Jewish survival; they feel that, in part at least, the world must be met with the ways of the world.

But in the main the tradition of anti-heroism continues to dominate Yiddish writing. *Dos kleine menschele,* the little man, appears again and again at the center of Yiddish fiction: it is he, long-suffering, persistent, lovingly ironic, whom the Yiddish writers celebrate; it is the poor but proud householder trying to maintain his status in the Jewish world even as he grows poorer and poorer who appeals to their imagination far more than might an Aeneas or an Ahab. Anyone, they seem to say, can learn to conquer the world, but only a Tevye or a literary descendant of Tevye can learn to live in it. The ordinary humble man becomes an almost legendary archetype in Abraham Reisen's little sketches, the very fragmentariness of whose form reveals the essence of their *Weltanschauung.*

From this central figure of Yiddish literature—one might call him the Representative Man of the *shtetl*—there emerges a number of significant variations and offshoots. One extreme variation is the wise or sainted fool who has often given up the householder's struggle for dignity and thereby acquired the wry perspective of the man on the outside. Another is the ecstatic wanderer, hopeless in this world because so profoundly committed to the other—as in I. J. Singer's novel *Yoshe Kalb* (in English, *The Sinner*).

The wise or sainted fool—to note a few of his appearances in this book—is seen full-face in I. Bashevis Singer's "Gimpel the Fool," where he acquires, with the piling up of his foolishness, a halo of comic sadness, and where, in the end, his foolish innocence triumphs over the wisdom of the world. Gimpel is the literary grandson of Peretz's Bontsha Schweig, whose intolerable humbleness makes even the angels in heaven feel guilty and embarrassed—though Bontsha, while an epitome of the type, is also meant as a harsh thrust against it. The wise or sainted fool also appears, somewhat muted, in Joseph Opatoshu's little story "May the Temple Be Restored," where his ignorance becomes the thread from which a devotion purer than his rabbi's is woven. And a more somber, less easily recognizable version of the type may be found in Moishe Kulbak's "Muni the Bird Dealer," where he barely speaks at all but ends with a gesture of despair that is terrible beyond the power of words.

Hand in hand with the anti-heroic Jewish hero, and more at the center of things than the sainted fool, goes the Jewish child, precocious, ingenious, deprived, yet infinitely loved. The completely carefree story about the adventurous boy, so favored in English, is virtually absent from the Yiddish, if only because that kind of boy could seldom survive in Jewish life. In the Yiddish story the child almost always carries a social burden heavier than we in America are accustomed to believe appropriate for children. Oppressed by this thought, Sholom Aleichem writes in his autobiography: ". . . this is not meant for you, Jewish children! Yellow sunflowers, sweet-smelling grass, fresh air, fragrant earth, the clear sun—forgive me, these are not meant for you. . . ." This note of deprivation winds through almost all Yiddish children's stories. Too young, far too young, they become *kleine menschelach,* little men—pale and bent scholars who do not see the sun, premature wage-earners scurrying for a piece of bread.

Yet they seem to bear these burdens, at least in the literature, with spirit and even joy. For in Yiddish literature the family is generally shown as a still cohesive unit; fathers may be strict, mothers tearful, brothers oppressive, but love breaks through and beneath the barriers of ritual. If there are few carefree children in Yiddish literature, there are few unloved and brutalized children. A story like Henry James's "The Turn of the Screw" would have puzzled Jewish readers who had been brought up on Abraham Reisen's tender sketches of childhood or Sholom Aleichem's loving stories about Mottel the cantor's son. They would have had difficulty in grasping the moral assumptions behind James's story. How, one can hear them asking, does a father leave his children in the hands of strangers to begin with? The many works in English, from Dickens to Graham Greene, about children hated and exploited do not find an equivalent in Yiddish. There children may have it very hard, but never from coldness. For whatever the deficiencies of Yiddish culture, the power of love remains: for the child, the poor, the weak, for the insulted and injured everywhere. It is the power at the heart of the Yiddish tradition.

Throughout this essay we have spoken repeatedly about the role of tradition in Yiddish literature. In America the idea of tradition has become an icon of literary criticism, and "traditional," though properly a neutral term, now serves for implicit praise. But if by traditional we mean not merely a writer's sense of continuity with the writers who have preceded him but also his sense of being part of a living culture and intimately related to an active audience, then it is in Yiddish literature—far more so than in modern English or American literature—that tradition has been a sustaining force. A writer like Sholom Aleichem could assume that his readers knew not only the world he described but every nuance that could be wrung from his plays of language; he had no need for depth psychology or a minute analysis of character, for his readers lived next door, as it were, to the people who lived in his books. He could count, above all, on one of the main resources of tradition: the powers of implicit communication among members of a coherent group. And he could assume that most of his readers knew that his stories, while immensely entertaining, were far from mere entertainments; that they understood because he felt no need to explain.

The Waste Land is far more recondite than any of Sholom Aleichem's stories, but the footnotes T. S. Eliot felt obliged to append suggest that he was writing in a society where tradition had been disrupted, where tradition had become a problem, *a subject for discussion.* By contrast, the coherence of Sholom Aleichem's stories indicates how much he could demand from his readers. Imagine Sholom Aleichem appending footnotes that explained to his readers how, for comic purposes, he had mangled Biblical and Talmudic texts! He had no need to foreshorten plots or seek fresh devices by which to avoid boring his audience; he was as sure of his readers as of his materials; and how many Western writers have been able to enjoy such advantages?

But it is in the work of another writer that one can most fully see the sustaining power of tradition. A reader coming to Yiddish literature from a distance may wonder at the very high estimate its critics place on the fragile little sketches of Abraham Reisen. In the hundreds of stories he wrote—without dramatic accent or visible plot line, they sometimes read like muted prose lyrics—Reisen has provided one of the truest and fullest portraits that we have of Jewish life in Eastern Europe. His sketches depend so heavily on the tacit cooperation of the audience, they assume so deep a sharing of values and knowledge, that to the unfamiliar reader they may sometimes seem more like literary clues than literary embodiments. Concerned not with events but with situations and predicaments, Reisen writes in a manner that reminds one of those stage designers who, by manipulating a few sticks of wood, create the illusion that a bare stage is really Lear's palace. And this is possible not merely because Reisen is a skilled writer—though it would be a mistake to underestimate the quality of feeling and perception beneath his mildly ironic surfaces—but because he is in complete rapport with his audience. (Some of his poems have almost become folk songs and are often sung by people who would be astonished to learn that they were composed by a twentieth-century poet.) The result is a kind of literary shorthand, a flash of communication achieved through a few phrases, a faint touch of color, a shrug or two—and the Yiddish reader understands and responds. We are not saying that Reisen is the best or the most exciting Yiddish story-writer; we are merely saying that he is in the mainstream of the Yiddish tradition, and that any reader who would savor the particular quality of *Yiddishkeit* will find it embodied with complete purity in his work.

Almost any story in this book could illustrate the living impact of tradition in Yiddish literature, but here we would mention a few examples of how that impact may be apprehended as a literary value. Jonah Rosenfeld's "The Sick Goose," which portrays an old man's dying night, seems at first glance to be a story that could come out of any literature. A closer reading suggests, however, that its swaying prose rhythms are distinctly Yiddish, recalling the rhythms of religious discourse. Thus, in drawing a chiaroscuro of death that might pertain to any old man, the author has endowed it with a unique cultural quality by using rhythms specific to Yiddish life. In Jacob Glatstein's "The Return," the author, while describing his visit to a Jewish family in Poland, brings his account to an end by mentioning, rather casually, that all through the visit he was not wearing a hat but that none of his friends brought this to his attention. The literary appropriateness of this ending rests upon the ritual significance of the Jewish male's wearing a hat; given this awareness, one quickly senses the implicit power of the story's ending. And in Isaiah Spiegel's "A Ghetto Dog" the climax is reached when an old woman, preparing to let herself and her dog be slaughtered by the Nazis, winds his leash around her arm in the way phylacteries are wound by pious men. This bit of symbolic action, which to the Yiddish reader bears the profoundest and most affecting associations, becomes the dramatic center of the story: the traditional symbol is the literary climax.

At this point, however, a qualification needs to be made. In America, at the present moment, most uses of the term "traditional" tend to suggest political and moral conservatism, a wish to return to some earlier and presumably better state of things. In the Yiddish context, however, tradition is almost always bound up with moral and social rebelliousness, for the mere existence of Yiddish literature is itself a rebellion against the assumptions of Jewish orthodoxy. Had the Yiddish writer remained entirely rooted in the orthodox community, he would never have turned to imaginative composition at all. Once he began to write in Yiddish, he implicitly acknowledged that his main desire was to communicate with man as well as God. The mere act of using the untamed secular "jargon" meant a worldly temptation, and it hardly mattered that some of the Yiddish writers were personally devout. Inevitably a good many of the early Yiddish writers came from the yeshivas, where they had been subjected to the long exhausting grind of rabbinical study, and now, in reaction, turned not to the gentile world but to the painful effort to understand their own world in purely human terms. The spokesmen for orthodoxy warned that once Jewish youth began to write stories and verses in Yiddish they would feel a desire to emulate the themes and forms of the West—and they were right enough in a way. What they failed to understand was that the choice had already been made. Slowly, gradually, the Yiddish writers began to disengage themselves from their social-religious community, to acquire a sense of group identity, to read the works of Western writers and find in them models of craft and skill they could find nowhere else. The sudden growth of a formal Yiddish literature in the late nineteenth century was a symptom that the Enlightenment was finally establishing itself in the world of the East European Jews.

This rebelliousness was quickened by more immediate, ideological stimulants. Both Zionism and Socialism offered visions of the good life, or at least a better life; both made it seem legitimate to compare the condition of the Jews with the condition of other peoples, a comparison that radically undercut the earlier assumptions of the Jewish milieu; and both brought with them the Western traits of restlessness, self-scrutiny, impatience. Once the Yiddish writer liberated himself from the hold of religious orthodoxy, he could no longer blink the appalling misery and degradation of life in *this* world by keeping his head in the clouds of Messianic expectation. He still loved his folk, and perhaps in his growing loneliness he loved it more than ever; but in his judgment of its condition he could not help applying, almost unwittingly, the standards of the West. That is why the introduction of naturalism into Yiddish literature came as an elemental revolution, a harsh and violent gesture repudiating the tradition of *edelkeit* (refinement, delicacy), from which had stemmed the writings of Mendele, Sholom Aleichem, and, to a lesser extent, Peretz.

Yet the possibilities for revolt were severely limited. The Yiddish writer could not cut himself off from the people: there was no place else to go. He could not find shelter in a bohemia or solace himself with dreams of "the happy few." His world lacked the range to permit him to live apart from or "above" the folk. One cannot imagine in the Yiddish literary life of three or four decades ago a figure like Stefan George, proclaiming an aristocracy of the word, or even like T. S. Eliot, launching a desperate raid upon an alien tradition. Here and there a Yiddish writer may have tried to adopt an aristocratic or aesthete's pose, but the only result was that he made himself seem pitiable. The Yiddish writer had to remain in intimate relation with the folk even if it turned its back upon him; he had to engage it in a dialogue even if the only answer was his echo.[8] But during the "classical" period of Yiddish literature and for some time afterward

[8] The briefest notice of the tie between Yiddish writers and their audience should include a word about the Yiddish theater as a force bringing the two more closely together. Beginning with the wandering troupes of Eastern Europe, and particularly Rumania, the Yiddish theater quickly became a popular institution, in fact, the major cultural outlet for the Jewish masses. Not only did professional playwrights like Abraham Goldfaden and Jacob Gordin write for it, but many Yiddish poets and novelists were tempted by the mass audiences it could provide in such centers as Warsaw and New York. To be sure, the Yiddish theater was often sentimental, crude, and melodramatic, but at its occasional best it released an enormous creative and emotional energy. And so long as it flourished, the slow insidious process of alienation between writer and audience, which had already begun in the career of Peretz, could never quite reach its painful finish.

there was a remarkably close tie between author and audience; and the literature that came out of that moment was a literature of affection and intimacy, affection even in complaint and intimacy even in despair.

There is no better way to discover the inner qualities of a literature than to translate from it. Among American Jews who retain vague memories of Yiddish as the tongue of their parents, there has arisen a legend that Yiddish is untranslatable. Such people always ask, with an air of suppressed triumph, how do you translate this or the other idiom? That is no problem at all: most Yiddish idioms, like most French or American idioms, are untranslatable and the translator is under no obligation to try the impossible; he need only hunt for vivid equivalents.

The truth is that all translation involves losses, and the job of the translator is to measure one loss against another: literal meaning against English idiom, original flavor against economy in the new version. But the idea that Yiddish is somehow uniquely untranslatable may very well arise from a hidden sentimental desire to keep it so, to preserve it as a soft sweet haze of memory.

Some of the difficulties in translating Yiddish are "technical," similar to difficulties in translating from any other language. By the standards of modern English, for example, many Yiddish writers have only the haziest notion of syntax and punctuation. The translator must therefore try to break up what seem to be endlessly winding sentences; yet if he does so he runs the risk of losing the reflective or dialectical qualities of the original Yiddish. Similarly, parts of speech enjoy a fluidity in Yiddish that is almost impossible to render in English. In one story that the editors translated, a goose is described as having *beryed* herself toward a food pail. The word *berye* is a noun referring to a super-efficient, even fanatical housewife—its origin is Hebrew, but that is a complication we shall let pass. The author, by twisting *berye* into a verb that describes the busy movements of a goose, has brought to the sentence an aura of suggestiveness that may be said to give the natural environment a distinctive Jewish shade. The best equivalent we could find was "bustle," but it was hardly very brilliant.

In Yiddish, too, there is a frequent use of the "reflexive" voice, about halfway between the active and the passive, which gives a strangely animated effect: the background of the story seems to dance about while the characters stand still. There is no satisfactory equivalent in English. And then there is the problem of diminutives, which barely exist in English but are numerous and rich in Yiddish, where they suggest the compression, intimacy, and vulnerability of East European Jewish life.

One problem in translating from Yiddish, however, *is* unique. Maurice Samuel has discussed the way Hebrew phrases form a sacred canopy over the profane action of Yiddish writing and sometimes become twisted into a backdrop of complex irony. "The fusion of the secular and sacred in Yiddish," he writes, "makes possible a charming transition from the jocular to the solemn and back again. Well-worn quotations from sacred texts mingle easily with colloquialisms, and dignified passages jostle popular interjections without taking or giving offense. There is about it all a suggestion of an oriental bazaar." But if one translates into a language that does not have these two levels of meaning and suggestion, that cannot make a complex point simply by repeating a phrase, first on a sacred and then on a profane level, clearly there will be a serious loss in translation. Such losses occur most of all when translating the work of the "classical" writers, in whose use of Yiddish the Hebrew component, with all its national and nostalgic reverberations, is very strong.

This linguistic problem reflects another and still more serious problem—and here it is surely correct to say that translating from the Yiddish is more difficult than from, say, the French. In translating from French a certain community between French and English culture can safely be assumed, while in translating from Yiddish it is necessary not only to present a rough facsimile of a verbal sequence, but somehow to summon a world that exists beneath the words. Inevitably, though at great risk, the translator becomes a tacit social historian.

One of the most trying experiences of the translator is the story that reads splendidly in the original Yiddish but that in English seems to have turned pallid. Aside from the limitations of any translator, this kind of disappointment may be put down to certain peculiarities of pace and tone in Yiddish literature.

We Americans are accustomed to the well-made story, the efficient narrative that achieves a hard, precise climax by grouping words into a pyramid of impressions. This kind of "art" story is written by only a few Yiddish writers, generally the later ones. The bulk of Yiddish fiction veers toward one or another extreme: toward an accumulation of sensuous impression or of winding oral narrative, which would seem highly wasteful to most American and English writers; or toward the bare little story in which characters are merely glimpsed, conflict is hardly present, and nothing seems to be happening. What is crucial, for both translator and reader, is that both kinds of Yiddish stories move far more slowly than the usual American story; they reflect a society in which time has not yet become an obsession; they are often monologues or conversations as much as they are narratives, and if the Yiddish writer like Sholom Aleichem wants to stop at a by-way for a chat, why not?

With this problem of pace goes the problem of tone. In the thin, bare, eventless little story favored by so many Yiddish writers, what matters most is the *nigun,* the undercurrent of melody or the humming undertone, which becomes the ultimate carrier of meaning. In such stories one is aware, above all, of the rhythm of a voice, sometimes the voice of the speaker in the story and sometimes the voice of the author himself. Everything depends, in translating such a story, upon hitting the proper key at the very beginning and not deviating from it, not allowing any fancy variations or flourishes. It is a problem in literary discipline; the translator must strictly subordinate himself to the material. And that is hard.

One final problem in reading or translating Yiddish literature needs to be mentioned, the vexing problem of sentimentality.

Sentimentality is defined by Cleanth Brooks and Robert Penn Warren as an effort to evoke an "emotional response in excess of the occasion." John Crowe Ransom, in a somewhat different approach, relates sentimentality to "certain inferior performances" in art: "The artist has the right sentiment for the object, but articulates the object no better than a man who has merely the sentiment. Unable to communicate the precise object, he would communicate at least his feeling for it, or his election of it as an object, and he is right in assuming that feelings are contagious among spontaneous persons. So he points reverently to it, and indicates the state of his own affections, and leaves us to explore the object mostly for ourselves."

Both statements are helpful, and the difference between them is probably due to their being focused on slightly different problems. The Brooks-Warren definition seems to emphasize the idea that an author *exploits,* with some degree of deliberateness, those emotions in his audience he knows to be all too readily available. The Ransom definition stresses sentimentality as the familiar outcome of an honest or respectable failure.

Both views are pertinent to a discussion of Yiddish literature. The

Brooks-Warren approach recommends itself particularly to an age of mass culture in which the responses of an audience are played upon with scientific malice; the Ransom approach points to the high cost of artistic effort at any time. As it happens, however, the sentimentality that exploits the emotions of a vulnerable audience is relatively infrequent in Yiddish literature (it can be found to a far greater extent in the Yiddish theater), if only because the blight of mass culture, which is the blight of an industrialized society, did not attack the Yiddish world until rather late, and then with little of the virulence it spent upon American or English literature. Yiddish writing, to be sure, had its servant-girl novels and still has its tear-jerking newspaper serials; but it is relatively easy to segregate such trash from serious work in a way that becomes increasingly harder to do in American literature. Far more prevalent in Yiddish literature is the kind of sentimentality described by Ransom, the kind that results from indicating an object with "reverent pointing" instead of embodying it imaginatively.

Now a reader who has been raised exclusively upon "modern" twentieth-century literature—let us assume such a deprived unfortunate exists only as a useful straw man—may well find a large amount of sentimentality in Yiddish literature. He is not likely, however, to do more than declare his gesture of dismissal, secure in the knowledge that once a piece of writing has been called sentimental nothing more need be said. But no easy gesture, whether of acceptance or rejection, will quite do. There *is* a considerable streak of sentimentality in Yiddish culture—it is a major deficiency; and one or two stories in this book can be seen as sentimental even by Yiddish standards. More important, however, is that area of Yiddish writing which may seem sentimental to readers who approach it with alien expectations but which is not at all sentimental when seen in the context of Yiddish.

For how can we tell when a piece of writing is sentimental and when it is not? Any definition assumes a set of common emotional and perhaps philosophical attitudes at the base of a given culture. Suppose, however, what is indeed the case: that the attitudes governing one culture are very different from those of another. Suppose that what seems, for one culture, "an emotion in excess of the occasion" is not at all so for another culture. Suppose what may seem, for one culture, a sufficient evocation or a delicate embodiment will for another be merely a "reverent pointing." And suppose that in Yiddish culture there is a greater emotional permissibility, a greater readiness to welcome tears or laughter, than in American culture. The desperate reliance upon blandness and composure, the cult of understatement, the assumption that it is good to feel but bad to show one's feelings—these attitudes, familiar enough to us, are quite alien to the Yiddish ethos. Perhaps this means that the Yiddish is more primitive. Perhaps it means that the Yiddish is healthier.

We must remember that the vocabulary of literary criticism rests largely upon such unexplored assumptions of value; that such notions as "sentimentality" are not eternal constants but are radically shaped by the context of the culture in which they are used. Cultures which have learned to enjoy the taste of worldly dominance and success, which have been able to acquire a sheen of assurance and elegance, will naturally tend to favor different criteria for establishing the margin of permissible emotionality than those which live in the aura of suffering and martyrdom, concerned not with the style of this world but the promise of the next.

A mature literary taste will be open to both varieties of expression; will welcome the possibility of responding to new standards of feeling; will be more than cautious in assuming that a judgment of preference is necessary or easily made.

V: THE "CLASSICAL" PROSE WRITERS

The main lines of Yiddish literary history are firmly drawn: almost everything in the modern era stems from the "classical" trio of prose writers, Mendele, Sholom Aleichem, and Peretz. So dominant are their literary personalities, so powerful the thematic and stylistic precedents they established, that even those later writers who try to break away from them generally succeed in doing little more than confirm the very influence they would reject. The most important work of the "classical" trio was in prose—only somewhat later does poetry become a major force in Yiddish literature. And since this anthology is devoted to Yiddish prose, the role of poetry must, in any case, be scanted here.

Mendele Mocher Sforim (which means Mendele the Bookseller) is one of those transitional figures who appear at the beginning of all literatures: he gradually moves from critical exposition to imaginative narrative. His fiction, mainly short novels, is a blend of the satiric and didactic, written always with the intent of purifying the spiritual life of the Jews. Strongly influenced by the Haskalah, or Jewish Enlightenment, he tries to forge, like Joyce's hero, "the uncreated conscience of [his] race"—a phrase that might have alarmed him in its grandeur though it would more likely have elicited one of his satiric quips. In Jewish history this task had, to be sure, been undertaken many times before, but it is in the nature of human life, and especially of literary life, that it must always be done again.

Mendele said of himself that he was split between the pious Jew of the synagogue and the skeptic of the Enlightenment. In a revealing joke, bitter as only Jewish jokes can be bitter, he added that only God above hated the Jews as much as he below. The pioneer Yiddish critic, Baal Machshoves, has analyzed this two-sidedness of Mendele with considerable insight and sympathy:

> His best work has a kind of dual feeling: every line echoes with disdain for the Jewish life that is past and every chapter ends on a note of sadness that cries out with compassion. Mendele was repelled by the foolish and terrible life of the ascetic who is drawn to experience yet disdains its pleasures. He was repelled by the Jewish masses clinging to the dead past. He disdained a Jewish collective that could not produce a healthy Jewish individual. He saw everything. He observed every movement of the Jewish body, portrayed it in the most minute detail, ridiculed the behavior and appearance of his heroes. Nothing escaped him. But with all his disdain of the Jew toward himself, toward his way of earning a living, toward his whole mode of life, beneath all this one feels compassion, and not the compassion of the strong for the weak, the physician for the sick; it is the compassion of the mother for her child, ready to forgive him, while all she can do is to help him weep, hold him close to her heart, and suffer along with him.

Mendele's formulated purpose was to establish contact with the Jewish masses, to lift them out of the spiritual lethargy to which centuries of isolation had brought them. Like Chekhov, a writer with whom he had little else in common, his stories keep telling people, Live better. Mendele wrote:

> The life of the Jews, although it seems outwardly ugly and dark in color, is inwardly beautiful; a mighty spirit animates it, the divine breath which flutters through it from time to time. . . . Israel is the Diogenes of the nations; while his head towers in the heavens and is occupied with deep meditation concerning God and His wonders, he himself lives in a barrel. . . .

The sudden leap in this passage from celebration to mockery, perhaps the mixture of the two throughout the passage, is characteristic of Mendele's complex attitude toward the East European Jews. Unlike many Yiddish writers who follow him, Mendele never romanticizes, never glorifies, seldom succumbs to the idyllic mode. Yet of all the Yiddish writers he is the most deeply rooted in the Jewish world and the most firmly grounded in the Jewish tradition. His desire for spiritual renovation is motivated by a total and unambiguous devotion to the idea of Judaism—and this can hardly be said of the many Yiddish writers who were later to attack him for being so critical of Jewish mores and manners. Even the frequent acridness of his tone is a sign of a total commitment, of disappointed or despairing love. By contrast, a writer like Peretz, who returns to such folk materials as the Hasidic tales, is actually much further away from common Jewish life than the caustic, sharp-tongued Mendele.

Of the major Yiddish writers Mendele is perhaps least accessible to an alien reader: he is almost entirely an *internal* writer, so acutely conscious of his immediate audience and of the urgency of communicating with it that he takes more for granted, culturally speaking, than an alien reader is likely to grasp. His style is slow, meandering, reflective, and mock-ironic; it mirrors, with satiric faithfulness, the club-foot tempo of the *shtetl.* Yet it is Mendele who first forges Yiddish into a modern literary instrument, who creates the characteristic imagery of Yiddish literature, who teaches the Yiddish writers how to make the Hebrew component of the language do the work metaphor does in other literatures. His imagery is traditional, organic, deeply consistent with the life he depicts. When he describes a natural scene, it takes on, magically, a Jewish face: the trees sway like men in prayer, the woods become metamorphosed into a synagogue, everything is seen in terms of the traditional spirit. And never does he feel the modern need to separate himself from his materials or to write as if he were grandly dead, refraining from direct address to his readers: he is a man of powerful will, a serious man with serious ideas.

In Mendele's novels there are a wider range of typical *shtetl* character and a more complete notice of its typical experience than in any other writer. Somewhat surprisingly, he uses his own version of the picaresque: he was much influenced by Cervantes. Traditionally, picaresque portrays a vertical journey, a social ascent of the outsider who storms society by disregarding its formal morality. In Mendele, and later in Sholom Aleichem, picaresque is more restricted, charting primarily a *horizontal* journey that seldom goes beyond Jewish limits; the outer precincts, with their lures and threats, are superbly suggested but seldom presented—and this, again, because of the economy possible to a writer who works within a living tradition. Mendele has little interest in plot or structural niceties; his novels, which are sometimes organized around a contrast between a Yiddish Quixote full of spiritual grandiosity and a Yiddish Panza trying to find the unfamiliar earth, are strings of anecdote, occasionally varied by a use of pastoral to point up his criticism of a stultifying orthodoxy. In a way special to Yiddish literature, Mendele is a great writer, though the very elements that make him so valued in his own culture probably prevent his recognition in any other.

Sholom Aleichem, by contrast, is a man without didactic intentions or social ideology, one of those rare storytellers whose work sums up the outlook of a whole culture. Few writers have so completely captured the imagination of their people as Sholom Aleichem has that of the Jews. He is the property of the Jewish people as a whole, known and loved even by those on the borderline of literacy. He is the only writer of modern times who may truly be said to be a culture-hero—far more so than Mark Twain or Dickens,[9] whose popularity hardly rested upon any feeling among their readers that they were moral spokesmen; and certainly far more so than T. S. Eliot, about whom it should be said that the claims entered by his admirers have yet to be recognized by his culture.

In his humorous yet often profoundly sad stories, Sholom Aleichem gave to the Jews what they instinctively felt was the right and true judgment of their experience: a judgment of love through the medium

[9] Sholom Aleichem is regularly compared to Mark Twain and Dickens, but for no compelling reasons. Mark Twain is a humorist, so is Sholom Aleichem, so are many other writers. But in terms of local quality the two are very different; as, similarly, are Dickens and Sholom Aleichem. The only useful comparison to be made here is that between Sholom Aleichem and Dickens as public literary figures.

In both Dickens and Sholom Aleichem the gap between their best and inferior work is so wide that it cannot be put down to the usual variations of achievement to which any writer is subject; it must be seen as the price both of them paid for being simultaneously major artists and popular entertainers. This split is neither so deep nor disastrous in Sholom Aleichem as it is in Dickens, if only because the circumstances causing this split in Sholom Aleichem's world were not yet so deep and disastrous as those in Dickens' world. Despite his fabulous popularity Dickens did not enjoy so central a position in English culture as Sholom Aleichem did in the Yiddish, for by the mid-nineteenth century England had already become too heterogeneous, too industrialized, to allow any single writer to speak fully or comfortably in its name. Toward the end of Sholom Aleichem's career one can see, however, those very factors at work which had made for the astonishing split between the Dickens of *Bleak House* or *Hard Times* and the Dickens who immortalized Little Nell.

of irony. Sholom Aleichem is the great poet of Jewish humanism and of Jewish transcendence over the pomp of the world. For the Jews of Eastern Europe he was protector and advocate; he celebrated their communal tradition; he defended their style of life and constantly underlined their passionate urge to dignity. But he was their judge as well: he ridiculed their pretensions, he mocked their vanity, and he constantly reiterated the central dilemma, that simultaneous tragedy and joke, of their existence—the irony of their claim to being a Chosen People, indeed, the irony of their existence at all.

Sholom Aleichem's Yiddish is one of the most extraordinary verbal achievements of modern literature, as important in its way as T. S. Eliot's revolution in the language of English verse or Berthold Brecht's infusion of street language into the German lyric. Sholom Aleichem uses a sparse and highly controlled vocabulary; his medium is so drenched with irony that the material which comes through it is often twisted and elevated into direct tragic statement—irony multiplies upon itself to become a deep winding sadness. Many of his stories are monologues, still close to the oral folk tradition, full of verbal by-play, slow in pace, winding in direction, but always immediate and warm in tone. His imagery is based on an absolute mastery of the emotional rhythm of Jewish life; describing, for example, the sadness of a wheezing old clock, he writes that it was "a sadness like that in the song of an old, worn-out cantor toward the end of Yom Kippur"—and how sad that is only someone who has heard such a cantor and therefore knows the exquisite rightness of the image can really say.

The world of Sholom Aleichem is bounded by three major characters, each of whom has risen to the level of a Jewish archetype: Tevye the Dairyman; Menachem Mendel the *luftmensch;* and Mottel the cantor's son, who represents the loving, spontaneous possibilities of Jewish childhood. Tevye remains rooted in his little town, delights in displaying his uncertain Biblical learning, and stays close to the sources of Jewish survival. Solid, slightly sardonic, fundamentally innocent, Tevye is the folk voice quarreling with itself, criticizing God from an abundance of love, and realizing in its own low-keyed way all that we mean, or should mean, by humaneness. As the Yiddish critic I. I. Trunk has put it: "The greatest merit of Sholom Aleichem is that he succeeded in embodying the idealistic element of Jewish history in the character of the *shtetl* folk—the ordinary little Jewish people."

Tevye represents the generation of Jews that could no longer find complete deliverance in the traditional God yet could not conceive of abandoning Him. No choice remained, therefore, but to celebrate the earthly condition: poverty and hope. For if you had become skeptical of deliverance from above and had never accepted the heresy of deliverance from below, what could you do with poverty but celebrate it? "In Kasrilevke," says Tevye, "there are experienced authorities on the subject of hunger, one might say specialists. On the darkest night, simply by hearing your voice, they can tell if you are hungry and would like a bite to eat, or if you are really starving." Tevye, like the people for whom he speaks, is constantly assaulted by outer forces. The world comes to him, most insidiously, in the form of undesired sons-in-law: one who is poverty-stricken but romantic; another who is a revolutionist and ends in Siberia; a third—could anything be worse? —who is a gentile; and a fourth—this *is* worse—who is a Jew but rich, coarse, and unlearned.

Menachem Mendel, Tevye's opposite, personifies the element of restlessness and soaring, of speculation and fancy-free idealization, in Jewish character. He has a great many occupations: broker, insurance agent, matchmaker, coal dealer, and finally—it is inevitable—writer; but his fundamental principle in life is to keep moving. The love and longing he directs toward his unfound millions are the love and longing that later Jews direct toward programs and ideologies. He is the utopian principle of Jewish life; he is driven by the modern demon. Through Tevye and Menachem Mendel, flanked by little Mottel, Sholom Aleichem creates his vision of the Yiddish world. Tevye, writes Samuel Niger, "is Sholom Aleichem's Sabbath; Menachem Mendel his workday week." Perhaps so; it is a lovely way of saying it. But what would Tevye be without Menachem Mendel, or Menachem Mendel without Tevye?

There is a strong element of fantasy, even surrealism, in Sholom Aleichem. Strange things happen: a tailor becomes enchanted, a clock strikes thirteen, money disappears in the synagogue during Yom Kippur, a woman's corpse is dragged across the snow, a timid little Jew looks at himself in the mirror and sees the face of a Czarist officer. Life is precarious, uncertain, fearful, yet always bound by a sense of togetherness and affection.

Middleton Murry once said of Thomas Hardy that "the contagion of the world's slow stain has not touched him." This magnificent remark must have referred to something far more complex and valuable than innocence, for no one could take Hardy to be merely innocent; it must have referred to the artist's final power, the power to see the world as it is, to love it and yet not succumb to it; and this is the power one finds in Sholom Aleichem.

Peretz is the most programmatic writer of the "classical" trio, the ideologue of Yiddishism, the student of European thought and literature. His home in Warsaw was the informal center of Yiddish literary life, to which all the young writers came, seeking advice, guidance, inspiration. Where Mendele and Sholom Aleichem were loved by the masses, Peretz was the hero of the intellectuals. He was fortunate enough, however, to live at a time when the divergence in taste between the masses and the intellectuals had not yet gone too far, so that if not quite so popular a folk hero as Mendele or Sholom Aleichem, he was still greatly honored and respected. As the Yiddish writer who most creatively balances himself between the claims of the traditional and the modern, Peretz stands halfway between those writers who retain a firm hold on the popular audience and those who no longer retain any sense of audience at all. With the passage of time he seems constantly to gain in stature.

Concerned with the reconstitution of the Jewish community, which he saw turning from the Divine Presence to a secular European perspective, Peretz wished to find mundane equivalents for those values that the sacred tradition could no longer sustain. His nationalism was no longer dominantly religious, nor based on the usual sanctions of the national-state; it was a culture-nationalism, and his vision of the "good Jew" is similar in quality to the nineteenth-century idea of the "good European." Peretz represents, at its highest level, a Yiddish version of that liberal humanism and secular idealism which characterized the best minds of Europe in the late nineteenth century. But it must be remembered that the nineteenth century, as we think of it, did not yet exist for the East European Jews: it had to be created for them. As the Yiddish poet Jacob Glatstein remarks in a brilliant essay, Peretz brought into Yiddish life "that restlessness, that fever, that coil of problems" we associate with the nineteenth century. And Peretz understood very well the special responsibilities and burdens that his status as cultural innovator placed upon him. One reason he served most of his life as an official of the Warsaw Jewish community was his belief that the cultural leader must submit himself to the check of those he leads. "All of us can be criticized publicly, especially the writer," he once said, "for he speaks to the public and therefore belongs to the public. It used to be said that the work and not the author should be criticized. But the public has the right to demand that from time to time the supplicant remove his prayer shawl so that it can see who prays in its behalf and who blows the *shofar* for it."

In his earlier stories Peretz faced both ways: outward, toward the skills of European literature, which he appreciated more than any of his Yiddish contemporaries; and inward, toward the heritage of the folk, which he would soon rework with fascinated eagerness. His earlier stories are mostly realistic, reminiscent of Chekhov though more lyrical and virile in tone. His style represents a distinct break from that of Mendele and Sholom Aleichem. Gone is the rich accumulation, the slow and leisurely winding. Peretz writes with the plastic rapidity, the transparent nervousness, that characterize so many modern authors. The rhythm of Mendele and Sholom Aleichem is the rhythm of a sleepy *shtetl;* the rhythm of Peretz is the rhythm of Jewish Warsaw.

In these early stories, often colored by themes of social revolt or of indignation over the decay of Jewish communal life (see "The Dead Town"), Peretz comes closer to individual characterization than any of his Yiddish contemporaries. The community, the mass, recedes into the background, and in its place he focuses upon *typical individuals,* though not yet the fully and uniquely individualized figures of modern literature. His people stand somewhere between the archetype and the fully formed character: a hopeless youth, as in "The Mad Student," torturing himself with his inadequacy, a pair of young lovers dreaming of happiness in a dismal Gorki-like cellar, a gentile doctor exhausting his rationalist ideals in a conflict with a backward *shtetl.*

In Peretz's later and more important stories he reworks folk and Hasidic themes in a way that appears to be folklike but is actually the product of a sophisticated literary intellect. As he retells and deepens these stories, Peretz the modern intellectual, the man who measures the distance between himself and the pieties to which he turns, is always, though unobtrusively, in sight. Peretz's use of Hasidic materials has been excellently described by Isaac Rosenfeld:

> The pragmatic stamp is on every word. The tone of wonder is given by the intelligence and not by the Hasidic awe it represents. Peretz shares the faith of which he writes but at a considerable remove, and it does not rest for him in the objects or efficacies of the Hasidic mystique, nor does it express a natural piety of utterance, as with prayer; his is a borrowed piety, taken from the intelligence, adept at translating one mode into another.

But in the end Peretz must always part company with the Hasidic wonder-workers, for he cannot really share their oneness of vision.

His story "If Not Higher" reads like a parable of his own literary situation: the skeptical Litvak, who may be seen as a persona of Peretz himself, finally recognizes the saintliness of the Hasidic rabbi, but he sees it as a *secular* saintliness; he worships the rabbi as a moral hero rather than as an accomplice of God, and this is very likely a kind of discipleship the rabbi would not accept. The Hasidic emphasis on joy Peretz would make his own, but he cannot really give himself to the source and spring of Hasidic joy.

Accordingly, to quote Isaac Rosenfeld again, Peretz "took the Hasidic ecstasies not as ultimate things, visions in the midst of appearances . . . but rather as the immediate phenomena in a radiance of this world." His vision, that is, was strictly historical, even though he dealt with materials their Hasidic authors would have insisted were profoundly non-historical. From Hasidism, Peretz tried to extract its life-strength, without finally crediting its source. The attempt was impossible, but because he so thoroughly knew this, Peretz transformed these seemingly simple folk stories into fascinating parables of a dilemma that was not his alone.

For analytical purposes it is possible to speak of Peretz the early realist, Peretz the Yiddishist, Peretz the Jewish communal leader, Peretz the reteller of Hasidic stories. To us, these roles would seem inevitably to require a fracture of literary personality or at least a strain so intolerable as to exact a painfully high price. But it is a testimony to the integrity of Yiddish culture, and to Peretz's own integrity, that he was able to integrate these roles in a unified public personality. He was the last Yiddish writer to be equally at home in the past and the present, the traditional and the modern, the folk and the literary. It did not, and could not, happen again.

VI: LATER GENERATIONS, LATER STYLES

Since this Introduction does not profess to be a history of Yiddish literature or an outline for such a history, there is no need to follow the many paths that were soon beaten from the central tradition of Mendele, Sholom Aleichem, and Peretz. Despite its youthfulness and the constrictions of its setting, Yiddish literature has managed to take over almost every Western literary mode and style. Examples of naturalism, impressionism, surrealism, expressionism, and traditionalism can all be found in the Yiddish prose and poetry of the past fifty years. Whether these terms mean very much when applied to Yiddish literature is another matter. For in the process of borrowing there is a transmutation so complete that these categories of Western writing are seldom helpful to a study of Yiddish literature. It therefore seems more profitable to notice the later developments of Yiddish prose in terms of literary generations and national centers.

The generation that followed the "classical" trio was remarkable first for its sheer creative energy and productivity, and then for its readiness to expend that energy in a passionate struggle with the very tradition which formed it and to which it remained tied with bonds of filial love. Such writers as Sholem Asch, David Pinski, I. M. Weissenberg, and Zalman Schneour appeared on the Yiddish literary scene only a short time after Peretz became its dominant writer and spokesman; many of them were directly encouraged by him and regarded him as their master; but almost all broke from his tutelage and tried to find ways of discarding the thin elegiac style, the bare linear story, the leisurely winding rhythm, the ethic of *edelkeit,* the anti-heroic Jewish hero—in short, the kind of sweetly ironic pantomime that Abraham Reisen, among this generation of Yiddish writers, was to make uniquely his own. There were many important differences of outlook and method among these writers, and a close study would have to focus upon these differences; but for our present sketch they may be seen as a fairly homogeneous generation that brought to Yiddish prose a number of new elements:

A wider range of subject matter, including themes borrowed from Western literature and not significantly present in the work of Mendele, Sholom Aleichem, and Peretz.

The discovery of social layers in the *shtetl,* which the earlier writers had passed by, and of the whole new world of Jewish big-city life.

A readiness, and sometimes an eagerness, to expose themselves to the influence of modern European writing as a counterforce to their native tradition.

A willingness to deal not merely with Jewish experience in Eastern Europe but also with universal themes that transcend or undercut the Jewish experience.

A celebration of energy as a principle of human life, and particularly of Jewish life, in opposition to the attachment of the earlier writers to the values of reflectiveness and endurance.

At about the turn of the century there appeared two Yiddish novelettes, both called *Dos Shtetl.* One was written by Sholem Asch, the other by I. M. Weissenberg. The Asch novelette, though at least a step removed from the manner of Mendele or that of Peretz, still portrayed the *shtetl* in romantic, idyllic terms: a patriarchal air prevails, nothing has really changed. The Weissenberg novelette opened a new world: Jewish workers come together to express their discontent, issue proclamations, organize strikes—the social struggle has begun to creep into the moldy villages of the Pale. A few years later David Bergelson, who came of age shortly after the turn of the century, was writing his exquisite short novels in which the *shtetl* has begun slowly to decay: the old aristocracy is now aware of its own obsolescence, a class of vulgar *nouveau riche* is pushing its way to the top, uprooted intellectuals float along the shores of social life—it is the familiar modern world, gray and desperate.

Other innovations in subject matter came rapidly, and with them a new Yiddish style: coarse, vivid, thick, erotic. Sholem Asch and Joseph Opatoshu turned to the life of the Jewish underworld, Asch in his episodic novel *Mottke Gonef* (*Mottke the Thief*), and Opatoshu in a group of stories about Jewish horse thieves. These works oscillated rather curiously, and sometimes charmingly, between realistic and romantic motifs: on the one hand, the desire to portray the Jewish underworld in all its blunt misery, and on the other, a sense of how exciting and exotic it was that there should be a Jewish underworld at all. David Pinski wrote tender little stories that introduced the new Jewish proletariat of the towns and cities, bewildered and broken by poverty and uprootedness. His characters ranged from *shtetl* Jews forced to become workers yet struggling to preserve the psychology of the *shtetl* householder, to militant proletarians who celebrate May Day with revolutionary ardor. Zalman Schneour was one of the first to introduce themes of erotic passion into Yiddish literature. In his book of connected stories *Shklover Yidden* (*Jews of Shklov*) he showed Jews in the grip of animal instincts, a theme that did not figure prominently in the writings of Sholom Aleichem and Peretz. And a host of writers introduced romantic love, not, however, with very great success.

Sholem Asch discovered new human resources among the East European Jews. His story "Kola Road" has become famous in Yiddish literature as a celebration of the *proste,* the common folk, and the *grobe yungen,* the vulgar and ignorant who live at the bottom of the Jewish world. I. M. Weissenberg joined in this celebration not from any particular sense of social vindication but from his love for the humorous and promiscuous energy of these little-noticed Jews, the butchers and porters and teamsters, with their physical prowess and passions, so striking in their contrast to the pale little heroes of Peretz and Reisen. Zalman Schneour, always ready to praise the release of impulse, has written a preface to his novel *Noah Pandre* that is a kind of ode to the under-half of the *shtetl:*

Where are you now, you Jews like oaks, with your broad-capped jack boots and squashed, burned noses like those of lions? You coachmen, butchers, water-carriers, plasterers, hewers of wood. . . .

You were always redolent of forests, cart grease, corn flour, fresh hides. Even on the Sabbath eve, after you had come from the baths and had crept into your fine cloth gaberdines and surtouts—grown tight since your wedding day—you gave off a smell of birch and bark and the plenty of a full week. You held your prayer books gingerly as if they were fluffy yellow chicks, held them with the tenderness and compassion of strong men, and piously swayed over them. And with the same callused and scarred fists you tossed five-hundredweight loads out of the barns onto your carts and from your carts into the barns as if they were balls of wool. . . .

They called you ignoramuses. You sat meekly and submissively by the western wall of the synagogue, next to the door. You waited for years before they called you up to the Law, a gift flung down at you from the reading desk like a well-gnawed bone. . . .

If drunken peasants started a fight on market day you ran to help the poor weak shopkeepers, you defended the widows who sell gingerbread and vegetables . . . and then you went to jail because you had protected the others.

It has become the custom, in speaking of this generation of Yiddish writers, to describe many of them as naturalists. Yet one may wonder whether this term has any pressing relevance to what these writers were actually doing. If by naturalism one means the effort to write a novel upon "scientific" principles in the manner of Zola or those theories of biological and social determinism associated with Dreiser, then few, if any, of the Yiddish writers who appeared during the first two decades of the century qualify as naturalists. For where Western naturalism implied a closing in upon life by forces beyond human control, these Yiddish writers were concerned with expressing their sense of an opening up of life, a joyous primitive discovery of new possibilities in physical impulse, personal experience, and social struggle. If by naturalism one means the literary strategy of relentless accumulation, then again few of these Yiddish writers could be called naturalists: Jewish life was not socially "thick" enough to require naturalistic documentation. Only if subjects of social rebellion and settings of plebeian squalor are meant—but surely this is not confined to any literary mode!—can writers like Asch, Weissenberg, and Schneour be spoken of as naturalists. They simply cannot be placed intelligently if one uses ready-made categories of European literature. Their work must be understood, first of all, as a complex and uneasy response to the major tradition of Yiddish prose, and, second, as an effort to bring into Yiddish literature wider ranges of modern experience.

But even as these writers drew away from the Yiddish masters, they remained far more subject to the "classical" tradition than they supposed. Like Sholom Aleichem and Peretz, they simply could not conceive of literature as a mere exercise in objective portrayal; they continued to think of it as a moral release, a collective expression. But now they chose new objects for celebration. Where Peretz celebrated, in his story "The Cabalists," a pious student who fasted to death in search of the Godhead, Asch and Schneour celebrated the lusty Jewish roughnecks who ate with iron appetites. These writers felt that the time had come to put blood and muscle into Jewish life, to revive the idea of heroism and battle. Whether they were right or wrong does not matter; what matters from a literary point of view is that in turning their eyes downward, to the lower depths of the Jewish world, they wrote with the same commitment to the idea of consecration that characterized the work of Peretz when he turned his eyes upward. In both instances the romantic impulse, which can never be entirely absent from the literature of an oppressed people, was deeply at work.

In retrospect, the prose writers who first came to prominence during the early years of the twentieth century appear to be the sacrificial generation of Yiddish literature. They rebelled; they experimented; they turned outward, away from the staleness of the *shtetl* and toward the fresh air of the fields and the excitement of the cities; they sought new sensations, new experiences; they opened themselves to history. And unavoidably they paid a price. Today the work of Sholom Aleichem and Peretz seems fresher and more immediate than the work of many Yiddish writers who were swept away by the European *Zeitgeist* of fifty years ago. A good portion of the writing of that time, which once seemed so bold, now seems merely of historical interest. Whenever Yiddish writers tried to do what the Western writers had long been doing they seldom did it quite as well, and even if they had, the result would not have been as interesting. To be sure, the work of such writers as Asch, Weissenberg, Schneour, and Opatoshu is firmly embedded in Yiddish literature. And such writers as David Bergelson and Lamed Shapiro have become major figures in modern Yiddish prose, successfully blending traditional themes with sophisticated techniques. But upon the generation as a whole, despite its very great talent, time has left a mark.

With World War I, Yiddish literature reached a turning point. The three dominant literary figures—Mendele, Sholom Aleichem, Peretz —died during the war years; old age had come to them, and the new times seemed bewilderingly alien to every standard by which they had lived and worked. Their funerals occasioned spontaneous outbursts of the love the Jewish masses felt for them. More than seventy-five thousand people came to Peretz's funeral in Warsaw, a similar number to Sholom Aleichem's in New York. In no other modern culture did the death of its leading writers arouse so intimate a response; in no other modern culture did the leading writers still *matter* so deeply.

Once the Russian empire was broken up, Yiddish literature split into three main sectors: Polish, Russian, and American. Paradoxically Yiddish literature of the "classical" period, though barely subsisting in the crevices of Czarist Russia, had nonetheless managed to express an international—or at least a non-nationalist—outlook. Mendele and Sholom Aleichem set their novels and stories in poor provincial villages, but by virtue of a symbolic concentration these villages came to stand for *a* human condition. The muddy streets, the shabby huts, the dilapidated synagogues—these enclosed both the reality and the aspirations of Jewish life. Precisely because the world they described was still outside or barely on the margin of modern history, Mendele and Sholom Aleichem were not stained by the idea of European nationality. Their work drew its impetus from the sublime incongruity between Jewish experience and Jewish ideal; hardly at all from the inhibiting prejudices of a fractured Europe.

Now, however, Yiddish literature began to take on special and distinct traits in each of its three national centers.[10] For one thing, the

[10] Efforts were made to improvise Yiddish cultural centers in various other countries, but despite certain individual achievements these usually came to little. As S. Niger has written: "Unfortunately the naturalization papers, which the Jewish immigrant hastens to procure, do not quite carry with them an acquisition of the nature of the new land or people, and in the Mexican or Cuban landscape which he paints lurk the hills, if not the mudflats, of his native Bessarabia or Poland. The very natural desire of the Yiddish writer to take root as quickly as possible in his new soil often leads to artificiality and to the very opposite of this desire, namely to superficiality." ("New Trends in Post-War Yiddish Literature," *Jewish Social Studies,* July 1939.)

free movement of Jewish populations was no longer possible: immigration to America was sharply curtailed, while Russia permitted neither immigration nor emigration. In Russia, except for brief intervals of tolerance, the Yiddish writers were cut off from every manifestation of Yiddish culture in the outer world. By contrast, the Yiddish writers of Poland and America maintained close relations with one another; the Yiddish press in America provided one of the main literary markets for the writers living in Poland, and a good many of the latter migrated to America as the possibilities for working or even surviving in Eastern Europe kept drying up. But despite an inevitable overlapping of subject and style, the distance between Yiddish writing in America and in Poland grew steadily larger.

Until the Nazi invasion, Poland remained the world center of Yiddish culture. Jewish life in Poland between the wars had something of the brilliant feverishness, the violent mixture of material poverty and intellectual restlessness, that we associate with life in the Weimar Republic. Always on the edge of dispossession and terror, the Jews strove to maintain their integrity as a people who could claim to have developed one of the most remarkable, if also most neglected, cultures of our time; and the very sharpness of the ideological and literary disputes that tore at the Jewish community of Poland testifies to the fact that life and passion and creative energy were still there.

The winds of literary modernism kept coming steadily from the West. Paralleling the rise of expressionism in postwar Europe, one group of Yiddish writers founded the magazine *Die Chaliastre* (*The Gang*) in which Yiddish approximations of the expressionist style were to be found. Another group, calling itself "Young Vilna," responded eagerly to the postwar European temper of restlessness and homelessness. Other young writers turned to a realistic documentation of Jewish working-class life in the large Polish cities. Perhaps the major literary achievement of the period—though it can be put down to the credit of American Yiddish writing as well, since the leading figures lived in both countries—was the creation of the full-scale modern Yiddish novel. I. J. Singer in *The Brothers Ashkenazi* and Sholem Asch in *Three Cities* set the pattern for those massive architectural novels through which Yiddish writers have since tried to portray the historical sweep and social density of East European life. These writers, though they focused upon the Jewish milieu, did not confine themselves to it. Like the social novelists of Europe, they tried to see modern society as a complex organism, with a "life" of its own, a destiny that superseded and sometimes canceled out the wills of its individual members.

At the same time Yiddish writing in Poland retained far more of the traditional manner and emphasis than Yiddish writing in either Russia or America. Despite its technical experiments, its turning to themes not exclusively Jewish, its readiness to share with other European literatures in the postwar moods of nihilism and bleakness—despite all this, Yiddish literature in Poland, particularly the prose, still showed the firm paternal influence of the "classical" writers. And for one reason above all: the *shtetl* continued to be the main setting, and therefore the dominant theme, of Yiddish fiction in Poland. The *shtetl* experienced a miniature revolution, it shook and trembled before the blows of the modern world, it was no longer the moldy *shtetl* of Mendele or the idyllic *shtetl* of Sholem Asch, but somehow it survived. The younger Yiddish writers spared it not an ounce of bitterness or harshness, yet it remained the fundamental unit of Jewish life, and of Yiddish literature, in Poland. As long as it survived, the *shtetl,* in the words of I. I. Trunk, was "the symbolic fatherland of Polish Jewry." And so long as that "symbolic fatherland" figured as the dominant image, if only as an object to attack, Yiddish literature necessarily retained something of its earlier "classical" tone.

In Russia everything was different. After the February Revolution of 1917, Russian Jewry no longer had to suffer the humiliation of the anti-Jewish laws, which two years earlier had been made so severe as to prohibit the publication of books with Yiddish characters. Until the end of 1924 Yiddish literature developed in an atmosphere of relative freedom, and it is no exaggeration to speak of a flowering of Yiddish poetry and prose during those years. Yiddish literary groups were formed in Moscow, Minsk, Kharkov, and Kiev, of which the last and most important was headed by David Bergelson. From 1922 to 1924 a magazine called *Shtrom* (*Stream*) was published in Moscow; it declared itself "a literary and art monthly . . . containing contributions from the best Yiddish writers, poets, and artists from Moscow, Kiev, Warsaw, Berlin, and New York. *Shtrom* aims to unite all responsible Jewish creative elements that are today forging the aesthetic values of our epoch." What seems most remarkable in this statement is that, in sharp contrast to the Russian campaign against "cosmopolitanism" during the late 1940s, a Yiddish magazine in Moscow could openly declare its solidarity with the Yiddish writers of Warsaw and New York—which meant, unambiguously, to recognize the existence of an international Yiddish literature with norms and themes not necessarily determined by the Russian revolutionary experience. Partly because it was still possible, in the era of revolutionary internationalism, to maintain a free exchange of ideas and impressions with Yiddish writers in the non-Soviet world; partly because the Yiddish writers in Russia were not yet strangled by dictatorial political censorship; partly because the Russian Revolution aroused the hope in many Yiddish writers that it would root out the causes of anti-Semitism—for these reasons, but not for these alone, Yiddish literature thrived. During its two years *Shtrom* reached a level of quality and sophistication that Yiddish writing in Russia never saw again.[11]

At the end of 1924, however, sweeping changes occurred: the era of Neanderthal party literature began. Not only was the content of Yiddish literature controlled with the same lumbering fanaticism as the content of Russian literature, but measures of exceptional severity were taken to root out the "petty bourgeois psychology" that was said to be especially strong among Yiddish writers. An attempt was made to cleanse the Yiddish language of its traditional and bourgeois locutions. Phrases recalling religious ceremony, terms drawn from Hebrew, words suggesting the life of commerce, were all proscribed. A deliberate and successful effort was made to seal off the Yiddish writers from their colleagues abroad. As N. Osylander, a Yiddish critic, wrote: "Why continue to weave the thread of a universal Yiddish literature when the Revolution has shattered the whole traditional Jewish social structure?" Yiddish literature soon became subject to the corrupting formula, "Socialist in content, national in form," which in practice meant party propaganda in emasculated Yiddish.

Nonetheless, the talent of the more important Yiddish writers was so genuine, the afterglow of the *Shtrom* period so attractive, that certain impressive achievements must be credited to those Yiddish literary men who struggled to remain writers in Russia between 1924 and 1941. Of these David Bergelson and Moishe Kulbak have been included in this book. Bergelson, who did his finest work during the pre-revolutionary period, again emerged as a major figure, writing several novels that demonstrate his absolute mastery of Yiddish prose. Kulbak wrote a novel called *Zelmenyaner,* a wry account of the way a Jewish family tries and fails to adapt itself to the new regime. Though

[11] The facts about Yiddish literature in Soviet Russia are to be found in Elias Schulman's "Die Sovietishe-Yiddishe Literatur, 1918–1948," in *The Jewish Book Annual,* Vol. 9, 1950–1951. Also see the same author's "Yiddishe Literatur in Sovieten Farband," in *Getseltn, a Yiddish Review,* Winter 1949.

far from indulgent in his treatment of this family, Kulbak, as a writer of severe integrity, could not avoid a certain veiled ridicule of the regime—and probably for this unspeakable crime he was among the first to disappear when the Stalinist government began purging Yiddish writers during the late 1930s.

During World War II, Yiddish literature was granted a provisional reprieve. Between 1941 and 1946 Yiddish writers turned out standard poetry and prose about heroic guerrilla fighters, Nazi atrocities, and Russian patriotism. Many of these, no doubt, were produced upon government demand, but some quality of raw feeling does come through, if only because Yiddish writers did not need to be prodded into hatred of Hitler. For all their earnestness, however, the Yiddish writers produced very little work of literary distinction—and the exceptions are almost all the work of older writers who had retained a certain sense of literary complexity and subtlety. Isolated for almost two decades, the Yiddish writers of Russia fell behind those of Poland and America. The development of Yiddish literature in the West was barred to them, and as a consequence their work was usually primitive in both content and technique. Literature may not always need complete freedom to survive, but it needs *some* freedom; it cannot, in any case, survive in the atmosphere that led Itzik Feffer, the commissar of the Yiddish literary world, to write:

> When I mention Stalin—I mean beauty,
> I mean eternal happiness,
> I mean nevermore to know,
> Nevermore to know of pain.

Which did not, of course, prevent Feffer's being purged together with the other Yiddish writers.

In the late 1940s Yiddish literature in Russia suffered a fate almost as terrible as that which it had suffered several years earlier at the hands of the Nazis. The drive against "cosmopolitanism," with its sickening anti-Semitic undertones, soon put an end to Yiddish literary activity. The publication of Yiddish books ceased. Most of the Yiddish writers disappeared. Nothing remained, nothing but silence.

There is still, however, a flicker of Yiddish literary activity behind the Iron Curtain, if not in Russia itself. In Rumania some Yiddish schools are tolerated, and in Poland about thirty Yiddish books were published in 1953, including works of Sholom Aleichem and Peretz—

with the predictable introductions by Stalinist critics. Whether this remnant of Yiddish literature will be allowed to survive, or will be doomed to the fate it has suffered in Russia, remains to be seen.

America has now become the last stronghold of Yiddish culture; here poets and novelists work without impediment and sometimes, alas, without an audience. A few of the Yiddish writers who managed to escape the holocaust of Europe have settled in Israel, but most have come here. Yiddish literature now has its international center in New York.

Yiddish writing in America first began to appear during the last few decades of the nineteenth century. Barely influenced by or aware of the Yiddish masters in Eastern Europe, the early writers were frequently sweatshop workers in New York and almost always extremely poor. Many were socialists or anarchists who used their verses, with an innocent didacticism, to rouse the exploited Jewish garment workers. They seldom wrote about the old country, for they seldom had any roots in traditional Yiddish culture. They sacrificed their genuine talents on the altar of their idealism. Such writers as Z. Libin and Leon Kobrin, in their ashen portraits of the Jewish worker, and Morris Rosenfeld, in his frequently stirring lyrics, tried to rouse the social consciousness of their haggard audience, to stir a spark of rebellion in its heart. These writers were close to the Jewish masses—indeed, part of their trouble as writers was that they were too close. Their work seldom achieved any aesthetic distance from the world it described; it reflected with a dismal, sinking literalness the spiritual impoverishment of Jewish life in late nineteenth-century New York. Still struggling for command of the word, these writers were overwhelmed by their subject, their environment, their problem. Some talented work remains, above all the lyrics of Morris Rosenfeld, but too much of it was marked by its special moment to have survived it.

Another and far more important generation of Yiddish writers appeared in America shortly before World War I. Floating on the surf of mass migrations from Eastern Europe, they enjoyed a deeper sense of the Yiddish tradition than the writers of the Rosenfeld-Libin generation. Where the earlier Jewish immigrants had been cut off from both old world and new, those who came to America between the turn of the century and World War I were so numerous and so coherent in their cultural attitudes that they re-created, in the dark tenements of the Lower East Side, something of the old country. Soon, of course, the Lower East Side, which was to become the heart of American Yiddish culture, acquired a quality of its own: it blazed with an intense literary activity, a mass socialist movement, and a profound striving for education and "improvement." The writers who were spiritually akin to this new wave of immigrants, and who profited from the excitement and vitality of its life, knew the "classical" Yiddish masters and were familiar with the more recent developments in European Yiddish writing. They stood at a crossroads in Yiddish culture: between *shtetl* and tenement, Europe and America, and both lent color and tension to their work. Their writing was characterized by a note, almost always satisfying, that was to be heard again and again in American Yiddish writing: the sense of belonging to two cultures, of having two homes, the old and the new. Writers like Yehoash and A. Lyessin not only became more conscious of their Jewish heritage but also began to experiment with poetry more personal in tone.

Many of the most gifted among them banded together in a group that called itself "Die Yunge" ("The Young Ones"). Influenced by the symbolist and impressionist schools of both Germany and Russia, they rejected the monolithic social emphasis of the earlier Yiddish writers in America, as well as the ethic of *edelkeit,* the bequest of the "classical" Yiddish writers. They insisted upon the autonomy of the creative experience, the necessity for each writer to discover his own theme and his own style, and the possibility of exploring areas of subject matter not previously touched by Yiddish writers. "Die Yunge"—which included the poets Moishe Leib Halpern, Mani Leib, and H. Leivick, as well as the prose writers Joseph Opatoshu, David Ignatoff, and A. Raboy—spoke in the name of "pure art" or aestheticism, but in retrospect the formal terms of their revolt did not express its actual meaning. Rather, they were rebelling along lines significant mainly to Yiddish literature itself, rebelling, that is, against the abstract didacticism of earlier Yiddish writing in America and working toward a new style that would break away from the "classicism" in Europe. Their modernism, often accompanied by the hijinks inevitable in any group of lively young writers, was far from unconditional; each of these writers, as he later went his independent way, retained something of what he learned from his youthful brush with modernism, yet almost all of them returned to traditional Jewish themes. Yiddish culture, by the very terms of its existence, allows only a limited receptivity to modernism, and many of the Yiddish literary revolts conducted in its name actually have had little to do with the avant-garde experiments of Western literature.

During the twenties and thirties the generation of "Die Yunge"—the group itself had disappeared—reached its creative maturity and did some of the best work American Yiddish literature can claim. Other literary groups also sprang up. The "In Sich," or Introspectionist poets, headed by A. Leyeles, Jacob Glatstein, and N. B. Minkoff, rebelling against the lyricism of "Die Yunge," employed free verse and preferred cosmopolitan themes. A "proletarian" tendency appeared during the thirties, producing work similar to that written in English. Meanwhile, of course, many Yiddish writers—like Lamed Shapiro and Peretz Hirschbein—went their own way, publishing their books, trying to survive, struggling with the terrible problem of writing for a constantly shrinking audience.

Though such important Yiddish novelists as Asch, Singer, Opatoshu, and Schneour have spent part of their time in America, it is in poetry that recent Yiddish literature in America has excelled. If such Yiddish poets as Moishe Leib Halpern, H. Leivick, J. I. Segal, Melech Rawitch, Itzik Manger, Jacob Glatstein, and Aaron Zeitlin—to mention only a few—were known in adequate translation, they would be discussed with the intensity that students of literature reserve for European and American poets.

Why recent Yiddish prose has not quite kept pace with Yiddish poetry is a problem requiring a fuller discussion than is here possible. But one hypothesis may be suggested: the Yiddish prose writers of the past two or three decades have found it increasingly difficult to locate their subject matter. In America they find themselves trapped between two subjects: the old world that has been obliterated, the new world they do not always firmly command. And the blunt truth is that Yiddish prose in America has scored greater successes in drawing recollected portraits of *shtetl* life than in its efforts to capture the elusive qualities of Jewish experience in America. But now that the *shtetl* is gone . . . For the poets this dilemma provides a usable and moving theme; but prose needs more than a theme. It needs a "world" that can be circled and probed and shaped.

The recent years have been painful and hard for the Yiddish writer. Yiddish literature has not recovered from the Nazi experience, and it is doubtful that it ever will or has any right to. When the Jews of Eastern Europe were being destroyed by the millions, the Yiddish writers drew together, not from a blasphemous belief that such horrors could be "dealt with" in literature, but in an instinctive gesture of solidarity and mourning. The Yiddish writers returned, along the path of nostalgic romanticism, to the world that had been destroyed.

Still numbed by the Hitler experience, Yiddish writers have suffered another blow, not comparable in kind or severity but in some ways even more painful, since it has come from within the Jewish world. The creation of Israel as an independent state, though it aroused great political hopes among Yiddish writers, brought intense disappointment and controversy. For the State of Israel, through a variety of semi-official devices, has discouraged the use of Yiddish among its citizens. The language is looked down upon for the very reason that Yiddish writers cling to it so fiercely and with so desperate an affection: because it is the language of the Jewish "dispersion," stained by exile, defeat, and martyrdom.

Nonetheless, Israel remains an important center of Yiddish culture. Over half a million Jews who live there still speak Yiddish, and about half of the Israeli population understands it. A number of important Yiddish writers—A. Sutzkever, David Pinski, Isaiah Spiegel, and many others—now live in Israel, and an excellent Yiddish literary quarterly, *Die Goldene Kait,* edited by the poet Sutzkever, is published there.

Yiddish literature survives. In New York, in London, in Tel Aviv, in Paris, in Buenos Aires, in Mexico City, in Johannesburg, Yiddish books and magazines continue to be published. The Yiddish audience makes up for its smallness by its admirable devotion. But it is a final tragic irony that a literature which began with the most fluent intimacy between author and audience should survive as the property of isolated circles of authors and readers, who cling to a language which for them is not only history but the answer to history.

What the future of Yiddish as both language and literature will be, no one really knows. Prediction and speculation are possible, but this is not the place for either. Our concern here is not with the future, not with prophecy. It is with the past, with the life and the warmth that come to us when we turn to the pages of Mendele, at the beginning, and Chaim Grade, at the end. Whatever the future, their past is certain. They wait for us, ready to speak, if we will only hear them.

IRVING HOWE
ELIEZER GREENBERG

Notes on the Authors

Mendele Mocher Sforim (1837-1917)

MENDELE MOCHER SFORIM ("Mendele the Bookseller") was the pen name of Sholom Jacob Abramovitz, the patriarch of Yiddish literature. Born into a Lithuanian rabbinical family, he received a traditional Jewish education at various yeshivas. At seventeen he broke away from the life of pious scholarship and joined a group of wandering beggars with whom he visited many communities in the Pale. Somewhat later he settled in the town of Kamenets Podolsk, where he completed his education and became a partisan of the Haskalah, or Jewish Enlightenment.

Mendele's literary career falls into three stages. After writing in Hebrew for a decade, he began to feel a need for employing the language that the masses of East European Jewry used in their daily life —Yiddish. After 1864, while continuing to work in Hebrew, he wrote regularly in Yiddish, despite the fact that many of his intellectual contemporaries looked upon Yiddish as a corrupt jargon unworthy of serious uses. The very pen name he chose indicated his desire to penetrate the minds and hearts of the Jewish masses, for in those days the traveling bookseller was often a carrier of knowledge, both religious and secular, as well as a kind of living newspaper.

Mendele then proceeded to write a series of short novels, which were to prove a decisive influence upon Yiddish literature. (For a critical discussion of his work see the Introduction.) His more important Yiddish novels include *Dos Kleine Menshele* (*The Little Man*), a sharp satire on Jewish community life; *Die Takse* (*The Tax*); *Fishke der Kruhmer* (*Fishke the Lame*), in which he drew upon his experience with the wandering beggars; *Die Klyatsche* (*The Mare*), an allegory of Jewish history; and *Benyomin Hashleshi* (*Benjamin the Third*), a satirical novel about Jewish idealism.

Because most of Mendele's writings are too long for inclusion in this anthology, it is impossible to provide an adequate selection of his work. But "The Calf" does show his typical blend of idyll and allegory. Beneath the surface of the story there churns a barely suppressed bitterness, a resentment against the deprivations suffered by Jewish boys who, like himself, had been taken away from the fields to bend and yellow over religious tomes. The death of the calf thus becomes equivalent to the death of spontaneity and youth.

Sholom Aleichem (1850-1916)

THE GREAT natural genius of Yiddish literature, Sholom Aleichem, was one of the very few modern writers who could be said to speak for an entire people. (His real name, by the way, was Sholom Rabinowitz; Sholom Aleichem, his pseudonym, means "Peace be unto you" in Hebrew and is traditionally used as a greeting among Jews.) Born in Russia, he began writing in Hebrew at the age of fifteen; two years later he was supporting himself as a teacher of Russian; at twenty-one he was appointed "Rabbiner"—government rabbi, a post seldom making great demands on piety—in a town in the province of Poltava.

He married the daughter of a wealthy landowner, and after his father-in-law's death became the administrator of a large estate, which brought him into close relations with the upper-class Jews of Kiev. In 1900 he retired from business to devote himself entirely to his writing. After the 1905 pogrom in Kiev, he left Russia. For a time he lived in Switzerland and made extensive lecture tours through Europe and America. When World War I broke out he fled to Denmark, and from there to America, where he settled in 1914. He died two years later.

Sholom Aleichem's literary production was enormous. From his first Yiddish story, "Tzvei Shteiner" ("Two Stones"), published in 1883, until the autobiography upon which he was working at the time of his death, there was a steady stream of some forty volumes of stories, novels, and plays. (For a critical discussion of his work, see the Introduction.)

The seven Sholom Aleichem stories in this book have been chosen with an eye to presenting a variety of his themes and manners. "On Account of a Hat," here translated into English for the first time, shows his gift for making a seemingly innocent anecdote into a remarkably shrewd and poignant evocation of the whole social position—the constant burden of peril—of the Jews. In "Eternal Life" he tells a profoundly skeptical story about the wages of altruism, which contains a strong undertone of the gruesome as a parallel to the comic surface; at least in the original Yiddish one can detect a touch of the Gogol influence that threads its way through most of his work. "Hodel" is taken from Sholom Aleichem's masterpiece, the series of stories built around the figure of Tevye the Dairyman; it exemplifies his highly disciplined gift for blending the comic and pathetic into a tone of humaneness. This humaneness—one might speak of irony as humaneness—also characterizes the little story called "Dreyfus in Kasrilevke," which shows the innocent Jews of Kasrilevke (the imaginary site of many Sholom Aleichem stories) simply unable to believe that the world could harbor so much injustice as to allow the conviction of Dreyfus. And in "The Search," Sholom Aleichem has written a complex story about the relationship between worldly and other-worldly values in *shtetl* society: the young man subjected to the search is disgraced at the end, yet his disgrace is used to point up a triumph of other-worldliness.

The last two Sholom Aleichem stories in this book represent additional modes of composition. "The Pair," translated here for the first time into English, displays an experimental side of Sholom Aleichem that is little known: Sholom Aleichem the allegorist, trying to communicate through symbolic indirection what many of his stories present directly. And "A Page from the Song of Songs," which is part of a group of children's stories, is Sholom Aleichem at his most purely lyrical, celebrating Jewish childhood.

I. L. Peretz (1851-1915)

ISAAC LEIB PERETZ stands at the intellectual center of Yiddish culture and literature. Born in Poland, he was exposed while still a boy to that conflict of ideas and impulses which was to dominate his mature life as writer and intellectual leader: the conflict between traditionalism, as embodied in a powerful Hasidic inheritance, and modernism, the new trend of secular-progressivist thought that was beginning to sweep through the world of East European Jewry. Peretz began his career as a lawyer and maintained a prosperous practice for almost a decade. At twenty-seven he published his first book, a volume of Hebrew poems, and from then on he devoted himself increasingly to literature. Though he became the guiding spirit and architect of modern Yiddish literature, he never abandoned Hebrew, and as a matter of fact was thoroughly at home in the literatures of several languages.

In the 1880s Peretz settled in Warsaw and became an official of the Jewish community. For the rest of his life he remained active in Jewish affairs, often to the detriment of his writing: he toured the provinces of Russia and Poland to collect statistics about Jewish economy, he participated for a brief time in the Jewish Socialist movement, and he served as editor of the *Yiddishe Bibliothek,* an important annual that published a wide range of articles on secular subjects.

The Peretz stories chosen for this anthology help suggest something of the scope and quality of his work. "Devotion without End," one of his longest narratives, is a lovely fable, written in somewhat archaic Yiddish; it serves both as a consummate expression of the values that dominate Yiddish literature—the love of Torah, the ineradicable possibility of forgiveness, the necessity for moral resurrection—and as a major example of Peretz's gift for enriching and complicating folk themes. This gift is also to be seen in "If Not Higher" and "Bontsha the Silent," two of his best-known stories, which are folk tales in origin yet clearly reveal the hand of a sophisticated artist—in the subtle distance from faith that is maintained in the first story and in the desperation with which the second one ends. "The Cabalists" also shows the writer's feeling of tension with regard to a tradition he can neither wholly accept nor reject.

"The Dead Town," one of Peretz's earlier stories, begins in a somewhat Chekhovian manner but quickly moves into something else, a kind of grotesque fantasy; it is one of the most mordant criticisms ever made of Jewish life by a Jewish writer. In another early story, "The Mad Student," Peretz has tried to blend religious materials with psychological themes; using the monologue form and employing a half-brilliant, half-mad dialectic that is extremely difficult to render into English, he set a tone which was later to be echoed by those Yiddish writers employing psychological realism.

Of the remaining Peretz stories, "Rabbi Yochanan the Warden" is a wry little morality; "Ne'ilah in Gehenna" is cleverly humorous; and "The Golem" is a cryptic little parable on the decline of faith, the loss of ancient wisdom, the dust of skepticism.

David Pinski (1872-)

PLAYWRIGHT, novelist, and storyteller, David Pinski was born in Russia. After a youth spent in Moscow and Vienna he went to Warsaw, where he came under the personal and literary influence of I. L. Peretz. Pinski was one of the first Yiddish writers to identify himself with the Jewish Socialist movement and to portray the life of the Jewish working class as it was beginning to emerge in such cities as Warsaw and Lodz at the end of the nineteenth century. Later he emigrated to America, where he was active in the Labor Zionist movement. He now lives in Israel.

After his early proletarian stories Pinski turned to erotic themes, writing stories and plays about the power of passion to shape and misshape human life. Some of these plays were widely produced; one of them, *The Treasure,* was staged by Max Reinhardt in 1911. Pinski also used historical Jewish subjects, seeking to find in them the distinctive element of Jewish heroism. More recently he has written stories about the destruction of the Jewish community in Europe.

Pinski's historical importance in Yiddish literature is considerable: he was a pioneer in introducing new subject matters. Reread today, it is his earliest stories that seem most fresh. "And Then He Wept" is an example of the compassionate tenderness the young Pinski was sometimes able to communicate in writing about the Jewish poor.

Mordecai Spector (1858-1925)

MORDECAI SPECTOR was one of those Yiddish writers who, in another cultural situation, might have published best-sellers. After rejecting an almost fanatical Hasidic background, Spector turned to writing Yiddish tales and novels. His first book, *A Roman un a Nomen* (*A Novel without a Name*), appeared when he was twenty-five, and from that time on his popularity among plain Yiddish readers grew rapidly. Toward the end of his life Spector left Eastern Europe and came to America, where he worked for several Yiddish papers.

Spector had a gift for homely colloquial expression, and this made him a favorite with readers for whom Peretz was too cryptic and Mendele too bitter. Most of Spector's writing lacks intellectual edge, and his Yiddish is often crude and impure; but amid the half-forgotten mass of his popular pieces there are a few, like "A Meal for the Poor," which strike an authentic note of Yiddish humor and suggest that his popularity was not merely that of the popularizer.

Sholem Asch (1880-)

SHOLEM ASCH, the most widely translated and most controversial figure of contemporary Yiddish literature, was born in Poland. Like many other Yiddish writers, he began writing in Hebrew as a youth, but under the influence of Peretz he turned to Yiddish at the age of twenty, and from then on has employed Yiddish as his means of literary expression.

Asch soon broke out of the boundaries of the distinctively Yiddish manner: his *shtetl* is not the *shtetl* of Peretz or Sholom Aleichem; it is no longer seen in exclusively Jewish terms. Asch brought to Yiddish literature the idea, or impulse, of soil romanticism; he was one of the first, indeed one of the few, Yiddish writers to value passion as a desirable quality in itself. As a stylist he is far from being in the first rank of Yiddish prose writers. His use of Yiddish is often clumsy and impure, being too heavily alloyed with Germanic elements.

A tremendously prolific writer whose work includes novels, plays, stories, and essays, Asch achieved his first major success in 1904, when he published *Dos Shtetl* (*The Town*), a rich genre picture of typical Jewish life in Eastern Europe. Asch's literary development has gone through many stages. Among his earlier, and perhaps his best, works are *Mottke Gonef* (*Mottke the Thief*), an episodic and somewhat picaresque novel about the Jewish underworld, and *Kiddush Hashem* (*Sanctification of the Name*), a narrative of Jewish heroism and martyrdom. Later he turned to social novels, moving far beyond his original *shtetl* locale, as in *Three Cities,* a panoramic account of Jewish life in pre- and post-revolutionary urban Russia. More recently he has written such best-sellers as *Mary* and *The Nazarene,* efforts to find a religious reconciliation between Judaism and Christianity, which have made him a highly controversial figure in the Jewish world. Simply as novels, and quite apart from their religious intention, these later books do not compare very favorably with Asch's early work. It is only fair to add, however, that the Judaeo-Christian tinge of his recent books, which has evoked such sharp criticism from Jewish circles, can be found embryonically in his earliest work.

Asch acknowledges Dickens and Tolstoi as his masters, but it is only occasionally that one can detect the influence of either. He seems to have been most influenced, once he ceased being a strictly Yiddish writer and became an international one, by the general conception of the social novel that prevailed in European literature some four or five decades ago. He builds his novels—even his stories—on an epic scale, striving most of all for elemental sweep and movement; he is a thoroughly romantic writer.

The first Asch story chosen for this anthology, "Sanctification of the Name," is a dramatic legend celebrating Jewish martyrdom: it concentrates into a few pages a recurrent theme of Yiddish literature. The second story, "Kola Street," is also typical of Asch's earlier work, reflecting the rebellion, by the generation of Yiddish writers following Peretz and Sholom Aleichem, against what they felt to be the excessive refinement and thinness of their predecessors. In "Kola Street" it is rough —yet Jewish—brute strength that is apostrophized, the energy of the Jewish artisans and storekeepers, their readiness to meet the enemy on the enemy's terms. The third, "A Quiet Garden Spot," is a little sketch, almost a fable, of the typical patterns of immigrant family life in America.

Abraham Reisen (1876-1953)

ABRAHAM REISEN, born in Russia, came from a family with a strong intellectual tradition and from a culture where adult responsibilities had to be assumed in early or middle teens. In his youth Reisen identified himself with the Jewish Socialist movement, and many of his lyrics sound a gentle note of protest. He died in New York, an undisputed favorite among Yiddish writers.

The hundreds of stories Reisen wrote—he was published at an early age—are mostly in the tradition of *edelkeit,* a tradition of moral refinement and delicacy. The central figures of the stories are more often archetypal than individual—for example, the poor but proud householder struggling to maintain himself in the life of the *shtetl.* In "The Big Succeh" we see him enjoying a brief victory; in "Tuition for the Rabbi" he suffers from a moral quandary; in "The Poor Community" his traits are distributed among several characters. The mood of "The Ascetic" is somewhat darker and more dramatic, as if to acknowledge those depths and passions that seldom fully appear in Reisen's stories.

Reisen's work is notable for a fragile delicacy of tone. He does not use a heavy pencil, he evokes rather than portrays. Some of his little stories—muted, barely plotted, without verbal tinting—have become almost legendary materials, or hints, of the Jewish imagination.

I. M. Weissenberg (1881-1937)

IN HIS youth Isaac Meier Weissenberg was an ordinary workman in Warsaw and Lodz. Stimulated by the renaissance of Yiddish literature in Poland at the beginning of the twentieth century, Weissenberg turned to writing stories; he was soon welcomed as a powerful and genuine voice from the depths of Jewish life. Weissenberg remained a poorly educated man throughout his life and developed theories by which to justify his strong suspicion of intellectuality. His stories are elemental explosions of feeling that remind one of the stories Gorki wrote as a young man.

Some critics describe Weissenberg as a realist or naturalist, but neither term is quite accurate. When he stops to portray misery, he does seem to have some affinity with naturalism, but anyone who reads "Father and the Boys"—a story that created an uproar in the Yiddish world when it first appeared—will see that his work is streaked with a naïve romanticism, a sense of the perpetually wonderful in a newly discovered world.

Once the reader puts aside expectations of structural unity and tonal consistency—expectations Weissenberg cannot satisfy and hardly cares to—it is possible to enjoy "Father and the Boys" as a half-violent, half-comic protest against the tone of restraint and refinement that dominated Yiddish literature in its "classical period." Instead of piety and ethical reflection, Weissenberg exalts instinctual energy; the *Yiddishe mame* becomes a blowzy, baby-smothering hag; the Jewish patriarch is transformed into a good-natured lout. But even as he rebels against the traditional modes of Yiddish literature, Weissenberg betrays a charming, sometimes humorous innocence, and in his sketch "Mazel Tov" this tenderness is fully released.

Zalman Schneour (1887-)

LIKE A number of other Jewish writers, Zalman Schneour writes in both Yiddish and Hebrew. Born in White Russia, Schneour began writing at nine; by fifteen he was publishing Hebrew poems. His best-known Yiddish works include *Shklover Yidden* (*Jews of Shklov*), a group of related stories about *shtetl* life, and *Noah Pandre,* a picaresque novel about a Jewish tough. Schneour now divides his time between Israel and America.

Unlike most of his predecessors in Yiddish literature, Schneour concentrates on the life of the senses rather than the life of contemplation, on violent action rather than delicate analysis. He was one of the first writers to introduce sexual themes into Yiddish literature; and he was one of the first to relish the coarse, peasantlike ways of the unlearned Jews, those *grobe yungen* who lived at the bottom of the *shtetl* world and were so seldom noticed by Sholom Aleichem, Peretz, and Reisen.

"Revenge," a story about the aftereffects of a pogrom, may seem melodramatic to some tastes, but one must remember that its theme is terribly real to both Yiddish readers and Yiddish authors. The story is distinguished by a bitter ironic climax, the very ineffectuality of the narrator's hope for revenge providing the necessary aesthetic and moral comment on the emotional accumulation of the bulk of the story. "The Girl," Schneour's second story in this anthology, also has a suggestive ending, this time a hint of sexual deviation, which complicates the meaning of the story and points to a possible Western influence. What might have been a dreary report of human squalor is given a certain carefreeness by Schneour's zest for the amoral vitality of his characters.

Lamed Shapiro (1878-1948)

ONE OF the most meticulous craftsmen in Yiddish literature, Lamed Shapiro wrote relatively little, but the stories he finally consented to publish after much revising and refining immediately established him as a major force among the younger Yiddish writers. Born in the Ukraine, Shapiro published his first story in Warsaw at the age of twenty-five. Later he went to London, and in 1906 emigrated to the United States. His first book of stories, *Oifn Yam* (*On the Sea*), which appeared in 1910, was strongly influenced by the Scandinavian realists. During the early stages of his career Shapiro was known primarily as the author of violent pogrom stories, such as "Der Tselem" ("The Cross") and "Der Kush" ("The Kiss"); but he came to feel that these and similar pieces were too crudely written, and he gradually widened the range of his subject matter and perfected his style.

Shapiro was one of the first "art" writers in Yiddish prose, one of the first, that is, to study and model himself after such masters of European Impressionism as Chekhov and Flaubert. From Chekhov he learned the possibility of employing tone as the unifying principle of a story; from Flaubert he learned the virtues of objectivity and economy. Shapiro's best stories are remarkable for their tightness of structure, their electrical terseness of style, their power of compressed metaphor. While many of them deal with *shtetl* life, they are far removed from the folk manner of early Yiddish literature. Their subject matter is rooted in the past; their mode of organization is entirely modern.

In "The Rebbe and the Rebbetsin," Shapiro evokes—through traditional Yiddish idyll but with a compression quite foreign to it—the aura of an entire way of life. "White Chalah" is a story of a pogrom seen not through the eyes of Jewish victims but as a sternly objective report on a tongueless peasant who comes to seem the personification of primitive violence. "Smoke," in a few sharply elliptical pages, presents the Jewish merchant of half a century ago, one foot in the synagogue and the other in the city. And in the long story "Eating Days" we see the richest and most mature expression of Shapiro's talent: a story that records the breakup of the traditional Yiddish world through the sufferings of a yeshiva student torn between spiritual and worldly appetites.

Moishe Kulbak (1896-?)

ONE OF the most gifted and enigmatic of Yiddish writers, Moishe Kulbak is known for both his poetry and prose. Born in Russia, he studied at various yeshivas, and in his youth began writing poems. He moved on to novels, stories, and plays. In 1920 Kulbak went to Berlin, where he lived in great poverty, haunting the museums and libraries. Three years later he became a teacher in Vilna, and in 1928 he went to Soviet Russia. Kulbak kept publishing until 1936, almost always in a tone certain to irritate the Russian officials and their representatives in the Yiddish cultural world; all of his writings contained an edge of satire and independence that marked him off from those Yiddish writers who merely repeated the current variation of the party line. In 1937 Kulbak disappeared, apparently "liquidated." No word has since been heard about his fate.

In tone if not technique, Kulbak was strongly influenced by Mendele Mocher Sforim. Though he abandoned Mendele's slow oral narrative, he retained the older writer's bitterness, his power of wry criticism.

Kulbak is sometimes classified as an expressionist, and in his splendid novel *Montik* (*Monday*)—a slyly satiric picture of how the Russian revolution descends upon a sleepy *shtetl*—there is something of that selective distortion one associates with expressionism. But no literary tag does much justice to his work, which is a highly individual and rather strange mixture of realism and fantasy, wry comedy and subdued mysticism.

"Munie the Bird Dealer" suggests something of Kulbak's characteristic sense of the way the human creature proves himself both ridiculous and tragic. Similar in theme but not in treatment to Bashevis Singer's "Gimpel the Fool," it depicts the collapse of a Jew whose life is almost indistinguishable from the peasants among whom he lives. The portrait of the bird dealer gains its strength from the elements that surround him—from the constant chirping of the birds, which suggests the meaningless continuity of animal life, and from the blows of the weather, which are described in powerful metallic images, to suggest the abrasive pressure of the non-human upon the human.

I. J. Singer (1893-1944)

ISRAEL JOSHUA SINGER is the author of a series of massive social novels about Jewish life in Eastern Europe, the best known of which have been translated into English as *The Brothers Ashkenazi* and *East of Eden*. Another of his novels, *Yoshe Kalb* (*The Sinners*), a portrait of a sainted fool, was dramatized with great success by the Yiddish Art Theatre in New York.

Born in Poland, the son of a rabbi, Singer was brought up in traditional Jewish fashion. His first book of stories, *Pearls,* came out in 1923 and attracted wide notice among Yiddish readers throughout Europe. A steady output of novels followed, each encompassing a major arc of Jewish experience. Singer came to America in 1939 and died five years later.

Singer's books are built upon spacious architectural principles. One of the more "modern" Yiddish writers, he organizes his work in a way that satisfies the usual Western expectations as to literary structure. His novels resemble the kind of family chronicle popular in Europe several decades ago, but because of the youthfulness of Yiddish literature and its relative indifference to formal experimentation, one does not feel in Singer's work that he is employing a literary mode close to being exhausted.

In his use of Yiddish, Singer avoids both the rhetoric "elevation" and the colloquial scrappiness that sometimes beset Yiddish fiction. His prose is polished, smooth, and even-textured. Among modern Yiddish styles, his comes closest to setting the standard for an accomplished "middle" style—and in a language that has seldom reached stability this is a genuine achievement.

The two stories by Singer in this anthology diverge somewhat from the norms of his larger works. "Sand" is a sumptuous piece of writing, rather loose in structure, but vivid in its painterly rendering of small-town Jewish life. "Repentance" is sparer in style and subtler in content. On one level this story celebrates the earthiness and joy of the Hasidic rabbi and his followers, but through the fine suggestiveness of its ending it shows that the Hasidic rabbi has become so obsessed with the *idea* of joy that he is ruthless in his devotion to it. "Repentance" thus becomes one of the subtlest criticisms of Hasidism to be found in Yiddish literature.

Jonah Rosenfeld (1882-1944)

IN THE work of Jonah Rosenfeld the problems of abnormal psychology, which have so absorbed modern writers, receive perhaps the first sustained treatment to be found in Yiddish literature. Rosenfeld was born in Russia, orphaned as a child, and apprenticed as a turner in Odessa. He worked for some years without showing literary inclinations, but in his early twenties, encouraged by Peretz, he began to write. His first sketch, dealing with Jewish working-class life, appeared in 1904; eight years later he published his first full-length novel, *In der Shtil* (*In the Quiet*). In 1921 he came to New York, where he lived until his death.

Almost all of his writings are deeply embedded in moods of anxiety. Fear, madness, horror, foreboding, the destructive powers of erotic obsession—these are among Rosenfeld's characteristic themes. The sense of collective consciousness, so dominant in the work of the founding fathers of Yiddish literature, gives way to a sense of irrevocable aloneness. Rosenfeld's interest in pathology is not, however, clinical; it is the result of an implicit conviction that men are driven by instinctual forces they can neither understand nor control.

The narrator-hero of "Competitors" is a "superfluous man," a descendant of those pious Jews who allowed their wives to become the breadwinners so they could devote themselves to the study of the Torah undisturbed. But now the husband has neither social nor religious place: even his role of attendant is being challenged by his daughter. Harsh and grim, the story flits unevenly, like a scarred film, from synoptic scene to synoptic scene; a particularly powerful moment is the one in which the narrator goes through his pantomime to suggest his need for new clothes. "The Sick Goose" is not distinctively Jewish in subject matter, but the treatment does show qualities unique to Yiddish literature. One begins by expecting a mood painting, somewhat like Sherwood Anderson's "Death in the Woods"—night, fear, death, a gray chiaroscuro. These elements are certainly present, but Rosenfeld avoids the expected dramatic accumulation and prefers to let the rhythm of his story rock back and forth, as if swayed by an argumentative undertone, a pattern of Talmudic discourse dimly present in some recess of the central character's consciousness.

I. Bashevis Singer (1894-)

THE YOUNGER brother of the novelist I. J. Singer, Isaac Bashevis Singer was born in Poland, received an orthodox Jewish education, and in 1926 became a journalist for the Yiddish press in Warsaw. Nine years later he published *Shotan in Goray* (*Satan in Goray*), which contains a number of highly imaginative stories as well as the title novelette, an account of false Messianism in seventeenth-century Eastern Europe so rich in internal references as to be virtually untranslatable. Bashevis Singer has also written a long novel, which appeared in English as *The Family Moskat*, and has translated many books into Yiddish from Hebrew, Polish, and German, among the last Thomas Mann's *The Magic Mountain*. Since 1935 he has lived in New York.

His stories are like a series of sudden illuminations of grotesque elements in experience, of the eerie and the wildly fantastic. Deeply learned in Hasidic and cabalistic lore, he brings to play upon Jewish life of several centuries ago—as upon contemporary Jewish life—a mind that reveres and delights in religious customs and emotions, yet is simultaneously drenched in modern psychological skepticism. His style is swift and dramatic, avoiding the oratorical sententiousness to which Yiddish literature is sometimes prone. He is at his best in short forms, exciting bursts and flares of imagination.

"Gimpel the Fool" begins as comedy but soon rises to a deep sadness and tragic statement. The story has an obvious kinship with Peretz's "Bontsha the Silent," but Bashevis Singer has taken the theme of the sainted fool—a favorite theme in Yiddish literature—and made it uniquely his own. "The Little Shoemakers" sums up the whole of contemporary Jewish experience: from tradition to modernity, from the old country to the new, from the ghetto to the camps. A blend of nightmare and fantasy, the story is a kind of dramatic poem commemorating the death of a civilization.

Joseph Opatoshu (1887-)

IN HIS highly productive career Joseph Opatoshu has lived through almost all the phases and mutations of the brief history of Yiddish literature. Born in Poland, Opatoshu received a Jewish education from his father, and attended a commercial school in Warsaw. In 1907 he emigrated to the United States. Seven years later he was awarded an engineering degree, but his career as a writer, which was soon to absorb his full energies, had already begun: he published his first story in 1910, and from then on wrote many stories and novels. He now makes his home in New York City.

Opatoshu began his career by writing harshly naturalistic stories about the coarsening of Jewish morality on the Lower East Side and somewhat romanticized though highly vigorous narratives about the Jewish underworld in Poland before World War I. Later he turned to historical novels; in the 1930s he wrote proletarian fiction reflecting the mood of the time; and more recently he has written many short sketches, bare to the point of fable, which have as their aim a spiritual renovation of Jewish life in America. His best-known novel, *In Poilishe Velder* (*In Polish Woods*), which has appeared in English, Polish, German, and Hebrew translations, is a sweeping account of Jewish life in mid-nineteenth century Poland; *A Tog in Regensburg* (*A Day in Regensburg*), written in archaic Yiddish, is one of the few fictional attempts to capture the Jewish experience of the Middle Ages; and *Pundika Retivtah* (*The Inn*) is set in Palestine during the Roman occupation.

The two sketches chosen for this anthology can hardly suggest the range of his effort, but they do contain themes typical of his later writings. "The Eternal Wedding Gown" expresses a yearning, common to many Yiddish writers, for the survival of the traditional religious values; while "May the Temple Be Restored!" is a subtle variation on a major theme of Yiddish literature: the virtues of the fool. This time the fool is the Jewish horse-dealer whose belated grief over the fall of the Temple betrays his ignorance but also demonstrates his capacity for spontaneous religious emotion.

Moishe Nadir (1885-1943)

MOISHE NADIR was a highly versatile writer who specialized in mocking feuilletons, surrealist comedy, sharp polemic. He was blessed with a highly cultivated sense of the absurd—and did not hesitate to use it.

Nadir, whose real name was Isaac Reiss, left his native Galicia for America at the age of fourteen. His vast output—he was published at seventeen—includes verse, dramatic criticism, stories, reportage, and translations into Yiddish from Hauptmann, Heine, Anatole France, and Peter Altenberg.

Though he lacked the self-discipline that might have made possible a full climax to his career, Nadir made a major contribution to Yiddish literature: he glorified and enriched the language. He was a master of Yiddish vernacular, and precisely for this reason his work is extremely difficult to translate, being full of puns, neologisms, jokes, and word plays that depend for their meaning on an intimate knowledge of Yiddish. But he did demonstrate to colleagues sometimes too concerned with theme and not enough with technique that written Yiddish could be an infinitely plastic and colorful medium of expression—as plastic and colorful as spoken Yiddish itself.

"My First Love" shows Nadir relaxing into romantic nostalgia and then quickly tensing into irony. While telling this mock idyll about six little boys who loved the same little girl, Nadir also delivers some sharp blows against the *shtetl*—his powerful chalk-white images suggesting the deprivations of a life he felt had been too frequently idealized. The little sketch that appears in a later section of this book is more characteristic, an example of his weird and caustic imagination.

Itzik Manger (1901-)

ITZIK MANGER, born in Rumania, is known to Yiddish readers primarily as a poet. At fourteen he was apprenticed to a tailor. At seventeen he was writing Yiddish verses, and soon he became one of the best-known Yiddish poets in Europe. Blending traditional Jewish themes with a highly sophisticated, modern sensibility, Manger has used the ballad form with particular effectiveness, sometimes making of it a kind of dialogue between past and present, promise and reality. Since the rise of nazism, Manger has led a wanderer's life, living for a time on the Continent, then in England, and more recently in New York.

"The Adventures of Hershel Summerwind" is part of a projected group of tales in which Hershel is to recall his scrapes as a boy in the world of East European Jewry. As the ending of the story indicates, Manger has used the traditional form of oral Yiddish narrative, but he largely eliminates the traditional religious and didactic elements. The story stands in sharp contrast to most Yiddish writing about children (see "A Page from the Song of Songs" by Sholom Aleichem and "My First Love" by Moishe Nadir in this book, with their undercurrents of sadness and bitterness). Manger, almost alone, writes about Jewish childhood in the accents of lightheartedness.

David Bergelson (1884-?)

THOUGH hardly known to the non-Yiddish public, David Bergelson is a major figure in modern Yiddish literature. He is a novelist and stylist of remarkable gifts.

Bergelson was born in Russia, the son of a well-to-do merchant. His early stories were too subtle in content and style to receive immediate recognition. But while a student at the University of Kiev he wrote *Arum Vokzal* (*Near the Railway Station*), a novelette that quickly brought him to prominence in the Yiddish literary world. In 1913 he published the novel *Noch Alemen* (*After All*), unquestionably an outstanding achievement of Yiddish prose. It is the story of the slow disintegration of a wealthy Jewish family in a Ukrainian town; its heroine, restless and "modern," is treated somewhat in the manner of Flaubert's Madame Bovary.

In 1921 Bergelson left Russia and settled in Berlin to become a regular correspondent for the New York *Jewish Daily Forward.* In 1926 he started *In Shpan,* a journal that maintained that Yiddish literature must be inseparable from the Jewish working masses.

After his return to Russia in 1933 Bergelson tried to write "positive" stories about Jewish life in the "new world." Many of these have a certain technical finish, but they lack the inner conviction, the aura of creative integrity, that shine through his earlier portraits of social decay. There are extant, however, two volumes of an unfinished trilogy, *Penek*, which deals with the post-revolutionary period in a manner that brings into sharp juxtaposition an imposed ideology and Bergelson's own acute sense of human loneliness and division.

During World War II he produced "patriotic" fiction according to the formula of "socialist realism." In recent years Bergelson, together with many other Yiddish writers, has disappeared from the Russian scene. Where he is now, whether he is still alive, remains unknown.

Most of Bergelson's best work is set in pre-revolutionary Russia. Influenced by Knut Hamsun but more frequently resembling Chekhov in his ability to evoke the atmosphere of decay through delicate understatement and indirection, Bergelson is a master at depicting the gradual breakup of the Jewish middle class and intelligentsia in provincial Russian towns. The story translated for this anthology, "In a Backwoods Town" is characteristic of this phase of Bergelson's career. In this world of moral twilight, all the leading characters have been touched, or bruised, by urban manners; yet they return, in their sloth or avarice, to a crumbling, corrupted *shtetl,* where the forms of piety prevail but the content has been eaten away. In status the leading character of the story is a rabbiner, or government rabbi, but in condition he is a *déclassé* intellectual.

Bergelson's effects depend not on plot or action but on a beautifully controlled style, quiet and subtle, barely ironic in its undertones, entirely free from rhetoric and flamboyance. He is outstanding among Yiddish writers for his sure sense of syntax and phrasing, and his mastery of its untranslatable inflections and rhythms.

Isaac Metzker (1901-)

ISAAC METZKER, born in eastern Galicia, came to the United States at the age of twenty-three. He lives in New York City and contributes fiction to the Yiddish press. His writing—perhaps his best-known work is the novel *Erd un Zun* (*Earth and Sun*)—is notable for the low-keyed lyricism and affection with which he treats rural life.

Metzker is one of the few Yiddish writers to describe the experience of Jewish farmers in Eastern Europe, and, in doing so, he reveals a strong feeling for the soil. His most recent novel, *Dem Zehden's Felder* (*Grandfather's Acres*), continues in this vein.

"To the New World" presents characters who also feel a strong bond with their native place; but gradually there appear alien and disrupting forces, the village community begins to lose its sense of identity, and as a result the first wave of emigration to America can be seen slowly taking shape.

Pesach Marcus (1896-)

BORN in Lithuania, Pesach Marcus came to the United States as a young man and embarked on a dual career of businessman and writer. He has published two books of short stories, and is currently working on a long trilogy about Jewish life in Lithuania. The first volume of the trilogy, *The Vilna Goan,* has appeared in book form and the second volume has been serialized in the Yiddish press. Marcus's writing is steeped in knowledge of traditional Jewish piety and lore.

In the story "Higher and Higher," Marcus has attempted a condensed expressionist portrayal—it cannot be understood in ordinary realistic terms—of a whole span of Jewish experience in America, the experience of the man who climbs the economic ladder only to find himself falling into the depths.

Jacob Glatstein (1896-)

JACOB GLATSTEIN came to New York from Poland at the age of eighteen and was educated at New York University. He is a versatile writer who has published several volumes of distinguished poetry, a book of critical pieces, a good many stories, and two highly regarded personal narratives describing his return to Poland in the late thirties, *Ven Yash Iz Geforen* (*When Yash Went Away*) and *Ven Yash Iz*

Gekuhmen (*When Yash Arrived*). This narrative, which is to form a trilogy, includes reflections, reminiscences, autobiography, interwoven stories, and sketches of Jewish life in Poland before World War II. They reveal Glatstein as a writer of considerable intellectual power, as does, incidentally, his poetry—he was one of the founders of the Introspectionist (*In Sich*) group. His book of criticism, *In Tokh Genuhmen* (*Sum and Substance*), is one of the few serious efforts to deal with Yiddish literature in strictly aesthetic terms.

"The Return" is taken from *Ven Yash Iz Gekuhmen.* Through the frail figure of the precocious Hasidic student the story suggests that even before Hitler invaded Poland the Jewish community was beset by the same crises of belief that have troubled the Western world. The young Hasid thinks he has found the way to the Jewish masses, but it is only a hallucination; over his brilliance hangs the threat of tomorrow's concentration camp; and meanwhile the more he goes into ecstasies about the beauties of faith, the more precarious does his faith seem.

The figures summoned by the boy in his fantasies are historical: the Bratzlaver, a saintlike leader of Hasidism; Jacob Frank and Sabbattai Zevi, false Messiahs of the seventeenth century who ended as apostates.

Isaiah Spiegel (1906-)

ISAIAH SPIEGEL is one of the very few Yiddish writers who lived through the martyrdom of Polish Jewry under the Hitler occupation. He published his first book of poems at the age of twenty-four, and since then he has issued five volumes of short novels and stories. Spiegel spent the war years in Poland, part of the time in concentration camps and part of the time in the Warsaw ghetto. Somehow he managed to survive the holocaust, and is now a citizen of Israel.

During the past decade he has written stories that deal mainly with the destruction of the Polish Jews. His work is notable for its restraint in handling the most terrible subject matter of our time and for mirroring the destruction of a people in the tragedies of individuals.

Like most of Spiegel's stories, "The Ghetto Dog" does not actually portray the massacre of the Polish Jews but registers it indirectly, through the impact on two women, both marginal to the Jewish world, of the strange behavior of a dog. The story reaches a climax at the moment when the old woman brings the dog to be shot by the Nazis and winds its leash about her arm in the manner that phylacteries are wound—a powerful instance of symbolic action.

Chaim Grade (1910-)

WITH A distinguished record as a Yiddish poet, Chaim Grade has only recently begun to write prose. "My Quarrel with Hersh Rasseyner" is his first published story. Born in Vilna, Poland, Grade studied at various yeshivas, among them that of the Mussarists, the ascetic sect described in his story. "My Quarrel with Hersh Rasseyner," which draws upon Grade's own experience, might be described as a philosophical dialogue, its main source of interest being the conflict of ideas between the secularized narrator and his believing friend. Grade has succeeded, however, in lifting the dialogue from the level of abstract colloquy to that of emotional confrontation, for he commands the rare gift of being able to dramatize ideas.

Before the war Grade belonged to the "Young Vilna" writers group —Vilna was a traditional center of Jewish scholarly and intellectual activity. He published his first book of poems in 1936, and since then has written prolifically. His verse includes both lyrics and long narratives, the latter often interspersed with reflective passages. Highly trained in Jewish lore and dialectic, Grade is particularly gifted at evoking the inner spiritual struggles of the East European generation that lived through the recent decades. A resident of New York since 1948, Grade has now begun to write prose regularly, and a book of his stories, *Mein Mame's Shabbosim* (*My Mother's Sabbaths*), is in preparation.

Part One
THE FATHERS

The Calf

MENDELE MOCHER SFORIM

1.

SHORTLY after the heroine of this story was born, something happened to her mother that caused a tremendous stir in our village.

Her mother was a handsome and well-bred beast—though her breeding was not of the obvious kind that goes with a pedigree. She did not have a full face or heavy body or plump udders, and her tail did not swing behind her like the train of a matron's dress. No, her beauty consisted solely in virtuous ways: mildness, patience, and humility. Like a true Jewish cow, she did penance for being in exile. Lacking a permanent lodging, she roamed the streets and slept wherever she could lay her head. On the rare occasions when the cold became intolerable, she was admitted to the dark outhouse, where she spent the night surrounded by an overflowing swill bucket, heaps of moldy rags, blocks of rotting wood, and the fresh stench of manure.

When it came to fasting, our cow was a paragon. She could fast for days without effort. She was simply not the glutton that gentile beasts are. Through sincere piety she gradually broke herself of the habit of feeding and would accept anything at all as food, and in any quantity. To paraphrase the saying about the woman of valor: "Many were the Jewish beasts that did valiantly, but she surpassed them all."

When the former owner of the cow had sold her to my mother, he proclaimed the beast to be overflowing with milk. This turned out to be not quite true, but it would be doing the cow a great injustice to blame her. In the first place, she was not guilty of withholding what she had, since she had nothing, and secondly, she received, as far as feed went, much less than her legitimate due. Besides, such mutual deceptions are common among Jews—deceptions based not so much on what is actually said as on what is imagined or predicted. This state of self-delusion being so widespread, all sales must be final.

Nor could the cow have been said to lack dignity. She did, it is true, wander about the market place, thrusting her chin into the peasants' wagons and sticking her tongue into this and that. But what would you have a poor beast do—drop dead in the middle of the street? Canvass any Jewish town and you'll find that all the Jewish beasts support themselves in the same way. And if our cow did manage to steal a lick from some peasant's wagon she was well rewarded—with a shower of blows and lashes, a deluge of vulgar insults from the mob.

So much for good looks and breeding. As for mildness, patience, and humility—half the Jewish population in the village could testify to that. On dark nights many a Jew staggered and fell over her as she lay sprawling in the mud of the market place. Another beast would have bellowed, "What's the idea, climbing over me in the middle of the night!" and would have reared up and thrown the poor man over her head. But our beast rose meekly to her feet and ambled away, her unexpected visitor perched gingerly on her back, until he fell of his own accord.

Our cow had her share of vices too. But where is the creature free of moral blemish? Is there a nobler beast than the bull, with his great head and big belly, or the he-goat, foremost of the village herd? Yet both those imposing creatures suffer from an unmentionable urge: neither can be permitted a female's stall without the presence of a watchman.

2.

Early one winter morning, as I lay huddled beneath my comforter, snatching the last few precious winks before going to study at the *cheder,* a hand shook me. "Hurry! Hurry and get up!" I opened my eyes and saw my sister, then about nine years old, standing near my bed. Her face was glowing, her eyes were burning with a peculiar light, and a fixed smile played on her lips. She was trying to say something, but her breath would not come. She made an inarticulate sound and pointed.

I looked. And just as I was, barefoot and naked except for my shift, holding one hand over my head (I had no time to look for my skull-cap), I jumped up and ran to the calf. My joy was indescribable: it was as though the world were now entirely mine and everything in it shared my jubilation. The sun shone more brightly, the dawn was less chilly, the air filled with a holiday spirit. Everything seemed to beam at me, crying, "Congratulations to you, boy, on a new calf!"

I squatted on the floor near the new arrival and studied her closely. She was a pretty beast, egg-yellow, with a white spot that resembled a silver cockade on her forehead. Gradually I became bolder and moved closer. First I touched her gingerly, and then, probing with one finger, I looked her in the eyes. Finally I became very chummy and gave her a hearty welcome with my whole hand.

The calf did not appreciate a boy's notion of a hearty welcome. Affronted, she gathered all her strength and tried to get up. She began with her backside, which she raised by cautiously rising on her rear legs, resting meanwhile on the knees of her forelegs. Then she got up on all fours, teetering like a shaky table. A cord hung from her navel. For a moment she stood this way, trembling, gawky, her calf-eyes protruding. Then she unexpectedly lifted her tail and started galloping through the room. The milking stool fell, the chickens were frightened and perched, with furious cackles, on table and bench, dishes were broken and pots upset. My mother, who was with the cow in the outhouse, rushed breathlessly into the room, and wrath descended on my head.

What a day I had of it! Slaps and blows at home, blows and slaps at *cheder*—may God preserve you from such a fate.

I left for the *cheder* with my head full of calf. Everyone I met on the way was told the glad tidings: our cow had calved! Beaming like the host at a celebration, I regaled my chums with praise of the calf and promised those lucky enough to be on close terms with me that they would be able to see it and even play with it in my company. I took as advance payment a pair of bronze buttons with eagles on them and a few pieces of cracked glass, swearing on my honor, as I held the fringes of my prayer vest, that each would be allowed the first ride on the calf. These items of business made me late for the *cheder;* I received an appropriate reward.

The Talmud lay open before me, but all I could see was the calf: small chin, tiny perked-up ears, delicate neck. The *rebbe* droned on, intoning the Talmudic singsong: I heard the cow mooing to her calf. The *rebbe* rose from his chair: the calf clambered to her feet. The *rebbe* lifted his arm: the calf lifted her rear—he to slap and she to run. The *rebbe* was furious. Wordless, I held my cheek. Suddenly the door opened and my rescuer appeared. Long life to the *rebbe*'s wife! But she stalked away empty-handed, slamming the door behind her, and the *rebbe,* completely losing his temper, took out his misery on me.

That I reached home with a whole skin was a miracle.

My first thought was for the calf. On tiptoe, like a lover spying on his beloved, I stole over to the corner where my mother had led the calf for fear of an evil eye. And the morning's episode was repeated: my approaches, the calf's flight, my mother's fury.

Yet my love for the calf grew daily, together with the sufferings it brought me. My childish heart froze with anguish at the dealings that took place over its body. They were going to slaughter the poor creature, they were casually dismembering it while it was still alive, counting on their fingers: so much for the hide, so much for the forequarters, so much for each limb. And all the while the innocent beast looked on, licking my mother's hand affectionately while she dickered over the price of its tongue.

At that time I was untutored in the world's subtleties. It never occurred to me that something might be amiss with the order of things; that the wisdom which had come down from time immemorial might be folly; philosophy, mere sophistry; conventional piety, unfeeling and cruel. So I was unhappy with my unhappiness, regarding it as the work of the Evil Spirit. I remembered how our *rebbe* had once explained the Biblical passage, "Go not after your own heart," as meaning that a boy ought not to allow himself strong desires.

I was deeply troubled. I struggled to remove all thought of the calf from my mind and told myself that it was sinful of me to feel compassion for a mere beast. Was I obliged to sacrifice my soul for her, to place myself in jeopardy of the fires of hell? But the more I strove to forget, the more her fate preyed upon me.

Unhappy and perplexed, I was ashamed to look either the calf or my mother in the eyes. God knows what might have happened to me had there not occurred something completely unexpected.

3.

It was a March night, cold and bitter. A wind raged outdoors, as though a thousand demons were celebrating their nuptials. Snowflakes danced through the air in weird, distorted shapes. Roofs shook; chimneys moaned; windowpanes crackled and buzzed. Not a soul was abroad.

Our cow, still recuperating, had spent the night in the filthy, drafty outhouse. What does a beast do in such a place? She chews her cud, regurgitating the sour stuff, and every once in a while she quietly sighs.

Early the next morning I was awakened by my mother's loud laments. The beast had died!

Everyone in the house was dejected; even the cock stood still, head downcast, neglecting his harem. A hen fluttered around, cackling, looking for a spot to set, but no one troubled to cover her with the sieve. Another hen flew out from under the bed and perched on a bench with her head high, as if to announce, "Congratulate me! I've laid an egg!" But no one noticed her. We all stood around disconsolate, including the neighbors, who had come running at my mother's outcry.

My mother launched into a funeral oration, describing the infinite virtues of our cow, her yield of cheese and butter (items I had never seen). She continued with a detailed account of how she had come in at daybreak to milk the cow; how she had found the beast covered with the snow that drifted in through the crevices in the outhouse walls; how she had set down the milk bucket, taken a broom, and swept the snow off the cow's back. Then for the first time she had seen that the beast was stark dead. At first my mother had been astonished, but now the reason was clear to her.

"Listen everyone," said my mother, piously raising her eyes to the ceiling, "this is God's handiwork. I realize it now. The beast has died as an atonement for us, she has taken our sins upon her. For there is a curious tradition in our family. My saintly forefather commanded his children and their children to commemorate the second day of the new moon of the month of Adar with a special feast, a sort of special *Purim,* in remembrance of a miraculous escape from death once granted him on that date. He pronounced a curse on any descendant who neglected this duty. Yesterday was that day, and I forgot to celebrate it. This beast, I tell you, is our atonement. Why else should a cow die so soon after having calved?"

While my mother was delivering this learned oration the calf rushed into the room, her head and tail up, crying, "Moo-moo!" The sight of the orphan broke our hearts, for the meaning of her "Moo" was plain enough. The poor thing was hungry and was lowing for her mother's teats. All the women wiped their noses, shuffled their feet, and began to move their lips. One of them, more learned than the rest, who was constantly citing the sages, particularly a certain Reb Bachya, was the first to lift her voice.

"The Eternal One, blessed be His name, which I am not worthy to mention!" She compressed her lips and wrinkled her face into a patchwork of piety. "The Almighty, who is exalted among His angelic hosts, is righteous, and His ways are righteous. Now the sages have declared —and in particular Reb Bachya—that there are times when a beast must die in atonement for his master's evil. May this beast atone for you and your household, O Yente" (addressing my mother), "cleansing you and all Israel of impurity, like unto the Red Cow of atonement.

"And now, O Yente," continued the female oracle, "this is my counsel. Let this calf, the fruit of the dead beast's womb, serve as a living memorial, that never again may you transgress against the vow of your saintly forefather. May she be reared in your household and may He who feeds all things, from the eagle on high to the lowliest worm, provide her sustenance: at times potato skins and at times bread crumbs. Consider her as you would a yeshiva student. What does an extra spoonful of soup or a slice of bread mean to a good housekeeper? And after all, a calf turns into a cow, and a cow is always useful, particularly for Jews."

All the women nodded their agreement with this pious and practical counsel. My mother allowed herself to be persuaded; and a stone fell from my heart.

The story of the cow's unprecedented death, so contrary to the laws of nature, created a great stir in the village. People kept dropping into our house to look at the calf, which was given the name of The Special *Purim* Calf.

For three days the village was filled with a terrible howling. The dogs that had gathered in the field were bidding the cow farewell by the customary rites of laceration.

4.

During the first days of mourning the calf yearned loudly for her mother's teats. Various means were tried to silence her: mushes of corn and bran, pieces of bread, even hay. She came into the world with eight fine, white teeth—I counted them myself. The calf used these teeth to chew whatever she was given, making small unhappy noises. Everything went into her mouth—handkerchiefs, tablecloths, old socks —her taste was truly catholic. People bore with her only out of respect for her mother's memory. One Sabbath eve she almost choked to death on the rag that served as the oven damper. Luckily someone saw her— it was necessary to turn the roast—and managed to extract the rag from her gullet just in time.

I alone sincerely loved and pitied the poor orphan. I took her part and bore the blows intended for her, and I loved her all the more. For we had this in common, that we were both persecuted by those stronger than we. It was not so much our physical suffering as the injustice of it all that pained me and drew me close to our calf.

And she seemed fond of me too. She would let me stroke her head, embrace her, grab her by the ears. At such moments she would lick me and look at me with her mournful eyes, as though trying to convey her melancholy to me. For my part, I sensed the unspoken words that the dumb, licking tongue could not utter.

I was a child, and like a child thought that the whole world was a copy of my village, that all places were the same and there was only one way of doing things. Everywhere people prayed, recited psalms, studied the *Mishnah,* pored over the *Gemarah,* sat in small stores, yawned, chatted, gossiped, leaned on canes. Human beings and beasts were part of the same order. Boys were led off to *cheder,* beasts led out to pasture. The *rebbe* had his plaited whip, the shepherd his crook. The one remedy for a slap or a blow was to play with a chum, whether boy or calf it did not matter, so long as it was a living thing. Lucky the boy who could gain the favor of some mongrel, which would follow him around, bark when told, attack at command. Every boy was ready to give up not only his noonday meal but his very soul for such a dog.

But all this is beside the point.

5.

Passover came to an end. Vacation time was over. The herd was led to pasture, and tiny children were carried to the *cheder,* still sleepy, dozing on their older brothers' shoulders. Yet our calf, who was well developed and able to get about on her own feet, remained at home. She was still too tender to join the herd, the shepherd said. There was time enough for her to learn what a beast needs to know: how to graze and chew the cud. So the calf remained at home. Her life was hardly a pot of honey. One of her tutors taught her the virtue of continence by stuffing her mouth with whatever was handy; another taught her good manners and decorum by a liberal use of the rod. Despite all the pains that were taken with her education, she was always hungry and lost considerable weight after her mother's death.

Luckily for her, my *rebbe* soon reached the point where he had nothing more to teach me. I was put on my own and assigned certain hours of individual study at the synagogue. And at the same time I was appointed guide and mentor to the calf. This was a wonderful stroke of luck for both of us.

A new world opened up for us, such as neither I in the *cheder* nor she in the outhouse had ever imagined.

"Come, my beloved," I would cry, picking up the rope that hung around her neck. "Let us go forth into the field!"

The green grass was a revelation. Everything was alive. We met God's creatures, previously unknown to us: every manner of bird and insect. They flew through the air, glided in the grass, singing and humming and buzzing. My eyes were dazzled by the bright colors of the flowers. I felt alive myself, alive inside. For once I could breathe freely. I turned somersaults in high spirits. Tired, I stretched out on the grass, belly up, and squinted into the sun, which smiled at me as though to say, "Well, young fellow, having a good time?"

Spontaneously I sang a hymn of thanksgiving in the traditional Jewish tremolo. The calf turned her head and mooed, which was her way of inquiring, "What's the matter?"

I jumped to my feet. She was right. Why this melancholy? I spat three times, to avoid an evil eye, and stopped singing.

The calf grazed zealously at my side. Watching her, I was reminded of the patriarch Jacob and how he had tended the flocks of Laban the Aramaean. I thought too of Jacob's happy encounter with Rachel at the well, how they had kissed and embraced. Suddenly my heart began to pound.

That was the work of the Evil Spirit: it was he who brought to mind the memory of a pretty girl who had been my playmate until I had suddenly grown bashful, without knowing why. But now I understood the reason for my shyness and felt miserable. The Good Spirit reproached me, crying, "See, this is where that charmer Nature leads you! She is a witch who puts lewd thoughts in a fellow's head." Nor did the Good Spirit spare the calf either. "A Jewish boy and a calf spending their time together! No good will come of this. Get back to the synagogue!"

But the Evil Spirit is far more cunning than the Good Spirit. Once a lad steps outside the synagogue walls, once he sees what God's fine world looks like, it is almost impossible to bring him back. Once drawn away from his studies and started along the downward path, he keeps to it on his own.

Where did I go? To the woods, of course, and the calf came with me. A short distance from the village we found a wood where ancient and full-grown hardwood trees pointed to the sky, gnarled roots naked at their feet, their tangled green crowns forming a green sea roof overhead. Near the wood a thicket of short saplings lay among fragrant grasses and flowers. Beyond the thicket fields of wheat and barley stretched as far as the eye could see, and beyond that the ground sloped down to a valley where a clear stream sparkled in the sun, as lively and playful as a child, hiding momentarily among trees thick with leaves, only to reappear in the distance, where it ran downhill murmuring over small stones.

Occasionally a bird would appear, perch on a branch, look at me surreptitiously, as though wondering what manner of creature I was, suddenly bow his head, flutter his tail, move his wings, and—farewell! He was off! Or another bird would turn up on the other side of the valley and face us, standing on his long crimson feet, his silver-white throat and red maw thrust upward, motionless, for a long time. Suddenly he would clop-clop with his beak and speed away over the swamp.

At other times the wood would resound to the neighing of horses pulling the peasants' wagons and the chatter of peasant women gathering mushrooms.

And there I lay at my ease, smiling with pleasure. I looked at the calf and thought to myself, How lucky we both are! We have each other to thank for being here. If not for me, you'd still be languishing in the outhouse, and if not for you, I'd be languishing in the synagogue.

I spent many days lazily enjoying God's world and enjoying my calf, which became my closest friend. I was constantly amused by the enthusiasm that set her dancing, raising her backside in a calf's frolic. At other times she would stretch out her neck to me, exactly like a child reaching to its mother, and plead, "Scratch me right here."

That summer saw a complete change in both of us. The calf put on flesh; she shed her old hide and hair, and the new came in fresh and gleaming. I too came into my own, with a sunburned complexion and a tremendous appetite. Study had as much attraction for me as straw and potato peels for the calf when she came home at night well fed.

My mother, who was not slow to notice this transformation, was not very pleased. "As far as the calf is concerned, a beast is a beast. But as for you, my fine young man, what is to become of you? Just look at you now! You've lost all your Jewish refinement. Your face is red, like a peasant's. And the way you gorge yourself! That's what you get from going to the woods. I tell you, nothing good will come of this." And then the invariable conclusion: "There's only one remedy. The only place that can make a 'real person' of you is the yeshiva."

6.

My life at the yeshiva, or rather my sufferings there, do not really belong to this story. After all, the calf is our subject, and my career only an appendage to hers. But since we have come this far, I may as well tell you something about it.

What my mother said was quite true: the yeshiva was a remedy. In a short time it turned me into a "real person," with a genuine pallor and ludicrous mannerisms. If I had stayed there for years, as my colleagues did, the yeshiva would have made me as real a person as any of its products. But, unfortunately, I was sinful and could not complete my education. I was badly tormented by the Evil Spirit, which assumed the shape of a calf and of grass and of trees. It was they who had spoiled me, who had turned my head, and now kept me from becoming the model of a "perfect vessel."

Looking at a brother monk—I mean, another yeshiva student—I would be reminded of the calf. When one of my fellow students would scratch himself, which happened often enough, I saw the calf scratching herself. When a student had no steady place to eat one day a week, which also happened often enough, I remembered how the calf had once roamed the house looking for her mother's teats. Wandering restlessly through the yeshiva with my fellows, sleeping on hard benches or on the ground, bitten by fleas, I would conjure up vistas of trees and crops and flowers and hillocks and valleys and a golden sun and a blue sky. When the boys snored in their sleep I heard bees droning. Their noisome breaths set me dreaming of fragrant flowers. There were times when I awoke in the middle of the night, empty with longing.

At such moments I would lose myself in grief and would silently address my unhappy companions. "Brothers, lost and far from home, woe unto us, and all the days of our years! How long shall the ground be our bed, the yeshiva our grave? The devil take us and our studies!"

But my friends slept on, dead to my cry. Regretting my bitterness, I begged their pardon. "Brothers, forgive me. I have had evil thoughts about you. Sleep on, sleep in peace, and may God have mercy on you."

"Dear Mother," I wrote one fine summer day, "yesterday we finished the Talmudical tractate of Baba Metzia. I am getting along pretty well in my studies. Still, I am very homesick for you, Mother, and for everyone at home. (I was ashamed to single out the calf.) Oh, please let me come home for a few days. There'll be no expense. I'll go on foot —all the boys do it. We go barefoot, with a stick in our hands and a pack on our shoulders. As for the few pennies for the trip, I've had them since *Purim*. Please let me come home!"

And without waiting for a reply I set out a few days later. Was there anyone in the whole world happier than I at that moment? Merchants may travel by coach, noblemen on horseback—but their comfort is nothing compared to the elation of a barefoot student fleeing the stench of the yeshiva for the fresh air. I started out very early, took the bypaths that led through fields of barley and corn, and walked all day, reaching home at the time of the late afternoon prayers, when the beasts return from the pasture.

I saw my calf, and she had grown in my absence. Her udders were firm, her horns had sprouted, and she was being courted. A pair of bucks escorted her to the edge of the garden behind our house, wooing her on the way, showing her how delightfully they could lick her, and leaping on her back. With all proper deference to the suitors, I drove them off with a stick and stationed myself in front of the prospective bride.

"Hello there," I said and tried to stroke her neck. But she turned her head away and lifted her small pointed horns like threatening spears, as though to say, "Hands off! Who are you to stroke me, fellow?"

I was more than a little taken aback, but I decided to try again.

"My, my," I said, holding a handful of grass before the beauty's nose. "Here's a present for you." She sniffed the grass, wrinkling her nose, and looked at me with wonder.

"Don't you recognize me?" I smiled somewhat bitterly.

Looking at her for a few minutes, and comparing her well-fleshed body with my own emaciated figure and sunken face, I could not help sighing for my wasted youth. "Almighty God, is it really your will that a human being be cooped up like a goose from childhood on, never to see the world, and to stuff his mind with such nonsense as mine is full of?"

But the calf had apparently recognized my voice, for now she became more friendly and put out her neck for me to scratch, as in the old days. She stood there quietly, looking at me through half-closed eyes, and mooed deep from her chest. I sensed what she meant. She was pleading,

"Scratch me, scratch me, for thy scratches are more pleasing to me than green grass." She was asking, "Where had my beloved disappeared to?" And she was condoling, "How you have changed for the worse!"

My mother, on the other hand, was quite taken with my appearance. It proved to her that I was studying diligently; my face was now that of a virtuous Jewish child, pale and refined, and, God willing, it would serve me well in securing a bride. For it turned out that two prospective fathers-in-law were already bidding for me. They kept whispering to my mother, nodding in my direction with appraising gestures and furrowed brows, like merchants haggling over a piece of cloth.

But the Evil Spirit doth not sleep and came to me early and late, urging me to go forth to my beloved Nature on the pretext that it was healthier out of doors, and that being in the fresh air would further my welfare. And then he began to question all the benefits of my newly won learning, my occupation, my purpose in life. He mocked me bitterly, calling me boor and barbarian. Things came to such a pass that the Evil Spirit began to subvert the yeshiva.

"You are nothing but a—did you think I was going to say 'beast'? Far from it! A beast is himself—he lives the life God has created him for, attends to his wants, follows his instincts, without evasions. But human beings like you are fools and distort their God-given natures. You live according to an idea of what life should be like, not what it really is. A fool, not a beast, is what you really are."

I was convinced, yet it did no good.

"Need breaks iron," goes the folk saying, and even the iron of the Evil Spirit could not withstand the need in my home. It was simply impossible for me to remain with my mother, a poor widow with many little mouths to feed. I bade farewell, farewell to the fields and the forests, farewell to the calf, to all my beloved. And I set out on foot for the yeshiva.

7.

The year that followed was much harder than the first. It was a year when householders were reluctant to give us "eating days," and I suffered hunger. The sages say that the misery of others is half a consolation. If so, I should have been consoled, at least by half, since so many of the other students at the yeshiva went hungry with me. According to the sages and ordinary common sense, that is the way it should have been, but in this case, unfortunately, theory and practice did not coincide. I not only found it difficult to bear my own suffering, I also suffered agonies over the misery of my companions.

Now, looking back, I can admit that the yeshiva life filled me with anger that year, tempting me to consign the whole business of learning to the devil. But that was only at first. After a while, when I grew used to the yeshiva, eating ceased to matter. Nor did I care about my torn shoes, ragged coat, frayed elbows. My chums and I would frequently poke fun at such inconsequential details, competing with one another in raillery. Only later did I perceive wherein the great virtue of the yeshiva lay: the paupers whom the yeshiva graduates are jolly paupers; its alumni—the *cheder* rabbis, the religious hangers-on, the general ne'er-do-wells—are unconcerned with worldly matters. And for Jews who must live in exile that is a saving virtue.

"Congratulate me, son," wrote my mother after a long silence. "Congratulate me on my cow. Don't you understand what I mean? Your calf has dropped a calf, and now she's a proper cow. There's milk at home—and after selling it in the market there's some left for us. Ah, if only you too were the cause of congratulations! It's a good cow, but she won't let me milk her—jumps and screams whenever I go near her. She is simply wasting away after her slaughtered calf. Have you ever heard of such a thing—a cow that won't forget her calf? She always was difficult; you were the only one who could handle her. Well, you brought her up properly, I see. It would be better if you had taught her less and yourself more. Study, my child, study, and, God willing, you'll become a proper man. Yes, no one can deny it, it was a really tender calf. The slaughterer paid me a good price for her. I'm sending you a few gold coins and a piece of broiled liver, by hand of Chayeh Hinde, as recompense for the trouble you once took with her mother. It seems that . . ."

I could not read on. I saw black, my head began to spin, and I fainted. My companions had to throw a bucket of water over me before they could bring me to my senses. They stood before me and asked what was the matter. Had someone become sick at home or, Heaven forbid, died? I could not answer. How could I tell them that I was sick at heart for a beast in whose company I had spent the happiest moments of my life? Tell them that my blood ran chill at the thought of a cow whose first-born calf had been slaughtered? I would have been a laughingstock!

8.

The slightest word is enough to upset a yeshiva student, to call his fantasy into play. This is particularly true of one who lacks "eating days," whose body is wasted by the strain of his studies and the stress of his hunger. My mother's few words were enough to inflame my imagination, already taxed by the mental flights of my studies, and soon my sleep was troubled with fearful hallucinations. No sooner did I lie down on the yeshiva floor than a curtain lifted before my mind's eye.

First to appear is my old playmate, the calf, now a cow, and her child, a tiny delightful thing. The calf approaches her mother, sucks at her teats, pushes against the udders, and merrily swishes her tail. The mother is ecstatic. Bending her head to her offspring, she licks it again and again, with a low murmur of love. I look at the mother with rapt attention, and she returns my gaze. As always, there is complete understanding between us. She stands there glowing, and her warmth sets the whole scene a-quiver with sympathy; my heart is so light, so happy.

Abruptly the scene changed. The stage darkened. Mother and child disappeared. Nothing remained.

I felt cold. There was an insurrection in me, whose battle cry was "Food!" I had visions of milk, sour cream, cheese, a whole loaf of bread spread with butter. Then I conjured up a roast, with chunks of meat sautéed in fat and onion. I grew faint with hunger. I could no longer bear it. I tossed about on the floor, turning from side to side. A bell rang in my ears: the second act.

A young calf, about eight days old, struggles out of the slaughterer's hands and runs off, crying bitterly, the slaughterer in hot pursuit. The calf cries desperately for her mother, but she is in the pasture and cannot help. The calf tries to hide under someone's coat tails. But the slaughterer drags her out, repeating the words of Rabbi Judah the Prince: "Go! This is what you were born for!" The slaughterer casts her to the ground, presses her down with his knees, pulls her neck taut, raises the knife, begins the benediction, "Blessed art thou, Master of the Universe," and strikes. Blood, a hoarse cry, a shudder, the death rattle.

I am blinded by colors, red and blue and purple. I wipe drops of blood from my forehead.

From that moment on I lost control of my bodily functions. I could no longer distinguish between dream and reality. Sweetmeats hung over my nose, made up of the calf's roasted liver and lungs. I was being slapped, pricked with needles. Burning coals scorched my pocket. Two gold coins sprang out. I looked at them—and a pair of blood-swollen calf's eyes stared back at me.

The same day they carried me off to the hospital, babbling incoherently, a letter arrived from my mother:

"My son, try hard to become a proper man. Devote yourself only to the yeshiva and your studies. Your poor mother is desolate, all her means of livelihood are gone. She has lost her last support, because of her sins.

"The cow, your calf, has died."

Translated by Jacob Sloan

On Account of a Hat

SHOLOM ALEICHEM

"DID I hear you say absent-minded? Now, in our town, that is, in Kasrilevke, we've really got someone for you—do you hear what I say? His name is Sholem Shachnah, but we call him Sholem Shachnah Rattlebrain, and is he absent-minded, is this a distracted creature, Lord have mercy on us! The stories they tell about him, about this Sholem Shachnah—bushels and baskets of stories—I tell you, whole crates full of stories and anecdotes! It's too bad you're in such a hurry on account of the Passover, because what I could tell you, Mr. Sholom Aleichem—do you hear what I say?—you could go on writing it down forever. But if you can spare a moment I'll tell you a story about what happened to Sholem Shachnah on a Passover eve—a story about a hat, a true story, I should live so, even if it does sound like someone made it up."

These were the words of a Kasrilevke merchant, a dealer in stationery, that is to say, snips of paper. He smoothed out his beard, folded it down over his neck, and went on smoking his thin little cigarettes, one after the other.

I must confess that this true story, which he related to me, does indeed sound like a concocted one, and for a long time I couldn't make up my mind whether or not I should pass it on to you. But I thought it over and decided that if a respectable merchant and dignitary of Kasrilevke, who deals in stationery and is surely no *litterateur*—if he vouches for a story, it must be true. What would he be doing with fiction? Here it is in his own words. I had nothing to do with it.

This Sholem Shachnah I'm telling you about, whom we call Sholem Shachnah Rattlebrain, is a real-estate broker—you hear what I say? He's always with landowners, negotiating transactions. Transactions? Well, at least he hangs around the landowners. So what's the point? I'll tell you. Since he hangs around the landed gentry, naturally some of their manner has rubbed off on him, and he always has a mouth full of farms, homesteads, plots, acreage, soil, threshing machines, renovations, woods, timber, and other such terms having to do with estates.

One day God took pity on Sholem Shachnah, and for the first time in his career as a real-estate broker—are you listening?—he actually worked out a deal. That is to say, the work itself, as you can imagine, was done by others, and when the time came to collect the fee, the big rattler turned out to be not Sholem Shachnah Rattlebrain, but Drobkin, a Jew from Minsk province, a great big fearsome rattler, a real-estate broker from way back—he and his two brothers, also brokers and also big rattlers. So you can take my word for it, there was quite a to-do. A Jew has contrived and connived and has finally, with God's help, managed to cut himself in—so what do they do but come along and cut him out! Where's Justice? Sholem Shachnah wouldn't stand for it—are you listening to me? He set up such a holler and an outcry—"Look what they've done to me!"—that at last they gave in to shut him up, and good riddance it was too.

When he got his few cents Sholem Shachnah sent the greater part of it home to his wife, so she could pay off some debts, shoo the wolf from the door, fix up new outfits for the children, and make ready for the Passover holidays. And as for himself, he also needed a few things, and besides he had to buy presents for his family, as was the custom.

Meanwhile the time flew by, and before he knew it, it was almost Passover. So Sholem Shachnah—now listen to this—ran to the telegraph office and sent home a wire: *Arriving home Passover without fail.* It's easy to say "arriving" and "without fail" at that. But you just try it! Just try riding out our way on the new train and see how fast you'll arrive. Ah, what a pleasure! Did they do us a favor! I tell you, Mr. Sholom Aleichem, for a taste of Paradise such as this you'd gladly forsake your own grandchildren! You see how it is: until you get to Zlodievka there isn't much you can do about it, so you just lean back and ride. But at Zlodievka the fun begins, because that's where you have to change, to get onto the new train, which they did us such a favor by running out to Kasrilevke. But not so fast. First, there's the little matter of several hours' wait, exactly as announced in the schedule—provided, of course, that you don't pull in after the Kasrilevke train has left. And at what time of night may you look forward to this treat? The very middle, thank you, when you're dead tired and disgusted, without a friend in the world except sleep—and there's not one single place in the whole station where you can lay your head, not one. When the wise men of Kasrilevke quote the passage from the Holy Book, *"Tov shem meshemon tov,"* they know what they're doing. I'll translate it for you: We were better off without the train.

To make a long story short, when our Sholem Shachnah arrived in Zlodievka with his carpetbag he was half dead; he had already spent two nights without sleep. But that was nothing at all to what was facing him—he still had to spend the whole night waiting in the station. What shall he do? Naturally he looked around for a place to sit down. Whoever heard of such a thing? Nowhere. Nothing. No place to sit. The walls of the station were covered with soot, the floor was covered with spit. It was dark, it was terrible. He finally discovered one miserable spot on a bench where he had just room enough to squeeze in, and no more than that, because the bench was occupied by an official of some sort in a uniform full of buttons, who was lying there all stretched out and snoring away to beat the band. Who this Buttons was, whether he was coming or going, he hadn't the vaguest idea, Sholem Shachnah, that is. But he could tell that Buttons was no dime-a-dozen official. This was plain by his cap, a military cap with a red band and a visor. He could have been an officer or a police official. Who knows? But surely he had drawn up to the station with a ringing of bells, had staggered in, full to the ears with meat and drink, laid himself out on the bench, as in his father's vineyard, and worked up a glorious snoring.

It's not such a bad life to be a gentile, and an official one at that, with buttons, thinks he, Sholem Shachnah, that is, and he wonders, dare he sit next to this Buttons, or hadn't he better keep his distance?

Nowadays you never can tell whom you're sitting next to. If he's no more than a plain inspector, that's still all right. But what if he turns out to be a district inspector? Or a provincial commander? Or even higher than that? And supposing this is even Purishkevitch himself, the famous anti-Semite, may his name perish? Let someone else deal with him and Sholem Shachnah turns cold at the mere thought of falling into such a fellow's hands. But then he says to himself—now listen to this—Buttons, he says, who the hell is Buttons? And who gives a hang for Purishkevitch? Don't I pay my fare the same as Purishkevitch? So why should he have all the comforts of life and I none? If Buttons is entitled to a delicious night's sleep, then doesn't he, Sholem Shachnah that is, at least have a nap coming? After all, he's human too, and besides, he's already gone two nights without a wink. And so he sits down, on a corner of the bench, and leans his head back, not, God forbid, to sleep, but just like that, to snooze. But all of a sudden he remembers—he's supposed to be home for Passover, and tomorrow is Passover eve! What if, God have mercy, he should fall asleep and miss his train? But that's why he's got a Jewish head on his shoulders—are you listening to me or not?—so he figures out the answer to that one too, Sholem Shachnah, that is, and goes looking for the porter, a certain Yeremei, he knows him well, to make a deal with him. Whereas he, Sholem Shachnah, is already on his third sleepless night and is afraid, God forbid, that he may miss his train, therefore let him, Yeremei, that is, in God's name, be sure to wake him, Sholem Shachnah, because tomorrow night is a holiday, Passover. "Easter," he says to him in Russian and lays a coin in Yeremei's mitt. "Easter, Yeremei, do you understand, *goyisher kop?* Our Easter." The peasant pockets the coin, no doubt about that, and promises to wake him at the first sign of the train—he can sleep soundly and put his mind at rest. So Sholem Shachnah sits down in his corner of the bench, gingerly, pressed up against the wall, with his carpetbag curled around him so that no one should steal it. Little by little he sinks back, makes himself comfortable, and half shuts his eyes—no more than forty winks, you understand. But before long he's got one foot propped up on the bench and then the other; he stretches out and drifts off to sleep. Sleep? I'll say sleep, like God commanded us: with his head thrown back and his hat rolling away on the floor, Sholem Shachnah is snoring like an eight-day wonder. After all, a human being, up two nights in a row—what would you have him do?

He had a strange dream. He tells this himself, that is, Sholem

Shachnah does. He dreamed that he was riding home for Passover—are you listening to me?—but not on the train, in a wagon, driven by a thievish peasant, Ivan Zlodi we call him. The horses were terribly slow, they barely dragged along. Sholem Shachnah was impatient, and he poked the peasant between the shoulders and cried, "May you only drop dead, Ivan darling! Hurry up, you lout! Passover is coming, our Jewish Easter!" Once he called out to him, twice, three times. The thief paid him no mind. But all of a sudden he whipped his horses to a gallop and they went whirling away, up hill and down, like demons. Sholem Shachnah lost his hat. Another minute of this and he would have lost God knows what. "Whoa, there, Ivan old boy! Where's the fire? Not so fast!" cried Sholem Shachnah. He covered his head with his hands—he was worried, you see, over his lost hat. How can he drive into town bareheaded? But for all the good it did him, he could have been hollering at a post. Ivan the Thief was racing the horses as if forty devils were after him. All of a sudden—tppprrru!—they came to a dead stop, right in the middle of the field—you hear me?—a dead stop. What's the matter? Nothing. "Get up," said Ivan, "time to get up."

Time? What time? Sholem Shachnah is all confused. He wakes up, rubs his eyes, and is all set to step out of the wagon when he realizes he has lost his hat. Is he dreaming or not? And what's he doing here? Sholem Shachnah finally comes to his senses and recognizes the peasant—this isn't Ivan Zlodi at all but Yeremei the porter. So he concludes that he isn't on the high road after all, but in the station at Zlodievka, on the way home for Passover, and that if he means to get there he'd better run to the window for a ticket, but fast. Now what? No hat. The carpetbag is right where he left it, but his hat? He pokes around under the bench, reaching all over, until he comes up with a hat—not his own, to be sure, but the official's, with the red band and the visor. But Sholem Shachnah has no time for details and he rushes off to buy a ticket. The ticket window is jammed, everybody and his cousins are crowding in. Sholem Shachnah thinks he won't get to the window in time, perish the thought, and he starts pushing forward, carpetbag and all. The people see the red band and the visor and they make way for him. "Where to, Your Excellency?" asks the ticket agent. What's this Excellency, all of a sudden? wonders Sholem Shachnah, and he rather resents it. Some joke, a gentile poking fun at a Jew. All the same he says, Sholem Shachnah, that is, "Kasrilevke." "Which class, Your Excellency?" The ticket agent is looking straight at the red band and the visor. Sholem Shachnah is angrier than ever. I'll give him an Excellency, so he'll know how to make fun of a poor Jew! But then he thinks, Oh, well, we Jews are in Diaspora—do you hear what I say?—let it pass. And he asks for a ticket third class. "Which class?" The agent blinks at him, very much surprised. This time Sholem Shachnah gets good and sore and he really tells him off. "Third!" says he. All right, thinks the agent, third is third.

In short, Sholem Shachnah buys his ticket, takes up his carpetbag, runs out onto the platform, plunges into the crowd of Jews and gentiles, no comparison intended, and goes looking for the third-class carriage. Again the red band and the visor work like a charm, everyone makes way for the official. Sholem Shachnah is wondering, What goes on here? But he runs along the platform till he meets a conductor carrying a lantern. "Is this third class?" asks Sholem Shachnah, putting one foot on the stairs and shoving his bag into the door of the compartment. "Yes, Your Excellency," says the conductor, but he holds him back. "If you please, sir, it's packed full, as tight as your fist. You couldn't squeeze a needle into that crowd." And he takes Sholem Shachnah's carpetbag—you hear what I'm saying?—and sings out, "Right this way, Your Excellency, I'll find you a seat." "What the Devil!" cries Sholem Shachnah. "Your Excellency and Your Excellency!" But he hasn't much time for the fine points; he's worried about his carpetbag. He's afraid, you see, that with all these Excellencies he'll be swindled out of his belongings. So he runs after the conductor with the lantern, who leads him into a second-class carriage. This is also packed to the rafters, no room even to yawn in there. "This way please, Your Excellency!" And again the conductor grabs the bag and Sholem Shachnah lights out after him. "Where in blazes is he taking me?" Sholem Shachnah is racking his brains over this Excellency business, but meanwhile he keeps his eye on the main thing—the carpetbag. They enter the first-class carriage, the conductor sets down the bag, salutes, and backs away, bowing. Sholem Shachnah bows right back. And there he is, alone at last.

Left alone in the carriage, Sholem Shachnah looks around to get his bearings—you hear what I say? He has no idea why all these honors have suddenly been heaped on him—first class, salutes, Your Excellency. Can it be on account of the real-estate deal he just closed? That's it! But wait a minute. If his own people, Jews, that is, honored him for this, it would be understandable. But gentiles! The conductor! The ticket agent! What's it to them? Maybe he's dreaming. Sholem Shachnah rubs his forehead, and while passing down the corridor glances into the mirror on the wall. It nearly knocks him over! He sees not himself but the official with the red band. That's who it is! "All my bad dreams on Yeremei's head and on his hands and feet, that lug! Twenty times I tell him to wake me and I even give him a tip, and what does he do, that dumb ox, may he catch cholera in his face, but wake the official instead! And me he leaves asleep on the bench! Tough luck, Sholem Shachnah old boy, but this year you'll spend Passover in Zlodievka, not at home."

Now get a load of this. Sholem Shachnah scoops up his carpetbag and rushes off once more, right back to the station where he is sleeping on the bench. He's going to wake himself up before the locomotive, God forbid, lets out a blast and blasts his Passover to pieces. And so it was. No sooner had Sholem Shachnah leaped out of the carriage with his carpetbag than the locomotive did let go with a blast—do you hear me? —one followed by another, and then, good night!

The paper dealer smiled as he lit a fresh cigarette, thin as a straw. "And would you like to hear the rest of the story? The rest isn't so nice. On account of being such a rattlebrain, our dizzy Sholem Shachnah had a miserable Passover, spending both Seders among strangers in the house of a Jew in Zlodievka. But this was nothing—listen to what happened afterward. First of all, he has a wife, Sholem Shachnah, that is, and his wife—how shall I describe her to you? *I* have a wife, *you* have a wife, we all have wives, we've had a taste of Paradise, we know what it means to be married. All I can say about Sholem Shachnah's wife is that she's A Number One. And did she give him a royal welcome! Did she lay into him! Mind you, she didn't complain about his spending the holiday away from home, and she said nothing about the red band and the visor. She let that stand for the time being; she'd take it up with him later. The only thing she complained about was—the telegram! And not so much the telegram—you hear what I say?—as the one short phrase, *without fail.* What possessed him to put that into the wire: *Arriving home Passover without fail.* Was he trying to make the telegraph company rich? And besides, how dare a human being say "without fail" in the first place? It did him no good to answer and explain. She buried him alive. Oh, well, that's what wives are for. And not that she was altogether wrong—after all, she had been waiting so anxiously. But this was nothing compared with what he caught from the town, Kasrilevke, that is. Even before he returned the whole town

—you hear what I say?—knew all about Yeremei and the official and the red band and the visor and the conductor's Your Excellency—the whole show. He himself, Sholem Shachnah, that is, denied everything and swore up and down that the Kasrilevke smart-alecks had invented the entire story for lack of anything better to do. It was all very simple —the reason he came home late, after the holidays, was that he had made a special trip to inspect a wooded estate. Woods? Estate? Not a chance—no one bought *that!* They pointed him out in the streets and held their sides, laughing. And everybody asked him, 'How does it feel, Reb Sholem Shachnah, to wear a cap with a red band and a visor?' 'And tell us,' said others, 'what's it like to travel first class?' As for the children, this was made to order for them—you hear what I say? Wherever he went they trooped after him, shouting, 'Your Excellency! Your excellent Excellency! Your most excellent Excellency!'

"You think it's so easy to put one over on Kasrilevke?"

Translated by Isaac Rosenfeld

Devotion without End

I. L. PERETZ

THERE once dwelt in Safed a Jew of great wealth and good fortune, who traded in jewels, diamonds, and other precious stones. He was truly a man of great wealth, not like the upstarts of our day.

This Jew lived in a palace of his own, with windows that shone like gleaming eyes upon the Sea of Galilee; and about this palace bloomed a magnificent garden with all manner of beautiful trees and fruits. Songbirds sang in the sky, and on the earth there grew aromatic herbs that were a joy to behold and of much use in healing. Wide paths, strewn with golden sand, wound through the garden, and over these paths the crowns of the trees wove into one another to form a canopy of shade. Little arbors in which one could rest lay scattered along the edges of the garden, and in the ponds, which glistened like mirrors, there swam the rarest and whitest of swans. It was an earthly paradise.

The Jew had his own mules and camels with which to cross the desert;

and for sailing the sea he had his own ship, with his own crew and captain. Would that all Israel knew such blessings!

Nor was this Jew miserly with his wealth. He married his children into rabbinical families and into the families of the learned in both Babylon and Palestine; he sent his sons to study Torah, and when the time came for his sons to leave he would joyfully give to each of them his share of the inheritance. In time there remained at home only his youngest child, the beloved Sarah, whom he treasured above all others.

Sarah was exceedingly beautiful, a maiden soft in heart and sweet in temper.

And when the time came he presented his youngest daughter with a wonderful gift, brought from the Babylonian yeshiva: a youth named Chiya. The head of the Babylonian yeshiva wrote to the Rabbi of Safed that Chiya was no less than "the crown of my head" and "the crown of the yeshiva." And as for lineage, Chiya's was the finest, the very finest in Israel.

Rumors soon spread through the world that Chiya came from a princely line; but the records of his descent had been destroyed in the siege of Babylon, where Chiya had lost mother and father, brothers and sisters, and had himself been saved only through a miracle. Of this none ever knew for certain, since Reb Chiya, in his great modesty, never spoke of it. But it is known that when people saw the lad Chiya walking in the street they would gaze upon him as upon a radiant picture, and some would even stop to recite a blessing over his loveliness. For Chiya had a truly royal face: the Divine Presence shone down upon him.

Chiya settled with his father-in-law at Safed, devoting himself entirely to the study of Torah. Soon, however, his life of seclusion and repose came to an end, for his father-in-law died shortly after the wedding. The young man had no choice but to take over the worldly affairs of the family and to make journeys to every corner of the earth. So it was that he became one of the greatest merchants of his time.

But this, God forbid, did not tempt him to relinquish his study of the Torah. When Reb Chiya rode upon his camel in the desert, a servant would lead the animal by the reins, while he kept his eyes fastened upon the sacred book that lay in his hand. And in his ship there was a separate cabin where he would sit in privacy, giving himself unto Torah, both to that which is revealed and that which is unrevealed.

Reb Chiya even found time to devote himself to the Seven Wisdoms of the old sheiks whom he met on his journeys in the desert: to the science of medicine, to the language of the birds and the beasts, even to astrology.

His deeds of charity were numberless, and wherever he went his hand gave freely to those in need. Not only did he put aside a tenth of his earnings for the poor, he also ransomed captive Jews of whose plight he heard while traveling in distant lands. And so it came about that Reb Chiya performed many a great deed in behalf of the people of Israel.

Since Reb Chiya dealt in diamonds and pearls, he met many princes and their ministers during his travels, and through his beauty and honesty—or perhaps it was still more through his wisdom—he gained favor in their eyes. These princes and ministers had faith in his word, and were always ready to grant him mercy for a fellow Jew.

Thus did Reb Chiya become a spokesman for his people. Merely by giving his word, he could obtain the annulment of evil decrees, save Jews from the chains and lashes to which they had been unjustly condemned, and more than once snatch a victim from the hangman's rope. Many, too, were the souls that he rescued from the still worse fate of forced apostasy.

During the lengthy months and years that Reb Chiya was absent from home, his good wife Sarah would maintain the kind of household that did honor to a man of his standing. Reb Chiya had complete faith in her. He knew that the hungry would leave her door sated and the thirsty refreshed. And he knew that Sarah would raise their only daughter in the ways of piety and goodness.

So, indeed, it was. The palace was always full of guests, the poor and the learned, beggars and rabbis. Whenever the heads of the yeshivas traveled abroad to seek help, they would stop at the House of Reb Chiya's Wife—for so it had come to be called—and there she would receive them with generosity and joy. She would ask for one thing only: that they place their hands on the head of Miriam, her daughter, and give her their blessing. Nor were the blessings in vain, for Miriam was like a gift from heaven, a child of loveliness. All of Safed basked in her beauty and goodness, saying, "Reb Chiya's daughter is radiant as the sun. She moves with the grace and charm of Queen Esther."

But the ways of God are beyond understanding, and as King Solomon once said, "Whomever God loves, him does He chastise." Often the Almighty tests the pious by visiting many sorrows upon them to see how deep and strong is their faith. Be that as it may, the virtuous Sarah suddenly fell sick. Reb Chiya received the news in a distant corner of the earth, and in his heart he knew that the worst had come. Quickly he abandoned all his affairs and hastened home over mountains and valleys, seas and deserts. Many were the obstacles he encountered: mules and camels fell beneath him in the desert, the storms of the sea beat wildly against his ship—yet God did not forsake him. Reb Chiya overcame all these troubles and reached his home in safety. Sarah was close to her end. When the pious wife looked upon her husband, she gathered together all her strength and sat up in bed, murmuring her gratitude to God for listening to her prayer and allowing her to see once more the face of her beloved husband. She turned to Reb Chiya and consoled him, saying that she accepted the coming of death in a spirit of readiness; and then she spoke to him of their daughter Miriam. Reb Chiya vowed that he would be both father and mother to the child, that no strange hands would be allowed to bend or twist or, heaven forbid, break their tender plant. And the dying Sarah promised that in the world above she would not forget her husband Chiya or her daughter Miriam; she would beg the heavenly powers to send their daughter a husband of honor and virtue. If ever there should be any perplexity with regard to the child, she, Sarah, would beg permission to appear before Chiya in a dream and there tell him what must be done. So it was that she bid farewell to Reb Chiya. She recited the *Shma Yisroel* once more, and then she cast loving eyes upon the face of Reb Chiya and begged him to accept the will of heaven. She slid down from her pillow, drew up her feet, turned toward the wall, and rendered her spotless soul unto God.

No sooner were the thirty days of mourning at an end than Reb Chiya, without a moment's hesitation, disposed of his pearls and rubies and diamonds and settled once again to a life of study and good deeds. He transformed his palace into a yeshiva, and from among the Jews of Safed and its vicinity he brought together the most gifted youths, whom he taught each day another portion of holy wisdom. These youths drank from his wisdom with eagerness, and those who were poor he maintained in his palace, lodging two or three to a splendid room and clothing them as if they were the sons of the wealthy. Nothing could escape Reb Chiya's foresight: he even thought to give them pocket-money, so that the poorest among them might enjoy an occasional innocent pleasure and not be shamed before their wealthier companions.

Whenever one of these poorer students reached the age for marriage, Reb Chiya would send messengers in search of a suitable bride.

He would provide the dowry, the wedding clothes, and at least half the cost of the wedding; he would conduct the bridegroom to the wedding canopy; and he would himself give the wedded pair his blessing. As for his beloved daughter Miriam, he hoped that the day would come when there would appear for her a youth among youths, one who would find favor in the eyes of man and in the eyes of God.

It was on this theme that he once wrote to the head of the Babylonian yeshiva, a sage with whom he corresponded on all matters holy and profane. He wrote in that flowery Hebrew which is only proper for such subjects, and as we transpose it here into profane Yiddish it must lose much of its sweetness:

"With the help of Him whose name is sweet I have planted a lovely garden (the yeshiva) in which many trees bear fruit (the students), and once the fruit ripens (the students who reach the age of marriage) I seek to find for it a worthy buyer (a good father-in-law) and tell him to say the blessing over the fruit (the wedding ceremony). And if God will look upon me with favor and show me a citron without blemish, that citron shall be for my beloved Miriam, long may she live."

To which the head of the Babylonian yeshiva replied in his usual concise way: "Can it be that in your yeshiva there are no scholars of sufficient distinction?"

And then it was that Reb Chiya hinted that something other than scholarship was troubling him.

"The Torah," he wrote in his metaphorical style, "is like a stream, yet not all streams have their source in Paradise—not all men study Torah in a spirit of purity. One man studies Torah only to slake his vanity: his sole desire is to surpass and humiliate his fellows. A second studies for the sake of reputation: his desire is not to honor the Torah but that the Torah honor him. A third brings to the Torah still another kind of lust: he enjoys disputation for its own sake; his delight consists not in reaching toward the wisdom of God but in displaying the cleverness of his mind, his little novelties of interpretation, his paltry twisting of texts. To prove his cleverness he is even ready to distort the visible meaning of the Torah. And others are still more gross: the Torah becomes for them a spade with which to dig the ground, to find a wealthy father-in-law, a fat living, and, at the end, an inheritance! Even if a student may be found who desires learning for its own sake—still his soul is marred by some stain, some imperfection. Of citrons there are many, but Reb Chiya desires for his Miriam only one that is pure within and pure without. Nor is that so easy to find, for the heart of man is deep and devious. As the Talmud says, honor a man and beware of him."

Again the head of the Babylonian yeshiva replied with his customary terseness: "Search and thou shalt find."

But where is one to search?

Reb Chiya used to say: "One might imagine that a man's true character could be discovered in his eyes. The soul lies imprisoned in his body, and the Creator of the Universe, in His infinite mercy, has built two windows in the walls of this prison. These are the eyes, and through them the soul looks out upon the world and may, in turn, be seen by the world. But these windows, alas, have curtains; and a man whose soul is flawed tries to keep it from sight—even as a bride with a defect is kept from sight before the wedding. And just when the soul is ready to let itself be seen, he lowers the curtain, presumably from modesty."

It would be easier, claimed Reb Chiya, to recognize a man's character by his voice. And about this Reb Chiya had a theory of his own.

"Man may be compared to an earthen pot. The ordinary soul is but a piece of broken pottery, while the extraordinary soul is like an earthen pot which can receive the waters of the Torah without losing a drop. But this is possible only when the pottery is whole and uncracked. How then can one be certain that the pottery is not flawed, even if flawed so slightly as to escape the eye? You need only tap the pot with your finger, and if its ring is clear and full, all is well. If not . . .

"A man who is not whole may have a voice that is high or low, a voice that is broken or a voice that trembles; but he will never have one that is clear and true. Between a man and a pot, however, there is this difference: if you tap a man whose voice is defective, he has the ability to imitate, in the manner of a parrot, the voice of a stranger. Have you sometimes heard from a distance the voice of a bird and then, upon coming nearer, discovered that it was the mimicry of a parrot?"

These notions Reb Chiya would put to the test in the following manner.

It was his custom to teach the day's lesson in the morning. Later, in the afternoon, he would release his students to enjoy the shade of the trees, taste the fruit, and say the blessing over it. As they walked through the garden they would rehearse the lesson of the day or discuss some obscure problem of the Torah; or even if they engaged in some innocent chatter on a secular topic, that too was no fault. Reb Chiya would shut himself away in his study and pore over the unrevealed portions of the Torah. Over a window of this room looking out upon the garden, there hung a thick silken curtain. From time to time Reb Chiya would drop his spectacles, lay them on the prayer book before him, cover it with his scarf, and on top of all place his little snuff box. He would walk over to the window and stand near the curtain, listening to the voices of his students, who were walking about in pairs or in groups and talking freely to one another.

What they said he neither could nor wished to hear; only the sound of their voices reached him, never the words. And as the months passed Reb Chiya, never once hearing a true voice, fell into a deep sadness.

Once he went so far as to complain. "Master of the Universe, the birds in the garden that have but the souls of animals sing thy praises; my pupils, each of whom has a unique soul, study thy Torah. Yet, why is it that the voice of the birds is pure and whole, while the voices of my students . . ."

Reb Chiya did not finish; it would be unseemly to speak ill of his own pupils. But the sadness in his heart remained.

From time to time new pupils arrived, and with them new voices, yet there was not a voice of perfect quality among them.

Once he stopped his daughter Miriam, looked upon her with love and pity, and asked, "My daughter, do you ever visit your mother's grave?"

"Yes," she answered.

"And what do you pray for at your mother's grave?"

Lifting her faithful eyes, she replied, "I pray for your health, my father. At times you seem so sad, and I, alas, know not how to gladden you. She, my mother, knew how. So I pray to her that she shall teach my heart, or tell me in a dream."

Reb Chiya patted her silken cheeks and told her, "My health, praise be to God, is as it should be. There is something else that you must pray for at your mother's grave."

"And that is—?"

"Beg her to help bring to pass that which I have in mind for you."

"I shall, my father."

It happened once, before the evening prayer, that Reb Chiya heard a loud quarrel in a distant part of the house. He could hear two voices, the angry voice of his assistant and the other, young and strange. The unfamiliar voice astonished Reb Chiya: this was the voice for which he had hoped and prayed. Closing the book he had been studying, Reb Chiya heard how the pleading young voice was slowly drowned out by the wrathful voice of his assistant. Reb Chiya rapped on his table to call his assistant, who came running, frightened and alarmed. His aged face was still pale, his eyes still flashed darts of fire, his nostrils still danced—so angry had he been.

Reb Chiya warned him: anger is a sin more terrible than idolatry.

"No, Rabbi," the old man said sulkily, "the Messiah must be here—that's the only explanation for such insolence from a mere youth."

"Well, all right—but what does he want?"

"A trifle—just to be admitted to your yeshiva!"

"Well?"

"So I ask him, 'Do you know the Talmud?' He answers, 'No!' '*Mishnah* at least?' 'No,' he says again. So I try a joke. 'Can you at least say the prayers?' And again, 'No!' He bursts into tears. What then? Well, he can read the words of the prayers but has forgotten their meaning. 'Numskull, what do you want from us?' He wants Reb Chiya. 'Why?' To beg you to let him sit in the yeshiva and listen to the lessons, so that perhaps God will help him remember."

"That means he knew and forgot," mused Reb Chiya. "He's sick. Why be angry?"

"Why be angry? I say to him, 'All right, I'll let you see Reb Chiya.' But the youth is dressed in rags, with a rope around his loins, and he carries a staff in his hand, as if he were a thief—a peeled branch of an almond tree. I tell him, 'You can see Reb Chiya, but first change your clothes. Have you others?' He neither has nor wishes to. He's not allowed to, he says. 'At least put your staff away.' Not that either. He's not allowed to part with it, neither in the day nor at night. He sleeps with it!"

Reb Chiya, realizing that this must be a penitent, said, "Send him in."

A pale slender youth entered, dressed just as the assistant had said, and remained standing at the door.

Reb Chiya asked him to come nearer, extended a hand of welcome, and prevented him from kneeling or kissing his hand. Seeing that the youth did not lift his eyes, Reb Chiya asked, "My son, why do you not look at me? Are you hiding your soul from my eyes?"

"Yes, Rabbi," answered the youth, "my soul is sinful, my shame is great."

Replied Reb Chiya, "Our sages say that no man may speak against himself. I ask you to lift up your eyes."

The youth obeyed. And Reb Chiya, looking into his eyes, was seized with a violent trembling: before him he saw a soul that had been cursed.

"Tell me, my son, who has cursed you?"

"The head of the Jerusalem yeshiva."

Knowing that the head of the Jerusalem yeshiva had died only recently, Reb Chiya asked, "When?"

"Two months ago."

Correct, thought Reb Chiya. Two months ago he was still alive. Aloud he asked, "Why?"

"About that I have been directed to confess to you."

"Good. And your name?"

"Chananiah."

"Well, Chananiah," said Reb Chiya, rising, "let us say the evening prayers and then you will be shown your place at the table. After you have eaten, go to the garden, where I shall hear out your story."

Reb Chiya took the youth by the hand and led him to the little synagogue by the side of the yeshiva.

And while they walked, these were the thoughts that ran through Reb Chiya's head: So young and such a voice . . . and a penitent . . . a curse in his eyes . . . wondrous are the ways of the Almighty.

It was late in the evening when Reb Chiya and Chananiah walked through the garden. Reb Chiya would cast glances at the sky, seeking some sign or omen; but the sky was veiled with a gray and silent mist; a night without a moon, without stars. Only the windows of the palace gleamed with little lights, and by these Reb Chiya led the youth Chananiah to an arbor.

Reb Chiya began, "There is a Hebrew proverb, *'D'aga b'lev ish—yeshina.'* "

"What does that mean, Rabbi?"

"It means: *d'aga*—sorrow (Chananiah repeating each word); *b'lev*—in the heart; *ish*—of a man; *yeshina*—he shall tell another. That is, a man with a heart of sorrow shall pour it out to another." And though the youth understood only the translation his pale face began to flush, as if he had fainted and only now was his soul gradually returning to his body.

Reb Chiya, filled with pity for the youth, told him, "Open your lips, my son, and may your words enter the light. Speak to me, my son."

And this was the strange tale that Chananiah told him.

The youth had been born in Jerusalem, the son of a wealthy widow who dealt in spices. Of her two children, the woman favored Chananiah over his elder sister Esther, for it was he who would someday say

Kaddish in her memory, and he, moreover, who quickly showed himself to be a prodigy.

Even when Esther reached the age of sixteen the mother remained untroubled by the fact that her daughter had not yet married. And when the neighbors reminded her that the time for marriage had come, the mother had a ready answer: "The girl's hair has not even turned gray." The mother's heart was wholly given over to her son Chananiah. She hired excellent tutors for the boy, and since, as a distant relative of the head of the Jerusalem yeshiva, she had entry into his house, she would bring Chananiah to be examined by him every few Sabbaths.

The youth impressed the head of the yeshiva greatly, and the mother would be beside herself with joy as she stood listening near the door, peering through a crack and seeing how the rabbi pinched the boy's cheek fondly and gave him the best apple from the Sabbath fruit bowl. Still greater was her joy when the rabbi's wife told her that the boy would be accepted by the Jerusalem yeshiva—though to this she did not agree, for she was unwilling to part from her son. She wished to keep her darling at home, so that she could entrust her shop to a neighbor for a moment and hurry into the house to embrace her child. She therefore engaged a more learned scholar who would study with the boy at home.

And it was this teacher who caused her downfall.

He was one of those false scholars who come to the Torah not for its own sake or from love of God but out of a lust to shine in their own right; and he soon led Chananiah along his false path. He taught the boy nothing but the devices of sophistry, the art of negating all things; and in the boy's heart he planted the bitter herbs of pride and presumption. Chananiah soon learned all of his tricks, for such knowledge is, in truth, a mere trickery, not the wisdom of the Torah—it was not this that was meant at Sinai. But neither the mother nor the neighbors understood this; and so they praised the boy still more. And the mother—for what can one expect from a foolish woman?—swelled with pride.

The time came when Chananiah had absorbed all that his teacher could offer, and he told his mother that he could now study on his own. The foolish woman felt that the gates of heaven had opened for her.

Chananiah now trod the false path by himself, engaging in disputes with the students at the yeshiva and with older scholars, whom he always put to shame and made seem mere ignoramuses. So it continued until word reached the head of the yeshiva, who said, "Youthful foolishness! But he will grow out of it," and then sent word to Chananiah's mother that she should punish the boy. "A mother," he added, "is allowed to."

But instead the mother gave Chananiah a kiss and bought him a costly present.

Encouraged, Chananiah strayed still further, running about in all the synagogues to display his tricks. He would interrupt the studies of pupils, asking them questions about the passages they were reading and then destroying the answers they gave him. So it continued until the student would become bewildered, and Chananiah had proved to everyone that the student was worthless.

Sometimes it happened that when a youth was explaining a passage of the Torah or a scholar was preaching—and this hardly before the speaker had finished—Chananiah would spring onto the pulpit and ridicule the explanation or cut the sermon into ribbons, as if with a scissors, ripping through it as through a cobweb and making the other seem a mere fool.

Again, word was brought to the head of the yeshiva, who now issued a stricter judgment: "Tell his mother that I have asked her to punish him severely." And again, instead of beating Chananiah, she rewarded him with kisses and gifts, so that he went still further along the paths of evil. When word was brought once more to the head of the yeshiva he sighed, hesitating to do that which should be left to a mother. But once he was told how the mother responded, he ordered that Chananiah be brought to him. The youth came, flaming with pride. And when the head of the yeshiva began to speak of Torah, he interrupted with needling questions, questions upon questions that were meant to show the prowess of his mind.

But the head of the yeshiva was truly a saintly man, and without a trace of anger he quietly replied, "Hear me out, Chananiah! All your knowledge can do is to negate—you have nothing but the power of saying 'no'—which means that you do not possess the Torah whole. For the Torah is made up of two parts, the one that allows and the other that forbids, the one that says 'Thou shalt' and the other 'Thou shalt not.' And you, Chananiah, have only the second half of the Torah. More than half you shall never have. And here is proof: say something of your own that carries the power of 'yes.' "

Chananiah was silent: his strength lay solely in destruction. He tried to justify himself. "But this I did not learn from my teacher."

Answered the head of the yeshiva, "Your teacher, Chananiah, is dead, and the fires of hell have wrapped themselves around him. His kind of Torah cannot save him. He will burn, Chananiah, until you root out from your heart the weeds he planted. You must take pity both on your soul and on his; come, repent, study the Torah in its purity."

Chananiah quickly ran off to the cemetery to see whether his teacher was really dead. There he was told, "Yes, the funeral took place yesterday," and they led him to the grave. He saw that overnight the grave had been covered with foul and ugly weeds. And Chananiah, knowing what this meant, decided to repent.

But something happened to interfere, alas, with Chananiah's resolve.

There lived in Jerusalem in those days a retired butcher, to whom the Jewish authorities had once sent a learned Jew to see whether he sold defiled meat as kosher; and when this learned Jew tried to carry out his task faithfully and appeared unannounced at a slaughtering, the butcher seized an ax and hurled it at his head. It was a miracle that the man survived; and a great commotion followed in the city. The Jewish authorities announced that the butcher's meat was not kosher, worse even than the flesh of swine. But since the butcher had by now become wealthy from his illicit trade, he closed his shop and became a usurer and an informer for the government. He complained against the Jewish authorities, who were thereupon cast into prison and banished. And since he no longer sold meat to his fellow Jews there was nothing they could do to him. They merely thanked God that this scoundrel had done no more damage than he had and hoped that he might now be quiet.

The wealthy butcher, who possessed the heart of a miser, did not enjoy his wealth; he neither ate nor drank, he dressed shabbily, and he raised fierce dogs to keep beggars from his door. He had no sons and but one daughter, whose name was Hannah. When this only daughter was born, his wife, a good and pious woman, fully realized the evil of her husband's ways and prayed to God that her womb be closed, for she did not desire sons who would follow in their father's footsteps. So it came to pass: she had but one daughter, and all her efforts to lead her husband to the path of virtue failed. As her life became unbearable to her, she prayed for an early death; and this prayer too was granted. Before she died she begged her relatives to bury her in secrecy, so that her husband would not know the place of her grave.

Thus it happened that the tyrant became a widower. And since no father would entrust him with a daughter, he did not remarry but lived alone with his only child Hannah. By some miracle he loved his daughter with all his heart and was ready to bestow upon her all the pleasures he denied himself—even though money was dearer to him than his soul. But Hannah refused everything, living by her mother's command that she accept nothing from her father but bread and water. Nor did the girl need expensive clothes, for she never left her father's house, not wishing to hear him cursed and abused in the streets of Jerusalem. Yet the less she desired the use of his money, the more did the father wish to heap favors upon her.

When he saw that his daughter remained stubborn in her ways the father decided: One favor she will accept; a husband who is a great scholar.

As soon as Hannah approached the age for marriage the father began to seek a husband for her. He wanted a scholar surpassing all other scholars; he hired marriage brokers to scour the land, and he himself rushed through Jerusalem, searching in all the yeshivas and promising a generous dowry to the youth who might be chosen. But it was all in vain. No one wished to be related to the wealthy butcher—and as for his daughter, her true worth remained unknown.

The man grew angry, and angrier still when a marriage broker once told him to put aside his pride and make the best of things by accepting the one man who was available, a poor carpenter who earned his bread honestly and who wanted Hannah for her own sake.

The wealthy butcher hit upon the plan of sending through the length and breadth of the land, especially to the distant corners where his name was not known, two poverty-stricken scholars whom he paid for two years in advance. Being poor, the two scholars could not refuse, and so they traveled the length and breadth of Israel—but to no avail.

Nor was it difficult to discover the reason for their failure. They spoke of a dowry and of maintenance for the future husband and of gifts, but of Hannah's father they said not a word. When they were asked about him they pretended not to hear, for they were honest men who did not wish to lie. And thus it became clear that something was very wrong, and no one wanted the match.

The two years passed, and now, before the gates of Jerusalem, the two learned Jews stood empty-handed, trembling with fear. Had they not left behind them wives and children they might have gone to some other country, for they knew that their employer would refuse to believe them and would think they had failed to do as he had told them. Perhaps he would even go so far as to turn them over to the government. The two learned Jews gave way to lamentations.

And as they sat before the gates of Jerusalem, lamenting their fate, they were accosted by a poor youth dressed in sackcloth, with a hempen rope around his loins and a staff cut from an almond tree in his hand; and this youth came to them, greeted them, asked if they wanted to drink, and inquired why they sat in such dejection; and he told them that he lived in the nearby desert and knew of a well from which they could drink. If they wished he would lead them. But the two learned Jews were not thirsty; they were worried. They asked the youth who he was, and he answered that he was a homeless orphan, living apart from all other men and subsisting on wild grasses.

"And have you no wish to study Torah?"

But he did study Torah, he replied. Every night, when darkness came over the desert, an old man appeared before him and taught him the Torah by word of mouth. He could see this old man from afar, his eyes sparkling like the stars in heaven and his white beard shining like snow, and each night the old man sat beside him, teaching him both Torah and its commentaries.

When they questioned the youth to see if he were truthful, pearls of wisdom seemed to fall from his lips. Then they asked him why he had abandoned the desert and come to sit by the gates of Jerusalem, and he answered with simple honesty that on the previous night the old man had bade him farewell, saying that they had met for the last time, and had directed him to the holy city where he would find both bride and fortune. "And I must obey the old man," added the youth.

As soon as the two learned Jews heard this story they were filled with joy and said to the youth, "Come with us, we know the bride for you." And he went with them.

They took him directly to the wealthy butcher and said, "Do not be concerned with the appearance of this youth. For he is truly wise: Elijah the Prophet has taught him in the wilderness." Without delay or question, the rich man accepted the youth, and fearful that a long delay might result in someone's casting an evil eye or at least spreading malicious gossip, he arranged for a marriage in two weeks. First of all he took the rags off the back of the youth and took the staff from his hand, and then he gave him new clothes such as are suitable for the son of a rich man. The old clothes he kept, however, hoping to sell them for a few coppers after the wedding. The news of this match spread quickly through the town, and some said the biggest dog gets the best bone; while others contended that it was the doing of the bride's mother, who had interceded in heaven. Still others remarked that the ways of God are beyond human comprehension.

The two weeks passed without incident and the day of the wedding came near. For the sake of his daughter the old miser forgot his niggardliness and arranged a feast such as the world has seldom seen. And to honor the bridegroom, all the distinguished Jews of Jerusalem came to the wedding, as did also the students of the yeshiva. While the bride was being prepared for the wedding, the bridegroom discoursed among the men on an esoteric point of Torah.

In the other room, the bride has been made ready. The musicians have begun to play. The chief rabbi and the head of the yeshiva, who are to conduct the groom to the canopy, hold candles in readiness for the wedding procession. And from the groom's lips the wisdom of the Torah continues to flow like a river of myrrh and frankincense, while his eyes gleam like the stars of heaven. All stand gaping with admiration, and Chananiah among them, silently, with no thought of envy or contradiction. On the contrary, he rejoices at the thought that he will now have a companion in study, a friend with whom to discuss all matters of learning. And he is flooded with love, a warm love for the bridegroom. He yearns to get up, to embrace him. He begins to move forward—and then the terrible thing happens.

Passing through the crowd, he hears one yeshiva student tell another, "The bridegroom is a better scholar than Chananiah," and the second one replies, "Of course, Chananiah is a blockhead by comparison." And this proves too much for Chananiah. It seems as if his heart is bursting, as if a wound has opened, as if a serpent has stung him—the Evil One, his own evil spirit. He stops, he rises on tiptoe, he begins suddenly to speak, and from his mouth there pours a stream of pitch and brimstone, contradiction and desecration. He senses that he is betraying his soul, that he is desecrating the wisdom of Elijah the Prophet, the wisdom of the Torah itself, that he is piercing the heart of the Torah with spears and with swords, he is murdering the Torah. Frightened, he wishes to cease, but he cannot—something outside of his will, a devil, speaks through him, something against his will. He sees the bridegroom turn pale with fear, stagger, collapse.

The wedding chamber becomes a living hell. The old miser, enraged, roars like a wounded lion, "Swindled! I've been swindled!" He rushes about like a madman, finds the two learned Jews who were his emissaries, beats them, and tears out their beards. He throws himself upon the musicians, wrenches the instruments from their hands, and smashes them into pieces. He runs to the bride and drags her away from the wedding canopy. He dashes out to another room and comes back with the bridegroom's old clothes: sackcloth, hempen rope, and staff. Tearing the new ones from the bridegroom's back, he hurls the youth into the street, and his clothes after him. The dignitaries of Jerusalem flee in terror. Only Chananiah remains. He stands in the same spot as if paralyzed and hears the old miser scream, "I won't waste this wedding feast! Bring the carpenter! Let him marry my daughter!" And only now does Chananiah manage to escape from the house.

In the street he encounters the head of the yeshiva, who takes him by the hand and says to him, "Chananiah, your evil is enough to destroy a world! Far better that you forget all you have learned."

"It was at this moment," continued Chananiah, "that something snapped in my brain, and I became as empty as a cage from which the birds have fled. The Torah had taken flight from me. I fell at the feet of the head of the yeshiva and begged for atonement, but he could only sigh. 'Who knows if there is any for you?'

"I began to sob wildly, and he pointed to the bridegroom, who stood not far away, bewildered in the strange city.

" 'As a first step,' said the head of the yeshiva, 'you might beg his forgiveness.'

"I was afraid, but he prodded me, 'Go, ask him to go home with you. I will come later.'

"I went to the bridegroom I had shamed, and before I could say a word he ran up to me and cried out, 'You are forgiven, forgiven! The match was not destined for me.'

"I would have preferred a beating, and he comes up to me, his hand on my shoulder, and calls me friend!

" 'But what sort of friendship,' I replied, 'can there be between an ignoramus and a scholar?' He looked at me, amazed, and then I told him of the curse the head of the yeshiva had placed upon my head. And he said to me, 'If ever again there appears before me my old teacher'—he meant Elijah the Prophet—'I will beg him to help you.'

"I brought him to my mother, suffering all the while the agonies of the damned. He spoke to me of Torah and I understood not a word. My heart wept with yearning for the Torah . . . darkness and desolation flooded my soul, as in a ruin at night. And when we came to my mother's house, I fell upon her neck with the cry, 'Mother, Mother, God has punished us. Your son no longer has a word of learning!'

"She cried out in fright, 'What do you mean? Who has cast a spell upon you?'

"And then I told her the whole story, pointing to the bridegroom I had shamed. She wept bitter tears, and my sister Esther turned her face to the wall, weeping. But at this moment there came the head of the yeshiva, and it was to Esther that he spoke first. 'Hear me, my daughter, go to the kitchen and prepare food for this scholar'—pointing to the youth who stood beside me—'and if fortune will shine upon you, he will prove to be your destined mate.'

"With dismay Esther glanced at the shamed bridegroom, but she obeyed the head of the yeshiva.

"And then he turned to my mother and said, 'This is no time for tears. You too have sinned in not providing for Esther and not punishing Chananiah.' And when my mother sobbed still louder, he continued, 'Not tears are needed now, but acts. Will you do as I tell you?'

" 'Yes,' sobbed my mother, 'I shall, I shall!'

" 'First marry Esther to this youth, for he is her destined mate.'

"A cry broke out of my mother's heart. 'This beggar in rags?'

" 'This is the youth to whom Elijah the Prophet taught the Torah. Is that how you obey me?'

" 'Forgive me, Rabbi! I obey, I obey!'

" 'And your son,' he continued, 'must crawl through the lands of exile, until the mercy of the All-Merciful shall be awakened in his behalf. He too will bring you happiness, but later. Esther is the older one!'

" 'And as for you,' he said to me, 'atonement for your dreadful sin might not have been possible had you not been fortunate. The marriage was not a destined one, and what you did has proved to be good for both bride and bridegroom.'

" 'Even the bride?' wondered my mother.

"To which the head of the yeshiva replied, 'It is known that Hannah, the daughter of the old miser, is good and pious. Her saintly mother pleaded for her in heaven and won for her one of the Thirty-Six Secret Saints upon whom the earth rests. And he is the carpenter whom the old miser dragged to the wedding canopy so that his feast might not go to waste. But this you must keep secret until he reveals himself.'

" 'God's miracles,' said my mother, somewhat relieved.

" 'And now,' he said to me and to the bridegroom, 'now, my dear children, each of you must take the other's clothes.'

" 'And you,' he added to me, 'must begin your wanderings in exile. Take the staff and guard it as the apple of your eye. At night, when you sleep, you shall place it beside your head. And I will pray that help may come to you and that the staff may blossom, so that your soul too will blossom, and then you will remember all that you have forgotten. But remember that only then may you wear other garments. And now go, without saying farewell to anyone.'

"I quickly dressed in the clothes of the bridegroom I had shamed, and at that very moment my sister entered with a plate of food. Seeing us now, she dropped the plate in astonishment. It broke with a loud noise, and the head of the yeshiva cried out, *'Mazel tov, mazel tov!'*

"More I did not hear, for I was already on my way."

As soon as he left Jerusalem, said Chananiah to Reb Chiya, he lost his way in a desert, where neither bread nor water was to be found. But he knew no desire for bread or for water, and he satisfied the wants of his body with the wild grasses that lay scattered in the desert. Throughout his wanderings he was in constant danger from the wild beasts, yet they harmed him not. When he came near them they would growl and then turn from his path. Chananiah understood that they had no power over him, for he was not yet fated to die. Once it seemed to him that a voice called out, "He belongs to . . ." But to whom it was that he belonged he could not hear.

And so he wandered in exile, through the days and through the nights, mourning over his youth that was being wasted without Torah, without a light or a ray for his darkened mind. If only he could have heard one word of Torah, one word . . .

Once, continued Chananiah with his story, he poured a handful of sand upon his head and then, in self-castigation, he stood on one leg, crying out toward heaven, "Torah, Torah." He cried with earnest devotion, on and on, until the sun sank, and then he fell to the earth and slept. In his sleep he saw again the head of the Jerusalem yeshiva, dressed in the clothes of the grave and with a golden crown upon his head. And the head of the Jerusalem yeshiva said to Chananiah, "Arise, Chananiah, for the time of your redemption is at hand. God has heard your prayer, and Elijah the Prophet has interceded for you. Arise and go forward, till you reach the city of Safed, where you shall go to the good man Reb Chiya and make full confession to him of all that you have done. You shall beg him to let you enter his yeshiva, and he will not refuse you. And when you reach the age of eighteen, he will find your destined bride and he will pray for you. His prayers, you shall remember, are hearkened to in heaven. And besides that, the ceremony of marriage and the blessings that follow it will also help you. On the eighth day after the wedding you will arise in the morning and will see that the staff by your head has begun to blossom and to sprout almonds; so too will your soul bloom and sprout. Then you will remember everything but the evil that was in you, and you will recite for Reb Chiya a portion of the Torah, but now it will be a Torah pure and without defilement. Reb Chiya will rejoice in you, but whether you will live long after that I cannot foretell."

With these words the head of the Jerusalem yeshiva vanished from Chananiah's dream. Chananiah awoke and began his journey.

"And now, Reb Chiya, I have come to you." So said Chananiah.

Reb Chiya looked upon him with great sadness and asked, "How old are you, my son?"

"Seventeen years and ten months."

"To be cut off so young," mused Reb Chiya.

Chananiah raised his big imploring eyes to Reb Chiya's face and pleaded in a voice that was trembling, "Rabbi, will you take me into your yeshiva?"

An empty soul, thought Reb Chiya, a stranger to the Torah—and yet from his throat one hears a voice like King David's violin. Aloud he said, "Sleep now, my son. Tomorrow I shall answer you."

Chananiah left him, and Reb Chiya remained for a while in the arbor, gazing up at the sky and wondering, Is this the youth for whom I have so long been waiting?

But the heavens were clouded and did not speak.

The next morning, once they were alone, Reb Chiya said to Chananiah, "Know, my son, that for my part I am ready to grant your request, but—"

Chananiah began to tremble. "Rabbi," he begged, "let me sit somewhere in a dark corner, at the back, farthest away from you. I will listen only to what you tell your pupils, I will do nothing but listen."

"I am willing," Reb Chiya comforted him, "but I fear that my students, being young and mischievous, may mock you. And let us not delude ourselves—they know a good deal while you, for the time being . . . The scorn of the learned for the unlearned is large, and you, my son, will suffer."

Joyously Chananiah cried out, "But I must suffer, Rabbi, I should suffer, and the more I am shamed the sooner will my curse be lifted."

"That may be," said Reb Chiya, "but I am afraid that your presence will harm the others. For is it not written"—he continued in Hebrew —"that those who shame others before the world shall lose their portion of Paradise?"

These words were now beyond Chananiah's understanding, but when Reb Chiya translated them he was still happier: "It means that even if the curse is lifted from my head I shall still have no share of Paradise, so that if I study the Torah it can be only for its own sake, without hope of reward."

To Reb Chiya these words were a delight and a balm. But he continued, "They, my pupils, how can I allow them to lose their share of Eternal Life?"

Chananiah remained silent for a moment and then replied, "And if I forgave them beforehand?"

Reb Chiya's answer was to take Chananiah by the hand, lead him to the yeshiva, and seat him, as the youth had requested, in a corner, apart from the students.

While Reb Chiya was expounding a passage of the Torah he cast an occasional glance at Chananiah and saw that the youth sat with eyes closed and ears attentive, his face flushing with happiness when the meaning of a word became clear to him and paling with anguish when he failed to understand. Sometimes a pall of fear would descend upon him: he could not make out even a word in translation. To Reb Chiya he seemed like a bewildered creature, lost and stumbling in the desert, parched with thirst yet brightening with hope at the sound of distant water.

Reb Chiya would frequently overhear his students whispering among themselves about Chananiah, taking his name in slander and contempt, and though this brought sadness to his heart he did not rebuke them, for he also saw that Chananiah returned their glances of evil with glances of love, as if they were bestowing a great favor upon him. And so Reb Chiya continued to speak of the Torah.

After Reb Chiya spoke, the students would ask questions and he would answer them. Only Chananiah remained mute, not a word of assent or denial passing his lips. But the devotion—a devotion without end—that he gave to every word glowed upon his face. When the class was done Chananiah would be the last to leave, and, still a solitary, he would spend his afternoon hours walking along the most distant and neglected path, which led to an abandoned hut amidst oleander trees. And there he would sit, lost in meditation, until the time for prayer.

Once, at prayer time, Reb Chiya went to the hut where Chananiah sat and inquired as to the progress Chananiah had made in his studies.

"My knowledge," answered Chananiah, "has yet to be restored to me, but now I do hear the words and I hear them with increasing clarity, and sometimes I can even remember their meanings in translation."

Reb Chiya sighed and remained silent.

"Rabbi," begged Chananiah, "you once used the word *yeshina*—let him tell another. This word has lived in my memory, lighting up the darkness of my soul. Let me speak to you!"

"Of course," said Reb Chiya.

"Sitting alone in this hut, I sometimes surrender myself to meditation, and it seems to me at times that I have been like a cage, full of songbirds that sang God's glory and celebrated His Sabbath. But then there came a magician who cast a spell upon the birds, and they began to sing other melodies, melodies insolent and dissolute. The mob did not understand this and praised both the cage and the birds in the cage, until there once passed through a learned man who paused to listen. He quickly caught the true drift of the melody, the undertones of error and deceit, and he went to the birds and said, "Rather than sing as you do, may you be stricken dumb!" He blew a harsh blast of cold and angry air into the cage, and then, as if by a miracle, the birds were silent. They fell to the bottom of the cage as if they were frozen, and there they still lie with wings folded, beaks closed and eyes shut, like the dead.

"And now, when I listen to your discourse and snatch a meaning from one or another word, each of your words seems to waken in me another bird. It opens its little eyes and its mouth and it begins to sing with a soft voice, a quiet voice, but the melodies are good, pious, and truthful melodies, and its wings begin to stir. Soon, soon it will fly."

"You see," comforted Reb Chiya, "God has mercy."

But Chananiah would not be comforted. "All this happens during the day. As soon as the sun goes down, the shadows of night settle again upon my soul. The cage is silent and frozen, the birds that have stirred their wings are lamed once more, and they fall as if dead, with their mouths closed and their eyes shut."

Reb Chiya, from his sadness, could only say, "Go, my son, to the prayers. I shall remain here and pray for you."

Gazing upon Reb Chiya with love and gratitude, Chananiah left.

Reb Chiya remained alone, reciting the evening prayers. As he was leaving the hut, intending to offer a prayer for Chananiah in the open, he saw two snakes twined about oleander trees, with their mouths drooping toward each other so that their venomous tongues almost met.

Reb Chiya was familiar with all the creatures of his garden, those that fly into the heavens, those that slumber on the branches of trees, and those that crawl on the ground. One of the snakes he quickly recognized, but the other, of the species called Achnai, seemed a stranger. But even as he grew curious as to why this snake had come to his garden, he overheard the familiar one ask the visitor this very question.

"I have come to sting someone."

The familiar snake smiled. "Your troubles are in vain. It is many years since I settled here, and when I came I too was a fiery and venomous snake. Frequently would I sting the students of the yeshiva. But with time I ceased. And do you know why? Because Reb Chiya, who is the head of the yeshiva, was once a merchant who traveled over the length and breadth of the world, and from the wise old sheiks whom he met in the deserts he learned many arts, not least of all the art of healing. I would sting and then he would apply the herbs that cured the stings. So I realized that my efforts were being wasted and I simply ceased working."

"Foolishness!" sneered the visiting snake. "Reb Chiya's herbs help only when a snake bites from innate malice, because of the ancient enmity between man and snake. It is well known that the Creator of the Universe prepares a cure for each plague when the plague is not yet visited, and even before he created the venom of snakes he had decreed that the earth should yield its remedies. But I do not fear this, for I come not of my own will and I shall sting not from the animosity of the snake. I come rather as the servant of the Angel of Death, and I come to carry out a sentence against a man who has been condemned."

"How is that possible?" asked the familiar snake with wonderment. "Here there are only the learned and pious students of Reb Chiya."

"It is Chananiah for whom I come, the youth who meditates here each day."

"But why?"

"This youth once publicly shamed a pupil of Elijah the Prophet. For that sin he was cursed by the head of the Jerusalem yeshiva with the curse of forgetfulness, and it was further decreed that he wander in exile, clad in sackcloth and with an almond staff in hand. Not till the staff blossoms can he again remember the Torah."

"That means—never."

"Who can know?" answered the stranger. "In heaven this sentence was found unsatisfactory; some said it was too mild and declared that Chananiah should be deprived of his share of Eternal Life. But the Master of the Torah was obdurate; he insisted that the youth be permitted to atone for his sins. A compromise was reached. The youth was to marry a pious daughter of Israel and on the eighth day after the wedding he would die. Half of his sin would be atoned for by the blessings of marriage, and the other half by his death. And since the young woman would be left a widow so quickly, she would be blessed with a son who would become a light of wisdom and a comfort to the world."

The snake grew weary of discourse, never before, perhaps, having spoken at such length. He begged his companion to lead him to water, whereupon the two snakes uncoiled from the trees and glided away. Reb Chiya remained standing, struck with fear.

For Reb Chiya now found himself in a terrible dilemma. If he did nothing to further the marriage of Chananiah, he would be contesting the will of Paradise and Chananiah would never recover the Torah. If he helped Chananiah to marry, he would be destroying the youth with his own hands and would, furthermore, be helping to condemn a Jewish daughter to early widowhood.

Reb Chiya searched the heavens; and the heavens kept silent. But his heart began to pound, and a voice within him said, "Chiya, sacrifice thy only daughter Miriam. Father Abraham would not have hesitated."

But it is not so easy to give up one's only daughter. And at this moment Reb Chiya remembered that his sainted wife Sarah had promised that, when need be, she would appear to him in a dream, and so he raised his eyes imploringly. As he prayed, the clouds vanished from his sight and millions of stars came out, promising him that all would yet be well.

His prayer was soon heeded. Once, toward the end of a fast day, Reb Chiya grew faint; his eyes began to close and he fell asleep. In his dream he saw his beloved Sarah, her eyes still shining with the love she had always borne him. As she placed her hand on his right shoulder, she said to him, "Fear not, Chiya. The life of our daughter shall be as bright as the light of the sun. Have faith."

He would have asked her more, but Sarah faded from his dream, and he felt himself being awakened. As Reb Chiya opened his eyes he saw before him his daughter Miriam, her hand on his right shoulder. "Forgive me, Father," she said, "but the sun has long since set, the moon has come into sight, and the stars are shining. It is time for you to break your fast."

Reb Chiya, seeing before him the climax of his dream, took her lovingly by the hand, drew her to his heart, and said, "I shall not break my fast, my daughter, until I have asked you and you have spoken the truth."

And when he saw the color spread across his daughter's face, he said, "My daughter, it is the custom that a young girl should unburden her feelings only to her mother. But you are an orphan, and I must be to you both mother and father. Therefore speak to me in honesty and leave nothing hidden in your heart."

Miriam buried her face in his breast and whispered, "Ask, my father."

"You see that the years pass by and I grow no younger. My beard has become as white as the snows of Mount Hebron. And how shall it be when I am called to my judgment? With whom shall I leave you?"

"Speak not of this, my father. I shall always heed you."

And so he asked, "Would you wish, my daughter, to be more righteous than Rebecca?"

"Not at all." She smiled.

"When Eliezer, the servant of Abraham, came to propose the marriage between Isaac and Rebecca, the Bible says that he was met with the words, 'We shall inquire of her wishes.' Nor was she shamefaced, for she answered, 'Yes, I do.' "

"Ask, Father, and I too shall answer."

"Tell me truthfully, which among my students would you desire as a husband?"

"Chananiah," answered Miriam softly, so softly that only a father's ear could have heard the name.

Amazed at the answer, Reb Chiya asked again, "And why does he please you above all others? Have you ever spoken with him?"

"God forbid," she replied. "And besides—would he have answered me?"

Reb Chiya smiled. "What then is it? Tell me." And when he saw that she found it difficult to speak he added, "I command it of you, Miriam, by my right of fatherhood."

And then it was that she told him why Chananiah pleased her above all others, and pleased her from the very first moment. "It was his voice, which flows into my heart with sweetness; and then—it was his strength."

"His strength?" wondered Reb Chiya.

"Surely it shows strength for a youth to go about in sackcloth among the well-clad students and to feel neither shame nor fear."

"And anything else?"

"And for the goodness of his heart, which glows from his eyes whenever he lifts them from the ground. And for his sadness—"

"But he is a penitent, a great sin burdens his soul."

"God will forgive him, He must forgive him!" she cried out. "There have been times when I passed his hut and heard his prayers. Is it conceivable that such heart-rending prayers will not be answered?"

"Our God, Miriam, is a God of Mercy."

"Of his sins I know not, but his atonement is deep. So much regret, so much pain, are cut into his face, and sometimes so much melancholy. One must pity him."

"Is it only pity that you feel?"

"At the beginning that was all. I used to think that if I were you I would constantly pray for him. Afterward the thought came to me: were I his brother I would surrender my life in his behalf. And then—you have asked me to be truthful—a warm stream of blood would rush into my heart. It seemed to me that the deepest sacrifice is possible only to a wife. Since you have commanded me, I speak.

"And once it happened, dear Father, I dreamed—it was on the holiday that you and your pupils went sailing. Chananiah also went—you asked him to—and I, watching through the window, saw the sadness on his face as he followed you. I remained alone in the house—it seemed so sad and lonely. I went into the garden. There too it was quiet; not a bird sang. And I became strangely weary. I looked at the flowers, and they too were drooping. The day was hot; I lay down near the white lilies, my hands folded beneath my head, and gazed at the sky. I slept and I dreamed.

"I dreamed that a dove was flying through the air, so white and gentle and sad. Beneath the dove there flew a black bird of prey, with a sharp beak that sought to stab it. My heart filled with pity for the dove, and I cried out in warning. The dove did not hear me, it continued to fly, but the black bird heard me and, for a moment, made off in alarm. Soon it came back, flying still faster and coming closer to the dove. I felt myself overcome with pity, and I cried still more loudly. Again the black bird grew frightened and turned aside, and again it returned to the chase. This happened several times, until the dove heard me and glided down to ask in tones of sadness, 'Why do you cry, child?' I answered, 'There is a black bird chasing you but you do not see it, and I am trying to frighten it away.' The dove said mournfully, 'It does not *want* to kill me; it *must* kill me. I am condemned to death, and the black bird will carry out the sentence unless someone sacrifices his life for me. And who will do that?' 'I will do it,' I cried to the dove. 'And you will feel no regret?' he asked. 'No, I swear it, I shall never regret.' The dove made signs of affection, stayed for a few moments, and then flew away. And when I awoke I understood what the dream had meant. I knew that the dove was he—Chananiah. I knew that true devotion, devotion without end, can be shown only by a wife. I have sworn, Father, I have sworn!"

Reb Chiya listened, and then he sadly asked, "And how would it be, my daughter, if Chananiah were destined to die in his youth? If he were destined to beget a son who would become a great scholar, but he himself were to leave this world at an early age?"

"Whatever the number of years decreed to him, they shall be happy."

Once more Reb Chiya's eyes grew sad, and again he asked, "And how shall it be if Chananiah is destined to bring forth a great scholar—a truly great one—but his life is reckoned not in years but, from the moment of his wedding, in days?"

"Days then, but days of happiness."

"And you would become a widow in your youth?"

"A widow, but a widow blessed by God."

Reb Chiya remained silent, unable to fathom the strength of his child. A deed of heaven, he thought.

Once again Miriam placed her hand on his shoulder. With eyes uplifted and in a voice that seemed prophetic she said, "I live in the hope that the sentence that hangs over him will be removed. I shall offer my life for his."

"But how, my daughter?"

"I do not know, since the sin for which he suffers is unknown to me. Later he will tell me."

In Reb Chiya's heart there could remain no doubt that this was a destined marriage. God tries me, he thought, and I shall endure the trial. To his daughter he said, *"Mazel tov,* my child. With God's blessing, we will arrange the betrothal tomorrow."

Miriam bent to kiss her father's hand, and when she rose Reb Chiya could hardly recognize her, so transported had her face become with happiness and joy.

"You have no fear, Miriam?"

"No, I wait upon God's word." Her voice rang as clear and pure as crystal.

But after Miriam left, Reb Chiya could not quiet his fears and he dispatched letters to the head of the yeshiva in Jerusalem and to the head of the Jews in Babylon. To them he poured out all his woe and perplexity.

"Tomorrow we shall mark the betrothal of my daughter Miriam, may God grant her long life. There are moments when it seems that I am placing a crown upon her head, and moments when I feel that I am leading my only child, my little white lamb, to the slaughter. Yet I do not wish to oppose the will of God. I shall set the date of the wedding for a month from this day, and during this month I shall wait for word from you, for your counsel and your wisdom. And I beg you to pray for me, to pray for my daughter and for the penitent youth as well."

The next day the betrothal took place. Everyone gasped, and the students of the yeshiva were beside themselves with astonishment: that such good fortune should befall Chananiah! But out of respect for their teacher they said not a word.

So the month passed. No letter for Reb Chiya came from Jerusalem or Babylon, which seemed to him an evil omen. On the day of the wedding he drew Miriam aside and said to her, "Do you know, my child, that your beloved Chananiah is fated to leave this world on the eighth day after the wedding?" And then he repeated what the snake had said and told her that he had not yet heard from Jerusalem and Babylon. If there was a speck of uncertainty in her heart, she could still withdraw.

Miriam replied, "I am certain and my heart is certain. Now that I know the sentence I know how to undo it."

"You! By what virtues and by what powers?" wondered Reb Chiya.

"By the power of my faith, and by the virtue of my mother, may she rest with God, and of you, my father."

The wedding canopy was made ready.

The bridegroom came in his sackcloth, with a hempen rope about his loins and in his hands a staff made from a peeled almond branch. Since he could not speak, Reb Chiya delivered the wedding sermon for him, and Chananiah listened with joy and with sorrow.

And when the bridegroom was led to his bride, she awaited him in workday clothes, with a drab kerchief covering her hair, so that she would not place herself above him.

And when the time came for the bride to be unveiled, her face shone like the sun and her eyes were clear and trusting and quiet, yet happy beyond measure.

And the bride was led around the bridegroom seven times, dressed as she was in her workday clothes, so as not to burden the heart of her beloved. Reb Chiya watched, with pride and with tears.

When Chananiah was asked to repeat the Hebrew words of the marriage ceremony he asked, "What do the words mean?"

Reb Chiya translated from the Hebrew, word for word.

All Safed gasped. And they gasped still more when the groom spoke not a word of Torah at the wedding feast.

The ceremony of the Seven Blessings that followed the wedding was held in the garden. The bride sat among the women like an orphan among the wealthy, and the groom like a dullard among scholars and rabbis discoursing upon Torah. Reb Chiya, no matter whether he spoke himself or listened to others, sat nervous and ill at ease, his eyes searching through the garden. Not that he regretted the wedding! He was, rather, looking for the strange snake, and soon he saw how Achnai glided silently among the guests, seen by none of them, never taking his eyes off its victim, the youth Chananiah.

On the evening of the seventh day of the Seven Blessings, Reb Chiya drew his daughter to his side and in a strained voice said to her, "Tomorrow is the day of judgment. Be strong, my daughter!"

"I am strong," replied the young wife, "for I am blessed by God. And I will redeem my husband from death."

"God be with you," said Reb Chiya, his eyes filling with hot tears.

"But remember," added Miriam, "tomorrow the miracle must occur. The staff must bloom and so must his soul! He must recite to you a portion of the Torah! Come to us early, dear Father."

The next morning, when Reb Chiya came to them, Miriam was already dressed but Chananiah still lay in bed. "Forgive me," he said to his father-in-law, closing his eyes, "I do not feel well."

Reb Chiya, however, was staring at the white staff that stood by Chananiah's bed. For the staff was slowly turning green, veins were beginning to course through it and tiny blossoms to appear. As Reb Chiya drew closer to gaze upon this miracle, he saw that Chananiah's face was also undergoing a transformation. Slowly it took on color, and the eyes, when Chananiah opened them, were clear and tranquil, untroubled by any curse. Reb Chiya turned to his daughter, to see whether she too had noticed this miracle, but Miriam was no longer in sight. Soon, however, Reb Chiya forgot his daughter and the miracle of the staff and even the snake Achnai, the messenger of the Angel of Death; for Chananiah had opened his lips and the words had begun to flow. They flowed like pearls of wisdom, wisdom that lighted up the Torah and the inner secrets and mysteries of the Torah. Chananiah, as he spoke, opened for Reb Chiya the gates to a new world, a paradise where the tree of knowledge and the tree of life and many other marvelous trees were blossoming. The clear light of the first seven days shone upon this paradise as with rays of gold; among the leaves sang a multitude of birds, and on every side there was a blossoming and burgeoning of life. Chananiah spoke; and to Reb Chiya it seemed that the soul of the world was speaking. Straining ears and eyes, Reb Chiya drank in every word that streamed from Chananiah's lips, and a great bliss, silent and holy, spread through his whole being.

The secrets and the mysteries of the Torah, as Chananiah unfolded them to Reb Chiya, were later recorded in the Book of Chananiah, which Reb Chiya issued with bindings of gold. But since these are wonders not to be described, let us leave the sages of the Torah and turn to the blessed Miriam.

Once she had seen her father gazing upon the miracle of the staff, Miriam snatched up her husband's sackcloth and ran from the room. Quietly and lightly she went through the palace, the thick carpet muffling her steps, and once alone she quickly threw off her clothes. "Forgive me, my God," she murmured, "forgive me if I violate the law that forbids a woman to wear the dress of a man, but a life is at stake." And she lowered Chananiah's sackcloth over her body and ran into the garden. She remained there quietly, staring at the path that wound its way from the door of the house far, far into the distance, until it disappeared among the oleander trees.

Murmuring prayers to the Almighty that he accept her sacrifice, Miriam saw the messenger of the Angel of Death, Achnai, uncoil itself from an oleander tree, and she quickly covered her face with her hands so as to seem to it like the fated victim Chananiah. Between the cracks of her fingers she watched the snake approach her, gliding slowly and with assurance, for it knew that its victim could not flee.

When the snake saw Chananiah (as it supposed) sitting calmly, waiting with his face covered, it thought, My victim waits and his heart is filled with foreboding. He is praying or perhaps confessing. The snake uncovered its fangs of venom. Miriam saw how Achnai began to move faster, now that its appetite was aroused. She heard the rustle of its skin over the ground. And when it had come so close that she could see the spots on its skin, Miriam closed her fingers and prayed silently in her heart, Lord of the Universe, accept my sacrifice! Quietly, without taking breath, she began her last confession, and not once did her lips tremble. Before the prayer was done she felt the sting of the fangs—and fell to the ground with the cry, "O Lord of the Universe, forgive me for the great scholar with which you were to bless me. May Chananiah live in his place!"

The death struggle followed, and it was with great pain that the soul tore its way out of her body.

But our God is a God of Judgment.

When Miriam's soul rose to heaven, the saints of Paradise were waiting for it, or more exactly, they were waiting for the soul of Chananiah. And when she was led to the Seat of Judgment she was asked, merely for the sake of custom, since the answer was known to all, "Were your dealings on earth honest?"

Answered Miriam, "I had no dealings on earth."

"Did you study the Torah?"

She smiled charmingly. "Lord of the Universe, have you ever directed the daughters of Israel to study your Torah?"

A tumult broke out. "Who are you? Who are you?"

"Miriam, daughter of Sarah and Chiya, wife of Chananiah!"

Consternation! The heavenly host realized that she had sacrificed herself, from devotion without end, for her husband, and that Achnai, the messenger of the Angel of Death, had been deceived.

So they cried out to her soul, "Return, quickly! Return to your body before it is moved."

No, said Miriam, and refused. To suffer twice the agonies of death, she declared, is beyond the burden placed on man. Unless of course, she said, they would accept her death in place of Chananiah's. For he must live.

"Agreed, agreed!" rose the cry in heaven. They were fearful of delay.

And at that very moment Miriam's soul returned to her body, and she rose from the ground without even a wound. With great joy she ran to tell her husband and her father what had happened, and as she entered the palace there arrived two messengers, one from the head of the yeshiva of Jerusalem and the other from the head of the Jews of Babylon. Both letters said only: *"Mazel tov!"*

About the great scholar that was born to Miriam, and of the satisfaction he brought to Reb Chiya, we may, with God's help, speak another time. Here it need only be added that the snake Achnai, the messenger of the Angel of Death who had let himself be deceived, was promptly dismissed and has never been heard from since.

Translated by Irving Howe and Eliezer Greenberg

Part Two

PORTRAIT OF A WORLD

Eternal Life

SHOLOM ALEICHEM

IF YOU like, I'll tell you a story of how I once took a burden upon myself and came close, perilously close, to misfortune. And why, you may wonder, did it happen? Because I was very young, neither experienced nor shrewd. It's possible, of course, that I'm still far from wisdom, for if I were clever, wouldn't I be rich? If you have money you're clever and handsome, and you can sing too.

In short, I was a young man, living, as the custom was, off my in-laws, sitting at my studies, dipping into forbidden books on the sly when my father-in-law and mother-in-law weren't looking. My father-in-law wasn't so bad. It was she, the mother-in-law, who made the trouble; she wore the pants; she was boss! All by herself she ran the business, made matches for her daughters—everything singlehanded. She picked me too; it was she who examined me in the Law; it was she who brought me to Zwihil from Radomishli. I'm from Radomishli myself—surely you've heard of Radomishli! It was written up in the papers not so long ago.

Well, so there I was in Zwihil, living off my in-laws, sweating over Maimonides' *Guide for the Perplexed,* hardly stepping across the threshold of the house, you might say, until the time came to register for military service and I had to bestir myself, arrange my papers, figure out a way of getting an exemption, obtain a passport, and all the rest of it. This, you might say, was my first journey into the world. To show that I was now a man I went to the market all by myself and hired a conveyance. God sent me a bargain, a lucky find—a peasant from Radomishli with a sleigh, a broad red sleigh with two wings on the sides, like an eagle. I never even noticed that he had a white horse, and a white horse, said my mother-in-law, means bad luck. "May I be lying," she said, "but I'm afraid this journey will end in trouble." "Bite off your tongue," exclaimed my father-in-law and regretted it immediately, for he soon got what was coming to him. But to me he said on the sly, "Women's superstitions."

I began to prepare for the trip—prayer shawl and phylacteries, cakes made with butter, a few rubles in my pocket, and three pillows: one to sit on, one to lean on, and one for my feet. But when the time came to say good-by the words stuck in my throat. It's always like that with me: I lose my tongue. What does one say? I don't know! To me it's always seemed rather coarse to turn your back on people and leave them, just like that. I don't know how you feel about it, but farewells for me are, to this day, a torment. But I seem to be losing the thread of my story. . . . I was on my way to Radomishli.

It was the beginning of winter; the snow was thick and made excellent going for the sleigh. White though it was, the horse ran like a song, and the peasant I had drawn was a silent one, the kind that answers "Eh-heh," meaning Yes, or "Ba-nee," meaning No. If you threatened him with the cholera you couldn't get another word out of him. Having eaten well, I departed happily, settled cozily in the sleigh, a pillow under me, a pillow at my shoulders, a pillow at my feet.

The nag leaps ahead; the peasant clucks; the sleigh glides; the wind blows. Snow whirls in the air and floats down upon the great wide highway. My heart is full of a strange, outlandish joy. For the first time I am going into God's little world, all by myself, my own master. And I lean back and stretch my legs in the sleigh, as proud and easy as a squire.

But in winter, no matter how warm your clothes may be, you want to stop, to catch your breath and warm your sides before you go on. I began to imagine a warm inn, a blazing samovar, a roast with hot gravy. These dreams pressed upon my heart—that is, they made me hungry. So I took up the matter of an inn with my peasant. "Ba-nee" he said, meaning No. "Is the inn far?" I asked. "Eh-heh" he drawled, meaning Yes. "How far?" But that I couldn't pry out of him. And then I began to think: Imagine if the driver had been a Jew instead of a peasant! He'd have told me not only where the inn was, but who was the owner, what he was called, how many children he had, how much he had paid for the inn, how much he earned by it, how long he's been there, and whom he had bought it from—he'd have recited me an epic. A strange people. Our Jews, I mean, God bless them.

So I dreamed on about my inn and the hot samovar and the little delicacies to eat. Until God took pity on me. The peasant clucked to his nag, turned the sleigh off to a side, and there stood a small gray hut covered with snow, a country tavern. Standing alone on the white snowy plain, it seemed strangely solitary, like a remote and forgotten gravestone. We drove up to it as grand as you please, and my peasant took the horse and sleigh to the stable while I went right into the tavern, opened the door, and remained standing on the threshold, perplexed. Why, you wonder? It's a pretty story, and a short one. In the middle of the floor, on the ground, lay a corpse covered with black. At its head stood two brass candlesticks with tiny candles. Tattered children sat beside it, beating themselves on their heads with their tiny hands, weeping, yammering, crying, "Ma-ma! Mama!" And a tall, long-legged man in a torn, summer-thin, loose coat paced back and forth, wringing his hands and muttering to himself, "What's to be done? What can I do?"

Seeing this, my first thought was to escape. "Noah," I said to myself, "clear out!" I began to back away. But the door closed behind me and something soldered my feet to the threshold. I couldn't move from the spot. Catching sight of me, the long-legged man rushed over to me with arms outstretched, like someone begging to be rescued. "What do you say to this misfortune!" he cried, showing me the weeping children. "Their mother has left them. What shall I do? What's to be done?"

"Blessed be God's righteousness," I said to him and wanted to console him with kind words, as the custom is among us. But he interrupted me and said, "It's an old story, you understand. She's been all but dead this past year. It was the true blessing, consumption. Poor thing, how she begged and prayed for death! But what shall we do, here in the middle of this barren field? What's to be done? If I go to a farm and hire a wagon to take her to town, how can I leave the children? And night is coming on. What's to be done!"

With these words my long-legged Jew burst into a strange tearless weeping, almost like laughter, and sounds resembling coughs came from his throat. "Oohoohoo! Oohoo!"

I forgot my hunger, my cold, I forgot everything and said to him, "I'm traveling from Zwihil to Radomishli and have a fine sleigh. If the village you speak of is not far, I can lend you the sleigh and wait here. If it won't take too long."

He threw his arms around me and almost kissed me. "Oh, long life to you for this good deed! You'll gain Eternal Life! As I am a Jew, Eternal Life! The village isn't far from here. Four or five miles, no more. It will hardly take an hour, and I'll send your sleigh right back. It'll bring you Eternal Life, I swear it, Eternal Life! Children, get up from the ground and give thanks. Kiss this young man's hands and feet. He's given us his sleigh, and I will take your mother to the consecrated ground. Eternal Life! As I am a Jew, Eternal Life!"

You could scarcely say there was rejoicing. The children, when they heard their mother was to be taken away, fell upon her with still more tears. All the same, these were good tidings. Someone—a man, myself—had turned up to do them a mercy; God alone had sent him there. They looked at me as though I were a redeemer, a sort of Elijah the Prophet, and to tell the honest truth I began to see myself as no ordinary person. Suddenly I grew in stature before my own eyes, becoming what some people call a hero. At that moment I was ready to lift mountains, to overwhelm worlds. Nothing seemed impossible. So I blurted out, "You know what? I'll take her myself, with the help of my peasant, so you won't have to leave the children alone at such a time."

The more I talked this way, the more they all wept. They wept and they looked at me as if they were seeing an angel that had come down from heaven. In my own eyes I kept getting bigger by the minute, unbelievably great, so much so that I forgot I had always lived in terror of corpses, being afraid even to touch them. With my own hands I helped carry out the body and put it in the sleigh. I promised my peasant an extra half-ruble and a shot of brandy. He scratched his head doubtfully and mumbled under his breath, but after his third drink he grew more reasonable, and the three of us—the peasant, the corpse, and I—were off. Her name was Chava Nechama, daughter of Raphael Michael. I remember this name as if I had heard it today, because I kept repeating it to myself, Chava Nechama, daughter of Raphael Michael. Her husband had taken great pains to make sure I got it correctly, since the burial service could not be performed properly unless her full name was invoked. So I kept repeating, "Chava Nechama, daughter of Raphael Michael."

And as I was doing this I forgot her husband's name! If you threatened to cut my head off, I couldn't remember what he called himself. He had told me his name and assured me that as soon as I came to the village I had only to mention it and the body would be taken from me, so I could continue my journey. He was well known in the village, he went there on the High Holidays, he was a liberal contributor to the synagogue and to such good causes as the ritual bath; to hear him tell it, he was virtually a legendary benefactor. He stuffed my head with instructions and directions, where to go and what to say. But I forgot every word of it. Nothing remained with me. Nothing! All my thoughts were centered on one thing only: I had a corpse on my hands. And this caused me so much tumult and panic that I nearly forgot *my* name. From early childhood I have dreaded the sight of the dead. It seemed to me, as we drove along, that the half-closed frosty eyes were looking at me and that the locked dead lips might soon open and some strange subterranean voice issue from them. Just to imagine such a sound would be enough to make you lose your senses. Not for nothing are stories told among us of people swooning or even losing their minds from fear of the dead!

We drove on with the corpse. I gave the dead woman one of my pillows; she lay there at my feet. To avoid weird and oppressive thoughts I looked toward the heavens and began to repeat silently, "Chava Nechama, daughter of Raphael Michael, Chava Nechama, daughter of Raphael Michael," until the names grew confused in my mind and I found myself saying "Chava Raphael, daughter of Nechama Michael" and "Raphael Michael, daughter of Chava Nechama." I failed to notice that it had been growing darker, the wind was blowing fiercely, and the snow fell and fell until it covered the road marks. The sleigh now seemed to be gliding forward at random into a white waste. The peasant grumbled more and more loudly; I could have sworn he was heaping threefold blessings upon me. "What's the matter?" I asked. He spat with rage—may God defend me! He opened his mouth and pelted me with words. I was leading him to ruin, he said, him and his horse too. Because of the corpse in the sleigh the horse had lost its way, we had lost the road, night was coming on, and soon we would be utterly forsaken.

When I heard this I was ready to turn back with the corpse and undo my good deed. But the peasant said there was no going back; there were no longer any recognizable signs; we were circling about, lost in the fields. The road was snowed under, the sky was dark, it was night, the little nag was tired to death. "May a filthy end overtake the innkeeper and all the innkeepers of the world!" cursed the peasant. "If only he had broken his leg," he continued—and by "he" he meant himself—"before he decided to stop at that inn! If only the first drink had choked him before he let himself be talked into this folly of taking a calamity into his sled, all for a few dirty coins, and being lost to the devils, nag and all, in these fields." About himself, he said, he didn't complain; maybe it was fated so. But the little nag, this innocent creature that knew nothing, what had it done to deserve such a fate?

I could have sworn that there were tears in his voice. I promised him another half-ruble and two more glasses of brandy to make him feel better, but this only made him furious, and he said that if I didn't keep quiet he'd throw the corpse out of the sleigh altogether. And I thought to myself, What will I do if he does throw out the corpse, and me with it, leaving the two of us there together in the snow, the corpse and me? Can anyone tell what a peasant will do when he becomes angry?

I grew dumb. I huddled into the pillows and tried to stay awake. After all, how can you fall asleep with a corpse in front of you? And besides, I had often heard that one must not sleep in the winter frost; from such sleep one may never waken. But my eyes began to droop. At that moment I would have given anything to be able to drop off, but I fought against it and held my eyes open with my fingers. Nevertheless they kept closing, again and again, while the sleigh flew across the soft white deep drifts, and a curious sweetness poured through my limbs. I experienced a strange, close pleasure, and I wished this sweetness to last forever, but some power kept waking me, cruelly rousing me, poking me in the sides and saying, "No, Noah, don't sleep. Stay awake!" And I forced my eyes and found this imagined sweetness to be a terrible chill that crept through my bones, and I began to know a deep fear—terror! May God have mercy on me! I imagined that the corpse stirred, uncovered itself, and looked at me with those frosty half-open eyes as though to say, "What are you doing to me, young man? Destroying a daughter of Israel who has died, the mother of tiny children, not bringing her to rest in consecrated ground?" The wind howled in my ears as if it were a human voice, and hideous thoughts ran through my mind. I saw us all under the snow, buried there, the horse, the peasant, the dead woman, and myself, the living frozen to death and only the corpse, the innkeeper's wife, come to life.

Suddenly I heard the peasant urge his horse on more cheerfully, thank God. He crossed himself in the dark with a sigh. It was as if he planted a new soul in me. Far off a tiny fire could be seen; it appeared, disappeared, and then we saw it again. A settlement, I thought, and I gave thanks to God with a full heart. To my peasant I said, "Apparently we've found the way. That's a town we're approaching, isn't it?"

"Eh-heh," said the peasant, without anger and in his usual laconic style. Right then and there I wanted to embrace him, to kiss him on the back for his good tidings and for his laconic "Eh-heh," which was dearer to me than the cleverest sermon.

"What's your name?" I asked, wondering why I hadn't thought to ask before.

"Mikita."

"Mikita!" I repeated, and found a rare charm in the sound.

"Eh-heh!" he said, and I wanted him to say more, at least a few words, for Mikita had become so dear to me, and his horse too, lovely little nag. I spoke to Mikita about him. "That's a fine little horse," I said.

"Eh-heh," answered Mikita.

"Fine sled too."

"Eh-heh."

And more than that, though you broke him into a dozen pieces, Mikita wouldn't say.

"Don't like to talk, do you, Mikita my heart?"

"Eh-heh."

I laughed. I felt gay, happy. If I had found a treasure or a juicy piece of news the world had never heard of I couldn't have been happier. In short, I felt lucky—oh, so lucky! Do you know what I wanted? I wanted to raise my voice in song. That's my nature, I sing when I'm happy. My wife, who knows me inside out, will ask, "Well, what's happened now, Noah? How much money have you made that you're singing so loud?" Women, with their women's brains, seem to think that a man is happy only when he's making money. I wonder why it is that our women are so much more concerned with money than we, the men. Who works for it? We or they? But there, I've fallen off the track again.

So, with God's help, we arrived in the village, and it was still quite early. The place was still deep in slumber, there were many hours before day would come, and nowhere was a fire to be seen. I caught sight of a wide-gated house with a little broom hung on it, to signify a hotel. We stopped, crawled down, and began to beat with our fists upon the gate. We knocked and we knocked, and finally we saw a little light in the window; then we heard someone scuffing his feet and a voice came from within: "Who is it?"

"Open up, uncle," I shouted, "and you'll win Eternal Life."

"Eternal Life?" came the voice from behind the gate. "Who are you?" The lock began to turn.

"Open up," I said. "I've brought a corpse."

"A corpse? What do you mean, a corpse?"

"A corpse means someone who has died. The body of a Jewish woman from the country. From an inn."

Silence on the other side of the gate. I heard a lock turn and feet scuffle away into the distance. The light went out. What was I to do!

The whole thing angered me so that I called my peasant to help me, and we beat so hard that at last the lamp reappeared and we heard the voice again.

"What do you want from my life? What kind of plague are you?"

"In the name of God," I pleaded as with a bandit. "Take pity. I have a corpse here."

"What kind of a corpse?"

"The innkeeper's wife."

"What innkeeper?"

"I've forgotten how he calls himself, but her name is Chava Michael, daughter of Chana Raphael—Chana Raphael, daughter of Michael Chava—I mean, Chana Chava Chana—"

"Get away from here, you *shlimazel,* or I'll pour a bucket of water over you."

That's what the innkeeper said. He clumped away from the window and put out the light. There was nothing we could do.

About an hour later, when the dawn began to show, the gate opened a bit. A black head streaked with pillow feathers looked out and said, "Was it you, pounding on the windows?"

"Of course. Who else?"

"What did you want?"

"I've brought a corpse."

"A corpse? Take it to the *shammes* of the Burial Society."

"Who is this sexton of yours? What's his name?"

"His name is Yechiel. You'll find him down the hill, not far from the bath."

"And where is your bath?"

"You mean to say you don't know where the bath is? I guess you don't live here. Where do you come from?"

"From Radomishli. I'm a Radomishler myself, but now I'm coming from Zwihil, and I've brought along the corpse from an inn not far from here. It's the innkeeper's wife—she died of consumption."

"A pity. But what's that to do with you?"

"Nothing, nothing at all. I was just passing through and he asked me —the innkeeper, that is. He's all alone out there in the fields, with little children, and no one to leave them with. So he asked me. And since it was a chance to win Eternal Life, I thought, why not?"

"There's something fishy about your story," he said to me. "You'll have to see the Burial Society. I mean the officers."

"Who are these officers? Where can they be found?"

"You mean to say you don't know? Reb Shepsl, one of them, lives on this side of the market place, and Reb Eliezer Moishe, another one, lives right in the middle of the market place, while Reb Yosi is near the old synagogue. The most important one is Reb Shepsl. He's the boss. He's a hard man, I may as well warn you. He won't be easy to get around."

"Thanks," I said. "May you live to give better tidings. When can I meet them?"

"When? What sort of a question is that? Why, in the morning of course, after prayers."

"Great," I said. "And in the meantime, let me come in to warm myself. What kind of a town is this anyway, a Sodom?"

Hearing these words, my host quickly locked his gate again, and the silence of a cemetery descended on the street. What could we do now? We remained standing by the sleigh, in the middle of the road, as Mikita murmured angrily, scratching his head, spitting and cursing. "May this innkeeper and all the innkeepers of the world meet a foul end. For himself," he said, meaning himself, personally, "he won't complain. But this little nag of his—what do they have against such a sweet little nag that they try to kill it with hunger and cold? An innocent creature, a beast of the field that has never sinned."

I felt ashamed. "What," I asked myself, "must he be thinking in that head of his about us Jews? How must we look—we the merciful and sons of the merciful—to peasants like this, coarse and boorish, when one Jew shuts the door against another and won't even let him in to warm himself on a freezing night?" It seemed to me then that our fate, the fate of the Jews, made sense after all. I began to blame every one of us, as usually happens when one Jew is wronged by another. No outsider can find more withering things to say of us than we ourselves. You can hear bitter epithets among us a thousand times a day. "You want to change the character of a Jew?" "Only a Jew can play such a trick." "You can't trifle with a Jew." And other such expressions. I wonder how it is among the gentiles. When they have a falling out, do they curse the whole tribe?

In any case, we sat in the sleigh in the middle of the market place and waited for daylight to bring a sign of life. By and by we heard doors creaking, the occasional groan of a windlass as a bucket was hauled from the well; smoke rose from chimneys, and the crowing of cocks grew stronger and livelier. Presently all doors opened and God's creatures appeared in a plenitude of forms: cows, calves, goats, and also Jews, women and girls wrapped in warm shawls and bundled up like dolls, bent triple and as frozen as winter apples in the cellar. In short, the town had revived from its cold sleep. The inhabitants awakened and poured the ritual water over their fingers before saying the prayers. The men were off to their labor of worship, prayers, study, and chanting of psalms; the women to their ovens, kneading troughs, and the tending of cows and goats.

I began to inquire after the officers of the Burial Society. "Where does one find Reb Shepsl? Where does Reb Eliezer Moishe live? Reb Yosi?" Those whom I asked, asked me in turn, "Which Reb Shepsl? Which Eliezer Moishe? What Yosi?" There were several Shepsls and several Eliezer Moishes and even several Yosis in the town, they told me. And when I said that I was looking for the officers of the Burial Society, they grew frightened and wanted to know, "Why does a young man like you need the Burial Society so early in the morning?"

Well, I didn't give them time to feel me out and come at the facts gradually. I told them my story at once, straight from the heart, and revealed what a burden I had taken upon myself. You should have seen what happened! Do you think they set about helping me in my misfortune? Nothing of the sort! They all ran to the sleigh to peer into it and see for themselves whether I really had a corpse. A crowd formed around us, a changing crowd; because of the cold some spectators left, others came over, looked into the sleigh, shook their heads, shrugged their shoulders, inquired of one another whose corpse that could be, and from where it had come, and who I might be, and how I happened to have brought it. But of help they gave me none whatever. It was only with the greatest difficulty that I persuaded someone to show me the house of Reb Shepsl.

I found him facing the wall, standing, wrapped in his prayer shawl and phylacteries, and praying, so sweetly, so melodiously, so raptly, that the very room seemed to sing with him. He snapped his fingers, bumbled harmoniously, twisted his trunk back and forth, made many queer and pious gestures. I had the double satisfaction of watching this extraordinary prayer—I love to listen to spirited praying—and of warming my frozen bones at the same time. And when at last he twisted his head around to me, his eyes were still full of tears and he had, for me, every appearance of a godly man, a man whose soul was as far from earth as his round fat body from heaven. And because he had not yet finished his prayers and didn't want to break off in the middle, he communicated with me in the holy tongue—that is, by means of winks and twirling of his fingers, shrugs, movements of the head, and twitching of the nose, with a few words of Hebrew thrown in for good measure. If you like, I can report our conversation word for word.

"*Sholom aleichem,* Reb Shepsl."

"*Aleichem sholom. Iyo*—sit. Sit down."

"Thanks. I've had enough sitting."

"*Nu? Ma?* What, what?"

"I've come to you on a great errand, Reb Shepsl. You'll win Eternal Life."

"Eternal Life? Good! But what? What?"

"I've brought you a corpse."

"A corpse? What corpse?"

"Not far from here there's an inn, and there lives a poor man, pitifully poor, and this poor man has lost his wife—she died of consumption—and he is left with small children. A great pity. If I hadn't taken pity on them I don't know what he would have done, this poor man, out there in the fields with an unburied corpse."

"Blessed be God's righteousness! But *nu?* Money? The Burial Society?"

"What money? He's poor as a mouse. Down to nothing. Burdened with children. Reb Shepsl, you'll gain Eternal Life."

"Eternal Life? But what? What? Poor folk, poor Jews here too. *Iyo nu? Feh!*"

And because I hadn't quite grasped his meaning he turned angrily to the wall once again and resumed his prayer, much less ardently this time, squeaking somewhat and rocking himself swiftly in a sort of galloping courier's tempo. He then threw off his prayer shawl and phylacteries and turned to me with great heat, as though I had spoiled a sale for him at the fair.

"Look here," he said to me, "this is a poor town and has enough of its own paupers who have no shrouds when they die. We have to hold collections for them. And still people come here from everywhere, from the very ends of the earth. Everyone has to die here!"

I defended myself as well as I could. I said I was innocent of any design against his town, that I was merely performing a good deed. "As though," said I, "one had found a corpse in the street! It's entitled to decent burial and last rites. You're an honest Jew, and a pious one. You can win Eternal Life by this deed."

He became even more furious. You might almost say he nearly

drove me out—that is, he didn't literally drive me, but pummeled me with words. "Is that so! You are a young man representing Eternal Life? Go and make a little inspection of our town. See to it that people are prevented from dying of hunger and cold and *you* will win Eternal Life. Eternal Life indeed! A young man who trades in Eternal Life! Go, take your goods to the shiftless and the unbelievers, and peddle your Eternal Life to them. We have our own charities, and if we develop a craving for Eternal Life we'll know where to find it. What do we need you for?"

So spoke Reb Shepsl, and angrily escorted me to the door, which he loudly slammed after me.

I swear to you that from that morning I took a rooted dislike to those people who are always worshiping and conversing with God. You will tell me that modern unbelievers are even worse than the orthodox old-fashioned communers-with-God, but I disagree. Now at least the hypocrisy is less glaring.

Well, Reb Shepsl had shouted at me and shown me the door. What should I do now? I turned to the others, his colleagues. But at this point a miracle occurred, a miracle straight from heaven. There was no need for me to seek them; they had come looking for me. We met nose to nose, at Reb Shepsl's door.

"Do you happen to be the young man with the goat?" they asked.

"What goat?"

"The young man, that is, who brought the corpse to our town? Is it you?"

"Yes, it's me. I'm the one."

"Come in with us to Reb Shepsl's and we'll talk it over."

"What's there to talk about? Take the corpse off my hands and you'll gain Eternal Life."

"No one's keeping you here," they said to me. "You can go any time you wish. You can even drive your corpse to Radomishli and gain our thanks for it."

"Many thanks for the advice," I said to them.

"You're welcome," they said to me.

So we made our way into Reb Shepsl's house, the three of us, and they began to dispute among themselves, quarreling, disagreeing, all but cursing one another. The two newcomers declared that Reb Shepsl had always been a hard man to deal with, a stickler for the letter of the law, a literalist. For his part, Reb Shepsl twisted to and fro, hitting back with quotations from Scripture. *The poor of your city have prior need.* But the others attacked him with strong arguments. "So? Does that mean that this young man should be turned away with his corpse?"

"God forbid!" said I. "Go off again with this dead woman? Why, I barely made it here alive. We were nearly lost in the storm. The blessed peasant wanted to throw me into the snow. I beg you, take pity. Free me from this burden. You will purchase Eternal Life."

"Eternal Life, that's quite a mouthful," answered one of the two, a tall, lean, long-fingered Jew, the one they called Eliezer Moishe. "We'll take the corpse from you and see that it's properly buried. But it'll cost you a little something."

"What do you mean?" I said. "Isn't it enough that I took this good deed upon myself, nearly perished in the field, was almost thrown from the sleigh by the peasant? And you still speak of money?"

"But you'll be winning Eternal Life, won't you?" said Reb Shepsl with such an ugly face that I loathed his soul. Only by a great effort did I hide my feelings—after all, I was at the mercy of these people.

"Listen to us," said the one called Reb Yosi, a little Jew with a meager beard, half plucked out. "You'd better realize, young fellow, that there's another obstacle. You have no burial papers."

"What papers?"

"We don't know who this corpse is. She may not be the person you say she is," said the lean one with the long fingers, Eliezer Moishe.

I stared from one to the other, and the long-fingered Eliezer Moishe pointed at me and said, "Yes. Who knows? Maybe you killed a woman somewhere. Maybe she's your own wife, whom you brought here with a story about a poor innkeeper, the innkeeper's wife, little children, consumption, and Eternal Life."

Apparently I myself looked like a corpse when he said these things, for the little one they called Reb Yosi began to console me, explaining that they had nothing against me. Why should they have? They didn't suspect me of a crime. They knew I wasn't a murderer or a thief. Nevertheless, he said, I was a stranger, and a corpse is no mere sack of potatoes. A human being is involved, a corpse. They had a rabbi, they gave me to understand, and a police official. One had to think of protocol.

"Yes," said Eliezer Moishe, pointing at me and looking me up and down as if I had already been convicted of a crime, "there's protocol."

I was struck dumb. Sweat started forth, my forehead grew cold, and I felt ill, as if I were going to faint. I understood my situation only too well. I saw how I had been snared. Shame, sorrow, and heartbreak overcame me. But I thought, Why enter into long negotiations with these three? I took out my small purse and said to them, "Listen to me. This is how matters stand. I see that I have gotten myself badly tangled. It was just my luck to have gone to that inn to warm myself right after the death of this innkeeper's wife, and to have listened to the pleas of the poor widower with children who promised me Eternal Life if I would give him a helping hand—and the upshot is that it's going to cost a pretty penny. All right, here's my purse. I have some seventy rubles in it. Take what you want. Just leave enough to get me to Radomishli. But relieve me of the corpse and let me go."

I must have spoken with great emotion, for the three of them exchanged looks, refused to touch my money, and said that after all this town was not Sodom. True, it was poor, with more paupers than rich men, but to fall upon a stranger like robbers, no, that wasn't their way. They had no intention of abusing me. They would take whatever I felt I could offer in a spirit of good will, but not a penny more. Still, I would have to contribute something, it was such a poor town. The beadles, the pallbearers, the shrouds, the plot, brandy for the services—all cost money. Naturally they didn't expect any extravagance. You start to spend carelessly on an occasion like this and there's no telling how much money may spill between your fingers.

Well, what else can I tell you? Even if the innkeeper had been a man of great wealth his wife's funeral couldn't have been more impressive. The townspeople came out in droves for a sight of the young man who had brought a corpse. The rumor spread, increasingly detailed and complicated, that I was a wealthy young man who had brought the body of his mother-in-law, a woman of vast fortune, to be interred—where did they get the idea she was my mother-in-law? Crowds came into the streets to welcome me, the wealthy mourner with the rich mother-in-law. I was said to be flinging money to the poor by the fistful. People pointed at me from all sides. And the poor—an endless multitude! Never, never have I seen such a quantity of paupers. Not even on the eve of Yom Kippur was there ever so great a throng before the doors of the synagogue. They snatched at my coat, they nearly tore me to pieces. After all, an immensely rich young man pouring money! It was no ordinary thing. Luckily the officials of the Burial Society were there to protect me. They prevented me from giving away all of my money, especially the tall sexton who kept by my side all the while and kept admonishing me with his long finger. "Young man, don't throw your money away. There's no end to this." And the more he admonished, the more the beggars crowded me and tore at my flesh. "It's all right!" they cried. "When you bury a rich mother-in-law you can afford to spend a few more pennies. She's left him plenty—plenty! Wishing him no bad luck, *we* should have as much as he's inherited."

"Young man," shrieked one of the beggars as he tugged at my coat, "give up half a ruble for two of us here! Or forty kopecks at least. We're two born cripples, one blind and the other lame. Give us fifteen kopecks at least for the two. Two cripples are always worth that much!"

"Cripples," shouted another beggar as he kicked the first one out of the way. "You call these cripples? My wife, there's a cripple for you! No hands, no feet, nearly lifeless, and with sick little ones. Give me five kopecks, will you, and I'll say *Kaddish* for your mother-in-law and brighten her Paradise."

Now it's easy to laugh, but it was no laughing matter at the time, for the poor multiplied all around me. They covered the market place within half an hour, like a plague of locusts. The pallbearers couldn't move forward. The officials had to beat the beggars off with sticks, and a free-for-all broke out. Peasants too began to collect around us, and at last the police took action. The inspector himself appeared, mounted and sporting a whip, and with a single glare and several lashes he scattered them all as if they were sparrows. Then he dismounted and approached the casket. He began to make inquiries. Who was it that had died? Of what illness? And why such disorder in the market place? It pleased him to begin with me. Who was I? What was my business here? Where was I bound to? I was terrified. I lost all power of speech. Why it is I don't know, but whenever I see a policeman I fall into a cold terror. I've never harmed a fly, and I know that a policeman is, after all, merely a mortal. I'm even acquainted with a man who is on friendly terms with a policeman; they visit each other; the policeman eats fish with him on High Holidays, and he is received as a guest in the policeman's house, where he feasts on eggs. This Jew is forever telling everyone what a gem his policeman is. But all the same, when I see a policeman my impulse is always to run. Perhaps it's hereditary, for I myself, you must remember, am a descendant of pogrom survivors from the days of Vailchikov. About those days I have heard stories and stories to tell you, but enough—I've fallen off the track again.

The inspector gave me a thorough grilling. I had to tell him who I was and what I was doing and where I was going, details about details. How could I explain that I lived with my in-laws at Zwihil and had to journey to Radomishli to obtain some papers? I was deeply thankful to the officers of the Burial Society for disentangling me. One of them, the fellow with the half-plucked beard, called the inspector aside and the two of them conferred in whispers full of secrecy, while the tall one with the thin fingers coached me meantime, half in Hebrew and half in Yiddish, telling me what explanations to make. "You will say you live a short way from town. And that is your mother-in-law who just died. And you've come here to bury her. And while you slip him a few rubles, invent a name straight from the *Haggadah*. Meanwhile we'll get your driver away and give him a glass of spirits, and keep him out of sight. Everything will be fine."

The inspector took me into a house and began to examine me. I'll never be able to repeat what I told him. I don't remember what I said; whatever came into my head, that's what I babbled. He took everything down.

"Your name?"

"Moishe."

"Your father's name?"

"Itzko."

"Age?"

"Nineteen."

"Single?"

"Married."

"Children?"

"Children."

"Occupation?"

"Merchant."

"Who is the corpse?"

"My mother-in-law."

"Her name?"

"Yente."

"Her father?"

"Gershon."

"Her age?"

"Forty."

"Cause of death?"

"Fright."

"A fright?"

"Yes, a fright."

"What sort of fright?" he said, putting down his pen, smoking his cigarette and glaring at me from head to foot.

My tongue seemed to stick to my palate. I decided that, since I had begun with lies, I might as well continue with lies, and I made up a long tale about my mother-in-law sitting alone, knitting a sock, forgetting that her son Ephraim was there, a boy of thirteen, overgrown and a complete fool. He was playing with his shadow. He stole up to her, waved his hands over her head, and uttered a goat cry, *Mehh!* He was making a shadow goat on the wall. And at this sound my mother-in-law fell from her stool and died.

As I wove this tale he kept looking at me, never once dropping his gaze. I mumbled, repeated myself, lost the sense of what I was saying. He heard me out, spat, wiped his red mustachios, accompanied me to the casket, raised the black lid, looked at the face of the dead woman, and shook his head with suspicion. He said to the three officials, "Well, you can bury the woman. But I'll have to detain this fellow while I investigate his story and find out whether she really is his mother-in-law and really died of fright."

You can imagine how I felt. I turned aside and burst into tears, the tears of a very small child.

"What are you crying for, young man?" said the one called Reb Yosi. He consoled me: I had nothing to fear. If was I innocent.

"If you've eaten no garlic your breath will be clean." Reb Shepsl smiled with such a grin that I wanted to slap both his cheeks.

Why had I let myself be so misled as to tell such a tale and involve my mother-in-law? To make things worse, it would now reach her ears that I had killed her with a fright and buried her alive.

"Don't be afraid. God is with you. The inspector isn't a bad sort. Just slip him something and tell him to drop the whole thing. He's a clever man. He knows you've told him a yarn." So spoke Eliezer Moishe as he pointed his long fingers at me. If I could, I would have torn him to pieces, the way one tears a herring.

I can relate no more. What happened afterward I hardly remember. The rest of my money was taken away, I was put in prison, and there was a trial. But all this was nothing compared with what happened when my in-laws discovered that I was in prison because I had somehow acquired a corpse. They came at once and declared that they were my father-in-law and mother-in-law—and things really began to boil. On one side the police kept asking, "Now that we know your mother-in-law is alive, this one who says she is Yente, tell us who the dead woman was." And on the other side my mother-in-law kept demanding, "There's only one thing I want to know. What did you have against me that you wanted to bury me while I was still alive?"

At the trial I was, naturally, found to be innocent. But it cost a lot of money. Witnesses were brought. The innkeeper and his children appeared, and I was freed. But what I had to endure from my mother-in-law—I wouldn't wish it on my worst enemy.

From then on, when anyone mentions Eternal Life, I run.

Translated by Saul Bellow

Hodel

SHOLOM ALEICHEM

YOU LOOK, Mr. Sholom Aleichem, as though you were surprised that you hadn't seen me for such a long time. You're thinking that Tevye has aged all at once, his hair has turned gray.

Ah, well, if you only knew the troubles and heartaches he has endured of late! How is it written in our Holy Books? "Man comes from dust, and to dust he returns." Man is weaker than a fly, and stronger than iron. Whatever plague there is, whatever trouble, whatever misfortune—it never misses me. Why does it happen that way? Maybe because I am a simple soul who believes everything that everyone says. Tevye forgets that our wise men have told us a thousand times: "Beware of dogs . . ."

But I ask you, what can I do if that's my nature? I am, as you know, a trusting person, and I never question God's ways. Whatever He ordains is good. Besides, if you do complain, will it do you any good? That's what I always tell my wife. "Golde," I say, "you're sinning. We have a *midrash*—"

"What do I care about a *midrash?*" she says. "We have a daughter to marry off. And after her two more are almost ready. And after these two, three more—may the evil eye spare them!"

"Tut," I say. "What's that? Don't you know, Golde, that our sages have thought of that also? There is a *midrash* for that too—"

But she doesn't let me finish. "Daughters to be married off," she says, "are a stiff *midrash* in themselves."

Try to explain something to a woman!

Where does that leave us? Oh yes, with a houseful of daughters, bless the Lord, each one prettier than the next. It may not be proper for me to praise my own children, but I can't help hearing what the whole world calls them, can I? Beauties, every one of them! And especially Hodel, the one that comes after Tzeitl, who, you remember, fell in love with the tailor. And Hodel—how can I describe her to you? Like Esther in the Bible, "of beautiful form and fair to look upon." And as if that weren't bad enough, she has to have brains too. She can write and she can read—Yiddish and Russian both. And books she swallows like dumplings. You may be wondering how a daughter of Tevye happens to be reading books when her father deals in butter and cheese? That's what I'd like to know myself.

But that's the way it is these days. Look at these lads who haven't got a pair of pants to their name, and still they want to study! Ask them, "What are you studying? Why are you studying?" They can't tell you. It's their nature, just as it's a goat's nature to jump into gardens. Especially since they aren't even allowed in the schools. "Keep off the grass!" read all the signs as far as they're concerned. And yet you ought to see how they go after it! And who are they? Workers' children. Tailors' and cobblers', so help me God! They go away to Yehupetz or to Odessa, sleep in garrets, eat what Pharaoh ate during the plagues—frogs and vermin—and for months on end do not see a piece of meat before their eyes. Six of them can make a banquet on a loaf of bread and a herring. Eat, drink, and be merry! That's the life!

Well, one of that band had to lose himself in our corner of the world. I used to know his father—he was a cigarette-maker and as poor as a man could be. But that is nothing against the young fellow. For if Rabbi Jochanan wasn't too proud to mend boots, what is wrong with having a father who makes cigarettes? There is only one thing I can't understand: why should a pauper like that be so anxious to study? True, to give the devil his due, the boy has a good head on his shoulders, an excellent head. Pertschik, his name was, but we called him Feferel—Peppercorn. And he looked like a peppercorn, little, dark, dried up, and homely, but full of confidence and with a quick, sharp tongue.

Well, one day I was driving home from Boiberik, where I had got rid of my load of milk and butter and cheese, and as usual I sat lost in thought, dreaming of many things, of this and that, and of the rich people of Yehupetz who had everything their own way while Tevye, the *shlimazel,* and his wretched little horse slaved and hungered all their days. It was summer, the sun was hot, the flies were biting, on all sides the world stretched endlessly. I felt like spreading out my arms and flying!

I lift up my eyes, and there on the road ahead of me I see a young man trudging along with a package under his arm, sweating and panting. "Rise, O Yokel the son of Flekel, as we say in the synagogue," I called out to him. "Climb into my wagon and I'll give you a ride. I have plenty of room. How is it written? 'If you see the ass of him that hateth thee lying under its burden, thou shalt forbear to pass it by.' Then how about a human being?"

At this the *shlimazel* laughs and climbs into the wagon.

"Where might the young gentleman be coming from?" I ask.

"From Yehupetz."

"And what might a young gentleman like you be doing in Yehupetz?" I ask.

"A young gentleman like me is getting ready for his examinations."

"And what might a young gentleman like you be studying?"

"I only wish I knew!"

"Then why does a young gentleman like you bother his head for nothing?"

"Don't worry, Reb Tevye. A young gentleman like me knows what he's doing."

"So, if you know who *I* am, tell me who *you* are!"

"Who am I? I'm a man."

"I can see that you're not a horse. I mean, as we Jews say, *whose* are you?"

"Whose should I be but God's?"

"I know that you're God's. It is written, 'All living things are His.' I mean, whom are you descended from? Are you from around here or from Lithuania?"

"I am descended," he says, "from Adam, our father. I *come* from right around here. You know who we are."

"Well then, who is your father? Come, tell me."

"My father," he says, "was called Pertschik."

I spat with disgust. "Did you have to torture me like this all that time? Then you must be Pertschik the cigarette-maker's son!"

"Yes, that's who I am. Pertschik the cigarette-maker's son."

"And you go to the university?"

"Yes, the university."

"Well," I said, "I'm glad to hear it. Man and fish and fowl—you're all trying to better yourselves! But tell me, my lad, what do you live on, for instance?"

"I live on what I eat."

"That's good," I say. "And what do you eat?"

"I eat anything I can get."

"I understand," I say. "You're not particular. If there is something to eat, you eat. If not, you bite your lip and go to bed hungry. But it's all worth while as long as you can attend the university. You're comparing yourself to those rich people of Yehupetz—"

At these words Pertschik bursts out, "Don't you dare compare me to them! They can go to hell as far as I care!"

"You seem to be somewhat prejudiced against the rich," I say. "Did they divide your father's inheritance among themselves?"

"Let me tell you," says he, "it may well be that you and I and all the rest of us have no small share in *their* inheritance."

"Listen to me," I answer. "Let your enemies talk like that. But one thing I can see: you're not a bashful lad. You know what a tongue is for. If you have the time, stop at my house tonight and we'll talk a little more. And if you come early, you can have supper with us too."

Our young friend didn't have to be asked twice. He arrived at the right moment—when the borscht was on the table and the knishes were baking in the oven. "Just in time!" I said. "Sit down. You can say grace or not, just as you please. I'm not God's watchman; I won't be punished for your sins." And as I talk to him I feel myself drawn to the fellow somehow; I don't know why. Maybe it's because I like a person one can talk to, a person who can understand a quotation and follow an argument about philosophy or this or that or something else. That's the kind of person I am.

And from that evening on our young friend began coming to our house almost every day. He had a few private students, and when he was through giving his lessons he'd come to our house to rest up and visit for a while. What the poor fellow got for his lessons you can imagine for yourself, if I tell you that the very richest people used to pay their tutors three rubles a month; and besides their regular duties they were expected to read telegrams for them, write out addresses, and even run errands at times. Why not? As the passage says, "If you eat bread you have to earn it." It was lucky for him that most of the time he ate with us. For this he used to give my daughters lessons too. One good turn deserves another. And in this way he almost became a member of the family. The girls saw to it that he had enough to eat and my wife kept his shirts clean and his socks mended. And it was at this time that we changed his Russian name of Pertschik to Feferel. And it can truthfully be said that we all came to love him as though he were one of us, for by nature he was a likable young man, simple, straightforward, generous. Whatever he had he shared with us.

There was only one thing I didn't like about him, and that was the way he had of suddenly disappearing. Without warning he would get up and go off; we would look around: no Feferel. When he came back I would ask, "Where were you, my fine-feathered friend?" And he wouldn't say a word. I don't know how you are, but as for me, I dislike a person with secrets. I like a person to be willing to tell what he's been up to. But you can say this for him: when he did start talking, you couldn't stop him. He poured out everything. What a tongue he had! "Against the Lord and against His anointed; let us break their bands asunder." And the main thing was to break the bands. He had the wildest notions, the most peculiar ideas. Everything was upside down, topsy-turvy. For instance, according to his way of thinking, a poor man was far more important than a rich one, and if he happened to be a worker too, then he was really the brightest jewel in the diadem! He who toiled with his hands stood first in his estimation.

"That's good," I say, "but will that get you any money?"

At this he becomes very angry and tries to tell me that money is the root of all evil. Money, he says, is the source of all falsehood, and as long as money amounts to something, nothing will ever be done in this world in the spirit of justice. And he gives me thousands of examples and illustrations that make no sense whatever.

"According to your crazy notions," I tell him, "there is no justice in the fact that my cow gives milk and my horse draws a load." I didn't let him get away with anything. That's the kind of man Tevye is. But my Feferel can argue too. And how he can argue! If there is something on his mind he comes right out with it.

One evening we were sitting on my stoop talking things over, discussing philosophic matters, when he suddenly says, "Do you know, Reb Tevye, you have very fine daughters."

"Is that so?" say I. "Thanks for telling me. After all, they have someone to take after."

"The oldest one especially is a very bright girl. She's all there!"

"I know without your telling me," say I. "The apple never falls very far from the tree."

I glowed with pride. What father isn't happy when his children are praised? How should I have known that from such an innocent remark would grow such fiery love?

Well, one summer twilight I was driving through Boiberik, going from villa to villa with my goods, when someone stopped me. I looked up and saw that it was Ephraim the matchmaker. And Ephraim, like all matchmakers, was concerned with only one thing—arranging marriages. So when he saw me here in Boiberik he stopped me.

"Excuse me, Reb Tevye," he says, "I'd like to tell you something."

"Go ahead," I say, stopping my horse, "as long as it's good news."

"You have," says he, "a daughter."

"I have," I answer, "seven daughters."

"I know," says he. "I have seven too."

"Then together," I tell him, "we have fourteen."

"But joking aside," he says, "here is what I have to tell you. As you know, I am a matchmaker; and I have a young man for you to consider, the very best there is, a regular prince. There's not another like him anywhere."

"Well," I say, "that sounds good enough to me. But what do you consider a prince? If he's a tailor or a shoemaker or a teacher, you can keep him. I'll find my equal or I won't have anything. As the *midrash* says—"

"Ah, Reb Tevye," says he, "you're beginning with your quotations already! If a person wants to talk to you he has to study up first. But better listen to the sort of match Ephraim has to offer you. Just listen and be quiet."

And then he begins to rattle off all his client's virtues. And it really sounds like something. First of all, he comes from a very fine family. And that is very important to me, for I am not just a nobody either. In our family you will find all sorts of people—spotted, striped, and speckled, as the Bible says. There are plain, ordinary people, there are workers, and there are property owners. Secondly, he is a learned man who can read small print as well as large; he knows all the commentaries by heart. And that is certainly not a small thing either, for an ignorant man I hate even worse than pork itself. To me an unlettered man is worse, a thousand times worse, than a hoodlum. You can go around bareheaded, you can even walk on your head if you like, but if you know what Rashi and the others have said, you are a man after my own heart. And on top of everything, Ephraim tells me, this man of his is as rich as can be. He has his own carriage drawn by two horses so spirited that you can see a vapor rising from them. And that I don't object to either. Better a rich man than a poor one! God Himself must hate a poor man, for if He did not, would He have made him poor?

"Well," I ask, "what more do you have to say?"

"What more can I say? He wants me to arrange a match with you. He is dying, he's so eager. Not for you, naturally, but for your daughter. He wants a pretty girl."

"He is dying? Then let him go on dying. And who is this treasure of yours? What is he? A bachelor? A widower? Is he divorced? What's wrong with him?"

"He is a bachelor," said Ephraim. "Not so young any more, but he's never been married."

"And what is his name, may I ask?"

But this he wouldn't tell me. "Bring the girl to Boiberik, and then I'll tell you."

"Bring her? That's the way one talks about a horse or a cow that's being brought to market. Not a girl!"

Well, you know what these matchmakers are. They can talk a stone wall into moving. So we agreed that early next week I would bring my daughter to Boiberik. And, driving home, all sorts of wonderful thoughts came to me, and I imagined my Hodel riding in a carriage drawn by spirited horses. The whole world envied me, not so much for the carriage and horses as for the good deeds I accomplished through my wealthy daughter. I helped the needy with money—let this one have twenty-five rubles, that one fifty, another a hundred. How do we say it? "Other people have to live too." That's what I think to myself as I ride home in the evening, and I whip my horse and talk to him in his own language.

"Hurry, my little horse," I say, "move your legs a little faster and you'll get your oats that much sooner. As the Bible says, 'If you don't work, you don't eat.' "

Suddenly I see two people coming out of the woods—a man and a woman. Their heads are close together and they are whispering to each other. Who could they be? I wonder, and I look at them through the dazzling rays of the setting sun. I could swear the man was Feferel. But whom was he walking with so late in the day? I put up my hand and shield my eyes and look closely. Who was the damsel? Could it be

Hodel? Yes, that's who it was! Hodel! So? So that's how they'd been studying their grammar and reading their books together? Oh, Tevye, what a fool you are!

I stop the horse and call out, "Good evening! And what's the latest news of the war? How do you happen to be out here this time of the day? What are you looking for, the day before yesterday?"

At this they stop, not knowing what to do or say. They stand there, awkward and blushing, with their eyes lowered. Then they look up at me, I look at them, and they look at each other.

"Well," I say, "you look as if you hadn't seen me in a long time. I am the same Tevye as ever; I haven't changed by a hair."

I speak to them half angrily, half jokingly. Then my daughter, blushing harder than ever, speaks up.

"Father, you can congratulate us."

"Congratulate you?" I say. "What's happened? Did you find a treasure buried in the woods? Or were you just saved from some terrible danger?"

"Congratulate us," says Feferel this time. "We're engaged."

"What do you mean, engaged?"

"Don't you know what engaged means?" says Feferel, looking me straight in the eyes. "It means that I'm going to marry her and she's going to marry me."

I look him back in the eyes and say, "When was the contract signed? And why didn't you invite me to the ceremony? Don't you think I have a slight interest in the matter?" I joke with them and yet my heart is breaking. But Tevye is not a weakling. He wants to hear everything out. "Getting married," I say, "without matchmakers, without an engagement feast?"

"What do we need matchmakers for?" says Feferel. "We arranged it between ourselves."

"So?" I say. "That's one of God's wonders! But why were you so silent about it?"

"What was there to shout about?" says he. "We wouldn't have told you now either, but since we have to part soon, we decided to have the wedding first."

This really hurt. How do they say it? It hurt to the quick. Becoming engaged without my knowledge—that was bad enough, but I could stand it. He loves her, she loves him—that I'm glad to hear. But getting married? That was too much for me.

The young man seemed to realize that I wasn't too well pleased with the news. "You see, Reb Tevye," he offered, "this is the reason: I am about to go away."

"When are you going?"

"Very soon."

"And where are you going?"

"That I can't tell you. It's a secret."

What do you think of that? A secret! A young man named Feferel comes into our lives—small, dark, homely, disguises himself as a bridegroom, wants to marry my daughter and then leave her—and he won't even say where he's going! Isn't that enough to drive you crazy?

"All right," I say. "A secret is a secret. But explain this to me, my friend. You are a man of such—what do you call it?—integrity; you wallow in justice. So tell me, how does it happen that you suddenly marry Tevye's daughter and then leave her? Is that integrity? Is that justice? It's lucky that you didn't decide to rob me or burn my house down!"

"Father," says Hodel, "you don't know how happy we are now that we've told you our secret. It's like a weight off our chests. Come, Father, kiss me."

And they both grab hold of me, she on one side, he on the other, and they begin to kiss and embrace me, and I to kiss them in return. And in their great excitement they begin to kiss each other. It was like going to a play. "Well," I say at last, "maybe you've done enough kissing already? It's time to talk about practical things."

"What, for instance?" they ask.

"For instance," I say, "the dowry, clothes, wedding expenses, this, that, and the other—"

"We don't need a thing," they tell me. "We don't need anything. No this, no that, no other."

"Well then, what do you need?" I ask.

"Only the wedding ceremony," they tell me.

What do you think of that! Well, to make a long story short, nothing I said did any good. They went ahead and had their wedding, if you want to call it a wedding. Naturally it wasn't the sort that I would have liked. A quiet little wedding—no fun at all. And besides, there was a wife I had to do something about. She kept plaguing me: what were they in such a hurry about? Go try to explain their haste to a woman. But don't worry. I invented a story—"great, powerful, and marvelous," as the Bible says, about a rich aunt in Yehupetz, an inheritance, all sorts of foolishness.

And a couple of hours after this wonderful wedding I hitched up my horse and wagon and the three of us got in, that is, my daughter, my son-in-law, and I, and off we went to the station at Boiberik. Sitting in the wagon, I steal a look at the young couple, and I think to myself, What a great and powerful Lord we have and how cleverly He rules the world. What strange and fantastic beings He has created. Here you have a new young couple, just hatched; he is going off, the Good Lord alone knows where, and is leaving her behind—and do you see either one of them shed a tear, even for appearance's sake? But never mind—Tevye is not a curious old woman. He can wait. He can watch and see.

At the station I see a couple of young fellows, shabbily dressed, down at the heels, coming to see my happy bridegroom off. One of them is dressed like a peasant and wears his blouse like a smock over his trousers. The two whisper together mysteriously for several minutes. Look out, Tevye, I say to myself. You have fallen among a band of horse thieves, pickpockets, housebreakers, or counterfeiters.

Coming home from Boiberik, I can't keep still any longer and tell Hodel what I suspect. She bursts out laughing and tries to assure me that they are very honest young men, honorable men, who were devoting their lives to the welfare of humanity; their own private welfare meant nothing to them. For instance, the one with his blouse over his trousers was a rich man's son. He had left his parents in Yehupetz and wouldn't take a penny from them.

"Oh," said I, "that's just wonderful. An excellent young man! All he needs, now that he has his blouse over his trousers and wears his hair long, is a harmonica, or a dog to follow him, and then he would really be a beautiful sight!" I thought I was getting even with her for the pain she and this new husband of hers had caused me. But did she care? Not at all! She pretended not to understand what I was saying. I talked to her about Feferel and she answered me with "the cause of humanity" and "workers" and other such talk.

"What good is your humanity and your workers," I say, "if it's all a secret? There is a proverb: 'Where there are secrets, there is knavery.' But tell me the truth now. Where did he go, and why?"

"I'll tell you anything," she says, "but not that. Better don't ask. Believe me, you'll find out yourself in good time. You'll hear the news—and maybe very soon—and good news at that."

"Amen," I say. "From your mouth into God's ears! But may our enemies understand as little about it as I do."

"That," says she, "is the whole trouble. You'll never understand."

"Why not?" say I. "Is it so complicated? It seems to me that I can understand even more difficult things."

"These things you can't understand with your brain alone," she says. "You have to feel them, you have to feel them in your heart."

And when she said this to me, you should have seen how her face shone and her eyes burned. Ah, those daughters of mine! They don't do anything halfway. When they become involved in anything it's with their hearts and minds, their bodies and souls.

Well, a week passed, then two weeks—five—six—seven—and we heard nothing. There was no letter, no news of any kind. "Feferel is gone for good," I said and glanced over at Hodel. There wasn't a trace of color in her face. And at the same time she didn't rest at all; she found something to do every minute of the day, as though trying to forget her troubles. And she never once mentioned his name, as if there never had been a Feferel in the world.

But one day when I came home from work I found Hodel going about with her eyes swollen from weeping. I made a few inquiries and found out that someone had been to see her, a long-haired young man who had taken her aside and talked to her for some time. Ah! That must have been the young fellow who had disowned his rich parents and pulled his blouse down over his trousers.

Without further delay I called Hodel out into the yard and bluntly asked her, "Tell me, daughter, have you heard from him?"

"Yes."

"Where is he, your predestined one?"

"He is far away."

"What is he doing there?"

"He is serving time."

"Serving time?"

"Yes."

"Why? What did he do?"

She doesn't answer me. She looks me straight in the eyes and doesn't say a word.

"Tell me, dear daughter," I say, "according to what I can understand, he is not serving for a theft. So if he is neither a thief nor a swindler, why is he serving? For what good deeds?"

She doesn't answer. So I think to myself, If you don't want to, you don't have to. He is your headache, not mine. But my heart aches for her. No matter what you say, I'm still her father.

Well, it was the evening of *Hashono Rabo*. On a holiday I'm in the habit of resting, and my horse rests too. As it is written in the Bible: "Thou shalt rest from thy labors and so shall thy wife and thine ass." Besides, by that time of the year there is very little for me to do in Boiberik. As soon as the holidays come and the *shofar* sounds, all the summer villas close down and Boiberik becomes a desert. At that season I like to sit at home on my own stoop. To me it is the finest time of the year. Each day is a gift from heaven. The sun no longer bakes like an oven but caresses with a heavenly softness. The woods are still green, the pines give out a pungent smell. In my yard stands the *succeh* —the booth I have built for the holiday, covered with branches, and around me the forest looks like a huge *succeh* designed for God himself. Here, I think, God celebrates His holiday, here and not in town, in the noise and tumult where people run this way and that, panting for breath as they chase after a small crust of bread, and all you hear is money, money, money.

As I said, it is the evening of *Hashono Rabo*. The sky is a deep blue and myriads of stars twinkle and shine and blink. From time to time a star falls through the sky, leaving behind it a long green band of light. This means that someone's luck has fallen. I hope it isn't my star that is falling, and somehow Hodel comes to mind. She has changed in the last few days, has come to life again. Someone, it seems, has brought her a letter from him, from over there. I wish I knew what he had written, but I won't ask. If she won't speak, I won't either. Tevye is not a curious old woman. Tevye can wait.

And as I sit thinking of Hodel, she comes out of the house and sits down near me on the stoop. She looks cautiously around and then whispers, "I have something to tell you, Father. I have to say good-by to you, and I think it's for always."

She spoke so softly that I could barely hear her, and she looked at me in a way that I shall never forget.

"What do you mean, good-by for always?" I say to her and turn my face aside.

"I mean I am going away early tomorrow morning, and possibly we shall never see each other again."

"Where are you going, if I may be so bold as to ask?"

"I am going to him."

"To him? And where is he?"

"He is still serving, but soon they'll be sending him away."

"And you're going there to say good-by to him?" I ask, pretending not to understand.

"No. I am going to follow him," she says. "Over there."

"There? Where is that? What do they call the place?"

"We don't know the exact name of the place, but we know that it's far—terribly, terribly far."

And she speaks, it seems to me, with great joy and pride, as though he had done something for which he deserved a medal. What can I say to her? Most fathers would scold a child for such talk, punish her, even beat her maybe. But Tevye is not a fool. To my way of thinking, anger doesn't get you anywhere. So I tell her a story.

"I see, my daughter, as the Bible says, 'Therefore shalt thou leave thy father and mother'—for a Feferel you are ready to forsake your parents and go off to a strange land, to some desert across the frozen wastes, where Alexander of Macedon, as I once read in a storybook, once found himself stranded among savages . . ."

I speak to her half in fun and half in anger, and all the time my heart weeps. But Tevye is no weakling; I control myself. And Hodel doesn't lose her dignity either; she answers me word for word, speaking quietly and thoughtfully. And Tevye's daughters can talk.

And though my head is lowered and my eyes are shut, still I seem to see her—her face is pale and lifeless like the moon, but her voice trembles. Shall I fall on her neck and plead with her not to go? I know it won't help. Those daughters of mine—when they fall in love with somebody, it is with their heads and hearts, their bodies and souls.

Well, we sat on the doorstep a long time—maybe all night. Most of the time we were silent, and when we did speak it was in snatches, a word here, a word there. I said to her, "I want to ask you only one thing: did you ever hear of a girl marrying a man so that she could follow him to the ends of the earth?" And she answered, "With him I'd go anywhere." I pointed out how foolish that was. And she said, "Father, you will never understand." So I told her a little fable, about a hen that hatched some ducklings. As soon as the ducklings could move they took to the water and swam, and the poor hen stood on shore, clucking and clucking.

"What do you say to that, my daughter?"

"What can I say?" she answered. "I am sorry for the poor hen; but just because she stood there clucking, should the ducklings have stopped swimming?"

There is an answer for you. She's not stupid, that daughter of mine.

But time does not stand still. It was beginning to get light already, and within the house my old woman was muttering. More than once she had called out that it was time to go to bed, but, seeing that it didn't help, she stuck her head out of the window and said to me, with her usual benediction, "Tevye, what's keeping you?"

"Be quiet, Golde," I answered. "Remember what the Psalm says: 'Why are the nations in an uproar, and why do the peoples mutter in vain?' Have you forgotten that it's *Hashono Rabo* tonight? Tonight all our fates are decided and the verdict is sealed. We stay up tonight. Listen to me, Golde, you light the samovar and make some tea while I get the horse and wagon ready. I am taking Hodel to the station in the morning." And once more I make up a story about how she has to go to Yehupetz, and from there farther on, because of the same old inheritance. It is possible, I say, that she may have to stay there through the winter and maybe the summer too, and maybe even another winter; and so we ought to give her something to take along—some linen, a dress, a couple of pillows, some pillow slips, and things like that.

And as I give these orders I tell her not to cry. "It's *Hashono Rabo,* and on *Hashono Rabo* one mustn't weep. It's a law." But naturally they don't pay any attention to me, and when the time comes to say good-by they all start weeping—their mother, the children, and even Hodel herself. And when she came to say good-by to her older sister Tzeitl (Tzeitl and her husband spend their holidays with us), they fell on each other's necks and you could hardly tear them apart.

I was the only one who did not break down. I was firm as steel—though inside I was more like a boiling samovar. All the way to Boiberik we were silent, and when we came near the station I asked her for the last time to tell me what it was that Feferel had really done. If they were sending him away there must have been a reason. At this she became angry and swore by all that was holy that he was innocent. He was a man, she insisted, who cared nothing about himself. Everything he did was for humanity at large, especially for those who toiled with their hands—that is, the workers.

That made no sense to me. "So he worries about the world" I told her. "Why doesn't the world worry a little about him? Nevertheless, give him my regards, that Alexander of Macedon of yours, and tell him I rely on his honor—for he is a man of honor, isn't he?—to treat my daughter well. And write to your old father sometimes."

When I finish talking she falls on my neck and begins to weep. "Good-by, Father," she cries. "Good-by! God alone knows when we shall see each other again."

Well, that was too much for me. I remembered this Hodel when she was still a baby and I carried her in my arms, I carried her in my arms. . . . Forgive me, Mr. Sholom Aleichem, for acting like an old woman. If you only knew what a daughter she is! If you could only see the letters she writes! Oh, what a daughter . . .

And now let's talk about more cheerful things. Tell me, what news is there about the cholera in Odessa?

Translated by Julius and Frances Butwin

The Search

SHOLOM ALEICHEM

"NOW, LISTEN to *me,*" said a man with round bovine eyes, who had been sitting in a corner by the window, smoking and taking in stories of thefts, holdups, and expropriations. "I'll tell you a good one, also about a theft, which happened in my town, in the synagogue of all places, and on Yom Kippur too! You'll like it.

Our Kasrilevke—that's where I come from—is a small town and a poor one. We have no thieves and no stealing, for there is nobody to steal from and nothing to steal. And aside from all that, a Jew just isn't a thief. I mean to say, even if a Jew is a thief, he is not the kind of thief who sneaks in through a window or goes at you with a knife. He may twist you and turn you, outtalk you and outsmart you—granted; but he won't crawl into your pockets, he won't be caught red-handed and led down the street in disgrace. That may happen to a thieving Ivan but not to a Jew. Imagine, then, someone stealing in Kasrilevke, and quite a bit of money too—eighteen hundred rubles at one stroke!

One day a stranger arrived in our town, a Jew, some sort of contractor from Lithuania. He appeared on the evening of Yom Kippur, just before the time for prayer. He left his bundle at the inn and hurried out to look for a place to pray and found the old synagogue. He arrived in time to attend the evening prayer and ran into the trustees with their collection box.

"Sholom aleichem!"

"Aleichem sholom!"

"Where are you from?"

"From Lithuania."

"And what's your name?"

"What difference does that make to your grandmother?"

"Well, after all, you've come to our synagogue!"

"Where else do you want me to go?"

"You surely want to pray here?"

"Have I any choice?"

"Then put something in the box."

"Of course. Did you think I was going to pray for nothing?"

Our stranger took three silver rubles out of his pocket and put them in the box. Then he put a ruble in the cantor's plate, gave a ruble for the rabbi, another for the school, and threw half a ruble into the poor box; in addition, he handed out coins to the beggars standing at the door—we have so many poor people in our town, God bless them, that if you really went at it you could distribute Rothschild's fortune among them.

When we saw the kind of stranger he was we gave him a place right at the east wall. You will ask how one could be found for him when all the places were occupied. Some question! Where does one find a place at a celebration—a wedding, say, or a circumcision feast—after all the guests have been seated at the table and suddenly there is a commotion—the rich guest has arrived! Well, all the others squeeze together until a place is made for the rich man. Jews have a habit of squeezing—when no one else squeezes us, we squeeze one another."

The round-eyed man paused for a moment, looked at the audience to see what impression his quip had made, and resumed his tale.

In short, the stranger occupied a place of honor. He asked the *shammes* for a prayer stand and, donning his cloak and prayer shawl, began to pray. Bending over his stand, he prayed and prayed, always on his feet, never sitting down, let alone lying down. He did not leave his stand for a minute, that Litvak, except when the Eighteen Blessings were recited and everyone had to face the Ark, and during the kneeling periods. To stand on one's feet on a day of fasting without ever sitting down—only a Litvak can do that.

After the *shofar* was blown for the last time, and Chaim-Chune the teacher, who always conducts the first night prayer after the holiday, began to chant, *"Ha-mai-riv a-a-arovim,"* we suddenly heard a cry, "Help, help, help!" We looked around and saw the stranger lying on the floor in a faint. We poured water on him to bring him to, but he fainted again.

What had happened? A fine thing! He had on him—the Litvak, that is—eighteen hundred rubles; and he had been afraid, so he said, to leave his money at the inn. You think it's a trifle, eighteen hundred rubles? To whom could he entrust such a sum in a strange town? Nor did it seem right to keep it in his pocket on Yom Kippur. So, after thinking the matter over, he decided quietly to slip the money into his stand—yes, a Litvak is quite capable of such a thing! Now do you understand why he did not leave his stand for a minute? Someone had apparently snatched his money during the Eighteen Blessings or one of the kneeling periods.

In short, he screamed, he wept, he lamented—what would he do now without the money? It was, he said, someone else's, not his, he was only an employee in some office, a poor man, burdened with many children. All he could do now, he said, was to jump into the river or hang himself right here in the synagogue in front of everybody.

On hearing such talk the whole congregation stood paralyzed, forgetting that they had been fasting for twenty-four hours and were about to go home to eat. It was a disgrace before a stranger, a shameful thing to witness. Eighteen hundred rubles stolen, and where? In a place of worship, in the old synagogue of Kasrilevke! And when? On Yom Kippur! Such a thing was unheard of.

"Shammes, lock the door!" our rabbi ordered. We have our rabbi—his name is Reb Yosefel—a true and pious Jew, not oversubtle but a kindly soul, a man without gall, and sometimes he has brilliant ideas, such as wouldn't occur even to a man with eighteen heads! When the door was locked the rabbi addressed the congregation. His face was white as the wall, his hands were trembling and his eyes burning.

"Listen carefully, my friends," he said. "This is an ugly business, an outrage, unheard of since the creation of the world, that in our town, in Kasrilevke, there should be such an offender, such a renegade from Israel, who would have the impudence to take from a stranger, from a poor man, a supporter of a family, such a large sum of money. And when? On a holy day, on Yom Kippur, and perhaps even during the closing prayer! Such a thing has been truly unheard of since the creation of the world! I can't believe such a thing is possible, it just can't be! Nevertheless—who can tell?—some wretched man was perhaps tempted by this money, particularly since it amounted to such a fortune. The temptation, God have mercy on us, was great enough. So if it was decreed that one of us succumb to the temptation—if one of us has had the misfortune to commit such a sin on a day like this—we must investigate the matter, get to the bottom of it. Heaven and earth have sworn that truth must come to the top like oil on water, so we must search each other, go through each other's garments, shake out the pockets of everyone here—from the most respectable member of the congregation to the *shammes,* sparing no one. Begin with me: here, my friends, go through my pockets!"

Thus spoke our rabbi, Reb Yosefel, and he was the first to open his caftan and turn all his pockets inside out. After him, all the members of the congregation loosened their girdles and turned out their pockets, and each of them in turn was searched, and felt all over, and shaken out. But when they came to Laizer Yosl he turned all colors and began to argue. The stranger, he said, was a swindler; the whole thing was a Litvak's trick, no one had stolen any money from him. "Can't you see," he said, "that the whole thing is a lie, a fraud?"

The congregation broke out in loud protests. "What do you mean?" they said. "Respectable citizens have submitted to a search—why should you be excepted?" The whole crowd clamored, "Search him, search him!"

Laizer Yosl saw that things were going badly for him, and he began to plead with tears in his eyes, begging that he be spared. He swore by every oath: may he be as pure of all evil as he was innocent of stealing. And on what grounds was he to be spared? He couldn't bear the disgrace of being searched, he said, and implored the others to have pity on his youth, not to subject him to such an indignity. Do anything you want, he said, but do not go through my pockets. How do you like such a scoundrel? Do you think anyone listened to him?

But wait a minute, I have forgotten to tell you who this Laizer Yosl was. He was not a native of Kasrilevke; he came from the devil knows where to marry a Kasrilevke girl. Her father, the rich man of our town, had unearthed him somewhere and bragged that he had found a rare gem, a real genius, for his daughter, a man who knew by rote a thousand pages of the Talmud, who was an expert in Scriptures, a Hebraist, and a mathematician who could handle fractions and algebra, and who wielded the pen like nobody's business—in short, a man with all seventeen talents. When his father-in-law brought him, everyone went to look at this gem, to see what kind of rare bargain the rich man had acquired. Well, if you just looked at him he was nothing special, a young man like many others, fairly good-looking, only the nose a little too long, and a pair of eyes like two glowing coals, and a mouth with a sharp tongue in it. He was examined; they made him explain a page of the Talmud, a chapter from the Bible, a passage from Rambam, this and that, and he passed the test with flying colors—the dog was at home everywhere, he knew all the answers! Reb Yosefel himself said that he could be a rabbi in any Jewish community—not to mention his vast knowledge of worldly things. Just to give you an idea, there is in our town a subtle scholar, Zeidel Reb Shaye's son, a crazy fellow, and he doesn't even compare with Laizer Yosl. Moreover no one in the world could equal him as a chess player. Talk about cleverness!

Needless to say, the whole town envied the rich man such a genius, although people said that the gem was not without its flaws. To begin with, he was criticized for being too clever (and what there's too much of isn't good), and too modest, too familiar with everyone, mingling too easily with the smallest among the smallest, whether it be a boy or a girl or even a married woman. Then he was disliked because of the way he walked around, always absorbed in thought. He would come to the synagogue after everyone else, put on his prayer shawl, and page the *Well of Life* or *Ebn Ezra,* with his skullcap on askew—never saying a word of prayer. No one ever saw him doing anything wrong; nevertheless it was whispered that he was not a pious man—after all, no one can have all the virtues!

And so when his turn came to be searched his refusal was at once interpreted as a sign that he had the money on him. "Make me swear an oath on the Bible," he said. "Cut me, chop me to pieces, roast me, burn me alive, anything, but don't go through my pockets!"

At this point even our Rabbi Yosefel, though the gentlest of men, lost his temper and began to scold. "You so-and-so," he cried, "you deserve I don't know what! What do you think you are? You see what all these men have gone through—all of them have accepted the indignity of a search, and you want to be an exception! One of the two—either confess and give back the money, or show your pockets! Are you playing games with an entire Jewish community? I don't know what we'll do to you!"

In short, they took this nice young man, laid him on the floor by sheer force, and began to feel him all over and shake out his pockets. And then they shook out—guess what?—chickenbones and a dozen plum pits; everything was still fresh, the bones had recently been gnawed, and the pits were moist. Can you imagine what a pretty sight it was, all this treasure shaken out of our genius's pockets? You can picture for yourselves the look on their faces, he and his father-in-law, the rich man, and our poor rabbi too. Our Reb Yosefel turned away in shame; he could look no one in the face. And later, when the worshipers were on their way home, to eat after the fast, they did not stop talking about the treasure they had discovered in the young man's pockets, and they shook with laughter. Only Reb Yosefel walked alone, with bowed head, unable to look anyone in the eyes, as though the remains of food had been shaken out of his own pockets.

The narrator stopped and resumed his smoking. The story was over.

"And what about the money?" we all asked in one voice.

"What money?" the man said with an uncomprehending look as he blew out the smoke.

"What do you mean, what money? The eighteen hundred—"

"O-o-o-oh," he drawled. "The eighteen hundred? Vanished without a trace."

"Vanished?"

"Without a t-r-a-c-e."

Translated by Norbert Guterman

Dreyfus in Kasrilevke

SHOLOM ALEICHEM

I WONDER if the Dreyfus affair made such an impression anywhere in the whole world as it did in Kasrilevke.

Paris, they tell me, boiled like water in an overheated kettle. Newspapers wrote, generals shot themselves, Frenchmen ran about the streets like crazy people, throwing their hats in the air. One Frenchman screamed, "Long live Dreyfus!" Another screamed, "Long live Esterhazy!" And as for the Jews, while all this was going on, they were smeared with mud by everyone, exactly as usual. But the agony, the pain and despair that Kasrilevke lived through from all this, that, I tell you, Paris will never match, not until the coming of the Messiah.

How, in Kasrilevke, did they ever find out about Dreyfus in the first place? Don't ask me! How, for instance, did they find out about the war of the English against the Boers? How do they know what's going on in China? What kind of an alliance does Kasrilevke have with China? Are they drawn together because of the great commerce that Kasrilevke carries on with China? No. Tea Kasrilevke imports, not from China, but from Wissotsky in Moscow, and as for the airy summer stuff that the Chinese call pongee, who in Kasrilevke could ever find enough in his pocket to put silk on his back? Let's thank God, if, in summer, they can afford a shirt of cotton! For, if not that, they'd have no choice at all, they'd simply have to walk around with nothing on!

So the mystery remains: how, in Kasrilevke, did they find out the entire story of Dreyfus?

From Zaidle, they found out, Zaidle, the son of Shem.

Zaidle is the only one in town who receives a newspaper, and everything that goes on in the great world outside they discover from him. That is, not from him but, truthfully, through him. Zaidle can read. He reads to them, he translates to them, and through him they learn the meaning of the pages with the black print; yes, he gives them exactly what's in the newspaper—and, do you know, they often give his words exactly the opposite meaning! Why? Because they understand everything better!

One day Zaidle, the son of Shem, rose in the synagogue to tell a story from his paper: how, in Paris, a certain Jewish captain, Dreyfus, had been imprisoned because he had handed out some secret papers of his country. This story, Zaidle will tell you, simply passed in one ear and out the other.

One of them said, shrugging his shoulders, "What a Jew won't do for business!"

Another said bitterly, "It serves him right! A Jew who tries to crawl all the way up there to the highest places and mix with the royalty!"

But later on, when Zaidle came again to the synagogue and told them a whole new story, that it was all a falsehood, that the Jewish captain, Dreyfus, the one who had been imprisoned, was the soul of innocence, and the whole business was just a plot of a bunch of generals who were fighting one another, then the entire little village instantly took Dreyfus to heart. He became one of theirs, a Kasrilevker. Wherever there were two, Dreyfus was the third.

"Did you hear?" one asks.

The other answers, "I heard!"

"Sentenced for life!"

"For nothing! For nothing! For a lie!"

And later on, when Zaidle came again to the synagogue and told them that there was a possibility that Dreyfus might be given a new trial and that somehow the world had turned up good, kind, decent people who took it upon themselves to prove that the whole thing was a mistake, the whole entire thing—then Kasrilevke began to talk again.

First of all they said, "Dreyfus is one of us." And then they asked, "How is it possible that such a dirty business can happen there in Paris? Pfui! It's not one bit nice for the French people!" And it went on in that way, discussion, disagreement, without end. They even made bets on it. One said there would be another trial, another said no, there wouldn't, once such a trial was lost it was lost for good.

But after a while they didn't have the patience to wait until Zaidle got ready to come to the synagogue and give them news of Captain Dreyfus; no, they had to go straight to Zaidle's house. And finally they didn't have the patience even to go to his house. No, they must go straight to the post office, get the paper right there, read it right there, and there discuss it over and over, scream, disagree, and argue, everyone at the same time, exactly as usual. Every now and then the postmaster would give them just a hint, you understand, in a very nice polite tone of voice, you understand, that the post office wasn't a place for carryings-on, it wasn't the synagogue.

"What," they cried, "compare a post office to a synagogue! Sacrilege!"

And only then did the postmaster mutter in Polish, "Pfui, you dirty Jews, so you really think the post office is your Jewish synagogue to carry on your Jewish business in!"

Yes, they heard him and they paid no more attention to him than to a fly buzzing about their earlocks; yes, he insulted them, and they went on reading the paper and discussing the affair of Captain Dreyfus.

But it wasn't only Dreyfus that Kasrilevke discussed. Every minute, it seemed, someone new came into the case. First General Esterhazy, then General Mercie, then General Pely, then Gansy—or so Kasrilevke heard it and gradually came to the conclusion that with the French there must be a law that as soon as there's a name ending in the sound "e," its owner becomes a general!

But there were two other men whom the Kasrilevkers really came to love. They gave themselves up completely to them, they rejoiced in them: Emil Zola and Lambori. For Zola everyone in the village would have laid down his life. What happiness it was just to speak out those two words: Emil Zola! If Emil Zola would only have come to Kasrilevke the whole town would have turned out with a wild welcome, they would have carried him on their backs through the dirty, muddy streets!

"What do you think of Emil Zola's letters?" one asked the other.

"Pearls! Diamonds! Rubies!"

As for Lambori, they counted out to one another his virtues, they gave thanks for him, they found happiness in the very thought of him, they devoured, they smacked their lips over his oratory. Of course no one in Kasrilevke could actually hear him make his speeches but they knew anyway that his must be a voice of gold.

I wonder if Dreyfus's own family in Paris looked forward to his return from the island with as much joy as did Kasrilevke. I tell you that from the moment he left that island in the middle of the sea, each one of them was swimming alongside him. Ah, now a storm arises and shakes the sea to pieces . . . the terrible waves rise higher and cast his boat about like a piece of wood . . . higher the waves rise . . . higher and higher . . . higher and higher! Merciful God!

Merciful God, they prayed, bring him safely back there to his trial, open the eyes of the judges and clear out their brains so that they may find the guilty one and the whole world behold our vindication! Amen!

On the great day when the news came that Dreyfus had arrived safely over the ocean, Kasrilevke declared a feast day. And if they hadn't been ashamed to, they'd have closed down all their businesses.

"Did you hear? He has arrived!"

"Safely!"

"Thanks be to God and His name!"

"How I would have wanted to be right there in the room to see how it was at that first meeting with his wife!"

"How I would have wanted to be right there to see how it was when the little children were told, 'Your father is here!' "

Women who, at that holy moment, were sitting here in Kasrilevke, hid their faces in their aprons so that they could blow their noses in peace and no one know that they were crying. Kasrilevke is a very poor little village; still, I tell you, there wasn't one who wouldn't have sold his very last rag if that could only have bought him a ride to Paris and he could have looked upon all those joyous sights, even from afar.

When the trial began a frenzy broke out in Kasrilevke. They tore Zaidle's newspaper to pieces; they choked over their food; at night they couldn't sleep—would they live through the night to see the next morning, and the morning after that, and still the morning after that! And so it went, day by day.

And then, all at once, a fearful cry went up from Kasrilevke, a clamor, a lamentation: "Holy! Holy!" The lawyer Lambori had been shot; the outcry of Kasrilevke should have been heard around the world.

"Why? What for?"

"Such a brutality, and for nothing! For nothing at all!"

"Worse! Worse! Worse than any sin ever sinned in Sodom!"

That same gun had been pointed at their breasts, that same bullet had penetrated their own hearts, that assassin had laid low each Kasrilevker!

Almighty God, Kasrilevke prayed, show Your wonders now. You know very well how to make a miracle if only You want to. Perform the miracle now that Lambori may live! And God, all blessings unto Him, performed the miracle and Lambori lived!

And so, at last, the trial came to its final day, and this final day worked upon Kasrilevke like a seizure of epilepsy. They quaked, they shook, they twitched. If only they could have fallen asleep and slept through a whole twenty-four hours, and waked up exactly at that moment when Dreyfus, with God's help, would at last be free. But as though out of spite, not one of them could close an eye. All night they tossed from side to side, quarreled with the bedbugs, waited in agony for the first light of dawn to show.

And when at last that first light showed, they leaped from their beds and ran to the post office, but it was still closed; even the gate was locked. They gathered, one after another, around the post office until the street overflowed. They paced back and forth, yawned, stretched, scratched their earlocks, murmured, "Hallelujah!"

When Yarmo, the janitor, unlocked the gates of the post office they all rushed inside at once. Yarmo became very angry—he'd show them who was boss here—and he drove them, with curses and insults, out into the street. And there in the street they waited and waited for Zaidle to make his appearance. And when at last Zaidle appeared, and when at last he picked up the paper and read aloud to them that nice passage about Dreyfus, there arose such a roar, such a protest, that the very heavens must have split. And this protest was not against the judge who had judged so badly; it was not against the generals who had sworn so falsely nor against the Frenchmen who had covered themselves with so much shame. No, this protest was against Zaidle, who read to them.

"It can't be!" Kasrilevke screamed with one voice. "It can't be! The heavens and the earth have promised that the truth must always come out on top, just as oil comes to the top of water! What will you tell us next? What lies? What stories?"

"Idiots!" shouted poor Zaidle with all the strength of his lungs, and he pushed the newspaper right into their faces. "Here! See what it says here in the paper!"

"Paper!" cried Kasrilevke. "Paper! And if you stood here with one foot in heaven and one foot on earth we still wouldn't believe you. Such things cannot be! No, this cannot be! It cannot be! It cannot be!"

Well, and who was right?

Translated by Hilde Abel

The Pair

SHOLOM ALEICHEM

1.

IT WAS a damp and dreary spring night. The world slept in darkness and in silence. It was a night for weird dreams.

The dreams that troubled our hero were violent. All night long his mind was disturbed by chickens, geese, and ducks. And in his dream one rooster figured with special prominence, a red bird, young and insolent, who refused to fade away. Persistently he remained in the foreground and provokingly chanted a nonsensical ditty:

Cockadoodledo-o-o-o . . .
They will catch you too-oo;
They will beat you,
They will eat you,
They will slit your throat too-oo-oo.

And each time the red rooster concluded his chant, all the chickens, geese, and ducks would make an unbearable noise.

Our hero was preparing to teach this audacious young rooster a lesson when suddenly there was heard a stamping of feet. A light appeared. Wild unfamiliar voices shouted in unearthly tones, "Not this one—the other—grab him—don't let him get away—tie him—careful with his legs, don't break them—ready?—get a move on—into the wagon with him—"

A pair of powerful hands seized our hero, bound him, twisted his legs, and thrust him into a roomy wagon. In the dark he could discern another creature, apparently female, crouching in the corner and trembling. Two people were puttering about the wagon. One was a savage-looking individual with head bare, the other equally savage but with his head covered by a fur cap. The bareheaded one carefully examined the wagon and the horses. The one with the fur cap leaped savagely onto the wagon and landed on the feet of the prisoners with such force that their heads reeled.

"Be careful now that they don't get untied and escape. Hear me?"

The admonition came from the bareheaded one, but the other did not trouble to answer. He merely lashed the horses and they were off.

2.

That they survived the night was itself a miracle. They had no idea where they were, to whom they were being taken, or why.

Because of the darkness they could not see each other very well. Only after dawn could they make each other out and converse quietly.

"Good morning, madam."

"Good morning."

"I could swear you're one of our kind—"

"There's no need to swear. You'll be believed without an oath."

"I recognized you at once, by your beads."

"That shows you have a good eye."

Some minutes passed and he spoke again. "How do you feel?"

"I could wish my feelings on my worst enemies."

Another pause, and then he whispered into her ear, "I want to ask you something."

"Yes."

"What are you accused of?"

"The same as you."

"I mean, what have you done wrong?"

"The same as you."

"It strikes me that you're annoyed about something."

"Annoyed! The boor! He plants himself on my feet and then complains that I'm annoyed."

"What are you saying? I, on your feet?"

"Who else?"

"It's he, that savage with the fur cap, may the devil take him!"

"Really? And I thought it was you. Forgive me if I hurt your feelings."

They could say no more, for the man in the fur cap roused himself and began whipping the horse furiously. The wagon leaped forward. The two prisoners listened to the quivering of their vitals. Suddenly the wagon came to a halt, and they beheld something they had never seen before.

3.

For the first time in their lives they saw a tremendous gathering of horses, cows, calves, pigs, and people. There were wagons with hoods raised, filled with goods, loaves of bread, and living creatures—chickens, geese, and ducks piled on top of one another. To one side a bound pig lay on a wagon, and his screeches of protest were deafening, yet no one paid any attention to him. Everyone was excited, everyone talked at once, everyone bustled about—it was a regular fair.

It was to this place that the fur-capped savage brought them. He lowered himself from the wagon and began puttering around with his prisoners. They awoke, strangely excited. What would be done with them now? Would they be untied? Or would he free them and let them go at will?

But their joy was short-lived. He merely moved them somewhat higher on the wagon, probably so that they could be seen better. A terrible humiliation! And yet one could think of it in another way. Perhaps it would be better if everyone could see them. Let the world see! Some kind soul might take their part and demand an explanation from the savage: Why? For what?

Thus the innocent prisoners reasoned, and it seemed that they reasoned well, for a kind soul did appear, a thickset woman in a Turkish shawl. She approached, felt around in the wagon, and asked the fur cap, "Your pair?"

"Any of your business?"

"How much do you want?"

"Where will you get so much money?"

"If I had no money would I talk to a lout like you?"

Such was the conversation between the Turkish shawl and the fur cap. They haggled for a long time. The savage in the fur cap remained cold and indifferent. The woman in the Turkish shawl grew excited. She turned away as if to leave, but came back at once and the bargaining resumed. This went on so long that the fur cap grew angry and the two started cursing each other. Meanwhile the prisoners exchanged a few words.

"Do you hear, madam?"

"Of course. Why shouldn't I?"

"Is it likely we are about to be ransomed?"

"It certainly looks that way."

"Then why does she bargain over us as if we were geese?"

"The humiliation!"

"Well, let them quarrel, just as long as we go free."

"Amen! I hope so."

The Lord be praised! The Turkish shawl dipped her hand into her pocket and took out the money.

"You won't let the price down?"

"No."

"Perhaps—all right, all right, just look at him rage. Here's your money."

And the pair passed from the savage in the fur cap to the fat woman in the Turkish shawl—that is, from one bondage to another.

4.

At the new place the prisoners were untied. Joyfully they felt the ground beneath them. They stretched and paced back and forth to make sure their feet still served them. In their happiness, however, they neglected to notice they were still far from free. Indeed, it took them a while to realize that they remained prisoners. They found themselves in a dark corner, with a warm oven on one side, a cold wall on the other, and an overturned ladder barring the exit. Food and drink had been left for them, and they were now alone, at God's mercy, so to speak. After examining their new dwelling they stood eying each other for a long time, as strangers will, and then they turned each to his own corner, where each surrendered to his own thoughts.

But they were not allowed to think for long. The door of their prison opened, and a crowd of women headed by the Turkish shawl came in.

The Turkish shawl led the women to the prisoners, pointed at them, and, her face aglow, asked, "How do you like these two?"

"How much did you pay for them?"

"Guess."

All of them guessed and all were wrong. When the Turkish shawl named the price they clapped their hands in amazement.

Envy crept into their faces. Their cheeks grew flushed, their eyes gleamed, but from their mouths flowed a stream of well wishing.

"Use them in good health! May you enjoy them! May you be as lucky all year! Together with your husband and children!"

"Amen! The same to you. The same to you."

The women left, and a moment later the Turkish shawl returned, leading in tow a man, a strange creature whose face was matted with red hair. Her face beamed with pride as she led him up to the prisoners.

"Now, *you* are a man of understanding, what do *you* think of this pair?"

The hairy person stared wildly. "I, an expert? What do I know of such things?"

"You're a scholar, and where there is learning there must be wisdom. Shouldn't God grant us a kosher Passover? Isn't it all for the sake of His precious name?"

The hairy person passed his hand over his beard, gazed heavenward, and intoned piously, "May the Almighty grant a kosher Passover to all Jews!"

The Turkish shawl and the hairy man departed, leaving the pair alone. For a moment they stood speechless, still wary of each other. Then she uttered a strange cry that was a cross between a cough and a scream.

He turned toward her. "What ails you, madam?"

"Nothing. I was thinking of home."

"Nonsense. You must forget that. We'd do better to get our bearings and consider what to do."

"Get our bearings? It's clear enough. We're in trouble, great trouble."

"For instance?"

"Don't you see we've been sold to savages just as one sells domestic beasts?"

"What will they do to us?"

"Plenty. When I was still a little bit of a thing I heard a lot of stories about what these savages do to those of our kind who fall into their hands."

"Nonsense! You mustn't believe in fairy tales."

"These aren't fairy tales. I heard it from my own sister. She said they are worse than wild beasts. When one of us is caught by a beast he is devoured, and that's all there is to it, but if—"

"There, there, my friend, it seems to me that you take too pessimistic a view of the world."

"Too which?"

"Too pessimistic."

"What does that mean, pessimistic?"

"It means, well, that you look through dark glasses."

"I don't wear glasses."

"Ha-ha."

"Why do you laugh?"

"Madam, you are a—"

"A what?"

He wanted to tell her, but the door suddenly opened and—

Better read on.

5.

The door opened wide, and a mob of small fry charged in like a whirlwind. Their cheeks flushed and their black eyes eager, they dashed toward the oven.

"Where are they? Where? Here they are, right here. Yankel! Berel! Velvel! Elie! Getzel! Quick! Over here!"

Only now did the pair discover what hell really meant: torment, suffering, endless humiliation. The small fry fell upon them like savages in the jungle. They skipped around them, examining them from all sides and loudly ridiculing them.

"Yosel, just look at that nose!"

"A schnozzle, Berel, a real schnozzola."

"Velvel! Pull his nose."

"No, by the mouth, Elie, like this!"

"Pull harder, Getzel! Make him holler!"

"You're all crazy. They holler only when you whistle at them. They can't stand whistling. Want to see? I'll whistle: Pheeeeeeee."

Ruffled, the prisoners blushed, lowered their heads, and exclaimed in unison, *Halder! Halder! Halder!*

The small fry picked it up and savagely mocked them. "Hold him! Hold her! Hold 'em."

Further enraged, the prisoners shouted louder. The youngsters were delighted. Convulsed with laughter, they mocked still louder. "Hold him! Hold her! Hold 'em!"

This competition resulted in such a racket that the Turkish shawl, God bless her, came charging in, grabbed the small fry, and tossed them out one by one, giving each a few sound slaps. This procedure she concluded with an all-round curse. "May a stroke descend on you, O Lord of the World, a fire and a plague and a cholera. May it seize you and shake you one by one, together with all the apostates, dear God, and may not one of you remain to see the Passover, dear merciful God."

Once rid of this torment, the prisoners did not regain their composure for some time. The savage outcries, the whistling, the laughter of the little barbarians rang in their ears. Later our hero came gradually to realize that it was pointless to continue grieving on an empty stomach, and he slowly approached the food.

"Madam," he said to his companion, "how long will you keep worrying? It's time to eat. The heavens haven't caved in, believe me, and we haven't had a bite all day."

"Eat well. I don't care for any."

"Why not? Are you fasting?"

"No. It's just that I don't care for any."

"Perhaps you want to teach them a lesson? Go on a hunger strike? You'll only succeed in doing yourself harm—that's all the good it will do."

"I don't see how one can possibly eat anything. It just won't go down."

"It'll go down, it'll go down. The first bite acts like a drill."

"A what?"

"A drill."

"You do use such strange words."

"Ha-ha!"

"Laughing again? What's the occasion?"

"I remembered the small fry."

"That's no laughing matter."

"What do you want me to do? Cry?"

"Why didn't you laugh when they were here?"

"What did I do?"

"It seemed to me you screamed."

"I screamed? I?"

"Who else? Maybe I did?"

"You were the first to start crying *halder, halder, halder."*

"Excuse me, but it was you who first cried *halder, halder."*

"So what is there to be ashamed of if I was the first?"

"And why should I feel ashamed if I was the first?"

"If there is nothing to be ashamed of, why have you lowered your nose?"

"I lowered my nose?"

"Who else?"

"Oh, it's so easy to notice someone else's nose!"

It was a pity that this interesting conversation could not be continued, but they were interrupted by the Turkish shawl, the mistress of their prison—as will be related in the next chapter.

6.

The Turkish shawl, as it turned out, was not their only mistress. They were fated to make the acquaintance of still another strange creature, a girl with a greenish complexion and a red kerchief. The two entered with arms full of good things: a bowl of rice mixed with beans and peas, a plate of boiled potatoes, chopped eggs, and an apronful of sliced apples and nuts.

As soon as they came in the greenish maid with the red kerchief pointed to the pair and addressed the Turkish shawl. "Look, they haven't even touched the food."

"Let's feed them now. I'll hold them and you put it in their mouths. Well? Why are you standing there like a dummy, with your teeth hanging out?"

"Why do they scream so when they look at me?"

"Silly girl! Take off that kerchief—they can't stand red."

"May all my troubles descend on their heads!"

"On your own head, silly—you come first. Why don't you put some rice and beans into his mouth?"

"Mistress dear, may you live long! I don't like the way he stares. Be careful that he shouldn't, God forbid, choke."

"You choke—you come first! All of a sudden she talks of choking, as if it were the first time I've done this. Stuff it down his throat—this way! I've been a housekeeper for twenty-one years, thank God. Now put a piece of apple and a nut in his mouth. More, more, don't be stingy!"

"I begrudge him? Why should I? It isn't mine. It's simply a pity, the way he suffers!"

"What do you say to this girl! A pity, she says. Am I doing him any harm? I'm only feeding him. And for whose sake? For the sake of God! For the sake of the holy Passover! The Almighty help me, I have fattened more than one pair for Passover. Let's have another nut and make an end of it. He's had enough for now. Now her. Begin with rice and beans."

"Good health to you, mistress, but how can you tell which is he and which is she?"

"May all my evil dreams descend on your head! She's asked to do one thing and her mind is the devil knows where! Wait till you get married, silly girl, and become a housekeeper, then you'll ask. Meantime do as you are told. More, more, don't be stingy! It's for the sake of nobody, except His Precious Name. For Passover! For Passover!"

Finished with their task, the women went off and the tortured prisoners remained alone. They staggered into a corner, rested their mournful heads upon each other, and surrendered themselves to thoughts of sadness, such as come very rarely, perhaps only a few minutes before death.

7.

Nothing begets friendship so readily as trouble. The two unfortunate prisoners are the best proof of this. During the brief term of their imprisonment they became as one, they began to understand each other at a mere hint, they were no longer bashful before each other, and they gave up addressing each other with the formal "you." They became, indeed, like one soul. She would address him as "My dear," and he would counter with "My soul."

Whenever the Turkish shawl and the red kerchief came with the food they could not admire the pair enough.

"What do you say to my pair?"

"A delight."

"Just feel them. Now what do you say? Some flesh, eh? Now shouldn't God help me because of the pair I fattened for Passover?"

When their work was done the wild women left, and the couple pondered the meaning of the Turkish shawl's remarks that she "fattens them for Passover" and that God should help her. Why should He? They thought hard and discussed the matter.

"Dearest, what is Passover?"

"Passover, my soul, is a sort of holiday among them, a holiday of freedom, of liberation."

"What does that mean—liberation?"

"Let me explain it to you. They consider it a great good deed to catch one of our kind and fatten him until this holiday Passover comes around, and then they let him free. Now do you understand?"

"Is it long till this Passover?"

"According to what I overheard the Turkish shawl say, it shouldn't be more than about three days."

"Three days!"

"What scared you so, you silly? The three days will pass like a dream, and when the dear Passover comes, they will open the doors for us and, 'Out you go, back where you came from.' Will we make tracks!"

"Dearest, you say such wonderful things. If only it were as you say, but I am afraid of one thing—"

"Sweetheart, you are always afraid."

"My dear, you don't know these savages."

"And where did you learn about them?"

"I heard plenty about them, dearest; when still at home I heard tell such stories about them! My sister told me she saw it herself."

"Again your sister's stories? Forget them."

"I would gladly forget them, but I can't. I can't get them out of my head by day or out of my dreams by night."

"And what are these stories that bother you day and night?"

"Darling, you won't laugh at me?"

"Why should I laugh?"

"Because you are like that. Whenever I tell you something you laugh and call me a silly goose or a foolish turkey or some other name."

"I promise not to laugh. Now tell me what you heard from your sister."

"My sister told me that people are worse than beasts. When a wild beast catches one of us it devours him and that's all, but when people catch one of us they imprison him and feed him well until he gets fat."

"And then?"

"And then they slaughter him and skin him and cut him to pieces and sprinkle salt on him and soak him."

"And then?"

"And then they make a fire and fry him in his own fat and eat him, meat, bones, and everything."

"Fairy tales, nothing to it, a cow flew over the moon. And you, you silly, you believe all this? Ha-ha-ha!"

"Well? What did I say? Didn't I say you'd laugh at me?"

"What else did you expect me to do, when you don't understand anything at all? It seems to me you must have heard a hundred times that the Turkish shawl said she was feeding us for the sake of no one but God."

"So what of it?"

"Just this, darling, that you are a silly goose."

"That is your nature! Right away you become insulting."

"Who do you mean by 'you'?"

"I mean all of you men!"

"All men? I am curious to know how many men you have known."

"I know only one, and that's quite enough for me."

"Oh no, you said 'men,' and that means you knew others besides me."

"What will you think of next?"

"Now you are angry again. Come here, I want to whisper something to you."

This loving scene was suddenly interrupted by the gang of small fry outside the window. They were not permitted inside, so they came each day to the window, and there they made strange gestures, stuck out their tongues, and shouted *halder, halder, halder*. The two would naturally respond, not as angrily as they had the first time, but more in the way of a greeting.

There is nothing in the world to which God's creatures can't become accustomed. Our prisoners had grown so used to their troubles that they now thought things were as they should be, just like the proverbial worm that has made its home in horseradish and thinks it sweet.

8.

There came a foggy morning. Inside it was still dark. The pair was immersed in deep sleep. They dreamed of their old home—a broad, unfenced out-of-doors, a blue sky, green grass, a shining brook, a mill that turned around, made noise, and splashed water. Ducks and geese splashed near the bank. Hens scratched, roosters crowed, birds flew about. What a beautiful world God had made for them. For them? Of course. For whom else were the tall, broad-branched trees under which one could stroll? For whom else was the mill where their entire family fed without letting anyone else near? For whom the round light in the sky that dipped into the river each evening? What wouldn't they give now for just one more look at the beautiful warm sun! at the big, free, light out-of-doors! at the mill and everything near it!

In the very midst of these sweet dreams they were seized and carried out. The fresh air of the foggy morning hit them full force. Another instant and they would take off and fly away over roofs and gardens and forests to where their home had been. There they would meet their own kind. "Welcome home, where have you been?" "Among wild people." "What did they do with you?" "They fed us for Passover." "What is Passover?" "It's a sort of holiday among people, a fine, dear holiday of freedom and liberation."

This is how they dreamed as they were taken to a narrow, dank alley where they were dropped in the mud. The wall was spattered with blood and many bound fowl lay on the ground in pairs and even in threes. Alongside stood young women and girls chatting and giggling. The pair looked about. Why had they been brought there? What were all the bound fowl doing there? What were the women and girls giggling about? And what was the meaning of the bloodstained wall? Was this the dear, good holiday of Passover? And what about freedom? And liberation?

Thus did the pair reason as they examined the bound fowl that lay quietly without asking any questions, as if this were the natural order of events. Only one loud-mouthed hen did not rest. Straining with all her strength, she flapped her wings in the mud and raved insanely. "Let me go! Let me go! I don't want to lie here! I want to run! Let me go!"

"Cockadoodledooo," a red rooster bound to two hens responded. "What do you say to this smarty? She doesn't want to lie here! She wants to go, she wants to run. Ha-ha!"

Our hero raised his head, carefully examined the insolent red rooster, and felt the blood rushing to his head. He could have sworn that he knew the fellow; he had seen him somewhere, had heard him before, but where? He couldn't remember. Yet wasn't there something hauntingly familiar about him? In heaven's name, where had he seen him? He raised his head a little higher, and the rooster noticed him and intoned in his high soprano:

Cockadoodledooo . . .
You were led
And you were fed,
Now you're tied,
Soon you'll be fried—

The red poet had no chance to finish. Someone's hand grabbed him with such force and so unexpectedly that he suddenly lost his voice.

The one who grabbed the rooster was an uncouth fellow with sleepy eyes, tall, thin, with long earlocks, his sleeves rolled up and his coat tails tucked in. In his hand he held a black shiny knife. Without delay he drew the rooster to himself, pulled up his head, looked briefly into his eyes, plucked three small feathers from his neck, and, *fft,* he passed the knife over his throat and tossed him back into the mud. For a moment the rooster lay motionless, as if stunned, then he got up and started running and turning his head back and forth as if looking for someone, or as if he had lost something. Our hero looked at the rooster and recognized him; it was the same one he had seen in his dream, and he recalled the song the rooster had sung. Now he could not say a word to his beloved, who lay close to him, trembling in all her limbs.

Meanwhile the savage with the shining knife proceeded with his work, unconcerned, like a true executioner. One after another the fowl flew from his hands, each first being tickled on the throat with the knife before being tossed into the mud. Some stretched out their legs, trembled, and kicked as they lost blood. Others flapped their wings. And every minute more victims joined them with cut throats. The women and girls observed all this yet did not seem to mind. On the contrary, some of them seized upon the still living fowl and started plucking their feathers, meantime chatting and joking and giggling as if it were water that flowed instead of the blood of living creatures. Where were their eyes? Where were their ears? And their hearts? And their sense of justice? And their God?

Our two bound prisoners watched the terrible scene, the horrible carnage at daybreak. Could it be that they too had been brought here for the same purpose as the chickens, ducks, and geese? Could it be that aristocrats, who haled from among the Indians, would share this terrible end with ordinary beings? Was it really true, what they had been told about these savages? And the prophecy of the red rooster, was that also true?

They began to understand the cold, bare truth and to comprehend everything they had seen and heard. One thing only they could not fathom. Why had the Turkish shawl boasted that God would reward her for fattening such a pair for Passover? Was that what their God wanted?

A few minutes later our loving pair, the prisoners, lay on the ground. Their still warm throats rested on each other, and from a distance it might have seemed they were asleep and dreaming beautiful dreams.

Translated by Shlomo Katz

The Dead Town

I. L. PERETZ

WHILE traveling through the provinces to take a Jewish census, I once saw a Jew stumbling painfully across the thick sand. He seemed to be sick; he could hardly drag one foot after the other. Taking pity, I asked him into my coach. The Jew climbed up, greeted me with a *sholom aleichem,* and began asking after all the latest news.

I answered, and ended with a question. "And where are you from?"

"From the dead town," he murmured.

I thought he was joking. "And where is this dead town? On the other side of the moon?"

"No," he said, smiling, "it's right here, in Poland."

"A dead town in Poland?"

"Of course. The gentiles don't know it and have never given it a name, but it's there. A Jewish town, an eminently Jewish town."

"What do you mean?"

"Just what I say! You have studied geography and think it includes everything. But we Jews dispense with geography. Our town isn't listed, yet people make long journeys to it and from it. What do we need geography for? Every driver knows the way. You don't believe me?"

I remained silent.

"But it's true. Our local rabbi exchanges letters with the wise men of the world. Back and forth fly questions and answers concerning the most vital problems of life: everything is taken care of. Not long ago, for example, a grass widow was relieved of her marriage ties, though it happens she had already lived most of her life in loneliness. Well, to be sure, the important thing wasn't the grass widow but the idea of the grass widow, the pleasure of the dialectic."

"This is the first time I ever heard of a dead town."

"That's odd! I suppose you don't get around much. It's a genuine Jewish town, a true haven of Israel. It has everything a town needs, even two or three madmen. And it's known for its commerce too."

"Are things brought in and out?"

"What's that?" asked the Jew, as if not quite able to grasp my question. "You mean merchandise—goods taken in and out?"

I nodded.

"Of course!" he answered. "We export phylacteries and import little sacks of holy earth from Palestine. But that isn't the main thing. The main thing is the commerce within the town. Taverns, guest houses, old clothes—that's the way we Jews get along."

"A poor town?"

"What's poor and what's rich? We make a living. The paupers beg in the town or in the countryside, but mostly in the town. Whoever stretches out his hand gets something. Others look for a soft touch; for example, a middleman haunts the streets in search of a bargain. The Almighty does not desert us. Orphan boys have their "eating days" at the tables of householders and study at the synagogue. Orphan girls become servants and cooks, or go elsewhere to earn their bread. Widows, divorcées, grass widows, sit over their fire ovens and with their heads circled by smoke dream that fully baked rolls grow on trees. Others live quite well."

"On what?"

"On what everyone lives. A pauper lives on hope; a merchant on air; and the man who works the soil—the gravedigger, I mean—he never lacks."

Is he mocking me, this bag of bones, this dried-out little Jew with deep-sunken eyes that flame like strange little fires? But not a smile creeps over his bony face, which looks as if it were covered with a sheet of yellow parchment. Yet that voice . . .

"All the same," I asked him, "what kind of town is it?"

"What do you mean? A town like every other town. We have a synagogue. Once, they say, there were paintings of the beasts and birds on the walls. On the ceiling were pictures of all the instruments King David played. Of course I never saw them, but the old people talk about it."

"And now?"

"Now? Dust and cobwebs. A wooden chain, carved out of one piece, still hangs from the ceiling, falling, charmingly, to one side of the Holy Ark. No one remembers who made the chain, but it must have been a master. A remarkable chain!

"In the synagogue," continued the Jew, "only the common folk come to say their prayers, only the artisans. They can hardly read Hebrew! The tailors have their own congregation, and the butchers and teamsters have hired a hut for their separate service. The more distinguished householders gather in the House of Study, a very imposing building—many tomes! And the Hasidim, they go off by themselves."

"Do you have many disputes?"

"As long as men live. . . . But in the cemetery there is peace. One burial place for everyone. And we also observe equality in the ritual baths."

"What else do you have?"

"What else do we need? Once we had a hostel for travelers but gave it up. Travelers can sleep in the House of Study—it's empty at night. We also have a place for the sick."

"You mean a hospital?"

"No, not a hospital. Just a hut with two rooms. It used to be the house of the ritual-bath attendant, but then the town decided that the attendant would be satisfied with one room and the other could be used for the sick. Besides, no more than three sick women stay there. One is an old crone with paralyzed legs, bedridden forever. Another's legs and arms are paralyzed. And the third is an insane grass widow. The beds occupy three of the corners and a stove fills the fourth. In the middle we have a little morgue, just in case—"

"You're making fun of me, my friend," I interrupted. "The town you describe is Tzachnovka! Tzachnovka with its affairs and its charities and good deeds! But why call it a dead town?"

"Because that's what it is. I speak of a town which from its inception has hung by a thread, and now that the thread has been broken floats in midair. And because it hangs by nothing it has become a dead town. If you like I'll tell you about it."

Meanwhile night had fallen. One part of the sky, as the sun set, had become bloody, fire-red. On the other side, the moon came swimming out of a light mist, like a bride peering from beneath her white veil. The beams it cast on the earth blended with the trembling shadows of the still, sorrowful night.

We drove into a small wood. The moonbeams stole after us, sliding past the trembling leaves. Below, among the fallen leaves and twigs, little circles of light danced about, like silver coins. The glimmering night and the quiet breath of the wood seemed magical.

I glanced at my neighbor. His whole appearance had changed. Now his expression was simple and without irony, his face suffused with an earnest melancholy.

"From its first moment," he continued, "the town hung by a thread, for it was built on land on which the law said no Jew could live. When enough of them had come together to form a congregation they held a meeting. It was decided to declare themselves part of a neighboring town, and on this basis they built themselves a synagogue, ritual baths for the men and women; they even bought a piece of earth for the cemetery. Only after they had done all this did they send influential emissaries to have the existence of their town recorded."

"And these messengers went with heads bent low?"

"Do we ever do anything but with heads bent? Could we do it any other way?"

"You're asking me?"

"Anyway, that's how it happened. And it wasn't quite as devious as you may suppose. There was a wealthy Jew in the town, and this wealthy Jew, as is usually the case, was thick with the authorities. So everything was signed over to him. His synagogue, his ritual baths, even his cemetery! The police kept silent. He was a man of influence. The plan was that as soon as the papers came from the authorities he would sign them over to the town and we could stop paying bribes."

"I suppose your rich man said, 'Put it in my name anyway'?"

"No, my friend, in those days such rich people were not yet the fashion. But listen—listen to what can happen to a Jewish town in this world. Not the rich Jew but his messenger caused all the trouble. On the road this messenger decided to abscond with the money and the papers. And he left the town a grass widow with living orphans."

"Did they send another messenger?"

"So quickly? Before they found out about it, before this and before that, the rich man died and left as his heir a little orphan. He wasn't allowed to sign anything until he was twenty-one."

"Didn't they try to hurry things up?"

"Certainly. When he was approaching twenty-one they would send another messenger, perhaps two."

"And meanwhile this was noted in the communal records?"

"Exactly! But the records remembered and the people forgot. Some say the records were burned, that the warden of the synagogue took the records, recited the blessing for the departure of the Sabbath over them, stoked himself with a little brandy, and disappeared.

"Meanwhile the community kept growing. Jews, the Lord be praised, multiply. They also come from other towns: one brings his son-in-law, another a daughter-in-law. In a word, the town grew. And as if in spite, the rich man's relatives disappeared. His widow remarried and left us, one son after the other left to wander across the seven seas. Only the youngest son remained. The community made him an official, married him off, and provided him with an experienced business partner."

"Who led him around by the nose?"

"According to the Law of Moses! Our young man had troubles with his partner and even more with his wife; and since he also signed a false note, he soon pulled a disappearing act—a total bankrupt. Townsmen and strangers raised a cry; the case went to court, and a bailiff was appointed. Not a penny was left—the wife hid the belongings. So the bailiff attached the synagogue and the cemetery!

"It was as if thunder had struck the town, suddenly pealing from a clear, unclouded sky. For, you understand, the story was kept secret from most of the townspeople until the last minute. And now, suddenly, the community hung, as I have mentioned, by a thread!

"What could be done? Off they went to the lawyers. And what could lawyers advise in such a case? To hold an auction. The bailiff would sell everything and the community would buy it back. This, to be sure, would be expensive, very expensive! Meanwhile, however, the community was no community, the papers had long since disappeared. So they had to find another rich man and buy things back in his name. The main thing this time was not to delay until the rich man died or left the town.

"At first glance it didn't seem a bad way out. The town had grown used to the loss of money. But by now there was more than one rich man in the town, there were several. And messengers—without number! In whose name should the purchase be made? And who should be our envoy? All were willing and all might easily be offended. So a meeting was held, and they pondered. They pondered so long that a quarrel broke out. And when we have a quarrel, it isn't settled the next morning. Sometimes it seems—aha, it's peaceful again, the flames are dying down; but then a peacemaker comes along, pours oil on the fire, and it burns all the brighter!"

The Jew wiped his pale forehead and continued with his story.

"Meanwhile something happened that would make one's eyes pop out —something you could hardly believe. But," he added, smiling, "it is night, and the creature that strolls across the sky at night"—he pointed to the moon—"we call Faith. At night, especially such a quiet night, one may believe everything."

"To be sure," I agreed, though not without hesitation.

"And the story is really quite dreadful. The bailiff stepped onto the holy ground of the cemetery. The corpses, hearing this, grew quite angry. The tombstones fell off the graves, the corpses crept out. You believe me?"

"I am not, God forbid," I told him, "a free thinker. I believe in an after-life. Only—"

"Only what, my friend, only what?"

"I always imagined that nothing but the soul survives, the soul that makes its way to heaven. The body that is lowered into the grave rots. In any case, without the soul it cannot move, it cannot rise again."

"Well said," the Jew praised me. "It's pleasant to know that you are among the learned. But you have forgotten, my friend, the world of illusion. The soul, you say, goes to the other world. But to which part? Paradise or Hell? Paradise is for saints and Hell for sinners. The first, for their good deeds, receive their share of the holy wine, and the second, for their evil, are thrown into boiling pitch. But that is only a way of speaking about reward and punishment. And why reward and punishment? Because a man, as long as he lives, has his choice. If he wishes to he does good, and if he wishes otherwise he does evil; and whichever way he makes his bed, that's how he lies, doesn't he?

"But suppose the man was no man, his life was no life, and he did neither good nor evil, because he could not do anything, because he had no choice and slept away his whole life as if in a dream? What shall be done with such a soul? Hell? For what? He never harmed a fly. Paradise? For which good deed? He never troubled himself to do anything."

"What happens to such a soul?" I asked.

"Nothing! It merely survives in the world of illusion. It remains attached to the body, but where it used to dream that it lived on the earth, now it dreams that it lives in the earth. And since no one in our town had really lived, hardly anyone really died. Neither good nor evil, neither sinners nor saints! Only daydreamers in a world of illusion! And when such a daydreamer enters the grave he remains a daydreamer; all that has changed is his lodging, nothing else.

"That's why dying among us was simply a comedy. For even if a feather were placed under the nose of a living man, do you think he would bother to remove it? Or to brush aside a troublesome fly? Soon they stopped worrying about livelihood—and then. . . .

"So it was. The same dream, the same world of illusion. It's that way in many towns. And if sometimes it happens, as it did among us, that a corpse creeps out of his grave, he does not even begin to remember that he has already recited the last confession, gasped his final breath, and died. As soon as the potsherds fall from his eyes, he goes straight to the House of Study or to the ritual bath or home for supper. And everything is again the way it was."

I don't know whether it was the fault of the moon or that I was not quite myself that evening, but I listened, I believed, and I even asked, "Well, did all of them, all the corpses, rise?"

"Who knows? Do they keep a directory? Perhaps there were a few free-thinkers who thought the day of resurrection had come and decided, out of sheer spite, to remain below. But a whole community rose up! Rose up and fled from the bailiff to the nearest woods."

"Why to the woods?"

"Because they couldn't go to town. It was still daylight, and according to the Law one shouldn't appear in one's shroud during the day. A town full of pregnant women, who might, God forbid, be frightened by the corpses into giving birth to corpses of their own."

"True. And the bailiff?"

"You're surprised at a gentile? He sensed nothing whatever. Maybe he was drunk, but he saw nothing. He kept right on with his inventory."

"And sold everything?"

"Not yet. So far he can't find a customer."

"And the corpses?"

"Ah, the corpses!"

The Jew rested himself for a moment and continued, "As soon as night fell, the corpses returned to the town. Each went to his own home, stole in through a door or a window or dropped down a chimney, hurried to a closet, took out some clothes, dressed himself, yawned, and stretched out to sleep. The next morning there was a townful of corpses."

"And the living, they said nothing?"

"They didn't even notice it, they were so busy quarreling. Everyone's head was simply bedeviled with quarrels. For that matter, how can you tell the difference between a living corpse and a corpse that has shed its winding sheet? It's not so easy!

"A son saw his father, spat three times, and burst out, 'Here I dreamed I had said *Kaddish* over my father and received his inheritance! May such dreams tempt my enemies!'

"A widow saw her husband and gave him a fine talking to! He had fooled her, the scamp, made fun of her, and she, foolish woman, had even prepared a new shroud for him."

"Suppose she had married again in the meantime?"

"Impossible! During our quarreling someone had set fire to the synagogue, together with the House of Study and the wedding canopy. Everything was burned to the ground. And almost everyone was accused in turn."

"And then?"

"Nothing. The corpses came to life, the living began to die out, for lack of space, of air, and most of all from hunger."

"A famine too?"

"As everywhere else. The corpses would sit down to their places at the prayers and at the dinner table as well. No one knew why, but suddenly spoons were missing. A housewife knows she has as many spoons as mouths to feed, so she thinks, A thief! The pious say, Devils! But when they realized that things were missing everywhere and there wasn't enough food to go around, they said, A year of famine, and they starved and continue to starve.

"And soon the corpses overpowered the living. Now they constitute the community and are its leaders. True, they do not beget children in the natural way, but whenever someone dies they steal him off his slab or out of his grave, and soon another corpse is wandering about the town.

"And what do they lack? They don't need to worry about death, they feel no fear. They eat merely to say the blessing, for they need no food, they have no sense of hunger. As for lodgings, a hundred corpses can live in one room, they don't need any air!

"And they have no sorrows. For what is the source of human sorrow but knowledge? *He who increases knowledge increases sorrow; the dead man knows not of sorrow*. The dead man neither wishes nor needs knowledge: it's not his affair. He merely wanders about in a world of illusion.

"These risen corpses keep themselves apart from all living things: they have no questions to ask, no doubts to ponder, no heartaches to suffer. And who do you think is now our rabbi? Once the rabbi was a living person; now he is a corpse wandering through the world of illusion. And who are his assistants? Creatures like himself—half-rotted corpses!

"These are the people who issue verdicts for the living and the dead, who know and do everything, who say the blessings and unite couples in wedlock.

"Who stands before the altar? A corpse! He has the face of a corpse, the voice of a corpse, and if by chance a cock suddenly crows he flees headlong from the altar.

"And our rich men, our philanthropists, the leaders of the community, the whole jabber of them, what are they? Dead, long dead and buried!

"And because of this the synagogue, the bath, and the streets are filled with an overwhelming stench. Everywhere, corpses."

"And you, my friend, what are you?"

"I?" answered the Jew as he leaped out of the carriage and disappeared among the trees. "I am half dead."

Translated by Irving Howe

Ne'ilah[1] in Gehenna

I. L. PERETZ

THE TOWN square . . . an ordinary day, neither a market day nor a day of the fair, a day of drowsy small activity. . . . Suddenly there is heard, coming from just outside the town, approaching nearer and nearer, a wild impetuous clatter, a splutter and splashing of mud, a racket of furious wheels! In-ter-est-ing, think the merchants, wonder who it is? At their booths, at their storefronts, they peer out, curious.

As the galloping horse, the thundering wagon, turn into and careen through the square, they are recognized! The townsfolk recoil, revulsion and fear and anger upon their faces. The informer of the neighboring town is at it again! Posthaste to the capital! God alone knows on whom he is going to do a job now.

Suddenly a stillness falls upon the market place. Reluctantly, with

[1] *Ne'ilah*—the last of the five services held on the Day of Atonement.

loathing, the townsfolk look around. The wagon has come to a halt. The horse is lazily nuzzling in the mire of the wheel ruts. And the informer, fallen from his seat, lies stretched out on the ground!

Well, even an informer has a soul; they can't just let him lie there, so the townsfolk rush forward to the body, motionless in the mud. Dead—like every other corpse! Finished! The members of the Burial Society make ready to do the last rites for the deceased.

Horse and wagon are sold to pay for the funeral expenses; the informer is duly interred; and those little imps of dispatch, who crop up just there where you won't see them, snatch up his soul and bear it off to the watchers of the gates of Gehenna.

There, at the gates, the informer is detained while the fiend of reception, he who keeps Hell's register of admission and discharge, wearily puts the questionnaire to him and as wearily, with his leaking pen, enters the answers: Who, When, How.

The informer—in Hell he feels cut down to size—respectfully answers: Born in such and such a place; became a son-in-law in such and such a place; was supported by father-in-law for such and such a number of years; abandoned wife and children; pursued, in such and such places, his chosen profession, until, his time having come, as he was passing with horse and wagon through the market place of Ladam—

At the mention of this name the fiend of reception, in the middle of a yawn, pricks up his ears. "How do you say it? La-ha—"

"Ladam!" [1]

The fiend goes red in the face, little lights of puzzlement twinkle in his eyes, and he turns to his assistants. "Ever hear of such a town?"

The assistant imps shrug their shoulders. Their tongues stuck between their teeth, they shake their heads. "Never heard of it!"

"*Is* there such a town?"

Now in the records of Gehenna every community has its own file, and these files are all alphabetically arranged, and every letter has its own filing cabinet. So a careful search is made through L—Lublin, Lemberg, Leipzig, they're all there—but no Ladam!

"Still, it's there," the informer persists, "a town in Poland."

"Contemporary or historical?"

"Founded twenty years ago. The Baron built it up. It boasts, in fact,

[1] The original Hebrew has L H D M, which are the initial letters of the phrase *"lo hoyu dvorim m'olam,"* meaning, "these things never were," "a pure fiction."

two fairs a year. Has a synagogue, a House of Study, a bathhouse. Also two gentile taverns."

Again the registrar addresses himself to his assistants. "Any of you remember—did we ever get anybody here from Ladam?"

"Never!"

Impatiently they turn to the informer. "Don't they ever die in this Ladam of yours?"

"And why shouldn't they?" he answers Jewish-wise, by returning a question. "Close, congested hovels that stifle you. A bathhouse where you can't catch your breath. The whole town—a morass!"

The informer is now in his element.

"Never die!" he continues. "Why, they have a completely laid-out cemetery! It's true that the Burial Society will flay you for the costs of burial before they bring you to eternal rest, but still they do have a cemetery. And not so long ago they had an epidemic too."

The interrogation at an end, due judgment is rendered concerning the informer, and concerning the town of Ladam due investigation is instituted. A town twenty years old, a town with an epidemic in its history—and not one soul landed in Gehenna! This was a matter one couldn't let drop.

The imps of inquiry are sent forth diligently to search the thing out.

They return.

True!

And they report as follows: That in the realm of Poland there is indeed a town called Ladam; that it is still extant; that it boasts its tally of good deeds and admits to a quantum (greater) of misdeeds; that its economy presents the usual occupations and the usual struggle; and that the Spirit of Evil representing Hell's interest in the said place, he too is not unemployed.

Why, then, have there never been any candidates for Gehenna from Ladam?

Because Ladam has a cantor! There lies the explanation! And what a cantor! Himself he's nothing! But his voice! A voice for singing, so sweet, so poignant-sweet, that when it weeps it penetrates right into hearts of iron, through and through; it melts them to wax! He has but to ascend the prayer stand, this cantor, and lift his voice in prayer, and behold, the entire congregation of Ladam is made one mass of repentance, wholehearted repentance, all its officers and members reduced, as if one person, to singlehearted contrition! With what result? With the result that, Up There, Ladam's sins are nullified, voided, made of no effect! With the result that for Ladam the gates of Paradise —because of this cantor—are forthwith flung apart! When somebody comes before those gates and says he's from Ladam—no further questions asked!

It was easy to see that, with such a cantor in the vicinity, Gehenna would have to operate in Ladam at a loss. Accordingly the matter was taken over by That Certain Party himself! Head of Hell, he would deal with the cantor personally.

So he orders that there be brought to him alive from the regions mundane a crowing Calcutta rooster, with comb of fiery red.

Done.

The Calcutta cock, frightened and bewildered in its new roost, lies motionless on the satanic altar, while he—may his name be blotted out!—circles around and around it, squats down before it, never taking his eye off it, his evil eye upon that bright red crest; winds around it, encircles it, until, the spell having worked, the red crest blenches and pales and grows white as chalk. But suddenly, in the midst of this sorcery, an ominous rumbling is heard from Up There. The Holy One, blessed be He, waxes wrathful! So he—may his name be blotted out!— in alarm desists, but not before he spits out a farewell curse:

"Cock-crow, begone! Begone his singing voice! Until the hour of his death!"

Against whom he really launched this curse, you, of course, have already surmised, and indeed even before the blood returned to the crest of the comb of the Calcutta rooster, the cantor of Ladam was minus his voice. Smitten in the throat. Couldn't bring out a note.

The source and origin of this affliction was known, but known, naturally, only to truly holy Jews, and even of these perhaps not to all. But what could one do? One couldn't, of course, explain it; the cantor just wouldn't understand. It was one of those things. Now, had the cantor himself been a man of good deeds, worth, and piety, one might perhaps have interceded for him, hammered at the gates of Heaven, clamored against injustice, but when the cantor was, as all knew, a man of insignificant merit, a trifle in the scales, a nothing, why, then . . .

So the cantor himself went knocking at the doors of the great rabbis, soliciting their help, imploring their intervention before the Heavenly Throne.

To no avail. It couldn't be done.

At last, winning his way into the court of the *zadik* of Apt, he clings to the *zadik,* won't be sundered from him, weeps, begs, and, unless and until he is helped, won't budge a step from the court. It is a most pitiable thing to see. Not being able to suffer the poor cantor's plight any longer, the *zadik* of Apt reluctantly decided to tell the cantor the irrevocable, but not without mixing in it some measure of consolation. "Know, Cantor," he says, "that your hoarseness will persist until your death, but know also that when, at the hour of your death, you come to say the Prayer of Repentance, you will say it with a voice so clear, you will sing it with a voice so musical, that it will resound through all the corridors of Heaven!"

"And until then?"

"Lost!"

The cantor still refuses to depart. "But Rabbi, why? Rabbi, what for?"

He persists so long that at last the *zadik* tells him the whole story—informer, rooster, and curse.

"If that's the case," the cantor cries out in all his hoarseness, "if that's the case, I—will—have—my—revenge!" And he dashes out.

"Revenge? How and from whom?" the *zadik* calls after him.

But the cantor is gone.

This was on a Tuesday, some say Wednesday; and that Thursday, in the evening, when the fishermen of Apt, out on the river to catch their fish for the Sabbath, drew up their nets, they drew forth the drowned body of the cantor of Ladam!

A suicide! From the little bridge over the river! For the saying of the Prayer of Repentance his singing voice had indeed come back to him, even as the *zadik* of Apt had promised, the learned *zadik* interpreting the words of That Certain Party and stressing them, *"until* the hour of his death"—but not *the* hour of his death.

Yet despite this assurance the cantor—and this was his revenge, as you will soon see—purposely, in that last hour, both on the bridge and in the water, refrained from saying the Prayer of Repentance!

No sooner is the cantor buried, according to the rite of suicides, than the imps are at his soul and to Gehenna he is brought. At the gates the questions are put to him, but he refuses to answer. He is prodded with a pitchfork, stimulated with glowing coals—still he keeps silent, won't answer.

"Take him as is!"

For these questionings in Hell are but a matter of form; Hell's own agents have all these years lain in wait for the unsuspecting cantor; Hell knows in advance the answers to Who, When, What for. The cantor is led to his proper place. A caldron seethes and boils before him.

But here, here the cantor at last permits himself the privilege of his voice. Clear and ringing he sings it forth: *"Yis-ga-da-al . . ."*

The *Kaddish of Ne'ilah!*

He intones it, he sings it, and in singing his voice grows bolder, stronger . . . melts away . . . revives . . . is rapturous . . . glorious as in the world aforetime . . . no, better . . . sweeter . . . in the heart, deeper . . . from the depths . . . clamorous . . . resurgent. . . .

Hushed are all the boiling caldrons from which up to now there had issued a continual sound of weeping and wailing; hushed, until, after a while, from these same caldrons, an answering hum is heard. The caldron lids are lifted, heads peer out, burned lips murmur accompaniment.

The fiends of calefaction stationed at the caldrons, refuse, of course, to make the responses. Bewildered, abashed, they stand there as if lost, one with his fagots for the fire, another with his steaming ladle, a third with his glowing rake. Faces twisted . . . mouths agape . . . tongues lolling . . . eyes bulging from the sockets. . . . Some fall into epileptic fits and roll, convulsed and thrashing, on the ground.

But the cantor continues with his *Ne'ilah.*

The cantor continues, and the fires under the caldrons diminish and fade and go out. The dead begin to crawl forth from their caldrons.

The cantor sings on, and the congregation of Hell in undertone accompanies him, prays with him; and passage by passage, as the prayer is rendered, hurt bodies are healed, become whole, torn flesh unites, skin is renewed, the condemned dead grow pure.

Yes, when the cantor comes to the verse where he cries out, "Who quickeneth the dead," and Hell's poor souls respond, "Amen, Amen," it is as if a resurrection, there and then, is taking place!

For such a clamor arises at this Amen that the heavens above are opened, and the repentance of the wicked reaches to the Heaven of Heavens, to the Seventh Heaven, and comes before The Throne itself! And, it being a moment of grace and favor, the sinners, now saints, suddenly grow wings! One after the other out of Gehenna they fly . . . to the very gates of Paradise.

Thereafter there remained in Gehenna only the fiends, rolling in their convulsions, and the cantor, stock-still at his stand. He did not leave. True, here in Hell he had brought, as he had brought on earth, his congregation to repentance, but he himself had not known a true repentance. That unsaid Prayer of Repentance . . . that matter of suicide. . . .

In the course of time Gehenna was filled again, and although additional suburbs were built, it still remains crowded.

Translated by A. M. Klein

Cabalists

I. L. PERETZ

WHEN TIMES are bad even Torah—that best of merchandise—finds no takers.

The Lashtchever yeshivah was reduced to Reb Yekel, its master, and an only student.

Reb Yekel is a thin old man with a long disheveled beard and eyes dulled with age. His beloved remaining pupil, Lemech, is a tall thin young man with a pale face, black curly earlocks, black feverish eyes, parched lips, and a tremulous, pointed Adam's apple. Both are dressed in rags, and their chests are exposed for lack of shirts. Only with difficulty does Reb Yekel drag the heavy peasant boots he wears; his pupil's shoes slip off his bare feet.

That is all that remained of the once famed yeshivah.

The impoverished town gradually sent less food to the students, provided them with fewer "eating days," and the poor boys went off, each his own way. But Reb Yekel decided that here he would die, and his remaining pupil would place the potsherds on his eyes.

They frequently suffered hunger. Hunger leads to sleeplessness, and night-long insomnia arouses a desire to delve into the mysteries of Cabala.

For it can be considered in this wise: as long as one has to be up all night and suffer hunger all day, let these at least be put to some use, let the hunger be transformed into fasts and self-flagellation, let the gates of the world reveal their mysteries, spirits, and angels.

Teacher and pupil had engaged in Cabala for some time. Now they sat alone at the long table. For other people it was already past lunchtime; for them it was still before breakfast. They were accustomed to this. The master of the yeshivah stared into space and spoke; his pupil leaned his head on both hands and listened.

"In this too there are numerous degrees," the master said. "One man knows a part, another knows a half, a third knows the entire melody. The rabbi, of blessed memory, knew the melody in its wholeness, with musical accompaniment, but I," he added mournfully, "I barely merit a little bit, no larger than this"—and he measured the small degree of his knowledge on his bony finger. "There is melody that requires words: this is of low degree. Then there is a higher degree—a melody that sings of itself, without words, a pure melody! But even this melody requires voicing, lips that should shape it, and lips, as you realize, are matter. Even the sound itself is a refined form of matter.

"Let us say that sound is on the borderline between matter and spirit. But in any case, that melody which is heard by means of a voice that depends on lips is still not pure, not entirely pure, not genuine spirit. The true melody sings without voice, it sings within, in the heart and bowels.

"This is the secret meaning of King David's words: 'All my bones shall recite . . .' The very marrow of the bones should sing. That's where the melody should reside, the highest adoration of God, blessed be He. This is not the melody of man! This is not a composed melody! This is part of the melody with which God created the world; it is part of the soul which He instilled in it.

"This is how the hosts of heaven sing. This is how the rabbi, of blessed memory, sang."

The discourse was interrupted by an unkempt young man girded with a rope about his loins—obviously a porter. He entered the House of Study and placed a bowl of grits and a slice of bread beside the master and said in a coarse voice, "Reb Tevel sends food for the master of the yeshivah." As he turned to leave he added, "I will come for the bowl later."

Shaken out of his reverie by the porter's voice, Reb Yekel rose heavily and, dragging his feet in his big boots, went to wash his hands at the basin. He continued his remarks, which now lacked enthusiasm, and Lemech from his seat followed his voice with great eagerness.

"But I," Reb Yekel's mournful voice trailed, "have not even merited to understand to what degree that melody belongs, through what gate it emerges. See," he added with a smile, "but I do know the fasts and 'combinations' required for this purpose, and I may even reveal them to you today."

The pupil's eyes bulged. His mouth opened in his eagerness not to miss even a word. But the master broke off abruptly. He washed his hands, wiped them, pronounced the benediction, and, returning to the table, recited with trembling lips the blessing over the bread.

With shaking hands he raised the bowl. The warm steam covered his bony face. Then he replaced it on the table and took up the spoon in his right hand, warming his left hand against the bowl. His tongue pressed the first bite of salted bread against his toothless gums.

Having warmed his face with his hands, he wrinkled his forehead, pursed his thin bluish lips, and blew upon the bowl.

All this time the pupil regarded him intently, and as the master's trembling lips stretched to meet the first spoonful of grits Lemech's heart seemed to contract. He covered his face with both hands and seemed to shrink all over.

Some minutes later another young man came, carrying a second bowl of grits and bread. "Reb Yosef sends dinner for the pupil," he announced. But Lemech did not remove his hands from his face.

The master put down his spoon and approached his pupil. For a moment he looked at him with loving pride; then he wrapped his hand in the wing of his coat and touched his shoulder.

"They brought you dinner," he reminded Lamech gently.

The pupil slowly removed his hands from his face, which was now even paler, and from his eyes, which burned with a still wilder fire.

"I know, *Rebbe,* but I will not eat today."

"The fourth fast in a row?" the master wondered. "And you will fast alone? Without me?" he added with a touch of resentment.

"This is a different kind of fast," the pupil answered. "It is a penitence fast."

"What are you saying? You, a penitence fast?"

"Yes, *Rebbe,* a penitence fast. A moment ago, when you began to eat, a sinful thought flitted through my mind, a covetous thought."

Late that night the pupil woke his master. They slept on facing benches in the House of Study.

"Rebbe, Rebbe!" he called in a weak voice.

"What is it?" The master awoke in fright.

"Just now I attained a high degree . . . ."

"How?" the master asked, still not entirely awake.

"Something sang within me."

"How? How?"

"I hardly know myself," the pupil replied in a still weaker voice. "I couldn't sleep and I pondered your words. I wanted to know the melody. I grieved so at not knowing it that I began to weep—everything within me wept, all my limbs wept before the Almighty.

"And even as I wept I made the combinations you had revealed to me. It was strange, I did not recite them by mouth, but somehow deep within me, as if it happened by itself. Suddenly there was a great light. My eyes were closed but I saw light, much great light."

"And then?" The master bent down to him.

"Then I felt so good because of the light; it seemed to me that I had lost all weight, that I could fly."

"And then, then what?"

"Then I felt very gay and cheerful so that I could laugh. My face didn't move, nor my lips, yet I laughed. It was such joyous, good, hearty laughter."

"Yes, yes, from joy."

"Then something within me hummed, like the beginning of a melody."

"Well? And then?"

"Then I heard the melody sing within me."

"What did you feel? What? Tell."

"I felt as if all my senses were deadened and shut off, and that something within me sang, the way it is necessary to sing, but without words, simply melody."

"How? How?"

"No, I can't describe it. I knew it before. Then the song became—became—"

"What became of it? What?"

"A kind of music . . . as if I had a violin within me, or as if Yonah the musician was within me and he was playing as he does at the rabbi's table, except that he played still better, more delicately, with more spirit. And all this time there was no sound, no sound at all, pure spirit."

"You are fortunate! You are fortunate! You are fortunate!"

"Now it's all gone," said the pupil sadly. "My senses are awake again, and I am so tired, so tired . . . so that . . . *Rebbe!*" he shouted suddenly and grasped at his chest. "*Rebbe!* Recite the confession with me! They came after me! A singer is missing in the heavenly host! A white-winged angel! *Rebbe! Rebbe! Shma Yisroel!* Hear, O Israel! *Shmaaa* . . . Yis . . ."

The entire town was unanimous in wishing for themselves a death such as this. Only the master of the yeshivah was not satisfied.

"Only a few fasts more," he said, sighing, "and he would have died with the Divine Kiss!"

Translated by Shlomo Katz

Bontsha the Silent

I. L. PERETZ

HERE ON earth the death of Bontsha the Silent made no impression at all. Ask anyone: Who was Bontsha, how did he live, and how did he die? Did his strength slowly fade, did his heart slowly give out—or did the very marrow of his bones melt under the weight of his burdens? Who knows? Perhaps he just died from not eating—starvation, it's called.

If a horse, dragging a cart through the streets, should fall, people would run from blocks around to stare, newspapers would write about this fascinating event, a monument would be put up to mark the very spot where the horse had fallen. Had the horse belonged to a race as numerous as that of human beings, he wouldn't have been paid this honor. How many horses are there, after all? But human beings—there must be a thousand million of them!

Bontsha was a human being; he lived unknown, in silence, and in silence he died. He passed through our world like a shadow. When Bontsha was born no one took a drink of wine; there was no sound of glasses clinking. When he was confirmed he made no speech of celebration. He existed like a grain of sand at the rim of a vast ocean, amid millions of other grains of sand exactly similar, and when the wind at last lifted him up and carried him across to the other shore of that ocean, no one noticed, no one at all.

During his lifetime his feet left no mark upon the dust of the streets;

after his death the wind blew away the board that marked his grave. The wife of the gravedigger came upon that bit of wood, lying far off from the grave, and she picked it up and used it to make a fire under the potatoes she was cooking; it was just right. Three days after Bontsha's death no one knew where he lay, neither the gravedigger nor anyone else. If Bontsha had had a headstone, someone, even after a hundred years, might have come across it, might still have been able to read the carved words, and his name, Bontsha the Silent, might not have vanished from this earth.

His likeness remained in no one's memory, in no one's heart. A shadow! Nothing! Finished!

In loneliness he lived, and in loneliness he died. Had it not been for the infernal human racket someone or other might have heard the sound of Bontsha's bones cracking under the weight of his burdens; someone might have glanced around and seen that Bontsha was also a human being, that he had two frightened eyes and a silent trembling mouth; someone might have noticed how, even when he bore no actual load upon his back, he still walked with his head bowed down to earth, as though while living he was already searching for his grave.

When Bontsha was brought to the hospital ten people were waiting for him to die and leave them his narrow little cot; when he was brought from the hospital to the morgue twenty were waiting to occupy his pall; when he was taken out of the morgue forty were waiting to lie where he would lie forever. Who knows how many are now waiting to snatch from him that bit of earth?

In silence he was born, in silence he lived, in silence he died—and in an even vaster silence he was put into the ground.

Ah, but in the other world it was not so! No! In Paradise the death of Bontsha was an overwhelming event. The great trumpet of the Messiah announced through the seven heavens: Bontsha the Silent is dead! The most exalted angels, with the most imposing wings, hurried, flew, to tell one another, "Do you know who has died? Bontsha! Bontsha the Silent!"

And the new, the young little angels with brilliant eyes, with golden wings and silver shoes, ran to greet Bontsha, laughing in their joy. The sound of their wings, the sound of their silver shoes, as they ran to meet him, and the bubbling of their laughter, filled all Paradise with jubilation, and God Himself knew that Bontsha the Silent was at last here.

In the great gateway to heaven Abraham, our father, stretched out his arms in welcome and benediction. "Peace be with you!" And on his old face a deep sweet smile appeared.

What, exactly, was going on up there in Paradise?

There, in Paradise, two angels came bearing a golden throne for Bontsha to sit upon, and for his head a golden crown with glittering jewels.

"But why the throne, the crown, already?" two important saints asked. "He hasn't even been tried before the heavenly court of justice to which each new arrival must submit." Their voices were touched with envy. "What's going on here, anyway?"

And the angels answered the two important saints that, yes, Bontsha's trial hadn't started yet, but it would only be a formality, even the prosecutor wouldn't dare open his mouth. Why, the whole thing wouldn't take five minutes!

"What's the matter with you?" the angels asked. "Don't you know whom you're dealing with? You're dealing with Bontsha, Bontsha the Silent!"

When the young, the singing angels encircled Bontsha in love, when Abraham, our father, embraced him again and again, as a very old friend, when Bontsha heard that a throne waited for him, and for his head a crown, and that when he would stand trial in the court of heaven no one would say a word against him—when he heard all this, Bontsha, exactly as in the other world, was silent. He was silent with fear. His heart shook, in his veins ran ice, and he knew this must all be a dream or simply a mistake.

He was used to both, to dreams and mistakes. How often, in that other world, had he not dreamed that he was wildly shoveling up money from the street, that whole fortunes lay there on the street beneath his hands—and then he would wake and find himself a beggar again, more miserable than before the dream.

How often in that other world had someone smiled at him, said a pleasant word—and then, passing and turning back for another look, had seen his mistake and spat at Bontsha.

Wouldn't that be just my luck, he thought now, and he was afraid to lift his eyes, lest the dream end, lest he awake and find himself again on earth, lying somewhere in a pit of snakes and loathesome vipers, and he was afraid to make the smallest sound, to move so much as an eyelash; he trembled and he could not hear the paeans of the angels; he could not see them as they danced in stately celebration about him; he could not answer the loving greeting of Abraham, our father, "Peace be with you!" And when at last he was led into the great court of justice in Paradise he couldn't even say "Good morning." He was paralyzed with fear.

And when his shrinking eyes beheld the floor of the courtroom of justice, his fear, if possible, increased. The floor was of purest alabaster, embedded with glittering diamonds. On such a floor stand my feet, thought Bontsha. My feet! He was beside himself with fear. Who knows, he thought, for what very rich man, or great learned rabbi, or even saint, this whole thing's meant? The rich man will arrive, and then it will all be over. He lowered his eyes; he closed them.

In his fear he did not hear when his name was called out in the pure angelic voice: "Bontsha the Silent!" Through the ringing in his ears he could make out no words, only the sound of that voice like the sound of music, of a violin.

Yet did he, perhaps, after all, catch the sound of his own name, "Bontsha the Silent?" And then the voice added, "To him that name is as becoming as a frock coat to a rich man."

What's that? What's he saying? Bontsha wondered, and then he heard an impatient voice interrupting the speech of his defending angel. "Rich man! Frock coat! No metaphors, please! And no sarcasm!"

"He never," began the defending angel again, "complained, not against God, not against man; his eye never grew red with hatred, he never raised a protest against heaven."

Bontsha couldn't understand a word, and the harsh voice of the prosecuting angel broke in once more. "Never mind the rhetoric, please!"

"His sufferings were unspeakable. Here, look upon a man who was more tormented than Job!"

Who? Bontsha wondered. Who is this man?

"Facts! Facts! Never mind the flowery business and stick to the facts, please!" the judge called out.

"When he was eight days old he was circumcised—"

"Such realistic details are unnecessary—"

"The knife slipped, and he did not even try to staunch the flow of blood—"

"—are distasteful. Simply give us the important facts."

"Even then, an infant, he was silent, he did not cry out his pain," Bontsha's defender continued. "He kept his silence, even when his mother died, and he was handed over, a boy of thirteen, to a snake, a viper—a stepmother!"

Hm, Bontsha thought, could they mean me?

"She begrudged him every bite of food, even the moldy rotten bread and the gristle of meat that she threw at him, while she herself drank coffee with cream."

"Irrelevant and immaterial," said the judge.

"For all that, she didn't begrudge him her pointed nails in his flesh—flesh that showed black and blue through the rags he wore. In winter, in the bitterest cold, she made him chop wood in the yard, barefoot! More than once were his feet frozen, and his hands, that were too young, too tender, to lift the heavy logs and chop them. But he was always silent, he never complained, not even to his father—"

"Complain! To that drunkard!" The voice of the prosecuting angel rose derisively, and Bontsha's body grew cold with the memory of fear.

"He never complained," the defender continued, "and he was always lonely. He never had a friend, never was sent to school, never was given a new suit of clothes, never knew one moment of freedom."

"Objection! Objection!" the prosecutor cried out angrily. "He's only trying to appeal to the emotions with these flights of rhetoric!"

"He was silent even when his father, raving drunk, dragged him out of the house by the hair and flung him into the winter night, into the snowy, frozen night. He picked himself up quietly from the snow and wandered into the distance where his eyes led him.

"During his wanderings he was always silent; during his agony of hunger he begged only with his eyes. And at last, on a damp spring night, he drifted to a great city, drifted there like a leaf before the wind, and on his very first night, scarcely seen, scarcely heard, he was thrown into jail. He remained silent, he never protested, he never asked, Why, what for? The doors of the jail were opened again, and, free, he looked for the most lowly filthy work, and still he remained silent.

"More terrible even than the work itself was the search for work. Tormented and ground down by pain, by the cramp of pain in an empty stomach, he never protested, he always kept silent.

"Soiled by the filth of a strange city, spat upon by unknown mouths, driven from the streets into the roadway, where, a human beast of burden, he pursued his work, a porter, carrying the heaviest loads upon his back, scurrying between carriages, carts, and horses, staring death in the eyes every moment, he still kept silent.

"He never reckoned up how many pounds he must haul to earn a penny; how many times, with each step, he stumbled and fell for that penny. He never reckoned up how many times he almost vomited out his very soul, begging for his earnings. He never reckoned up his bad luck, the other's good luck. No, never. He remained silent. He never even demanded his own earnings; like a beggar, he waited at the door for what was rightfully his, and only in the depths of his eyes was there an unspoken longing. 'Come back later!' they'd order him; and, like a shadow, he would vanish, and then, like a shadow, would return and stand waiting, his eyes begging, imploring, for what was his. He remained silent even when they cheated him, keeping back, with one excuse or another, most of his earnings, or giving him bad money. Yes, he never protested, he always remained silent.

"Once," the defending angel went on, "Bontsha crossed the roadway to the fountain for a drink, and in that moment his whole life was miraculously changed. What miracle happened to change his whole life? A splendid coach, with tires of rubber, plunged past, dragged by runaway horses; the coachman, fallen, lay in the street, his head split open. From the mouths of the frightened horses spilled foam, and in their wild eyes sparks struck like fire in a dark night, and inside the carriage sat a man, half alive, half dead, and Bontsha caught at the reins and held the horses. The man who sat inside and whose life was saved, a Jew, a philanthropist, never forgot what Bontsha had done for him. He handed him the whip of the dead driver, and Bontsha, then and there, became a coachman—no longer a common porter! And what's more, his great benefactor married him off, and what's still more, this great philanthropist himself provided a child for Bontsha to look after.

"And still Bontsha never said a word, never protested."

They mean me, I really do believe they mean me, Bontsha encouraged himself, but still he didn't have the gall to open his eyes, to look up at his judge.

"He never protested. He remained silent even when that great philanthropist shortly thereafter went into bankruptcy without ever having paid Bontsha one cent of his wages.

"He was silent even when his wife ran off and left him with her helpless infant. He was silent when, fifteen years later, that same helpless infant had grown up and become strong enough to throw Bontsha out of the house."

They mean me, Bontsha rejoiced, they really mean me.

"He even remained silent," continued the defending angel, "when that same benefactor and philanthropist went out of bankruptcy, as suddenly as he'd gone into it, and still didn't pay Bontsha one cent of what he owed him. No, more than that. This person, as befits a fine gentleman who has gone through bankruptcy, again went driving the great coach with the tires of rubber, and now, now he had a new coachman, and Bontsha, again a porter in the roadway, was run over by coachman, carriage, horses. And still, in his agony, Bontsha did not cry out; he remained silent. He did not even tell the police who had done this to him. Even in the hospital, where everyone is allowed to scream, he remained silent. He lay in utter loneliness on his cot, abandoned by the doctor, by the nurse; he had not the few pennies to pay them—and he made no murmur. He was silent in that awful moment just before he was about to die, and he was silent in that very moment when he did die. And never one murmur of protest against man, never one murmur of protest against God!"

Now Bontsha begins to tremble again. He senses that after his defender has finished, his prosecutor will rise to state the case against him. Who knows of what he will be accused? Bontsha, in that other world on earth, forgot each present moment as it slipped behind him to become the past. Now the defending angel has brought everything back to his mind again—but who knows what forgotten sins the prosecutor will bring to mind?

The prosecutor rises. "Gentlemen!" he begins in a harsh and bitter voice, and then he stops. "Gentlemen—" he begins again, and now his voice is less harsh, and again he stops. And finally, in a very soft voice, that same prosecutor says, "Gentlemen, he was always silent—and now I too will be silent."

The great court of justice grows very still, and at last from the judge's chair a new voice rises, loving, tender. "Bontsha my child, Bontsha"—the voice swells like a great harp—"my heart's child . . ."

Within Bontsha his very soul begins to weep. He would like to open his eyes, to raise them, but they are darkened with tears. It is so sweet to cry. Never until now has it been sweet to cry.

"My child, my Bontsha . . ."

Not since his mother died has he heard such words, and spoken in such a voice.

"My child," the judge begins again, "you have always suffered, and you have always kept silent. There isn't one secret place in your body without its bleeding wound; there isn't one secret place in your soul without its wound and blood. And you never protested. You always were silent.

"There, in that other world, no one understood you. You never understood yourself. You never understood that you need not have been silent, that you could have cried out and that your outcries would have brought down the world itself and ended it. You never understood your sleeping strength. There in that other world, that world of lies, your silence was never rewarded, but here in Paradise is the world of truth, here in Paradise you will be rewarded. You, the judge can neither condemn nor pass sentence upon. For you there is not only one little portion of Paradise, one little share. No, for you there is everything! Whatever you want! Everything is yours!"

Now for the first time Bontsha lifts his eyes. He is blinded by light. The splendor of light lies everywhere, upon the walls, upon the vast ceiling, the angels blaze with light, the judge. He drops his weary eyes.

"Really?" he asks, doubtful, and a little embarrassed.

"Really!" the judge answers. "Really! I tell you, everything is yours. Everything in Paradise is yours. Choose! Take! Whatever you want! You will only take what is yours!"

"Really?" Bontsha asks again, and now his voice is stronger, more assured.

And the judge and all the heavenly host answer, "Really! Really! Really!"

"Well then"—and Bontsha smiles for the first time—"well then, what I would like, Your Excellency, is to have, every morning for breakfast, a hot roll with fresh butter."

A silence falls upon the great hall, and it is more terrible than Bontsha's has ever been, and slowly the judge and the angels bend their heads in shame at this unending meekness they have created on earth.

Then the silence is shattered. The prosecutor laughs aloud, a bitter laugh.

Translated by Hilde Abel

If Not Higher

I. L. PERETZ

EARLY every Friday morning, at the time of the Penitential Prayers, the Rabbi of Nemirov would vanish.

He was nowhere to be seen—neither in the synagogue nor in the two Houses of Study nor at a *minyan*. And he was certainly not at home. His door stood open; whoever wished could go in and out; no one would steal from the rabbi. But not a living creature was within.

Where could the rabbi be? Where should he be? In heaven, no doubt. A rabbi has plenty of business to take care of just before the Days of Awe. Jews, God bless them, need livelihood, peace, health, and good matches. They want to be pious and good, but our sins are so great, and Satan of the thousand eyes watches the whole earth from one end to the other. What he sees he reports; he denounces, informs. Who can help us if not the rabbi!

That's what the people thought.

But once a Litvak came, and he laughed. You know the Litvaks. They think little of the Holy Books but stuff themselves with Talmud and law. So this Litvak points to a passage in the *Gemarah*—it sticks in your eyes—where it is written that even Moses, our Teacher, did not ascend to heaven during his lifetime but remained suspended two and a half feet below. Go argue with a Litvak!

So where can the rabbi be?

"That's not my business," said the Litvak, shrugging. Yet all the while—what a Litvak can do!—he is scheming to find out.

That same night, right after the evening prayers, the Litvak steals into the rabbi's room, slides under the rabbi's bed, and waits. He'll watch all night and discover where the rabbi vanishes and what he does during the Penitential Prayers.

Someone else might have got drowsy and fallen asleep, but a Litvak is never at a loss; he recites a whole tractate of the Talmud by heart.

At dawn he hears the call to prayers.

The rabbi has already been awake for a long time. The Litvak has heard him groaning for a whole hour.

Whoever has heard the Rabbi of Nemirov groan knows how much sorrow for all Israel, how much suffering, lies in each groan. A man's heart might break, hearing it. But a Litvak is made of iron; he listens and remains where he is. The rabbi, long life to him, lies on the bed, and the Litvak under the bed.

Then the Litvak hears the beds in the house begin to creak; he hears people jumping out of their beds, mumbling a few Jewish words, pouring water on their fingernails, banging doors. Everyone has left. It is again quiet and dark; a bit of light from the moon shines through the shutters.

(Afterward the Litvak admitted that when he found himself alone with the rabbi a great fear took hold of him. Goose pimples spread across his skin, and the roots of his earlocks pricked him like needles. A trifle: to be alone with the rabbi at the time of the Penitential Prayers! But a Litvak is stubborn. So he quivered like a fish in water and remained where he was.)

Finally the rabbi, long life to him, arises. First he does what befits a Jew. Then he goes to the clothes closet and takes out a bundle of peasant clothes: linen trousers, high boots, a coat, a big felt hat, and a long wide leather belt studded with brass nails. The rabbi gets dressed. From his coat pocket dangles the end of a heavy peasant rope.

The rabbi goes out, and the Litvak follows him.

On the way the rabbi stops in the kitchen, bends down, takes an ax from under the bed, puts it in his belt, and leaves the house. The Litvak trembles but continues to follow.

The hushed dread of the Days of Awe hangs over the dark streets. Every once in a while a cry rises from some *minyan* reciting the Penitential Prayers, or from a sickbed. The rabbi hugs the sides of the streets, keeping to the shade of the houses. He glides from house to house, and the Litvak after him. The Litvak hears the sound of his heartbeats mingling with the sound of the rabbi's heavy steps. But he keeps on going and follows the rabbi to the outskirts of the town.

A small wood stands behind the town.

The rabbi, long life to him, enters the wood. He takes thirty or forty steps and stops by a small tree. The Litvak, overcome with amazement, watches the rabbi take the ax out of his belt and strike the tree. He hears the tree creak and fall. The rabbi chops the tree into logs and the logs into sticks. Then he makes a bundle of the wood and ties it with the rope in his pocket. He puts the bundle of wood on his back, shoves the ax back into his belt, and returns to the town.

He stops at a back street beside a small broken-down shack and knocks at the window.

"Who is there?" asks a frightened voice. The Litvak recognizes it as the voice of a sick Jewish woman.

"I," answers the rabbi in the accent of a peasant.

"Who is I?"

Again the Rabbi answers in Russian. "Vassil."

"Who is Vassil, and what do you want?"

"I have wood to sell, very cheap." And, not waiting for the woman's reply, he goes into the house.

The Litvak steals in after him. In the gray light of early morning he sees a poor room with broken, miserable furnishings. A sick woman, wrapped in rags, lies on the bed. She complains bitterly, "Buy? How can I buy? Where will a poor widow get money?"

"I'll lend it to you," answers the supposed Vassil. "It's only six cents."

"And how will I ever pay you back?" said the poor woman, groaning.

"Foolish one," says the rabbi reproachfully. "See, you are a poor sick Jew, and I am ready to trust you with a little wood. I am sure you'll pay. While you, you have such a great and mighty God and you don't trust him for six cents."

"And who will kindle the fire?" said the widow. "Have I the strength to get up? My son is at work."

"I'll kindle the fire," answers the rabbi.

As the rabbi put the wood into the oven he recited, in a groan, the first portion of the Penitential Prayers.

As he kindled the fire and the wood burned brightly, he recited, a bit more joyously, the second portion of the Penitential Prayers. When the fire was set he recited the third portion, and then he shut the stove.

The Litvak who saw all this became a disciple of the rabbi.

And ever after, when another disciple tells how the Rabbi of Nemirov ascends to heaven at the time of the Penitential Prayers, the Litvak does not laugh. He only adds quietly, "If not higher."

Translated by Marie Syrkin

The Mad Talmudist

I. L. PERETZ

1.

He rushes back and forth, alone, in the House of Prayer. It is noon time. Suddenly he stops himself.

Almighty God: who am I?

Who am I? They call me Berel, son of Chantsia. But is that what I am, the name? A sign is not yet the store. The house where the rabbi lives is called *Pod-karpiam,* and I—Berel Chantsia's!

In Tzachnovka everyone knows who Berel is; but in America? Suppose someone in America were suddenly to say, "Berel Chantsia's." Would anyone know he meant me?

Here it's different. They smile, shake their heads, make wry faces. "A familiar creature, this Berel." One thinks: the village Talmudist. Another: our madman. A third: who knows? And the fourth remembers that I'm named after my uncle Berel. When Teibele says this she sighs; she knows I'm an orphan. But in America, where no one knows Chana the marketwoman, or that once there was a hair-splitter named Berel who was my mother's brother, or that I am called madman, student, orphan, and perhaps hair-splitter too (I must take after my uncle)—what would they say there about Berel Chantsia's?

But I must have some idea as to who I am. I myself repeat the words: madman, student. So that's who I am!

Mad. Who else would stop to ponder: who am I? A man is a man! I'm a man and they call me Berel. If I were a house they might call me *Pod-karpiam*. If I were a prisoner I'd have a patch on my back with a number on it. If my father, instead of my mother, had been the breadwinner, they'd call me Berel Shmerl's. Of course it would be hard to pronounce Berel Shmerl's, but they'd have to! And they might not chatter about me all the time if my name didn't roll off their tongues so easily.

But no matter what they call me, I'm still a human being.

A human being, but also a student, an eternal student. Suppose a man becomes an orphan: does that mean he has to spend his whole life in the House of Prayer? I'm not a cripple; why couldn't I work like the others? Run errands, chop wood, become a servant. Then I'd have something to wear instead of these rags; I'd have bread every day instead of missing two days a week. And I wouldn't go around worrying my head about who I am.

If only I knew whose coat I wear; the devil take me if I know! A piece of Chaim's, a piece of Jonah's, and three-quarters rubbish. It's a blessing Teibele sews, otherwise I'd be naked as Adam.

But isn't it all madness, this endless probing, this endless hair-splitting . . . pointless . . . Shmerl, Chaim, Jonah . . . Is there a limit to the number of students I've seen go by? One is now a merchant, another a street porter, a third keeps an inn; one is a widower, and Shmerl has his third wife; all have children, work, things to do; good, bad, but busy; they feed themselves, they don't remain Talmudists all their lives. They're human beings. I too want to be a human being!

But what is a human being?

As sure as I'm a Jew, I'm not a human being.

A Jew, yes. Of course a Jew. But so is everyone else in Tzachnovka, and yet they're not me. I'm a man . . . all human creatures that aren't female are men. But they're not all Berel Chantsia's, are they?

No, brother Berel, don't fool yourself. You're a man, a Jew; but you aren't *that* man, you aren't *that* Jew. All that is added on, extra; it's not you. *You* are something else.

Talmudist, madman, orphan, unfortunate—but of Talmudists, madmen, orphans, and unfortunates there is no lack in this world . . . perhaps fewer of my kind, perhaps in another city, perhaps in America. But are they all alike? No, heaven forbid, each is different.

In that case, who the devil am I?

A *dybbuk* must have entered me, someone else, an Other who thinks for me—while I go around thinking it's I who do the thinking. The proof is, when I have strength (every day but Mondays and Tuesdays) the Other has no power over me; and then I think even less. How is it possible for a man in this world to understand himself? What does it mean to want to understand yourself? I want to tear myself out of my body, I want to stand apart from myself, or have the Other stand apart from me. Then "he" can look at me or I-he can look at him-I.

What is all this? Wait, let me think. Something is buzzing in my head.

He runs to the washstand and pours cold water on his face. He pulls out a rag from beneath the oven and binds it tightly around his forehead.

Good, now it will work. Let's try again. I want to know: who am I? I myself . . .

Where shall I look, up or down? right or left? After all, I live in myself. When I crawl on top of the Sacred Ark, I'm entirely up; nothing of me remains below. When I go to the cellar, I'm entirely down. So how can I find myself?

What is it that lives in me and thinks for me?

Something does live there, doesn't it?

I know this: when the sexton's wife didn't count the cookies and I hadn't had anything to eat for three days, I was terribly tempted to snatch one. But I said: no, you mustn't! they're not yours. And then I found a thousand excuses. "The sexton's wife can afford to give me a few." "If I asked her she'd let me have some." "With God's help I'll pay her back." But no: you mustn't! And so it remained: no!

At first everything followed in order: I asked the question and I answered it. But later something else happened, it became mixed up: Yes and No, No and Yes, and then again No! It became a debate, and No won. Not because I didn't want the cookies or had lost my hunger. It was just that my hand couldn't move; it didn't know whom to obey. The proof was, I became exhausted, just as after a fierce quarrel, or after a heated discussion with Jonah the Noodle, who tries to tell me that the Vilna Gaon, of blessed memory, sits in Paradise with his snotty beard simply because he stuck his tongue out at Hasidism!

Such a fool! But really I was tired. I remember so clearly. And the same thing on *Purim,* when I brought sweets from the merchant Feinholtz to the rabbi. My mouth watered, my tongue twitched just as I now jump around. My hands trembled; a piece of cake, macaroons, other sweets. The tempted "I" wanted to take; the honest "I" did not.

They talk about the Spirit of Good. All right, let it be so. But me, I'm nothing more than a house where two neighbors live, the Spirit of Good and the Spirit of Evil. Isn't that so? But here it is again, the same business with names. Who are they? And who am I?

I'm the house, I'm the good neighbor, I'm the bad neighbor. I'm all of them; yet who am I?

Yesterday everyone laughed because I stood on one spot for an hour. I *know* why I did that. I just couldn't move. Out in the yard they were chopping wood and I wanted to see whether I too could work. I had already begun to go out when I saw two benches: one on the left and one on the right. On this side they say the bathhouse is being heated, and my skin begins to itch, I want to run off to the bath. But on the right Zorach the teacher is telling Yankel that in the *Bal-Akeida* (the commentary on Abraham's sacrifice of Isaac) the chapter for the week is truly marvelous. So I begin to wonder what has moved Zorach to hurry over to the east wall and pull down the tome. Well, I remained standing; the feet didn't know whom to obey: the Berel who wants to chop wood, the Berel who wants to go to the bath because his skin itches, or the Berel who wonders what has struck Zorach the teacher. And I remained that way, standing still, until I remembered I hadn't said my evening prayers.

Now four people live in me: a wood-chopper, an Abraham sacrificing Isaac, a bather, and a man who says his evening prayers and drives the other three behind the oven so they shouldn't make a sound. He rules, the feet obey him. Proof is, I went to the east wall and prayed.

There's a bit of truth in all this. For the others didn't get lost, they just hid behind the oven and kept peeking out at me—they winked, they laughed. In the middle of the prayer I kept thinking about wood-chopping, switching to the highest step of the bathhouse, and the commentary on Abraham's sacrifice of Isaac too.

But what's the use of a Spirit of Good and a Spirit of Evil if sometimes I'm three and sometimes four!

Right now I feel as if I were not even alive, as if "I" am absolutely nothing. And even if I were alive, I would not get up from my bench in the morning, I would lie there like a *golem* till the end of the world. Indeed, I am a *golem,* I have no soul. Everything near me lives, everything has a soul, their souls send out long, narrow, pointed threads, rays that come to me, penetrate me, stir me, force me to my feet, order me to move, act, run. But I—I myself am nothing!

Who then does the thinking? What within me thinks? Again, a stranger? Not me?

All right, a stranger. But who? How does he get into me? Am I a cage and he a little bird? King David, of blessed memory, speaks of "my little dove"—is it the dove that wants to chop wood, go to the steam bath, steal a *Purim* sweet, snatch cookies from the sexton's wife, and at the same time ponder over a passage in the *Bal-Akeida?* No, little dove, that won't do. If that's what you are, you should be ashamed.

Ha! Berel Chantsia's is a little dove, a little bird; Berel has wings and a mouth, and someday Berel will fly out of the cage.

Well, Berel, will you then also wonder who you are? Also be an orphan? A student? A madman?

Master of the Universe! Who am I?

2.

The merchant Wolfe enters the House of Prayer.

Berel notices him and runs off to one side. Wolfe washes his hands, wipes them on his coat tails, pulls down a tome from the bookshelf, and begins to study. Berel does not take his eyes off him.

Who is he? *Berel asks and quickly answers,* Wolfe the merchant! *Meanwhile Berel pinches his cheek sharply.*

Fool! Donkey! Wolfe the merchant is just like Berel Chantsia's. That's his name—but who is he? Is he one, two, or three? How many birds chirp in his cage?

Let's think.

Right now he is one, Wolfe the merchant. He sits and studies, so absorbed he doesn't see me. He studies *Nedorim* (the Scripture of Vows); more than that he can't follow. Now he is a portion of *Nedorim* —but later, what will he be then? Later Wolfe the merchant will go into the street, sell his grain with false weights, cheat the length and breadth of Poland, go home to his wife, poor little Teibele, and beat her black and blue! Berel Chantsia's. You see that little lamb? See how it wrinkles its forehead? See those pious eyes? See, see! And you, Berel, you fool, you donkey, you want to tell me that this is the thief of the street, the brute of the house? No, Berel, you can't put that over on me; no, that's not the way a thief looks, or a brute.

I tell you, Berel, there are three Wolfes. One is a pious little lamb that sits and studies *Nedorim* and will continue to study it straight into the other world, no doubt with the commentary of the Almighty Himself. The second is a thief and will steal from the plates even in heaven. The third is a brute who beats his wife without mercy.

It stabs my heart—I often dream of her. At night sometimes, when I'm asleep, she pleads with me to rescue her. Not with her lips, of course; she says nothing. A daughter of Israel doesn't converse with a man. But she looks at me with such—with such a—such a sort of look.

God Almighty! She's allowed to look, isn't she? She can look at a man . . .

I, a man. Wolfe the merchant, may he rot in hell, he's a man. I eat in his house one day a week, but I'm his enemy. I would stab him—not the Wolfe who sits and studies, not even the thief, but the brute, him I'd kill! I can't do it myself, I have no power, I'm only a cage. I even have a pocketknife, a sharp pocketknife; it's so sharp you can cut your nails with it or shave.

I never use it, the edge mustn't get dull.

But I alone, by myself, can't. I need a voice to command me, a voice from heaven, someone, anyone, even Zorach the teacher. Even Wolfe himself! And if she asked me, quietly, in a dream at night! But she won't, a daughter of Israel won't. God forbid, I'd despise her if she even talked to me.

It's better this way; let her look, all night long, always; in the daytime someone might see us. It's enough to look at night.

But oh, how beautiful it would be! I'd take out my knife, sharpen it on my boots, once, twice, a third time—and finished!

How his guts would spill out!

Not you, I don't mean you, Wolfe the merchant, who sits there studying *Nedorim*. The other one, the other one, the brute—not you.

Listen, Berel Chantsia's, if you were a man and not a Talmudist, an orphan, a madman, a philosopher, everything would be fine. Teibele would cry, she'd be a widow, but in my dream I'd say to her, "Teibele, it's enough you have two husbands, one who steals and one who studies. What do you want with a third one? Do you really need three? To be beaten day and night?"

But perhaps he is really just one?

Berel, let's bet on it: there are three. Come, while he sits here and studies, come into the street and you'll see how the other one steals and later how he beats. Come, you'll see!

He gets up, runs on tiptoe to the door, pulls out the key, and locks the door from the outside.

3.

He returns, angry and pale.

They hid themselves, those scoundrels.

They have nothing else to do today, there's no fair. Some sort of holiday, flags hung out, no chance to cheat anyone. Teibele isn't home . . . must have gone to a neighbor . . . the door is shut. . . . Maybe both of them, the swindler and the brute, are hiding. When

I looked in through the window I thought something was stirring beneath the bed, a shadow was quivering on the floor. So that's the answer to the riddle! He sits here and studies while the other two hide under beds. Where else can they hide?

And Wolfe the merchant, that dunce who studies *Nedorim,* didn't even hear me get up and lock the door, he's so deep in his study.

But maybe he doesn't study, maybe it's the thief who sits here and tries to cheat both me and God.

Wolfe!

What is it?

Nothing.

Fool!

A minute later.

Wolfe!

What is it?

I have a pocketknife.

Good for you!

Want to see it?

No!

So don't.

A few minutes later.

Wolfe!

What?

Are you really studying or just making believe?

What do you care?

I've got to know. Honestly, I must know.

Be quiet, lunatic!

Still later.

Wolfe!

What is it now?

How many are you?

Wolfe the merchant grows angry, closes his tome, leaves the House of Prayer. Berel is alone.

Was it Wolfe I talked to? And what did I tell him? Why did he run away from me? How did I get out? What is this knife I'm holding?

Berel, you beggar! You cut the boots yourself! Do you have any others? Will Teibele give you another pair? Did she come by these so easily? You see, madman, someone else is living within you, it isn't you.

Let me see for myself what you look like, donkey, let me see what someone looks like who lets his boots be cut.

He runs over to the washstand, pulls the rag from his head, and begins to rub the brass basin.

Now I see something of you—wait, wait, I'll see you still better. I want to see your miserable face, your donkey's head.

He drops to his knees and rubs with all his strength. Suddenly he stops.

But who is polishing the basin? Is it I? Do I have the strength? Did I eat today, or even yesterday? What is today? Tuesday? Monday and Tuesday I have no place to eat. Who then does the rubbing?

He continues his work.

Whoever it is, let him rub: I, the bird, the dove, the Spirit of Evil or the Spirit of Good. But I must see this beggar's miserable face. I must see it—now, now!

He closes his eyes. He continues to rub vigorously. He opens his eyes and sees himself in the basin.

So that's how you look—a corpse, an utter corpse, ready for the grave! They can put the shards on your eyes.

You see, Teibele, you see how I look? And this, when you give me a piece of bread. If not for that . . .

He loses himself in thought, but remembers: A corpse! Yes, I Berel the student, Berel the orphan, Berel the madman! That's it! And yet: who am I?

He looks into the basin and sees himself: Where are the torn boots?

Angrily: A plague on you! A plague on you, you basin man! You too must have torn boots; if I have them, you must also!

He stretches out on the floor, props his head on the ground, and sticks his feet against the basin: I can't see, but you have them, you have the torn boots! Look!

Getting up is hard. He thinks the man in the basin is holding on to his feet. But he pulls them away, stands up, surprised and frightened.

Basin man! *he taunts himself, and yet is afraid to look in the basin. He runs over to the oven, smears his hand with lime, spreads it over the basin.*

There, lie in your misery, don't stare at me!

His head begins to hurt, his feet to wobble. Again he loses himself in thought.

I must remember something . . .

Now my head hurts . . . when the brute beats Teibele my head hurts . . . my legs hurt. When I pinch my cheek it burns—that means I have a cheek. I have hands and feet, a head, a heart, and maybe even a soul—everything. But I myself, what am I? Not the cheek or the feet, the head or the soul. What then? Nothing!

If I could kill myself and see what happened to me—what would remain of me when there were no longer a head, hands, feet, cheeks, torn boots—then I might know something! Maybe it would be good to try.

If only she commanded me . . . But perhaps I could try it on him.

Translated by Irving Howe and Eliezer Greenberg

Rabbi Yochanan the Warden

I. L. PERETZ

WEARY and exhausted from his work for the community, Reb Yochanan the warden came home. Entering the kitchen, he perceived the fragrance of food, of meat and stewed apples. He quickly went into the adjoining room, where his wife Ssoshe received him in not too friendly a fashion. No sooner did he appear on the threshold than she cried to him in an angry voice, "You idler!"

"Why do you scold?" Reb Yochanan asked, sitting down on a bench to rest himself.

"He asks why I scold! You're always taken up with the affairs of the community! When, good-for-nothing, will you ever do anything for yourself?"

"For myself?" the puzzled warden asked. "What do I have to do for myself? Our children are, thank God, independent, and we two lack for nothing. What is there left for me to do?"

He surveyed the room and added, "The bed is made without me; the dishes are washed without my assistance; I haven't so much as touched the walls and yet I see no trace of a spider's web. The table is laid, the cloth is white as snow, the silver gleams. On the table I see a dish made with horseradish, with fine grated horseradish, as well as a little bottle of brandy—"

"Stop your chatter and go wash, as the Law commands!"

"No, Ssoshe, I'm not going to wash until you yourself admit that I am right. Here at home there is nothing for me to attend to, but there's plenty to do in the House of Prayer. Who will devote himself to those matters if I don't? Yosske the tradesman, who barely has time to eat? Or Yechiel the peddler, who hastens to leave his house at the end of the Sabbath and doesn't get back home until the evening of the following Friday? Or maybe Reuben the moneylender, who runs about all day long to collect a few pennies of interest from his poor debtors? Or else the tradesmen who must work so hard to earn the necessities of life?"

"All right! Let be! I'm not angry any longer."

"Never mind that. I know you're not angry any longer. I'd simply like to prove to you that I am thinking of myself too. Look at me, Ssoshe; look at my white beard; look at my white earlocks. I'm not young any longer. And so it behooves me to prepare for my long journey."

"Your journey? What kind of a journey?" Ssoshe asked in a moment of amazement. But immediately thereafter she understood what he meant and cried out in fright, "For heaven's sake, don't give the Evil One an opening!"

"You don't have to be afraid, Ssoshe. You're a little beyond twenty too. And what are we two going to answer up there, in the world to come, when they ask us what we have done in *this* world? Are we going to say that we ate and drank? What will the Master of the World say to that? You, at least, will be able to plead that you devoted yourself to the society for providing poor girls with dowries—"

"Don't mention it," Ssoshe implored him. She was afraid of jeopardizing her reward in the world to come.

"By the same token I want a meritorious action to my credit too."

"Very well. Fine. Do whatever you like. But now go and wash!"

"One more thing," the warden continued. "Do you remember your silk bridal dress with the silver stripes?"

"How could I not remember it?"

"Would you be inclined to dedicate it to the House of Prayer so that a curtain for the Ark could be made of it?"

"I'd be glad to do that! I'll go look for it."

"Wait, Ssoshe, I've already taken it, and it's already hanging in front of the Ark."

"You rogue!" said Ssoshe, smiling.

Now at last Reb Yochanan proceeded to the ritual washing of his hands. He ate with a hearty appetite, said the grace after his meal, and went to bed.

He fell asleep promptly, and his soul ascended to heaven and he recorded his good deeds there in the Book of Good Deeds: "I, Yochanan, the son of Sarah, have been busy all day long with sacred matters. I said to myself: I and my wife Ssoshe dwell in a fine house, while the House of God, the holy House of Study, is rickety and in need of repairs. Therefore I hired workmen to begin the repairs. This very day two new benches and a new table have been brought in. I also gave orders to clean the floor and to shine up the walls and the furnishings and all the sacred objects. I have also had a new lamp hung on the eastern wall in front of the cantor's stand. But there were only three hundred gulden in the account of the House of Prayer. In order to pay for everything I had to take forty-five gulden and eighteen groschen out of my own pocket. For the profit of my wife, Ssoshe, I dedicated the silken curtain for the Ark. In addition, she is active in the society for providing dowries for poor girls. May God remember that in her favor! The repair of the House of Prayer was completed today. And I have given strict orders to the beadle that he is by no means to permit anyone to use the House of Study as a lodging for the night. It is no longer to be a bedroom for beggars. From now on the beadle is going to lock up the House every evening . . ."

Reb Yochanan's soul continued to write, while another soul came flying into heaven and made the following entry in its book: "I, Berel, the son of Judith, am now seventy years old. So long as I had the strength I earned my own livelihood. Now that I am old and weak and have lost my strength, I have had to go begging from house to house. In the beginning things were not too bad. The householders knew me, and I always had enough to eat. By and by, however, they got tired of me, and more and more rarely did they give me a piece of bread. Often, too, they gave me bread so stale and hard that my old teeth couldn't chew it any more. I saw that if I stayed in my own town I would perish of hunger. Therefore I left and came here. It is bitter cold tonight, and I wanted to go into the House of Study to pass the night, as is customary among Jews. But the beadle locked the door and wouldn't let me in. The warden gave him directions to let no one spend the night in the House of Study; it was not to be turned into an inn. So I sleep in the street, and the cold gnaws at the marrow of my old bones.

I am hungry and all but frozen. I ask Thee, Thou Master of the World, who stands in greater need of the House of Study—Thou or I?"

And there resounded from heaven the echo of a voice: "Both of these souls are to appear instantly at the Judgment Seat of the World Above!"

The next morning two men were found dead—Reb Yochanan the warden in his bed, and an old beggar frozen to death in the street next to the House of Study.

Translated by Ludwig Lewisohn

The Golem

I. L. PERETZ

GREAT men were once capable of great miracles.

When the ghetto of Prague was being attacked, and they were about to rape the women, roast the children, and slaughter the rest; when it seemed that the end had finally come, the great Rabbi Loeb put aside his *Gemarah,* went into the street, stopped before a heap of clay in front of the teacher's house, and molded a clay image. He blew into the nose of the *golem*—and it began to stir; then he whispered the Name into its ear, and our *golem* left the ghetto. The rabbi returned to the House of Prayer, and the *golem* fell upon our enemies, threshing them as with flails. Men fell on all sides.

Prague was filled with corpses. It lasted, so they say, through Wednesday and Thursday. Now it is already Friday, the clock strikes twelve, and the *golem* is still busy at its work.

"Rabbi," cries the head of the ghetto, "the *golem* is slaughtering all of Prague! There will not be a gentile left to light the Sabbath fires or take down the Sabbath lamps."

Once again the rabbi left his study. He went to the altar and began singing the psalm "A song of the Sabbath."

The *golem* ceased its slaughter. It returned to the ghetto, entered the House of Prayer, and waited before the rabbi. And again the rabbi whispered into its ear. The eyes of the *golem* closed, the soul that had dwelt in it flew out, and it was once more a *golem* of clay.

To this day the *golem* lies hidden in the attic of the Prague synagogue, covered with cobwebs that extend from wall to wall. No living creature may look at it, particularly women in pregnancy. No one may touch the cobwebs, for whoever touches them dies. Even the oldest people no longer remember the *golem,* though the wise man Zvi, the grandson of the great Rabbi Loeb, ponders the problem: may such a *golem* be included in a congregation of worshipers or not?

The *golem,* you see, has not been forgotten. It is still here! But the Name by which it could be called to life in a day of need, the Name has disappeared. And the cobwebs grow and grow, and no one may touch them.

What are we to do?

Translated by Irving Howe

And Then He Wept

DAVID PINSKI

BEREL the carrier, poor but cheerful, lived in a cellar. Its two small windows below the cobbled pavement of the courtyard were gray and muddy, scarcely admitting the sunbeams that sometimes reached them. Dampness leaked from the walls, mold glittered and sparkled in the corners.

A table stood near the wall, between the two windows. Two of the legs were its own, the others proxies—sticks of wood, which often disappeared when there was nothing else with which to heat the stove. At such times the table was shoved against the wall and remained standing, Berel said, "with God's help."

There were three white chairs as well, all without backs. As soon as a back toppled, Berel intended to hammer it into place again, but meanwhile the two sticks supporting the table had been burned up and no other firewood remained. So Berel would pull a solemn face and hand down a truly philosophical decision: one can sit on a chair even though it has no back, but potatoes must be cooked. And he would intone in a Passover voice, most impressively, while the chair-back entered the oven along with other scraps that Berel and his children had scavenged.

Two beds completed the furnishings. Rags, which Berel persisted in calling pillows and blankets, covered them, and under and near them stood boxes filled with more rags. Berel announced proudly that these were shirts, tablecloths—all sorts of household riches.

Did all this worry Berel? He laughed.

"What more do I need? Not a thing. As long as there's life . . ."

He had four children; two slept with him in one bed, two with the mother in the second bed. But he had no fear of more children. "Children," he said, "are a delight, a joy. Of course, they need a lot, but what's the difference? As long as I can come home and there's someone to play with, to make myself foolish with. What a pleasure! What a gang I have!"

Only his wife Bas-Sheve caused Berel dissatisfaction. He couldn't bear her moaning, her wailing and complaining.

"Eh," Berel said, shrugging, "my wife isn't fit for anything—always crying. She wants so much—what is there that she doesn't want? You'd think she had a contract with God, and He had promised to provide for her."

The tears had barely come to her eyes when Berel began to pose in front of her, his right hand against his cheek, his left hand supporting the right, his face twisted into woe and his head rocking back and forth. Bas-Sheve didn't find the imitation amusing. She grew angry. "All you do is laugh!"

"But I'm crying. Can't you see?" mocked Berel in his weepy voice.

"I wish we were crying for you, you great provider!" Her piece recited, she turned her back sharply. Berel wasn't insulted. Curses couldn't bother him. It almost seemed that without her curses life would be dull.

Only when she began to curse herself did Berel really become angry. "Almighty God," she cried out once when there was nothing to eat and a child was ill into the bargain (not at all a rare coincidence in Berel's house), "Almighty God, rescue me from this dark and bitter life!" Her voice trembled; she meant it in earnest. At that moment she had no fear of death, and Berel felt it. His ribs seemed to crack with anguish. Outraged, furious, he began to scream, "May your tongue wither!"

Bas-Sheve, reduced to silence, wept instead, while Berel cast angry glances at her. "What good does crying do? That's all I want to know. You fool!"

As far as Berel was concerned, a human being should never cry unless, God forbid, someone died. But once . . .

Once of an evening Berel played so hard with the children, wrestled and cavorted and carried on so lustily, that he plummeted onto his bed—and the bed exploded into bits.

He rose from the ruins, laughing. "Hoorah! Just wait, children. We'll deliver a funeral oration over the bed." Crouching like the humpbacked village orator, Berel made as if to speak. Bas-Sheve, clutching her head, broke into a wail. "It's too much—I can't stand any more. It's the last straw. I'll kill myself."

"Shh, let me say the eulogy." Berel tried to calm her, to draw her into the game. But she kept on moaning, "God in heaven, how can I be rid of this miserable life? At least we owned two beds, and now we don't even have that."

Berel grew angry. "Cow! What shall I do with you? Come on, cry some more. So the bed's smashed! You cow! Come on, moo-oo. Why aren't you bellowing?"

"May I bellow for the loss of your head!" She threw herself at him. "If only I could get rid of you I'd see daylight! Whenever you lift a finger it turns out a misfortune. Murderer, you're my private Angel of Death."

Berel's good humor was restored by the familiar accusations. "Come on, tell the truth—why all this uproar? Why upset the universe? What's a broken bed—a catastrophe? Has the sky collapsed? Listen. Think what might have happened to one of us, and instead it's happened to the bed!"

He remonstrated. She wept.

Blotting the tears with her apron, she thought of the future. No new shoes for the children. The first few pennies that came into the house would have to go for a new bed . . . though perhaps the old one could still be fixed. Meanwhile she and the two girls would sleep on the floor, and he—that foul hunk of disaster—he'd sleep in the remaining bed.

When Berel finished she answered tartly and with tears, "Sure, you have lots of beds, don't you? Go, crawl on the floor in the mud and the damp, and you'll learn how to laugh—may this be your last laugh!" Bas-Sheve glared at him.

Berel laughed. "What a joke!" Berel, that great gentleman, has to sleep on the floor. Come on, kids, drag down the mattress," he told the boys.

"Not while I'm alive will I let you sleep on the floor!" She leaped up and shielded the mattress with her body.

Berel was astonished. "What's wrong? Are you crazy?"

"When you're dead, then you can lie on the ground. Not now."

Berel grew stern. "Bas-Sheve, this is no time for foolishness. Let me get some sleep." He reached for the mattress.

She pushed his head away and pointed to the bed. "Lie down, and may you never get up."

"I don't sleep in women's beds," he joked. "Come on, let me get some sleep." He grabbed the mattress.

"I said no and I meant it," screamed Bas-Sheve, clutching the mattress with both hands.

"So I'll lie down without a mattress!" Berel laughed and took off his coat.

Bas-Sheve rushed at him with her nails. Her cheeks flushed, her eyes burned. Berel grew excited. It was his young Bas-Sheve again! Warmth flooded his heart, a smile flowed across his face. "Ah, my pretty wife," he called and wanted to embrace her. But she thrust him off, her hatred absolute. "Get away from me quietly. If you don't I'll break your head."

She turned her back and began to prepare the bed for him. In that instant he grabbed the mattress, spun it onto the floor near the stove, and threw himself on top of it.

"Come on, boys," he ordered, "let's get to sleep."

Bas-Sheve cried out in fury, "Get on that bed!"

"Tomorrow."

"Stop ordering me around—may you wither and rot."

He laughed.

"Get into that bed! Do you hear what I say?"

"Ho-hum."

Frenzied, she began to kick the one remaining bed with her feet. "There—take that! There!"

Berel and the children jumped up in horror while she kept kicking with all her strength.

Berel tried to control her, to soothe her. He caught and held her tightly. "Have you gone mad?"

She tore herself away. Her heart contracted, her head blazed. She wanted to smash, smash, smash . . . But he held her too strongly. She tried to bite him.

"Bas-Sheve! Look, Bas-Sheve," he stammered, twisting away from her teeth. He managed to lower her to a chair. Slowly Bas-Sheve calmed herself and began to weep. The children formed a chorus, wailing with fright.

Berel felt lost. He stood before Bas-Sheve and didn't take his sorrowful eyes off her. "Bas-Shevenke, little Bas-Sheve, stop, please stop!"

His voice twitched. "Bas-Shevenke," he pleaded gently, softly. His heart warmed with a marvelous tenderness, his throat seemed to choke and thicken. And that time Berel wept too.

Translated by Sarah Zweig Betsky

A Meal for the Poor

MORDECAI SPECTOR

I WAS invited to a wedding.

Not to any of your newfangled weddings where dowagers and pretty young girls in décolleté are surrounded by a halo of powder as they move like goddesses, or where gentlemen in frock coats, white gloves, and waxed black mustaches reek of scented pomade.

Not to a wedding, you understand, where one eats according to a printed timetable—Fish à la Prince So-and-So, Bouillon La Falutin, Meat Diplomatique, Salad Wiltedgreen, Dessert Fifi, Wine Antediluvian—that is to say, served in bottles plentifully smeared with last year's mud!

Not at all. I was invited to an old-fashioned Jewish wedding, a wedding, in other words, where respectable Jewish men and women gather together, dressed in the same holiday attire they use for going to the synagogue every Sabbath. The kind of wedding where the "smorgasbord" consists of home-made honeycake and strudel, followed by gefilte fish, warm fresh rolls, golden-yellow broth, stuffed spring chicken, roast duck, and wine drunk out of large, immaculate white jugs.

A wedding at which every last religious ceremony is observed, including, naturally, the one that commands the host to serve a free meal for the poor.

The host, Reb Yitzchok Berkover, had provided a free meal for the poor at the marriage of each of his children. And now it was the turn of his youngest daughter, his favorite child, and he had invited all the poor folk from the neighboring town of Lipowitz to the village in which he had lived all his life.

It was now the wedding day, two o'clock in the afternoon, and still no sign of the poor, for whom a servant in charge of three huge wagons had been dispatched that morning. Lipowitz was only a few miles away. What could the matter be? All the relatives and wedding guests were waiting impatiently for the ceremony to begin. At last the servant, out of breath and galloping on a horse that had been unhitched from a wagon, arrived by himself.

"What's this? Are you alone?" asked his master.

"They don't want to come," was the answer.

"What do you mean, 'They don't want to come'?" we asked in astonishment.

"They say that unless each one is promised a ruble, under no circumstances are they coming to the wedding."

We all burst into laughter, but the servant continued with his story. "You see, there's already been one wedding in Lipowitz today, complete with a free meal for the poor. So they're all full. Naturally they're in rebellion. If they're not given a ruble each they won't budge. The ringleaders you all know—there's that cripple with the crutches, and the lanky beggar, also Feitel Dragfoot, and Flatnose Jake. The rest would probably come, but these four won't let them. I wasn't sure what to do. After debating with them for an hour and coming to no conclusion, I took one of the horses and have come back for more instructions."

We roared with laughter at the thought of this bizarre uprising, but Reb Yitzchok went into a rage. "You bargained with them? They won't take any less?" he screamed at the messenger.

"Bargained, of course. They won't take a kopeck less."

"Their stock of merchandise must have gone up in price lately," snapped Reb Yitzchok with an angry laugh. "Then why did you leave the wagons behind? We'll do without the paupers."

"I wasn't sure what to do. I was afraid you would be angry. I'll run back this instant and bring the wagons."

"Wait a while. Don't be in such a hurry." And Reb Yitzchok began to discuss this unlooked-for problem with his guests and also with himself.

"Who ever heard of such a thing? Those ragamuffins are going to dictate what I should do? Bargain with me? Just because I want them to have a good free meal and a little donation besides. I must give each one precisely a ruble, they say! If I gave them a quarter of a ruble each, they couldn't afford to take it, of course! Their overhead is too high. The nerve of the beggars! I'll get along without them, they'll see. Fiddlers, strike up the tune! Where's the sexton? You can start the final preparations."

But immediately he changed his mind and waved his hands. "Wait a while. It's still early. What did I do to deserve such a fate? Is my whole enjoyment to be spoiled? Why shouldn't I have the pleasure of giving a free meal to the poor at the wedding of my youngest child? I'd be willing to give them half a ruble. Money's not the question. It's the principle. The nerve of them! To haggle with me! Well, let it go. I've done my share. If they don't want to come, that's their business. They'll be sorry later. Weddings such as this don't come every day. We'll get along without them!"

"Shall I prepare the bride?" asked the sexton.

"Yes, let them—no! Wait!"

The guests were unanimously in favor of forgetting the beggars, but Reb Yitzchok's face suddenly underwent a profound change. His rage subsided and he came to ask me and a few others to do him a favor. He requested us to go to the town and see if we couldn't manage to win over the poor. "He hasn't any sense. There's no use depending on him," he said, nodding at the servant.

They made another horse and wagon ready for us, and we rode away. The servant on his horse lagged behind us.

"A mutiny, a strike of the poor—how do you like that?" That's the tone we talked in the whole way. "I've heard of strikes by workingmen. They refuse to work. They demand higher pay. But a strike, an ultimatum by paupers—paupers demanding a higher scale of pay for coming to eat a free meal! That's something new."

Twenty minutes later we entered the town of Lipowitz. In the main square of the town, in the market place, stood three great peasant wagons filled with straw; the small horses were unharnessed and eating their bags of oats. Around the wagons were at least a hundred people—the lame, the halt, and the blind, and in addition half the loafers and urchins in town. They were making a terrific noise.

The cripple who had been described as one of the chief ringleaders was sitting in the driver's seat of one of the wagons and banging his crutches on the wood. The lanky beggar with a red plaster on his neck stood near him. The two were haranguing the crowd.

"Look," cried the lanky one triumphantly as soon as he caught sight of us, "they've come to beg."

"Beg!" called out the cripple, bringing his crutches down with a crash.

"Why aren't you at the wedding?" we asked them. "There'll be a good meal, and each of you will get some money to take home with him too."

"How much?" asked a chorus of voices.

"We can't tell exactly. But you'll take what you can get."

"A ruble maybe? If not, we stay put."

"The sky will fall in if you don't go!" mocked some loafers in the crowd.

The beggars raised their sticks and ran at their tormentors. For a minute it looked like a real riot, but the lanky one on the wagon stretched himself to his full height and thundered at them, "Quiet! Quiet, you miserable beggars! It's impossible to hear what these gentlefolk are saying to us. Listen to them!" He then turned to us. "Please realize, brothers, that unless we get a ruble each we don't move from here. We've no fear that Reb Yitzchok will marry off his favorite daughter without us. Where can he get another gang of paupers on the spur of the moment? Is he going to send to the next town for them? It'll be a lot more expensive for the wagons, and besides the wedding will have to be postponed."

"Do you think that just because we're poor they can do as they like with us?" cried one of the rebels perched on top of a wheel; he was completely blind in one eye, and he had a rag tied around his jaw as if to keep his teeth from falling out. "Nobody can force us to go. Even the chief of police and the governor general himself can't do anything to us. A ruble each or we don't go!"

"R-r-r-ub-bles," stuttered a beggar.

"Rubles," screamed the one with the flattened nose.

"Rubles," sang out two merry beggars, doing a dance.

"Rubles! Rubles!" screamed all the poor together.

All their lives they had been condemned to silence, forced to swallow with their spittle every insult anyone cared to offer them, anyone who had given them a kopeck or thrown them a crust of dry bread or a gnawed bone. Now for the first time they were tasting the same pleasure as the well-to-do. For the first time these beggars felt that the well-fed people needed them, and they were determined to gain their point. And sure enough, even as we were arguing with them, there came another messenger from Reb Yitzchok with word for the poor to set out at once and each would receive his ruble.

Bedlam broke loose, pandemonium. The three large wagons filled up in a twinkling. One pauper cried, "Oh, my broken back!" Another, "Oh, my arm!" A third, "My leg, my leg!" The merry beggars seated in the wagons started to jig with their feet. The horses were harnessed, and with much laughter the procession got under way. An escort of urchins accompanied us some distance, crying loudly, "Hooray!" Some of the hecklers fired a few rocks after the wagons amid hoots and whistles and catcalls. But to the beggars it was as if they were being pelted with flowers and accompanied by bursts of triumphant song, so happy were they over their victory.

For the first time and perhaps the last, they had spoken out in loud voices and succeeded in getting their way. They had done exactly as they wanted.

After the bridal ceremony, after the golden-yellow broth, the feast was served to the wedding guests and to the poor, seated at separate tables. Reb Yitzchok and his closest relatives observed the commandment to wait on the poor with their own hands and to anticipate whatever their hearts desired in the way of food or drink.

"Your health, Reb Yitzchok. We wish you long life, happiness from your children, and even greater wealth!" The poor men kept drinking toasts to him.

"And your health, your health too, brothers. Drink hearty. Long life to you. May God help the whole congregation of Israel, and you among the rest," Reb Yitzchok responded.

After the meal the musicians began to play again, and the poor danced around in a great ring, holding Reb Yitzchok by the hands. Reb Yitzchok danced out into the very center of the ring made by the poor. His satin coat tails flew like the wings of an eagle. His eyes, from which tears of joy were freely running, seemed to be staring straight upward, while his thoughts soared higher than the Seventh Heaven. He laughed and he cried at the same time, like a child. And all the while he kept embracing the poor, each in turn. He hugged them affectionately and kissed their cheeks.

"Brothers!" he cried out to them, dancing. "We must be merry! Let us be merry as only Jews know how to be merry! Fiddlers! Play something a little faster, louder, livelier, stronger!"

That is how a Jew is happy.

That is how a real Jewish wedding ought to be.

The poor, as well as the rest of the wedding guests, clapped their hands in time to the music.

In short, as I have already said, dear reader, I've been to a Jewish wedding.

Translated by Milton Hindus

Sanctification of the Name

A LEGEND

SHOLEM ASCH

White lies the snow on the roads and fields. The light of the moon is thrown back by great white stretches as by frozen seas; the stars are so densely sown in the heavens, they sparkle so restlessly, that you would think they are elbowing each other for room. And from the distance comes the sound of a Jewish melody, punctuated by the crack of a driver's whip:

Hey, hey, clear the way,
Jews are coming, stand aside,
Come, my friend, come, my friend,
Let us go to meet the bride!

Beards and earlocks, tangled gaberdines, shining eyes, merry voices —where are these Jews coming from? From a wedding, of course. The covered cart is jammed with celebrants, the father of the bride, the father of the bridegroom, the uncle of the bride, the uncle of the bridegroom—the four chief celebrants, they—and a host of other villagers.

In front and on top sits the driver, jovially tipsy. The whip curls and crackles in the air. "Hey, hey, clear the way, Jews are coming, stand aside!" His hat executes a dance of its own on his head. The horses, infected by their master's gaiety, forget the daily yoke; they feel they are coming from a wedding, it is proper to rejoice, to let go, to throw off the burden of care—and they cease to be drayhorses, they become racehorses, they streak down the white road like phantoms.

Inside, the celebrants, and anmong them the four chief celebrants—the two fathers, the two uncles—sit rocking, with arms interlaced, with beards waggling in the dark, with hats slipping to one side. They sing joyously. What do they sing? Songs of drink or of love, songs of youth or of the chase? Not they! They are Jews! And in a time of merriment they sing snatches of the Talmud, fragments of prayers, reminders of the sacred books and of the commandments.

From the sages let us learn,
From the holy men of old,
Let the fool for riches yearn,
Piety outshineth gold;
Come, my friend, come, my friend,
Let us go to meet the bride.

White shines the road, white lie the fields; and the melody of the Jews, half gay, half mournful, carries across the night.

Come, my friend, come, my friend,
Let us go to meet the bride.

Neither the driver on his seat nor the Jews rocking inside the cart see advancing toward them the carriage of the *Pan,* the nobleman of their village, the master and landowner; they do not hear the bellow of the driver behind the three horses harnessed in length: "Hey, filthy Jews, off the road! The *Pan* is passing!" They cannot hear the words because their hearts are full. And why should they not be full? One more Jewish pair wedded, in defiance of disaster! One more Jewish home set up, to be as the house of Jacob and as the house of Abraham, a place of learning and prayer! They do not hear, they do not draw off the road, they do not take their hats off with a frightened, "Yes, sir, good morning, sir, your servant, sir, excuse us, sir!" Still more loudly the postilion bellows: "Jewish dogs! Off the road when the *Pan* is passing!" Now they hear, and they stick their heads out. They answer him in their own tongue: "Who are you to bid the world off the road when you pass? We are the worshipers of the living God, you worship an image, an idol." They do not yield: it is the *Pan*'s carriage that must stand still while they pass. And back from the road drifts their melody:

From the sages let us learn,
From the holy men of old,
Let the fool for riches yearn,
Piety outshineth gold.

The next day the liveried servants of the *Pan* were in the village, seeking, questioning: "Who came back last night along the road in a cart? Whence came they? What were they doing?" They also brought report, true or false, of the body of a dead peasant, found that night in the empty inn along the selfsame road.

And before the day was ended five Jews had been carried off in chains and flung into prison: the fathers and uncles of the bride and bridegroom, the four chief celebrants, and the drayman who had driven them.

These four chief celebrants were the four leading householders of the Jewish community.

The Jews of the village are assembled in the synagogue. The tall white candles burn as on the Day of Atonement. From the women's gallery overhead comes a sound of stifled weeping, a continuous, subdued refrain. Now and again a voice rises above the chorus, the voice of the wife or mother of one of the prisoners.

The old rabbi, in white robe and prayer shawl, stands before the Ark and intones a Psalm: "Why do the heathen rage, and the people imagine a vain thing?"

The whole congregation, in white robes and prayer shawls, repeats tremblingly after the venerable rabbi, "Why do the heathen rage, and the people imagine a vain thing?"

There is sudden silence in the crowded little House of Prayer. A sound is heard by the spirit, the sound of passing souls. These are the souls of all the martyrs of all the generations, an invisible procession; for the Psalms are being said now for Jews who are being tortured to death.

In the prison human demons tear the flesh of the prisoners, to force a confession from them; in the synagogue Psalms are being said to strengthen the prisoners in their resistance, so that they may endure and not be broken, so that they may remember the Name of God and sanctify it. It is a bitter trial of alternating torment and temptation.

The *Pan* has promised that the first Jew to confess to the crime and to convert to Christianity will be rewarded as no man in these parts was ever rewarded before: he will be made the overseer of all the taxes paid by the Jews, he will be given the franchise of all the inns in the district, he will be made the ruler of all the Jews. And as for the rest, they will be beheaded, their corpses quartered and denied Jewish burial.

Behind the sound of the procession of the martyrs, the spirit catches another, horrible beyond endurance: it is the screaming of the men whose flesh is being torn from their bodies.

Concerning four of the tormented Jews there is utter certainty in the hearts of the assembled: these four will assuredly not desecrate the Name of God either to escape from passing pain or for the sake of the vanities and frivolities of this earth. In the lamentations of the wives and mothers of the tormented ones there is never a suggestion of a desire for such weakness; when their eyes have wearied of shedding tears they look forth into space with pride. And when the women about them dare to look at them, their eyes too betray pride, and even a reverent envy of the wives and mothers of the men who are sanctifying the Name of God.

But concerning one, the fifth among the prisoners, the drayman, the community is not sure. A gross, ignorant lad he is, the driver of the village; impious, God help us; more than once has he been known to desecrate the Sabbath in the sight of others. He is not seen every day in the synagogue for afternoon and evening prayers; but he has been seen, on a Sabbath, strolling down the village street with his horse. The rabbi has rebuked him more than once; and there was even talk once of imprisoning him for a few days in the vestibule of the synagogue, that he might learn godliness. But it is said that when this was threatened he threatened to run away to the Christians and have himself baptized. So they left him alone.

In a corner of the women's gallery the mother of the drayman stands alone, her kerchief drawn over her face, ashamed to look at the other women. But they cast glances at her, glances of pity and bitterness. "To have brought forth such a son!" For there is a rumor in the village that the drayman is ready to confess, that he has obtained a respite, that the wall of resistance is about to be broken. The mother of the drayman stands alone, for the others have withdrawn from her. She says no Psalms, for she does not know the text; she holds no prayer book in her hand, for she cannot read. But she murmurs a prayer of her own: "Father in Heaven, be his strength! Father in Heaven, be his strength!"

The tears run down her cheeks into the kerchief. No one sees her tears or hears her murmured prayer; for they have withdrawn from her and look at her with pity and bitterness. "To have given such a son to the Jewish fold!"

Once again the Jews are assembled in the House of Prayer. This day no Psalms are said. All are seated on the floor. The lecterns will not be used for study or prayer. The candles are ranged along the floor. The rabbi, in stocking feet—symbol of mourning—reads the Book of Lamentations—supreme utterance of mourning. The congregation repeats the words after him, quietly. For now it is the end, and the time of official mourning is at hand. The executioner's block stands in the market place; the men are being led out. Four memorial candles burn in the synagogue, and about each candle sit the martyrs' nearest of kin. In a corner of the synagogue, in a lowly place near the entrance, stands a fifth candle, which has not been lit. Near this candle sits the mother of the drayman. It is not known yet whether her son has withstood the trial, and whether he belongs to the martyrs. Still they look at the mother with pity and bitterness. "To have given us such a son!"

The murmurous repetition of the Book of Lamentations is suspended as the sound of hoofs comes closer down the street. Something is thrown down before the door of the synagogue, and a fist smites on the door. One, two, three, four—five. Five knocks. And at the sound of the fifth the mother of the drayman springs from her place by the unlighted candle and tears open the door. Five heads lie on the ground before the synagogue door.

She sought out the head of her son and lifted it in her hands. Holding it high before her, she entered the synagogue. It was as if she wanted the whole world to see. A fierce pride shone from her eyes. She had lifted the kerchief from her face, so that she might look back at everyone of the assembled. And the assembled moved away from her reverently, made a space for her, when she began to dance.

Lightly her footsteps moved over the floor as she danced with her son's head before the Holy Ark. She uttered no word, her lips were locked, but her eyes passed from face to face over all the assembled. And they all moved away from her reverently, envy and wonder on their faces.

"The mother dances with her son! The mother dances with her son!"

She laid down the head of her son at the foot of the Ark; she brought the memorial candle from its place by the door and placed it in the midst of the memorial candles in the center; and with her own hands she lit the candle, so that it burned among the others.

Translated by Maurice Samuel

Kola Street

SHOLEM ASCH

1.

THE WESTERN tip of Mazowsze, south of the sandy hills along the bend of the Vistula between Plock and Wloclawek, is a region poor in water and sparse in forests. The horizon extends endlessly, and there is nothing to stop the eye: long monotonous fields stretch for miles and miles, for the most part covered with scanty grain, and only occasionally cut by the white ribbon of a cart road bordered with infrequent weeping willows. This triangular area, which includes Kutno, Zychlin, Gostynin, Gombin, and a number of smaller towns, has none of the mysterious charm of its neighbor, the province of Kujawy, so rich in legends about the souls of the dead that haunt black lanes, wander in the fields, and lure people into the swamps; nor is it as rich in color and in sound as its other neighbor, the Duchy of Lowicz, which gave birth to the greatest Polish composer and creator of the mazurka, Chopin. Flat and monotonous are its fields, and the peasant who cultivates them is as plain as the potatoes they yield. Unlike the peasant of Lowicz, he does not deck himself out in white caftans and brightly colored trousers and hats adorned with ribbons and corals; nor does he go in for witchcraft like the peasant of Tall Poplars in Kujawy. Here the peasant is like a clod of earth into which God has breathed a soul, like the walking lime that grows in front of his house. He never quits his reed, on which he plays, far into the night, long formless tunes that have no beginning and no end, tunes that are like his long, broad, green-covered fields. He is a man without guile—"I am as God made me." When he is friendly he will give you his very shirt; but when he gets mad he will take his revenge, let it be at the cost of his life. He is devoted to his cow, which lives with him, and will never slaughter it for his own use. But above all he loves and cherishes his horse, which he never subjects to daily labor: to plow his field he would yoke his cow or his wife rather than his horse. He saves his horse for Sundays, to drive it to church, and to show it off when he goes to visit friends in a neighboring village.

The Jew native to this region partakes more of the flavor of wheat and of apples than of the synagogue and the ritual bath. The land is rich for grazing: the peasant breeds cows and oxen and sheep, and the Jew buys them from him to take them to Lodz or across the German border, which is nearby. Among the Jews there are the renowned fishermen of the Lonsk ponds, who supply fish to Lodz and the surrounding country in the Kalisz and Plock areas; the sturdy teamsters who take Litvaks to the frontier where the railway has not yet penetrated; and the big horse-dealers who sell the horses bred and nurtured by the peasants to Germans coming from Torun and Berlin. The poor Jews rent orchards from the peasant for the summer; in the winter they wash his pelts in the town pond and take them to the fair in Lowicz or Gombin. Throughout the week the Jew stays in the village, sharing the peasant's life. For the Sabbath he comes to town to attend services at the Three-Trade Synagogue, where fisherman, cattlemen, and teamsters divide the honors among them, and where they discuss the events of the week. On Saturday, after the Sabbath meal, they go into the field, where the horses are fed and the boys play games. After sunset they settle on benches in front of the houses, watch the promenading servant girls, and tell stories.

In one of these towns there was a street called Kola Street, so named because it lies on the road that leads from Zychlin to the neighboring town of Kola. The Three-Trade Synagogue was in Kola Street. This street was not in the Diaspora, as it were: there no Jew was ever beaten. If it happened that recruits passing through the town in the fall began to riot, members of the congregation would take matters into their own hands: armed with shafts torn from carts and iron bars wrested from shutters, they would go out into the streets and teach the hooligans a lesson.

The street of the scholars, the street where live the rabbi and the teachers, and where the bathhouse and the poultry slaughtering yard are situated, felt very much ashamed of Kola Street: "They're illiterates, butchers, fishmongers!" The scholars lived entirely on the festival money contributed by Kola Street; and whenever they were in trouble—whenever, for instance, a shepherd set his dog on a Jew or a drunken peasant started a row in their street—Jews, young and old, would run to Kola Street, crying for help. Nevertheless, at heart, the scholars condemned the Kola Street crowd. "Not at all like Jews," they would say to one another, "and when the Messiah comes, they will come to us for help." The upper-class people of Broad Street, such as Reb Berachiah the moneylender, also had the greatest contempt for them: "Savages, with no manners at all! But we need this rabble sometimes—for instance, to keep the recruits quiet and to stop them from smashing our windows."

Kola Street reciprocated the feelings of the gentry in the other streets, whom they called limp rags—"Jews soaked in water." But when they needed to appeal to heaven—to write a petition to a rabbi to pray for a sick child or to recite the Psalms (they were not too good at it themselves), they had to depend on the scholars. When the High Holy Days were close at hand the Kola Street crowd treated the scholars with the greatest respect—"Moses' bodyguard," they would call them. Sometimes, on the eve of Yom Kippur, a tall vigorous Jew, a teamster or a fisherman, would lie prostrate on the threshold of the synagogue, and then the street of the scholars scourged Kola Street in the sight of God in Heaven.

In Kola Street there stood a one-story house built of timber. It was known as The Benches, because of the long benches in front of it, on which the Three-Trade congregation used to sit. Israel Zychlinski lived in that house.

Reb Israel was the oldest and most respected inhabitant of Kola Street. He was a man in his seventies, yet he walked without a stick and did not wear glasses—a survival of bygone days when a five-kopeck coin could buy a quart of brandy. When a bull broke loose from his rope and Reb Israel, after chasing him for a couple of hours, finally caught him by the horns and bent the bull's mighty neck, he would groan and say with a little laugh, "Eh, my old strength is gone." He was an important cattle-dealer who bought up all the cattle in the surrounding country and sold it to the Germans by the thousand. Because he was a man who did not begrudge the other fellow his share, everybody, Jew and gentile, treated him with great respect. To him they gave their money for safekeeping, from him they borrowed money when they needed it, and to him they came for advice and to have their quarrels settled; and what Reb Israel said—that was final. Reb Israel could, if necessary, slap the face of the biggest and strongest tough. No one would dare disobey him. If anyone did, Kola Street might kill him on the spot. The ox-drivers who took the cattle to Lodz or to the German frontier always stopped at Reb Israel's, spending the night in the stables with the horses and cows. Food in his house was free for everyone. There was always bread and butter on the table—you came in, helped yourself, and went on your way. There was an abundance of everything—cows, oxen, horses, goats, sheep, geese, and helpers, Jews and gentiles. Nothing in Reb Israel's house was under lock—here no one would steal: that would mean death on the spot. When anyone was wronged in the town he came to Reb Israel to complain, and Reb Israel went out and slapped faces right and left.

One day the Hasid who was licensed to sell spirits had the house of a Jewish widow searched on a Sabbath eve. Brandy was discovered there, and the woman was thrown into jail. Reb Israel was summoned to intervene in her behalf. He took a stick and went to talk to the Hasid.

"Get the widow out of jail."

"Reb Israel, she is robbing me of my daily bread!"

Reb Israel said no more. He went home and sent two of his helpers to the tavern with sticks in their hands. They took two barrels of spirits, put them outside the shop, and opened the taps—help yourself, get your fill! And Jews had a Sabbath until they rolled in the streets. As for the licensed tavernkeeper, he got a black eye into the bargain and was promised more of the same next week—and he couldn't do a thing about it either.

One day a tough young fellow entered Reb Israel's house and stood there by the big wardrobe.

"What do you want?" said Reb Israel, going up to him and smacking him across the face. "I hear you think you're tough. You beat your mother. Don't you know who feeds you? And yet, if somebody else says a word to her, you're ready with a knife!"

"Reb Israel, it's my mother. I can beat her—she's *my* mother. But a stranger better watch out. I'll tear him to pieces. Isn't that as it should be, Reb Israel?"

"And what have you come for, Zirel?"

"Screwface, the Hasid who keeps the oil store, offered me a gold piece to climb the wall at night and have some fun with the oil barrels belonging to his competitor, Yoske's son-in-law."

"I'll break your head if you do. Take the gold piece and then do nothing."

"But he won't give me the gold piece before I've done the job."

"Tell him to deposit it with me. Then go to Yoske's son-in-law and tell him to raise a cry tomorrow, pretending that his barrels were opened. I'll give you the gold piece, and if Screwface has anything to say, knock his teeth out."

Every Friday evening Reb Israel, on returning home from the road, sat down on the bench in front of his house, with his pocket full of coins, and prayed to God in his heart: "Father, send me Jews who need money for the Sabbath." And he did not go in before distributing all his change among the poor. Then he washed himself, put on his best caftan, and went to the Three-Trade Synagogue to welcome the Sabbath. Wandering beggars took good care to stop in the town for the sake of Reb Israel's Sabbath—the taste of his *kugel* made their mouths water for the rest of the year—and the congregation was always full of them. Reb Israel would post himself at the door with the crowd of beggars—no Jews love having a poor man as guest for Sabbath more than cattlemen or fishermen—and took home all who were left over. The *shammes* of the congregation would call out, "Three gulden for a guest," auctioning them off just as he auctioned off the privilege of reading from the weekly chapter of the Torah in the synagogue—so many members of the congregation were eager to take a guest home. Next morning, when the rabbi expounded the *midrash* to the congregation, Reb Israel listened to him with tears in his eyes, and after the service he invited the worshipers to his home to toast the Sabbath over a glass of brandy. And while they drank one another's health he banged his fists on the table, urging them, "Drink, Jews! To our father Abraham! To our teacher Moses!" The whole house shook from the blows of his fist on the table.

Reb Israel could read his chapter of the Torah, and he was at home in the commentary of Rashi when it was free from Aramaic words. Reb Israel loved Rashi with all his heart, looking upon him as a near relative, a member of the family of all Jews. And there was another Jew whom Reb Israel loved—King David. His Psalms are so sweet that they melt every limb in your body—and he is just a Jew, King

David is. Reb Israel could imagine meeting him in the street and exchanging greetings with him—"How do you do, King David?" "How are you, Reb Israel?"—and then talking with him about the market.

Whenever a daughter of Reb Israel reached marriageable age, he went to the rabbi and said, "Rabbi, choose a son-in-law for me from among your pupils."

He took the son-in-law and set him up in his own house for the rest of his life. "Here is your food and your drink, your Sabbath clothes and your pocket money, and you, study the holy Torah!"

His sons-in-law with their great volumes of the Talmud inspired him with such awe that he walked on tiptoe before them. He reserved for them the best and most precious of his possessions, and when he heard the voice of the Torah resounding in his house the old man wept for joy.

Reb Israel's sons were real giants. "Zychlinski's bodyguard," they were called—and they were no scholars either. But Notte, the son of his old age, was stronger than any of them. Notte was a strapping young fellow who went out in the morning with Burek his dog, and Bashke his sheep, and his whistle. A pigeon perched on his shoulder. The whole street trembled before him as he stood in front of his house with his straw hat tipped rakishly on his head, his riding crop in his hand, whistling for his pigeons, which circled over his head. Josephine brought his horse from the stable; if it was not groomed to perfection, or if the mane was not well combed and braided with straw, he gave her a slash with his crop, so that her young blood spurted from her full red hand.

Josephine was a servant, a gentile girl who had been brought from the village and had been in Reb Israel's house since her childhood. Strong as iron, she fitted into the household; she was one of them, took part in discussions, gave her opinion, and voiced her displeasure when she did not have her way. Notte maltreated her, sometimes cruelly, but she never held a grudge against him for that. She would toss her head and stand defiantly. "Go ahead, hit me if you feel like it."

Half an hour later, when she saw him on his horse, she walked out in front of the house and stood with arms akimbo, her eyes smiling through the red and blue welts he had left on her face. "There's no rider like him!"

When he returned he beckoned to her with his finger. She at first pretended not to see, then she went up, pouting, and lazily took the reins. He winked at her and went up to the attic, to his pigeon cote. She briskly led the horse to the stable.

In the doorway she ran into the caretaker's wife, who asked her, "Who's marked your face up for you?"

"What's that to you? Whoever did it, did it." Josephine thumbed her nose at her and quickly followed Notte upstairs.

Notte kept a pigeon cote. The attic in which the oats for the horses were stored was traditionally used as a pigeon cote; wherever the pigeons were taken, on being set free they always flew back to the attic and settled on the roof. The gentile baker at the other end of the town also had a pigeon cote, and Notte and the baker were continually at war. Notte would release his pigeons, and the baker his; sometimes one side would take a pigeon from the other—a hen from one flock would come to court a cock from the other flock, trying to get him to accompany her to her home.

It was just such occasions that the gang lived for. For Notte had his gang of Jewish and gentile boys who spent the night in his house; just as the baker had his own gang of gentile baker boys. When one side won a pigeon from the other, it was as jubilant as if it had conquered the world, while the losers went about downcast, meditating revenge. This led to vicious brawls between the rival gangs, brawls from which God preserve us!

2.

It was a Friday afternoon in the summer. Reb Israel had just returned from the road. Casimir, the stable boy, led the horse to the pump to drink. Josephine removed the things from the carriage, including a goose, a turkey, and a bagful of fish that Reb Israel had bought on the way for the Sabbath. Suddenly one of Notte's boys rushed into the courtyard, stuck two fingers between his lips, and let out an ear-piercing whistle.

"What's the matter, you bastard?" said Notte, coming into the courtyard with Bashke.

"The baker let his pigeons loose. His entire flock is perched on a roof near the city hall."

In two leaps Notte was in the attic: he opened his pigeon cote and let out the pigeons.

With his crop in his hand, surrounded by his gang, Notte went into the street. Across the market square stood the baker and his gang, armed with sticks; overhead, high in the clouds, the pigeons hovered, fluttering their light wings, in two separate flocks. One flock flew into the other, and the two mingled for a short time, then separated again, swooping down to the market square or soaring upward. After circling above the market several times the pigeons settled on the roofs. High on one roof perched an isolated pigeon, as if cast out by his companions. A hen from Notte's flock flew up to him, and the two birds began to whisper. Notte's gang waited with baited breath for the moment when the pigeons would come to an understanding and fly together to Notte's attic.

Suddenly one of the baker's gang hurled a stone at the pigeons, which flew away. That was the signal for hell to break loose. One of Notte's boys went up to the offender and smacked him across the legs with his stick. The gentile boy fell to the ground, screaming. The baker's gang charged with sticks, and a vicious battle began. All you could see were sticks flying in the air and coming down on heads; Jewish and gentile boys lay on the ground with blood on their faces. The blind Leib came running from the slaughterhouse with a shaft in his hand, whirling it above the crowd.

Notte grabbed the baker, held his lapels with one hand to prevent him from running away, and with the other hand smashed into his face, his ribs, his stomach—each blow resounded loudly—and he kept pounding with his bare fist until his victim went down. All this time the pigeons were flying above them, one flock into the other, as if they knew that the fight was about them. They flapped their wings as they swooped down close to the combatants' heads, and then they soared into the sky.

With the baker out of the way the gangs separated, waiting for what would happen next. With the help of God the two pigeons had reached an agreement: the hen lured the cock into Notte's pigeon cote.

Notte's boys were beside themselves with joy. But the baker's gang laid plans for revenge.

That Friday night the baker sneaked into Reb Israel's attic, made his way to the pigeons, and proceeded to strangle one after the other. But he had miscalculated his chances. The pigeons, sensing a stranger among them, flapped their wings and flew from one end of the attic to the other, clucking loudly.

Josephine, who slept in a room under the attic, ran to Notte and pulled him by his hair. "Master, someone's in the pigeon cote!"

Notte grabbed an iron bar—there was always one lying next to his bed—and went upstairs.

As he rushed into the attic something struck his head so hard that he saw stars, but he took no notice and got hold of the intruder. Notte held the man's mouth to stifle his cries, and he hit him over the head and in the chest until he felt it was enough. Then he took him by the head, dragged him down the stairs, and deposited him in front of his own house.

A few days later Notte was taken to jail. But it is no easy thing to arrest a fellow like Notte. When the police officer came for him Josephine asked him to go with her to the stable under the pretext that she wanted to tell him something. He went quite willingly, but the boys were waiting for him in the dark and gave him such a thrashing that he was in no condition to return for Notte. Alarming rumors began to circulate in the town. It was said that Notte was going about the streets with his leaded crop, Bashke following him. Then he was caught by three jail guards and the two police officers stationed in the town and taken to jail.

In the meantime the baker died. The town lived in ever-growing fear. Various stories were told about peasants gathering here and there. Yechiel, the village peddler, reported in the synagogue that a peasant woman in a village had asked him to look into a mirror; he had seen the rabbi's head there, whereupon the woman had said that she had cast a spell. There were rumors of ritual murder, and reports came from neighboring villages that Jewish dairymen had been held up and robbed of everything. A town meeting was called in the rabbi's house and a day of fasting was decreed. The well-to-do Jews left town. The street of the scholars looked as if Death had swept it with his black wings. In the House of Study candles burned all day and Jews recited Psalms; the Psalm-readers stayed up all night. Mothers would suddenly grab their children coming home from school and hug them and lament over their young lives. Betrothals and weddings were postponed till "after"—when things would calm down. Jewish guards armed with heavy sticks patrolled the streets after dark.

Notte looked out from behind the tiny bars in the cell window giving on the market square. Each morning Josephine led his horse in front of the jail to show him that it was well groomed. All day Bashke and the dog Burek lay outside his window, and their master spoke to them through the bars. And each day his gang had to drive his pigeons past the jail, and Notte from behind the bars gave orders to his boys, telling them what was to be done.

The town was more and more in the grip of fear. The Jews went about looking like ghosts. Gentiles of the town with whom they associated the year round terrified them. The water carrier who supplied Jewish houses was said to have told a Jew that on St. John's Day they would go for Moshkowski's house. The synagogue candlelighter would become supervisor over the Jews; the gentile attendant at the graveyard would become governor and the Jews would have to pay him tribute. The Jews listened to these tales, and their hearts sank. Young children and girls were sent away from home, to stay with forgotten aunts and uncles discovered in other towns. The street of the scholars prepared for the worst. "God, we are under Thy protection, Thy will be done!"

Kola Street was calm, ignoring the whole thing. When one of them met a Jew from the street of the scholars walking with a gloomy face, he would say, "Hey, bigwig, have you prepared your mousehole at home?"

It was said that the day of judgment would be on St. John's Day. That is the day of one of the biggest fairs, when the peasants come to town for the first time after the harvest. Then the barns are full of grain, and potatoes and cabbages are piled high in the fields. The peasant comes to the fair with wife and children to buy them gifts. He sells the grown cattle and buys young ones to graze on the stubble. At the fair he meets his cronies, discusses the year's harvest with them, and then they all go to have a drink.

And that day to which the Jews had always looked forward with so much hope of good business, this year filled their hearts with terror, and they longed for it to be over as soon as possible.

When the day came Jews hurried to the synagogue early in the morning and began to pray. The rabbi stood at the lectern, and the entire congregation burst out weeping, as though it were the concluding prayer of Yom Kippur. After the service the rabbi opened the Holy Ark, and all the worshipers together recited the confession of sins which is usually said at the deathbed. The rabbi recited a verse, and then the congregation recited a verse. Before going home they said farewell to one another and voiced their hope that they would be alive to meet again on the morrow.

All this time they could hear peasant carts rolling over the bridge.

Carts arrived at the market square, and each sound of a cart was like Death knocking at Jewish hearts. It was as though the carts were rolling differently today, as though the peasants and their women were walking differently.

For a time the day wore on as usual. The peasants sold their wares, bargained hard about the price, gave in at the end, and then bought what they needed.

At first the Jewish stores remained closed. A peasant wanted to buy some herring, so a herring woman opened her stand just to sell him herring; but then a second peasant came, and a third one. When the storekeeper across the street saw a store open, he opened his too, and one after another all the stores opened. The day began to resemble all market days. The Jews regained confidence and held their ground more firmly when bargaining with the peasants. Then suddenly a boy came running from the horse market, crying, "Help, they're beating Jews!"

In no time all stores were closed, shutters down, doors locked. Men and women grabbed whatever was at hand—a baby, a lamp, a table, a blanket—and ran as though from a fire, but soon stopped, not knowing where to go. They crawled under their beds, lay there awhile, then thought better of it, crawled out, shoved aside wardrobes, hid behind them, then out again, and up to the attics. Some scrambled into cellars, some climbed up on stoves. Children cried, and mothers silenced them with pillows. Stragglers knocked at doors, begging to be let in; people sought shelter in strange houses, entering the first door they found open. Stranded fathers groaned over their children and pressed other people's children to their hearts.

When the news that Jews were being attacked reached Kola Street, Hershele Cossack ran out of his butcher shop, grabbed a bag, threw into it three ten-pound weights, and slung it over his shoulder. Come on, brothers! And all of Kola Street surged after him—butchers with cleavers and knives, teamsters with shafts from their carts, fishermen with grappling irons, horse-dealers with steel whips on their horses—all of them streamed to the horse market.

The big square at the intersection of the two roads was teeming with carts, carts, carts, which were surrounded on all sides and lost in a mass of horses, oxen, people, and pigs. It was a scene of many colors, and resounding with many cries. Drunken peasants with clubs in their hands were chasing Jews in long caftans, who were jumping frantically over carts, horses, and people. The horrible scream of a man leaping over a wagon and shouting desperately for help mingled with the wild laughter of a drunk. Horses reared and kicked, and under their hoofs people were rolling on the ground, and pigs were squealing. Sticks, earthenware, caps, were flying over people's heads. Frightened geese and chickens flitted around the carts, cackling and squawking, filling the air with feathers from their disheveled wings. Everywhere Jews in black caftans were darting in all directions, shrieking with terror.

Like a stream of glowing steel pouring into the deep cold sea, Kola Street plunged into the fray. In a minute the battle was joined. Bars of steel and iron slammed into human bodies, blood ran into eyes, down caftans, over carts and wheels. You couldn't see what or when; all was confusion, horses on top of men, men on top of horses. A bleeding peasant woman dragged her wounded husband while he kept punching her in the belly, trying to wrench himself free from her hands. Little children clung to their mothers' skirts. Fathers shoved their children away from them, and with tight lips and bloodshot eyes pressed into the melee. One man thrust his fist into another's mouth, trying to pull his tongue out, and then took him by the throat and strangled him to death. Two men set upon each other, got squeezed against a cart, and one of them smashed hard fists into his chest and stomach and bit him with his teeth. No one was fighting for any definite reason; all were seized by the same frenzy; the beast that slumbers in man was roused. They were one seething mass in the sight of heaven and God, and each was trying to eat the other alive.

3.

All day Notte looked out of the cell window. He did not regret the fun he had started—he was not the kind of man who is given to regrets. He had been waiting for the moment it would start. He had not formed any plan, he had not thought of how he would break out—he was not the kind of man who makes plans. For him, things had to come of their own accord, and when they did come, they burst into flame and broke forth like thunder.

Then he caught sight of people fleeing from the horse market. A boy ran with a bleeding head, women darted across the square to get their children. Stores were being closed. His lips tightened, and with bloodshot eyes he flung himself against the door. It was only a small-town jail, but the door was too strong to be smashed by a man's fist. He shook the bars at the window, and they bent under the impact, but they were cemented firmly in the wall. He seized his pallet and banged it against the stove—in a minute bricks and boards were smashed. Like thunder imprisoned in a room, he hurled himself against the walls. In the end he dug his teeth in his hands and, crouching with his head between his knees, began to howl, and his howling rose to the ceiling and surged against the bars and went out through the window.

He crouched like that for a long time. Then a voice called from outside, "Master! Master!"

He looked up and saw Josephine, her hair streaming.

"They're after your father," she cried, handing him an iron bar through the window.

In one jump he was at the door. He thrust the iron bar behind the door handle, leaned his chest against it, and pushed with all his strength. One, two, three—the door crashed open. A guard tried to intercept him, but a punch in the jaw knocked him off his feet, and he sprawled on the floor, drenched in blood. Notte rushed home to his father.

The peasants had set out from the horse market to Reb Israel's house. "To Zychlinski's! His son killed a peasant!" they shouted, brandishing spades and rakes.

As they swarmed into the courtyard and stood in front of the house with their weapons cries rang out, "They're at Reb Israel's!" And all of Kola Street, young and old, went into action. The blind Leib—a giant who could snap an iron bar—grabbed a three-pronged pitchfork in the stable. Kola Street surrounded the courtyard.

"What's this?" Reb Israel cried out. Holding the iron bar he sometimes used on the Lodz road against thieves, he came out to face the peasants all by himself.

"Whom have you come to attack?" he said. "Me? I have toiled for you all my life, buying your cattle from you, you dogs, paying in hard cash and taking it to foreign places! I have sweated for you on your roads, burned for you in the summer heat, frozen for you in the winter cold, to cram your pockets with money! Come on, you dogs! Here I am! I want to see who dares to lay his hands on me!"

The peasants stood silent. Then one of them said, "We've nothing against you, Zychlinski. We're only after your son, who killed one of our people."

"Here I am!" cried Notte, throwing open the gate and rushing into the courtyard. He grabbed the nearest peasant by the sides, raised him in the air, and banged him down on the ground, so that you could hear his legs cracking under him. The others flew at him like a whirlwind. But Notte seized another peasant by the head, lifted him up in the air, and used him as a living cudgel against the others. The Kola Street crowd swept forward with their pitchforks.

Reb Israel's voice rose above the tumult. "Stop, I tell you! He has killed a man! Let him defend himself alone."

And Notte defended himself alone. With one of the assailants in his mighty arms he slammed away at the others. Men dropped around him as ears of grain fall before the scythe. A peasant whacked him on the head with a shovel, and red blood poured down his face. Still holding his living club, he charged deeper into the crowd; then, snatching a spade from the hands of one of them, he struck out right and left, as though a demon had entered him, filling his mighty arms with blood so that the veins almost burst out of his skin. Another peasant behind him dealt him a savage blow in the side with an iron bar. He doubled up and remained motionless for a moment, and then lunged forward again. Someone caught one of his hands from behind, but he still kicked and bit. Then he doubled up again and held his side.

"You goddam sons-of-bitches!" Josephine emerged suddenly as though from under the earth, wielding a rake. "You've killed the young master!" She slammed at the head of the peasant who had caught Notte's hand and moved threateningly toward another. "I'll teach you!" Brandishing her rake, she drove the assailants away from Notte, who stood bent in half, almost touching the ground, holding his side with one hand and banging at the heads of the peasants trying to grab him with the other. Finally Josephine managed to lead him into the house and put him to bed.

The peasants wanted to follow, but, seeing the Kola Street crowd with their weapons, they fell back, some with bleeding heads and others with broken arms, muttering, "That bitch isn't even a Jew!" Seven or eight of their blood-drenched companions were left lying in the courtyard.

Now that market day was over the street of the scholars crawled out from behind stoves and wardrobes, from attics and cellars. Next morning they came to the synagogue, greeted one another, and loudly sang praises to the Lord. After the service they sent for cake and brandy, and resolved to meet again at night and hold a banquet. Kesriel and Ozer, Reb Israel's sons-in-law, promised to get him to contribute his youngest son's pigeons. Since the son was a mass of broken bones he would surely not resist, and it was certainly fitting that Jews should feast on the pigeons that had put the entire Jewish community in jeopardy, and thus get rid of the whole brood that had been the cause of so much affliction.

And so it was. The two young men, on returning from the service, discussed the matter with their father-in-law, and then they went up to the attic, took all the pigeons, and sent them to the slaughterer.

Notte lay on his bed, deathly pale. An icebag was placed on his head, which was wrapped in one large bandage; his lips were still clenched tight, and his chest was heaving. Josephine sat by his side, handing him whatever he asked for. He heard a noise in the attic, he heard the pigeons flapping their wings—the very thought lifted him from his bed, but he could not move. He kicked off his blanket and lay there listening.

The pigeons were flapping their wings—he looked at Josephine, pointing his finger at the ceiling.

Josephine went to the attic and came back holding in her arms three tiny fledglings, with scarcely any feathers, whose mothers had just been taken away from them to be slaughtered. They kept flapping their bald wings, looking for something. Their thin necks, with thin warm skin covering the delicate bone that could be snapped with a finger, were pulled in; their heads were hidden between their little wings, and their little wings were seeking something.

Notte took them in his hand, tightened his lips, and kicked away a chair that stood near his bed. The little birds were trembling softly in his hand, miserably seeking something. He tucked them under his shirt, held them against his bare breast, and warmed them. The fledglings quivered pitifully on his breast, begging for something, flapping their wings.

His face grew whiter. His eyes were glazed, sunk in their sockets; his nose grew longer, whiter and thinner, and his lips were pressed together so tightly that they seemed locked in a spasm.

The room was silent now. A light breeze trembled on the window-panes. Everyone had gone out, leaving the house to the thunder that was about to break forth in a fury of destruction.

He lay there and felt the helpless little birds quivering on his breast. His eyes bulged and filled with blood. He was silent.

He sat up on his bed and looked around him. He caught sight of some grains of wheat, chewed them into flour, thrust a fledgling's bill into his mouth, and fed the bird with his tongue. The thin little neck throbbed between his fingers and the wings pleaded.

"God!" he cried out. He grabbed the fledgling, gave a twist to its head (the little bird uttered one squeak, and a thin jet of blood sputtered into his face), and threw it away. He twisted the neck of the second fledgling, and threw it away. The third fledgling . . . Then he got down from his bed, snatched the mirror, and smashed it on the floor. He went up to the wardrobe, split it open, and flung it down. He went to the bed, ripped the bedding with his teeth, and the feathers flew in the air. With one blow he bashed in the table. He grabbed a chair and flung it at the stove, and the stove crashed to the ground. He tore his shirt and bit his hands. In the end he collapsed, and, lying amid the wreckage, he pressed his face to the floor and fell asleep, and slept long . . . long . . .

No one dared enter the room to rouse the sleeping thunder.

Translated by Norbert Guterman

The Poor Community

ABRAHAM REISEN

THE LITTLE town of Voinovke, which consists of forty houses and thirty-five householders, since five of the houses stand empty, rocked and rumbled and boiled like a stream on the eve of Passover, when the snow begins to melt. But it wasn't the eve of Passover. It was a week before Rosh Hashonoh, and the community had no prayer leader.

In the nearby town of Yachnovke, which is several times larger than Voinovke, one could not only get a prayer leader, but quite a good one—with a neck, a double chin, and in general a cantor's bearing, only he would want to be well paid, and that was the trouble! The town of Voinovke had already disposed of its few public rubles on a cantor whom, through ill luck, the past summer had brought; he had prayed a full Sabbath service with a choir of six. In a way, it had been worth it: since Voinovke had been Voinovke, it had not heard such beautiful singing. The synagogue, which is over two hundred years old, as the older folks tell it, barely survived the cantor and his choir. The windows trembled, the walls shook, and from the ceiling big chunks of plaster fell. In great wonderment the community gave this cantor and his choir all of its public money, and now, a week before Rosh Hashonoh, it suddenly realized that it didn't have a single penny with which to hire a prayer leader. So the townspeople gathered in the synagogue to discuss the problem.

"That was certainly one of the most foolish things in the world!" exclaimed Ariah Leib the tailor, who looks upon himself as a Jew of some standing, since he has a long beard and a little boy who studies in the Yachnovke yeshiva.

"What a thing to do! It could happen only with us," said Chaim the glazier in support of his friend. "In the middle of the year to give a cantor all of our money!"

"Foolishness! Sheer foolishness!" added Chanon the teacher, shrugging his shoulders.

"You know what my decision would be?" said Zorach the shoemaker, stroking his beard in the manner of a rabbi. "I would have those who hired the cantor pay for a prayer leader with their own money. That's my advice," he said gravely, as if everything depended on his advice.

"But go find out who hired him! All of us hired him," said Zalmon the smith. "All of us wanted at least once in our lives to hear some religious singing. It's hardly an unworthy desire. But when? When the town is rich! A Yachnovke can afford to spend a few rubles for a cantor in the middle of the year, but not we paupers."

"Well, what shall we do?" asked several voices in the synagogue.

"It's very serious," answered one.

"Chaikel Sheps, you will pray with the Sabbath tune," said Zorach the shoemaker to the leader of the Sabbath prayers.

Chaikel Sheps does have a bit of a voice but doesn't know any prayer tunes other than those of the Sabbath.

"Try, Chaikel, try!" said several of the householders. "Make up your mind!"

Chaikel Sheps got red in the face and weakly replied, "I am afraid."

"Try, try! *Ha-me-lech!*"—Zalmon the smith showed him how.

"Aye, you can do it all by yourself," chimed in Chanon the teacher and went on, *"Yo-shev-el-chi-seh ram-veh-noh-soh-oh-oh! Ai-ai-ai-ai-ai-aai!"*

The whole gathering joined in, and for a few minutes the synagogue rang with the tunes of the High Holidays.

"Now everybody knows it, but when Rosh Hashonoh comes nobody will remember," one householder remarked.

Everybody took this idea seriously, and the gathering settled into deep thought.

"You know, we have no one to blow the *shofar* either," announced the *shammes,* in the middle of everything, from the Torah-reading platform.

The group was startled.

"How come? Where is Nachman?"

It seems that Nachman, a pale thin young man of about twenty, who has "eating days" and is studying by himself, had for two years blown the ram's horn for nothing.

"This year I will blow in the village of Sosnovtchine. They're giving me three rubles—three rubles . . ." he managed to stammer, fearing for his very skin, which had been clothed by the community.

"You're a cheapskate!" someone called out.

"A ruffian!" another shouted.

"One who always eats without paying," a third said, sneering.

A torrent of words poured down on poor Nachman. He felt as if he were being pricked with needles. "I have to earn something for a winter coat. I cannot—" he pleaded. "Forgive me, but the winter is cold."

"What do people want from him really?" they asked, retreating. "He needs a winter coat. He is going around with nothing on, naked . . ."

"It really is so," everybody agreed.

"That means we have neither a prayer leader nor a *shofar* blower."

"It seems we have no Torah reader either," admitted the *shammes* from the platform.

"What do you mean?" They were startled. "Where is Old Peshes? Where is he? Where is he?"

"Old Peshes will also read in Sosnovtchine," confessed Nachman, as if he were somehow guilty. "He is getting two rubles."

The group was stricken. Some lowered their heads, as if looking for advice, while others lifted their heads toward the ceiling and stood deep in thought for a few minutes.

"What's there to think about?" asked one. "These High Holidays we'll pray individually. No more congregation."

"A pretty story, and a short one!" said another, laughing bitterly.

"This has to be written down in the permanent record."

"No more Voinovke!"

"Let's all chip in and hire someone with our own money," suggested Chanon the teacher, and was immediately taken aback by his own words.

"All right. Give me a ruble," said Zalmon the smith, extending his hand.

"I have none," said Chanon, shamefaced, "but there are householders who do have."

"Who has?"

"Nobody has!"

"The holidays that are coming—they're no trifle!"

The synagogue was in a turmoil. Everybody offered advice, but none of it was good.

Suddenly the old *shammes* banged the table on the platform, and everyone became quiet.

"I have a solution. Keep quiet awhile."

"Really? Really?" they all exclaimed impatiently.

The *shammes* inhaled deeply, took a powerful smell of snuff, wiped his nose, and finally spoke.

"This is the story. During the summer our community did something very foolish. We wasted our few rubles on a triviality. We forgot our poverty, our station, and we yearned to hear a cantor. Who knows really who he is! A cantor who rides from town to town can hardly be such a pious man. A worthy cantor sits home. But the story is—well, it is a thing of the past. The conclusion is: we are left without a prayer leader for the High Holidays, without a *shofar* blower, without a Torah reader—absolutely without a thing. And if you want to know something else, the *shofar* itself is not as it should be. Now it will still blow, one way or another; but when Rosh Hashonoh comes, there will have to be so much blowing—a *trooeh,* a *shvorim,* a *tekieh gdoleh*—it will surely falter. Even last year it hesitated, if you will recall—I recall very well—and Nachman is a good blower."

Everybody looked at Nachman, and he blushed.

"Therefore my advice is that this year we should become partners with the Sosnovtchine *minyan;* that is, we should all pray there this year. Walking is permitted, and altogether it is three and a half *versts;* it will be a pleasant walk. We shall all save ourselves headaches: where shall we get a prayer leader, a Torah reader, a horn blower and also a horn? Because the horn, I repeat, the horn will give up on Rosh Hashonoh. Surely it won't be able to manage a *trooeh shvorim*—it is too old and already has a few faults. All that remains for us is Sosnovtchine."

After the *shammes*'s talk they all began to grumble.

"From the town to the village, and on Rosh Hashonoh—no!"

"Let those yeshiva students come here!"

"What sort of high-and-mightys have they become?"

"In the past the yeshiva students used to come to us to pray."

"Now that they have learned Hebrew they make a *minyan* at home."

"Never mind the Hebrew, I'm sure they can count money."

"What do they lack? They have the best: bins filled with potatoes, with kraut, with chicken, with eggs—"

"Sour cream, butter and cheese—"

"May all troubles fall on their heads!"

"Sh-sh, don't curse them. It is the month of the High Holidays."

"Who is cursing? Who? Who?"

"Nobody, nobody . . ."

"Who has any complaints against them?"

"Berke of Sosnovtchine is a fine Jew; it will be a pleasure to pray in his home—a house as big as a field, three times the size of our synagogue."

"A fine Jew!"

"And what's wrong with the other yeshiva students? They're nice people!"

"Of course!"

"So it is settled that this year we'll pray in Sosnovtchine?"

"There is no other solution."

"A fine thing! As I'm a Jew, a mountain has lifted from my back!"

"What a mountain!"

"We must send someone to find out if he'll let us."

"What a question! It will be an honor to him!"

"It's no small thing! Townspeople coming to pray in a village!"

And the meeting ended in peace.

On the morning of the first day of Rosh Hashonoh, when the townspeople, on their way to Sosnovtchine, passed their old, dilapidated synagogue, standing there with cloudy eyes, woebegone and orphaned, their hearts felt sore and tight, and silently, without words, only with their eyes, they begged its forgiveness.

Translated by Charles Angoff

The Big Succeh

ABRAHAM REISEN

BARUCH's cottage was the smallest on the street. It was really more like a village hut than a town cottage. Only the roof with its rotting shingles showed that it belonged to the town, and the *mezzuzah* on the doorpost that it was a Jewish home.

The little cottage consisted of a single room. Baruch's older daughter once called the rear half, which was separated from the front by an unpainted wooden cupboard, "the dark chamber," but somehow she couldn't impress this name on the family. Twice she called it "the dark chamber," but when the others remained indifferent she began to doubt the propriety of her phrase and went back to calling it, like everyone else, "the dark corner."

In such a crowded cottage a cupboard is hardly a welcome guest. Tall, proud, wholly self-assured, it stood there in the middle of the single room, without regard to the discomfort it caused every member of the family. But the cupboard was an inheritance from Baruch's parents and had to be tolerated, though secretly everyone hoped it would somehow vanish.

The oven was an even greater nuisance, a tyrant that occupied almost three-quarters of the cottage. The cupboard was its close neighbor, but it was plain that between them little love was lost: they kept staring at each other like old enemies. Only on the eve of Passover, when Tsivyeh, the mistress of the house, would whitewash the front of the oven, would it deign to look upon its neighbor with any friendliness.

How such a huge oven had managed to squeeze into such a small cottage no one knew. The cottage must have been a hundred years old, but what its former proprietor could have had in mind was still a mystery. Anyway, its present owner hadn't bought the cottage himself. Right after Baruch's wedding his father had settled him there, and there Baruch had remained for some twenty years, never troubling to learn the history of the cottage. There were more important things to do: Baruch was a man with a wife, a man with many children and little income.

Naturally, one of the biggest troubles in his household is the overcrowding. His wife Tsivyeh is an able housekeeper, and their older daughter is an even better one; the two of them try hard to get some order and roominess in the cottage. But no matter how hard they work they seem to accomplish very little. Take, for example, what happens after a meal. The mother and daughter have worked themselves to the bone, cleaning up and making a sort of passageway to the table. But in less than ten minutes something generally falls to the floor, something that has not been firmly set, or the bench is accidentally moved, and again no one can make his way through the cottage: you have to leap if you want to get anywhere! For, naturally, besides the cupboard and the oven, there are two beds, a table, and two long benches, the longer of which, with its sharp edges, has made dents in the wall.

"Such a wonderful inheritance your father left us!" jeers Tsivyeh at her husband when the crowding becomes unbearable—when she makes the beds or bakes *chalah.*

Baruch never answers her, for he himself is not too happy about his inheritance. But at times he says to himself, Well, at least it's our own little place.

Not only did the crowding cause physical hardship to Baruch and his family, it also caused spiritual hardship, and indeed the spiritual was by far the greater.

Baruch, to be sure, was a poor Jew, and yet, as was fitting for a man of his origins, he was a householder. Itche Zlates, for example, was a close relative of his, and Itche was a wealthy man. Besides Itche, Baruch had many other relatives. Nor did Tsivyeh have anything to be ashamed of—her origins were also far from lowly. The two sides of the family had aunts, uncles, nephews, and nieces aplenty. And it was precisely because of these many relatives that Baruch, Tsivyeh, and their older daughter quarreled so often.

It happens, and not seldom, that Tsivyeh gives birth to a son, and naturally that's a time for celebrating—even if it's the third boy. In the cottage it's quite crowded, but for the first week the newborn baby lies near its mother and takes up little space. Even later, when it needs a crib, there is no problem. Tsivyeh has brought up all her children in hanging cribs, which take up room only in the air, forming a kind of second floor. But there is no room for the circumcision, not even for a quorum of men to hold the prayers. And, as has been mentioned,

Baruch and Tsivyeh both have large families, all of whom must of course be invited.

That's when the quarreling starts. The wealthier aunts and uncles, the shining lights of the family, are the first to arrive, and even they don't come in a group, but in pairs. Baruch apologizes to them for the lack of room, and he throws complaining looks at the walls, as if to say, Stretch, you oppressors, stretch!

Still more bitter is their humiliation during the holidays, when the relatives, as is the custom, invite one another to their homes.

"Remember now," they all say to Baruch, slapping him on the back after prayer. "Don't make me coax you to come with your whole family —remember, do you hear me?"

Baruch listens and wonders. What can he do? Not go, and create ill feeling in the family? So, of course, he and his wife and their children make the rounds of the relatives. They have a sociable drink and a bite to eat, and then, when the time comes to invite them to his house, which is the polite thing to do, his tongue loses the power of speech and he can only mumble, "It would be nice to ask you to my house, but—"

"Of course, when you have a bigger house. God will help."

Baruch would like to say, "Why not now? After all, in a happy home it's never too crowded." Could there be a cleverer answer? Yet it remains in his throat, never leaving his lips no matter how hard he tries.

Forgetting to thank his relatives for their hospitality, Baruch slinks out, his family trailing behind him, and he is plagued by the feeling that he has gone not so much for the holiday as to be given a meal by a rich man who pities him. And his face burns with shame.

In this way he visits a second relative, a third, and a fourth. What else can one do?

But to accept the hospitality of his relatives every holiday and never return it is simply unthinkable to Baruch. No matter how poor he is, that low he has not fallen.

Passover, Shevuoth, Chanukah with pancakes, *Purim* with its delicacies—out of the question, the cottage is simply too small. But that's why there is another holiday—*Succoth.* And on *Succoth,* Baruch has the laugh on the whole world.

His cottage, to be sure, is the smallest on the street, but the yard next to it is the largest. Nor is there a lack of vacant space. The trick is to build, and while Baruch hasn't the means to put up a big house he can patch together a *succeh* larger than any other. The rest of the year he may be cramped and miserable, but for these seven days he wants to live like a prince of the land. An hour of good living is worth while, but seven days! Think of it, seven days of comfort, when there is no need to be ashamed before one's relatives!

Right after Yom Kippur, Baruch begins to build his palace. First he sends his oldest boy to the garret, where there are four or five boards, also an inheritance from his father. Naturally, these boards wouldn't even "cover a tooth" on an ordinary *succeh,* least of all one so huge as Baruch plans. But one must remember that Baruch is a very thrifty planner. He does not build his *succeh* in the middle of the yard, where he would have to put up four walls; he builds it against a wall of his cottage. And since the *succeh* must be bigger than the cottage, he attaches the few boards to his wall so that they touch his neighbor's fence, which is, fortunately, also made of boards. Thus Baruch has two walls, almost ready-made, and he now has to build only another wall and a half. Then he takes down the three storm windows from the garret, the two doors of the cupboard, and borrows the rest of the necessary materials from his neighbors, who are already familiar with his plight and lend him this and that, as they have done before. Now the *succeh* has three-and-a-half walls and an opening for a door. The door is made not from wood but from quilts, actually two quilts, since a big *succeh* must have a big door, and one quilt would of course not be enough.

When the shell of the *succeh* is finished and there is no further need for man's work, the women go to it—that is, Tsivyeh and her older daughter. They sweep the ground, cover it with yellow sand, carry all the furniture from the cottage—that is, the table with the two benches and the two stools—to the *succeh*. The cottage is empty and feels offended, and the four walls can almost be heard to murmur, Eh, fancy people! But who has time to pay attention to the cottage, when in the yard stands such a grand *succeh*. Everybody laughs at the cottage and wants to forget that after *Succoth* they'll have to return to it.

Who, indeed, when things go well, considers what will come later?

The *succeh* is now the dwelling of the family, while the cottage serves merely as a kitchen. "As a kitchen," says Tsivyeh bitingly, "it is really quite large."

The cottage hears all this and almost bursts. The four walls think to themselves, Wait, wait, we'll settle accounts with you!

But who listens to them? Now the grand lady is the huge *succeh,* and the relatives will come to her, not to the cottage.

And, true enough, the second day of the holiday Baruch invites the shining lights of the two families.

"Will you see a *succeh!*" he says to them with a proud smile. "A *succeh*—a field! a prairie!"

"Yes, yes," say the various members of the family, "on *Succoth* you are king."

The family enjoys his lavish hospitality, which Tsivyeh has prepared with their last penny, and Baruch serves everyone, his face beaming. He just can't resist the temptation to say to at least one relative, "I incline to think that my *succeh* is bigger than yours."

The "incline," of course, is used merely out of politeness. Baruch is positive that his *succeh* is the biggest in town. And great is his joy when the wealthiest relative says to him, in a somewhat dejected manner, "My *succeh* is a bit of a thing. There's hardly enough room to move around."

This is the reply that Baruch remembers all year long, and it gives him the courage and the brass to accept the hospitality of his relatives on the other holidays. It's not so terrible—on *Succoth* he repays them many times.

Translated by Charles Angoff

Tuition for the Rebbe

ABRAHAM REISEN

"PAPA," Shloimke cried out, coming home from *cheder* in the evening. "The *rebbe* wants money!"

"Money again?" Chanon winced. "How long has it been since I sent three rubles with you?"

"He says that it's already the end of the term and you only gave seven rubles. There are eight more rubles coming to him," said Shloimke. "And he wants them!" he concluded, angrily scratching his head.

"Quiet! Just don't upset yourself, my treasure," Chanon said nervously, reminding himself that it really was a long time since he had sent any money. He became silent and in his despair began to tug at his beard, as if he were trying to get some advice out of it: Well, my dear beard, what do you think of this catastrophe?

Without waiting for an answer he began to rub his hand over his face, and when this did not help either, he started lifting his cap off his head and putting it back again, lifting it off and putting it on again. For a long while he held it in his hand. Then he replaced it. Finally, after he had done this several more times, his lined face brightened and his eyes lit up. Pleasantly, but without looking at anyone, he announced, "Tomorrow we sell a bag of seed."

"Then will you give me money tomorrow?" Shloimke asked.

"Not tomorrow, my son. But the day after."

"The day *after* tomorrow! The day *after* tomorrow!" Shloimke said in a tantrum. He could see himself marching right into school, looking his teacher in the eyes, and saying, "I didn't get it."

"Silence!" Chanon said grimly. "I told you the day after tomorrow. And the day after tomorrow is what I mean. When I say something, it's said."

"Really, Shloimke," his mother joined in, "you make such terrible faces for nothing. Where's the fire? Your father said the day after tomorrow, so he means the day after tomorrow."

Shloimke reconsidered, decided it was not so bad, and promptly forgot all about it. He demanded his supper.

"And what will you want next?" his mother said half-jokingly. "First it's money for the teacher, now it's supper. Maybe you ought to go out and earn some money."

"I'm too little."

"Too little"—his mother sighed—"a boy of twelve." She sighed again, without knowing quite why.

The next morning after his prayers Chanon went to the yard and opened the bin where the grain was kept. He looked over the bag of seed lying tranquilly in the corner. There were two other grain bins, both empty, and they seemed to regard Chanon with displeasure; it was a long time since he had something to put into them.

Chanon thrust his hand into the first bin and took out a handful of grain. "Beautiful," he said aloud. "Certainly first grade." Keeping the seeds in his palm, he stirred them thoughtfully with his finger: Not that it didn't cost me plenty. I paid good money for it. But try and convince the merchant Levine. He'll sniff and say "inferior merchandise" and cut off my nose and ears in the bargain. A merchant is a merchant.

Chanon sighed and began to calculate. The bag of seed cost him an average of seven gulden a pood. Even if the merchant gave him seven gulden and ten groschen, the most he could realize from a hundred pood would be a hundred times ten groschen, which came to only five rubles. Interest on the money came to two rubles, which would leave him, all in all, a clear profit of precisely three rubles. He sighed again.

He had to make at least ten rubles from this seed. He pulled his beard, rubbed his face, stirred the seed. Then he raised his eyes slowly to the hayloft of the barn. The hayloft held the answer. There were three sacks of cheap seed up there, bought at only one gulden a pood. To mix in three or four pood of this poorer seed—after the merchant had examined the good kind, of course—would bring him a few rubles profit. . . . But that was stealing. And Chanon wanted to be an honest businessman. Chanon stood in fear of God, of himself.

At that moment, however, he feared himself a little more than God. For his deed God might perhaps pardon him. God knew it was not his fault; poverty made him do it. But Chanon was less merciful. Instead of forgiving himself for such a deed, he would let it gnaw at him forever: What did you do, Chanon? Eh? Was it nice? Was it good? Was it honest? Think it over, Chanon. . . .

Chanon tore his eyes away from the hayloft where the cheap grain was stored. He had decided to do the honest thing.

"Honest," he cried. "Honest! *Honest!*"

He locked the bin and went to call the merchant.

Levine the merchant, a big Jew with a red face and little black eyes, rolled up his sleeves and shoved his arms into the bottommost corner of the bin.

But Chanon could not resist praising his merchandise even before it was examined. "First grade. There's nothing to discuss!"

The merchant was annoyed. A little worm like Chanon trying to grade the seed before Levine himself had examined it! He spoke coldly. "We'll soon see what grade it is."

Chanon's heart pounded with terror. Suppose the merchant decided the seed was not first grade. A robber of a Jew, he thought, asking himself the best way to soften him up with a good word.

"You, Pani Levine, no one has to tell. You always know, Pani Levine. All by yourself. If only I had a tenth of the seed you ship to Königsberg."

"Yes, indeed, brother, I don't blame you for wanting it," Levine said smugly, poking around in the seed. "But what would you have done with so much money?"

"Heh, heh, heh," Chanon laughed bitterly. "I'd know what to do. I'd trade, like you, with Königsberg."

"Grade of the seeds, two and a half. Two at the most," Levine said abruptly.

Chanon's agonized smile vanished. He was barely able to stand on his feet. "Pani Levine, what are you saying?"

"Exactly what you heard," the merchant replied coldly.

"And what are you paying me?" Chanon asked in a strangled voice.

"Ninety-eight kopecks, and I'm being generous. Grain is down now," Levine said calmly.

"Pani Levine," Chanon said pitifully, "you want me to lose money?" He longed to pierce him with a knife. Robber! he wanted to scream. You big fat robber!

"I'm not going to take a loss either," Levine said dryly, turning to leave.

"Add a little something," Chanon pleaded. Anyone but Levine could have heard the tears in his voice. Levine returned to the bin, rolled up the sleeves of his black coat again, and reached down to the bottom. "All right. You have two more kopecks—an even ruble. When you stick to somebody, you're like tar!"

"You're not giving me more?"

Levine scowled and failed to answer. His face frightened Chanon. If Chanon did anything, Levine would refuse to buy from him. With a glance at the hayloft where the cheap grain lay, Chanon gathered up his strength and tore the words from his mouth. "Of course, for you. . . . When will you take it?"

"I'll send my men up with drays at four o'clock."

"Good," Chanon agreed, looking up at the hayloft with trepidation. Just as the merchant was about to leave he cast his little black eyes around the bin. "But," he warned, "don't try to palm off any of the cheap seed on me. You people love to do that."

Chanon turned white, and to keep the merchant from guessing what was on his mind he began to swear. "I? May God keep me safe from such things. What are you saying?" Then, sensing that the merchant could read his mind, and anxious to dispel even the slightest suspicion, he forced himself to blurt out, "Here! You can even take my key. Keep it yourself until four o'clock."

Levine was pleased. "Wouldn't hurt at all. You're an honest man, but business, you know—business!"

"With the greatest of pleasure! With the greatest of pleasure!" Chanon cried out, sick with despair that he had ever proposed such a thing. His face burned, his temples pounded, and only the most violent effort kept him from screaming, Murder! Murder! Murder!

With trembling hands he locked the door, removed the key, and with a smile that could pierce a rib he turned to Levine. "Now the key is yours."

"Fine, fine," Levine said, hiding the key deep in his pocket.

"But, Pani Levine," Chanon said tearfully, "just try not to be late. Sometimes we need things in the bin. . . ." But Levine was gone. Chanon heaped reproaches on himself. Idiot, he thought, idiot! What did you do? You made yourself a pauper. Where will you get the *cheder* money now?

Chanon wrung his hands, seeing spots before his eyes. Remaining by the barn, he began to look for some way to get back in. But it was closed off on every side, except for a long narrow window without a pane. He stared at this little window, measuring it with his eye. He wondered if he could get himself through it. But it was impossible. Thin as he was, he was still too big for that tiny window.

At two o'clock Shloimke came back from *cheder*. "Well, Papa, are you giving the *rebbe* money tomorrow?"

Chanon did not answer. He narrowed his eyes and, deep in thought, stared at Shloimke.

"Papa, why are you looking at me like that?" Shloimke asked, laughing uneasily. He shoved his cap down and without looking at his father spoke again. "Well, tell me, will you have it?"

"Shloimke! You want to do something clever?"

"What?"

"Come into the yard. I want to tell you something."

Wondering, Shloimke followed his father into the yard. "What is it, Papa?"

Chanon led him to the barn and, pointing to the narrow window which was not very high up, said, "Could you creep through that little window?"

"What a question!" Shloimke said happily, realizing that his own father was encouraging him to be bad.

"Then crawl in, my precious," Chanon said, feeling ashamed for both of them. "And after that, climb up to the hayloft. The sacks of cheap seed are up there, you see—"

"I know! I know! The kind you mix in with the good stuff. I saw you do it once," Shloimke cried out, proud of his knowledge.

"Don't yell, stupid boy," Chanon said angrily. "Crawl up to the hayloft, untie a sack, and pour the seeds into the grain bin. But you have to mix it well after that. Can you do it?"

"Sure, I'll mix it with a shovel."

"So creep in. But be careful."

Shloimke pulled himself up and quick as a cat disappeared through the window. Chanon stood guard, facing the street. His heart pounded as he pictured Levine coming along with the key in his hand. After five minutes he went over to the little window. "Well, what's happening?"

"I'm mixing!" Shloimke cried out happily. "I've poured in two sacks already."

Trembling, Chanon called softly through the little window, "Robber! I'll kill you. You're ruining the seeds."

"I'm mixing it all up," Shloimke yelled. "You won't be able to tell the difference."

Well, thought Chanon, a child is a child. A painful elation shot through him. He tried to calm himself. After all, two sacks are two sacks. Maybe now there'll be a profit. What can one do?

After ten minutes Shloimke was shouting through the little window, "All done, Papa!"

"Well mixed?"

"Absolutely!"

A sweating Shloimke crawled out. His cheeks, usually pale and thin, were red, and his eyes sparkled. His whole young body showed his pride in having been trusted by his father to do the job. Taking a few seeds from his pocket, he showed them to Chanon. "Good?" he asked with satisfaction.

The devil take him, Chanon thought. He's good. That murderer—doesn't trust anyone, even takes away the key. He's a thief himself.

Shloimke looked at his father in bewilderment, unable to understand what disturbed him. "Well," he said, "will you have money for the *rebbe* tomorrow?"

"Naturally, my son," his father answered with assurance. "I'm giving you five rubles tomorrow."

And the next day Shloimke flew to *cheder* with a new five-ruble note in his pocket. The teacher pinched him on the cheek and called him a good boy. In his happiness Shloimke wanted to tell him about his great accomplishment. But he remembered that his father had warned him for the love of God not to tell anyone.

So Shloimke sat himself down to learn God's Torah, holding yesterday's secret deep in his young heart, where it pressed to be let out.

But how differently the secret pressed on his father, Chanon.

Translated by Anne and Alfred Kazin

The Recluse

ABRAHAM REISEN

IN THE synagogue the evening prayers are over. The miserly assistant sexton, a scrawny Jew with a pointed black beard, has darkened all the lights but one, which is turned very low. "Oil is expensive," he growls as he turns out lamp after lamp.

The few who have remained in the synagogue are squatters, and while they resent the despotic assistant sexton who has left them in almost total darkness, they do not dare to protest. Besides, they are too lazy to study. And how can they blame the assistant? His orders to economize come from the chief sexton, whose orders, in turn, come from the treasurer himself.

The dim light suits their mood. It is a few weeks after *Succoth*. Outside the cold rain strikes monotonously on the windowpanes. The faces of Moses and Aaron, carved in wood on the altar, stare, sterile and morose. Even the leopard placed between them, which the village woodcarver had hoped would blaze with life and brightness, droops wearily, dreaming perhaps of the forests of Lebanon from which it came.

The black curtain over the Holy Ark, donated by the rich woman of the village and made from one of her leftover dress lengths, breathes upon the old synagogue with sadness and yearning. On the wall the shadows cast by the few remaining people resemble corpses returned from the grave.

Five people are usually left in the synagogue each night, besides the assistant sexton. Two of them are yeshiva students who have been studying here for the last few years and are planning to move to a richer town if they ever find the energy. One of them—called the Zelver after his birthplace—is about twenty years old, with a long thin neck and a large Adam's apple that hops in time to every word that comes out of his wide mouth. The other is the Dohlinever, a year younger. He looks older than the Zelver because he doesn't believe very strongly in washing his face, which is also covered with a thick beard. But despite these differences in appearance, the two live peaceably together. They lend each other lumps of sugar. They share their cigarettes, even though the Zelver happens to smoke more. They disagree violently, however, about definitions of heaven. The Zelver says heaven is really here on earth, but not in the way it is usually imagined, in grossly material terms: the Messianic bull and Leviathan, he says, are merely symbols. Paradise, to quote Maimonides, is only for the spirit, and the spirit raises itself to the Seventh Heaven. But the Dohlinever, who is rather more practical, thinks that Paradise is for the body as well, and that the wild bull and whale are not symbols but solid facts. When their quarrel flames to real intensity, they smoke a cigarette together and thus come to some accord.

The third resident of the synagogue is the Recluse. He is a little over forty, and there are silver hairs twining through his thick beard. He became a recluse not through piety but from a desire for freedom. Or so he once told the Dohlinever.

"A man," he explained, "should not wear a yoke. He should be able to feel that he is always alive, and he can feel this only when he is free from the burden of labor. I realized as much when I was thirty. Now my only regret is for the years I lost keeping a store. Not only my clothes, but my spirit as well, stank of herring and oil in those days."

The Dohlinever was not too pleased with this explanation. "Suppose all men wanted to live as freely as you, what would the world come to?"

"Little fool," said the Recluse, laughing. "Who told you the world must come to something?"

Now the Dohlinever was truly distressed. "What do you mean—after all—the world! It's such a beautiful world." But he had no chance to argue it through with the Recluse, who was skilled in dialectic and could quote pages of Aristotle and Plato, of whom the Dohlinever knew almost nothing.

These profound discussions would always cost the Dohlinever a cigarette, for the Recluse, though not a regular smoker, had to have one after a sharp exchange. The Dohlinever would call over the Zelver, who acted as the communal tobacco pouch, and say, "Treat the Recluse to a cigarette."

Rolling the tobacco in a piece of paper, the Recluse would philosophize good-naturedly. "You say the world would not come to anything. True, true. But what of it? You think, children, that this is the first world that ever existed? There have been thousands of worlds already—read the books they've written. And they knew something too. Even more than our rabbi."

His free-thinking stabbed the two yeshiva students to the heart, but they never betrayed him. Somehow they felt pity for the Recluse and from time to time would give him a baked potato, a glass of tea, a cigarette.

The fourth inhabitant of the synagogue is called Yankel the Dog. A boy of eighteen, he wandered into town several years ago, and no one knows who his parents are or where he comes from. Terribly lazy, he idles about day after day and has finally taken the bench near the door as his bed.

At night other people appear. First, Chaim the teacher, a man who has lost his job and looks it. Despair itself. He stands near the pulpit, musing for a while, rouses himself, approaches the assistant sexton and asks for a pinch of snuff. The assistant glares at him but complies. Chaim the teacher sniffs, sneezes, and, his strength renewed, continues to the corner where the Zelver, the Dohlinever, and the Recluse are talking.

About seven o'clock Chieneh the widow appears with her apple basket. She is the only woman who is permitted to sell in the synagogue. Standing near the entrance, she eyes the emptiness of the place, thinking wryly, The luck I'll find here! She goes over to the oven and, feeling the cold of the white tiles, retreats in disappointment.

She smiles again. "Imagine, not to be able to warm up a bit even in the synagogue!" As the assistant sexton comes over she asks him familiarly, "What's the story, why is the oven so cold?"

"After all," he jokes, "why shouldn't you donate a wagonload of wood? They say you have plenty of money."

"Of course, I'm rich. Why not?"

The assistant sexton, a widower, scratches the back of his neck lustily. "The devil only knows—if I were sure you had money I'd court you myself."

"Well, are you going to buy something?"

"It's too expensive."

"Take some. For you I'll sell it cheaper."

He selects three spoiled apples from the basket. "And what, for example, would you charge for these?"

"You've picked the biggest apples, but since it's you—a kopeck."

"You're as expensive as a druggist," he complains. "Three tiny apples for a kopeck? And a groschen wouldn't do?"

The widow swears she can't.

"Just as you say," and he begins to put back the apples.

She thrusts another little one into his hand. "Here, now you have four."

He smiles. "In that case, make it five."

The widow hunts for a fifth little apple and hands it to him. "You've picked my bones bare," she says, groaning.

The Zelver points out Chieneh to the Dohlinever. "Look, the apples have come."

"They cost so much!"

"What's the difference?" says the Zelver stubbornly. "After all, we're no more than human."

"All right, buy some. I'll pay half."

The Recluse sighs quietly and walks over to the woman. His large eyes look straight at her. Their eyes meet. Abashed, she lowers hers.

The Zelver bargains for ten apples for two kopecks and returns with them to the Dohlinever. The Recluse remains alone, face to face, with the widow. "It's so late," he murmurs.

"What can one do?" she answers quietly. "One wants to sell."

"Yes," the Recluse says and looks at her more tenderly. "Selling . . . I understand." Instinctively he raises his eyes to the balcony where the women sit during services. "It's dark up there," he says as if to himself.

"What did you say?"

"I mean," he stammers, "it's completely dark up there, in the women's section."

"Why do you mention it?" the widow wonders.

"I only mean . . . they skimp so. A lamp should be burning there too. It's always so dark there at night." He looks about him. The assistant sexton is sitting in a dark, remote corner, chewing on his apple. The Zelver and the Dohlinever have also withdrawn to a corner and are sharing their apples. Chaim the teacher, his head propped on a bookrest, is snoring loudly. Yankel the Dog has left. The Recluse stands rooted to the spot, gazing at the window, and thinks, And why not?

The widow senses something. Shyly she tugs her kerchief tighter over her head and turns to leave.

"You're going already?" he stammers.

"What can one do? One must go."

"Far?"

"Yes, almost to the cemetery."

"A pity." He sighs. "Such a long way to go." Again he looks up at the women's section, where the little windows beckon with their dark eyes.

"Good night," calls the widow and leaves with her basket.

The Recluse stares after her for a long time and then returns with a sigh to the students. "What do you think that woman wants here anyway?" he asks.

"She wants to sell apples," answers the Dohlinever.

"And I"—the Recluse smiles oddly—"suspect it's for something else."

"You mean she comes to steal?" asks the Dohlinever hesitantly.

"Who knows—" replies the Recluse, stopping in the middle of his sentence. He walks away, over to the window, where his eyes follow the road to the cemetery.

The two young men bring him an apple. "Eat."

As if shaken from a dream he turns from the window. "Thanks."

Eating the apple calms him. He speaks quietly. "Once we were talking about the way of the world," he begins, wiping the moisture of the frozen apple from his mustache. "The way of the world is a deep secret, and not only the way of the world but of each man. Every man is a universe and his way a secret." He looks at them and laughs cheerfully.

Chaim the teacher snores heavily behind the bookrest. "Some snoring," remarks the Zelver.

"Let him be," says the Recluse amiably. "Happy is he who sleeps. In fact, I think I'll rest a bit. Somehow I feel very tired."

As he speaks he goes over to a corner bench, takes off his coat, makes a pillow out of it, and stretches out lengthwise.

In a few minutes he is asleep. In his dream he sees the apple woman.

He reaches out his arms and grasps a bookrest that stands near his head.

At first the bookrest sways back and forth, but soon it settles into balance and stands quietly, clasped by the sleeping man.

Translated by Sarah Zweig Betsky

Mazel Tov

I. M. WEISSENBERG

THE TOWN is ablaze: the rabbi is sinking rapidly—and it soon becomes clear that the doors of heaven are closed.

Heart-rending cries pierce the air. In the doorways of stores pale women stand weeping and look quietly and intensely toward the end of the street. Chave Gittel, who sells pots and pans, runs along excitedly, her face flushed. She meets another woman, whispers violently, waves her hands. Hirshl the teacher hurries by, his stringy neck protruding, his hands in his back pockets, his sharp elbows sticking out like the wings of a fleshless goose almost ready to fly. A small schoolboy, with tiny feet and flaming cheeks, runs after him.

"To the synagogue! To the synagogue!"

The synagogue overflows. Teachers and pupils from all the schools have poured together into one mass.

A Jew, covered with a red shawl, stands before the altar and with outstretched, imploring hands recites the *Tfila l'Mosha* in a whining voice, line by line. The crowd replies with such sorrow and dismay that the children watch with open mouths and staring eyes. Near the wall a man hides his face in the prayer book, sighs bitterly, raises his eyes to the ceiling and closes them once more. He remains motionless, his neck stretched out, like Isaac at the sacrifice. All are praying, repeating prayers; the rabbi's name has been applied to prayers over and over again, his initials placed before each sentence. The crowd prays on and on.

In the rabbi's yard men trample one another. Plain people, shoemakers, tailors—all stand staring. Young Hasidim pace back and forth, their dangling sashes tripping their feet, scarcely talking to one another. Teachers and pupils return from the synagogue. The teachers stand aside, quietly chatting. Schoolchildren, playful youngsters, climb the fence that surrounds the rabbi's garden. They crawl over the roof of the icehouse and stretch out upon it, lengthwise and crosswise, with their faces turned toward the windows of the rabbi's house. Sextons and disciples run in and out, confused. Young men trip over their feet. When one of them is asked what is new, he throws out his hands, sighs, and hurries away. A large crowd of women stands in a corner, grimacing at one another and holding their aprons, ready to cry.

Suddenly a wail rises from the house. The crowd stirs. The doctor calls out, Pray to the Lord! Someone shouts from the window. The crowd remains stupefied, the women break loose, cutting their way through the men, who make way for them. With a yell the women rush into the street, where still other women join them. On the way to the market place they break into two groups, one running toward the synagogue and the other toward the cemetery.

In the market place the men mill about like lost, silent sheep. The news comes. The crowd stands frozen. Trembling lips whisper, "Blessed be Thy judgment! Blessed be Thy judgment!"

And now the crowd is left with nothing at all, neither hope nor consolation. One thing remains: to bemoan the rabbi's wife and children. The people stumble to one side, abandoning themselves to God's will and the judgment they take for love.

The sextons run to the post office, carrying long written telegrams. The windows of the room in which the rabbi lies flame up and a thin cold rain drops from the dull sky. Women put up their collars and huddle their heads into shoulders. The teachers retreat into the large red shawls that bundle up their necks; their faces grow bluer, sunken. Lips tremble, eyes quiver.

At night the Hasidim begin to arrive from the nearby villages, and toward morning there is a vast commotion, the streets get no rest from the cabs and carriages. By dinnertime the stores are closed and the whole town gathers in the rabbi's yard.

Suddenly a cry is heard at the door: Open! Open! The coffin appears, the crowd begins to move.

They go to the synagogue to pray for the dead. There is not even room for a pin. Men stand close against one another; men and women together, and over the tables and the altar, everywhere, it is dense and black. The burning lights of the chandeliers throw their heat. Faces grow red, shiny with sweat; the air is hot, muggy, suffocating. The coffin is placed before the altar, and the Hasidim lift themselves on one another's shoulders, wishing to see over the mass of heads. They hang in the air, one on top of the other, all together. Then, quiet: all eyes turn to the center. Soon a thin little voice is heard: "Too great a penance you have taken, O Lord, for our sins! You have torn away our King of the Torah, you have taken away the tool without which we cannot build."

Again it becomes quiet, and among the women and girls, who stand with kerchiefs on their heads that partially cover their eyes, a suppressed sob breaks out.

The coffin is moved; the crowd begins to push through both doors and through the open windows.

The street is already blocked. A chain of Hasidim winds along one side while on the other the crowd accompanying the coffin stretches like a long belt of thousands of faces. All the way prayers are said. The son and heir follows the coffin, resting his forehead upon it and hiding his face in his hands.

On the blessed spot, among the trees, the grave is already dug and the coffin ready. While the rabbi is lowered into the open grave, the crowd bids him a final *mazel tov,* and then turns to the son: *"Mazel tov,* Rabbi! *Mazel tov."*

The grave is covered; the new rabbi says the prayer for the dead.

And a consolation, a new hope, begins to blossom. Faces lighten again, eyes glisten with new love, and everyone gathers around the rabbi to see the Divine Presence settling on his pale face.

In the cemetery all is quiet. The trees sway softly, in prayer.

Translated by Irving Howe and Eliezer Greenberg

Father and the Boys

I. M. WEISSENBERG

SHLOMO THE FATHEAD—so his wife, Channah Leah, calls him, and with good reason. Because on Friday nights, when all the other Jews are on their way to the synagogue, that's when he takes the pot of *tsimess* between his knees, summons his two sons, and all three dig in with wooden ladles, their faces flaming as though they were Turks, stuffing their snouts till there's nothing left for Channah Leah's Sabbath breakfast. On Sunday this same Shlomo the Fathead grabs pack and stick and, without even blessing himself, marches off to the village, together with his younger son, Moishele Brute. He wouldn't dare rouse the older boy, Pinchusel. This one, like a regular soldier—his mother actually calls him soldier boy—lies pillowed on a trough, on a couch made of chairs, covered with the boards used for cutting noodles, and fills the small gray room with his snoring. His naked elbows are flung over his head, and his nostrils gape at the ceiling.

"Let him sleep," says Shlomo to his younger son, laying a finger to his lips, as if to say, the hell with him. "C'mon, let's get out of here and go to the village. You'll have his share."

With pack and stick, the two breadwinners sneak out of the house on tiptoe, so quietly that Channah Leah, in her white nightcap, face buried in the pillow, does not hear the creak of the door.

All is quiet in the house. Day is breaking, the bluish dawn comes in through the windows, touching up the walls. Shlomo and son are on the loose.

"Look, Pa." Moishele Brute holds up a lacerated bare foot and hops on the other. "Look—I cut myself on a stone." He displays a bloody wound on a dirty sole.

"The devil take you!" says his father. "Serves you right. That's what you get for running around."

Moishele Brute tightens his belt and marches off with the old man, feeling that it is he, and not his brother Pinchus, who is his father's right-hand man. In his vest pocket he carries a thimble and a paper of needles, apprentice equipment, while his father carries the master's tools, measuring tape, scissors, and chalk. Moishele envies him. Just wait till he gets the hang of it from following the old man—then he'll get up of a Sunday morning and run off to the village. All alone, no one will know what's become of him. His mother will throw a fit—who knows, maybe her son got drowned, maybe the devils hauled him away to the woods and married him off to a calf? Who can tell what happened to him? While he, Moishele Brute, spends the week in the village, eating roast potatoes and sour milk, and does not return to the town till the following Friday night. The Sabbath candles are already shining through the windows, the women look out to see him come all sweaty and dusty from the road, and they turn their eyes to follow him, thinking, What a fine wage-earner that lad is! And then, as calmly as you please, he drops in on his mother, Channah Leah, throws off his pack, hands her five rubles, and says, "Here, Mama. It's for you." And what a Sabbath he'll have at home, with his mother shoving food at him, one dish after the other, while he acts so quiet and refined, never a great eater. . . .

Moishele's eyes glow with joy. He looks about him on the sandy road as he and his father climb the hill beyond the village, from which they can see the green fields and the far blue woods spreading out before them. The sun is rising and the eastern sky flares up in broad bands of red and brown. Moishele puffs out his cheeks and asks his father whether the village they are going to has caught fire during the night.

"Dumbhead," says his father. "Can't you see, the sun is rising?"

Moishele takes another look and catches sight of the sun, tucked behind a blue cloud bank. Rays of light, like long horns, point across the sky. Why, yes, his father is right.

How early it is! The stillness of night has not yet lifted, a dark silence lies over the distant woods. Deep in the valley he sees a pair of oxen and a peasant in a broad straw hat, his shirt hanging outside his trousers. There is something mysterious about the peasant and the oxen, standing under the blue sky as though someone had put them there for no apparent purpose. High against the cloud bank that circles the eastern horizon a bird rises, twittering and dipping its wings in and out of the clouds, and pours sweet music through the morning light. Higher and higher rises the bird until it becomes a black dot, and its chirping, coming from a great distance, can no longer be heard. In that very distance, above which the bird is now soaring, Moishele and his father will arrive two hours later. Looking down from the sky, the bird can already see the thatched roofs, whitewashed walls, and single windows that give on the sandy road. The bird is there already, but they won't be there till later.

How fine that will be, thinks Moishele. His father will put on the innkeeper's prayer shawl and phylacteries and say his prayers, standing at the window, and he too will say his prayers. Then the innkeeper will give them pot cheese to eat and a hunk of black bread—ah, what a life!

His father interrupts him, brushing against his sleeve. "Did you hear, Moishele, did you hear Mama this morning? Was she groaning?"

"Why should she groan?" asks Moishele, regarding his father with his mouth open and his lips puffed out.

"Answer me, did you hear her groan?"

"Groan?"

"Go on, you dumb ox!" He pushes Moishele away. Again, with a side-long glance, he asks, "Don't you know what I mean?"

Moishele plays dumb. He knows they are making another baby, and that his mother, Channah Leah, is expecting to drop it out of her belly any day now. But what's it to him? Let the old man think he doesn't understand such business.

They let the matter rest and go on, making tracks for the village.

"Shake a leg," says his father. "I'm a year or two older than you," says he, "and blessed be the Name, look at me!"

He takes bigger and bigger strides, his coat tails flapping against his boots. By the time he pauses on the grass to take off his boots, Moishele is so far behind he can no longer catch up. He hops after him, favoring his sore foot, and so they vanish over the fields.

Only now does Channah Leah awake. The first thing she sees when she raises her head is that the other bed has long been empty; and when she looks out the window and sees how high the sun has risen, she pictures to herself her two breadwinners striding barefoot over the fields, their caps rolled up on their foreheads, their faces reddened, and he, the old man, carrying his boots on his shoulder. She looks at her son, who is still snoring, at his healthy red face, the lips blowing, the nostrils flaring. A regular steam engine. God Almighty, she thinks, what have you wished on me? But when she sees his closed eyes she reflects, more calmly now, What a blessing it is that this bully sleeps at times. A blessing for the whole wide world.

For this is how Pinchusel operates when he is awake. In the morning he stuffs both pockets with rolls and, heigh-ho! off to the square, to his gang, the sweet doves. Or else he grabs a horse in broad daylight, right out in the market place, and gallops off with it, just like that, to bathe it in the river or pasture it all day in the field behind the mill. And never mind whose horse it is. Let someone come to look for it, or the boys run up to point him out—There he is! That's him!—Pinchus doesn't bat an eye. He stands there gazing out into the pasture. Not until he's in trouble for sure—say, the policeman is coming—does he get a move on, and then he calmly mounts the horse and takes off, free as the wind, and go do him something! If it pleases him, he'll bring the horse right back to the spot where he lifted it, even after the town has lost hope of seeing it again, and in all corners the cry is up—Pinchus has stolen a horse!

One day he played a dirty trick. This was on a peasant girl who, together with some other peasants, was coming from the priest, to whom they had gone with the first sprouts of their gardens to have them blessed for a good harvest. Pinchus grabbed the girl's bunch of greens and gave her a few good whacks besides. This was a little too much, and they all said, Now he'll catch it, wait, you'll see, he's not long for the light of day. But when his father threw it up to him—What's this, molesting girls in the middle of the street?— Pinchus shot right back at him—And what did you do before you married Ma? That's how he answered him. Father and son flew at each other like two goats locking horns.

But Pinchusel knows how to get around his father. He doesn't give a hang for Channah Leah, but he's not one for staying in bad with the old man.

With God's help, a carnival had once come to town. Pinchus took on new life. No sooner had the carnival boss, the troupe of peasant girls, and the dark woman in braids, who looked like a gypsy—no sooner had they set up the center pole in the middle of the market place than Pinchus was on hand, helping them fasten down the sides of the tent and hitching the wooden horses to the painted chariots. That Sunday, when the peasants from the neighborhood showed up with their girls, the carrousel was rigged up and all set to go.

Pinchus had already found favor in the boss's eyes. If he had joined the company—who knows?—he might also have had a peasant girl for a wife—he might even have started a carnival of his own. But something kept him from joining the troupe, although the boss urged him, and the oldest of the girls, a brunette with red lips, winked at him and looked him right in the eyes, an unmistakable invitation. All the same, he brought his father to the market place—at least let the old man see how his son rated with the carnival folk.

When Shlomo took in the round canvas top with a red flag flying from the center pole, the crowd of young men and women intermingled with the peasants from the villages and their girls with shiny parasols and blond curls standing out from under their white kerchiefs, the silks and satins hanging from the big tent and the battery of brass trumpets aimed directly at the market place, he was even more excited than his son. To think that such beauty could be found, right here in town, and at a carnival! It seemed to him that there would soon be some fine doings here, some really fine stunts.

"What's going on?" he asked his son.

"They're going to run the horses. Six cents for a horse ride, four for the chariots," Pinchus replied, precise and to the point.

Shlomo couldn't believe it: ride on wooden horses? And when he pushed deeper into the crowd and saw the horses hitched to the chariots and behind the chariots more horses, his mouth popped open.

"I helped them put it together," proudly declared his son. "Do you think they could have got it up so fast without me? Hey, Pa, do you want a ride? I can get you a ride for free. I should live so, free!"

Shlomo the Fathead gasped and smiled, and his goggling eyes were as glassy as the beads with which the satin hangings of the tent were embroidered.

"Wait," he said, glancing at his son. "Wait and we'll see." He stroked his beard.

When the shiny brass trumpets struck up a march, "Ta-ta-ta-raa! Ta-ta-ta-raa!" Shlomo could no longer contain himself, and he chimed right in, singing the march tune, which he learned on the spot, and to which, to this very day, he sings the Sabbath hymns, so that his wife, Channah Leah, bawls him out. "How can you be so shameless? Day and night, day and night, the same old tune!" But a lot Shlomo cares.

"Ta-ta-ta-raa!" sounded the trumpets, and he helped them out, "Ta-ta-ta-raa!" with his throat all puffed up, as though he would turn himself into a trumpet too. The carrousel was spinning round and round, the horses were chasing the chariots which were chasing the horses, and the hot faces and brilliant eyes of the gentile boys and girls, turning on the merry-go-round, were making Shlomo dizzy. He kept casting looks of love at his son; he was nearly out of his mind! At last the carrousel came to a stop. Pinchus led his father to a horse (with a wink at the ticket-taker's wife: this is my old man) and he himself climbed up under the canvas top to turn the crank and set the works aflying.

Shlomo's eyes were burning at the young women and the girls who were looking on, beholding the honor to which he had risen through his son. "C'mon, Pinchus!" he cried out. "Let's go!"

A bell began to ring somewhere under the satin canopy, which was decked out in white and blue beads. The passengers grabbed their tickets, mounted the horses, the womenfolk taking the chariots, and once again the trumpets sang out "Ta-ta-ta-raa!" Off flew Shlomo, round and round, together with the whole carrousel. Among all these flaming faces Shlomo's was the only Jewish one.

A gang of boys, who stood glued round the carrousel with sticks and whips in hand, at once fell to belaboring Shlomo's horse. "Giddy-app!" they cried. "Look at him ride!" Shlomo grew dizzy, his beard flew apart, streaming at either side of his face like a demolished broom, his eyes popped and sparkled, and the boys laid on, larruping his poor horse and ringing him round in laughter. Behold! Shlomo in full pursuit of a gentile girl!—she, with the tails of her babushka flapping in the wind, and he, with his venerable beard trailing over his shoulders. But no matter that the boys are laughing and shouting and walloping the wooden beast—on rides Shlomo in relentless pursuit! Or at least until his Pinchus up above turned sick from all this revolving and let heave right onto his father's head. Down over his face and beard ran a stream of everything Pinchus had eaten in the last ten years, and down came Pinchus himself, falling plop into the chariot with the peasant lass. The carrousel ground to a halt.

In utter confusion father and son ran away, with the gang of boys after them, shouting, "Shlomo the Fathead was chasing a *shiksah!*" But the Jews in the town took this accusation lightly; they knew it was just something to do with the carrousel. In fact, the shopkeepers appeared at their doors, smiling in their beards to see how Shlomo ran across the market place with his coat tails flying like a regular old devil, the Prince of Darkness himself, and after him his son, with the boys swooping down on them both.

Channah Leah, running out bravely with her arms spread wide, came to the rescue—God knows what they had been caught at, what crime or theft!—and whisked them into the house. There she learned that her Prince of Darkness had been riding the merry-go-round.

She shook her head and regarded her husband with profoundest pity: a grown man and a father, to be such a fool!

Shlomo reconsidered and saw that she was right—he really had done something foolish—so he blamed it all on his son. But Pinchus was beyond her powers. She had watched him go from bad to worse and was unable to do a thing, and on that day she completely despaired of him and admitted that no good would ever come of the boy.

Now, looking at him as he lies in bed with the sleeves of his nightshirt rolled up, she sees the soldier cropping out in his face—and she thanks God and praises Him that this murderer of hers goes to sleep sometimes. What a blessing for all Creation that is!

Channah Leah gets out of bed, throws on a shawl, and goes next door with a stove lid in her hand to fetch fire. Her neighbor lets her have a few live coals, and they fall to talking. Channah Leah pours out her heart on the subject of children, how little joy she has had in hers. And how are you coming along with the new one? asks the neighbor woman. Any day, answers Channah Leah, any day now. Actually she regrets the whole business. When she had Moishele she vowed, never again. She still remembers the time she had with him. A pair of her husband's trousers was hanging on the wall. Channah Leah ordered them taken out of her sight, and she cursed Shlomo for all she was worth—only to let herself get trapped again.

Her neighbor consoles her. God willing, she may have an easy delivery this time, and they go on talking of pregnancies and confinements, agreed that a woman's lot is a bitter one.

Channah Leah relates how, heaven protect us, she had a third child, between the first and the second, who was born the size of a six-month-old, may he rest in peace. And the neighbor woman tells her in turn how Tcheitel the kerchief-maker was sitting of a Saturday night beside a lamp at the window, sewing on a kerchief. Suddenly she saw a woman fly past the window with streaming hair, clutching a tiny baby to her bosom. It was Uta Mottel's daughter-in-law, God save us. . . .

Channah Leah spits three times and returns home.

When Pinchus wakes up she asks him to take down the *mezzuzahs* and have the scribe make sure they are all right.

She has laid in little blankets and shirts and has a clean sheet in readiness to hang over her bed. That night she would not go to sleep without putting a Bible at her head, and not her women's Bible, but Shlomo's, with the Hebrew letters.

And what do you suppose? On that very night the neighbor woman was already attending her, and at three in the morning they ran for the midwife. She gave birth to a boy with a mane of thick black hair. Not for nothing had Shlomo been anxious, as he climbed the hill, to know whether her pains had begun. He was counting on a happy Sabbath, hoping that when he returned, with God's help, on Friday, he would find his wife safely delivered.

Channah Leah lies in bed like a countess, curtained off behind a sheet, which hangs from a string, suspended from the ceiling; the sheet is covered with good-luck charms. Whenever she wants something she need only poke her nightcapped head out from behind the curtain, and it's handed to her. Her face is so much lighter, her voice softer and more tender than before. She has only one anxiety, that no harm should befall the baby, nothing of the kind, God forbid, that happened to her own unfortunate child, or the one that her neighbor told her about. She is determined not to let the child out of her arms for a moment, and when she sleeps to hold onto him with all her might and protect him with her whole body, like a good mother.

Thursday night came round. She fell asleep to the sweet thought of Shlomo's arriving the next day, and his surprise at seeing what a fine boy she had presented him with—and all without his expecting it.

She sleeps.

In her dream the Queen of Sheba comes to her with bare breasts and long hair and she is wearing a strangely shaped, old-fashioned dress, a crinoline of Turkish cut, covered in a design of flowers and eyes. The Queen of Sheba is crawling into her room through the half-open window. She keeps crawling and crawling, but she is having trouble getting through the window, the Queen is so heavy, so fat. Channah Leah is frightened; she calls out in a muffled voice and presses the child to her . . . and the poor thing will never want a better Queen of Sheba than the one she is providing him with.

Day is just breaking, the windows are turning light blue. Shlomo raps softly at the door, and Pinchus, half asleep, gets down to let him in. Shlomo enters on tiptoe, Moishele after him. He was too restless to sleep that night in town, and came running with the dawn. He sees the curtained bed and a smile appears in his eyes. Turning to his son, he nudges him and whispers, "What is it?"

"A boy," says Pinchus.

"A boy!" The smile spreads over his face.

Moishele joins in, hopping with joy. "There'll be a circumcision. And a basket of chick-peas, all for me!"

"Shut up, you brat! You'll wake Mama," says his father, giving him a poke.

"Shut up! The devil—" says Pinchus in support of his father.

"Mama must have just fallen asleep?" says Shlomo.

"No, she's been asleep all night."

"All night?" Shlomo is taken with fear. Softly, slowly, he moves up to the curtain. "Channah Leah, Channah Leah," he calls to her gently. "Channah Leah . . ."

Channah Leah goes on sleeping.

"Let me, I'll wake her," declares Moishele in a gruff voice.

"Keep still, you brat! You'll frighten her." And Shlomo silences him, a finger held between his teeth.

"Channah Leah, Channah Leah . . ."

"Huh-h-h?" A long-drawn-out murmur rises from behind the curtain.

"Channah Leah, where is the baby?"

"Oh, my God! The baby!" she cries out, bolting awake.

Shlomo, more dead than alive, plunges through the curtain. The boys stand paralyzed, staring at the sheet with glassy eyes.

"Oh, my God! The baby!" Channah Leah cries out again and lifts up the child by one hand, as if it were a dead gosling. His head dangles. Her eyes bulging with fear, she takes his face in her hands and begins to tear at it.

"May you die of cholera!" Shlomo pronounces over her in blessing and brings both fists down on her head. "Channah Leah'le, you butcher, you've already murdered one son of mine!" he cries, seeing that the child is not breathing, that it is lifeless and cold, like a chunk of dough. He steps away, his head lowered.

Channah Leah redoubles her outcries, and Shlomo, like a bear hunter, with sturdy, long strides, paces the floor, back and forth, back and forth, his glowing eyes on the curtain. The two boys are hiding in a corner and thanking God that they are in no way to blame.

Before long the neighbor women come running into the house to find out what is the matter.

Only now does Channah Leah really set up a wailing. "Oh, what a misfortune has fallen on me! It was the Queen of Sheba—the Queen of Sheba came crawling in through the window. Such great big tits she had. She smothered my child with her tits—"

"Tits!" cries Shlomo. "Who needs bigger ones than yours? To the rabbi, quick—I want a divorce! May you catch the first plague!"

"Shlomoshu, my dear one, what do you want from me?" she cries, turning her tears on him, but it doesn't work.

Later, when they came to take away the child, Channah Leah was obliged to remove the curtain, make the bed, and accompany her husband to the rabbi.

"Rabbi," pleads Shlomo, "she has ruined me. Two sons of mine she's killed. Two sons—"

"And you, woman, if you please, what have you to say?" asks the rabbi.

"Two sons, woe is me!" she wails in a most pathetic mama-voice.

"What do you want from her, Shlomo? A woman—she certainly wanted them to live," observes the rabbi.

"Father, you're coming home!" Pinchus marches into the rabbi's house with a thunderclap, nearly smashing the door, followed by Moishele, growling.

The rabbi throws up his hands in self-defense.

"So you're going to divorce my mother?" Pinchus bangs his fist down on the table. "Go on home, or I'll split you open!"

"There, you see, Rabbi! Go ahead and raise children," says Shlomo, pointing first to his son and then to Channah Leah's belly. Suddenly he rushes out, slamming the door.

"And you, Mama,"—Pinchus takes a coin out of his pocket—"here's a forty-cent piece. Go on home and make supper."

Channah Leah went home, dodging along the fence in the alley, for fear of meeting people. She had been shamed enough. All the way home, Moishele kept bothering her to put up the big pot, not the little one, and to fill it to the top with potatoes. The last time he had eaten was in town. So Channah Leah went home.

On the following Friday, Shlomo was again sitting with the pot of *tsimess* between his knees, and the two boys, the bulls, were snorting away beside him. All of them, with red, sweaty faces, like Turks, and huge wooden ladles in their hands. And once again Channah Leah was complaining that they never leave anything over for breakfast on the Sabbath.

But later the same night, when the candles were burning in the Menorahs, and Shlomo and his sons were sitting at the table, singing "The Sons and Sons of Sons," Channah Leah lost herself, staring at Pinchusel with tender eyes, and somehow, though she couldn't have said why, he seemed so much dearer to her. She was unaware of the tear that rolled down her cheek and splashed into her plate of bean soup. But Shlomo gave her a murderous glance: eighty-eight plagues on her. With four sons like these two he could have conquered the world. Sick of looking at her, he turned to the boys and gave them the sign: Let's go! And all three burst out singing the carrousel march, to the words of a Sabbath hymn.

Translated by Isaac Rosenfeld

Revenge

EXTRACTS FROM A STUDENT'S DIARY

ZALMAN SCHNEOUR

WHEN THE telegram—that frightful telegram—came from my village I was struck dumb. I could focus only on my dead father's portrait, hanging on the wall of my room. For several minutes I couldn't even remember what it was.

I read the wire over again, dropped it mechanically on the floor, stood mechanically over it. Suddenly I grabbed at a pile of books, flung them away, and ripped some newspapers apart, moaning all the while, short, throttled moans, as if a snake were biting my heart.

. . . I am lying on my bed, completely dressed. My room reeks of Valerian drops, my German landlady with her pale sharp nose stands at the window, whispering to a man whose bald spot refracts the light. His naked head nods heavily, his puffed lips murmur, "Horrible, horrible . . ."

On the second day, at noon, I arose, changed, washed my face, and sent for wine. When I had drunk so much that my eyes turned muddy I announced to my landlady that I was going home for several weeks. She was to keep my room for me.

I watched the mountains from the train window. The gray heads of the hills, their foreheads black and creased, jostled one another, danced away from me, and I thought how wrong the poets were when they called nature a "loving mother." No, these white-topped mountains had stood sedately, looking just as they did now, while over there—fire, murder, torture. The Rhine had gone on its way, rumbling and spuming, while people were being robbed and strangled, nails were being driven into skulls. The whole world was a sort of kennel. An angry God threw his children, the little weaklings as well as the great ruffians, into this kennel and locked them up forever. "Here," He said, "here are some pretty toys. Take these hills and forests and rivers; there is a moon, a sun, some stars—play, my darlings, and split your heads!"

The telegram trembled in my hand. "Pogrom. House looted and burned. Brother killed. Mother seriously wounded. Take courage and come home." Signed by a distant relative. Probably himself beaten, robbed, driven by disaster. Otherwise how could he have sent me such a telegram, unaware of its effect upon me?

The roaring train wheels drove the text of the wire from my thoughts. The wheels pounded and turned, smashing, scattering into fragments the message, the woods and the rivers through which the train raced, all into fragments.

A German, his beard and mustache neatly trimmed, had been sitting near me. He edged away, inspected me with astonishment, and smoked his cigar. He mouthed at it with fat lips—puff, puff, puff.

We have traveled far beyond the borderline. No more mountains and valleys, no more rivers foaming through black rocks. Cold-blooded, stupid firs shook their wet evergreen heads. Why were they shaking? Perhaps with pity for me? Whatever the reason, how could it help? This time too I had to cross the frontier illegally. Three years before I had stolen over on my way to Switzerland, escaping to a university and away from military service. Returning, I again had to sneak across, out of reach of the police. I was guided by a sallow Jew who overcharged me, fleeced me. "Over there they're beating us, and here you rob me, scum!" But I had said nothing.

Days had merged into years. For three years I had been gnawing like a mouse among the dusty books. When I wanted to torment myself I would lower my head softly into my arms and my fantasy would summon at once my dearest childhood memory, which I guarded in my heart as closely as a golden chest. The Vilner Gaon's picture, framed in black, floats toward me from the white east wall of our house. A handsome Jew, soft-eyed, white-bearded, he sits in his prayer shawl and phylacteries and writes with a goose quill. One Sabbath, when I was a small boy, a very small boy, I began scribbling away with a feather, looking up at the picture, imitating the way the "old Jew" wrote. My father scolded me lovingly: Jews must not write on the Sabbath, only Christians. I was shamed and hid behind my mother, thought a bit, then quietly tugged at her apron and pointed at the Vilner Gaon's picture. "Mama, why is that old Jew writing today? Why is he allowed to?" My father, blessed be his memory, laughed and stroked his beard, and my mother hugged and kissed me, kissed me and said nothing.

Whenever I remembered all this my heart grew serene and gentle, like the first snowfall. How could I imagine that this picture no longer existed, that it had been burned together with our house? I'm almost at home, here is our village, our house. I open the door, and my mother stands before me, her face radiant with pride under her black headdress. My brother Moishele sits over his books, as always, his curly black hair falling across his eyes. Before the greetings, before the kisses, before anything, I run straight to the room with the white picture in its black frame. Yes, he's here! The Vilner Gaon sits, just as he always does, writing with his goose quill.

The train had stopped at a station. A tall wrinkled Jewish woman with a face yellow as parchment entered the coach and tried to sell me milk, thrusting a blue bottle under my nose. I sprang up as if she had slapped me. "I don't want any," I screamed, and my whole body trembled. Her face dropped and she escaped quickly.

I ran after her and caught her as she went down the train steps. "Forgive me," I shouted after her, and my throat throbbed. "You understand? A pogrom—you understand? A murdered brother, a wounded mother, you understand?"

She faced me, shaking, retreated, eyed me again, retreated, looked. People were gathering around the coach.

The train went on, the fir trees had vanished, and now desolate fields stretched endlessly. It seemed that the train stood in one spot, and I would never reach home. Other Lithuanian Jews, probably from our district, were sitting in the coach. I wanted to talk to them, to hear the details of our pogrom. I controlled myself and kept my seat.

I forced myself to think again of my slain Moishele, of my mother. But only foolish and petty things crept through my mind. Once more the Vilner Gaon's picture, once more my childhood toys, my childhood memories.

I was eight years old. My father was already ill at that time, and my mother took me along with her to the *shochet* to have a hen killed. It was an autumn night, silent and dreary in our village; the mud underfoot spurted, and the bound hen in my mother's basket clucked as if she knew where we were dragging her.

The slaughterhouse was in a yard, and in the light of the yard lamp the young hen's golden-yellow feathers gleamed. As the slaughterer grabbed her she began screeching; he twisted her little head between her wings, flicked several golden feathers from her long reddish neck, and quietly, piously closing his eyes, made the blessing over her.

"Amen." My mother gently nudged me.

"Amen," I answered through shivering lips. It was the first time in my life I had seen it. Something short and metallic had coldly glowed, after that fingers had tightened, and then . . . wings were suddenly clapping.

Going home, it was quiet and dark; the mud spurted once more under our feet, but now the hen in the basket made no sound.

That night I couldn't fall asleep, thinking and thinking about the hen that hadn't known yesterday she was to be slaughtered today; thinking about human beings who, it seemed, must undergo the same fate. My childish heart wept without tears.

As I remembered, my blood grew fevered, and in place of the slaughtered hen I saw slaughtered people, people near and dear to me, slain. I tried to evoke them in stronger, clearer colors, as though intent on self-torture. The harder my heart ached and pounded, the more elaborate grew the frightful pictures I drew in my head. My teeth clenched with the effort.

. . . Our house is in flames. The Vilner Gaon's picture is blazing, his snow-white beard turns black, my father's holy books, guarded by my mother like the eyes in her head—they too are burning. And "they" are dragging my Moishele by his feet through the mud. He strains and twists, shouting, "Mama! Mama!" Here comes one of them, his eyes drunk with brandy and murder, a knife—no—not a knife—an ax! The ax glistens, swoops through the curly black hair. The crack of a human skull. A choked, weak groan . . . and a stream of blood flows lazily, braids itself through the curly hair, soaks into the earth, into the mud. It is a serpent, a reddish-black snake. Over there they are stabbing my mother. A blunt rusted knife slashes her breast, and something red, thick, snakes along her white apron.

Cold sweat covered my brow; everything about me swirled in mist. I felt my limbs swelling; each hair on my head seemed swollen and unbelievably painful.

But I will not remain silent. I return, and I shall take revenge. And what a vengeance it shall be! Set fire to their houses secretly, at night. Set fire to them, and in the midst of the tumult crack brains, shoot, strangle whole households. Smash everything! Cram their throats with broken glass! Butcher their flesh and drown it in acid! Yes, *smite the*

Philistines, smite their very souls! Damned along with them, but not accept my mother's lot.

The wheels snatched at my wild thoughts, caught them on the rails, sprayed the pieces upon forests and fields.

I shook with cold as the train approached my station on the third day of my journey. I put on my greatcoat and overshoes, but they could not stop my teeth from drumming.

The locomotive crawled into the small white station, coughing and snorting, an exhausted elephant. My teeth still clacking, I lowered myself softly to the platform. The platform was just as I had left it, and the waiting room was a waiting room. Porters scrambled, dragging baggage; Jews of every sort shoved toward the ticket window. Outside the waiting room the horses stood as always, Jewish horses, with sunken, mangy flanks. Drivers wrangled, cursing each other's ancestors, fought over passengers. Wasn't it exactly as it had always been?

And now I was sitting in the wagon of a tall dark Jew. The horse plodded through the usual mud up to its neck, scattering dirty black spray. My little suitcase danced crazily, banged at me—everything just as it used to be. Here was the blue pointed roof of the church. The early winter sun began to set, glazing the roof with cold fire. The church was a church. Nothing at all had happened—nothing. I was coming home. My mother would prepare supper; the first course would be chopped liver—yes, chopped liver with chicken fat . . .

"Where are you going, young man?" The driver's coarse voice suddenly reminded me that we were still far from the village, still following the field track through half-frozen, empty potato fields.

"Take you to the inn, young man?"

"Take me? Why, take me to Chayeh, to Chayeh Mendel's." My answer ripped out and floated over the field. I stood up in the wagon and clutched at the driver's hairy collar. My own words choked me. "Tell me, Reb Jew, how is she now, Chayeh Mendel's? Is she well again? Yes? Take me to her, that's where I'm going. To Chayeh Mendel's."

The driver halted his horse and dropped the reins. He eyed me anxiously and stammered, "Chayeh Mendel's? Bless us, then you're—that is—does it mean then that you're hers—her son, the student from abroad? Is that who you are? Greetings—ah, but after all it's not permitted, since you're a mourner."

"What!" I screamed and felt that the very next minute I would cover the naked fields with my cries.

"May long years be ours. A pious woman. Poor thing, how she suffered in the hospital. Buried just yesterday."

I sat in the wagon and glared at the driver.

"She kept waiting for you, wanted to see you before she died. And about your Moishele—I suppose you've heard about him?"

Without warning I rose and pressed my face against the driver's sheepskin coat, nuzzled against him, and wept bitterly, the first tears since the telegram. I sobbed like a child, pleading, protesting, mumbling meaningless words.

"Reb Jew, Reb Jew, Chayeh Mendel's is my mother. My mother!"

I fell silent. Warm, wormlike tears kept threading down my cheeks. The driver was distressed; he climbed down from the wagon and puttered about, trying to please me, like an adult with a weeping child. He rearranged the straw, prodded my suitcase into better position, all the while trying to show me the pity in his eyes. Finally his head dropped, his beard quivered. His voice was broken, hacked by sorrow.

"May God bless us all. Had a carriage . . . smashed to bits. So now there's a wagon stuffed with straw. Thank God, rescued the horse. Besides that—well, what is there to say? My daughter—what is there to say—my unfortunate daughter. Shamed, dirtied."

In the middle of that bleak field under that cold winter sky we both began to sob—he standing on the ground, whip in hand, and I sitting in the wagon; he, a Jew over forty, with a wrinkled face and long graying beard, and I, young, very young, with clean-shaven cheeks. He wiped his eyes with his thick, callused, tarred hand, I with my respectable, refined white hand, accustomed only to paper and to the smooth covers of books. Both of us wept quietly, almost inwardly, and neither knew which of us should be the first to comfort the other. And the sun shone calmly in its blood-smeared setting, and the winter sky coldly stared down on the desolate field.

Darkness fell as we entered the village. All the way in, the driver's cracked, torn voice had told how they had ruined him; worst of all, ruined his daughter. He told how they had fallen upon the village, devastated it; how the sheriff himself—may he be cursed—directed and helped them.

"Soon you'll see the chimneys that they—a pestilence on their heads —have left us." The driver's voice trailed off with these words; he turned to me and wanted to smile. The smile became a gnashing of teeth, and he began to beat his horse with all his strength, the whip-handle flailing its dirty, collapsed flanks.

Then he was silent.

My tear-filled eyes saw only his mute, bowed back, a thin Jewish back in a big sheepskin, belted with a knotted rope.

The driver brought me to a small filthy inn that had miraculously survived, along with twenty or so other houses. At the inn they discovered who I was and invited me to start the mourning rituals. I didn't even bother to answer them, washed my tear-streaked face, and escaped. The innkeeper, a short, sharp-eyed Jew, watched me leave. As I disappeared he shrugged his regret.

The ruined, muddy, half-frozen streets were dead, deathly silent. In their cremation the streets had lost their identities and had become a crazy sprawling community of red and white skeletons. They were skeletons of clay and tile ovens, sunk in cold ashes, black coals, ugly smoke-scorched boards and planks. Their futile, tall chimneys stretched red throats, lonely and dull, toward the gray sky and mutely begged for pity. The smoke-streaked, stark chimneys, the deserted black grates, peered out of the red ovens in the shape of great rectangular eyes, torn open by dumb fear. Or like gigantic mouths which cried without sound, "Save us."

Human shadows twisted around the chimneys, like mourners on the way to their ancestral graves, perhaps like wandering and sinful souls. One gray, bowed Jew carrying a prayer book passed me and, sighting an unfamiliar nose, scuttled off in fright, as if I were chasing him with a knife.

I recognized the chimney of our gutted house by the naked wild pear tree that grew nearby. Once we had knocked down its hard little pears and played ball with them. Now the tree stood stripped, half burned, its bark singed.

I started toward the chimney. Black, frozen coals crunched under my feet. The chimney, the half-consumed pear tree, looked at me and didn't recognize me. The oven was ajar, blackened: how many potatoes Moishele and I had roasted in it! Mother had made pancakes on it, brown, crusty pancakes. Winter evenings, home from school, I used to rub myself, warm myself, against this tiled oven; I still saw, in the air, the picture of the Vilner Gaon. Consumed by fire, it hung there still. If I had returned eight days ago I would have met wholeness: the walls, the shining yellow furniture, the Vilner Gaon sitting and writing, my mother dusting. No, this was all a dream, some dreadful nightmare of red chimneys.

Night had come. The red chimneys grew shapeless in the dark, uglier and more glowering than at twilight. Close by a little yellow fire was lit. By its glow I recognized a small gentile house—untouched, of course, by destruction. I remembered that a red-haired gentile lived there, a shoemaker with mean dogs, whom I had feared once, so long ago.

I was confident that this sweet neighbor of ours had burned and pillaged with his own hands. Even his house fire winked and teased with malice: "Ho, you have a house, have you?" Well, if I wished I could return the compliment, come at night and draw a hot bath for that gentile. Then he'd remember . . . crawl like an ape . . . one twist of blazing straw would be enough.

But I knew I wouldn't. The lust for revenge that had agonized me while I was on the train had disappeared, blown away in smoke.

My misery, my pain, were too deep for revenge. I would not sell my sorrow for a dirty act of vengeance. I was devoured with an odd, nagging, tragic pity for everything, for everyone.

"Caw, caw," a great crow cried, flying over the tall chimneys. Was it the black soul of a witch, gloating? "My prophecy came true! What did I tell you?"

And if I took revenge—upon whom? From whom? Where was this monstrous pogrom-beast? I hadn't seen her, I had seen only fragments of her. I had seen the gnawed bones she had discarded. As soon as she had glutted herself on human flesh she had split into single, tiny bits, and each bit in itself was nothing. A week ago these scattered shreds of hate and evil united and suddenly spawned a bloodthirsty beast with a thousand heads and teeth, a thousand sharp-pointed paws. But the beast had only one heart and one barbaric and wicked desire in that heart. Now that she had sated herself with blood, stuffed herself with limbs, she had fallen apart into little fragments. How could I hunt them out? From which scrap should I exact vengeance first?

I heard the thick growl of a dog.

Startled, I found myself still standing at the burned chimney. I was as foolish and forlorn as the chimney itself, and here a large dog was springing at me through the debris, howling wildly. His courage grew, and at every bark he tossed his head, obviously enjoying his lewd noises. How they rang and battered against the ruins! Their echo pounded into my frenzied brain like cold spikes. I recognized the dog, my childhood enemy, the shoemaker's dog.

I spat out my hatred at him, drove him away with a kick aimed into the darkness. Apparently he had been waiting for just this. He attacked me with frantic howls, as if I were killing him. He grabbed at my foot, reached the calf. Enraged, I ground my teeth in the dark and spoke slowly, evenly, with measureless hate.

"So, you've sniffed out a Jew? You've smelled a Jew?"

The dog hurled himself at me again. My throat gagged from a hot, corrosive wave of nausea. Somehow, in that darkness, my hands found a heavy length of charred wood, raised it with all their strength, and threw it powerfully, swiftly. The crack of a splintered bone, an unfinished, choked yelp—and silence. Only thin legs thrashing in the night, growing weaker, weaker. Mechanically I dropped the wood, approached, and bent down into the darkness. The dog lay with his belly up, and from his skull something trickled down and spread over the broken, frozen bricks, like blood from an unsanctified sacrifice on a crumbling altar.

Before I could understand what I had done, the door of the Christian house slammed harshly. The sound of coarse, scolding, heavy, hastening footsteps—the gentile must have overheard!

Translated by Meyer Levin

The Girl

ZALMAN SCHNEOUR

NO ONE could possibly call Brayne a girl—just the Girl. Her parents called her the Girl, her neighbors called her the Girl. Even strangers, seeing her for the first time, immediately thought of her as the Girl.

A hulking creature, she had fiery red cheeks under small greasy green eyes, and pendulous blue lips. Her fat hands were always red, as if she had just finished grating beets.

Tall, thick, unyielding, clumsy as a chunk of wood, she kneaded sweet gingerbread dough; winter-long, summer-long, she kneaded the dense dough. In the summer it was hard work. Simmering drops of sweat would crawl slowly down her forehead, down her face, and hang from the tip of her nose. Her nose cried out to be scratched, just to be swabbed with her sleeve—but there was no time, the dough must be kneaded. In the wintertime a bit of her neighbor's roof, covered with sober snow, showed through the window, and Hvedke the water carrier's beard was covered with ice fragments like the crystals of a luster. Then it was good to bend over the big mixing trough and knead the dough, sunning herself, as it were, in a private summertime. A sweet warmth crept through all her bones; her whole body grew lighter. Her shoulders seemed to move uncoaxed, and the dough rose and sank, sank and rose again, pliable as rubber.

Brayne's mother, Asne, aged and broken before her time, stood in the market square all day, selling gingerbread and roasted poppyseeds to the village peasants. She cursed and wrangled with her competitors over a penny sale, and then came home frozen, creased, on winter nights. Before the blueness of her body could fade she began her grumbling.

"Look at the Girl sitting home eating and drinking! If she only tried freezing all day in that market, then she'd know what life was really like. She'd learn what a big favor she does me by staying home and kneading! You'd think she was leading a hard life!"

This was the argument Asne muttered to herself as she blew on her icy hands and rubbed her feet together, trying to get warm. A thin woman, small, frostbitten, in muddied men's shoes, she looked like a stray bee deprived of her winter rest. Asne flew through the house, angry and buzzing, and aware that no one heard her and no one would help her.

Yet Brayne watched her, like a cow numb before the slaughter. Zavel, that old drunkard and gingerbread baker, would get off the sofa at the sound of his wife's voice and bow to her.

"Bless you, madam, give me a few cents for a drink, bless you."

Asne, bumbling about the room and blowing on her fingers, would ask, "And how would you like the plague?"

"Bless you, madam," Zavel answered, bowing again, "a Jew owes one hundred benedictions a day, and I haven't made one yet."

So Zavel joked, humoring his wife. But he did not humor his daughter. All day he sprawled on the straw sofa, his drunkard's head shaking, as he listened to the hissing of the thick honey-dough, to the quivering and crackling of the heavy chair and the deep trough moving under her strong, masculine fists. Sometimes a chicken duel or a goat battle outside the window would catch Brayne's attention, and her red hands would stick in the dough while her small eyes stared. Zavel would leap up, startled, like a child who is almost asleep until his mother stops singing. He missed the hissing of the dough, the tumult in the trough.

"Girl!" he would yell, hoarsely drunk and impatient. "Girl, knead! And may your bones rot!"

Zavel often failed to wheedle money out of his wife for his "benedictions." On those days Zavel seethed, and as soon as he saw Brayne's eyes wandering, he would sit up cautiously, pull a muddy shoe slowly and quietly off his foot, close one bleary eye for good aim—and fling the shoe right at Brayne's side or at her elbow or even at her head. Then he would croak happily, "Well, aha?"

"Ouch!" Brayne would squeak in muffled pain, hurling herself upon the dough, quickly, quickly, so forcefully that the windows shook.

She never said more than "ouch." She didn't even turn in the direction from which the shoe came—she knew what it meant. The dough kept up its hissing and the trough its creaking beneath her heavy pummeling. And Zavel sat on the sofa with one shoe on, scratching himself and listening to the dough's song; calmed himself and lay down again. But, remembering, he would heave himself up once more. "Girl, my shoe!"

Brayne would kick back her father's shoe, now an inert weapon, without even turning around. The shoe slithered swiftly over the flour-pasty floor and came straight at Zavel. Zavel caught it, pulled it on slowly, stretched out once more on the dusty straw sofa, and dreamed. He dreamed and listened.

Brayne could sense the times when her father was sound asleep. She would straighten up warily and gaze with shining eyes at the locked cupboard that stood near him. There lay the freshly baked gingerbread and the roasted poppyseeds she loved. Her broad nostrils trembled, but she was afraid to sneak over and pry the cupboard open with a knife. The memory of the beating she had received the last time she had tried was still strong. When her mother had returned home and found some of the poppyseeds gone, she attacked the Girl with unearthly curses and slaps at her face, while Zavel had hopped around her, thumping the Girl's sides.

"May the poppyseeds explode and leak out of you, you piece of flesh!" her mother swore, and struck.

"Amen!" Zavel gasped, swinging a shoe at Brayne's back.

Two little people danced about her: a skinny Jewish woman with cold wrinkled hands, and a small Jew with matted hair, one shoe in his hand and the other on his foot. Both cursed and beat her. She stood between these two creatures, large, weighty, guilty, red from head to foot, and accepted the blows, ignorant of any defense. All she did was blink her eyes, sweat and snuffle, an exhausted horse.

"Hit her? You might as well hit the wall," her mother screeched and delivered a stronger smack.

"Amen!" Zavel chimed in, gouging her so fiercely with the tip of his shoe that she groaned and had to retreat a step.

This particular blow Brayne couldn't forget. She became oddly terrified of her father's dirty shoes. Nor could she think of him any longer as "Father"—"Father," for example, "is sleeping," or "Father is awake." Now it was: "Zavel is awake," "Zavel sleeps," "Zavel quarrels." The locked cupboard whispered to her, the newly roasted poppyseed entranced her nose, but Zavel's shoes, Zavel's shoes . . .

On Saturday, Brayne, wearing a clean blouse, would sit at the window and watch the world go by. Her father and mother slept, and she alone was awake, sitting with her breasts pressed against the window, her hands more glaringly red than ever against the white blouse. Ducks waddled toward their bath. Soft white clouds swam slowly, Sabbath-like, soul-troubling, across the blue sky. A bird flew by, landing in the swamp on the other side of the river, while she sat and dully watched it all, like a deaf man in the midst of a conversation. Her greasy green eyes would light up only when they saw a gang of boys strolling with girls. She might see Velvel the shoemaker with his bride, or broad-shouldered Yankel the plasterer with his girl Dvoshe. Brayne's thick neck stretched, her red forehead pushed against the warm pane, her little green eyes blazed. If she noticed a boy grasping a girl's arm or waist, she broke into quiet, choked laughter. Inside of her something tugged and ached, and she laughed. Odd laughter—a queer noise from her chest and a stifled giggle—laughter like a hen's cries. Her mouth never opened to free the laughter, but it escaped through her nose as her sides and broad back and breasts tossed and leaped. How could such a small, smothered sound come from a great healthy cow like Brayne?

"Hneh, hneh, hn—"

"Girl!" Her mother was torn from her light sleep. "Girl!"

Brayne knew what her mother's warning meant. Zavel and his shoe might both awaken. But she couldn't control her laughter; something tickled and gnawed at her. Boys, and boys with girls, many betrothed couples, strolled down the street, and her laughter grew and grew. She was dying to laugh, to laugh forever. She knew Zavel had already dashed from his bed and was roaring right at her. She knew the heavy shoe was beating her in her new blouse. It hurt, it soiled the white blouse, but the laughter kept ripping her chest. Stronger and stronger, forcing the nostrils to shiver and itch.

"Hn, hneh, hn—"

Sleeping was uncomfortable, hot, after such a Saturday. Brayne usually slept like a stone, but on those nights she was restless. Zavel snored, her mother groaned, and the old furniture snapped in the darkness. The bed creaked under her heavy body as she turned. Somehow that creak made the gnawing at her heart start all over again, and she wanted to laugh. She tried to lie quietly, but it was hot, very hot, and she listened for the sound of the creaking bed, that crack of the mattress in the dark.

Benny Lip was known about town as a thief and a basket snatcher. Two teeth protruded through his harelip. Thin, hungry, nineteen or twenty years old, he had a nervy face and squint eyes with a queer white gleam. It was the gleam shared by professional thieves and spies. One fine day he showed up in town, and on the same day people began to frown at him sideways and to bar their doors against him. When he was hungry he dragged through the streets, crying in a crazily piercing voice, "Ah-oo, ah-oo, ah-oo." This was the sound of Benny's wrath, and woe to any irritable woman who bade him be silent. Then he would park himself in front of her window and grate for hours on end, out of spite, and there was nothing anyone could do about it.

Where did Benny live? Where did he sleep? Where did he eat? Sometimes a piece of scrapiron was visible under his jacket, sometimes an old broken candlestick, or even a bun. If anyone happened to stare at Benny chewing his bun, he rasped, "Ah-oo, ah-oo," and walked away.

Sometimes Benny came to Zavel's to buy a penny's worth of poppyseed, and as he dashed in he would pinch Brayne's arm and retreat to a corner. Brayne fell apart—fluttered and blinked and kneaded as if she were being whipped.

Zavel, scratching, lay on the sofa. "Well, bum?" he asked.

"Poppyseed, poppyseed!" Benny danced, his shoulders jerking, while

Zavel crawled reluctantly off his sofa and slowly unlocked the cupboard with rusted old keys. The dull knife with which he hacked at the black roll of poppyseed enraged him every time it slipped.

"How much do you want?"

"A few cents' worth." Benny sidled toward the cupboard.

"Get away from here, you!" Suspiciously Zavel protected the roll. "I can do without your help."

"Just look at the big fuss!" But Benny moved back.

As Zavel weighed out the poppyseed he called to Benny, *"Davai dengi*—let's see the cash." Whenever Zavel was really serious, really firm, he spoke Russian.

"Just look at all the fuss," Benny answered and handed Zavel the money. Only then did he get the poppyseed.

Standing, Benny ate it—he chewed and sucked with gusto. His shoulders, his nose, his white eyes—all moved and rolled as he bit at the black poppyseed, the healthy white teeth sticking out of his harelip. Zavel peered from under his shaggy brows as if he were at a sideshow. Brayne burned, kneading the dough or scraping the mixing trough as wildly as if her life depended on it.

"Give me another piece, Zavel. Tomorrow I'll pay you back, sure as I'm a Jew!"

Zavel didn't even bother to answer.

"Just look at all the fuss!" Benny said brazenly, and then turned to stare at Brayne. "Hey, Zavel, why don't you marry off the Girl? Give her to me for a wife—what about it?"

"Listen to him!" Zavel answered calmly and hunted for a stick. "Get out of here, you bag of bones!"

Benny sprang for the door, pinching Brayne again as he passed. He postured in the doorway, taunting Zavel with a throaty wheedle, "You'd like a brandy, eh? Dying for just a little one? Ah-oo, ah-oo!" And he ran away.

Zavel poured out his anger on the Girl: he beat her with his shoe, with the stick, and Brayne perspired. A few days later Benny would dash in again and the show would be repeated.

Once, when Zavel was returning from evening services where he had observed the anniversary of his father's death, he met Benny Lip in his hallway. Asne, of course, was at the market, and Brayne was home alone. Benny seemed flustered and tried to edge out into the street, but Zavel grabbed his collar. "Stand still!"

"Just look at all the fuss," Benny began in his normal fashion, but stopped and changed tactics. "Believe me, as I'm a Jew, Zavel, I've taken nothing."

Zavel clutched at Benny's collar with one hand while with the other he searched him carefully. The search over, Zavel shoved him away. "Well, you bag of bones, drag yourself out of here."

Benny needed no urging. Zavel watched from the hallway, waiting for Benny to begin jeering at him, to start his growl and his song of ah-oo, ah-oo. But Benny kept on running, and his frightened face looked back only once. Zavel wondered as he entered the house.

Zavel saw the Girl sitting near the trough, her arms half drowned in the dough, her hair wild, her cheeks horribly red. She sat and laughed quietly to herself, laughed like a hen clucking.

Zavel begrudged her the chair. He yelled hoarsely, "See how she lolls about! A fine way to knead! You're too sick to stand up?"

Still not satisfied, Zavel jabbed her in the side.

Brayne stood up and began kneading.

"What did that thief do here?"

Brayne laughed silently.

Zavel snatched off his shoe and began angrily to pound at her. "Girl, what did he do? What did he do here?"

Suddenly the most astonishing thing happened. Instead of humbly receiving the blows, Brayne ran about the room, her red dough-covered fists clenched, her teeth bared, and roared like an animal, "Oo-oo, oo!"

Zavel paled. For the first time he recognized in Brayne a creature stronger than himself. He hurriedly put on his shoe; his hands trembled and his voice trembled. "Go on, get along with the kneading. Don't you hear me? The ashes in the oven are waiting. What will become of you, damn you!"

No one knew quite how it happened, but after that incident relations among the father, mother, and the Girl changed. Zavel no longer threatened with his shoe—he cursed like a fishwife instead. After stuffing Brayne with all the oaths he could invent, he would stop, meditate for a while. Then he would spit in anger at himself and stretch out on the sofa.

Benny Lip never came there again. When he saw Zavel on the street he turned aside.

None of this sat well with Zavel. He began to suspect the Girl, but he was afraid to tell Asne. She might torture him, accuse him of not having watched carefully enough, and then she wouldn't give him any more money for liquor. So he hid his lonely doubts and waited, waited. He could control himself until he glanced at the reddened nape above the broad shoulders, shaking as they kneaded, and then he would grind his teeth and curse to himself, "Damn you, what's going to become of you? Damn you!"

Once he forgot the new order and began to beat her with his shoe. Brayne screamed crazily, shoved her kneading away, overturning the bench and the trough and the dough. She pushed her belly against the wall and howled like a maddened beast.

Zavel picked up the dough. He did not tell Asne.

The Girl became different. As soon as she saw her power over her parents she grew lazy, ate a lot, didn't knead or wash up or fire the oven as quickly as she had done before. She tired easily, and, even though she lay down to rest, blue patches appeared under her eyes, and the eyes themselves changed—they were no longer dreamy, no longer stupefied. In the middle of her work she would start wandering about the room, her sleeves still rolled, secretly snickering her wild henlike laughter. Once the laughter rose to a horrible pitch when she looked out the window. Her white horse teeth bit at the reddened hands: Benny Lip had passed. She rarely slept at night now, but tossed from side to side, choking with laughter.

Asne, listening in the dark, would whine to Zavel, "Do you hear? The Girl has given up sleeping."

"It's nothing," Zavel answered.

"Since you've started pampering her you ignore everything she does."

"To hell with her!" Zavel waved the problem aside and snored to convince Asne that he was unconcernedly asleep.

Zavel drank heavily. Brayne grew lazier and lazier. Asne stood all day in the market place, grumbled and swore when she came home, and, afraid to pick on the Girl, assaulted Zavel with her stored-up rage.

Dead drunk one night after his return from the tavern, Zavel hungered for his sofa. But before he could get through the hallway and collapse he heard his wife's voice. In the kitchen he found Brayne squatting on the floor and Asne standing over her, screaming and screeching.

"Carry that sack of flour out to the storeroom! Do you hear me?"

"Scared," the Girl stammered, crossing her hands over her heart.

"Carry it out right now—or you'll be carried out feet first!"

"Scared."

"And you old drunk, you!" Asne whirled upon Zavel. "Don't you see how she's tormenting me? Why don't you say something, you drunk? Say something, sot!"

Zavel automatically ripped off his shoe.

"Scared, scared, scared," droned the Girl and hugged her knees.

Zavel landed a blow.

Through the fog of brandy and noise Zavel saw Brayne suddenly lurch to her feet. Asne was already flat on her back, and a powerful hand clutched his windpipe, throttling him. The whole world shimmered. Only the Girl's voice existed, choked, frightful, bestial. "Ah—Zavel, ah-ah, Zavel."

Asne was barely able to save him from the Girl's hands.

All night Zavel lay sleepless, though he was drugged with drink. He feared the Girl might decide to finish strangling him. When he did doze off, at dawn, he was awakened by his wife's desperate cries.

"Help! Help! She's pregnant—God help her!"

"Amen." Zavel answered in his old accustomed manner, sleepily opening his eyes and sitting up in bed.

Asne, half-naked, wailed over him, tearing her hair with skinny, shivering fingers. "She's pregnant, she's pregnant, oh, God help her!"

"Amen," Zavel again supplied, bowing his head.

Asne was struck by his calm. Why, he sat quietly, as if nothing at all were happening! He had not even looked startled! She stood at the bedside, frozen, suddenly, despairingly, silent.

Her fixed silence muddled Zavel. Not knowing what to say, he began to stutter, "Dear madam, eh, blessings on you . . . eh, slip me a few cents . . . for a benediction . . ."

Translated by Sarah Zweig Betsky

White Chalah

LAMED SHAPIRO

1.

ONE DAY a neighbor broke the leg of a stray dog with a heavy stone, and when Vasil saw the sharp edge of the bone piercing the skin he cried. The tears streamed from his eyes, his mouth, and his nose; the towhead on his short neck shrank deeper between his shoulders; his entire face became distorted and shriveled, and he did not utter a sound. He was then about seven years old.

Soon he learned not to cry. His family drank, fought with neighbors, with one another, beat the women, the horse, the cow, and sometimes, in special rages, their own heads against the wall. They were a large family with a tiny piece of land, they toiled hard and clumsily, and all of them lived in one hut—men, women, and children slept pell-mell on the floor. The village was small and poor, at some distance from a town; and the town to which they occasionally went for the fair seemed big and rich to Vasil.

In the town there were Jews—people who wore strange clothes, sat in stores, ate white *chalah,* and had sold Christ. The last point was not quite clear: who was Christ, why did the Jews sell him, who bought him, and for what purpose?—it was all as though in a fog. White *chalah,* that was something else again: Vasil saw it a few times with his own eyes, and more than that—he once stole a piece and ate it, whereupon he stood for a time in a daze, an expression of wonder on his face. He did not understand it all, but respect for white *chalah* stayed with him.

He was half an inch too short, but he was drafted, owing to his broad, slightly hunched shoulders and thick short neck. Here in the army beatings were again the order of the day: the corporal, the sergeant, and the officers beat the privates, and the privates beat one another, all of them. He could not learn the service regulations: he did not understand and did not think. Nor was he a good talker; when hard pressed he usually could not utter a sound, but his face grew tense, and his low forehead was covered with wrinkles. *Kasha* and borscht, however, were plentiful. There were a few Jews in his regiment —Jews who had sold Christ—but in their army uniforms and without white *chalah* they looked almost like everybody else.

2.

They traveled in trains, they marched, they rode again, and then again moved on foot; they camped in the open or were quartered in houses; and this went on so long that Vasil became completely confused. He no longer remembered when it had begun, where he had been before, or who he had been; it was as though all his life had been spent moving from town to town, with tens or hundreds of thousands of other soldiers, through foreign places inhabited by strange people who spoke an incomprehensible language and looked frightened or angry. Nothing particularly new had happened, but fighting had become the very essence of life; everyone was fighting now, and this time it was no longer just beating, but fighting in earnest: they fired at people, cut them to pieces, bayoneted them, and sometimes even bit them with their teeth. He too fought, more and more savagely, and with greater relish. Now food did not come regularly, they slept little, they marched and fought a great deal, and all this made him restless. He kept missing something, longing for something, and at moments of great strain he howled like a tormented dog because he could not say what he wanted.

They advanced over steadily higher ground; chains of giant mountains seamed the country in all directions, and winter ruled over them harshly and without respite. They inched their way through valleys, knee-deep in dry powdery snow, and icy winds raked their faces and hands like grating irons, but the officers were cheerful and kindlier than before, and spoke of victory; and food, though not always served on time, was plentiful. At night they were sometimes permitted to build fires on the snow; then monstrous shadows moved noiselessly between the mountains, and the soldiers sang. Vasil too tried to sing, but he could only howl. They slept like the dead, without dreams or nightmares, and time and again during the day the mountains reverberated with the thunder of cannon, and men again climbed up and down the slopes.

3.

A mounted messenger galloped madly through the camp; an advance cavalry unit returned suddenly and occupied positions on the flank; two batteries were moved from the left to the right. The surrounding mountains split open like freshly erupting volcanoes, and a deluge of fire, lead, and iron came down upon the world.

The barrage kept up for a long time. Piotr Kudlo was torn to pieces; the handsome Kruvenko, the best singer of the company, lay with his face in a puddle of blood; Lieutenant Somov, the one with girlish features, lost a leg, and the giant Neumann, the blond Estonian, had his whole face torn off. The pockmarked Gavrilov was dead; a single shell killed the two Bulgach brothers; killed, too, were Chaim Ostrovsky, Jan Zatyka, Staszek Pieprz, and the little Latvian whose name Vasil could not pronounce. Now whole ranks were mowed down, and it was impossible to hold on. Then Nahum Rachek, a tall slender young man who had always been silent, jumped up and without any order ran forward. This gave new spirit to the dazed men, who rushed the jagged hill to the left and practically with their bare hands conquered the batteries that led the enemy artillery, strangling the defenders like cats, down to the last man. Later it was found that of the entire company only Vasil and Nahum Rachek remained. After the battle Rachek lay on the ground vomiting green gall, and next to him lay his rifle with its butt smeared with blood and brains. He was not wounded, and when Vasil asked what was the matter he did not answer.

After sunset the conquered position was abandoned, and the army fell back. How and why this happened Vasil did not know; but from that moment the army began to roll down the mountains like an avalanche of stones. The farther they went, the hastier and less orderly was the retreat, and in the end they ran—ran without stopping, day and night. Vasil did not recognize the country, each place was new to him, and he knew only from hearsay that they were moving back. Mountains and winter had long been left behind; around them stretched a broad, endless plain; spring was in full bloom; but the army ran and ran. The officers became savage, they beat the soldiers without reason and without pity. A few times they stopped for a while; the cannon roared, a rain of fire whipped the earth, and men fell like flies—and then they ran again.

4.

Someone said that all this was the fault of the Jews. Again the Jews! They sold Christ, they eat white *chalah,* and on top of it all they are to blame for everything. What was "everything"? Vasil wrinkled his forehead and was angry at the Jews and at someone else. Leaflets appeared, printed leaflets that a man distributed among the troops, and in the camps groups gathered around those who could read. They stood listening in silence—they were silent in a strange way, unlike people who just do not talk. Someone handed a leaflet to Vasil too; he examined it, fingered it, put it in his pocket, and joined a group to hear what was being read. He did not understand a word, except that it was about Jews. So the Jews must know, he thought, and he turned to Nahum Rachek.

"Here, read it," he said.

Rachek cast a glance at the leaflet, then another curious glance at Vasil; but he said nothing and seemed about to throw the leaflet away.

"Don't! It's not yours!" Vasil said. He took back the leaflet, stuck it in his pocket, and paced back and forth in agitation. Then he turned to Rachek. "What does it say? It's about you, isn't it?"

At this point Nahum flared up. "Yes, about me. It says I'm a traitor, see? That I've betrayed us—that I'm a spy. Like that German who was caught and shot. See?"

Vasil was scared. His forehead began to sweat. He left Nahum, fingering his leaflet in bewilderment. This Nahum, he thought, must be a wicked man—so angry, and a spy besides, he said so himself, but something doesn't fit here, it's puzzling, it doesn't fit, my head is splitting.

After a long forced march they stopped somewhere. They had not seen the enemy for several days and had not heard any firing. They dug trenches and made ready. A week later it all began anew. It turned out that the enemy was somewhere nearby; he too was in trenches, and these trenches were moving closer and closer each day, and occasionally one could see a head showing above the parapet. They ate very little, they slept even less, they fired in the direction the bullets came from, bullets that kept hitting the earth wall, humming overhead, and occasionally boring into human bodies. Next to Vasil, at his left, always lay Nahum Rachek. He never spoke, only kept loading his rifle and firing, mechanically, unhurriedly. Vasil could not bear the sight of him and occasionally was seized with a desire to stab him with his bayonet.

One day, when the firing was particularly violent, Vasil suddenly felt strangely restless. He cast a glance sidewise at Rachek and saw him lying in the same posture as before, on his stomach, with his rifle in his hand; but there was a hole in his head. Something broke in Vasil; in blind anger he kicked the dead body, pushing it aside, and then began to fire wildly, exposing his head to the dense shower of lead that was pouring all around him.

That night he could not sleep for a long time; he tossed and turned, muttering curses. At one point he jumped up angrily and began to run straight ahead, but then he recalled that Rachek was dead and dejectedly returned to his pallet. The Jews . . . traitors . . . sold Christ . . . traded him away for a song!

He ground his teeth and clawed at himself in his sleep.

5.

At daybreak Vasil suddenly sat up on his hard pallet. His body was covered with cold sweat, his teeth were chattering, and his eyes, round and wide open, tried greedily to pierce the darkness. Who has been here? Who has been here?

It was pitch-dark and fearfully quiet, but he still could hear the rustle of the giant wings and feel the cold hem of the black cloak that had grazed his face. Someone had passed over the camp like an icy wind, and the camp was silent and frozen—an open grave with thousands of bodies, struck while asleep, and pierced in the heart. Who has been here? Who has been here?

During the day Lieutenant Muratov of the fourth battalion of the Yeniesey regiment was found dead—Muratov, a violent, cruel man with a face the color of parchment. The bullet that pierced him between the eyes had been fired by someone from his own battalion. When the men were questioned no one betrayed the culprit. Threatened with punishment, they still refused to answer, and they remained silent when they were ordered to surrender their arms. The other regimental units were drawn up against the battalion, but when they were ordered to fire, all of them to a man lowered their rifles to the ground. Another regiment was summoned, and in ten minutes not a man of the mutinous battalion remained alive.

Next day two officers were hacked to pieces. Three days later, following a dispute between two cavalrymen, the entire regiment split into two camps. They fought each other until only a few were left unscathed.

Then men in mufti appeared and, encouraged by the officers, began to distribute leaflets among the troops. This time they did not make long speeches, but kept repeating one thing: the Jews have betrayed us, everything is their fault.

Once again someone handed a leaflet to Vasil, but he did not take it. He drew out of his pocket, with love and respect, as though it were a precious medallion, a crumpled piece of paper frayed at the edges and stained with blood, and showed it—he had it, and remembered it. The man with the leaflets, a slim little fellow with a sand-colored beard, half closed one of his little eyes and took stock of the squat broad-shouldered private with the short thick neck and bulging gray watery eyes. He gave Vasil a friendly pat on the back and left with a strange smile on his lips.

The Jewish privates had vanished: they had been quietly gathered together and sent away, no one knew where. Everyone felt freer and more comfortable, and although there were several nationalities represented among them, they were all of one mind about it: the alien was no longer in their midst.

And then someone launched a new slogan—"The Jewish government."

6.

This was their last stand, and when they were again defeated they no longer stopped anywhere but ran like stampeding animals fleeing a steppe fire, in groups or individually, without commanders and without order, in deadly fear, rushing through every passage left open by the enemy. Not all of them had weapons, no one had his full outfit of clothing, and their shirts were like second skins on their unwashed bodies. The summer sun beat down on them mercilessly, and they ate only what they could forage. Now their native tongue was spoken in the towns, and their native fields lay around them, but the fields were unrecognizable, for last year's crops were rotting, trampled into the earth, and the land lay dry and gray and riddled, like the carcass of an ox disemboweled by wolves.

And while the armies crawled over the earth like swarms of gray worms, flocks of ravens soared overhead, calling with a dry rattling sound—the sound of tearing canvas—and swooped and slanted in intricate spirals, waiting for what would be theirs.

Between Kolov and Zhaditsa the starved and crazed legions caught up with large groups of Jews who had been ordered out of border towns, with their women, children, invalids, and bundles. A voice said, "Get them!" The words sounded like the distant boom of a gun. At first Vasil held back, but the loud screams of the women and children and the repulsive, terrified faces of the men with their long earlocks and caftans blowing in the wind drove him to a frenzy, and he cut into the Jews like a maddened bull. They were destroyed with merciful speed: the army trampled over them like a herd of galloping horses.

Then, once again, someone said in a shrill little voice, "The Jewish government!"

The words suddenly soared high and like a peal of thunder rolled over the wild legions, spreading to villages and cities and reaching the remotest corners of the land. The retreating troops struck out at the region with fire and sword. By night burning cities lighted their path, and by day the smoke obscured the sun and the sky and rolled in cottony masses over the earth, and suffocated ravens occasionally fell to the ground. They burned the towns of Zykov, Potapno, Kholodno, Stary Yug, Sheliuba; Ostrogorie, Sava, Rika, Beloye Krilo, and Stupnik were wiped from the face of the earth; the Jewish weaving town of Belopriazha went up in smoke, and the Vinokur Forest, where thirty thousand Jews had sought refuge, blazed like a bonfire, and for three days in succession agonized cries, like poisonous gases, rose from the woods and spread over the land. The swift, narrow Sinevodka River was entirely choked with human bodies a little below Lutsin and overflowed into the fields.

The hosts grew larger. The peasant left his village and the city dweller his city; priests with icons and crosses in their hands led processions through villages, devoutly and enthusiastically blessing the people, and the slogan was, "The Jewish government." The Jews themselves realized that their last hour had struck—the very last; and those who remained alive set out to die among Jews in Maliassy, the oldest and largest Jewish center in the land, a seat of learning since the fourteenth century, a city of ancient synagogues and great yeshivas, with rabbis and modern scholars, with an aristocracy of learning and of trade. Here, in Maliassy, the Jews fasted and prayed, confessing their sins to God, begging forgiveness of friend and enemy. Aged men recited Psalms and Lamentations, younger men burned stocks of grain and clothing, demolished furniture, broke and destroyed everything that might be of use to the approaching army. And this army came, it came from all directions, and set fire to the city from all sides, and poured into the streets. Young men tried to resist and went out with revolvers in their hands. The revolvers sounded like pop guns. The soldiers answered with thundering laughter, and drew out the young men's veins one by one, and broke their bones into little pieces. Then they went from house to house, slaying the men wherever they were found and dragging the women to the market place.

7.

One short blow with his fist smashed the lock, and the door opened.

For two days now Vasil had not eaten or slept. His skin smarted in the dry heat, his bones seemed disjointed, his eyes were bloodshot, and his face and neck were covered with blond stubble.

"Food!" he said hoarsely.

No one answered him. At the table stood a tall Jew in a black caftan, with a black beard and earlocks and gloomy eyes. He tightened his lips and remained stubbornly silent. Vasil stepped forward angrily and said again, "Food!"

But this time he spoke less harshly. Near the window he had caught sight of another figure—a young woman in white, with a head of black hair. Two large eyes—he had never before seen such large eyes—were looking at him and through him, and the look of these eyes was such that Vasil lifted his arm to cover his own eyes. His knees were trembling, he felt as if he were melting. What kind of woman is that? What kind of people? God! Why, why, did they have to sell Christ? And on top of it all, responsible for everything! Even Rachek admitted it. And they just kept quiet, looking through you. Goddam it, what are they after? He took his head in his hands.

He felt something and looked about him. The Jew stood there, deathly pale, hatred in his eyes. For a moment Vasil stared dully. Suddenly he grabbed the black beard and pulled at it savagely.

A white figure stepped between them. Rage made Vasil dizzy and scalded his throat. He tugged at the white figure with one hand. A long strip tore from the dress and hung at the hem. His eyes were dazzled, almost blinded. Half a breast, a beautiful shoulder, a full, rounded hip—everything dazzling white and soft, like white *chalah*. Damn it—these

Jews are *made* of white *chalah!* A searing flame leaped through his body, his arm flew up like a spring and shot into the gaping dress.

A hand gripped his neck. He turned his head slowly and looked at the Jew for a moment with narrowed eyes and bared teeth, without shaking free of the weak fingers that were clutching at his flesh. Then he raised his shoulders, bent forward, took the Jew by the ankles, lifted him in the air, and smashed him against the table. He flung him down like a broken stick.

The man groaned weakly; the woman screamed. But he was already on top of her. He pressed her to the floor and tore her dress together with her flesh. Now she was repulsive, her face blotchy, the tip of her nose red, her hair disheveled and falling over her eyes. "Witch," he said through his teeth. He twisted her nose like a screw. She uttered a shrill cry—short, mechanical, unnaturally high, like the whistle of an engine. The cry penetrating his brain maddened him completely. He seized her neck and strangled her.

A white shoulder was quivering before his eyes; a full, round drop of fresh blood lay glistening on it. His nostrils fluttered like wings. His teeth were grinding; suddenly they opened and bit into the white flesh.

White *chalah* has the taste of a firm juicy orange. Warm and hot, and the more one sucks it the more burning the thirst. Sharp and thick, and strangely spiced.

Like rushing down a steep hill in a sled. Like drowning in sharp, burning spirits.

In a circle, in a circle, the juices of life went from body to body, from the first to the second, from the second to the first—in a circle.

Pillars of smoke and pillars of flame rose to the sky from the entire city. Beautiful was the fire on the great altar. The cries of the victims—long-drawn-out, endless cries—were sweet in the ears of a god as eternal as the Eternal God. And the tender parts, the thighs and the breasts, were the portion of the priest.

Translated by Norbert Guterman

Smoke

LAMED SHAPIRO

1.

AT THE first puff his face turned deep red, as if he were straining to lift a heavy load. He broke into a violent cough. Still, there must be something to it: the grownups smoked. He grew stubborn—and got used to it.

His father was a poverty-stricken teacher, and besides boys aren't supposed to smoke—so he picked up butts.

Later, studying in the synagogue, he would occasionally have a pack of tobacco. He never denied anyone a cigarette when he had it; he was never ashamed to ask for one when he didn't.

His name was Menasha.

From the synagogue he went as son-in-law to Reb Shoel Marawaner. Reb Shoel himself came to the synagogue with the matchmaker. The imposing Jew with the drooping eyes examined Menasha for a few minutes: a tall youth, broad and sturdy; the half-length frock coat of the Hasidic merchant will fit him perfectly. Reb Shoel peered into the book Menasha was studying, asked a few questions, began a casual conversation, and while glancing sideways listened with pricked-up ears to the youth's modest, somewhat cryptic replies. Rising suddenly from the bench, Reb Shoel ended the conversation with, "Bring your phylacteries."

2.

In one of their most intimate moments his young wife asked, "Tell me, what sort of taste do you get from your cigarette? Give me a puff—let me try it."

He took the rolled-up burning cigarette from his mouth and moved it to her lips. Etta's lips closed like two pillows over the cigarette.

"Phew!" she coughed. "It's only smoke."

Menasha smiled. "Smoke—but it's good."

"What's so good about it? It's bitter and gets in your eyes."

He laughed. "But it's good," he repeated, as a whirlwind of shame and shamelessness wrapped the two young people in its folds.

3.

He accepted the wealth of his father-in-law's household without betraying any of the pauper's greed. In only one thing did he indulge himself: he used the best tobacco that could be had. Knowing this, the younger people in the synagogue would frequently dip into his tobacco tin.

Once Reb Shoel's older son-in-law, Nehemiah, called Menasha aside. "Why do you let them smoke up your tobacco, those pigs? They themselves buy *mahorka*."

Menasha looked at him quietly. "How can you refuse anyone a cigarette?"

Nehemiah turned and glanced cautiously around the synagogue. One eye closed, the other lit up with wisdom. "Fool, don't you understand? Do as I do—two kinds," he burbled with a little laugh.

Menasha said nothing. But he did not introduce two kinds of tobacco.

He frequented the synagogue, studied at home, strolled about with a stick in his hand. Often he would sit quietly, listening to the business conversations Reb Shoel held with Jewish merchants. Those were the years of journeying to Danzig or Leipzig or Königsberg. Reb Shoel was one of the travelers to Danzig. For his older son-in-law Nehemiah he opened a dry-goods store: "Sit and measure linens." Nehemiah would have preferred to talk about Danzig, but Reb Shoel dismissed him with a wave of the hand. To Menasha he never said a word about business. And Menasha too was silent—until Etta was brought to bed and gave birth to twins, boys.

The evening after the double circumcision the father-in-law called Menasha into his room, handed him a packet of money, and said, "Go."

Menasha was a little frightened. "I don't even know where or what—"

"You'll learn. When you're rid of the money you'll know."

This took place during *Chanukah*. By Passover, Menasha was back. They celebrated the first two days of the holiday, and Danzig was never mentioned. Only on the evening of the second day did Reb Shoel invite Menasha to his room.

"What's new?"

"I've learned something," said Menasha, blushing.

Reb Shoel nodded.

After Passover, Menasha received another roll of bills and left for Danzig. From then on he would travel regularly for two or three months each year, and often twice a year.

4.

With the passage of the years children sprang up in every corner of the house. Some were getting older, others crawled around, new ones were born. Reb Menasha—in time he became "Reb" Menasha—looked on and laughed quietly. Reb Shoel was no more; his business had been taken over by Reb Menasha, as had the old house with the spacious rooms.

During the months Reb Menasha stayed home in Marawan he lived as before: visited the synagogue twice a day, studied in the afternoon, talked business in the evening. The outer world made one change in his habits: he smoked cigars.

"A cigarette is for a youngster," he explained, smiling. "A Jew with a beard, a father of children, has to smoke cigars. The Germans are no fools."

Cigars were not the only thing that the outer world had brought, but of this only Etta knew. That is, she did not know: she sensed. How did he live there, in that outer world? What was it really like? She did not think about this, but it seemed to her that her husband grew steadily broader and taller, and she wondered why the measure of his clothes did not change. He had a habit of smiling with his eyes alone, and this smiling glance wrapped her into itself, carrying her along in a flow that was peaceful, deep, and unceasing, as the river that passed by the town flowed, year in and year out, into the distant world. She was not frightened; on the contrary, she felt secure in this wide stream. And many times she curled up against her husband and even tried to take a puff from his cigar. But this only brought tears to her eyes and spasms of coughing. He would slap her lightly on the back and laugh.

5.

There were already a few sizable boys in the house, and a whole flock of half-grown ones and small fry were pushing after them.

Danzig was no longer the Danzig of old. Etta skimped—except for Reb Menasha's cigars, and in this one regard he did not oppose her. It went so far that the family had to leave the old house with its spacious rooms and rent another. At that time Reb Menasha sat down by himself in his room and became engrossed in the problem: what is wrong with Danzig? He sat there, looking through the window, smoking cigars, reflecting. The next day he left for the Don.

For several weeks he wandered about in the tumultuous region between the lower Don and the Caspian Sea, observing, considering, counting, measuring—and at the end he bent a finger of his right hand with his left and said, "Caviar." And he began to connect the Don with Danzig.

He was away for two years, and these were the hardest for the family at home. But after these two years, when he came home to rest for several months, people began to figure according to a new calendar: this or the other incident occurred "at the time Reb Menasha first went to the Don." And when he came home he bought back Reb Shoel's house and life continued as in earlier times.

He would now go to Danzig only once every two or three years, but for that very reason he spent two-thirds of his time on the Don. After caviar, he began to trade in smoked *wobla*—a local kind of sardine he had himself discovered. He earned much and spent much: one child after the other grew up, lived, and studied. In the end the father put each of them on his feet. For the wedding of the youngest he called together all his children. They celebrated in the old style, and at the end of the wedding meal Reb Menasha rose at the head of the table.

"Children, I shall no longer go to the Don. I have enough for myself and the old lady to live out our few years. The rest is for you. Go in good health, and may the Almighty let you live your years no worse than I have mine. You need not worry about us—we will not burden you."

6.

Life flowed like a river nearing its mouth: the wider and deeper, the more peacefully and quietly. Menasha's high smooth forehead showed only one narrow crease from temple to temple, his black hair had grayed in only a few places. In the early summer evenings, against the orange glow of the sinking sun, he would stroll, as always, with his stick in hand; and his step remained certain and measured, his back strong and erect. Only his eyes were absorbed, deeply absorbed.

In his middle years he had studied mainly with his eyes. But now, in the quiet afternoon, his voice would rise more frequently through the old synagogue, taking up the mild and sad melody of his youth, taking it quietly, still more quietly, until it sank into the surrounding stillness, like the reverberation of a string—and then rising again until it reached its full strength, sweet and bitter, like the tears of childhood.

He enjoyed spending his time in the synagogue with the younger students, discussing Torah and justice. About the outer world and his life away from home he said little.

"People live and die there just as they do here," he would answer shortly, smiling with his eyes. "A Talmud made in Slawite or in Danzig—what's the difference? Only the printing and the covers. The content on the other hand—" And he would stare at the thread of smoke, taking care that the white ash, which sat like a Cossack's hat on the head of his cigar, should not fall but remain there as long as possible.

Coming home one morning from the synagogue with his prayer shawl and phylacteries under his arm, he found Ziessel, his youngest son. "Ah! I knew you'd come."

The young man's face changed color.

"Now, now," his father soothed him. "I did not mean to shame you. Things don't go well, eh? But first wash, and then we'll eat."

Listening to his son's story, Reb Menasha nodded his head: a fine plan . . . who could have expected that . . .

"I knew you'd come. You're rash and a little hasty, but you'll learn. I put away a small sum for you. Not much, but you'll be able to start again; and keep your eyes open. Here, take it—and don't come for more: there isn't any. We are old, and if I die first your mother must not be left in want. She won't go to you children.

"And another thing—" He called back his son from the door. "Now it's not like the old days. In my time, when a Jew came to Danzig with a thick beard and a high forehead, it was enough; if the corn and wheat were good one sold them at a profit, if not, one had a loss. We didn't run our business, it ran itself. That the world is now different I needn't tell you—you're younger than I. Danzig is no longer Danzig, the beard and the forehead no longer assets. Nowadays business has to be conducted, you understand? Well, go in good health and may good fortune be with you."

7.

A summer and a winter passed, and then another summer. Again the winter came, early and bitter, with snows and frosts and wild angry winds. In December, Reb Menasha caught cold, coughed, and spat blood: it was the return of an old inflammation from the early days in Danzig, which was supposed to have left no scars. It spread quickly, and one gray morning, when the thin snowflakes melted in people's eyes and for no reason at all the air smelled different, his children came running from the outer world to stand by their father's bed. A few old friends and the rabbi had remained through the night.

For several hours the cough had not troubled the sick man and his temperature had fallen, but the young doctor did not leave. He sat not far away, at a table, and silently twisted his pencil between his nervous fingers.

Reb Menasha opened his eyes. It was hard to recognize him, but the eyes with their hidden smile had remained the same. He asked for a smoke.

"But Papa—"

The doctor's shrug cut short Ziessel's protest. He turned pale and handed his father a cigar.

"Not that," said the sick man. "Hasn't anyone a cigarette?" And his eyes smiled.

He took a puff from the thin little cigarette and called, "Etta . . ."

She lowered her hands from her eyes and dragged herself out of the corner. In recent years she had become rather fat and short of breath. Now her small round face was drawn together like a child's fist, and her glance seemed helpless and lost: the river, close to its end, threw her upon an unknown shore.

"Menasha, Menasha," she whispered.

"Want a puff?" He laughed. "Smoke . . . but it's good."

A whirlwind seized the old woman. She let out a cry, a laugh, a cough, all at the same time, as if smoke were choking her. Reb Menasha put aside the cigarette and winked to the rabbi, who went over to the bed and began reciting the last prayer with him. After the first few words Reb Menasha lost himself in coughing. The cough never ceased: it froze in the air, and there it remained.

Translated by Irving Howe and Eliezer Greenberg

The Rebbe and the Rebbetsin

LAMED SHAPIRO

ONCE UPON a time there were a *rebbe* and a *rebbetsin.*

When the *rebbe* studied Torah the *rebbetsin* would say she heard angels chanting, and when the *rebbetsin* cooked fish for the Sabbath the *rebbe* was certain that he smelled the odors of Paradise. Both the *rebbe* and the *rebbetsin* were equally good, pious, and wise. If there ever was a difference between them, it was that the *rebbetsin* could almost issue rabbinical judgments, while on the subject of cooking fish the *rebbe* claimed no knowledge.

God had closed the womb of the *rebbetsin.* The *rebbe* would sit in one corner, the *rebbetsin* in another, and they would plead to God in silence:

Creator of the Universe, heed the prayer of your servant and bless me with a son, so that I may teach him your Torah and good deeds . . .

Creator of the Universe, Lord of the World, hearken to the prayer of your servant and rejoice me with a child, so that I may plant good ways in him and teach him to do your will . . .

And the *rebbe* would sit down by the side of the *rebbetsin* and say, "When our son begins to talk, I will myself teach him how to read and the meaning of the words."

And the rebbetsin would add, "When our *Kaddish* awakens I will say morning prayers with him, and before he goes to sleep evening prayers."

And so the years flew by, and the townspeople began to whisper among themselves, "If a woman has no children after ten years of marriage, the husband must not live with her."

And this was told to the *rebbe,* and the *rebbe* answered, "I will not send my wife away, and God will yet give me a son."

The townspeople grumbled and thought of removing the *rebbe,* but later they decided that if the barrenness of his wife didn't trouble him, it certainly should not trouble them—and so the years went. The *rebbe* sat opposite the *rebbetsin* and they talked.

"When our child grows up, I will teach him the *Gemarah* and all the commentaries."

"When our son will come Fridays from the bath I will honor him with fresh fish, and when he returns from the synagogue on the Sabbath I will meet him with the sacramental wine."

And a while later the townspeople again remembered them and gave them advice. "Adopt a child and bring it up, and a hundred years from now it will say *Kaddish* for you."

The two of them shook their heads. The *rebbe* answered, "How can I instruct a strange child in Torah and good deeds if I am not responsible for his sins? And the *rebbetsin* said, "How will I be able to love a strange child if he has not cost me my blood?"

And both of them added, "No, God will bless us with our own child!"

The townspeople grumbled, called them stubborn, and in time forgot them once more.

And the two old people decided: When our treasure grows up he will issue rabbinical judgments and write holy books. . . . When our joy reaches eighteen, we will lead him to the wedding canopy. . . .

One after the other, in the flow of eternity, the years passed by. On a morning they were found dead. They were sitting on their beds, facing each other, in the same nightshirts, clasping their hands, like children, around their knees. Across their faces flitted a smile. And in the air of the old house, as though the words still hummed:

When our son will grow up . . .

When our *Kaddish* will grow older . . .

Translated by Irving Howe and Eliezer Greenberg

Munie the Bird Dealer

MOISHE KULBAK

1. MUNIE

MUNIE bred and sold birds. His moldy little house, covered with moss and sprouting with slippery little mushrooms, had gradually acquired the appearance of a chickencoop. The pigeons had sprinkled the walls, shelves, and tables with a thin coat of chalk. There was a smell of mildew and bird droppings, and the small dirty windowpanes admitted a sparse, cold, leaden light. From cages of every description came a continual shrill chirping; there was a hopping behind the wires and a tapping of beaks against various tin lids and other objects. Munie lounged on his heavy leather seat, crawled into the pigeons' cages, felt them with his hands, blew into their feathers, and quietly paired the various birds. Gentle tiny canaries, yellow as lemons, sang in little cages. Pigeons covered with feathers and strong as hens walked about the house. And in the half-darkness there always sat squat peasants with thick, potato-like noses, birdcatchers come from somewhere in the wet Byelorussian forests; they gabbled, jostled about, took naps on bags of potatoes in the corners, and sucked big old-fashioned pipes, blowing smoke like steam engines.

Deals were concluded in silence: plump red-breasted robins were bartered for broken cages, and finches of the color of dark camomile for mousetraps or threadbare old hats that had lain in the attic for years. Staring stupid eyes looked slowly from under thick eyebrows, like ponds overgrown with bushes, and occasionally a word was said, lazily and hoarsely, that sounded more like a cough or a groan.

Munie shuffled all over the place, occasionally slapping an ancient hand, and this meant that a silent peasant would set out for a birch wood the next day at dawn, and linger there for weeks on end, until he had finally lured a squirrel, or even a pure-feathered canary, into a cage. Surely songs about Munie were sung in the swamps and in all the remote woods of Byelorussia!

2. NECHE THE MARKET WOMAN

Hot, still summer days. Trees, cut out against the diaphanous brightness, stood shadowless. Not a bough moved. A magpie standing on a crossbar opened wide its black beak, amazed at the heat. Munie sat on the threshold of his house, waiting for a living soul. But no one appeared on the searing road. Only at sunset did Neche come to visit him.

She was only a market woman with a stand, but she had great experience in finding wives for bachelors. The birds hopped and sang in their cages. Munie sat at the table, prepared to listen. Neche talked in circumlocutions, drawing pretty parallels, and hinted that these days a man needed a wife to keep house. She too dealt in chickens, and she knew the work they made. Munie sat red-faced, looking less like a man than a piece of stone. He did not blink an eyelash, but every pulse in his body throbbed strongly, and Neche the market woman went on talking in circumlocutions, drawing pretty parallels.

The windows grew grayer, letting through the cool reflection of a dreary distant sunset without color and without warmth. Then Neche took a good look at Munie, and moved closer, and whispered into his ear words that opened him wide and poured fire into every last corner of his being.

Munie was silent, but that night he crawled slowly into the pigeons' cage and sat there till daybreak with his eyes open, thinking. In the morning the canaries sang more prettily. Munie washed himself in a basin. He combed his black forelock, twisted his mustache, and sat at the open door. By noon Neche the market woman had not shown up, and the clay-colored peasants were already napping inside, looking like patched old pots, holding their cages on their knees, senilely joking, and chattering with the merry birds. But Munie was in high spirits, he even whistled like a bird, and then he craned his neck, trying also to sing bass; but he could not sing.

With evening, thick shadows covered the walls. A peasant as old as the world came to spend the night. He had brought from his distant village a raven that he himself had kept for fifty years, and now he stood leaning on his two sticks, talking to the birds. Munie walked aimlessly about the house. He was at a loss, and he rubbed his forehead: he had just discovered important thoughts going on there.

When the peasant stopped his chatter for a moment Munie beckoned to him and then cried into his dirty hairy ear, "Is it possible for a man like me to take a woman into his house? Ha?"

"It's possible—why not?" The peasant hiccuped somewhere behind him. And then he wanted to laugh, but his efforts were of no avail. He looked like an old caved-in barn, where the wind blows and bangs the dried boards and shingles.

The birds were already drowsy; the peasant, who was only twice as old as his raven, wandered about the house, babbling and tottering, until he too fell asleep on a bag of potatoes. And so about five hundred living creatures slept together in the dark little house.

In the morning Neche the market woman came.

Since the birds could not be disturbed, the house would not be whitewashed, she said. But Munie must hang up a sign—Malkele, his fiancée, must be let know, after all, what kind of man her husband-to-be was. "And what do you keep in your trunk, Munie?" Neche darted back and forth in the house, peeping everywhere, pushing open windows; then she rolled up her sleeves, made a hand mop, and proceeded to clean up the place, wiping the benches, sprinkling water from her mouth, beating the pillows. Then she suddenly grabbed her basket and ran out.

Neche disappeared like the wind.

Munie went up to a nail-studded green trunk and with a long key that hung next to his skin slowly lifted the heavy oaken lid. Inside were Munie's possessions: coarse linen shirts with collars embroidered in peasant style, and at the very top of the pile a pair of pressed trousers, and even a pair of new patent-leather shoes. No one was in the house when he gently tapped the soles as one taps an earthenware pot, and no one was there—nor did anyone even look at Munie—later, toward the evening, when he walked home from the bathhouse all pink and steaming like a baked apple, with his shirt under his arm. No one turned to look at Munie.

3. MALKELE THE FIANCÉE

Neche the market woman helped Munie knot his flaming red necktie. The evening was white: the place where the sun was supposed to set stood empty and desolate, behind broken, hollow clouds, dilapidated, like scaffolding around a building that had never been completed. The two little windows now hung in the room like a useless pair of spectacles. But a lamp was lit, and Neche was helping Munie to knot his necktie. A cool snow-white cloth shone on the table. The samovar was bubbling. Transparent glasses filled with fragrant brown tea added to the festive air of the house; and stillness also spread over the freshly swept cages. Munie kept twisting his black mustache. Neche was busying herself about the house, going in and out again to see whether Malkele, the charming black-haired fiancée, was coming.

The lamp burned for a long time, and Munie's necktie glowed with rainbow tones. And then Neche slowly, with a deep bow, opened the door for the fiancée, who walked in slowly, and was silent—silent.

And here it is proper to stop to admire Neche's presence of mind —she at once began to talk with much feeling about the high cost of living. For Malkele—and this should not be held against her—was at first quite embarrassed; she did not even put her umbrella in a corner, as is the proper thing to do. Munie cleared his throat, as befits a male, stared, and pulled up his belt around his belly. Finally Malkele began to talk. As Neche assured us, pearls poured out of her mouth, while Munie sat, his face on his hand, listening, overcome with joy.

And then Neche said, "Munie, you won't be sorry. When Malkele wants to work, she is a demon."

In this way he realized that Malkele would be a good housekeeper. He sat silent, with a sharp twinge of joy in his heart, and waited.

A little later Neche left, and only then did Malkele talk about how respectable people lived and scolded Munie for not taking a glass of tea in the morning on an empty stomach. She even rose from her seat and showed him, pointing with her fingers, how she would arrange the furniture. That of course was right!

Daybreak was already graying. Malkele sat close to Munie; suddenly she pinched her fiancé exactly in his armpit and said, "Muninke, mind my words, I'll make a man out of you!"

In this way he realized that Malkele was very much devoted to him. His heart began to throb with ecstasy, he huddled close to her, and, already faint with desire, he began to dream in a low voice.

"Malkele, you'll make potato pancakes for me . . . you'll buy *shmaltz* herring at Channah Dvoire's . . ."

And they kissed too. First to wake up in the half-darkness was the old finch. He shook his warm camomile-colored coat and gave a leisurely whistle to greet the sun, which had just begun to spray the windowpanes with a rosy dew. There followed a clucking in the cages, and a vague dark cooing of pigeons in all the shadowy corners. And above all this rose the golden trill of the canary.

4. MUNIE AND MALKELE

The moldy house was soaking in the endless autumn rains. The roof, like a piece of wet mud, had slid downward, and the crumbly sprawling chimney smoked and stank. The crooked door creaked loudly on its one hinge, and all the way up, next to the roof, hung the new sign—the blue board showing a red-footed pigeon with an open green beak and a yellow eye, and under it, in fancy black letters:

PIGEONS AND OTHER BIRDS SOLD HERE

The wind shook the swollen roof, plucked at the wet ragged panes, and slapped the walls with long, watery hands.

Malkele stood at the burning stove. The room was stuffy, the birds were puffing themselves, making crackling noises with their beaks under their feathers. Peasants from the neighborhood sat quietly in their drenched sheepskins, stroking their mustaches and drying themselves. A blackbird had died in the morning; it lay rigid on the table, with its yellow feet stretched out and an open empty eye. Munie was busy at the cage. A hollow-boned peasant with a thin neck stood next to him, telling him something, clucking like a hen; in his canvas breeches he looked like an autumn scarecrow on a pole. Munie laughed himself sick at the peasant's stories, wiping his tears with his sleeve, and heaving on his leather chair. The raven, perched on the cornice above the stove, sleepily turned his back to the room and gave its tail an energetic shake.

Malkele clutched her cheek and cried angrily, "Munie, take away your raven! It's messing up my hair!"

She began to sulk. Some of the peasants, full of respect for Munie's wife, rose from their seats and waved their hands. "Shoo, shoo!" And then the raven, proud and calm, moved behind the stove as though to say, "You all mean less than nothing to me."

But Malkele continued her sulking. She did not talk, and later, when she happened to come near the table, she grabbed the dead blackbird and threw it on the floor. Munie was upset; he shambled over to the bird and put it in his bosom.

He should not have done it, for Malkele turned pale, ran up to him, and flung the crushed bird out the door. "Even without it you stink like a carcass, my handsome husband!"

That was what she said. Munie raised frozen eyebrows at her, looking foolish, but did not answer. Sheepish peasant eyes also wandered about the room, then slowly grew dim under the thick bushy eyebrows.

It was autumn. The light was clouded in Munie's house. The crooked autumn rains soaked and sapped the last traces of joy. Somewhere in a muddy field a tree dropped its last brassy leaf. Dirty mists hung over the roofs like torn rags.

It was autumn. Evenings dragged, thin and sad, starless, the poorest evenings in the world. Munie sat all the time, peeling his potatoes. The lamp smoked. It was during such long nights that Malkele used to darn Munie's socks, but now she sat with folded hands, dozing and dozing. The wind was playing with the rain, pulling it into streamers and spraying the walls.

It was autumn. Munie was sitting through the long, long evening when he suddenly heard a whistle outside the window. Someone had thrust a finger in his mouth and whistled into Munie's ear. Malkele started and grabbed her headkerchief.

Munie asked, "Malkele, who is whistling?"

"Look at him, look!" said Malkele. "It's Ziske Channah-Dobke's of course."

Munie felt a bit hurt at not having been able to recognize Ziske by his whistle, but he didn't mind, and asked again, "Who is this Ziske Channah-Dobke's, Malkele?"

"Look at him! Why, it's Ziske, one of the gang!" And she was out the door.

Munie scratched his head, cursed the world, and then, in the darkness, beat his breast with his fists. It was quiet around the house—Malkele had gone away with Ziske the thief. Somewhere the rain was dripping into a pail.

That night Munie crawled into his bed, buried his head in the blanket, and lay until daybreak with open eyes. Before sunrise the door creaked slowly. Malkele was back. She quickly threw off her dress, slipped quietly into the bed, and fell asleep at once. Munie lay next to the wall; he did not breathe, he feared to move a limb, it hurt him so. But in the morning Malkele was busy: the stove was lit, potatoes were steaming on the table, the birds were hopping and sipping clear water, and Malkele herself sang pretty songs.

Then Munie thought stealthily, It's true that she's a demon worker, but she shouldn't be going out with other men, should she?

5. ZISKE CHANNAH-DOBKE'S

Peasants with ratty beards and sheepskins brought the cold from Jadlow Forest. They came to Munie's to sell late-season birds. Crazy bluethroats tried to squeeze themselves through the wires of the cages; red-breasted autumn robins, like juicy ripe strawberries, smelled of bogs and moisture; and occasionally winds entered the house, winds saturated with the winy odors of gray apples. Out of the mists emerged a strong bloody autumn that lighted winy-fragrant fires in the neighborhood, and roared far and wide, with lashing winds over every thin glistening pond.

What was Munie to do in this drunken autumn when Malkele his wife went out almost every night? Those roaring autumn nights he lay on his bed like a dog in a kennel, listening for distant steps, holding his breath under his blanket, and waiting; and not until the frosty silvery morning would he shamble out to the yard, to the fountain, pour cold water over himself, and slowly recover from the desolation of the night. That was how Munie lived.

And one day Malkele said to him, "I'll tell you the truth, Munie, I'll tell you the truth. Ziske is too shy to come in."

Munie lowered his eyes, thought hard, and said, "What is there to be shy about? I'm not a bear."

A little later she brought him in, the shy Ziske Channah-Dobke's. He swaggered over, small, with a red neck, in a pair of shiny boots, and, still swaying and swaggering, shoved a cold butcher's hand into Munie's.

"How are things, Munie?"

Munie held the hand, heavy as a dressed rump of beef, and slowly stammered, "No complaints—everything's all right."

"And the birdies?"

"Thanks for asking."

And then Ziske sat down, sprawling comfortably, slapping himself on his strong neck, and pushing his cap over his eyes, as if he were bothered by the sun. Soon he talked only to Malkele.

Munie went quietly to the pigeons: it had slowly become clear to him that he was somewhat superfluous here—just as the belated song of a bird in some side cage had become superfluous now, in the violet autumn. The two windows that always let through only a thin leaden light now admitted the sparse glow of a sunset on the fields. Or was it a reflection of the red-veined roaring autumn that was trampling the roads with its copper feet?

That night Malkele made Munie's bed on the bench under the window. The fact is, he was a little ashamed when he later went to sleep on the bench like a bachelor. He lay through the dark night listening intently. What was Malkele up to? Nobody came that night. But Malkele slept restlessly, and at one point she cried wildly in her sleep, so that Munie had to crawl down from his bench and wake her.

And so night followed upon night, cursed, drained of all joy, as though the pulse of the world had stopped beating. Munie malingered, and went to bed late, waiting for Ziske. But Ziske did not come when he was expected. In the middle of one night he broke in suddenly, wild, carrying on like a *goy;* he took Malkele on his knees, and they drank, laughed, and even kissed. Munie said nothing. Suddenly Ziske blew out the lamp, and, still laughing, both tumbled into the bed.

Munie could scarcely sit up on his bench, and in a strangled, whimpering voice he asked in the dark, "What are you doing there? Ha?"

The laughter stopped at once. A little later Ziske's voice rose sharply, like a bare butcher knife being drawn from a boot. "Don't worry, brother, I won't skim off your cream."

And for a long time afterward the darkness was alive with ardent whispering; it hissed like a snake in this night that lay petrified in the room, silent and blazing like an overheated stove. Munie pressed himself into the wall, stopped his ears, and was petrified like the night, lying cold and rigid for hours, like a piece of hardened clay. He prayed for the day to come.

Only at daybreak did he crawl down from his bench. A dirty light was dripping from the panes, mingling with the thin shadows on the walls. The raven on the stove flapped its stiff wings and silently moved away behind the cornice. An empty bottle lay on the floor. In the bed Ziske lay next to the wall, his arm under his head, snoring and accompanying the snore with a thin whistle. Malkele came to slowly, rubbed her eyes, and, catching sight of Munie far in the corner, she yawned and said, "Munie, will you please get me a drink of water?"

He brought her the water. She drank thirstily, then handed back the tin cup and turned over.

The windows were gray, like cooling steel. A shabby dawn had entered the room. Munie shuffled over to the large wire cage, slowly opened the door, and crawled inside, to the warm pigeons. The startled birds flapped their wings, rose in the air, and immediately dropped on the boards and wires, huddled in pairs around him, and slumbered again.

Munie sat down with his hands on the floor, and remained there, motionless, not like a human being, but like a piece of broken gray stone.

Translated by Norbert Guterman

Repentance

I. J. SINGER

RABBI EZEKIEL of Kozmir and his followers were great believers in the divine principle of joyousness.

Reb Ezekiel himself was a giant of a man, standing a full head above his Hasidic followers, and broader in the shoulders than any two of them placed side by side. On Holy Days the court of Reb Ezekiel was crowded with visiting Hasidim, and in the synagogue the mighty head of Reb Ezekiel, swathed in the silver-worked headpiece of his prayer shawl, swam above all others, a banner and a crown, an adornment to the gathering and the symbol of its glory.

Reb Ezekiel is no more than a memory today, but there are still extant two of his possessions: an ivory walking stick and a white satin gaberdine, which fastens at the front not with buttons but with silver hooks and eyes. The grip of the stick is so high that no man is able to use it for walking. A certain grandson of Reb Ezekiel, inheritor of the dynastic rights of this rabbinic line, puts on Reb Ezekiel's garberdine once a year, on the New Year, when the ram's horn is to be blown for the opening of the heavenly gates; but if he tries to take a step in this mantle of his grandfather, he stumbles over the ends, which trail along the floor. To protect him not less than the illustrious garment, the followers of the grandson put down a carpet of straw on the floor of the synagogue for the two days of the New Year.

Rabbi Ezekiel and his followers believed not only in joyousness but in the virtue of good food.

Of the fast days that are sprinkled throughout the sacred calendar

Reb Ezekiel and his followers observed only the Day of Atonement. Even on *Tishe b'Av,* the Black Fast that commemorates the tremendous calamity of the storming of the Temple, Reb Ezekiel and his followers ate. If it came to pass that a fool of a Hasid, having had a bad dream, insisted on fasting, he had to leave the court and go across the Vistula to the village opposite Kozmir.

At the court of Rabbi Ezekiel there were always dancing and singing; there was perpetual drinking of wine and mead. It was a common saying with the rabbi, his children, the Hasidic followers, and visitors: "It is not the study of the Law that matters, but the melody that goes with the studying; it is not the praying that matters, but the sweet chanting of the prayer."

One day a strange thing happened. Rabbi Naphthali Aphter, the greatest opponent and critic of Reb Ezekiel, actually came on a visit to the town of Kozmir, for the Sabbath of Repentance.

Rabbi Naphthali Aphter was the exact opposite of Reb Ezekiel of Kozmir. He was a weakling, a pygmy of a Jew, skin and bones, something a moderate wind could carry away. He fasted every day of the week—from Sabbath to Sabbath, that is. He broke his fast evenings with a plate of soup, nothing more; and lest he should derive from the soup anything more than the barest sustenance, lest he should take pleasure in the taste of food, he would throw into the plate of soup a fistful of salt. On Saturdays he permitted himself meat and fish, in honor of the sanctity of the Sabbath; he ate the eye of a fish and a sinew of flesh. When he ate, every swallow of food could be traced in its passage down his slender, stringy throat. Further to mortify his body, Rabbi Naphthali slept no more than two hours a night; the rest of the time he sat before the sacred books. And when he studied he did not follow the traditional custom, which bids the student set his repetitions to a sweet chant; this he considered a sinful concession to the lust of his ears. He muttered the words dryly under his breath. In the night he held the candle in his right hand, to be certain that he did not doze. His hand trembled, and the drops of grease fell on the yellow pages of the pious books, which he turned with his left hand. The tears ran down his withered, parchment-like cheeks and fell side by side with the drops of grease on the ancient pages, which smelled of wax, tears, hair, and mildew.

He repeated for the thousandth time, in the harsh mutter of his study: "*Shivoh medurei gehinom*—there are seven chambers in the courts of hell. The fire of the first chamber is sixty times as hot as the fire we know on earth; the fire of the second chamber is sixty times as hot as the fire of the first chamber; the fire of the third chamber is sixty times as hot . . . and thus it follows that the fire of the seventh chamber is hotter by sixty times sixty to the seventh time than the fire which we know on earth."

He continued: "Therefore happy are those who are only transformed into fish and animals, into trees and grasses. And there are also human souls that wander in the wildness of space, and there are others that are flung about as with slings, and their plight is bitterest of all."

Rabbi Naphthali had sundered himself completely from the things of this world. He had even separated himself from his wife and knew her no more. But wicked thoughts, evil visitations, tormented him, especially in the nights, and gave him no peace.

And this was not only when he lay down for the two hours of slumber which he permitted himself. Even while he sat at his sacred books shapes and phantoms in the likeness of females surrounded him. It was useless to close his eyes to them, for with closed eyes he only saw them better. They penetrated his ears too. They shook down great masses of black hair, they sang with voices of piercing sweetness, they danced immodestly, and they flung their arms around him. They caressed his sparse little beard, they played with his stiff, flat earlocks, twining them around their fingers.

He fled from these visions and voices to the ritual bath, which lay in a corner of the yard of his house. He tore off his clothes, stumbled down the cold, slippery, stone steps, and flung his weak body into the black, icy water. But even then it seemed to him that he struck his head not against the harsh water but against silky cushions; and his body lay on soft down, tempting and exciting.

A naked woman, irresistibly beautiful, held him close in the hot bands of her arms. . . . He fled from the water and took vows to be harsher with his rebellious and pampered body. He halved his allowance of soup at the end of the day and doubled the salt with which he spoiled its taste. He wept day and night, and his eyes were never dry.

But the Evil Inclination, the Wicked One, whispered mockingly in his ear, "Fool that you are! You have separated yourself from your wife, who is a pure and good woman, to sin in secret with abominations of the night. You have left your simple couch of straw and feathers to loll on divans of silk and down . . ."

Rabbi Naphthali wept so long and so hard that at last the well of his tears dried up and his eyes gave out only a thin rheum. He longed to become blind, so that he might look no more on the sinful world.

But the Evil One read his thoughts and continued to whisper mockery into his ear. "Fool that you are! Why do you seek to rid yourself of the eyes of the flesh? Is it not because you know that with the eyes of the spirit and the imagination you can see sweet visions a thousand times more sinful?"

In the end Rabbi Naphthali decided to visit the rabbinic court of Kozmir. If fasting and mortification of the flesh will not help, perhaps Reb Ezekiel has better counsel, he thought.

He slung a sack over his shoulders, took his prayer shawl and phylacteries under his arm, and set out for Kozmir, planning to arrive there for the Sabbath of Repentance.

When they learned in the court of the Kozmir rabbi that Naphthali himself, the bitterest opponent and critic of Rabbi Ezekiel, had arrived on a visit, there was great rejoicing. Reb Mottye Godel, the chief beadle and grand vizier of the Kozmir rabbi, stroked his beard proudly and said to all the Hasidim, "This is a great victory. If Reb Naphthali himself comes here, the others will follow, and soon all the Jews will acknowledge our rabbi. I tell you, we will live to see that day."

Rabbi Naphthali arrived, of course, not on the Sabbath itself, but on the preceding day; and he asked at once to be admitted to the presence of Reb Ezekiel. But the Kozmir rabbi could not receive him. He was going, he declared, to the baths, to purify himself for the Sabbath. He remained in the baths longer than was his wont. In the steam room he climbed up to the highest and hottest level of the stairs and shouted joyously to the attendants to pour more water on the heated stones and to fill the room with more steam. His followers, who usually accompanied him to the highest steps, fled from him this time, unable to endure the heat.

The rabbi laughed loudly at them. "Fools," he cried, "how will you learn to endure the flames of hell?"

When he returned from the baths Reb Ezekiel lay down on the well-stuffed, leather-covered couch on which he rested in the daytime, and he seemed to have forgotten entirely about Reb Naphthali. After he had taken a nap he commanded that the Sabbath fish be brought in to him to taste, and then he remembered Reb Naphthali.

"Mottye," he said, "bring in the fish prepared for the Sabbath—and Reb Naphthali too."

It was a custom with Reb Ezekiel to taste the Sabbath fish the evening before. He said, "They that taste thereof have merited life, as the Holy Word says."

It was also his custom to sharpen the pearl-handled bread knife himself, and to slice the onions that were served with the fish on the Sabbath.

When Rabbi Naphthali entered, conducted by the chief beadle, Reb Ezekiel greeted him joyously. "Welcome, and blessed be thy coming," he exclaimed in a thundering voice, which sent tremors through Reb Naphthali. He put out his hand, seized Reb Naphthali's, and squeezed it so hard that Reb Naphthali doubled up.

"What good tidings have you for me, Reb Naphthali?" he asked happily.

"I have come to ask you for counsel on the matter of repentance," answered Reb Naphthali, trembling.

"Repentance?" shouted Reb Ezekiel, and his voice was as gay as if he had heard the sweetest tidings. "Repentance? Assuredly! Take a glass of brandy. What is the meaning of the word 'repentance'? It is: to turn! And when a Jew takes a glass of brandy he turns it upside down, which is to say, he performs an act of repentance."

And without waiting Reb Ezekiel filled two silver beakers with brandy in which floated spices and little leaves. "Good health and life, Reb Naphthali," he said and pushed one beaker forward.

Reb Ezekiel emptied his beaker at a gulp. Reb Naphthali broke into a stuttering cough at the mere smell of the drink, but Reb Ezekiel would not let him put it down. "Reb Naphthali, you have come for my counsel. The first thing then, which I will teach you, will be the mystery of eating and drinking."

He forced Reb Naphthali to swallow the brandy and then pushed toward him a huge piece of stuffed carp, highly seasoned. "This," he said with a smile, "comes from the hand of my wife. She is a valiant woman, a pearl of price, and her stuffed fish have in them not less than one-sixtieth of the virtue and taste of Leviathan himself."

The first piece Reb Naphthali tried to swallow stuck in his throat. But Reb Ezekiel would not be put off, and he compelled Reb Naphthali to eat. "Rabbi Naphthali, the road of repentance is not an easy one, as you see. But there is no turning back on it."

When it was impossible to make Rabbi Naphthali eat another bite, Reb Ezekiel took him by the hand, led him into the other room, and bade him stretch himself out on the well-stuffed leather-covered couch.

Rabbi Naphthali refused to lie down. "What?" he said. "Lie down and sleep in the middle of the day? And with the Sabbath approaching?"

"It is better to sleep two days than to entertain one thought," said Reb Ezekiel and closed the door on him.

During the Ten Penitential Days between the New Year and the Day of Atonement, Reb Ezekiel taught Reb Naphthali the mystery of food and the inner significance of joyousness. Every day there was another banquet in the rabbinic court, and wine and mead were consumed in barrelfuls. The singing in the court was heard throughout Kozmir; it echoed in the surrounding hills and carried across the Vistula.

"Well, Reb Naphthali, are you visited by thoughts, by fantasies?" Reb Ezekiel asked him every day.

"Less now," answered Reb Naphthali.

"In that case, here's another glass of mead," said Reb Ezekiel, and he saw to it that Reb Naphthali drank it all down.

And every day, when the banquet was over, he led his guest into his own room and made him sleep on his leather-covered couch. "Sleep!" he said. "Ordinary, unlearned Jews are permitted to sleep in the daytime only on Sabbaths. But good and pious Jews who are followers of a Hasidic rabbi are enjoined to sleep by daylight every day in the week."

When they all sat at the dinner which precedes the eve of the Day of Atonement, Reb Ezekiel kept closer watch than ever on the visitor. Not a minute passed but what he pressed on him another tidbit. "Reb Naphthali, eat, I say. Every mouthful you swallow is written down in your heavenly account as a meritorious deed. Eat heartily and swell the account."

In the court of Kozmir the Day of Atonement was the merriest day of the year. The rabbi himself stood at the pulpit and conducted the prayers. He did not let anyone replace him, but led the congregation from morning till evening, through all the divisions of devotion. He did not sit down for a minute, and his voice never ceased from singing.

All prayers were set to a happy chant in Kozmir, even the most doleful, even the martyrologies. The House of Prayer was jammed with Jews in prayer shawls and white robes. Above them all towered the rabbi, his head adorned with a skullcap wrought with gold embroidery, the crown and glory of the congregation. His voice rang as loudly in the closing prayer of the Day of Atonement as it had done in the opening prayer the evening before, though he had not tasted food or drink for twenty-four hours. Around him stood his dynasty, his sons and grandsons, all in silk and white satin, and their voices sustained him throughout the whole service. The melodious tumult of this choir was heard in town, in the hills, and in the village across the river; the congregation helped to swell it, and the day was observed with dancing as well as singing.

Around the door of the House of Prayer stood the feminine half of the dynasty, the rabbi's wife, his daughters, his daughters-in-law, his granddaughters. They too were dressed in silk and satin; on their bosoms shone gold-embroidered coverings; on their heads wimples glittered with precious stones; and their lips moved piously in whispered prayer.

Reb Naphthali bent down to the earth in the fervor of his devotions. He longed to squeeze at least one tear from his sinful eyes, but all his efforts availed him nothing. The riot of song all about him deafened him, and he could not concentrate on one miserable thought.

When the Day of Atonement was over, the congregants took the stubs of the burning candles from the boxes of sand and went out into the synagogue yard for the Benediction of the Moon. The moon swam luminously in a clear sky, and the congregants rejoiced in her light. "Welcome," they cried to her, dancing joyously. "Be thou a good sign and a bringer of good luck."

Reb Ezekiel stood in the midst of his Hasidim, radiant as the moon in the midst of the stars. "Welcome!" he cried thunderously to Reb Naphthali and took him by the hand as if he were about to draw him into a dance.

But in that instant Reb Naphthali was seized with a violent trembling, and before anyone could take hold of him he had slipped to the ground.

The Hasidim dropped to the ground beside him, but when they felt his hands and face, these were as cold as the damp grass on which he lay. There was no sign of breath in the frail body.

Panic seized the assembly. Hundreds of congregants tried to touch the body where it lay wrapped in prayer shawl and white robe. But those that were at the center lifted up the body of Reb Naphthali, carried it into the House of Prayer, and laid it down on the pulpit, where the Scroll is laid for the reading of the Law. Those that could not get into the House did not go to their homes but remained standing, petrified, and some of them began to weep audibly.

The panic lasted only a minute or two.

The door of the rabbi's room opened, and the rabbi, his face as radiant as when he had stretched out his hand to Reb Naphthali and the latter had fallen to the ground, looked out above the congregation. He had withdrawn for a moment, and now he was back with the congregation.

His voice rang out. "If anyone wants to weep, let him take a rowboat and pass to the other side of the Vistula. There is no weeping in Kozmir."

Amazed, silent, the Hasidim followed the gesture of the rabbi and filed into his room.

The table sparkled with gold and silver in the light of a hundred candles. Ranged along its center were dusty bottles of wine and mead, each surrounded by a heap of grapes and pears and pomegranates.

The Hasidim seated themselves. The rabbi drank, sang happily, and distributed morsels to his favorites. This night he was more generous than ever before. Children and grandchildren sat at the head of the table, snatched his gifts, and followed him in song.

The feasting lasted through the night, and only when the morning star was peeping in through the window did Mottye, the chief beadle, give the signal that the rabbi was now prepared to speak. The Hasidim crowded close to him, their hands on one another's shoulders.

Many minutes passed before the rabbi came to his pronouncement. He sat playing with the silver watch that lay in front of him on the table. He picked up a heavy bunch of grapes and moved it up and down as if he were estimating its weight. And throughout all this he chanted a Hasidic melody to himself.

When he had finished the melody and had let all the echoes die down about him, he opened his mouth and spoke. "I wanted to teach him the great mystery of joyousness, but he was unable to grasp it."

He looked out of the window toward the House of Prayer, where the little body of Reb Naphthali, wrapped in prayer shawl and white robe, lay on the pulpit, and he ended his pronouncement:

"He had sunk too far into habits of gloom, and there was no saving him."

Translated by Maurice Samuel

Sand

I. J. SINGER

1.

ON THAT afternoon of the Feast of the Pentecost the Jews of Podgurna did not, as was their custom, retire to sleep when the meal was over; instead they took off their high, dusty boots, gathered their wives and children about them, and streamed toward the hut of Pesach Plotnik.

Barefoot, and with shirt open at the throat, Pesach was standing by the low well, his open and bewhiskered mouth immersed in the bucket of fresh water he had just drawn up. With every swallow the thick veins throbbed on the hard, sunburned neck. Thin silvery threads of water ran down his vast, curly beard and found their way to his fleshy bosom under the open shirt.

"Reb Pesach! God have mercy! Do you want to drain the well dry?"

"The more you drink, the stronger you become," gurgled Reb Pesach from the bucket. He lifted his face for a moment to grin at the arriving guests and applied himself again.

The men sat down on the rotting foundations that peered out from under the walls of Pesach's hut. The women gathered in a group around a log, and the children lay down in the sun and dug their toes into the hot sand.

The early summer, which is Pentecost time, is hot in Podgurna. For miles to the north, east, and south there is nothing but white sand, and when the sky is clear, the vast arch that meets the horizon on every side seems to shut out or to annihilate the rest of the world. Only to the west is the monotony broken; there the Vistula passes among low, wood-covered hills, where the shepherd lads lie in wait for girls bathing in the river. Around the hills there are low forts covered with ivy; and in front of each fort there is an old gun on two wheels, a trophy from the Turkish war. Between each pair of forts a little soldier, rifle at shoulder, paces evenly back and forth. But Podgurna has no trees; its white sandy body lies naked to the heat of the sun.

On the wastes surrounding Podgurna you will find nothing but an occasional bucket, battered beyond use, an abandoned and tattered military drum, a few empty cartridge shells, and the whitened jawbones of horses and oxen. The village itself consists of a few huts huddling in a depression. The roofs are not of straw, like the roofs of Polish cottages, but of board, and the spaces around the windows are not tinted blue but red or brown, like the windows in big Russian villages near a railroad station.

On this afternoon the few young men of Podgurna are bored, as usual; and no matter how low they pull the shining visors of their dashing Russian caps over their brows, the sun still creeps into their eyes. A wind blowing from the river brings a suggestion of coolness and foam, and the young men want to steal away for a dip. But Pesach Plotnik holds them back. "Boys, don't leave. Reb Jonah will be here any minute."

The young men obey. They have no alternative when it is Pesach Plotnik, the most important householder in the village, who commands. Besides, the few dozen Jewish families of Podgurna are so interrelated by marriage that Pesach is a relative of almost everyone assembled at his house this afternoon; brothers- and sisters-in-law, aunts, uncles, and cousins direct or by marriage, one name or another fits nearly everyone present. So the young men, restrained by family duty as well as by respect, return to their seats, and the discussion is resumed on the subject of the latest quarrel with the Jews of the town of Grobitze.

There is bad blood between the villagers and the Jews of Grobitze.

When the Jews of Podgurna went to the services in the synagogue of Grobitze for the first time they were received with a mixture of astonishment and friendliness. Those were the days when the government first began to build forts along the banks of the Vistula. From somewhere in remote Russia came hordes of red-bearded, flaxen-haired peasants and they dug up the sands at the foot of the hills. The millionaire contractor who brought them to Podgurna was a clean-shaven man who wore gold-rimmed spectacles. Together with these hordes of peasants he brought some dozens of black-bearded men who carried whips instead of spades and shovels and who drove before them countless herds of big-horned oxen and woolly sheep.

In those days there was a great boom in Grobitze. The peasants bought great quantities of tobacco and herring and sold the shopkeepers their home-made wares of wooden spoons and platters. The soldiers who occupied the district brought stolen goods to the shopkeepers and practically gave them away. But when on the Sabbath morning the few dozen black-bearded Russes—as they were thought to be—marched into the Grobitze synagogue, with the clean-shaven millionaire contractor at their head, the assembled Jews were so astounded and delighted that they scarcely knew what to do. Young men even forgot themselves in the midst of the Prayer of The Eighteen Benedictions, which must be said in complete silence and absorption, body and head turned rigidly to the east; they interrupted their devotions to stare at the clean-shaven millionaire where he stood, his neat little prayer shawl slipping from his shoulders, his bare lips moving in prayer. They watched the Russes closely, to see whether they accompanied their prayers with the right gestures and whether at the end of the Eighteen Benedictions they took the three little steps backward in traditional style. Later, when the newcomers were called up to the pulpit, to be honored with a reading from the Pentateuch, some of them did not know the appropriate prayer by heart and had to be helped out by friendly householders of Grobitze.

A variety of marvelous stories was evoked by the coming of these black-bearded Jews from the interior of Russia.

Pious and learned citizens of Grobitze remembered what they had read in ancient books concerning legions of converts to the faith, the ten lost tribes, and the Sephardic Jews of the Yemen. It was generally accepted that these newcomers came from remote parts, somewhere near the borders of Persia, in the vicinity of Shushan, Ahasuerus's capital. Some of the younger people, less pious than the older generation but participants in the neo-Hebraic culture, surmised that these were Khazars, Russian converts of the eighth century. But whoever these Jews were, the community of Grobitze was mightily exalted by their coming. Whenever the clean-shaven millionaire contractor came riding through the town in his open carriage, a white-bearded Russian general seated beside him, a vast coachman in a shiny silk hat and red sash on the box, the Jews of Grobitze felt their respect for themselves take a sudden upward leap; and evenings they recalled stories of righteous kings who took Jews as their nearest advisers, of anti-Jewish decrees which were annulled, and of prosperous days in the House of Israel.

But all this was only at the beginning.

The work on forts along the Vistula stopped; the clean-shaven millionaire contractor climbed one day into his open carriage, drove off with his coachman in the silk hat and red sash, and never returned. The red-bearded peasants climbed into their long wooden carts and also drove off, never to return. But the couple of dozen black-bearded Jews who had come with the hosts remained. They took the barracks to pieces and put up small poor huts not far from the foot of the sand-hills. Then it was that the Jews of Grobitze realized that they too had been building castles on sandy foundations. The town sank back into its old humdrum existence; the big new ritual baths they had hoped the millionaire contractor would build for them disappeared with their other dreams; and the mysterious visitors from the ancient capital of Shushan turned out to be Siberian Jews—at least, such was the view now taken—Siberian Jews who had served terms for forgery, counterfeiting, incendiarism, and the like, ignorant boors who did not know the difference between a cross and the letter *aleph,* and, worst of all, paupers, absolute paupers.

Since the disappearance of the contractor and the withdrawal of the workers there had never been peace between Grobitze and Podgurna.

The Jews of Podgurna sit before the well and recall the humiliations and insults they have borne at the hands of the Jews of Grobitze.

They recall a certain morning of a Passover. The houses have been cleaned inside and out, as befits the holiday. There is a pleasant smell of borscht and goose fat in the air. The Jews of Podgurna, young and old, go several miles on foot to Grobitze, to the services in the synagogue. The road near the river leads through fresh meadows in which a few spring flowers lift their modest heads. The Jews march on, wetting their boots in the shallow ditches and stumbling over roots hidden in the grass. They are happy. A mild, sweet wind blows across their faces and plays with the locks of their newly trimmed beards. There is a holiday spirit in the air as well as in their hearts. But when they enter the synagogue of Grobitze they are greeted with hooting and reproaches and bitter laughter. Elderly Jews point scornful fingers at them; young people thrust them out of the synagogue. How did they dare to walk all that distance on a holiday, and to prayers at that, without the traditional precaution against infringement of the Law? Did they know the limitations on distances for the Sabbath and for Holy Days? Very likely not, stormed the Jews of Grobitze. But that was no excuse. They should not pray among decent people in the synagogue. Their place was in the little beggars' synagogue, whither they were dispatched. Arriving there, the Jews of Podgurna found waiting for them dirty old tables, covered with the grease of countless candles, at which to say their prayers. And later in the day the Jews of Grobitze sent them bundles of matzos, unleavened bread, and of dumplings, as if they were beggars picked up on the street.

Sitting near the well, the Jews of Podgurna remember many humiliating incidents: anniversaries for the dead delayed and forgotten, to the derision of the Jews of Grobitze; prayer shawls seized and examined and discovered to be ritually impure; the contempt of the older people, the shrill laughter of the young. And the Jews of Podgurna had suffered in silence, for they were at the mercy of Grobitze. Where else could a man go on the anniversary of the death of his father or mother to say the *Kaddish?* Where else could they send a boy to learn his Hebrew letters? Where else could they consult a learned man concerning the purity or impurity of an animal or a fowl? And where else, finally, could one of them be buried when he died? All of these considerations had held them in bondage to Grobitze; but ever since that last incident with Pesach Plotnik in the synagogue of Grobitze, not even these considerations were strong enough to maintain the tie. The time had come for the Jews of Podgurna to act.

This is how the thing had happened.

Jews of Podgurna were driving some hundreds of head of cattle to the garrison. It was a Friday afternoon shortly before the Pentecost, and the Jews were in a great hurry. They urged the beasts on, smote them on the rump, and broke their sticks on the horns. But the day was hot, and the oxen would not be driven too fast. They stopped every little while and huddled against one another; they dug their horns into the sand and would not be moved. And when at last they galloped across the market place of Grobitze, the Jews of that community were on their way to synagogue to welcome the Sabbath.

The next morning, the Sabbath, the Jews of Podgurna offered their most abject agologies; they also offered, in expiation, to make the full quota of the day's donations in the name of the Holy Law. But the Jews of Grobitze would not forgive; nor would they call up a single Jew of Podgurna to do some holy office.

The morning drew on. The sun was shining into the dusty synagogue, its rays becoming hotter as the hours wore on. The candles wilted in their sockets, and the burnished crowns on the Scrolls of the Law burned as if with an inward flame.

The climax of that morning's bitterness came with the washing of hands of the priests. The priests had removed their boots, according to the ritual, and Pesach Plotnik of Podgurna, who was also a Kohen—that is to say, a priestly descendant of Aaron, brother of Moses—took off his boots like all the others. But when he bared his arms and approached the Levites, who were pouring water on the hands of the other priests, they refused to serve him. The young men of Podgurna who saw this frightful insult felt the blood rushing to their cheeks. They threw their prayer shawls from their shoulders, they rolled up their sleeves, and they flung themselves at the Levites of the congregation of Grobitze. They seized two of them, little, frightened fellows, by the throat, dragged them over to the basin, and howled, "Pour water, you louse, pour water!"

The Levites poured water, but they were so frightened that more water fell on Pesach's bare feet than on his hands. In hoarse, angry tones Pesach blessed the community of Grobitze, and when he had finished the benediction he brought his fist down on the table with such force that all the candles in the synagogue danced. "If any Podgurna Jew crosses the threshold of this synagogue after today," he yelled, "I'll tear a leg out of his arse!"

The Jews of Grobitze howled back derisively, "You'll be coming here, you boors! You can't manage by yourselves."

But Pesach Plotnik called the Jews of Podgurna to a meeting; instead of going to bed after the Pentecostal feast, they were to assemble in front of his house.

Here they sat and talked while they waited for Reb Jonah, who at last was perceived crawling barefoot toward the company, his wrinkled old face beaming with good humor.

Reb Jonah is very old; but his great distinction is that he has been a Cantonist; that is to say, he was snatched from his parents in childhood and made to serve the Czar for twenty-five years. In all these years Reb Jonah did not once play the renegade to his Jewishness. They put him to the torture, but he would not yield. They made him kneel a whole day on hard peas, they made him run after wild horses, they put him in the guardhouse for refusing to say Christian prayers along with the other soldiers, but Reb Jonah held out. He said the Jewish prayers every day, and even now he can repeat them by heart from beginning to end. He also knows when the Holy Days are due, and he can twine the ritual fringes which all pious Jews wear. Not for nothing had he been made the beadle of the village synagogue in far-off Siberia when he had finished his twenty-five years of service.

Here he comes now, wearing even on this hot day the heavy Siberian hat that merchants wear only in the winter. He is in his shirtsleeves; his four-fringed garment lies over his shirt. Reb Jonah is fond of telling stories of his long service in the army, and he speaks disrespectfully of modern young men who have only three years and eight months to serve instead of a quarter of a century, like himself. But he likes the young people just the same. He greets them with a laugh as he approaches, his countless wrinkles, his white beard and whiskers, illumined by his cheerfulness.

The only man in Podgurna whom he treats with respect is Pesach Plotnik, the oldest resident of the village except for himself. And he listens now to what Pesach has to say; he listens, keeping his hand behind his ear and grunting every minute or two. "I hear you, Pesach."

Pesach speaks with him long and earnestly in the presence of the assembled village. Why should he, Reb Jonah, still go peddling in the villages at his advanced age? He is over eighty, may God spare him until his hundred and twentieth year. Would it not be better for him to remain henceforth in the village, to take these youngsters lying about in the sand and teach them to read from a prayer book? Would it not be easier, and also more becoming, for him to lead the congregation in prayer and to see to it that fringes and prayer shawls and the little *mezzuzahs* on the doors were all in order? The villagers would give him in return the very best they had, flour and milk, barley and good pieces of meat, so that neither he nor his granddaughter Mashka should want for anything. And in this way the congregation of Podgurna would be liberated from its bondage to those Grobitze stinkers.

Reb Jonah listens and finds that every word of Pesach's is brimful of wisdom. And when Pesach has finished, the congregation gathers around Reb Jonah and goes into a kind of chant.

"Reb Jonah, you'll be able to remind us when the anniversaries are due! Reb Jonah, we'll build a little synagogue for you!"

And the women add, "Reb Jonah, we'll sew dresses for your Mashka! We'll bring her skirts and pinafores!"

Reb Jonah is radiant and bewildered with happiness. He recalls how, in far-off days, he marched in line with the soldiers, and under the heathen hat of the Czar wore, in secret, the headpiece of his phylacteries—a little headpiece, the size of a walnut. He recalls the siege of Sebastopol and the maneuvers at which he saw the Czar in person; he also recalls that he has three medals, and that for many years he was the faithful beadle of a little synagogue in a Siberian village.

And old Jonah smites himself on the chest, and he growls from the thicknesses of hair surrounding his lips, "Everything you want, dear Pesach. I'll teach them to read in the prayer book; I'll twine the fringes for the prayer shawls. Twenty-five years I served in the army. I was in the war, and I never forgot my Jewish prayers."

There is joy among the Jews of Podgurna. Reb Jonah passes around his bone snuff box, the men take huge sniffs and sneeze contentedly. Reb Jonah himself takes the last pinch, bigger than all the rest, sniffs it up with a single breath, and shows all these young people how one takes snuff without sneezing. After which he imitates their pitiful, helpless sneezes: "Atchoo! Atchoo-oo!"

2.

In the early morning, when the sun begins to peep over the hills and the birds are flicking the sand over their bodies, Reb Jonah and his granddaughter Mashka are already up and busy.

Reb Jonah creeps barefoot from hut to hut and taps at the windowpanes with his long, hard nails, calling his young pupils to their lessons; he accompanies himself with a melody that is a mixture of some ancient Russian folk song and the traditional Jewish chant of a beadle waking Jews to their morning prayers.

"Get up, my little ones," sings Reb Jonah, "because if you don't there's a strap waiting for you."

Mashka stands at the door of their hut, one hand on her hip, the other arched above her eyes; she stares across the sandy wastes as if she is seeing them for the first time. She lifts up her head and looks at the clay-covered rafters, in which there are several nests; tiny swallows dance about in them, showing, not their beaks, but their stiff, colored little tails.

Soon the youngsters will be here, for the hut is now the village *cheder*. Mashka throws another look around the neat room and once more wipes the two wooden benches on which the children are to sit.

When Reb Jonah has collected all his pupils he arranges them in ranks. In one hand he holds his belt, which he has taken off and uses both as baton and whip; with the other hand he holds up his trousers, which otherwise would fall down. He walks through the ranks and sees to it that the boys stand properly at attention, with feet close together, shoulders drawn back, bodies leaning slightly forward. When he is quite satisfied with their bearing he takes out the fringes of his ritual garment, utters a single, firm "Hear, O Israel," and issues the command, "In single file, forward march! Each boy must kiss the fringes, march!"

He does not always teach inside the *cheder*. When the morning is mild and windless he prefers to range the children around him outside, while he sits down on a stone with an old and tattered prayer book open on one knee. He points to the big letters with the straw of a broom and chants, "Abrashka, a little square table with a leg chopped off—that's the letter *hai*."

"Moshka, a closed box with one side bulging out, that's the letter *samach*."

None of the grownups is in Podgurna these days. The men are out on the roads, driving oxen from village to village and from markets to the garrison slaughterhouse; they move about in great clouds of dust under the hot summer sky. The oxen lower their heads and fling the dust about with their horns. Now and then a gelded ox remembers the days of his masculine strength and turns in unprovoked fury on another ox; then the herdsmen bellow so loudly that their voices can be heard for miles around.

"Hey, Abrashka, hey, give him one over the head, the old skirt-chaser!"

Voices respond, "Give it to him, the one with the crumpled horn!"

The women are not at home either; they are peddling in the villages, making their way through fields of grain, along narrow, twisting paths leading from farm to farm.

"Do you need anything, Panie?"

In the village are left only those children who are too big to be carried along and too little to help father or mother. All day long they lie in the sun around Jonah's hut and dig their toes into the hot sand.

When Reb Jonah's throat goes dry with repeating the lessons, or his foot falls asleep from too much sitting, he ceases to play the schoolmaster and becomes the drill sergeant. He gives the boys sticks to put on their shoulders like guns, he teaches them to march in a straight line, and he slaps his thigh to keep them in step.

"One, two! One, two!"

The youngsters march. Abrashka, Pesach Plotnik's grandson, has the smoky chimney of a lamp; he puts this to his mouth and serves as company trumpeter.

Mashka stands at the door, sees the old man's joy, and shakes her head pityingly. "An old man is like a baby, just like a baby," she murmurs.

The day drags on, the sun crawls reluctantly across the sky, as if it hated to sink behind the fortresses on the hilltops; and Mashka comes creeping out of the house for the thousandth time to look at the sun. She does not know what to do with herself. Now she shifts the small square mirror, with the fly-spotted photographs stuck into the frame, from one wall to another; now she combs her thick chestnut hair into another style. She takes off the beads around her throat and counts them once more; then she breaks off this occupation suddenly with the look of a startled bird.

Sometimes, very far away across the sands, she sees a white something twinkling and trembling in the quivering air, and she cannot tell whether the something is approaching or retreating. It draws nearer, and at last she recognizes a soldier. Tired and dusty, he comes across the sands to the door of the hut, to ask for a drink of water. At rare intervals there comes an old, lame beggar, who takes off his hat and displays a shock of white hair. He opens a tattered sack and takes from it dry husks of bread; he lays his old military coat on the ground, sits on it in the shadow of the hut, and chews slowly. Then he gets up and goes. And again the long, dusty hours, the empty, dry, hot hours, pass slowly over Mashka's head, and it seems to her that they will always, always pass over her head like that, never changing, world without end.

Mashka goes out into the sand, pulls her dress up above her knees, and dances. There is no one to see. She opens her blouse and shows first the whiteness of her throat, and then one little breast, and, as her dancing grows wilder and her blouse opens more, the other little breast. She puts her hands up to her young breasts, very tenderly, as if she were holding two young kittens to her heart. Suddenly she sees her shadow on the sand, imitating every gesture of hers, and she is ashamed. She covers herself hastily.

Later in the day she goes down to the Vistula, finds a deserted stretch of bank, and slips into the water. But after she has been swimming awhile she thinks she can hear a whispering and muttering around her. She covers her nakedness with her hands; she steals back to the shore and hastily draws her shift over her.

Only in the evening does she sit down in front of the door of their hut; she is quiet now, meditative, contented, as though she were resting after a long day's work. A few shots come through the darkness from the forts on the hills, and in the distance a trumpet sends its ringing command through the dusty air. Mashka loves the sound of the trumpet in the evening, and she listens with strained attention until all the echoes have died away in the wilderness around her. She sits waiting for the voice of the trumpet, and also for the footsteps of a visitor who comes now and then from Grobitze and sometimes spends the night in the hut. When she thinks she hears him she puts her hand to her eyes and peers into the darkness.

The only Jew of Grobitze who does not share in the quarrel with the Podgurna community is Aaron, the son of the slaughterer of Grobitze.

Aaron is still a very young man. His little black beard is as soft as silk, and his pale cheeks as smooth and fresh as the cheeks of an only and spoiled child. And yet more than a year has passed since Aaron, who is a slaughterer in his own right, lost his wife in childbirth, and the prohibition to slaughter fowl and cattle which was then laid upon him has not yet been lifted, and he has nothing to do at home. Not that he lacks anything. His father has a fine, smooth slaughtering blade which he keeps in a silk sheath, and he is never short of work. Every time he kills an ox he receives a few coins, which he shoves into the back pocket of his greasy long coat. In the evening he comes home, opens the door, takes out the coins, and throws them into his wife's lap. Aaron's mother is always busy in the kitchen, which reeks of blood and is filled with chicken feathers.

Aaron has all that he needs, but he has a beautiful, light, keen slaughtering blade of his own. So he does not stay home but goes from village to village, between the waving fields of grain, seeks out the Jews who are too far from the town to bring their animals to be slaughtered there in proper ritual fashion, and asks gently, "Is there something to be slaughtered? Perhaps a little calf? Or maybe a chicken?"

Aaron likes slaughterer's work. He loves to see a healthy goat put up a fight with a farmer and refuse to be thrown. Then when the goat lies on the ground, its legs tied together, Aaron rolls up his sleeves thoughtfully and tests the glittering blade against his fingernail, seeing meanwhile the reflection of his face in the steel. Then he stoops over the goat and looks with smiling eyes into the eyes of the animal staring back at him stonily.

Aaron does not fail to visit Podgurna, among other villages. And as often as he comes he has this greeting for Reb Jonah: "Well, Reb Jonah, have your little rascals learned anything yet?"

"They're learning, they're learning, the young blackguards," Reb Jonah answers and smiles contentedly out of his vast white bush of hair.

Aaron remains sitting in Reb Jonah's hut a long time. He watches Mashka standing, silent and timid, over the dishes, and a light smile creeps in and out of his soft silken beard.

The very first time he stayed overnight in Reb Jonah's hut Aaron saw wonderful things, which had never gone out of his mind.

Mashka, who was preparing his bed for him, worked so hard shaking up the straw-filled mattress that her breasts stood out against her thin blouse and the ringlets danced and trembled on her soft, girlish neck. Then she lifted her hands to her hair, so that the wide sleeves slipped off her shoulders. She undid her braids and said, with the humility of a village girl, "You can go to sleep now. The bed is made."

Lying in the bed, Aaron felt the warmth Mashka had left in the pillows, pressing them to her breasts. He could not stop wondering why it was that he had never noticed his wife making the bed, and then a thought began to torment him: Have I really been a widower for a whole year?

After that night his visits to Red Jonah became more frequent.

Reb Jonah waits for him always. Having undertaken to keep the Jews of Podgurna informed of the exact dates of Holy Days and anniversaries, Reb Jonah has discovered that his skill with the calendar is largely imaginary. One Jew of Podgurna has already been misled and has failed to light the memorial candle for his dead father at the right time. But Aaron, the young slaughterer, knows everything; he can tell a man when his parents died as if he had been present at the funeral; nor does he ever make a mistake with the Holy Days. Reb Jonah is happy that Aaron does not notice how he is being pumped for information, and he always says to him, "Reb Aaron, stay the night with us, do. . . . Reb Aaron, it's dangerous to go home so late."

Mashka thumps and pulls and pushes the straw-filled mattress as if she wanted to destroy it. She holds the pillows against her breasts a long time and beats them into shape. Afterward Aaron lies there, rigid and awake. He throws the cover off his hot body, then pulls it on again. Reb Jonah's dull voice comes to him from the other room.

"Reb Aaron, last year there were two portions of the Pentateuch which fell on the same week, weren't there?"

"Reb Aaron, if you bury a man at night, do you reckon his anniversary from that day or from the day after?"

3.

The whole summer passes, and the Jews of Podgurna have not set foot in the synagogue of Grobitze; the Jews of Grobitze are eaten by rage and disappointment.

Things are not at all bad in the village of Podgurna. Contracts have been let to Jewish merchants of Plozk for the extension of the Podgurna fortress; the cattle for the workers and garrison come from surrounding villages, and all week long the Jews of Podgurna collect new droves for the slaughterhouse. Almost every day they pass through the streets of Grobitze with hundreds of head of oxen, raising a mighty dust and leaving behind little heaps of manure and fragments of horn. The women in the market place shove their baskets of vegetables against the wall till the drove of hungry oxen has passed by; mothers snatch their children to their bosoms, and menfolk stand by with brooms to sweep up what the cattle leave behind. They speak angrily.

"I hear they're making money hand over fist."

"I'm told they get ten kopecks for every head they drive in."

The Jews of Podgurna have put down the money for a Scroll of the Law, which is now being prepared for them, and there is a great story attached to this Scroll. Reb Jonah never fails to repeat it to Aaron whenever the latter comes on a visit.

One day a messenger came to the village of Podgurna, a mounted messenger in uniform, and in his hand he bore a letter from the High Command of the fortress of Podgurna. The Jews of Podgurna were frightened. They knew they had built their village on land that belonged, technically, to the fortress; and they also knew that this was forbidden to Jews. But they had ignored the law and put their trust in God, hoping that the transgression would be forgotten. Perhaps the authorities had indeed forgotten. Perhaps someone from Grobitze had sent in a little reminder—who could tell? The Jews of Podgurna donned their holiday clothes. Reb Jonah pinned his three medals on the lapel of his greenish coat, and put himself at the head of the procession.

"Forward, march!"

But the general had not been angry at all! He had received them with a smile, he had stroked his beard several times, and he had said, "My children, you are free to live even in the fortress itself if you want. That isn't why I sent for you at all. Not at all. It's something else. That contractor of yours, Moses Abramitch, gave me a hundred rubles for your community. I suppose you'll know how to spend it, eh?"

"God bless Your Highness," the Jews chanted and took three steps backward, as if they were finishing a prayer. They did not go straight home from this strange visit. They went in procession to a village where a pious scribe was known to live, and they put the money down for a Scroll of the Law.

The Jews of Grobitze were filled with fury when the story reached their ears. They had begun to see that Podgurna was not so helpless as they thought. It was rumored that after this extraordinary reception by the general the Jews of Podgurna had been emboldened to ask him for a little plot of earth to be set aside as the village cemetery. And if the general should grant this petition Podgurna would be able to spit at Grobitze: synagogue, teacher, cemetery—they would have everything of their own.

So there are many in Grobitze who now regret the whole business and say angrily, "We shouldn't have quarreled with them. The community will suffer for it."

Others, dignified and self-assured, refuse to be downcast. "Wait," they counsel. "Patience! They'll be coming to us yet in their stocking feet."

Meanwhile the only Jew of Grobitze to visit Podgurna is Aaron, the slaughterer's son.

Things are looking up for Aaron too. No sooner was work resumed on the fortress than the Plozk contractors put up several new slaughterhouses on the riverbank—long, low wooden buildings well smeared with shiny tar. Every day there is a great slaughtering of oxen, which the Podgurna Jews drive in from the villages. And Aaron, whom the Jews of Grobitze still keep from practicing his profession, spends the whole day in the fortress slaughterhouses, kneeling, blade in hand, over the bound animals.

The slaughterhouses are filled with tumult. Several dozen young men, all of them from Plozk, wrestle from morning till night with the lean, horned cattle. The oxen know before they enter the slaughterhouses what awaits them. They feel it in the smell of blood that permeates the air for miles around; they feel it in the packs of hungry dogs that follow them along the road, and in the heavy, bloated flies that settle on their skins. And as they draw near the barracks their fears are confirmed by the bellowing and screaming and choked gurgling that float from the tarred wooden buildings. When they are a few yards from the barracks they rebel; they lower their horns, open their nostrils wide, turn upon their drivers, and try to stampede. But the half-naked young men come out from the buildings, they tie ropes to the horns of the oxen, they drag them forward to the slaughter. There they lie in rows, their feet bound, their glassy eyes following the black man who moves quietly from row to row, the thin, flashing blade in his hand; something inside them turns over, their throats contract convulsively, and a choked screaming issues from between their clenched teeth and spends itself against the blood-bespattered, tarred walls.

A faint excitement stirs in Aaron. The oxen stretch in endless rows; the blade in his hand is so light, so fine, that he does not feel the weight of it. The glassy eyes of the oxen follow him wherever he goes. He too is stripped to the waist, and the sweating, shouting young men give him no rest.

"Faster there, Aaron! That's enough testing the knife on your nail! The soldiers don't mind how you kill."

He moves faster from one outstretched throat to another: a light swift motion of the knife, back and forth, then he tries to jump clear of the hot breath and the spouting blood.

The screaming and gurgling grow louder. Life runs out in thin, streaming rivulets, which spread on the cement floor of the barrack and drain into gutters leading to the river. Outside there is a throaty howling of dogs; and sometimes, when one of the men heaves a huge, bloody bone among them and breaks the leg or back of a dog, the howling changes to a long, trembling wail. Not far from the animals that still spout blood, barefoot village girls kneel with shallow tin bowls, catching whatever blood they can before it all runs away into the river. They carry the blood home and cook it. The young men take no money, but now and then one of them lays bloody hands on a girl and drags her away to a corner of the slaughterhouse. To get time for this byplay they must work all the faster, and so they harry Aaron and drag him from beast to beast. The sweat of their bodies beats into his nostrils. When they are not yelling at him to kill more swiftly, they nudge him, indicate the barefoot village girls, and ask in hoarse mockery, "Hey, Reb Aaron, what do you think?"

Then something boils up in Aaron; he feels the veins in his eyes growing hot, and there is a tingling at the roots of his hair. He sets his teeth and rolls his sleeves higher; he feels his anger rising at the sight of the outstretched throats and glaring eyes of the oxen, and his knife slides faster, bites deeper.

When the day's work is over he comes to Podgurna, to visit Reb Jonah.

The sun is still shining. Reb Jonah welcomes him from a distance with his broad, wrinkled smile. He shows off his pupils before Aaron; he makes them crawl on their bare knees in the hot sand, as he was forced to do in the army whenever he displeased his officers.

Mashka welcomes Aaron with a shake of her head, which sets her ringlets dancing. She is ashamed of her grandfather, playing soldiers with the little boys, and when Aaron comes near she lowers her eyes and murmurs apologetically, "An old man is just like a baby."

But Aaron smiles gently and answers, "It doesn't matter. When we're his age we'll be the same."

They smile at each other, and Aaron wants to laugh out loud at the thought that Mashka could ever be as old even as his mother, who waddles along, turning her hips right and left. And Mashka wants to laugh out loud at the thought that this young man could ever be as old as her grandfather, who has never been young, and that his soft black silken beard could ever become white and hard and bristly.

Aaron opens a package, takes out little squares of cheesecake, and eats modestly and slowly. Since he began working in the slaughterhouse he has been eating more. His mother bakes and cooks for him; she gives him fat food, roasts, giblets. His black silky beard is beginning to curl, his eyes are becoming narrower above his pale, high cheekbones; they are filled with a heavy dreaminess.

Mashka stands over the wash trough, her arms in water to the elbows. She feels his hot glance passing over her neck to her bosom. She pulls her blouse together and shivers.

Reb Jonah dismisses his pupils and sits down on the stone outside the hut. He wipes the sweat from his brow, as if he had just dismissed a company of soldiers. Aaron joins him and offers him a square of cheesecake. The old man breaks it in two, gives Mashka one piece and eats the other slowly, grinding it softly between his withered gums.

Mashka suddenly becomes very shy. She does not want to eat her piece of cake. She feels Aaron's eyes on her, and she burns from head to foot.

Aaron says, "You can eat that. It's good. Home baking."

Reb Jonah finishes chewing and swallowing, and he talks ceaselessly. He tells of the progress of the Scroll of the Law. The scribe has now reached the fourth book of the Pentateuch. When the Scroll is finished it will be brought to Podgurna and deposited in the back room in Reb Pesach's hut. Every day Reb Jonah will come and polish the golden crown of the covering. The Eternal Light will always be burning in Reb Pesach's room, as if the hut were a real synagogue. Women will come with long anniversary candles; as there are no candlesticks, Reb Jonah will prepare boxes of sand to serve as holders. He knows how to do things, he does; the community of Podgurna has elected him rabbi and teacher and beadle and guide, and he will do his duty by it. Twenty-five years he served . . . siege of Sebastopol . . . a synagogue in a Siberian village. . . .

Evening descends mildly on the village. The wind from the river stirs the soft silken beard of a young man and the ringlets of a young girl; it insinuates itself softly under her armpits and sends a wave of coolness over her breasts. Far away a circular framework of blue and violet rises about the world, the air becomes damp, and a cool, light dew settles on everything, bringing with it a universal laziness and sleepiness.

Later Reb Jonah lies in his tiny room, closes his eyes, but does not sleep. He sees before him the general, much impressed by his three medals. He thinks of his dead wife, tries to remember what she looked like, and cannot evoke her face. He sees the tall memorial candle that was entrusted to his care guttering and going out; he knows now for sure what he always suspected: namely, that a three-quarter-pound candle won't last twenty-four hours, from evening to evening; it must be a pound candle. He suddenly wants to make sure about a certain anniversary that is due one of these days for a certain Jew of Podgurna, and he calls several times, "Reb Aaron, are you awake or are you asleep?"

He turns his ear with his hand, but no sound comes to him, so he closes his eyes again and envies the young people who fall asleep the instant they get into bed. Later on, it seems to him that there is a slight noise from the kitchen, where Mashka is sleeping; a scraping and creaking penetrates to his deaf old ears. Sometimes the noises are clear and impudent, as if they did not care if he heard; at other times they sink into frightened silence. He listens intently, tries to catch the meaning of the noises, but fails. He picks up one of his boots standing by the side of his bed, bangs on the floor several times, and growls, "Scat! Whoosh-sh-sht! Get out!"

There is instant silence in Mashka's room—not the faintest sound. Reb Jonah is delighted at having routed the noises and mews like a cat: "Mia-a-ow, mia-a-ow!"

4.

White snow covers the wastes around Podgurna, hides the yellow sand completely, and makes the region look wider and more desolate than ever. The men of Podgurna stay away for weeks, snowbound in desolate villages in the company of their cattle; the women of Podgurna pass nights in the huts of the peasants.

But here, in Podgurna, Reb Jonah still makes the rounds every morning. Wrapped in his old overcoat, his feet thrust deep into Siberian boots, he staggers from hut to hut, taps on the windowpanes, and calls out, "Get up, you rascals! There's a strap waiting for you."

Desolation enfolds the village; the snow lies as level, as undisturbed, as though it were planned for an eternity. The days are short and dark. They are like reluctant visitors; they take one short look at the inhospitable earth and they withdraw. But the nights are long, dark, swollen, and hopeless. There is not one friendly human voice, there is no banging of doors, no baying of dogs.

Reb Jonah has lost his good humor. He still makes the youngsters stand in rows outside his hut and commands them as in the summer: "One, two! One, two!"

But the youngsters cry from the cold. They rub their ears and noses. And Reb Jonah is angry with them. Why, when he was their age, he was already a Cantonist; the Czar's emissaries had caught him and carried him away from home! He was in a Siberian village, the temperature was below forty, and still he did his daily exercises. In fact, he becomes so angry that he begins to take the leather belt from his trousers. Then the children cry, and Mashka calls angrily through the window, "Grandfather, they're freezing, do you hear? They're freezing!"

Thereupon Reb Jonah dismisses the children with an impatient gesture and creeps across the village to the little synagogue.

They never built a new synagogue—that is, from the foundations up. But there is a synagogue after all. The back room in Pesach Plotnik's hut was set aside, the walls were decently whitewashed, and a pulpit of new boards was put up. From the middle of the ceiling hangs a crooked brass candelabrum, and over the Ark that contains the Scroll hangs the Eternal Light, which is only a red porcelain lamp of the kind that may be seen in little provincial hotels and village churches.

Reb Jonah always finds something to do around the synagogue. He takes down the candelabrum and examines it closely for any evidence of candle-drippings, but it shines so brightly that Reb Jonah can see every hair of his face in it. However, he polishes it once more for good luck and replaces it. He takes down the smaller candelabrum from the pulpit and goes through the same performance. He climbs up on a ladder and peers into the Eternal Light, to make sure that there is plenty of oil in it, and he mutters, "Enough for another week."

He crawls into every corner of the room, looking for fragments of pages from prayer books. If he finds one he picks it up and kisses it, as he learned to do in his childhood days. Perhaps he finds only a straw; he picks that up too and carries it solemnly from the room. If he only weren't afraid he would take down the Scroll too, open it, and read it. But he knows that this is forbidden. All he permits himself is to approach the Ark, feel the soft woolen curtain, and kiss the velvet Shield of David three times, muttering meanwhile, "When Passover comes we'll buy you a new covering, white satin."

Then he retires from the room, taking backward steps away from the Presence in the Ark, and goes out into the snow.

When the winter was young Pesach and the other men of the congregation were still to be seen fairly frequently in the village. Evenings, they would return across the snow, and the first place they went to was not their homes, but the little synagogue. They would wash their hands in the snow, wipe the spots of blood off their sheepskin coats, and, once in the synagogue, they would count their numbers, to see if all who set out had returned. But since it is forbidden to Jews to count human beings, they would say, "Here's not one, not two, not three . . . not nine . . ."

But when winter deepened over the country and the Vistula froze over, the men of Podgurna stayed away weeks at a time. Reb Jonah, the only man in the village, recalled the anniversaries the men on the road should be observing, but he was never sure of his dates; and as the weeks passed he found less and less to do.

With their fathers away, the youngsters had given up attending Reb Jonah's *cheder*; they played on the snow-covered hills, tobogganed down their slopes, and threw snowballs at one another. When the Vistula froze over they improvised skates by tying hard wire to the soles of their shoes, and flew over the ice like swallows. They made a big snow man, put a stick into his hand, danced around him, and sang, "Forward, march! One, two! One, two!"

Reb Jonah is seldom at home. Only Mashka is there. She creeps through the rooms, peers through the frozen windows, does not know what to do with herself. When Reb Jonah returns he asks her to cook him a dish of noodles and honey. There's half a sack of flour in the kitchen and a whole jar of honey. But Mashka does not hear him; she keeps peering through the frozen windowpanes into the distance.

Reb Jonah looks at her wonderingly. Of late she has been very quiet. He talks to her, but she never answers. She only looks through the windowpanes.

He remembers that in the summer she was good to him. She always used to bake cheesecakes steeped in honey. She had always been so gay; she would run up to him, throw her arms around him, kiss him on the eyes and beard, and cry, "Granddaddy, darling, it's so good, it's so good!"

Now she does not even answer him, and he asks himself what he has done. It seems to him that he has done nothing; he has broken nothing, spoiled nothing. He goes up to her, puts a feeble hand on her warm neck, and asks, "Mashka, does anything hurt you?"

She trembles and cries sharply, "Oh! You've got such cold hands! I could die from them."

He says nothing more. He sits down near the stove and warms his feet.

Only in the evening do the children come to the *cheder*. They cluster around the stove and roast potatoes in the flames. Reb Jonah is not angry with them; he does not try to teach them; he only tells them stories of his military experiences. The children have heard the stories so often that they want to laugh. They thump one another in the ribs and turn their faces away from him. Reb Jonah tells them what tortures he had to suffer because he insisted on saying his Jewish prayers every morning; he compares himself with the Jews of the new generation, who serve only three years and eight months, and don't go into a synagogue even when they are on furlough. Those that don't serve in the army stay out on the roads for weeks and never visit their own little synagogue. It makes him very sad. He puts his finger meditatively to his nose, looks reproachfully at the youngsters, as though they were to blame, and says, "Children, we are too far from God's ways."

But this is too much for the children. They burst into shrieks of laughter. Hurt, Reb Jonah repeats the "Hear, O Israel" and sends the children home.

When night comes Reb Jonah lies down in his woolen underwear and his four-fringed garment. He lies awake for hours. Mashka is in bed in the next room, and dim though his hearing is, Reb Jonah is aware that she is not asleep, but tosses around in her bed. That is strange. At her age, he remembers, he slept like a log; and more than once he did not awaken until the corporal dragged him by the feet from his pallet, and he found himself lying on the floor of the barracks. He could still hear the angry voice: "Get up, you loon. It's four o'clock. Do you want to sleep all day?"

He stares at the dark walls and sees himself standing at attention with the rest of the regiment. The Czar himself is passing by; Reb Jonah's ear tickles him; he feels that if he does not put up a hand to scratch himself he will faint. But he is no longer with his regiment; he is in the Siberian synagogue; the watery sun shines through the windows; he must get up, make the rounds, call the Jews to prayer. He starts up—and he is in darkness again, and the night glimmers in through the windowpanes of his hut in Podgurna. The tiny flame of the night lamp burns blue; Reb Jonah is able to make out that the oil has not sunk at all, and he realizes that only a few minutes have passed; the eternity of the night still lies in front of him.

He rolls over on his side, puts his hand behind his ear, and listens. He thinks he hears noises in the next room, a shuffling and sighing, a moving of cushions. Hearing those noises in the summer, he used to think it was only a mouse nibbling at the skins hanging in a corner to dry, and then he would pick up a boot, bang it on the floor, and shout, "Scat! Whoo-sh-sht! Get out of there!"

But now it is not summer, and no skins are hanging to dry in the other room where Mashka is sleeping. So he crawls out of his bed and makes his way to Mashka. He stands over her in the darkness, shivering with cold and anxiety. He is afraid she is having a nightmare, so he wakens her and murmurs, "Mashka, come and lie in my bed."

She hears him and pulls the bedclothes tighter. He tugs at them again. "Mashka, you can do that. It's not wrong with a grandfather."

He feels the cold cutting his feet. He sits down on the edge of the bed, and then Mashka throws her warm arms around him, kisses him wildly, and weeps. "Granddaddy dear! Darling Granddaddy!"

Old Jonah is bewildered. He does not know why she should cry so.

She is telling him something, but in such a low voice that he cannot make out the words, and he is ashamed of his deafness. So he murmurs, soothingly, "I hear you, Mashka, I hear you."

But then Mashka takes her arms from around him, shakes him violently, and cries so loudly that now he can hear every word. "What do you hear? What did I say to you?"

He does not know what to answer. Mashka lets go of him, pushes him from the bed, and shouts angrily, "Go back to bed, you! Crawling around like that in the night!"

He goes back to bed, understanding nothing. Odd girl! Now she kisses him, now she thrusts him from her. If only he had someone to consult, to talk to about her! Pesach would be the man. But what's the good of Pesach, who's always away, with his oxen? Reb Jonah tries to remember on what day Pesach must observe the anniversary of his mother's death, because then Pesach will surely have to come home. But he can't reckon it out. If at least Aaron, the slaughterer's son, were here! Aaron could tell him. But it is months since Aaron has been this way. That's an odd thing too. In fact, only the other day he asked Mashka about it, but she answered him so angrily that he did not feel like asking again.

Something bad about that girl, he decides, and shuts his eyes tight, in the hope that he will fall asleep. But his eyes open again as if of their own accord. After a time he suddenly hears the hen clucking in the outhouse. It occurs to him that the poor creature must be perishing from the cold. Or maybe a skunk has sneaked in, and the hen is choking in the stink. He crawls out of bed again and goes to the door on tiptoe, so that Mashka should not hear him. He steps into the little outhouse and calls in a low voice to the hen, "Come in, chicky, come into the warm room."

5.

There are lively times in Grobitze.

Spring has come, and silver rivulets run through the narrow streets and wash the green sunken cobblestones. The water drips and pours from the roofs into big-bellied barrels. The damp clean air takes the first sunlight of the year, and there is a smell of melting snow and baking *matzos*. But what gives liveliness to all this is something else, something less usual and more interesting.

Strange stories have come to Grobitze from over there, from the village of Podgurna, which lies in the valley, soaking in the melting snow. Peasant women who have passed that way tell the stories.

There's a young girl there, they tell, not more than eighteen years of age; one fine day she went into a barn, lay down, and gave birth to a boy, a healthy little one, brown as a nut. Who the girl is they don't quite know, but it's certain that she's no stranger: she's from Podgurna. It appears, however, that she's an orphan. Groups of eager men and women, glad of the spring and of such a piece of news, gather outside. They point to Podgurna, rub their hands, and exchange ironic congratulations.

"Mazel tov! Good luck! Happy day!"

It is the young men who are most excited. They feel that their cynical views on womankind have been vindicated. The news adds to their stature and their impudence. They look the women boldly in the eyes. They ask them, with profound irony, "Well, what do you say to that?"

The younger boys, those who still go to *cheder,* catch vague echoes of the news. It is something mysterious, thrilling, and forbidden. The teachers in the little rooms are aware of an undercurrent of disturbance; cheeks are crimson, eyes sparkle, whispers pass from group to group. The air is laden with secrecy and sinfulness.

And older Jews scratch their beards thoughtfully and say, "Well, well, it's our turn now. They'll need us, those scholarly gentlemen of Podgurna."

They debate questions of punishment, of expiation, of fines, of ceremonies. What's to be done? How much is to be exacted? No one has any clear views; Grobitze has never faced such a question before. But that the punishment will be well thought out, that the fine will be heavy, there is not the slightest doubt. And behind the debates run little shivers of suppressed thought, queer visitations in elderly, pious heads.

It is quiet in Podgurna. Almost all the men have returned. The chimneys send curls of smoke into the sky; the homes are full. But Podgurna is quiet. The men keep themselves grimly busy. One mends an ax, another grinds a knife, a third hammers at a broken chair. And if one of the women, unable to endure the silence, breaks out with, "God help us all! That such a thing should happen in Podgurna!" her husband brings his fist down on the table and bellows, "Hold your tongue! Not a word, do you hear?"

When Podgurna first learned the news there was something like a panic—though only for a moment.

The men came home on a Friday evening. The Vistula had begun to break up, and animals could no longer be driven along the muddy roads. The men reckoned they would stay in the village until after Passover. When they reached the village, wading knee-deep through the half-flooded fields, they did not disperse to their homes but proceeded in a body to the little synagogue. They washed their hands in the snow, rubbed the bloodstains off their sheepskin coats, and went in to prayer.

The brightness and freshness of their synagogue was like an audible welcome. The brass tubes of the candelabrum shone with a hundred quiet points of light. The lion on the Ark of the Scroll put out a long, pointed golden tongue, and on the woolen curtain Pesach Plotnik's name twinkled in silver letters. The men took their places for the prayers, opened their books. And then Reb Jonah announced that, before the regular Friday-evening prayers, he would ask them to read a one-day portion—that is, a seventh part—of the Book of Psalms for his Mashka, who was sick.

The congregation was perturbed and astonished. They had heard nothing, of course; and somehow it was strange. What ailed the girl?

Reb Jonah himself did not know. They all looked anxiously at the candles, which were good for about an hour. If they were going to read a day's portion of the Psalms and then recite the prayers that usher in the Sabbath, they would have to work fast. But no one demurred, and they settled down to the reading of the Psalms, chanting them with a homely melody and uttering the words in their full, heavy, village way. The cheerful mood was a little chastened now, but not destroyed. In the deep pockets of their sheepskin coats they carried, every one of them, a package of greasy, stained banknotes, the fruit of a winter's labor. True, the district was flooded now, and it would be some time before they could resume work. But already the feel of the thaw was in the air, an odor of spring freshets and of rotting roots creeping from under their winter covering. Passover would come and go, the full spring and summer would follow. For Passover they had, this year, their own little synagogue; no need any more to depend on the moods of those Grobitze swine. On the way home they had discussed a number of projects intended to signalize their contentment and gratitude. They would perhaps get a new velvet covering for their Scroll of the Law, and a new curtain, velvet too, in place of the old woolen one. The time had also come to renew the petition for the piece of land for a Podgurna cemetery. Reb Jonah too ought to get something special for Passover, perhaps a new pair of trousers. He had done well by the synagogue; he had kept it spotlessly clean; and he taught the children devotedly. Nor would they forget Mashka, his granddaughter, who ought to get a new dress for the holidays.

And so the men said the prayers heartily, and the girl's name, Mashka, sounded loudly every few minutes in front of the opened Ark with its Scroll. But just as they reached the last invocation of "May it be Thy will," the door burst open, and a wild bevy of women broke in. They were wringing their hands, their voices raised in shrill lamentation.

"Stop! Don't pray for her! Don't utter her name! Reb Jonah, God help you, do you know what has happened?"

The congregation was petrified. The men stared open-mouthed, a half-finished "Almigh—" frozen in their throats. Before the women had spoken they suspected, they guessed.

It was a dreadful moment for all of them—the horror itself, the manner of its publication, the place and the time. The women who had first discovered it had lost their heads; some of them had harbored a secret rage against the old man and his granddaughter and were using this as their opportunity to strike. The synagogue was in a turmoil. The screaming of the women sounded amid the hoarse questions of the men; a panic was on.

And then suddenly Pesach Plotnik brought his mighty fist down on the pulpit and thundered, "Women and children, out of here! All of you, you bastards!"

Half a dozen men, Reb Jonah and Pesach Plotnik among them, made their way through the Sabbath twilight to Reb Jonah's hut, and there they cross-examined Mashka. And she told them simply how "he" had come every evening, to chat with her grandfather, to offer them pieces of cheesecake, and to remain overnight. She told them everything. And Reb Pesach tugged at his beard and breathed a deep sigh of relief. The worst fear was dissolved from his heart. It might have been one of those others, a soldier from the fortress. But if it was only one of the Grobitze swine, he, Pesach Plotnik, would show them what Podgurna could do. He ground his teeth and shook his fist at the wall in the direction of Grobitze. "Wait! Podgurna will show you!"

And then Pesach Plotnik sent word throughout the village, to all the women in particular, that Mashka was to be treated decently. They should help her as though she were a respectable wife who had just brought forth a legitimate son of Israel. Not a word was to be spoken against her, in her presence or elsewhere. He, Pesach Plotnik, ordered this, and he would tear a leg from the person who disobeyed him in the letter or the spirit.

The days pass, one by one; Podgurna does not talk; the men stay home, having no work. Only the Vistula is mightily occupied.

The waters are rising higher and higher against the hills on which the forts rear their heads. Vast fragments of ice rush seaward with a furious cracking and growling. At one moment they seem to be making a swift beeline for the port of Danzig, like boats driven by a fresh wind. But then suddenly they begin a stampede to the side, like a drove of frightened oxen. And, like oxen, they climb on one another's flanks. A white barricade piles up across the river, the waters gurgle at its base, try to race around it, rise higher and higher against the hills. On a high wall linking the forts soldiers stand behind guns. The guns turn, point to the mounting ice barricade, open their steel mouths, and spit hot steel. The barricade cracks and breaks up, the waters rush straight forward, the fields for miles around are deafened with the roaring of guns.

Podgurna, watching from its doors, is happy. If it were not for those soldiers behind the guns the river would overflow its banks, there would be no passing from hut to hut. The men put their hands to their ears, and with every boom of the guns they murmur cheerfully, "That was a good one. Again. . . ."

The little ones won't stay home. They gather at the end of the village to watch the firing of the guns from the fortress. They also know that there is something queer in Reb Jonah's hut these days. What it is they do not know, but they do know that there is no more need, these days, to go to *cheder*. They are free to run around all day, to watch the soldiers in the distance, to pass by Reb Jonah's hut in the hope of seeing the queer thing that they feel inhabits the place now. But they see nothing, they learn nothing, and they soon forget.

It is a Friday morning, the eighth day after the homecoming, and a long wagon, heavily laden with men and drawn by two horses, comes rattling into the market place of Grobitze. Pesach Plotnik leans back on the box, draws at the reins with all his might, jumps down, and turns his back ostentatiously on the men and women in the market place.

They come running out of their shops and glare suspiciously at the arrivals. They think at first that a peasant wedding party has arrived in town; it turns out to be nothing but Podgurna toughs—and what a way to come dashing into the market place! As if Grobitze belongs to them!

They don't know what to make of it. The youngsters who gather around the cart don't know whether to cheer or to throw stones—so they do nothing. There is the cart, right outside the house of the old slaughterer. The Podgurnians have flung the door open, they have crowded into the living room, they are already seated at the table with the old man. And Aaron is there too, white, frightened, speechless in the midst of this gang of hefty young Podgurnians.

People crowd at the windows and at the door, but they are not admitted. The gang comes out, without a word of greeting. The market place is paralyzed to see the Podgurnians mount their cart, turn it violently in the direction of the rabbi's house, and gallop up to the door without a word of explanation to anyone. Aaron is in their midst. They get down, storm the house, just as they did at the slaughterer's. Grobitze is profoundly alarmed. Nothing good can come out of Podgurna. And this time the men of Grobitze insist on listening in. But the young Podgurnians are at the door, and fists are driven into faces, cheeks are slapped with a sound like pistol shots.

Aaron stands in the middle of the room, a thin red trickle running down from one nostril into his mouth. Pesach Plotnik, his shirt open at the throat, his eyes flaming, his beard bristling, hammers on the table with both his fists and in a voice that comes out muffled between clenched teeth he rages, "You'll marry her, you bastard! You'll marry her now! This minute, I say. Get a canopy at once, or I'll tear a leg out of you!"

There is a scurrying to and fro, a frightened questioning and whispering; groups gather and dissolve, but no one does anything. Then they come out of the house: Pesach Plotnik, Aaron, the old slaughterer, the rabbi, the Podgurnians. They mount the cart; they are gone in a spatter of mud. The crowd in the market place watches the cart grow smaller in the distance, and they see the coat tails of the rabbi lifted in the wind.

Reb Jonah's hut is crowded and noisy. The candles bend from the heat of their own flames and of the men and women jostling one another in the small rooms. The canopy has been put up, the wedding has taken place. The circumcision too—a double event—has been ceremoniously carried out. But in the midst of the prayer that follows, Reb Jonah forgets the father's name and he prolongs the melody, waiting to be helped. "And his name shall be called in Israel, Abraham son of . . . son of . . . o-o-o-f . . ."

Pesach Plotnik bends over to him and prompts, "Son of Aaron the Levite."

The women form a thicket around the bed, which is heavily curtained and adorned, as becomes a new mother. The men lift up the glasses of brandy waiting on the tables, and they shout joyously, *"Mazel tov!* Good luck! A happy hour! *Mazel tov,* the father! *Mazel tov,* Rabbi! *Mazel tov!"*

As the bottles on the tables empty and the steam in the room grows denser, the Podgurnians warm up, and hands are put on shoulders for a round dance. They are ready to forget and forgive. After all, a human being is a human being and does human things. Aaron will go on slaughtering the oxen in the garrison slaughterhouses; true, the soldiers don't need a Jewish ritual slaughter—they could eat oxen slaughtered by a gentile butcher too. But Aaron is there, and he'll stay on. It never does a soldier harm to eat kosher meat.

The Rabbi of Grobitze does not forgive or forget so easily; nor does the old slaughterer. But the men of Podgurna, hot with brandy and the consciousness of merit, will have no sulking on this happy occasion. They draw the rabbi and the old slaughterer into the dance; they hold the two men in a viselike grip and drag them along in the stamping circle. The children press against the wall and watch delightedly the confusion of legs and feet, the massive boots of the Podgurnians, the slippers of the rabbi, the soft shoes of the slaughterer. The women cluster around the bed; they too have taken a drop of drink; their faces are red; they whisper to one another and to the bride-mother. They caress her face, they braid her hair, they offer advice on babies and husbands.

Mashka is happy and dazed. Through a narrow break in the curtains she catches now and again a glimpse of a black-bearded young man spinning around in the thundering circle of dancers, and a red tide washes over her face.

Her head is heavy with happiness. She lets it droop toward the baby that has just been initiated into the Covenant; it is sleeping now, drugged with the drop of wine that had been placed on its lips.

And Mashka sings softly, "Sleep, my little crown, sleep, my happiness. . . ."

Translated by Maurice Samuel

Competitors

JONAH ROSENFELD

TWO IRON beds, a faded mirror without a frame, a lemon crate for a dresser, a couple of bowlegged stools, and a table with a limp—that's my furniture.

Big mouth, blue lips, squeaky voice, and wet eyes always running with tears—that's my wife.

My other possessions—a daughter of ten with a mouth on hinges and eyes like a fox, as thin as a shaving, quick as a chick. A little boy of seven, who looks five. He's as bright as day, but he's as dry as a stick that's been left in the ground for a grave-marker, and just as skinny. The third one is two years old, no bigger than a newborn babe, but when it comes to screeching she doesn't go by weight.

As for me, I'm a runty little man with a sparse beard and tiny little dark eyes. Take a good look at me, the husband of my wife and the father of three children. Occupation? Nothing. I do my wife's work. Early in the morning, as soon as I'm up, I start the fire and set the kettle to boil, wake my wife, hand her a glass of tea, and see her off to the market place. Then I get to work on the kids, wash, dress, and feed them—which is easier said than done. The little one throws a fit and screams for her mama, and, as soon as she is going strong, my son and heir joins in to show what he can do along these lines. I take the baby in my arms and run to the window to distract her. I rap on the panes, hammer on the table, tap against a glass, cluck my tongue, and meanwhile I take care of the little boy too, playing horse with him. You should see us—sometimes he's the horse and I'm the rider, sometimes the other way round. Or else we play soldiers, barking commands at each other. "About face! Left march! One, two, three, four!" At last, thank God, they've shut up for a while. I run to make the beds, sweep the floor, and put up lunch, and as soon as lunch is ready I pour a portion into a pot, wash a bowl and spoon, and—run! I can't catch my breath with all this running. I have no watch, and I'm always scared to death that I'll be late. My heart is hammering. Finally I catch sight of the stalls and counters of the market place, heaped with mountains of onions, beets, cabbages, parsley, carrots, potatoes, horseradish, and other such delicacies. At one of these counters sits my wife.

Often while I run I spill soup over my coat. Do you think I'd notice it in time? Not till she pops out her calf's eyes and welcomes me with a choice, restrained curse.

"What's the matter?"

"Look at yourself!"

They are all laughing, fit to choke. One of them, a fat slob of a woman with a healthy red face, who sits opposite my wife, actually rocks from side to side, holding her belly in both hands—may she only live long! My old lady sets to pinching me and gouges chunks out of my hide.

I'm lucky to get off with a mere pinching. Most of the time, when she gets through pinching me, she adds a slap for good measure. And I ought to be thankful when it ends there. Because when she gets home from work, that's when she first sails into me—out of sheer gratitude, you understand, for whom else does she have to pick on? But I'm also no piker, I pay her back double, and we slug it out in earnest. She pushes me, I punch her; she lands one in my teeth, I give her a poke in the ribs; she sets up a scream, the kids chime in, and I run out of the house as fast as my legs will carry me. Gradually I slow down—I am hardly aware how I come to find myself standing still, looking at the ground, the sky, the houses, the people going back and forth.

Just as I come to a stop without being aware of it, so I am unconscious of the actual moment when I begin to drift back. I return with a heavy heart and head, loaded to the full; I walk slowly, a step at a time. When I reach the house I stand at the window and look in to see how my little one—that is, the big one, my ten-year-old daughter—is faithfully slaving away, helping her mother undress the children and put them to bed, and tugging at her mother's heavy boots, and I think —damn her, she's competing with me! I can tell she's glad to be rid of me, and that she's sidling up to Mama to show that they can get along perfectly well without me. When the fire is put out I press my face against the windowpane. I can see nothing in the darkness. All the same I picture the scene—a woman stretched out in bed, and next to her a small child; at their feet a girl of ten. In the other bed lies the husband, a lazy, good-for-nothing dog, of no use to God or man, and next to him their son. Every last one of them a skinny runt—melt them down and you can make one proper human being out of the whole damned batch.

I grow tired standing under the window and I turn around to the street, heave a sigh, look up at the stars, and lose myself among them, looking for a sign. The sky descends toward me—here it is, I can touch it, and before I know it I'm up in the sky, looking down on the earth. Now there's a great man for you! But the moment I enter the house I'm squelched. My mouth tightening, I steal up to the bread like a regular little thief and fall to, stuffing myself. My wife is a light sleeper; she hears me and lets me have a tongue-lashing. I come up to her and promise, honor bright, that it'll never happen again, from now on I'll behave. She shuts up—I'm forgiven. I undress and sneak into bed beside her. She plays dead, and I pretend I don't know what's going on. The hell with it, let her think she's fooling me! And so, half asleep, I've had three kids by her. We wake up angry, as usual.

One Thursday morning, after I had put up a pot of water, I went to undo my daughter's braids before washing her hair. She jumped like a rabbit and turned a red, puffed-up face at me. "What's the matter?"

Instead of answering, she looked at me in anger and puffed her face out all the more.

"Don't you want to have your hair washed?"

"I don't need your help," she replied, hanging her head, playing with her fingers.

"You don't want me to wash your hair?"

"No!"

All right. No is no. I could wash the hair of the two younger ones. When the water was warm I began to undress my little boy. But my daughter popped out of the ground, grabbed his hand, and pulled him away.

"Hey, what's this?"

She held his hand and wouldn't answer.

I tried to pull him away. She held on and mumbled, "I'll do it."

Can you imagine that?

"You'll do it?"

But I was beginning to catch on. I looked at her awhile and then I asked, "Where did you get that big idea? Who told you you could do the work in this house?"

"I feel sorry for Mama," she replied.

"What? You feel sorry—"

"I feel sorry for Mama. She slaves all day long to feed you."

"So?"

"So if I wash my own hair and dress Yankele and Mindele, you'll be able to go out and earn a living."

"What? You'll dress Yankele and Mindele? Feed them? Clean the house?"

"What's so hard about that? And then maybe you'll be able to earn a living."

So it's nothing to her! I drudge all day long—what don't I go through! The little one pulls my beard out ten times an hour, I lose my voice singing before I can put her to sleep, and she says it's nothing. She sends me out to earn a living! So I'm not earning my keep, I'm sponging off them. Oh, sure, she'll take over! And what'll become of me? Go be a wet nurse? Of course, a wet nurse—what else am I good for? Over my dead body! That little brat isn't driving me out of the house! If anyone goes, she will. No one's telling me how to earn a living.

"Come here, you! Did your mother tell you to say that?"

"No. I said it myself."

"What do you mean, yourself? Your mother didn't put you up to it?"

"No!"

"And I suppose you're not trying to kick me out of the house?"

No answer.

I grabbed her by the pigtail. "Do you happen to know who I am?"

She tried to break away.

"Do you know that I'm your father? And that I can do whatever I want with you? Even kill you. Do you know it's a father's duty to punish his child, and if she goes wrong he's even got the right to kill her? Do you know that?"

I must have been shouting—the baby woke up. My eldest tore herself away, ran to the baby, and began to rock it, singing the song I always sing. Here I really went mad. What right has she to rock the baby to sleep with *my* song, the song I made up myself? So . . . I walked right up to her, gave her a shove that sent her flying, and began to rock the baby myself.

Oy lu-lu, little girl,
Mama will make you a dress to wear,
Papa will wash and comb your hair,
Mama will bring you an apple to eat,
Shut your eyes and go to sleep.
Oy lu-lu, oy lu-lu.

I tell you, even if she lives to be a hundred, she'll never be able to rock a baby the way I do.

"Go away!" she cried. "I'm going to rock her!"

So that's your game. Well, I'll take care of you! I pulled off my belt and with all my might—over her head, her face, her back! Now you'll know how to talk back to your father! I'll give you something to remember!

The two young ones began to howl. I went wild and let all of them have it, laying it on as thick as the traffic would bear. Then I began to tear out my own beard. I wound up at the window, sagging on my elbows, and burst into tears.

When their mother came home that evening they fell on her, complaining how I had murdered them. This made them cry all over again. As she listened to them my dear wife sank down on the bed like a log, held her face in her hands, and every now and then threw me a glance that made my blood run cold.

"What's going to become of us?" she wailed, raising her head. Her eyes were full, like puddles.

I kept my own counsel.

"What'll become of us, I ask you?"

What could I say?

"You know you belong in a madhouse?"

I felt like asking her, What's so crazy about me? Is this the first time a father beat his children?

"Please, I've supported you so long. I've fed and clothed you, even bought your shoes. In all the eleven years that we've been married you haven't once earned enough for a single meal. I can't go on like this, I'm so weak, I'm exhausted. Are you trying to kill me? What do you want from me? Isn't it enough that I have to feed the children? Must I feed you too? Who ever heard of such a thing?"

Even my eyes filled with tears. She had never spoken to me like this!

"But Mirele," I cried, "she insulted me! She was driving me out of the house. It breaks my heart. After all, I'm her father! A child kick her own father out of the house? Who ever heard of *that?* Well, answer me!"

"And who ever heard of a man who sits at home and waits for his wife to come and feed him?"

"So—you told her to say that!"

She stared at me as if she didn't understand a word.

"Did you tell her to kick me out of the house?"

Silence, a sigh; but she looked at me in such a way that my blood froze.

"Did you tell her she could wash the children's hair? She! She's going to wash their hair! She can't even hold the baby straight."

"I can do it better than him!" cried my daughter.

"You should live so, you brat! All you're good for is to talk back to your father."

"And all he can do is beat her."

"Oh, so you don't give a damn! Next thing you know she'll be talking back to you. Let's see you give her a few slaps!"

"Please leave me alone! Do you hear me?" cried my wife.

That ended it. She sighed a few times and went to sleep.

And I kept my job. I didn't let the little one get near the baby or do a thing around the house. I wouldn't even let her wash her own hair. And when I used the comb on her, you can be sure I tore the hair out of her head.

Thank God, I'll be all right for a while. It was my only way out: my wife must have another baby. Then I would have nothing to fear from my rival. I knew what my dear daughter was after—she even let on why. She had been nagging her mother to make her a silk dress, and as her mother said no, she understood, young as she was, that this was because of me. She realized that if she were alone in the house, my wife would give in to her. And the truth is, I was afraid that sooner or later she'd have her way. But now I'm in clover—who's afraid of her? With my wife pregnant they won't be getting rid of me so fast. I saw to that. But it was far from easy—she kept pushing me away, and this time she didn't pretend she was asleep. "You beggar, you! Another litter?" she would say, doubling up so I couldn't get to her. I had my work cut out for me, but I made it. It has given me a tremendous satisfaction; I need no longer cower before my wife. I feel a sense of triumph when she stands before me with her pointed belly. I've shown her who wears the pants.

In great pride I take a walk every evening after supper. I fold my hands behind my back, thrust out my belly (it seems to me, all of a sudden, that I too have a big belly), and I walk slowly, mincing my steps, like this: one-two, one-two. I should worry—let it rain, let it snow, let the moon shine. It's all one to me. And even though it's cold I take off my hat and let the air get at my head. I don't despise my head—it's no fool, it understands a thing or two.

After my walk I return home, and not on tiptoe either, but right smack into the middle of the room, where I take account of my small fortune: one, two, three. . . . If not for me, these three little human beings wouldn't exist. These sleeping tots are mine, my own flesh and blood. They are me, and I am they. And my wife is also mine, she belongs to no one else but me. Inside her belly lies another bit of me. So altogether we are . . . one, two, three; my wife makes four; the child she's carrying, five; and myself, six. . . . I am six and the six are me. I take up the whole house. There's a man for you! Good night, ladies! Good night, all!

I was going about in rags. For quite a while I had been meaning to ask my wife to make me something to wear. Now the time was ripe; if I let this opportunity slip by, it would be gone for good. I kept postponing it, and my time was running short. Any day now she'd flop into bed, and then it would be too late. One day I swore, tonight's the night.

As soon as she came in I helped her off with her jacket and shook out the snow. I tell you, the greatest gentleman couldn't have treated his lady any better than I treated my wife that night. But still I said nothing. Go cut off my tongue to get a word out of me. When she began to undress for bed I went over to my wife and stood up to her like a soldier; after standing there awhile I called her attention to my clothes, from head to foot—in pantomime. She gave me an imbecilic look. Very well, she didn't understand. Again I indicated the condition I was in, bending down to my shoetops and sweeping my hand up to my head. Still an idiotic stare. I decided to go at it a little bit at a time: I raised one leg, revealed one shoe, then the other; I showed her the front of my trousers and then; peace be with you, presented the rear; then I held out my elbows, one at a time, for her to see how they had poked through the sleeves.

"Why are you standing there like a dummy?" she asked.

I kept still.

"What's the matter, are you paralyzed?"

I didn't move.

The little one suddenly began to cry in her sleep. My competitor and I made a dash for the cradle, but she got there first and began to rock it. I was left standing, neither here nor there. Now what? I saw she was doing an excellent job of rocking, just as if she'd been a mother all her life. I ran to the cradle and picked up the baby, though I knew that this would wake her. My daughter grabbed her out of my arms and ran to her mother. I held my tongue and went back to my post, trying to act unconcerned.

"Look how you're holding the baby!" I suddenly shouted, though she was holding her better than I did.

"None of your business," said she.

The nerve! "What do you mean, none of my business? You're twisting her hands!"

"What do you care?"

"What do *I* care? After all, I'm her father!"

"Well, well, well."

"I'll give you a well, well. Mindele, little darling, come to me!"

"Now what do you want? Why are you picking on the girl?" asked my wife.

"What do you mean? She's twisting the poor child's hands! After all, I'm a father. It makes my heart bleed!"

"Don't let it bother you."

"What!"

"Listen, will you please get out of here?"

"But look how I go around in rags!"

"I'm telling you, get out of my sight!"

"But look at me—"

"Look at *me!*" piped up my competitor. "I haven't a stitch to wear!"

The devil!

"You should only catch the plague!"

"Look how I go around!"

"I'm warning you, get out of here!"

I remained.

My wife wasted no time. She waddled across to the wall, took down the rolling pin, and raised it over my head.

The children began to scream. My competitor must have been frightened; she dropped the baby.

Good. Just what I was waiting for. I forgot about my wife and the rolling pin. I leaped at the girl, grabbed hold of her hair, and dragged her like a bitch down the whole length of the floor, pounding her on the back and shouting, like a devoted father, "There! Now you'll know how to hold a baby! Now you'll know!"

They squealed like pigs in the market. The little one and the big one lay on the floor, screaming at the top of their lungs. My little boy buried his face in his mother's skirts and yelled his head off, and she, my wife, stood there like a dunce and didn't know where to turn. Should she beat me? Should she pick up the baby from the floor, comfort her? Should she go up to the other one? She rolled her eyes insanely. Suddenly she burst out crying and began to tear at her hair. And I, thinking she was out of her mind, dashed to the window and set up a racket of my own. I beat on the windowpane and called for help.

This happiness of mine didn't last very long. The baby died three months after it was born. In fact, the first time I saw the little creature I knew in my bones that my happiness wouldn't last. The child was born with one foot in the grave.

He was circumcised a month late. My competitor wouldn't come near him till after the ceremony. The old woman ran home several times a day to nurse him, though the other children had not known the breast after the first eight days of confinement; I brought them all up on the bottle.

How happy I was on the day of the circumcision! Who could hold a candle to me? Everybody drank to my health: *L'chaim! L'chaim!* from all directions. I felt I had come alive; I too amounted to something in the world. If only I could have been happy a little longer!

The child grew worse after the circumcision. If not for my daughter, perhaps he would have dragged on for another half year. But she shortened his days. She was always opening and shutting the door, on purpose, and she was in no way disturbed when I cried, "Monster! Do you want to kill the baby?"

No, she kept right at it and would answer me, "And suppose I do? Who's afraid of you?"

In all this time I was the only one who looked after him; no one even came near the cradle. He was a disgusting thing, a loathsome sight: a long-drawn-out face, like a wrinkled sour pickle. There was not a bit of meat on his bones; pouches of skin hung all over him. When I held him, my fingers crawled through his flesh. I could bear to hold him only on a pillow.

But the night he died he acquired a strange beauty in my eyes. I no longer saw him as a child, but a grown man who understood everything.

Naturally I was afraid of him. I trembled when I stood near him, out of fear that he could guess what was going on in my mind. It seemed to me that he saw right through me—he knew that I could stand the sight of him even less than all the others in the house.

They were all asleep; it must have been about three o'clock. A dark night. A fearful wind blew, shoveling snow against the windowpanes.

As he was gasping his last breath I lighted a candle and looked right into his face. He lay quite still, but his heart was beating rapidly and his eyes were only lightly closed. The moment before he died he opened his eyes—such clear, black little eyes!—and looked up at me. "Forgive me!" I said to him. As soon as I said this his eyes clouded over. They remained open.

I covered the little corpse with a black shawl. I fixed the candle at his head, and all alone I began to pace the floor, with my head bowed; my feet were dragging.

Suddenly I flared with resentment. Why should I have to hang around a corpse all night long? I went to my wife's bed, gave her a poke, and cried, "Wake up! The baby died!" I thought she would go mad. Then I waked my competitor. "Get up! Your brother's dead!"

The mother uncovered the child and fell upon him, weeping softly. The young one's eyes were popping out of her head, and she was trembling with cold. I stood to one side, looked at the two of them, and smiled. Then I took my competitor by the hand, led her into the middle of the room, and stepped back, singing and clapping my hands for her to dance.

The old woman cried out, "Have you gone crazy!"

"Who's crazy? She killed the baby! He would have lived if she hadn't made him catch cold!"

"What are you talking about?"

"Oh, I know what I'm talking about! She left the door open on purpose!"

Again I began to sing and clap my hands.

"Help! Help! He's out of his mind! Stop that clapping!" cried my wife.

"On purpose! On purpose! Let him hear, let him know who killed him! If it hadn't been for her he would still be living!"

I went up to the baby and said, "Do you hear, Hershel, your sister Malke is to blame. She is your Angel of Death. I, your father, Maier b'rabbi Itzchok, I say to you that you must avenge your untimely death!"

They made such an outcry one would think the corpse had actually come back to life and gone to work on them. The mother fell upon the child, her whole body quivering; she was stamping her feet and babbling in distraction. My daughter leaped about the house, yammering, and the two younger ones woke up and also began to howl. By now I was completely bewildered. For a while I didn't know what I was doing, and in this half-conscious state I packed my few belongings. When I was done packing, I went up to the dead child and said, "May the light of heaven be yours, my dear son! Pray for your poor father, who is now going out into the world. . . ."

Then I took up my bundle and glanced in farewell at the two younger children. I went slowly out of the house and out into the black world.

Translated by Isaac Rosenfeld

The Sick Goose

JONAH ROSENFELD

UNPLEASANT as it was for the old man to crawl down from his oven in the early morning and go to the cold hut where he fed the geese, he was still glad to be of some help to his children. Not wanting to be a useless mouth, he had more or less taken this chore upon himself. The work itself was not really so hard, but getting up at dawn, crawling down from his warm oven, and carrying out the food he had prepared the night before and left standing in the kitchen so that it would not freeze—this he found very disagreeable. Yet once he had finished his work he had a feeling that reminded him of his younger years, long ago, when he had done things for his children. It seemed to him that his fatherly worries had crept into his old age—except that now the place of the children had been taken by winged feathery creatures to whom he was also a kind of father. For it was through him that the geese had come into the world.

During the summers he would set the geese on the eggs, then feed and nurse the goslings. Hovering over the goslings in the meadow, he felt that in his old age he was again bringing up children, children that did not belong to the human species. And this alone could explain why, when the time came for the geese to be slaughtered, the old man would sit distractedly on his oven, thinking of the gruesome day of judgment that awaited the unfortunate creatures he had helped raise only to see their flesh and their fat eaten.

Yes, he knew his work could have no other end, but, as he followed the geese in summer and watched over them in winter, he drove this thought out of his mind; he did not want to think about the fate of those for whom he had such a close, almost fatherly feeling.

Each time the old man entered the hut the geese would receive him with a tumult of cries. One after the other they would thrust out their little heads and their red beaks with the charming little nostrils that always caught the fancy of the old man. Their friendly welcome always pleased him . . . in just this way children greet their father when he brings something home for them.

After giving the geese their food and drink the old man rarely failed to converse with them or stroke one or another on the head. And when one of them wronged another by keeping it from the trough he would reproach her. "You rascal, why don't you let her get to the trough?"

Other times, when one of the geese began to choke from gulping too much food, he would say to her, "You see, God has punished you for not letting the other one eat."

Though he loved all the geese, it was to the submissive and the weaker ones that he felt closest, those which lagged behind and with helpless envy watched the stronger, more daring geese push toward the front, where food and drink were kept. There were always a few of this kind, and the old man would watch out for them, doing all that he could to help them reach the food.

All in all, he found pleasure in his work. He no longer felt so lost and alone, and thanks to these living creatures he could even gain a certain satisfaction from being a bit useful around the house.

But whenever he had to get up at dawn, crawl down from his oven, and go to the cold hut he felt intensely unhappy. To be sure, it was not too warm on the oven either, but by comparison with the hut it felt like Paradise. When the time came to crawl down from the oven, the old man would groan deeply, slowly begin fumbling for his clothes, and slowly gather them together. Even more slowly would he begin putting on his rags, and only when he was fully dressed would he lower his feet, letting them hang for a long time over the oven while he continued to groan. It seemed as if the groans were coming from the black chimney, from its utter blackness, which rose above the roof outside, where the cold and angry winds were howling.

One winter it happened that one of the geese took sick. The old man noticed that the goose seemed feeble and sad; she huddled in a corner of the cage and watched with a strange indifference the tumult of the geese being fed. The sick goose did not move from her place, and only when a rush began, when all the geese bustled to get ahead of one another, did she pick herself up or let herself be carried along by those that were scurrying back and forth; afterward she would remain by herself, staring indifferently, as though she were reflecting with disdain upon this goose riot.

At first the old man thought she was merely one of the submissive geese that lacked courage to fight for food; but later, after he had examined her more closely and noticed how pale her beak and legs were, he became convinced that the goose was sick and began to give her special care.

From time to time he would bring her a bit of mashed potatoes with flour, a dish which geese are very fond of, and sometimes he brought her leftovers from the house. But he could seldom reach the sick goose, for no matter which way he turned, the strong and courageous ones with their little heads and their red beaks would stand cackling in his way. Not only did he fail to feed the sick goose his tasty dishes, he also had to suffer from the scramble of the others. Watching her almost tore his heart: now she stands up, now she is pushed back by them, she sits down, stares indifferently with teary eyes, twists her yellowed beak, as though she asks nothing from life or geese but to be left alone.

When he saw that the sick goose showed no sign of getting better the old man decided to pull her out of the cage (even this he did not find very easy), coddle her with the tasty food, and then return her to the cage.

Had he been master of the house he would have taken the sick goose to the kitchen and kept her there till she became well. Even then, he realized, her life would be short; even if he could save her from death, the days of a goose are numbered. Well, he was used to this. Such is the fate of all domestic creatures. Man has his Angel of Death, and for geese the Angel of Death is man. And just as one is filled with pity at the sight of an unnatural death, so the old man pitied the sick goose, fretting over her to keep her from leaving the world in an unnatural way (which for her, however, would have been natural). In any case, there was nothing he could do to help her. *For this is their destiny: they shall be slaughtered and their flesh shall be eaten.* . . .

To crawl down from the oven was not very easy, yet it seemed much easier when he left his perch to visit the sick goose. Each visit saddened him: he would find her stuck away in a corner, almost ghostly, with slovenly, drooping wings and a mouth as yellow as the mouth of a man about to die.

One night the old man awoke with a pounding heart. He had been awakened, it seemed to him, by the beating of wings. True, the beating of wings could not be heard from the hut where the geese were kept. He knew this and it puzzled him. But at the same time, knowing that the sick goose lay in the hut, he let himself believe that, since she was indeed close to death, the sound of the wings had been her last fluttering. So he really had heard it. . . . But why *this* sound he did not understand. One way or another, he was certain that something was happening or had already happened, and that the sick goose was lying there, stretched out . . .

Well, good riddance. . . . He would have liked to believe this, but he could not. A heavy, painful sadness ate into his whole being, and he was drenched with fear. The beating of the wings stayed with him, and it frightened him far, far more than it should have. For if he really had heard what he imagined, if it was merely something that had happened to the sick goose, why was his fear so great?

He could not forget that from the tightly shut and distant hut no beating of wings could be heard. Perhaps he had only imagined it. And if he had only imagined it, it may have had nothing to do with the sick goose. Perhaps his worry about the sick goose was really a worry about himself. And if this were so, the beating of the wings which he thought had come from the hut had really come from the Angel of Death. . . .

The old man grew feverish. To calm himself he tried to believe that the beating of wings had indeed come from the hut, and that his fear was for nothing more than a goose. Of course . . . something had happened to her . . . he felt it. . . .

No matter how little he wished this to be true, the old man was still eager to believe that it was, simply so that he could find some peace. But he knew he would not rest until he went to the hut and saw the sick goose.

To crawl down from the warm oven in the middle of the night and go to the cold hut was not easy; not to go was worse.

The old man sat up and for a few moments lost himself in black thoughts. Then he slowly lowered himself to the ground. He felt about for a match, struck one on the shoulder of the oven, lit a piece of kindling, and took it to the hut.

As soon as he came in the geese, disturbed by this midnight visit, began a restless cackle. With his piece of kindling the old man went directly to the cage, sank down, and peered into it. The geese restlessly craned their necks over one another, blocking his way, but finally the old man found the sick goose. He was more than a little astonished to see that she was in the same condition as yesterday (or was it today? . . . he was not certain). And as always when he wanted to reach her, she stood up and sat down, stood up and sat down. Each time she was jostled by the fluttering geese she would stand up and sit down.

Only when the others had settled into a heap could the old man really examine the sick goose. She now seemed worse than usual, though still not close to death. The old man and the sick goose exchanged sympathetic glances, like old acquaintances who know each other well but have nothing to say. The sick goose twisted her neck from side to side, scrutinizing him first with one eye and then the other. It almost seemed as though she were not satisfied to study him with one eye at a time, she would have preferred to use both. . . .

The old man felt that her hours were numbered, and it occurred to him to take her out of the cage and carry her into the kitchen. He imagined that there, in the kitchen, death would come more easily to her. And a moment later he opened the door of the cage and pulled her out by a wing.

The flutter of wings blew out the kindling, and the old man was left holding the sick goose in the darkness of the hut, where pale gleams flickered from the white streaks of snow in the crannies of the wall. Once the kindling went out the old man quickly grew bewildered. A trembling fear came over him, and the snow which glimmered from all sides, cutting the darkness with light, began to dazzle him: it seemed as if each streak of snow gleaming in the air were a token of some dead white world buried in the depths of the blackness.

Holding the goose by a wing, the old man anxiously fumbled for the wall, where he knew he would find the door. He reached for it once and then a second time, but the door was not there. He became still more bewildered and frightened, and meanwhile the goose kept pulling at his arm with her whole weight and beating his legs with her free wing. Beating—all he could hear was the beating of wings, and the goose kept thrashing about only to beat his legs with her wing.

The longer the old man fingers the wall, searching for the door and not finding it, the more certain he becomes that he will never find the door. Yes, somewhere there is a door, but not here. . . . Or here, but not for him. . . . The door was here for getting into the hut, but now, for getting out, it is no longer here, it has disappeared. . . .

The goose grows heavier and heavier, she keeps beating him dumbly on the legs, not uttering a sound. . . . A thought springs into his head.

. . . It isn't a goose he is carrying. It was a goose, but no longer is. It is a wing, only a wing . . . wings without a goose and with a weight that drags his arm. It is . . . death . . . death with wings, whose beating he had heard in his sleep, lying on the oven.

The old man dropped the goose and with fresh anxiety began tapping on the wall where he knew the door should be. His nervous tapping was accompanied by a beating of wings. The white streaks gleamed more and more often. With lightning speed they appeared here and there, disappeared and appeared again, as if the whole black space were filled with angry devils that had lured him into the hut.

Each moment the old man grew more frightened. He ran back and forth, forgetting why and toward what he was running, sometimes forgetting where he was. It seemed as if he were racing through an endless distance, being chased and driven by the devils that had descended on the hut. Running about, he fell over something soft and felt that it was the same thing he had dropped from his hand. And as before, it beat its wings, silently, as if it were only beating and wings.

He wanted to get up but was paralyzed with fear. And somewhere in his mind that was not yet entirely paralyzed thoughts were leaping up like cold frogs: he is dead, and death is that which beats with a beating of wings. It seemed part of himself and yet fearfully strange. It was something that lives with a lifeless life. . . . It lives with death. . . .

When his daughter-in-law entered the hut in the morning she found the old man lying without a sign of life, and near him, without a sign of life, lay a goose.

Translated by Irving Howe and Eliezer Greenberg

Gimpel the Fool

I. BASHEVIS SINGER

1.

I AM GIMPEL THE FOOL. I don't think myself a fool. On the contrary. But that's what folks call me. They gave me the name while I was still in school. I had seven names in all: imbecile, donkey, flax-head, dope, glump, ninny, and fool. The last name stuck. What did my foolishness consist of? I was easy to take in. They said, "Gimpel, you know the rabbi's wife has been brought to childbed?" So I skipped school. Well, it turned out to be a lie. How was I supposed to know? She hadn't had a big belly. But I never looked at her belly. Was that really so foolish? The gang laughed and hee-hawed, stomped and danced and chanted a good-night prayer. And instead of the raisins they give when a woman's lying in, they stuffed my hand full of goat turds. I was no weakling. If I slapped someone he'd see all the way to Cracow. But I'm really not a slugger by nature. I think to myself, Let it pass. So they take advantage of me.

I was coming home from school and heard a dog barking. I'm not afraid of dogs, but of course I never want to start up with them. One of them may be mad, and if he bites there's not a Tartar in the world who can help you. So I made tracks. Then I looked around and saw the whole market place wild with laughter. It was no dog at all but Wolf-Leib the thief. How was I supposed to know it was he? It sounded like a howling bitch.

When the pranksters and leg-pullers found that I was easy to fool, every one of them tried his luck with me. "Gimpel, the Czar is coming to Frampol; Gimpel, the moon fell down in Turbeen; Gimpel, little Hodel Furpiece found a treasure behind the bathhouse." And I like a *golem* believed everyone. In the first place, everything is possible, as it is written in the Wisdom of the Fathers, I've forgotten just how. Second, I had to believe when the whole town came down on me! If I ever dared to say, "Ah, you're kidding!" there was trouble. People got angry. "What do you mean! You want to call everyone a liar?" What was I to do? I believed them, and I hope at least that did them some good.

I was an orphan. My grandfather who brought me up was already bent toward the grave. So they turned me over to a baker, and what a time they gave me there! Every woman or girl who came to bake a pan of cookies or dry a batch of noodles had to fool me at least once. "Gimpel, there's a fair in heaven; Gimpel, the rabbi gave birth to a calf in the seventh month; Gimpel, a cow flew over the roof and laid brass eggs." A student from the yeshiva came once to buy a roll, and he said, "You, Gimpel, while you stand here scraping with your baker's shovel the Messiah has come. The dead have arisen." "What do you mean?" I said. "I heard no one blowing the ram's horn!" He said, "Are you deaf?" And all began to cry, "We heard it, we heard!" Then in came Reitze the candle-dipper and called out in her hoarse voice, "Gimpel, your father and mother have stood up from the grave. They're looking for you."

To tell the truth, I knew very well that nothing of the sort had happened, but all the same, as folks were talking, I threw on my wool vest and went out. Maybe something had happened. What did I stand to lose by looking? Well, what a cat music went up! And then I took a vow to believe nothing more. But that was no go either. They confused me so that I didn't know the big end from the small.

I went to the rabbi to get some advice. He said, "It is written, better to be a fool all your days than for one hour to be evil. You are not a fool. They are the fools. For he who causes his neighbor to feel shame loses Paradise himself." Nevertheless the rabbi's daughter took me in. As I left the rabbinical court she said, "Have you kissed the wall yet?" I said, "No; what for?" She answered, "It's a law; you've got to do it after every visit." Well, there didn't seem to be any harm in it. And she burst out laughing. It was a fine trick. She put one over on me, all right.

I wanted to go off to another town, but then everyone got busy matchmaking, and they were after me so they nearly tore my coat tails off. They talked at me and talked until I got water on the ear. She was no chaste maiden, but they told me she was virgin pure. She had a limp, and they said it was deliberate, from coyness. She had a bastard, and they told me the child was her little brother. I cried, "You're wasting your time. I'll never marry that whore." But they said indignantly, "What a way to talk! Aren't you ashamed of yourself? We can take you to the rabbi and have you fined for giving her a bad name." I saw then that I wouldn't escape them so easily and I thought, They're set on making me their butt. But when you're married the husband's the master, and if that's all right with her it's agreeable to me too. Besides, you can't pass through life unscathed, nor expect to.

I went to her clay house, which was built on the sand, and the whole gang, hollering and chorusing, came after me. They acted like bear-baiters. When we came to the well they stopped all the same. They were afraid to start anything with Elka. Her mouth would open as if it were on a hinge, and she had a fierce tongue. I entered the house. Lines were strung from wall to wall and clothes were drying. Barefoot she stood by the tub, doing the wash. She was dressed in a worn hand-me-down gown of plush. She had her hair put up in braids and pinned across her head. It took my breath away, almost, the reek of it all.

Evidently she knew who I was. She took a look at me and said, "Look who's here! He's come, the drip. Grab a seat."

I told her all; I denied nothing. "Tell me the truth," I said, "are you really a virgin, and is that mischievous Yechiel actually your little brother? Don't be deceitful with me, for I'm an orphan."

"I'm an orphan myself," she answered, "and whoever tries to twist you up, may the end of his nose take a twist. But don't let them think they can take advantage of me. I want a dowry of fifty guilders, and let them take up a collection besides. Otherwise they can kiss my you-know-what." She was very plainspoken. I said, "It's the bride and not the groom who gives a dowry." Then she said, "Don't bargain with me. Either a flat 'yes' or a flat 'no'—go back where you came from."

I thought, No bread will ever be baked from *this* dough. But ours is not a poor town. They consented to everything and proceeded with the wedding. It so happened that there was a dysentery epidemic at the time. The ceremony was held at the cemetery gates, near the little corpse-washing hut. The fellows got drunk. While the marriage contract was being drawn up I heard the most pious high rabbi ask, "Is the bride a widow or a divorced woman?" And the sexton's wife answered for her, "Both a widow and divorced." It was a black moment for me. But what was I to do, run away from under the marriage canopy?

There was singing and dancing. An old granny danced opposite me, hugging a braided white *chalah*. The master of revels made a "God 'a mercy" in memory of the bride's parents. The schoolboys threw burrs, as on *Tishe b'Av* fast day. There were a lot of gifts after the sermon: a noodle board, a kneading trough, a bucket, brooms, ladles, household articles galore. Then I took a look and saw two strapping young men carrying a crib. "What do we need this for?" I asked. So they said, "Don't rack your brains about it. It's all right, it'll come in handy." I realized I was going to be rooked. Take it another way though, what did I stand to lose? I reflected, I'll see what comes of it. A whole town can't go altogether crazy.

2.

At night I came where my wife lay, but she wouldn't let me in. "Say, look here, is this what they married us for?" I said. And she said, "My monthly has come." "But yesterday they took you to the ritual bath, and that's afterward, isn't it supposed to be?" "Today isn't yesterday," said she, "and yesterday's not today. You can beat it if you don't like it." In short, I waited.

Not four months later she was in childbed. The townsfolk hid their laughter with their knuckles. But what could I do? She suffered intolerable pains and clawed at the walls. "Gimpel," she cried, "I'm going. Forgive me!" The house filled with women. They were boiling pans of water. The screams rose to the welkin.

The thing to do was to go to the House of Prayer to repeat Psalms, and that was what I did.

The townsfolk liked that, all right. I stood in a corner saying Psalms and prayers, and they shook their heads at me. "Pray, pray!" they told me. "Prayer never made any woman pregnant." One of the congregation put a straw to my mouth and said, "Hay for the cows." There was something to that too, by God!

She gave birth to a boy. Friday at the synagogue the sexton stood up before the Ark, pounded on the reading table, and announced, "The wealthy Reb Gimpel invites the congregation to a feast in honor of the birth of a son." The whole House of Prayer rang with laughter. My face was flaming. But there was nothing I could do. After all, I *was* the one responsible for the circumcision honors and rituals.

Half the town came running. You couldn't wedge another soul in. Women brought peppered chick-peas, and there was a keg of beer from the tavern. I ate and drank as much as anyone, and they all congratulated me. Then there was a circumcision, and I named the boy after my father, may he rest in peace. When all were gone and I was left with my wife alone, she thrust her head through the bed-curtain and called me to her.

"Gimpel," said she, "why are you silent? Has your ship gone and sunk?"

"What shall I say?" I answered. "A fine thing you've done to me! If my mother had known of it she'd have died a second time."

She said, "Are you crazy, or what?"

"How can you make such a fool," I said, "of one who should be the lord and master?"

"What's the matter with you?" she said. "What have you taken it into your head to imagine?"

I saw that I must speak bluntly and openly. "Do you think this is the way to use an orphan?" I said. "You have borne a bastard."

She answered, "Drive this foolishness out of your head. The child is yours."

"How can he be mine?" I argued. "He was born seventeen weeks after the wedding."

She told me then that he was premature. I said, "Isn't he a little too premature?" She said she had had a grandmother who carried just as short a time and she resembled this grandmother of hers as one drop of water does another. She swore to it with such oaths that you would have believed a peasant at the fair if he had used them. To tell the plain truth, I didn't believe her; but when I talked it over next day with the schoolmaster he told me that the very same thing had happened to Adam and Eve. Two they went up to bed, and four they descended.

"There isn't a woman in the world who is not the granddaughter of Eve," he said.

That was how it was—they argued me dumb. But then, who really knows how such things are?

I began to forget my sorrow. I loved the child madly, and he loved me too. As soon as he saw me he'd wave his little hands and want me to pick him up, and when he was colicky I was the only one who could pacify him. I bought him a little bone teething ring and a little gilded cap. He was forever catching the evil eye from someone, and then I had to run to get one of those abracadabras for him that would get him out of it. I worked like an ox. You know how expenses go up when there's an infant in the house. I don't want to lie about it; I didn't dislike Elka either, for that matter. She swore at me and cursed, and I couldn't get enough of her. What strength she had! One of her looks could rob you of the power of speech. And her orations! Pitch and sulphur, that's what they were full of, and yet somehow also full of charm. I adored her every word. She gave me bloody wounds though.

In the evening I brought her a white loaf as well as a dark one, and also poppyseed rolls I baked myself. I thieved because of her and swiped everything I could lay hands on, macaroons, raisins, almonds, cakes. I hope I may be forgiven for stealing from the Saturday pots the women left to warm in the baker's oven. I would take out scraps of meat, a chunk of pudding, a chicken leg or head, a piece of tripe, whatever I could nip quickly. She ate and became fat and handsome.

I had to sleep away from home all during the week, at the bakery. On Friday nights when I got home she always made an excuse of some sort. Either she had heartburn, or a stitch in the side, or hiccups, or headaches. You know what women's excuses are. I had a bitter time of it. It was rough. To add to it, this little brother of hers, the bastard, was growing bigger. He'd put lumps on me, and when I wanted to hit back she'd open her mouth and curse so powerfully I saw a green haze floating before my eyes. Ten times a day she threatened to divorce me. Another man in my place would have taken French leave and disappeared. But I'm the type that bears it and says nothing. What's one to do? Shoulders are from God, and burdens too.

One night there was a calamity in the bakery; the oven burst, and we almost had a fire. There was nothing to do but go home, so I went home. Let me, I thought, also taste the joy of sleeping in bed in midweek. I didn't want to wake the sleeping mite and tiptoed into the house. Coming in, it seemed to me that I heard not the snoring of one but, as it were, a double snore, one a thin enough snore and the other like the snoring of a slaughtered ox. Oh, I didn't like that! I didn't like it at all. I went up to the bed, and things suddenly turned black. Next to Elka lay a man's form. Another in my place would have made an uproar, and enough noise to rouse the whole town, but the thought occurred to me that I might wake the child. A little thing like that—why frighten a little swallow like that, I thought. All right then, I went back to the bakery and stretched out on a sack of flour, and till morning I never shut an eye. I shivered as if I had had malaria. "Enough of being a donkey," I said to myself. "Gimpel isn't going to be a sucker all his life. There's a limit even to the foolishness of a fool like Gimpel."

In the morning I went to the rabbi to get advice, and it made a great commotion in the town. They sent the beadle for Elka right away. She came, carrying the child. And what do you think she did? She denied it, denied everything, bone and stone! "He's out of his head," she said. "I know nothing of dreams or divinations." They yelled at her, warned her, hammered on the table, but she stuck to her guns: it was a false accusation, she said.

The butchers and the horse-traders took her part. One of the lads from the slaughterhouse came by and said to me, "We've got our eye on you, you're a marked man." Meanwhile the child started to bear down and soiled itself. In the rabbinical court there was an Ark of the Covenant, and they couldn't allow that, so they sent Elka away.

I said to the rabbi, "What shall I do?"

"You must divorce her at once," said he.

"And what if she refuses?" I asked.

He said, "You must serve the divorce, that's all you'll have to do."

I said, "Well, all right, Rabbi. Let me think about it."

"There's nothing to think about," said he. "You mustn't remain under the same roof with her."

"And if I want to see the child?" I asked.

"Let her go, the harlot," said he, "and her brood of bastards with her."

The verdict he gave was that I mustn't even cross her threshold—never again, as long as I should live.

During the day it didn't bother me so much. I thought, It was bound to happen, the abscess had to burst. But at night when I stretched out upon the sacks I felt it all very bitterly. A longing took me, for her and for the child. I wanted to be angry, but that's my misfortune exactly, I don't have it in me to be really angry. In the first place—this was how my thoughts went—there's bound to be a slip sometimes. You can't live without errors. Probably that lad who was with her led her on and gave her presents and what not, and women are often long on hair and short on sense, and so he got around her. And then since she denies it so, maybe I was only seeing things? Hallucinations do happen. You see a figure or a mannikin or something, but when you come up closer it's nothing, there's not a thing there. And if that's so, I'm doing her an injustice. And when I got so far in my thoughts I started to weep. I sobbed so that I wet the flour where I lay. In the morning I went to the rabbi and told him that I had made a mistake. The rabbi wrote on with his quill, and he said that if that were so he would have to reconsider the whole case. Until he had finished I wasn't to go near my wife, but I might send her bread and money by messenger.

3.

Nine months passed before all the rabbis could come to an agreement. Letters went back and forth. I hadn't realized that there could be so much erudition about a matter like this.

Meantime Elka gave birth to still another child, a girl this time. On the Sabbath I went to the synagogue and invoked a blessing on her. They called me up to the Torah, and I named the child for my mother-in-law, may she rest in peace. The louts and loudmouths of the town who came into the bakery gave me a going over. All Frampol refreshed its spirits because of my trouble and grief. However, I resolved that I would always believe what I was told. What's the good of *not* believing? Today it's your wife you don't believe; tomorrow it's God Himself you won't take stock in.

By an apprentice who was her neighbor I sent her daily a corn or a wheat loaf, or a piece of pastry, rolls or bagels, or, when I got the chance, a slab of pudding, a slice of honeycake, or wedding strudel—whatever came my way. The apprentice was a goodhearted lad, and more than once he added something on his own. He had formerly annoyed me a lot, plucking my nose and digging me in the ribs, but when he started to be a visitor to my house he became kind and friendly. "Hey, you, Gimpel," he said to me, "you have a very decent little wife and two fine kids. You don't deserve them."

"But the things people say about her," I said.

"Well, they have long tongues," he said, "and nothing to do with them but babble. Ignore it as you ignore the cold of last winter."

One day the rabbi sent for me and said, "Are you certain, Gimpel, that you were wrong about your wife?"

I said, "I'm certain."

"Why, but look here! You yourself saw it."

"It must have been a shadow," I said.

"The shadow of what?"

"Just of one of the beams, I think."

"You can go home then. You owe thanks to the Yanover rabbi. He found an obscure reference in Maimonides that favored you."

I seized the rabbi's hand and kissed it.

I wanted to run home immediately. It's no small thing to be separated for so long a time from wife and child. Then I reflected, I'd better go back to work now, and go home in the evening. I said nothing to anyone, although as far as my heart was concerned it was like one of the Holy Days. The women teased and twitted me as they did every day, but my thought was, Go on, with your loose talk. The truth is out, like the oil upon the water. Maimonides says it's right, and therefore it is right!

At night, when I had covered the dough to let it rise, I took my share of bread and a little sack of flour and started homeward. The moon was full and the stars were glistening, something to terrify the soul. I hurried onward, and before me darted a long shadow. It was winter, and a fresh snow had fallen. I had a mind to sing, but it was growing late and I didn't want to wake the householders. Then I felt like whistling, but remembered that you don't whistle at night because it brings the demons out. So I was silent and walked as fast as I could.

Dogs in the Christian yards barked at me when I passed, but I thought, Bark your teeth out! What are you but mere dogs? Whereas I am a man, the husband of a fine wife, the father of promising children.

As I approached the house my heart started to pound as though it were the heart of a criminal. I felt no fear, but my heart went thump! thump! Well, no drawing back. I quietly lifted the latch and went in. Elka was asleep. I looked at the infant's cradle. The shutter was closed, but the moon forced its way through the cracks. I saw the newborn child's face and loved it as soon as I saw it—immediately—each tiny bone.

Then I came nearer to the bed. And what did I see but the apprentice lying there beside Elka. The moon went out all at once. It was utterly black, and I trembled. My teeth chattered. The bread fell from my hands and my wife waked and said, "Who is that, ah?"

I muttered, "It's me."

"Gimpel?" she asked. "How come you're here? I thought it was forbidden."

"The rabbi said," I answered and shook as with a fever.

"Listen to me, Gimpel," she said, "go out to the shed and see if the goat's all right. It seems she's been sick." I have forgotten to say that we had a goat. When I heard she was unwell I went into the yard. The nannygoat was a good little creature. I had a nearly human feeling for her.

With hesitant steps I went up to the shed and opened the door. The goat stood there on her four feet. I felt her everywhere, drew her by the horns, examined her udders, and found nothing wrong. She had probably eaten too much bark. "Good night, little goat," I said. "Keep well." And the little beast answered with a "Maa" as though to thank me for the good will.

I went back. The apprentice had vanished.

"Where," I asked, "is the lad?"

"What lad?" my wife answered.

"What do you mean?" I said. "The apprentice. You were sleeping with him."

"The things I have dreamed this night and the night before," she said, "may they come true and lay you low, body and soul! An evil spirit has taken root in you and dazzles your sight." She screamed out, "You hateful creature! You moon calf! You spook! You uncouth mane! Get out, or I'll scream all Frampol out of bed!"

Before I could move, her brother sprang out from behind the oven and struck me a blow on the back of the head. I thought he had broken my neck. I felt that something about me was deeply wrong, and I said, "Don't make a scandal. All that's needed now is that people should accuse me of raising spooks and *dybbuks*." For that was what she had meant. "No one will touch bread of my baking."

In short, I somehow calmed her.

"Well," she said, "that's enough. Lie down, and be shattered by wheels."

Next morning I called the apprentice aside. "Listen here, brother!" I said. And so on and so forth. "What do you say?" He stared at me as though I had dropped from the roof or something.

"I swear," he said, "you'd better go to an herb doctor or some healer. I'm afraid you have a screw loose, but I'll hush it up for you." And that's how the thing stood.

To make a long story short, I lived twenty years with my wife. She bore me six children, four daughters and two sons. All kinds of things happened, but I neither saw nor heard. I believed, and that's all. The rabbi recently said to me, "Belief in itself is beneficial. It is written that a good man lives by his faith."

Suddenly my wife took sick. It began with a trifle, a little growth upon the breast. But she evidently was not destined to live long; she had no years. I spent a fortune on her. I have forgotten to say that by this time I had a bakery of my own and in Frampol was considered to be something of a rich man. Daily the healer came, and every witch doctor in the neighborhood was brought. They decided to use leeches, and after that to try cupping. They even called a doctor from Lublin, but it was too late. Before she died she called me to her bed and said, "Forgive me, Gimpel."

I said, "What is there to forgive? You have been a good and faithful wife."

"Woe, Gimpel!" she said. "It was ugly how I deceived you all these years. I want to go clean to my Maker, and so I have to tell you that the children are not yours."

If I had been clouted on the head with a piece of wood it couldn't have bewildered me more.

"Whose are they?" I asked.

"I don't know," she said, "there were a lot. . . . But they're not yours." And as she spoke she tossed her head to the side, her eyes turned glassy, and it was all up with Elka. On her whitened lips there remained a smile.

I imagined that, dead as she was, she was saying, "I deceived Gimpel. That was the meaning of my brief life."

4.

One night, when the period of mourning was done, as I lay dreaming on the flour sacks, there came the Spirit of Evil himself and said to me, "Gimpel, why do you sleep?"

I said, "What should I be doing? Eating *kreplach*?"

"The whole world deceives you," he said, "and you ought to deceive the world in your turn."

"How can I deceive all the world?" I asked him.

He answered, "You might accumulate a bucket of urine every day and at night pour it into the dough. Let the sages of Frampol eat filth."

"What about judgment in the world to come?" I said.

"There is no world to come," he said. "They've sold you a bill of goods and talked you into believing you carried a cat in your belly. What nonsense!"

"Well then," I said, "and is there a God?"

He answered, "There is no God either."

"What," I said, "*is* there, then?"

"A thick mire."

He stood before my eyes with a goatish beard and horns, long-toothed, and with a tail. Hearing such words, I wanted to snatch him by the tail, but I tumbled from the flour sacks and nearly broke a rib. Then it happened that I had to answer the call of nature, and, passing, I saw the risen dough, which seemed to say to me, "Do it!" In brief, I let myself be persuaded.

At dawn the apprentice came. We kneaded the bread, scattered caraway seeds on it, and set it to bake. Then the apprentice went away, and I was left sitting in the little trench by the oven, on a pile of rags. Well, Gimpel, I thought, you've revenged yourself on them for all the shame they've put on you. Outside the frost glittered, but it was warm beside the oven. The flames heated my face. I bent my head and fell into a doze.

I saw in a dream, at once, Elka in her shroud. She called to me, "What have you done, Gimpel?"

I said to her, "It's all your fault," and started to cry.

"You fool!" she said. "You fool! Because I was false is everything false too? I never deceived anyone but myself. I'm paying for it all, Gimpel. They spare you nothing here."

I looked at her face. It was black. I was startled and waked, and remained sitting dumb. I sensed that everything hung in the balance. A false step now and I'd lose Eternal Life. But God gave me His help. I seized the long shovel and took out the loaves, carried them into the yard, and started to dig a hole in the frozen earth.

My apprentice came back as I was doing it. "What are you doing, boss?" he said, and grew pale as a corpse.

"I know what I'm doing," I said, and I buried it all before his very eyes.

Then I went home, took my hoard from its hiding place, and divided it among the children. "I saw your mother tonight," I said. "She's turning black, poor thing."

They were so astounded they couldn't speak a word.

"Be well," I said, "and forget that such a one as Gimpel ever existed." I put on my short coat, a pair of boots, took the bag that held my prayer shawl in one hand, my stick in the other, and kissed the *mezzuzah*. When people saw me in the street they were greatly surprised.

"Where are you going?" they said.

I answered, "Into the world." And so I departed from Frampol.

I wandered over the land, and good people did not neglect me. After many years I became old and white; I heard a great deal, many lies and falsehoods, but the longer I lived the more I understood that there were really no lies. Whatever doesn't really happen is dreamed at night. It happens to one if it doesn't happen to another, tomorrow if not today, or a century hence if not next year. What difference can it make? Often I heard tales of which I said, "Now this is a thing that cannot happen." But before a year had elapsed I heard that it actually had come to pass somewhere.

Going from place to place, eating at strange tables, it often happens that I spin yarns—improbable things that could never have happened—about devils, magicians, windmills, and the like. The children run after me, calling, "Grandfather, tell us a story." Sometimes they ask for particular stories, and I try to please them. A fat young boy once said to me, "Grandfather, it's the same story you told us before." The little rogue, he was right.

So it is with dreams too. It is many years since I left Frampol, but as soon as I shut my eyes I am there again. And whom do you think I see? Elka. She is standing by the washtub, as at our first encounter, but her face is shining and her eyes are as radiant as the eyes of a saint, and she speaks outlandish words to me, strange things. When I wake

I have forgotten it all. But while the dream lasts I am comforted. She answers all my queries, and what comes out is that all is right. I weep and implore, "Let me be with you." And she consoles me and tells me to be patient. The time is nearer than it is far. Sometimes she strokes and kisses me and weeps upon my face. When I awaken I feel her lips and taste the salt of her tears.

No doubt the world is entirely an imaginary world, but it is only once removed from the true world. At the door of the hovel where I lie, there stands the plank on which the dead are taken away. The grave-digger Jew has his spade ready. The grave waits and the worms are hungry; the shrouds are prepared—I carry them in my beggar's sack. Another *shnorrer* is waiting to inherit my bed of straw. When the time comes I will go joyfully. Whatever may be there, it will be real, without complication, without ridicule, without deception. God be praised: there even Gimpel cannot be deceived.

Translated by Saul Bellow

May the Temple Be Restored!

JOSEPH OPATOSHU

IT WAS a night after the High Holy Days, a rainy night, a night in autumn, such a night as one can come upon only in small Polish towns, when the darkness is so intense that the downpour seems to consist of the blackest ink.

On such a night broad-shouldered Simcha, the drayman, was tossing in bed, unable to fall asleep. An atmosphere of prosperity pervaded the house. The warm, close air was redolent of ground coffee, of prunes, of almonds and dates. Sounds of snoring came from the smaller room, which served as sleeping quarters for Wolf and Fishel, the two sons of Simcha. They had wound up their work in connection with the recent building of the railway line between Warsaw and Berlin, and had come back from Voulke, a place about a mile from Mlava, which was a town on the border between Russia and Germany. The railway had brought prosperity to Mlava and to the draymen who transported goods from the station to the city; and the most prosperous among them was the broad-shouldered Simcha. The four of them—he and his two sons, together with Velvel, a youngster who worked for Simcha—could load plenty of goods on their huge drays. And it wasn't so much Simcha himself as his two sons who took a tithe of all these goods, but each tithe—a sack of almonds, say, or a sack of coffee, or a sack of prunes—would be stored in Simcha's house. And Simcha's wealth kept piling up. He had built himself a barn, with stalls where he kept his Percherons with their leonine manes. And Simcha's sons, who inspired everybody at the railway terminal with fear and trembling, weren't the sort to let anybody put one over on them.

But at the very height of his prosperity, when the whole town was envying Simcha, his best dray horse—the dappled gray—dropped dead. And not in the line of duty, but in its stall, apparently poisoned by some enemy! And before Simcha had a chance to buy himself another, his three-year old bay had also pegged out in its stall.

Simcha felt certain by now that both horses had been poisoned; he had as many enemies as there were draymen at the railway terminal. And all this, mind you, was due to his two sons, who were so handy with their fists.

As the father with his sons and their young helper stood over the fallen horse he remarked, "Listen, my lads—even if they were to poison one of our horses every week we would still have the whip hand over them. But as long as I don't catch one of them red-handed I've got to keep my mouth shut. From today on, however, we mustn't take our eyes off our horses at the terminal. And you, Velvel, will sleep in the barn to be near them."

As soon as those two horses dropped dead something began to brew in Simcha. He was the kind of man who would break before he would bend. And so Simcha did not bend. He kept up his pride as before, and he was now in the market for two dray horses—and they had to be good horses, at that.

But at night, as he tossed and turned on his bed, he felt much aggrieved because God was picking on him, of all people. Why? True enough, Simcha was a simple sort, hardly able to say his prayers, and what praying he did was mostly by heart rather than from his prayer book. Yet who contributed to the synagogue as handsomely as Simcha? Not a Sabbath passed but that a poor Jewish guest or two sat down at his table. And whenever the rabbi called for contributions Simcha never gave less than a silver ruble.

Why, then, was the Lord chastising him so?

It was past midnight, yet Simcha could not sleep. He stared into the darkness, which was filled with snoring as grating as a sawmill going full blast. Had Simcha been able to read he would have got out of bed, lit a candle, and sought enlightenment in some Talmudic tome. But instead, after a sigh or two, he began to dress in the dark. And when he had put on his boots the floor started to creak under him.

"Where are you going, Simcha?" his wife asked.

"Something won't let me stay in bed, Hannah," Simcha answered. "I'm going to take a look at the horses."

"You don't think I've slept a wink either, do you?"

Simcha ignored her remark. He drew his trouser-belt tighter, picked up a whip, and went out of the house. A cold drizzle was coming down; the sky was all blackness. Simcha entered the barn, where an oil lantern was flickering. The horses sprawled out in their stalls raised their heads, eying their master; Simcha patted one, then another, then the third. Velvel turned over on his pile of hay and asked, "Who is it?"

"It's me, Velvel. Go back to sleep."

Simcha left the barn and, using his whip as a pointer, counted his drays: one, two, three. He would be able to use only two of them. In his vexation he spat, swished his whip, and started walking. The darkness—a raw darkness, at that—looked like a wall to Simcha. He halted with closed eyes, listening to the mingled sounds of the wind and the rain, and he thought he heard muffled weeping. He turned from Pottery Street and proceeded along Plotsk Street toward the market place. The weeping became more distinct. A tiny light flickered in the dark. Where could that light be coming from? The rabbi's, perhaps?

Simcha paused before the rabbi's house. From the rabbi's study, where a light flickered in the window, came the sounds of subdued lamentations. Who could it be? The rabbi's wife? An ailing child, perhaps? They might need help. Simcha, clutching his whip, mounted the dark, creaking steps. Only now did it strike him that the rabbi himself was crying. A shudder ran through Simcha's body: the rabbi was weeping! And this rabbi, Reb Wolf Lipshitz, was famous almost throughout Poland. Not just anybody, but Rabbi Wolf, at one time Rabbi of Warsaw, now Rabbi of Mlava. His elder brother, Reb Moishele, was the Rabbi of Lodz, and their sister Priva was the wife of the Rabbi of Kutna.

As Simcha opened the door he was awed by the scene he saw: the Rabbi of Mlava seated on the floor, holding a lighted candle in one hand and a volume of the Talmud in the other, and intoning in a weeping voice.

"What's happened, Rabbi?" the drayman exclaimed, raising his whip. "Is the Rabbi mourning for someone?"

"No, Simcha. I am merely reciting the midnight prayers, the *tikun chtzoss*—"

"And what is *tikun chtzoss*?" Simcha asked, spreading his palms in bewilderment.

"Our Holy Temple has been destroyed; the Divine Presence is in exile," the rabbi explained, still in the same tearful tone of voice. "Hence the Jews have to pray, weep, and mourn aloud—"

"Woe is me!" Simcha clutched his head with both hands. "The Holy Temple has been destroyed—woe is me!"

The drayman broke into loud wailing, as if he were hearing about the destruction of the Temple for the first time. He began to beat his head with his fists. If the Rabbi of Mlava was weeping, why should Simcha the drayman keep quiet? And he refused to do so; he took to pounding his head against the wall so hard that splotches of blood appeared on his forehead. The rabbi scrambled to his feet in dismay. Putting his hands on the drayman's shoulders, he began to pacify him.

"You may do yourself serious injury, Simcha. You're actually bleeding! There, you'd better sit down."

The rabbi made him take a seat, wiped off the blood with his handkerchief, and asked him repeatedly if he would like a glass of water.

"No, Rabbi," the drayman declined, feeling embarrassed by the fuss the rabbi was making over him. "I don't want any water. If anything, I'd like a drink of something stronger. It would ease my aching heart."

"Where would I get you a drink?" the rabbi countered, as if embarrassed at not having any liquor in the house. But when the rabbi started rummaging for a bottle, Simcha left, only to return shortly with a demijohn, which he placed on the table. Then, pouring out two tumblers, he observed, "If my heart ached over the destruction of the Temple, then yours, Rabbi, must have been actually breaking. Let's have a glass on it then."

As the two downed their drinks Simcha became quite animated. After the third glass the rabbi also grew jolly; his astute eyes were smiling as he pushed away his tumbler and said, "That will be enough, Simcha."

"What do you mean by *enough,* Rabbi of Mlava?" the drayman countered as he downed his fourth glass, and then the fifth, and the sixth. "How can you say *enough,* Rabbi, at a time when we Jews are beset with trials and tribulations? The Temple has been destroyed . . . God has sent a curse upon my house. . . . Inside of a fortnight two of my horses—my best horses—have dropped dead. God wants to bring me down a peg or two, it seems. So you see my position, Rabbi of Mlava," Simcha maundered on as he poured a seventh glass out for himself. "I feel like wailing and weeping. . . . The Temple has been destroyed . . . Simcha the drayman is left with nothing but his whip, no longer well-to-do, no longer on good terms with God—"

"Now, now, Simcha." The rabbi led his guest to a sofa. "Where will you go in such a downpour? Spend the rest of the night here. There, lie down. Good night, Simcha!" And the rabbi covered him with an overcoat.

He paused for a moment in the doorway. In one hand he was holding what remained of the candle, and in the other a folio of the Talmud. And, as Simcha turned over toward the wall, the rabbi walked out of the room.

Translated by Bernard Guilbert Guerney

Part Three

JEWISH CHILDREN

A Page from the Song of Songs

SHOLOM ALEICHEM

BUZIE is a name. It is a diminutive of Esther-Libbe. First Esther-Libbe, then Libuzie, then Buzie. She is a year older than I, or maybe two years, and together we are not quite twenty years old. Now, I ask you, how old am I and how old is she? But that is not important. Instead let me give you a short sketch of her life.

My older brother Benny lived in a village, where he owned a mill. He was a wonder at shooting, riding, and swimming. One summer day while bathing in the river he drowned. Thus the old adage that the best swimmers drown was borne out. He left the mill, two horses, a young widow, and a child. The mill was abandoned, the horses were sold, the widow remarried and moved to some distant place, and the child was brought to us.

That child was Buzie.

That my father should love Buzie as his own is easy to understand, and that my mother should watch over her like an only daughter is natural. In her they found a comfort for their great sorrow. But that has nothing to do with me. Then why is it that when I come from *cheder* and find Buzie not at home my food is flat and tasteless? And why is it that when Buzie comes in the darkest corners are suddenly lit up? And why is it that when Buzie speaks to me I drop my eyes? And when Buzie laughs at me I weep?

And when Buzie . . .

All through the winter I had been looking forward to the Passover holidays. Then I would be free from *cheder,* free to play with Buzie, free to run outdoors with her. We would run down the hill to the river's edge, where I could show her how the ducklings learn to swim. When I try to tell her about it she only laughs at me. Buzie doesn't believe a thing I tell her. She doesn't believe that I can climb to the top of the highest tree—if I only wanted to. She doesn't believe that I can shoot—if I only had a gun to shoot with. She never says she doesn't believe, she only laughs at me. And I hate nothing more than to be laughed at. But when Passover comes, the beautiful, free days of Passover, when we can run outdoors, away from the watchful eyes of my parents, then I will show her such wonders that they will take her breath away.

The wonderful time, the most joyous time of the year, has come.

Buzie and I are dressed in our holiday clothes. Everything we have on twinkles and shines and crackles. I look at Buzie and I am reminded of the Song of Songs, which I studied before Passover with my rabbi. Verse after verse, it comes back to me:

"Behold, thou art fair, my beloved, thou art fair; thy eyes are as doves, thy hair is a flock of goats that comes down from Mount Gilead.

"Thy teeth are like a flock of white lambs that come up from the river, all are alike; the same mother bore them.

"Thy lips are like a thread of scarlet; thy speech is full of sweetness."

Why is it that when you look at Buzie you are reminded of the Song of Songs? Why is it that when you study the Song of Songs, Buzie comes into your thoughts?

We are ready to go. I can hardly stand still. My pockets are full of nuts. My mother gave us all we wanted. She filled our pockets and told us we could play with them to our hearts' content. But she made us promise not to crack any before Passover.

"Are you ready?" says Buzie.

I jump for the door. Away we go. The nuts make a drumming sound, they rattle as we run. At first we are dazzled by the brilliance outside. The sun is high up already; it is looking down on the other side of town. The air is free and fresh, soft and clear. Here and there on the hill beyond the synagogue there sprouts the first grass of spring, tender, quivering, green. With a scream and a flutter of wings a straight line of swallows flies over our heads and again I am reminded of the Song of Songs: "The flowers appear on the earth; the time of the song of birds has come and the voice of the turtle is heard in our land."

I feel strangely light. It seems to me that I have wings. Any minute now I will rise into the air and fly.

From the town strange sounds arise—a roaring, a boiling, a seething. It is the day before Passover, a rare and wonderful day. In one instant the world is transformed. Our yard is a king's court. Our house is a palace. I am a prince and Buzie is a princess. The logs of wood piled about our door are the cedars and cypresses of the Song of Songs. The cat that lies near the door warming herself in the sun is a roe or a young hart in the Song of Songs. The women and the girls who are working outdoors, washing and cleaning and getting ready for the Passover, are the daughters of Jerusalem. Everything, everything is from the Song of Songs.

I walk about with my hands in my pockets, and the nuts rattle. Buzie follows me step by step. I cannot walk slowly, I am treading on air. I want to fly, to swoop, to soar like an eagle. I start running, and Buzie runs after me. I leap onto the pile of logs and jump from one log to another. Buzie jumps after me. I jump up, she jumps up; I jump down, she jumps down. Who will get tired first? I guessed it.

"How-long-will-you-keep-it-up?" asks Buzie all out of breath.

And I answer her in the words of the Song of Songs: " 'Till the morning breeze come and the shadows flee away.' There! You are tired and I am not!"

I feel proud that Buzie cannot keep up with me. I gloat over her and at the same time I am sorry for her. My heart aches for her, because I imagine she is unhappy. That is Buzie—full of gaiety one moment, and the next she is hiding in a corner, quietly weeping. At times like these nothing helps. No matter how much my mother tries to comfort her, how much my father caresses her, she continues to cry. For whom does she cry? For her father who died when she was a baby? For her mother who married and went off without as much as a good-by? Ah, that mother of hers. When you mention her mother Buzie's face turns fiery red, as though she were ashamed of her. She never says an unkind word about her, but she looks unhappy. I cannot bear to see Buzie looking so wretched. I sit near her on the logs and try to distract her thoughts.

Rolling a few nuts about, I say, "Guess what I could do if I wanted to."

"What could you do?"

"If I wanted to, all your nuts would be mine."

"Would you win them away from me?"

"No. We wouldn't even start playing."

"Well then, would you take them away from me?"

"No. They would come to me by themselves."

She raises her eyes to me, her blue eyes, eyes straight out of the Song of Songs. I say, "You think I am joking. Well, I know a certain language, I know some magic words . . ."

She opens her eyes wider. I explain, feeling grown and important, all puffed up with pride. "We boys know a lot of things. There is a boy in *cheder,* Shaike, who is blind in one eye—he knows everything. He even knows Cabala. Do you know what Cabala is?"

"No. How should I know?"

I am suddenly lifted to the Seventh Heaven because I can give her a lesson in Cabala.

"Cabala, silly, is a useful thing. By means of Cabala I can make myself invisible. With Cabala I can draw wine from a stone and gold from a wall. With the help of Cabala you and I, just as we are sitting here, could rise to the clouds and above the clouds . . ."

To fly up to the clouds with Buzie and above the clouds, and fly away with her, far, far off over the ocean—that has been one of my fondest dreams. There, beyond the ocean, begins the land of the dwarfs who are descended from King David's time. These dwarfs are kindly little people who live on sweets and almond milk, play all day long on little flutes and dance in a ring, are afraid of nothing and are kind to strangers. When someone arrives from our world they give him food and drink and shower him with costly garments and gold and silver ornaments, and before he leaves they fill his pockets with diamonds and jewels, which lie about in their streets as trash does in ours.

"Really? Like trash in the streets?" asked Buzie wonderingly when I once told her about the dwarfs.

"Don't you believe it?"

"Do you?"

"Why shouldn't I?"

"Where did you hear about it?"

"In *cheder,* of course."

"Oh, in *cheder*!"

Lower and lower sinks the sun, painting the sky a fiery gold. The gold is reflected in Buzie's eyes. They swim in molten gold.

I want very badly to impress Buzie with Shaike's ability and with the wonders I can perform by means of Cabala. But Buzie won't be impressed. Instead she laughs at me. She looks at me with her mouth half open and all her pearly teeth showing, and laughs.

Annoyed, I ask, "Don't you believe me?"

Buzie laughs again.

"You think I'm boasting. That I'm making up lies."

Buzie laughs harder.

I have to repay her for this. I know how, too. "The trouble with you is that you don't know what Cabala is. If you knew you wouldn't laugh.

By means of Cabala, if I wanted to, I could bring your mother down here. Yes, I can. And if you begged me very hard I could bring her tonight, riding on a broomstick."

At once she stops laughing. A cloud crosses her lovely, bright face and it seems to me that the sun has suddenly disappeared and the day is done. I have gone too far. I have wounded her. I am sorry I ever started this. How can I make up to her now? I move closer to her. She turns away from me. I want to take her hand and speak to her with the words of the Song of Songs: " 'Return, return, O Shulamite!' Turn back to me, Buzie . . ."

Suddenly a voice calls out, "Shimek, Shimek!"

Shimek—that's me. My mother is calling me, to go to the synagogue with my father.

To go with Father to the synagogue on the eve of Passover is one of the pleasures of life. Just to be dressed in perfectly new clothes from head to foot and to show off before one's friends. And the services—the first evening prayer, the first benediction of the holiday season! What delights the Lord has provided for His Jewish children.

"Shimek! Shimek!"

My mother is in a hurry. "I'm coming! I'm coming right away. I just have to tell Buzie something, just one little thing!"

I tell her just one thing. That what I told her was not true. To make other people fly by means of Cabala is impossible. But I myself—I can fly, and I will show her right after the holidays. I will make my first attempt then. I will rise up from these very logs where we are now sitting, and in one moment I will be above the clouds. From there I will turn to the right—there, see—there where everything ends and the Frozen Sea begins . . .

Buzie listens, absorbed in my story. The sun, about to sink, sends its last rays to kiss the earth.

"What," asks Buzie, "do you mean by the Frozen Sea?"

"Don't you know what the Frozen Sea is? That's far in the north. The water is as thick as jelly and as salty as brine. Ships cannot go there, and people who are caught in it never return."

Buzie looks at me wide-eyed. "Then why are you going there?"

"Am I going to touch the sea, you silly thing? I'll fly high up over it, like an eagle, and in a few minutes I shall be on dry land. That is where the twelve high mountains that belch fire and smoke begin. I shall stop on the tip of the twelfth mountain and walk from there for seven miles till I come to a thick forest. I will cross several forests till I come to a small lake. I shall swim across the lake and count seven times seven. Out of the ground will spring a dwarf with a long white beard. He will say to me, 'What is your wish?'

"And I will say to him, 'Lead me to the queen's daughter!' "

"Which queen's daughter?" asks Buzie, startled.

"The queen's daughter," I explain, "is the beautiful princess who was snatched away from under the wedding canopy, bewitched, and carried far, far away and locked up in a crystal palace for seven years—"

"What is she to you?"

"What do you mean—what is she to me? I have to set her free, don't I?"

"You have to set her free?"

"Who then?"

"You don't have to fly so far, believe me. You don't have to fly so far," says Buzie and takes my hand. Her small white hand is cold. I look into her eyes and see in them the last faint reflection of the gold that is draining from the sky.

Slowly the day is going; the first beautiful day of spring is passing away. Like a spent candle, the sun goes down. The noises that we heard all day are dying too. There is hardly a person to be seen in the street. From the windows of the houses there wink the flames of candles lit for Passover eve. A strange, a holy stillness surrounds us, and Buzie and I feel ourselves slowly merging with this stillness.

"Shimek! Shimek!"

This is the third time my mother has called me. As if I didn't know myself that I had to go to the synagogue! I'll stay only another minute, not more than a minute. But Buzie hears her too, pulls her hand out of mine, jumps to her feet, and begins to push me.

"Shimek, your mother is calling you. You'd better go. It's late. Go."

I am getting ready to go. The day is done, the sun has been snuffed out. All the gold has turned to blood. A cool breeze has sprung up. Buzie keeps pushing me toward the house. I throw a last quick look at her. Her face has changed, and it has a different, an unearthly beauty in the twilight. The thought of the bewitched princess flits through my head. But Buzie won't allow those thoughts. She keeps pushing me ahead. Slowly I start to go, and I look back just once at the bewitched princess who has now completely merged with the strange Passover twilight, and I stand rooted in one spot. But she waves her hand at me, bidding me to go, to go quickly.

And it seems to me that I hear her speaking in the words of the Song of Songs: "Make haste, my beloved, be thou like a gazelle or a young hart upon the mountain of spices."

Translated by Julius and Frances Butwin

My First Love

MOISHE NADIR

THIS IS the story of a first love, and it's not very new and perhaps not very interesting. Dear God, who has not written and rewritten and poured out in hundreds of chapters the sorrows and joys of his first love! And the world is already so old! It has heard so much about love and lovers, about loves happy and unhappy, about loves that end with marriage and loves that end with carbolic acid! Indeed, is there anything at all the world hasn't already heard about? It's fortunate, then, that my story is about the love of a twelve-year-old boy, who loved, not alone, but in partnership with five comrades. This, it seems to me, sets my story a little apart from all other romances. I shall tell how these six students of the Talmud in Galicia tried to find a path into the stony heart of their beloved, who was called Surele and always wore white gloves.

My story, I must warn you, will not instruct or educate you. Nor will it pick you up—that is, uplift you—and carry you away to a better world. If there's anything I hate it's to pick up strangers and carry them away. I once knew a Jew who was so uplifted by a certain story that to this day his wife is still looking for him. Disappeared! Gone! I mean to say, he's here all right, but not with his wife. No—with someone else's!

My love story, really, is written for myself alone, a cozy little story, but if you've nothing better to do at the moment, and if your mind is at ease, sit down and read about a boy, a girl, and a love that took place somewhere in Galicia, in an isolated village that few people know and even fewer know of.

I cannot say that that far village cradled me. Rather did it coffin me, for I slept in a small narrow wooden box; my mother couldn't afford the luxury of a cradle. In our village, there is no lake, but only a little brook, which courses drowsily through the gardens of hops and slowly on toward the foot of a white cliff, where, oddly, the brook turns yellow and changes its direction, and from here no one knows where it wanders. In summer the little brook plays gently over the pebbles. Now and then a covey of ducks chases a tattered leaf that drifts on the surface. Now and then a Polish peasant beats her wash with a wooden paddle. Now and then a Jewish girl washes a window that she has simply plucked out of its frame and brought from home.

This stream ices over with the first frost, and you simply don't know what's become of it. It's so shallow that even children can't swim on their stomachs. That's why, in our village, you find so many Jews who can swim only with their noses stuck up; so to say, on their backs.

Ours is a tiny, dirty, lonely, frightened, neglected, and lovable village; it's a blessing from God in the summer, and a curse from God in the winter. Why do I say a curse in the winter? Simply because it was in winter that my—or better said, our—first romance began. Whatever you say, I was not—God forbid!—a lonely lover. No, I was never lonely. My first love was shared, with my full knowledge, by five other lovers, all of whom wore the same little jackets, the same little round hats, and curly earlocks that hung down our cheeks as still as little glass bottles.

But let's get back to the village. If it can be said that a village just lies down, then you can certainly say that about my village. It lies down and doesn't move. It lies down and sleeps away the years amid high cliffs of chalk that embrace it like the white hands of a sick God. The cliffs are white, the mud is white, and white, too, are the people, white and frightened.

There you have a brief description of my village, which lies down among the chalk cliffs and sleeps and dreams. Of what does it dream? Of white bread and butter, of coffee and cream and all those delicacies that are good for village folk and not at all bad for city gentry.

Apart from the white hills, our village enjoys a privilege others don't. The hops fields! Almighty God! Eternal God! Even now, at this moment, the fragrance of the hops tickles my nostrils and mingles with the fragrance of fresh chalk and white earth and thin young trees with their thin branches.

Pretty, beloved, dirty village in Galicia. . . .

My father went away to America, and my mother wept. And I? I too wept, shriller than my mother; it was ear-splitting. The whole Sabbath night before he left I cried, I and my beloved mother. We took him, with so many others, to the stagecoach, and when my father was gone my heart was very heavy. Did I say heavy? No, light, light as a feather. Something had been torn out of my heart—and so quickly! I moped around, a boy without a heart. Have you ever seen such a boy? I would sit with my mother, looking up into the great empty sky and yearning. It was not my heart that yearned, but—oh, I don't know what myself. And I would grow weary of looking up into the empty distant sky, and I would turn back to the earth and tear up the little field flowers that grew on the hills, and rip the white petals from the little yellow cores, and I would count, one . . . two . . . three hundred . . . and yearn. And, in all, I was no more than twelve small years.

Summer went—an entire summer yearned away. Winter came, and my mother sent me to the school of Reb Chaim, the *shochet*. A big school with big boys like myself. We learned exactly how to draw the blade across the calf's throat, exactly how to let the blood out of the slaughtered innocent, we learned how to make off with the dried pears that the *rebbetsin* had stacked away in the attic against the winter. We learned everything—except what we had been sent there to learn, Torah and Talmud, which our *rebbe* tried to knock into our heads by sheer force.

Our *rebbe* was a short man who wore a flowered robe, and his little beard sprang directly from his mustache and did not quite reach the tip of his chin, which looked, scandalously, as if it had been shaved. What a bad-tempered man, God spare us! When he was angry he knocked the Talmud into you with a blow, a slap, and a pinch at the same time, or he knocked the *Gemarah* into you with a kick that caught you right in the heart. Fortunately for me, I was a boy who no longer had a heart. His anger and his temper were not so much the result of a bad disposition, I came to learn, as of a bad digestion. He was a slave to mineral water, and if the bottle was full all was well; but if the bottle was empty, watch out for your life!

All the same, we liked him and were proud of him. We liked him because he was often called away, to slaughter a calf. Sometimes he was even called away for a day or two, and then we liked him very much. We were proud of him because he was known in our parts as the best teacher and the worst-tempered man. And because of this unending fury we were even proud of ourselves, noble uncomplaining martyrs!

It was during this time that I fell in love with Surele. Who was Surele? She was two years older than myself, fourteen, and she wore shoes with high heels, a blue ribbon in her hair, and, winter or summer, white gloves. Was she pretty? I really can't say. What does that mean, pretty? It means to have a pale aristocratic face, like that of the landlord's daughter. Surele certainly didn't have a pale face; on the contrary, she had a round red shining face. Thus I never could be certain if she was pretty, but, pretty or not, Surele wore gloves, white aristocratic gloves. That was enough for me; I fell in love with her. Really in love, deeply in love, mortally in love, immortally in love. My soul was one glowing fire; it burned and burned, like the bush in the desert that was not consumed. Day and night, at the academy and at our Jewish school, at home and in the synagogue, my soul was possessed by Surele and Surele's white gloves.

The academy was the Polish school near Surele's home. When I realized that I could not live without her, worldly things no longer meant anything to me and I dedicated myself to school and never missed a day. Passing Surele's house on the way to school, I would stop a moment and look up at her window and then bound away with a heart full of joy. I begged my teacher to let me come early and ring the schoolbell. I was certain that if Surele passed and saw me pulling the bellrope, she would have to admit that I was no ordinary boy but one whom she must admire and respect, and, yes, even try to win for her own.

Alas for my hope! As with the hopes of all unfortunate lovers, it melted away like snow under a hot sun. Month after month, day in and day out, I pulled at that bellrope, and there was no change in Surele's feelings for me. No, nothing would come of bellringing! I would have to find some better way to her heart.

Among Reb Chaim the *shochet*'s six pupils was Hershele, who was like a rabbit, small and quick, and, like a cow, he was always butting you with his head. Oh, he was a real mischief-maker! He was like a weed: wherever you didn't plant him, there he sprang up, and when he sprang up you had to cut him down. To slap Hershele was almost considered a good deed. But God knows that our Hershele was a fine lad and an absolute master at carving whistles out of new green branches.

Hershele and I became great friends. I regretted that he always butted me with his head, less because it hurt than because it wasn't dignified for a student of the Torah and the Talmud. Still, I became accustomed to this habit and even took it up myself, and with that our friendship became absolutely cemented.

One night I asked Hershele to go down to the brook with me to find new green branches for whistles. It was on that night that I entrusted him with my secret, the burdensome, bitter, unbearable secret of my soul: my love for Surele.

Hershele listened. Then he butted me with his head, just like that, and cried out joyfully, "What are you talking about!" He revealed that he was not at all indifferent to her himself, and that as he grew in size, so would his love grow. Moreover, not he alone, but every boy in Reb Chaim's school was in love with Surele—every single one.

As he spoke I felt very lonely, and yet happy too. And, not knowing what else to do, I bent over like a cow and butted him with my head. Just like that!

Winter came, and with it the white nights and the lighted lanterns, the going home from school with lanterns in the dark and the calling out in the stillness, "Good night! Good night!" Winter came, and with it the bright running of skates, of sleds, and the need to do something wild, something crazy, something fantastic, that seizes upon young lads in the wild white nights in a desolate village among white hills.

The secret of my love was made known by Hershele to our comrades, and this made us all feel very close to one another. Slowly each one unburdened his heart, and we agreed to be in love cooperatively. For if we were united, no one could speak, no one could give away the secret. But what, actually, were our plans? How far did our love go? What form should it take? And how, after all, did one go about the business of loving? This we didn't know, and we didn't worry about it. We knew only that we carried a deep and serene love for Surele. Together, collectively, we would talk about her and think about her and dream about her, wild dreams, and we were as happy as it is possible to be.

Thus passed several weeks during which we, collectively and individually, hovered around Surele's house and gazed up at her window. We heard the cat meow—it was Surele's cat—and we were filled with joy. We heard the rustle of a tree in the garden—Surele's plum tree—and our souls shook with bliss. Over the house we saw a star fall from the sky—Surele's star—and our souls were struck down with sadness. And these emotions consumed us like a fever, and they were as unknown and frightening as the white nights among the white hills, and we did not know how anything would begin or how anything would end.

The great snow storms came. On the thatched roofs of the little houses snow sparkled in the cold winter sun and at night glittered like jewels against the sky. Our village seemed to have gone into hiding. If anyone passed along the street he heard only his own footsteps, as though he were a lost soul forever wandering over the earth.

Everything was as white and fresh and light as our own hearts, the six foolish hearts of six foolish boys collectively in love with Surele.

Once on such a night, when there was a stormy meeting in the synagogue, concerning, I think, what to do about the poor, we six lovers met before the great bookcase of the synagogue. The chair of Elijah the Prophet was empty, and we sat on it—we!—and then we crept behind the bookcase, to hide from the congregation. There, with pounding hearts, knowing that we were criminals, sinners, we pulled out the fringes of the prayer vest from under our jackets, and on those fringes we swore our eternal love for Surele, our Surele.

During this small meeting, which was held in the very midst of the large meeting that raged about us, concerning the poor, we kept the secret of our love by not even breathing the words "she" or "her," lest in this holy place of the bookcase and Elijah's chair we cast a shadow on our honor as decent boys who obeyed their fathers and their mothers.

To strengthen our bond we decided that each of us should write one letter of her name, with a piece of our native chalk, on the left—the heart—side of the bookcase. There were six letters in her name, six boys, six lovers. Awe-stricken, and with trembling fingers, knowing that we were committing an unforgivable sin, we each wrote a letter until—there stood her name, S-u-r-e-l-e. Then we swiftly erased it with our sleeves and went out into the winter night to dream our dreams.

How we could come closer to our beloved was a problem that constantly troubled us. Each day Surele grew more beautiful, more desirable, and more precious to us. In my mind, her round shining face rose ever higher, like a moon rising across the sky. Yet, more splendid than the moon, more glorious, more brilliant was Surele! Each day we would gather in the same holy place, behind the bookcase, and exchange news about Surele. Hershele had seen her out strolling with her mother. Moishele had bumped into her at the post office, and she had been wearing her white gloves. Feivel had caught a glimpse of her as she went into the baker's for rolls. Aristocratic rolls! But gradually these stories lost all color, all charm. There was no real news. Each day there was the same little meeting; each night the same walk over the white mud street past her house and then back home again. What would the outcome be? Was this romance? Well, we could buy ourselves a novel and find out. And that's how things stood: we'd buy a novel of love and study it.

In our village, pack peddler means just one thing: the man who carries books on his back—books about marriages and such. From time to time he simply descends on us from out of nowhere, like the snow, cold and angry. He sits at a long table, pulls out a small parcel, unties a black bread wrapped in a red handkerchief, cuts off little slices, impales them on the tip of his knife, salts them delicately, and then, as delicately, pops them into his big bearded mouth. Talking is not his business, and when some boy asks him how much his books cost, he barks fifteen pennies, or ten, whatever it is, and picks up his stick and drives the boy away, simply to save himself talk.

It was from this pack peddler, when he finally appeared among us, that we bought the love story *Ziliabor*—for ten pennies. How we held it in our hands unopened and looked at it again and again! How we read it over and over, sighed with the lonely Jadrina, the unfortunate countess, and wept when the hero at last turned her down! But still we found no solution to our problem. The only resemblance between our Surele and the unhappy Countess Jadrina was that they both wore white gloves. Nothing else. Well then, what could we learn from this novel of love? Nevertheless, as you will see, we did hit upon a plan.

This plan, a very simple one, sprang from the brain of our admirable Hershele. It was only this: in another month a fair would visit our village, with the exalted one who was both baker and confectioner. Until then we would save money, save out of the pennies that we were given for the school feasts, save out of our own tiny allowances for sweets, so that when the confectioner at last opened his booth we could buy a really magnificent box of candy.

The month passed slowly. Oh, how long a month was! But as the time went by we six lovers saved. We saved out of necessities, out of luxuries, until we had accumulated a capital. This we hid in the basement of the synagogue while we waited for the opening of the fair, the coming of the confectioner, and the solution to the problem whose name was Surele.

At last the time came when we six met and asked, "When will the day of deliverance come? Who among us shall make the purchase? Who shall be entrusted with the money?" It was decided that since Hershele and I had been the first to fall in love we should be the chosen ones.

The fair opened. Early in the morning the town was already like a barnyard, geese cackling, pigs grunting, calves lowing. The fair spread over our whole little village and climbed the hills; the tumult increased and the uproar of the animals cast everything into disorder. The village burst with joy, the market place rocked with life. Famished men with straw in their mouths and straw in their earlocks ran about and grabbed for food; they spoke Yiddish, Polish, quarreled and mocked one another, laughed, joked, slapped one another on the back, shook hands with unknown Polish peasants, who wore peculiar red scarfs and hats tipped way back on their heads. Near the confectioner's booth a beggar sat, a cripple, and he turned the handle of some strange musical instrument and sang a melancholy song. A Jew wearing a skull-cap and with a yardstick in his hand stood in front of his tiny store and insulted a peasant, shouting that the peasant was no gentleman. Oh, but the peasant was indignant and shouted back that he *was* a gentleman—wasn't the proof his pocketful of money? Nearby a wagon was drawn up, and from every inch of it hung boots—magnificent boots with red laces, shining soles, and bright-colored tongues, enormous boots, tiny boots, in unending array. A red-headed man sat in the wagon, and he too seemed to be made of leather, and he shouted, "Everyone walks! Everyone needs boots!" An officer with a plumed hat strolled past, glared angrily at the crowd, and the black shiny rim of his hat glittered with all the pleasure and pride of being an officer.

And there, there at last, was the confectioner's booth, the desire of our hearts, the hope of our happiness. On a long table covered with bright paper lay gingerbread, honeycake, chocolates, bonbons, caramels, whistles made out of candy, even sausage made out of candy. Hershele and I looked around nervously, to see that no one was watching us. Then hastily, with shaking, icy fingers, we put down our fortune, our silver sovereign. The confectioner was astounded. Stammering, we told him, "A box—a box of candy." He packed a box, tied it up with a red string, gave it to us, and said respectfully in Polish, "Thank you, gentlemen."

And so at last we held in our hands a box of candy, a gift. What to do now? But before we could consider further steps, there were our four lovelorn comrades to think of. They were waiting in the synagogue. We must let them know what we had accomplished, whether we had bought or not, and what we had bought.

"Bought?" they cried, running to us.

"Bought!"

"For how much?"

"For a sovereign."

"Good things?"

"We didn't look."

"Open up!"

We opened the package, and it was at that moment that we discovered what wonders the world can offer. Sparkling little sugar candies, caramels, and candy sausage that looked exactly like the real thing! And milk chocolate!

"We should taste a piece," Hershele said.

"God forbid!" the others cried. "Every piece is for her, for Surele!"

"Just one," begged Hershele and began to butt us with his head.

"Not even half a candy, not even a quarter, not even this much," said Moishele, measuring out the tiniest tip of his little finger.

With the greatest care we wrapped the candy up again, tied the red string back around it, and hid it in the basement of the synagogue until we two, Hershele and I, should find the opportunity to present it, with our own hands, to Surele.

I simply haven't the power to describe to you what we lived through during those next days until we were to present our gift. Not I, not any other person, could tell you, I think, except perhaps an angel with wings. Our tremblings, our burnings, our longings, our hopes, the fantasies we wove with the golden thread from that great spool called childhood, would be too much even for an angel with wings to describe to you.

I can only say that though you too may once have been innocent and young and in love, it would still be difficult for you to understand what we felt.

It was the end of winter now, the nights were still cold and frosty but quiet, without wind and without the sting of wind, and the sky was as clear and transparent as a crystal bowl. The white fields beyond our town, the chalk cliffs that, covered with snow, were once again white, the white chimneys and the poor little cottages, all looked back at the frozen moon and wondered if on the moon too it was so cold, so strange. It was on such a night that Hershele and I went forth on our mission of love.

Surele's parents are well-to-do people. Her father is a man of learning, respected, who always wears a black velvet tie under his white collar. He has built a house just out of town near the Polish academy, a little removed from the common herd. Not far from his house is that plot of earth where the sleepers lie and the crosses grow straight up from the earth, and a little farther along is the church with its great archways in which hang bells whose worn clappers are like tongues sticking out of a witch's mouth.

At times the wind steals through the archway, stirs the bell, and it trembles, gently, gently, and you can't quite be sure whether the bell is ringing or not. All around the bell tower grow mountain ash, whose red bitter fruit ripens only when the frost bites them, and the fruit looks like bright frozen drops of blood.

Emboldened, with joyful steps, I strode along with Hershele. Under my jacket was the precious gift, the box of candy that we six comrades were offering to the god of love. The night was fresh and clear. We hurried, although it was still early. Surele had just left her father's store and was on her way home. We had seen her. We had seen the blue ribbon in her hair flutter through the window of her father's store. We hurried to get ahead of her. We walked faster! Faster! Our boots crunched the snow, and somewhere in my heart that same sound echoed. Now at last we were near her home. Surele was still far off. We stood a little way from her house. It was dark. Here was the cemetery whose stone crosses stuck up straight out of the earth. And now the little bell shivered. Perhaps someone was pulling the worn chain. No. It was only the wind . . . only the wind. And she—where was she? Ah, there she came—nearer and nearer. We could see the white gloves showing from the sleeves of her black jacket. And now she came nearer still. So near! I felt as though something in my heart was ringing, as though in my heart someone was pulling a bell. My hand, holding the gift, trembled. Oh, oh, the gift was falling! And Hershele went completely to pieces. He babbled.

Now at last she was upon us, face to face. Tenderly Hershele and I blocked her way.

"What do you want?" she demanded harshly.

"Surele—dear one—Surele—" I stammered and took the gift from under my coat. "Surele, beloved, this is for you. Take it!" Hershele bent his head as if to butt her, then caught himself.

But Surele didn't understand our secret at all, didn't understand our deep love for her, didn't understand anything. And therefore, innocently, she asked, "Why do you give me this?"

"For nothing, Surele," I assured her. "I swear on my life, for absolutely nothing," and into her hands I put the little package with its gift of love.

"Are you crazy?" she burst out. "For heaven's sake!" And she threw the gift down and flew into the house as swift as an arrow shot from a bow.

Quietly, with bowed head, I bent and picked up the little box from the snow and wiped it off with a corner of my new jacket, and, still with bowed heads, like mourners, Hershele and I went back with our gift to our four comrades, who had remained a little way off, near a mound of snow-covered stones, like a grave, and waited for us.

"Well?" they clamored as we came into sight. "Accepted?"

"Not accepted!" we both exclaimed bitterly, and Hershele butted one of our comrades-in-love, not, any longer, like a cow but like a violent raging bull.

"Now what will happen?" I asked, and tears choked my voice. "We'll have to eat the candy ourselves."

And that night the old moon, silent and sorrowful, looked on as six little boys held a funeral feast, and the large beautiful candies were drenched with even larger childish tears.

Translated by Hilde Abel

The Adventures of Hershel Summerwind

ITZIK MANGER

THESE stories were told to me by Hershel Summerwind in Pantule's Inn, where the Jewish porters, water-carriers, and ordinary laborers would gather to drink tea in the late afternoon. All of Hershel's stories were outlandish, yet all were true, for they had really happened to him.

If you still see the stars in heaven, do you know whom to thank for that? No one but Hershel Summerwind!

It took place once upon a time when he, Hershel, was still a snip of a schoolboy, not more than eleven. Hershel was the greatest prankster in the world: he earned an endless number of slaps from the rabbi and was always the first to taste each new cat-o'-nine-tails. But the rabbi's slaps were nothing at all compared to his stepmother's pinches. Hershel was born an orphan—his mother had died in childbirth—and his stepmother, whom his father brought from another town, wasn't exactly wild about him. Some folks even said she had her reasons.

All day long Hershel made life miserable for her. If she sent him on an errand he'd make tracks and return only for supper. When his father came home from the market place, worn and weary, his stepmother would pour out a heartful of complaints: Hershel did this and Hershel did that.

But his father, who was sweet-tempered by nature, never beat him. True, he was upset by Hershel's pranks, but after the stepmother had finished chanting Hershel's praises the father would smile sadly. "You'll see, Zlate, our Hershel will make good. But how good that will be, God alone knows!"

When she saw that her husband dismissed the problem as a joke, the stepmother took things into her own hands. She was good at pinching, so she pinched. And each time she pinched him, Hershel saw Cracow and Lemberg spring up before his eyes. His answer to her pinches was still more tricks and pranks.

That's the sort of fellow he was—the biggest prankster in the world.

In the house a rooster roamed about, behaving as if he owned the place, doing whatever he wanted and dirtying up wherever he liked. No one asked him any questions, no one bothered him. Hershel, the stepmother would treat like a dog, but the rooster she cuddled as if it were a pigeon.

The stepmother, who believed in ghosts, spirits, and transmigration of souls, became convinced that the rooster was none other than a reincarnation of her first husband Mendel. She recognized him by his profile and the way his head trembled: her Mendel to the marrow!

When no one was home she actually called him "Mendel," and, wiping her eyes on her apron, she would say, "You're paying, Mendel, you're paying! You had to become a rooster, woe is me! Who told you to chase the girls, Mendel? I warned you, and now you've come back as a rooster."

A minute later: "It's lucky you fell into my hands and I recognized you. Some place else you'd have been slaughtered long ago."

In turn Mendel seemed clearly to feel that the stepmother was his friend. Whether he also recognized her as his wife, Hershel Summerwind doesn't know to this day, and whatever Hershel doesn't know he isn't the man to talk about.

No matter how many roosters were slaughtered, Mendel remained alive, guarded and cherished by the stepmother. That Hershel Summerwind hated Mendel goes without saying, and whenever he could he made life miserable for him. Tearing out feathers one by one, that too goes without saying. If the rooster fell into a doze Hershel would wake him up. If he met the rooster in the yard Hershel chased him until he fluttered onto the fence, hoarsely crowing and pleading for help.

When the stepmother heard Mendel's anguished cries she would rush out, more dead than alive, to save him from Hershel's vengeance. And each time she heard the rooster crowing, it seemed to her still another sign that she had come upon a reincarnation of her first husband, blessed be his memory. For that was just the way *he* used to crow when called upon to recite a chapter from the Torah on the Sabbath!

Once it happened that the devilish Hershel was chasing the rooster through the yard. Seeing the rooster flee, his wings stiff with terror,

Hershel felt a tremendous pleasure, and as he scampered after Mendel he chanted a rhyme of his own composition:

"Mendel, may your growth be stunted,
I hope you'll be forever hunted!"

In the face of such danger the rooster jumped onto the fence, crowing and begging the stepmother for help, but even then Hershel did not leave him alone. Besides, this time the stepmother wasn't home, having gone out to buy something and having stopped on the way to chat with Gittel the soothsayer about ghosts, spirits, and the transmigration of souls. When she came home she found Hershel aflame with excitement, happily chasing the rooster, who seemed scarcely able to catch his breath. That Hershel got his goes without saying. The stepmother twisted his ears with a vengeance; he barely escaped with his life. Running away, he stuck out his tongue at her and burst into loud song:

"Mendel, may your growth be stunted,
I hope you'll be forever hunted!"

The stepmother pressed the rescued rooster to her bosom and murmured, "You're paying, Mendel, you're paying!" And to the fleeing Hershel she cried out, "Wait till you come home for supper! Wait!"

Hershel didn't, of course, come home for supper. Hungrily he wandered through the streets, and in his imagination he saw Mendel the rooster pecking grains of food while the stepmother encouraged him, "Eat, Mendel, eat! May you grow fat and healthy!"

By now Hershel regretted the whole thing: what was the good of it? Hunger gnawed at him, but he was afraid to go home. Only at night, when everyone was asleep, did Hershel return, quietly, on tiptoe; he crept up to the garret and went to bed on an empty stomach.

He had a strange dream. He is a young rooster himself, a trickster. The stepmother, a fat respectable hen, takes him to school for the first time, and the teacher—heaven forbid!—is Mendel the rooster. Mendel, as usual, holds his head to one side. He asks Hershel, "Which is the *aleph?"* Immediately afterward he pecks at Hershel's head. "Which is the *gimmel*?" And again he pecks at Hershel's head.

Frightened, Hershel woke up and looked around him. Yes, he was still in the attic, it was only a dream. He caught his breath and cocked his ear. Who was pecking now?

Slowly he crawled over to the attic window and stuck out his head. At first Hershel was stunned. The sky was full of stars, but on the black chimney stood Mendel the rooster, pecking at the stars with his sharp beak, thinking apparently—the foolish rooster!—that the stars were grains of food.

Hershel immediately sensed the danger. If he allowed Mendel to keep pecking at the stars, the rooster would spoil the whole starry night—and not only this one, but all starry nights, for as is well known, one night bequeaths the stars to the next.

Hershel climbed out of the attic window and on his belly slowly edged his way up the chimney, so that Mendel should not hear him. And Mendel was so absorbed with his gluttony that he heard nothing at all.

Suddenly Hershel grabbed Mendel by the wings—and the rooster became so frightened that he threw up all the stars he had already swallowed!

Twirling the frightened rooster around his head, Hershel sang a new rhyme that suddenly came into his head:

> "Mendel munches stars like mutton,
> He has no rival as a glutton."

The stars in heaven winked slyly, and Hershel understood their meaning: "Hershel, we'll never forget you for this favor."

At first the rooster was stunned. The meal of stars he had been devouring with such zest came to an end so quickly he hardly knew what was happening to him. Only when Hershel began to twirl him through the air and dance around the chimney like a wild Indian did Mendel set up a fearful crowing.

All the roosters of the town answered him, as is the custom of roosters, and there was such a bedlam that the people of the town awoke, thinking it was already dawn, and began the ceremony of washing their fingers before eating.

Hershel's stepmother, when she heard the desperate cries of her reincarnated Mendel, rushed to his rescue. In her nightgown, with a rake in hand, she climbed up to the attic and barely squeezed herself through the little window. What Hershel caught you can imagine for yourself; the stepmother wasn't miserly.

To this day Hershel Summerwind can show you the black and blue marks of those blows. But it was worth it, he added. "After all, I saved the stars."

From that night on Mendel began to ail. In a few weeks he shook his head for the last time in a corner of the yard, and into what kind of creature he has since been reincarnated no one knows. But Hershel survived his stepmother's blows. Proof? He is still alive to tell us true stories of things that happened to him.

For example, the story of the birds.

It was years ago. Hershel was a youth of eighteen or nineteen, the picture of health. His younger sister Eidel had already married, but the stepmother continued to grumble, "In some families such a boy is already a father, but this one hangs around, idle and empty-handed, chasing the girls. You'll have the same end as my Mendel, mark my words!"

But who cares if a stepmother grumbles? She had never been a friend of his, and since Mendel the rooster died—even less of a friend!

Incidentally, every year on the day of Mendel's death she donates candles for the synagogue and hires Oyzer the *shammes* to say *Kaddish*.

In short, Hershel's younger sister Eidel was happily married and within the year had a son. Two days before the circumcision Hershel's father called him aside and said, "Harness the horse, my son, and ride to Daraban. Tell Zalman the innkeeper to give you a barrel of wine he put aside for me twenty years ago. And with God's help, tell him, the day after tomorrow will be the happiest day of my life—the first grandchild! Take the whip, harness the horse, and come back quickly with the barrel of wine, so we can carry off the circumcision in grand style."

Twenty years ago when Hershel's father and Zalman the innkeeper had met after a long separation—they were old pals, one body, one soul!—Zalman had lowered a barrel of wine into the cellar, and, clapping his friend on the back, had told him that the wine would be his when the happiest day of his life arrived. And for almost twenty years the barrel of wine had been waiting in Zalman's cellar.

Hershel hitched up the horse and wagon, took the whip with the red handle, and sang out, "Giddap, Brownie, we're off to Daraban!"

The road to Daraban was long, uphill and downhill, fields and woods. Trees along the way, birds and golden sun. The horse trotted quickly, not waiting for Hershel to prod him with the whip.

Hershel felt gay. He flourished his whip in the air. On his lips danced a rhyme:

"We speed along to Daraban,
We speed along our joyous trip,
Says the horse, 'Don't spur me on.
Hershel, throw away your whip.' "

Hershel felt the whip was useless—that's why he made up the rhyme. Perhaps, too, because with a rhyme it's less lonely on the road.

That night when Hershel arrived at Daraban, Zalman the innkeeper was overjoyed to see him. No small thing, the only son of his oldest friend. He slapped Hershel on the back. "How's your father? Getting on, eh?"

And when Hershel told him his mission, Zalman slapped his back again. "That means we have to celebrate. You may be sure the barrel is waiting. With the years it's become better." Sighing, he said, "Ah, if only man were like a barrel of wine."

Hershel unharnessed the horse. He had brought a sack of oats from home, but Zalman would not let him open it. "You'll use your sack on the way home. Today your colt is the guest of my colt. They'll eat from the same trough. My colt likes having guests. Takes after his master. Understand, Hershel?"

Zalman the innkeeper invited Hershel into the dining room, poured out two glasses of wine, and said, "Long life, Hershel, and may your father have joy of you."

Hershel was tired and hungry from the long trip. Noticing this, Zalman cried, "You're hungry, Hershel! My old lady should be back any minute—she went to a funeral."

Hershel knew that Zalman's wife, Ziessel, never missed a funeral. Coming home from a funeral she would always say, "May all Jewish children enjoy such a funeral." That's why she was nicknamed "Ziessel-may-all-Jewish-children."

As soon as Ziessel came home she immediately began to prepare dinner, saving her account of the funeral for later. But once everyone was at the table she could no longer restrain herself and began, "May all Jewish children enjoy such a funeral . . ."

Hershel didn't relish his food. Wearily he fell upon his bed, and in his dream he saw a funeral. Four Jews carry a coffin. The father follows, downcast. Sighing, he says to the stepmother, "No more Hershel!" The stepmother gibes, "Some bargain, your Hershel . . ." Suddenly, as if from the earth, Ziessel the innkeeper's wife appears. She points to the coffin. She shouts at the top of her voice, "Such a funeral our Hershel had, may all Jewish children enjoy such a funeral."

The funeral vanishes. It never happened, it's really a circumcision—Hershel's circumcision. Everyone joins in the ceremony. They drink wine, eat cake. Hershel sees Itche the circumciser, a knife between his teeth, prepare for the ritual. Hershel wants to cry out that he's already been circumcised, but he can't. He wants to run away, but his feet are heavy as lead.

Hershel woke up and spat three times to ward off the evil eye. In the street people were already at work. Peasants were sitting in the inn, drinking wine and smoking *mahorka*. Quick as a flash, Hershel dressed himself, said his prayers on the run, and hitched up his horse. Zalman the innkeeper helped him lift the barrel of wine onto the wagon, then sang out, "Giddap, Brownie!"

Only after he had left Daraban did the shadow of last night's dream disappear. Here was the windmill, here he turned to the open road—uphill, downhill, through fields and woods, all the way home. The whip was again unnecessary, but, having brought it, Hershel carried it back.

It was a hot summer day. The road was dusty. Hershel took off his jacket. "Ah, a pleasure." But the farther he went, the more the sun burned. His throat became so dry he could hardly catch his breath. Suddenly it occurred to him that he was indeed a fool: in the wagon lay a barrel of wine, while he was expiring from thirst. True, it was for the circumcision, but what would be the harm in taking a sip and slaking his thirst? And without a second thought Hershel pulled the cork out of the barrel, bent down, and took a good long drink.

The wine was old and rich. After one gulp Hershel's head began to swim; his eyes began to close; and he was soon asleep.

How long he slept there Hershel Summerwind does not remember, but when he awoke he saw a strange picture indeed: scattered around the wagon lay more than a hundred birds, all dead drunk.

Only then did Hershel remember that he had forgotten to cork the barrel. While he slept the birds must have gathered, sipped the wine, and fallen to the earth, drunk.

Hershel sprang down from the wagon, afraid the birds would fly away once they became sober. A shame—so many beautiful birds. It will be a real celebration when they start singing tomorrow at the circumcision.

Hershel found a thread in his pocket, and one by one he bound the little feet of the birds, who were still soundly sleeping. When he had finished binding their feet, he wound the thread around his belly and made a strong knot. Now they wouldn't be able to fly away even when they became sober. Hershel Summerwind, pleased with this piece of work, took another good long drink from the barrel of wine and again fell fast asleep.

When he woke, his feet were fluttering through the air and his head was touching the clouds.

While he had been sleeping so soundly, the birds had sobered up, shaken the sleep from their wings, and flown off with Hershel Summerwind—up, up, to the clouds that were sailing through the sky.

Hershel's heart pounded with fear. Below, his horse was neighing. It called to him, reminded him, that the wine was unprotected, that tomorrow was the circumcision, his father's feast would be spoiled.

"A pretty story," Hershel reproached himself. "What did you need birds for, eh? Now you're in for it, Hershel Summerwind. They're carrying you off the way the devil carries a thief. And who knows where they'll take you?"

But his reproaches didn't help. It was too late.

Hershel shouted down to the horse, which stood patiently in the middle of the road, not knowing what to do. "Take home the barrel of wine, Brownie! You know the way. Farewell, Brownie, and regards to my father. A *mazel tov* to my sister, and a fig to my stepmother!"

The horse lifted its ears, to make out what Hershel was shouting from the clouds. He must have understood, for he soon began to pull the wagon and started off without master or whip.

The birds that were carrying our Hershel higher and higher burst into song. A delightful melody, a song sweeter than all songs, a song for the sun, for the winds and the clouds. Hershel listened to the song for a while and then joined in himself. His voice was a good one. The birds were astonished and talked it over among themselves.

"It's a strange bird that flies with us, but he certainly can sing."

"Of course it's a strange bird," called out another, "and his song is entirely different. Reminds me of ripe red cherries."

"Red cherries," chimed in a youngish bird. "I love red cherries."

"Listen to the wizard," jeered a middle-aged bird. "Who doesn't like to pick cherries? Only a fool."

"Know what, fellows?" said an elderly bird. "Let's fly to Zeinvel's orchard—the cherries must be ripe by now."

"To the cherry orchard! To the cherry orchard," piped all the birds and quickly took off for Tziganesht, where Zeinvel's orchard lay.

The birds, Hershel tells us, made a mess of the orchard. The scarecrows were helpless.

But thanks to this flight Hershel's life was saved. The flying frightened him, his head grew dizzy, his eyes teared, his ears were humming.

But as soon as the birds descended to the first cherry tree, Hershel cut the thread in half and sprang down from the tree, jumped over the fence, and set off for home. It was only four miles. He ran without stopping to catch his breath, and after the evening prayers were done he staggered, half alive, into his father's house. The horse was already waiting there, in front of the door, with the barrel of wine—so no one guessed what had befallen our Hershel.

The next day, at the circumcision, Hershel told the story of the birds and the great miracle that had followed. And so that all should know he was telling the truth Hershel Summerwind sang the song the birds had sung when they carried him through the air.

From this story you can see what a great and good God we have. For if He helped such an idler as Hershel Summerwind, He will certainly help all faithful and God-fearing Jews, who follow His commandment and live by His word.

Translated by Irving Howe

Part Four
BREAKUP

Eating Days

LAMED SHAPIRO

1.

I WAS ON eating days at that time, and Tuesday was a blank in my schedule.

The full name of the little town was Zagorie-Vitrok (or, Beyond the Windmill Hills), but the Jews had shortened and changed this to Zahoria.

When I came into the street the first afternoon of my arrival, the tiny place lay suffocated under the July sun. Jewish men and women sat dozing in the doorways of their shops. Near the meat market the dogs were lying with their tongues hanging out, their glazed eyes looking upon the world without any interest—not even for the bloody sides of beef that hung in the windows of the little butcher shops. Strewn over the ground of the market place and glinting yellowly were loose sheaves of straw left over from the last fair day. The wind, the chief—and sole—sanitary inspector of the town, had not yet swept them away. On the principal street all the shutters were closed—shutters gray, white, green, all kinds of shutters, a long row of them, and all closed. Everything was so still that Zahoria, as I eagerly took in the new scene, looked like a town in a dream.

2.

"This yeshiva," the student from Berdichev told me, "was once quite big."

The yeshiva was located over the women's section of the small synagogue; the high-ceilinged House of Prayer was divided into floors toward the back, and this upper floor, with a separate outer staircase, was where we did our studying. It was a long narrow chamber, running the width of the synagogue, with ten windows distributed along the three outer walls. In the fourth, the interior, wall was a tiny window, little more than a slit, facing the Holy Ark. There were two long tables for collective study and a dozen lecterns at which the older boys could study by themselves. Ranged along the walls and at the tables were long benches, and upon these several students, I among them, used to sleep.

Another young student—he came from Stavisk—called me aside, lifted his right index finger impressively, and gave me to understand: "The yeshiva may not look like much now, but it was really big at one time. There used to be a hundred and fifty students here, poring over Holy Writ day and night. In those days the yeshiva was still in the building where the old synagogue is now; and even later, during the first years under Nissel, the assistant rabbi, when he wasn't so hard a drinker, from sixty to eighty students would sit down to study the Talmud with him."

A hundred and fifty . . . eighty . . . sixty . . .

"Now there are twenty-three or twenty-four of us, at all the tables and lecterns," the Stavisker went on. "The yeshiva has been going down for several years; it's falling lower and lower—nobody knows why. The town has no love for us; it has no faith in our studies nor in our fear of God. We're a burden on them, the way a chronic old invalid is to his family; he sinks before their eyes but won't die. The people in the town are not eager to invite us to their tables; whoever can manage to avoid it by contributing a few pennies does so. A great many of us miss one or two eating days—on such days we get seven kopecks for food. When it comes to a place to sleep it's still worse, and getting a clean shirt for the Sabbath is worst of all."

3.

The student from Krutogor told me in confidence, "Do you think our yeshiva was always the way you see it now? You should have been here years ago, you would have seen something then."

He too? What was the yeshiva to him? The Krutogorer was a big robust fellow without a sign of beard or mustache on his smooth womanish face. He had great, liquid, bulging eyes and a child's smile on his rosy, fleshy lips—lips like little sausages. He didn't really have a bad head on his shoulders but he had no inclination for study. To make up for that, he excelled in another respect: he could not talk for two minutes without going off into smut. He was an inexhaustible spring of stories, riddles, witticisms, not one of which but concealed under its surface a sexual meaning. His stories somehow were repulsive—deliberate, without warmth, and even without vulgarity, yet always with insinuations, puns, and double meanings. If you wanted them to, they had a meaning, but an ugly one; if you weren't after a meaning, there wasn't any at all—they were mere pointless stories. When you persuaded yourself that the fellow was up to no tricks he seemed to be speaking casually—too casually—and the childlike smile on the rosy, moist little sausage lips was somehow too childlike. You felt yourself taken in, mocked; you became angry. But he, the simple fellow, couldn't understand why you were angry since, after all, he hadn't meant any offense, and—

"*Sha*! You know what? I've got a wonderful story to tell you—"

The Krutogorer had already acquired a disciple, a brilliant lad of fourteen—Ariah Leib's little Chaim. Chaim too had a good head: he was genuinely fond of tackling some abstruse tractate of the Talmud or of joining in some profound discussion on the Talmudic commentators, but the Krutogorer was leading him astray, and the youngster whinnied like a colt at his tutor's stories; now and then he would interpret some passage or homily in a way that turned one's stomach. Both master and disciple made life miserable for the student from Warsaw.

4.

The Warshaver did not really hail from Warsaw. He came from a town somewhere in Poland the name of which was almost impossible to remember, and so he had been nicknamed after Warsaw. How he had ever got here from remote Poland no one knew, nor did anyone take any pains to find out. The students were all strangers to one another, and none of them cared to talk about where he had come from or to what family he belonged: most likely there was little worth remembering.

The Warshaver was the oldest student in the yeshiva, well over thirty. He was narrow-boned and spare, lanky rather than tall. His cheeks were pocked with acne; his eyes were black and glowed as if in fever. The nape of his neck was very hairy—the nape of his neck only: his face was beardless—and he wore a tiny Polish cap, the only cap in the whole town with a narrow visor on it. He had a "hard" head: studying did not come easy to him, but he was most diligent and pious. He was forever studying; you never saw him without some tome in his hands, and he generally did his studying aloud, swaying to and fro with closed eyes, which he opened only occasionally to glance at the *Gemarah*. He went often to the ritual baths. The two days that were blank on his eating schedule he had designated as his permanent fast days; and there were those who held that he mortified his flesh in still other ways.

The Krutogorer made a point of harassing the Warshaver, in which he was abetted by little Chaim. Their scheme was to take a position not far from the lectern of their victim and then proceed to study aloud some tractate from the Talmud—the one on the Sabbath, let us say—with a great show of zeal. The Warshaver tried to stop his ears; but if he did so he could not hear his own chant and consequently was hardly able to understand what he was studying.

"You ugly beasts!" he screamed at them. "Adulterers! Apostates!"

He threatened to complain to Reb Zalman, a meat inspector who acted as our dean; he cursed them in his quaint Polish-Yiddish dialect. But they went right on with their beloved studying as though they were in no way at fault, apparently engrossed in the complicated passages of their tractate, until at last the Warshaver fled from the synagogue, his eyes blazing with rage and his lips twisted in pain.

5.

Nissel, the assistant rabbi, was giving us a Talmud lesson.

Nissel did not look like a Jew at all. His heavy, massive body, his beetling bushy eyebrows, and his red nose with its cross-hatching of tiny blue veins made him look like the coarsest of old peasants—one of those who worked at night on the barges that plied the river. He had a red eczema, quite extensive, on the back of his left hand: when studying, he kept this hand concealed under the Slavita tome of the Talmud. His small skullcap perched close to the nape of his neck, and he wore spectacles.

The yeshiva lads spoke of him under their breath, as though they were perplexed about him. He was a great drunkard—a Jewish drunkard, that is: he did not wallow in the gutter, but he took a drink whether anyone was celebrating or not. He walked around in a daze, wrapped up in himself, as indifferent to his studies as to his pupils. Now and then, when he came to a Talmudic session deeper in his cups than usual, we leaped on our benches with enthusiasm: profound expositions and comments, razor-keen innovations issued from his mouth like fireworks. On the other hand, if once in a great while, God forbid, he put in an appearance altogether sober, it was impossible to stand him: he would curse and revile everyone in angry, vulgar, and barbed words. He had been deprived of his status as an assistant rabbi a long time ago; all he found to do now was to hold the Talmudic sessions in our yeshiva and give a two-hour weekly lesson to the son-in-law of the local Croesus. Because of his sharp tongue he was at odds with the town and the rabbinical court. The overpious Hasidim suspected that he hailed from Lithuania, and the townsmen would shrug their shoulders. "Well, what can you expect from a Litvak!"

Because the yeshiva sessions, except on those rare occasions when he was far gone in drink, held very little interest for him, he finally hit on a new plan: let the students learn by heart. In other yeshivas, now, there were students who could recite hundreds of pages of the Talmud from memory.

"There are scholarly heads for you!" he exclaimed, his small evil eyes looking daggers at his hearers, so that one could not make out whether his words were meant to praise or to damn. Let the students tackle the Baboth tractate, to begin with: it was neither too difficult nor too easy. This would enable him to give a real discourse, to present a new interpretation—whenever he could get around to it and felt so inclined.

6.

In the night we used to hear the steamboats paddling down the river, about a mile away. Those of us who slept in the yeshiva could by now recognize the boats that plied our stretch of the river.

"That's the *Imperator*," somebody on one of the farther benches would remark, his cigarette glowing in the darkness. The *Imperator*, its low-pitched whistle wheezing like some substantial householder, was the newest steamboat on the river; it had all the latest improvements and had been built somewhere outside of Russia.

"Fee-fee-ee-ee!" Someone else among us would announce with a laugh that it was the *Pushkin*—a small boat, narrow, long, and moving through the water as nimbly as a pen over paper.

A far-flung throaty roar, prolonged and hoarse as that of some beast in agony, meant the approach of the *Dominion*, the oldest and biggest tub, broad-beamed, unwieldy, drowsy, and slow.

In the dead of night, after the first siren had made one's ears alert, one could hear the steamboats distinctly as they approached our landing, then slowed down and became quiet. We held our breath and could almost see the boat with all its lights, the people running up and down the gangplank, the strange, gay, animated scene. Within two minutes a second whistle sounded, then a third, and one's ears caught the gasping of the steam, the renewed beat of the paddles, growing stronger, more powerful and impetuous. At a certain point the noise came echoing back from the hills along the riverbanks with special clarity: one could have sworn that the vessel was advancing upon the town. Before long, however, the noise subsided, as though a kettle had been put over it: fainter, more distant. Shh . . . one moment you still heard it, then you didn't. Silence.

The silence lasted quite long—until the Krutogorer started in. "I'm going to ask you a riddle—"

"Stop annoying us!" I would become resentful. "We know every riddle of yours by heart."

"All the same, try to guess this one—"

"Not interested—some other time," I could not help telling him.

Sometimes he subsided, sometimes not.

7.

My eating days had not come to me easily or all at once. My Sundays and Mondays changed several times: my hosts on these days made no particular impression on me.

The Wednesday meals I had at the house of a butcher known as Buni the Redhead. The rusty, bristly hair on his face grew almost to his eyes—murderous and arrogant eyes—and his voice was gruff. This Jew didn't even know how to pray properly, and there was talk in the town that he beat his wife. Why should he want a yeshiva student? But he himself hailed Reb Zalman, our dean, in the street one day. "Send over one of your shnooks to my house and let him stuff his guts."

For food, Wednesday was my best day. Buni's wife was attractive in a swarthy sort of way, but a sloven. She had apparently never heard of a tablecloth—she put a loaf of bread and a bowl of warm food right on the bare wood: "Eat to your heart's content!" The food itself was heavy, filling—stuffed derma, beet soup with fat meat, baked sheep's head, the roast neck of a kid slithery with grease. And she served meat at both my meals.

The whole family sat down together to the evening meal: Buni, Buni's wife, and their only child, a girl of about sixteen, with her body just emerging from adolescence and a face of piety: white and translucent, somewhat sickly, the nose well shaped, and the eyes large and shiny, like a calf's. But I rarely found Buni home when I came, and either his wife or daughter would serve me my meal.

A totally different sort of household was that of Isser Tabachnik, where I ate on Thursdays. It was situated on the other side of the market place, where the principal street began, and had lacquered floors, lace curtains on the windows, and potted plants on the window sills. The family lived in grand style, keeping a cook and a country girl for the youngest child. My meal was served at a separate table in the kitchen, while the cook bustled about with her pots and pans, and the time assigned to me was an hour after the family had eaten.

Isser Tabachnik traded on a big scale in grain, timber, and beets for the sugar refineries. He was a personable man: tall, broad-shouldered, with a potbelly, a smooth skin, and a beautiful, well-groomed dark beard. He wore a fine knee-length overcoat and a soft hat with a deep crease. He had an important air about him, and his word was his bond. A man who knew his own worth.

Shaina Leah, his wife, came of a more aristocratic family than her husband's; she was not so obtrusive as he and seemed to be good-natured. There was also a girl in the house, about twelve, thin, swarthy, ugly, and ill tempered; at the least provocation she would throw herself on the floor and start kicking the walls or the furniture. Then there was a little boy of three, and somewhere out in the world Isser and his wife had married daughters.

My breakfasts weren't worth talking about. And my two Friday meals I had at Stissy the Widow's.

Stissy was tall, of a dark complexion; she had narrow Tartar eyes, was clever and not much given to talk. The peasants respected her. She ran a dry-goods and notions store, catering chiefly to the women-folk of the surrounding countryside. The stock consisted of multi-colored wool and cotton fabrics, bright ribbons, gimcrack jewelry and strings of beads, headkerchiefs, sashes, and kindred items. She wasn't rich, but she did have a fair income and a house of her own on Rabbi's Street. The house was old and none too big, but well built—that is, it had hardwood floors, a tin roof, and even window shutters. The household was run by her daughter Tzirel, a girl along in years, rather dumpy, not good-looking, with a complexion none too clear or healthy; her dark eyes, however, were quite decent—beautiful, in fact.

I was still shy one eating day though—that same Tuesday.

8.

Those were the years when the world crumpled and twisted my soul like a nervous hand impatiently pulling a glove on the other hand. Each day had a flavor all its own. The sun, for instance, shone differently after a meal on the Sabbath than after a meal on a weekday. And merely crossing Rabbi's Street to get back to the market place was like making a journey to another town. Just the sight of the rich man's house, its walls painted a roseate hue and a green balcony on the second floor, was as exciting to me as meeting a guest from afar.

There was a chunk of plaster missing on one of the outer walls of the synagogue, and each time I chanced to pass by I looked at the ugly gaping hole with hatred.

On an empty lot not far from the yeshiva four charred girders stuck up out of the ground—all that was left of a house that had burned down. They were an eyesore. Blackened, weather-beaten, gaunt, they mournfully stared at me—at me alone—and frightened me.

Summer, winter, snow, rain, frost, heat—all plucked at me like fiends and pulled me in all directions.

At that time other things also piled up on me.

Once, at the time of my evening meal in Isser Tabachnik's house, a pan with strudel had been left on the kitchen table, just out of the oven. The aroma of cinnamon and raisins titillated my nostrils. Some liquefied brown sugar had run out at one end of the strudel and formed a glazed jelly. As the pastry cooled it crackled softly and faintly from time to time, as if someone were snapping matchsticks. When the cook left the kitchen for a moment I hurriedly broke off two jagged pieces of the strudel and slipped them in my pocket. After finishing my meal hastily I returned to the synagogue, and in a corner I devoured the cake stealthily. I bit off large chunks, hardly chewing them, so that tears came, and for some time the strudel stuck in my throat.

The whole thing had come upon me so unexpectedly that it seemed to have happened not to myself but to someone else. I was, in other words, a thief and a glutton. A thief? No, not a thief! I had stolen, of course, but then I would never steal again—I wouldn't. A glutton—yes, I had gobbled the cake down like a glutton, without even enjoying its savor. And the terrific stupidity of it all!

Next Thursday I did not come for my meal at Isser Tabachnik's house. The Thursday after that I hung around his door for several minutes, with my heart palpitating, and then, setting my jaw, opened the door at last. All through the meal it seemed to me that the cook was banging her dishes more than usual. I also had the impression that the good Shaina Leah had met me with a smile in her eyes—a clever and restrained smile—but just the same I dawdled over washing my hands and ate slowly and stubbornly. And within me the turmoil was great.

The incident of the strudel was still fresh in my thoughts when I happened to come upon the scene as Buni and his wife were beating their daughter. This girl with the pious face was run after by all the apprentices in town, to say nothing of a few young men from among the local elite, and even a couple of gentile boys. She was friendly with all, spending her time with anyone. With the coming of dusk it was impossible to keep her in the house. That day her parents had caught her—not for the first time—with one of the boys, and they were squaring accounts with curses and fists. Through the tears her eyes glistened with a moist brilliance; her fresh lips pouted like a child's as she softly, dejectedly, kept pleading, "What *do* you want of me? What *do* you want of me?"

The scene harrowed me. Once, as I was leaving the butcher's house, I came upon the girl in the dark anteroom. I stopped her, stretched out my hand, and touched her—not respectfully. Whereupon she looked at me with her big dismayed eyes and then, lowering them, froze into a mute, sheepish submissiveness. I immediately released her and dashed out. But even then I felt that neither the deep fear of Buni the Redhead nor my dread of the disgrace if I were caught would keep me away from this girl, from the mature face on the half-ripe, tantalizing adolescent body.

I was a low creature—a low creature.

Since such was the case, I locked myself in Stissy the Widow's privy one Saturday afternoon and, rolling a cigarette, had a smoke. When I came out my legs were wobbling. I had never dreamed a cigarette could be so delectable. The savor of the transgression and the pungency of my dissoluteness intoxicated me like strong wine.

The range of my lusts, like the range of my ambitions, was rather small. But the Evil One had swooped down upon me like a tempest, suddenly and from all sides. I was living as if in a fever, my heart in incessant ferment.

9.

I did just what the Warshaver had done: I turned my blank Tuesday into a fast day. Of the seven kopecks allowed me for food on that day I squandered two on tobacco and saved five.

On this day I used to study by myself in the synagogue proper. I usually got there when the worshipers had just dispersed after the morning service. Paying little attention to my assigned lesson, I browsed instead through various tomes of Holy Writ, humming as I did so and pausing to meditate between my studies. My stomach was empty and felt hollow; the tobacco smoke was pungent. A strange silence reigned in the high-ceilinged synagogue, where ordinarily the slightest sound gave birth to echoes. Yet on the verge of this silence hovered the dormant sounds and sights of another world: a world not so substantial as the one around me yet hardly less real.

Ruth and Naomi trudged forever through the cornfields on their way to Boaz, under a summer sky—around the fifth hour after noon. Jacob pastured the sheep for Laban—and I saw distinctly the rods of green poplar and hazel and chestnut which Jacob had set before the flocks in the gutters of the watering troughs, that the flocks should conceive when they came to drink: he had peeled white strips in the rods and made the white appear which was in them—and that white was moist from the sap. On a night when the wispy clouds could not hide the light of the moon, Sulamith went about the city in the slumbrous streets, knocking on doors and gates, questioning the watchmen that go about the city: "Saw ye him whom my soul loveth?" Esau had just come from his hunting, his hairy garments still redolent of the fragrance of the fields; he sat eating his dearly bought pottage of lentils, and the delicious steam of the lentils blended with the smell of the goatskins upon the luckless Esau. Amid the desert sands the tabernacle curtains of fine twined linen fluttered and bellied in the wind. The ground plan of the tabernacle was not quite clear in my mind, but the "blue, and purple, and scarlet" floated before my eyes; I had a distinct image of the curtains of goats' hair, and of fine twined linens, wrought with cherubs of cunning needlework. . . .

The faint hum of a life pattern ancient yet present reached me like a song from afar. And on Tuesdays I rested from myself and my world.

10.

As early as the Ten Days of Repentance the skies became overcast; the Day of Atonement was chill and depressing, and on the Day of Hosannas for the Torah an intermittent drizzle dampened the gala mood of the town. After that the sky remained overcast, the rain came oftener and fell more heavily. Of nights the raindrops pattered on the roofs in the same monotonous beat. This went on for ten nights or so, night after night. Before long autumn brought its mud; then the first snow fell, followed by a second snowfall that blended with the slush and turned it into icy gruel. Melancholy, the great melancholy of autumn, settled in a heavy pall over Zahoria—and over my heart.

On the way to my meals I had to slog through the mire (I would rather not talk about what my shoes were like); but whether I was traversing the market place or some other thoroughfare my eyes kept hungrily seeking something, since a great fearfulness pressed on me. Jewish heads—men's heads, women's heads—peeped out of the doorways of the little shops like mice out of their holes. They had a sad, patient, stubborn look about them, these heads. What were they looking for, would you say?

A Jewish crone, all bundled up in shawls, sits near a stall with apples—little apples, frozen apples, all in a heap. She sells them to the children, at a penny an apple. How many children pass by here each day, and how many day after day? How many of them have a penny in their pockets, as well as a lust for her little apples? How much do those little apples cost her, and how much gain can they bring in for her own subsistence? And how many mouths does she have to feed day after day, selling little frozen apples?

At the far end of the market place stands an old wooden store; it has all but tumbled down. Its stock consists of a sack of oats and three bundles of hay: just that and nothing more. Zussi, the son of Michlie, huddles in the doorway, staring straight ahead. He is wrapped in a brown coat, with an upturned collar the shade of rusty tin. His face is small, birdlike, hemmed in by a short, stiff, sandy-hued beard, and his small round hen's eyes of the same hue look out upon the world listlessly. No matter when I pass by, Zussi is huddling there in that unvarying position. A mixture of dislike and fear, originating somewhere deep within me, wells up in my throat. A dead man, keeping vigil. They had forgotten to put shards over his glazed eyes: so he huddles there and stares.

The town's pothouse marks the beginning of the gentiles' quarter. Their principal thoroughfare and side streets engirdle the town.

The gentiles have a world all their own. A sort of perverse Sambation River, which does not desist from flinging stones even on the Sabbath, and a man—a Jew, that is—cannot cross it except at the risk of his life. Take the gentiles now: for what earthly reason were they ever put into the world? The way things look, they were created expressly to be a scourge against men—against Jews, that is—like pestilence and famine. On the other hand, during fair days, they pour into town and inundate it like torrential waters—and provide Jews with a livelihood. On such days one can earn something—and on those same days the air is permeated with menace that lurks in ambush like a ravening beast. The Almighty, in other words, has many uses for his creatures. Strange! You take the gentiles now—it's hard to make them out. There they were, celebrating weddings and holding wakes, worshiping their idols, going to and fro in their fields and their orchards, and, in general, following all sorts of callings that had little to do with Jews. . . . The whole subject was hazy. A complex enigma indeed.

The steamboats kept getting fewer and fewer on the river. And around the time of *Chanukah* their whistles and the beat of their churning paddles in the night ceased altogether. In the dead of night, when it was very quiet, one occasionally heard a whistle, high and piercing—but it was the whistle of a locomotive on the railway twelve miles beyond the river. Next summer (word of this had been going around the town for twenty years) the railway would be extended to Zahoria. Meanwhile the locomotive whistle was far off and hard to believe in. I lay on my bench, covered with a few rags, my ears on the alert as they waited in vain for some other sound. From time to time the dead thud of some heavy object against a soft surface came from a courtyard nearby. It was the clumping of Blind Itzi's horse in its stable. Now and then the poor nag let out a whinny: it was afraid of the rats. And then —again the silence.

In the month of January, under the icy breath of two or three cold spells, the mud solidified into clods. Then the cold blew in gusts from the north, sweeping through the town and changing into a three-day blizzard that piled up in drifts reaching to the window sills.

Late one Thursday night I was awakened by the unusual quiet and bitter cold. A green star twinkled in what I could see of the sky through my window, and the bones of the old synagogue crackled softly as it moaned in the arms of a deathly silent and searing frost.

When I came to the market place in the morning the world was all new—never had there been such a world! A great reddish-yellow sun was hanging over the hills; pillars of smoke rose like trees from the house chimneys, and fleecy white coats—so white that they were blinding—had been flung in loose folds over the houses, fences, stores, and the whole world, to its very ends. From all the gates heavily loaded peasant sleighs, their bells jingling, were heading for the fair, and wagons, their axle-grease frozen, groaned and screeched over the snow. Cows mooed; new earthen pots rang and sang under the taps of testing fingers, and the babel of human voices was so great it jarred the ears, like water pounding one's head after a deep dive. The air was as heady as home-brew and full of fiery needles that quivered in the rays of the sun and pricked one's face. My fingers were numbed from the frost, my ears froze instantly, as though turned into paper, tears came to my eyes from the cold—and from joy at being alive.

11.

Over at Stissy the Widow's they began giving me the big copper ewer.

Even before that Tzirel had asked me to come for an additional meal on Friday, about noon. Her mother would still be in her little shop at that time, and it was Tzirel who generally served me. She would spread a snowy white tablecloth and then bring on a fresh loaf and a deliciously browned beef stew. As I ate she went quietly and unobtrusively about her household tasks.

On the eve of the Sabbath, upon my coming from the synagogue, both women acknowledged my "Good Sabbath" greetings most cordially, and I noticed that the beautiful eyes of the daughter's plain face grew bright, as serene and sanctified as the Sabbath candles themselves. An antique silver beaker damascened with black designs and filled with raisin wine stood ready, as always, for the *Kiddush* prayer, and though mother and daughter washed their hands before the meal in a tin basin, I was given the old two-handled ewer of copper, which, scrubbed and polished, usually lay atop the commode, next to the brass samovar, both flanked by two silver candlesticks. It had roosted there, most likely, ever since the death of Stissy's husband.

When the fish was served the choice bits always went to my plate.

It was warm in the house, and the air was satiated with appetizing odors. I hummed the Sabbath tunes at my ease, and as Tzirel busied herself with washing the dishes between the fish and soup courses, her clever mother sounded me out cautiously.

"So, whose son are you in Tarashcha, did you say?"

I ought to bring my laundry to them, she suggested. They had a peasant woman who did washing for next to nothing, so if I wished . . .

Tzirel very rarely spoke to me, and if she had to ask me something she would address me indirectly, as though speaking to the wall.

I began to bring them my small bundles of wash, and on getting them back I was surprised to find missing buttons sewed on and the holes mended with neat darning or still neater patches. From time to time I found a new shirt in my bundle, or a pair of new socks, or an extra handkerchief.

I felt as if threads were being spun about me. That is, no one really spun them—the spinning came about of itself, as it were, yet I felt, somehow, uneasy.

Later on the widow happened to remark to me, with a smile in her narrow Tartar eyes, "Women, now—you would hardly class them on a par with men, would you? Take the benediction of the outgoing of the Sabbath, for instance. Why, we never even get the chance to hear it. If it isn't too much trouble, perhaps you'll come over on Saturday night, after the last prayer?"

I began going over on Saturdays, after the evening prayers. The commode yielded a small, ancient spice-holder of silver filigree: this container still gave off a faint fragrance, a reminder of the days of antiquity. Tzirel held the twisted white and green candle for the *Habdalla* prayer for me. She strained like a child and tilted it, the hot wax dripping on her fingers. This made me smile, and yet I was touched.

Inwardly I began to yield a little. Looking at it from another angle —why not? A fine household and good people. They were not without livelihood. The mother was favorably disposed, the daughter liked me. The only drawback was—well, she was not exactly a beauty. And she was such a quiet thing—such a quiet thing!

12.

On the eve of *Purim* the Warshaver was caught with a gentile girl. That same night he hanged himself with his trouser belt from a chandelier in the women's section of the synagogue. Two fingers of his right hand were caught in the belt noosed about his neck. His trousers had slipped over his thin hips and had bunched up around his feet. The lower half of the body, which men feel so ashamed of and go to such pains to hide from strange eyes, was outlined against the thin, dirty underwear, and the gray-blue stiffening flesh peeped through a rent. As the body was being taken down from its gibbet little Chaim broke into bitter wailing; he sobbed and hiccuped for hours; it was impossible to quiet him.

Aside from us, his fellow students, no one came to the Warshaver's burial. Carrying the coffin on our shoulders, we plowed through the icy slush, and the butcher boys jeered, shouting something after us which we could not make out—nor wished to make out. The dead man was buried as befits a suicide: close to the fence and on the far side of a small ravine.

Ariah Leib's Chaim was taken out of the yeshiva. The Krutogorer quieted down and, before long, disappeared. Nissel, the assistant rabbi, now snarled at everybody like a mad dog. The students began to desert the yeshiva one by one, on the pretext of going home for the holidays but with no intention of coming back. Only fifteen or sixteen of us remained for the next term.

The yeshiva began to disintegrate, as though devoured by maggots. And I was terrified—truly terrified.

13.

The spring nonetheless rushed in with the speed of a young colt. The bearers of *Purim* presents still had to slog along muddy roads, and keep the white napkins protecting their trays from getting spattered; but a little later other Jews, bending under wickerwork baskets that spread the delectable aroma of oven-fresh matzos, could pick out a dry spot here and there to step on. Jews bustled about in the stores with eager faces. And once I chanced to see Zussi, the son of Michlie, chatting with a neighbor—and there was a smile trembling on Zussi's lips—a smile that seemed pitiful, dusty, and insignificant, but a smile just the same. A smile—I saw it with my own eyes!

In the far upper reaches of the Dnieper huge masses of snow thawed; the flood waters broke up the thick ice all the way down the river and overflowed the Zagorie valley, almost up to the town limits. One could again hear the steamboats whistling on the river; the hills all around turned green again. Sweet, fresh, moist odors spread through the air, and the sun once more gave forth its warmth. Two weeks before the coming of Passover the river reverted to its banks, the mud dried, the lilac was in full bloom—and the sun grew warmer and warmer. By the time the white blossoms had covered the cherry trees in the gentile quarter we were running each day to the river to bathe. The dust on the highways swirled in pillars; spring galloped on until summer took over the reins with a strong and firm hand.

During a hot spell guests from Cherkassy arrived at Isser Tabachnik's house: a daughter and her baby, which she was still nursing. I heard a strange voice in the living room.

"My mother-in-law said not to wrap the baby in swaddling clothes."

Whereupon a shudder ran down my spine, as if a drop of rain had worked its way inside my shirt collar. It was a rather low voice, throaty, husky, insidious—as if a pane of glass were faintly vibrating within her. And the voice said, "My mother-in-law said not to wrap the baby in swaddling clothes."

I made up my mind not to leave until I had seen the newcomer, and my wish was realized sooner than I expected. Within a few moments she came into the kitchen and, without taking any notice of me, started hunting for something in the cupboard. I had time to catch a glimpse of a towering mass of bright hair and a soft, lithe body in a loose dress of rustling black silk. Suddenly she caught sight of me and her great eyes regarded me in surprise. The food stuck in my throat. She left the room immediately, and although my eyes had been fixed on my plate I had managed to catch a smile lurking in a corner of her beautiful mouth.

I stumbled out of the room.

A mound of red cherries was flaming on a stall in the center of the market place and I bought some for a few pennies. At the entrance to the yeshiva I ran into the Stavisker.

"Would you care to pronounce the benediction over the first fruits?" And I held out the cherries to him.

He looked at me in astonishment. "Where did you get those cherries?"

"The mother-in-law said not to wrap the baby in swaddling clothes," I told him.

"What did you say?"

"Not to wrap the baby in swaddling clothes, the mother-in-law said. No swaddling clothes for the baby, said the mother-in-law—"

"You're crazy!" the Stavisker assured me. "Come on—how about a dip in the river?"

"No, I'd rather get back to studying."

I did not study, however. Instead I wandered from the yeshiva to the synagogue, from the synagogue to the rabbi's court, and all the while kept repeating to myself the words of the mother-in-law as if they were a verse from one of King David's Psalms. Such common words! Not in vain does the Talmud say: *The voice of a woman is of itself a seduction.* Seduction? For shame! Seduction is such an ugly word. On the contrary, such a voice as hers was . . . was as the cooing of a dove. Would the cooing of a dove be deemed unseemly before the Lord? And yet, what a head of hair! Bright yellow, piled high, like a haystack. Woman's hair—there, that was also forbidden, another seduction, a word that was like spitting in someone's face. And the silken rustle of the dress about the body it concealed—a body that rippled like a river under a light wind, like grain in a field when a breeze springs up. . . . A slight tremor ran through my body. My God, Thy hand smote me suddenly—and hard!

14.

In the evening I could hardly wait for the prayer to end. As soon as it was over I dashed off for my supper. There were no lights in Isser Tabachnik's house to greet me. The tall windows stared blindly at the western sky. A sadness came over me.

The cook was in the kitchen, however; she was alone in the house. She served me without much ceremony. After supper I paced up and down before the house for a long time, but it remained cold and aloof. There was still not a glimmer of light in the windows, and I returned to the yeshiva.

The week dragged on. I lost all zest for studying, and as soon as I opened some Talmudic tome I would slam it shut again. Whoever heard of such stuff? "If one rides astride a cow, and another leads it, and each claims the animal as his"—so? How did that concern me? How did it affect me, a young man from Tarashcha, whose life had so far gone thus and so, and would go on so and thus? But then, indeed, what shape and form would it assume henceforth? What would become of me? What would become of Stissy the Widow's daughter, the decent Tzirel? Of the synagogue . . . the dry-goods store . . . Zussi, the son of Michlie?

The next Tuesday was not of much help to me either. The words from the past, the bygone world, suddenly became remote—very remote indeed; they lost whatever little substance they had retained before. The colors of the past faded away, its odors evaporated. That Tuesday I neither ate nor fasted; it proved to be the worst day of my week.

But the worst thing of all was my having forgotten her face—the face of Isser Tabachnik's daughter, I mean. I had hardly had a good look at her in that fleeting moment in the kitchen. All I could recall was the high-piled hair, the color of straw—that, and the voice with the glassy ring which re-echoed within me, and still another thing which tormented me like a festering thumb. I felt like one who had found something only to lose it the next moment. Several times during that week I prowled around her house in the dark, but in vain. But when Thursday came at last and I showed up for a meal she was not there. The others were at home; there were some visitors too, and the talk revolved around her (or so I thought), but she herself was not there. I ate—ate again, prayed—prayed again, it might have lasted an hour—not a sign. Dejected, I rose from the table—only to collide with her in the doorway. I sprang back.

She came upon me like a rare and luscious fruit, sleek, roseate and white, bedded in green silk trimmed with point lace; her hair was braided like a wreath about her head and almost touched her brow; her green-gray eyes were like two ripening berries, and there was a celestial fragrance about her.

I stood there, startled and dazed; she stepped aside to make way for me; I did precisely the same thing at the same moment, thus blocking her. She then took a step in the other direction—and so did I—whereupon she burst into laughter, and once again I caught that glassy undertone in her throaty laugh. Confused, I hopped from side to side, still barring her way.

Her laughter echoed after me even when we had somehow disentangled ourselves and I had dashed out of the house.

15.

At night the *Dominion* churned down the river, bellowing long and piteously, like an animal in birth pains.

Heavy clouds had hung over the city since nightfall, but no rain had fallen. Now and then the clouds would squeeze out a few orphaned drops that fell among the trees in the rabbi's orchard, but there the matter ended, and a strain of wishing and being unable hung in the air. I tossed upon my bench and my flesh tormented me.

So she laughed at me, laughed so heartily yet heartlessly that my own heart both wept and laughed. And why shouldn't she laugh? Not so long ago I had taken a peep in a mirror at Stissy the Widow's and had caught sight of a nose as blunt as a saddle pommel, dark stubble smeared like mud over gaunt cheeks, and bulging delirious eyes—the eyes of a madman or a drunkard. And a body (this I knew without the aid of any mirror) like that of some hairy beast, patched up from bones and hide!

Perhaps they had even told her the story of the strudel? I suddenly sat up on the bench where I slept, then slumped down again. Nonsense! Whoever paid any attention to me? Who was interested in remembering and repeating what I did or failed to do? Did they as much as notice me? They minded me no more than some stray cat that snatched a bone at their kitchen door.

But, whether the story had been repeated to her or not, had I stolen the strudel or hadn't I? I had, and I had choked on it in secret, and spittle had trickled down my beard. That's the sort of creature I am. And I sinned my sins in a dark anteroom or in the stench of a privy.

On the other hand, what was she, when you came right down to it—an angel? After all, she had a husband, she had a child—and to beget a child one must ——. The coarse word would have eased matters for me, would perhaps have brought her closer to me. But, oh! I didn't have the heart to use it.

A fortnight went by without my seeing her at all—nor had I been too anxious about it—and once I even skipped a meal at the house where she was staying. I was tired—very tired.

Buni the butcher's daughter put herself in my way quite often, but now I would pass her by as though I didn't even see her. Tzirel, Stissy's daughter, had become even more silent. Had she sensed something?

But on Thursday *she* herself served me a meal. The cook had gone off somewhere, the mother was evidently indisposed, so the daughter set the table for me and motioned to me to wash my hands. My weariness had not left me, and for that very reason, instead of keeping my eyes fixed on my plate, I let them follow her about and wondered why she now seemed entirely different. She was wearing a loose garment, a robe of some sort, with brightly colored birds and flowers on it. Her hair, done in a single braid, came over her shoulder and fell on her bosom; her face seemed pale, somewhat off-color, puffy. I suddenly noticed a resemblance to her mother, to the good, genial Shaina Leah, something I had failed to see before. It was better that way, more pleasant—and yet, what did it matter?

She became fidgety and lifted her eyes to look at me, but I did not lower mine. This lasted for some time, until the perplexity in her eyes changed to embarrassment.

"Pardon my inquisitiveness," I remarked calmly, "but what is your name?"

A blush started from below her neckline and made its way up her throat, mantling her whole face.

"Why do you ask?"

"Just so. I merely wanted to know."

She contemplated me awhile. Then, lowering her eyebrows, she said, "Hannah. My name is Hannah." And she went out of the kitchen quietly.

I left shortly afterward and followed a side lane to the rear of the house. Then I made my way into the courtyard and saw that my conjecture had not deceived me: the window of her room looked out on the yard, and through the transparent curtain one could easily see what was going on within the room, though it was only dimly lit by a small lamp on a night-stand near the bed. She—Hannah herself—was rummaging in her wardrobe. Then a high-pitched wail, like the piping of a small bird, reached me from within. Before long she sat down on the bed, picked up her baby, talking to it with pursed lips, the way women always do when the baby is very young, unbuttoned her robe—and a full, round, white breast nuzzled the tiny face.

Without any sensuality, only with some such sensation under my heart as that of the suckling baby, I satiated my eyes for several minutes. Then I dashed over the fence and came back to myself.

Could human flesh be so exquisite, so white and serene—and so—so rich?

16.

On the next Tuesday I made an effort to regain that peace of mind which this day usually brought me. I went without food; all I did was study, in the synagogue proper. I studied unctuously—I chanted. The singsong outweighed the words, and the studying was meant to calm my feelings rather than to enrich my mind.

The following day when I arrived for supper at Buni's house I found the butcher pummeling his wife. So, those rumors making the rounds of the town were true. She was running around the table and screaming, "You heathen! You filthy peasant! May the Lord strike you down! May you perish from the earth!" But he merely kept after her with a stick.

Disgusted and frightened, I ran out of the house. I decided never to set foot there again. And, at the same time, I would be getting rid of the butcher's daughter, who had become used to waylaying me with downcast eyes, while I, both indignant and guilty, tried to avoid her.

Within a few hours, however, Buni showed up at our yeshiva. My heart sank. His roving eyes singled me out and he came over to me.

"Why did you run away?" he shouted and cuffed me a couple of times; then he grabbed me by the ear and led me out of the synagogue, demanding that I go with him and eat at his house. All the students had run out to witness my humiliation. At first I tried to resist, but I was too afraid of him. When he brought me to his house he placed a dish of meat before me and ordered me to eat. I did as I was told, choking on every mouthful, while he stood over me all the time. His wife, her face bound up, kept pacing the kitchen without a word. The girl was evidently not in the house.

When my plate was empty Buni insisted that I wash my hands before saying the prayer after meals.

"And then you may go to the devil," he snapped. "And don't let me catch you around here again!"

I withdrew from the rest of the students. In the dead of night I tossed on my bench and moaned as though in pain. As for taking further meals at Isser Tabachnik's house—I could not even think of it. It seemed to me that the whole world must by now be aware of my shame.

During the Sabbath meal Stissy the Widow kept glancing now at me, now at her daughter, but she did not say a word.

That same Sabbath I heard (it was a small town) that Isser Tabachnik's daughter was returning on Sunday to her home in Cherkassy.

The blow must have been stunning: I went about as if in a daze. But I came to my senses in the middle of the morning service on Sunday. I snatched off my prayer shawl and phylacteries and all but ran to the river.

It was nearly too late. People were already running up and down the gangplank. I elbowed my way with difficulty into the enclosure. My eyes found her almost at once in the throng on the upper deck; she was exchanging farewells with her mother and her little sister on the landing. She was a changed being: this time she was in a gray outfit, the jacket tailor-made, something like a student's tunic; her hat was of black straw, wide of brim, with a jaunty feather. Erect, sure of herself, and with an altogether different voice—from head to toe the rich daughter-in-law. The chasm that had divided us before was now yawning between us more widely than ever.

Had my stare attracted her? She turned her head in my direction and for some minutes looked straight into my eyes. Then she turned her head away abruptly, took her baby out of the crib standing alongside of her, put it back again, and called down, "Keep well, keep well! Temke, be a good girl—don't make Mother worry!"

The whistle drowned out her voice. The gangplank was hauled away. The whistle spewed more steam, and the next moment the black water widened between the boat and the landing. Half a mile down the river the steamboat disappeared.

The place where we went swimming was not far from the landing, and I dragged myself there, undressed, and sat down on the sandy bank. Far off across the river something like a huge tuft of cotton-wool formed in the air, then it disintegrated in the sunlight and a new tuft rose up farther away, followed by still others: clouds of smoke from a passing locomotive. But no sound accompanied them.

"The sound will never reach here," I said rather loudly.

The sun shone brightly, the river was ablaze, mirroring its radiance, and I, a naked mortal, sat on the sand with my head sunk on my knees. I sat for a long time, very likely pondering something or other, and, I think, even dozed off for a few moments.

Then I got dressed without having taken a swim.

On my way back I stopped at Stissy the Widow's. "Tzirel," I said, "I've come for my few pieces of laundry. I'm leaving."

Her cheeks and forehead paled.

"Yes," I added, "I am being called home. My father is ill—very ill."

The beautiful eyes in the plain face became still larger. "Your father? But you said you have no father—that you are an orphan—"

"Is that what I said? Well, if I said so, then I must be an orphan. I'm going away, Tzirel, I'm going away. Be well."

I was already in the street when she came out with a parcel in her hand and called after me, "You forgot your laundry!"

"My what?" I said.

She stood there with tight lips, holding out the parcel.

"Good-by, Tzirel," I said in a softer tone. "Good-by."

She said nothing but nodded her head.

An hour later I was back at the landing, standing before the ticket-agent's little window. The ticket-agent, a middle-aged Pole with sullen eyes and an aristocratic blond mustache, asked, "Where to?"

He caught me off guard and stood there impatiently. Let's see: Cherkassy was down the river, wasn't it?

"Up the river," I said.

He eyed me for some time with a sour expression. "As far as Kiev?"

"Yes—yes, as far as Kiev."

I came out on the landing itself. It was early for the next boat and no passengers were yet in sight. The sun was already behind me and the shadow of the landing lay sharp and black on the water. Farther out it was yellow, and over the entire width of the river full-bodied, swollen waves were gliding along—gliding from one end of the world to the other.

Translated by Bernard Guilbert Guerney

In a Backwoods Town

DAVID BERGELSON

1.

IT WAS almost by chance that the thirty-year-old Burman, who had the clean-shaven face of an actor and had at one time been a student, found himself in Dubrovich, a godforsaken little town lying close to the border. More by way of a joke than anything else, he had let himself be chosen as Rabbiner, the government rabbi, who generally had more liberal leanings than a rabbi of the old school. Then he had grown drowsy and indolent, had ceased writing to his only sister, a hunchbacked masseuse, and had let his blond mustache grow long and his chance to finish at the university go by forever.

That summer he used to go swimming twice a day with the local officials in the chill stream that wound like a serpent past the little town; he had, together with the sot who acted as county clerk, falsified various military service papers, and had gone walking with Manya Rimmer, a girl whom he had tutored at one time. She was the only student in the locality and had married curly-headed Froika Cherkiss on the Sabbath after the Feast of Tabernacles. During these walks Manya, who was brown as a gypsy, had confided to Burman that she was not overly in love with her husband, that the printing shop he had opened here with her three thousand rubles was not to her taste, and that in all likelihood she would not listen to him but return to her studies next winter. She was in earnest: what was the good of sticking here?

Burman had listened to everything and reflected that just a year ago this young woman who was now talking to him had been a prize shared by himself and Froika, that each of her lovers could then pinch her plump arms in secret. But now she was married to Froika, and everything was somehow so odd; Froika was living with her in three small furnished rooms, while he, Burman, was left all to himself, still in his bachelor quarters.

When the chill month of September rolled around Manya left the house more and more rarely. Tongues began to wag in the little town that she was not on good terms with her husband, and absolutely nothing remained for Burman to occupy himself with. He grew still more slovenly, drowsy, and indolent, and took to calling on the wealthy widow Perliss and her timorous red-haired daughter, who had eight thousand rubles for a dowry and a purchased high-school diploma. The little town had already decided, on several occasions, that Burman would marry the girl.

Every day, in the afternoon, when the elderly widow was asleep in the quiet of her bedroom, where even to this day there were two beds and the atmosphere of an elderly couple still lingered, Burman would make his way through the garden and the kitchen. He paid no attention to the maid, who was washing up after the noonday meal, and lost no time in sinking into a wickerwork easy chair in the parlor. For hours on end the red-haired girl sat there with him amid the overstuffed furniture and the potted plants, both plants and furniture once the property of an old general who had gone bankrupt. She would read to Burman some new book, paper-bound and extremely boring. She read very badly, in a quavering voice, and kept thinking, even as she read in her bashful and dull way, that Burman had at one time been her tutor and might now marry her. Her voice quavered as he listened and corrected her mistakes; her voice quavered when Burman, letting his head drop on his chest, dozed off with a hazy awareness that the autumn which prevailed in his rabbinical soul was now coming into being out of doors, and that somewhere beyond the godforsaken little border town there must surely be great bustling cities where men were active and alive. But now it was all the same to him: he would never again experience any joy in life. He dozed on.

Once, when the weather was inclement, as he opened his eyes after such dozing, he found that the windows looking out on the widow's garden seemed much darker than they usually were at that time of day and that raindrops, dewy and like tears, were pelting the panes. He saw the girl's downcast head but could not at first make out where he was. The lamp was already lit in the adjoining dining room. By the table, at the simmering samovar, sat the widow, who had just got up. She was staring out of the window at the weepy November garden and was musing about Burman, who was the town Rabbiner, about her daughter, who had eight thousand rubles in dowry, and that if there was to be an engagement party, the thing to do would be to invite the other rabbi, the *shochet,* and the cantor, as well as all the kin, and then shatter the symbolic plate by the glow of many candles. But she had neither the energy nor the ability to relate these disjointed thoughts. Because of the tranquil and hermetic way of life that had become normal to her she had long since lost the urge to think in an orderly fashion, to raise her voice, to seek contact with other people in the town, or to take an interest in anyone else's troubles.

"Sheba, daughter," she called into the parlor in a singsong, breaking voice, "ask Burman to come to tea."

At that point Burman's eyes found the girl's, glowing in the dark like little red flames and fixed longingly on his face.

"Burman!" she said tremulously, out of her longing. "You must have been sleeping, I think."

He felt himself irritated by a drowsy dislike for her voice, for her red hair, and for her hands, which still held the book. At the next moment he felt her stroking his hand in the dark, losing it and finding it and stroking it again.

From that day he desisted from going to the widow's house. He sat at home in his bachelor quarters. There everything was dusty and drab; drab were the walls, the ceiling; drab were the heaps of theological books that stared at him from the table so woefully, as though they were warning him: "So, Burman, you're frittering away your time, are you? You won't come to a good end, Burman!"

He took note of all this and was forever trying to make up his mind as to whether he could marry the widow's girl. With a half-smile hovering about his long blond mustache he pondered whether or not to ask—in a light vein—for the opinion of his sister, the hunchbacked masseuse. "Dear Sister," he would jest in his letter to her, "looking back over my whole life . . ."

2.

Melech the Goy, the town Croesus, died about this time, and Elisha Asness, his grandson, a sturdy and wiry fellow of twenty-nine, came back from Nikolaev. He sported a new gray suit, with a heavy gold watch-chain across the vest. He had fallen heir to Melech's big house with a lot of greenery around it and windows that looked out on the common at the very edge of the town, to a loan office with a gentile patronage, to the post of communal tax collector, and to more than ten thousand rubles in cold cash. Almost immediately he quarreled with the whole Jewish community, since the town had refused to bury his grandfather unless he, Elisha, came across with a contribution of four thousand rubles for local Jewish charities. The corpse lay unburied and rotting for three days and nights; at that point Elisha had called in the commissioner of rural police and, with the help of two police guards, had buried the corpse himself.

Thereupon the local tradespeople had taken to egging on the local meat dealers against him and had prevailed upon them to stop slaughtering their cattle in his district, thus inflicting a loss of two hundred rubles a week on Elisha.

"Wait!" the eminent and well-to-do citizens consoled themselves. "If it's the will of the whole town that Melech the Goy's grandson should go around begging for bread, then with God's help the thing will come to pass."

Elisha, however, did not lose heart. He threatened to spite the local tradesmen by opening a dry-goods store and another printing shop, and often stood at the window of the house he had inherited and balefully glared at the Jewish houses that sprawled out toward the circular market place.

"It'll get tired of this, will this filthy town. It'll get tired!"

Elisha had always been a jolly sort of fellow. Besides that, the town knew that not so long ago he had married a girl from Medzhibozh, a notorious character, that he had not gotten a copper of dowry with her, and that he was about to bring her to Dubrovich, as soon as the furniture he had ordered from out of town should arrive.

One day, meeting Burman in the street, he bowed to him, took him in with a glance, and called out quickly, "God be with you, Pani Rabbiner! How's the election coming along?"

Just then the smoke from his cigarette got into Burman's eye; with the other he studied Elisha with a surprised and somewhat quizzical smile. There really were unpleasant rumors about the election of a new rabbi. But since he was hardly acquainted with this new tax collector he did not know what answer to make and felt extremely awkward.

By this time Elisha had caught sight of the curly-headed Cherkiss, on his way home from his shop, and had his gray eyes fixed on Froika's pallid face. "Froika the Simple!" he brought up the nickname of some twenty years ago, when both had been going to the same Hebrew school. "Just look at him! He's become quite a man—won't even bother to turn around!"

Froika, a shade too shrewd and always on the parsimonious side, had by now lost all touch with the townspeople. Some two or three months before his wedding he used to run to Burman's lodgings several times a day, and had a habit of pinching Burman's plump breast and shouting so loudly that all the neighbors could hear, "Just take a look—it's like a girl's! Like a girl's, as sure as I'm a Jew!"

But now his unshaven face had a haggard, toilworn look, and he was kept busy day after day in his printing shop. On rare occasions he was seen strolling with his wife at dusk, and even then, if anyone stopped him, he would take her arm as if it were some sacred object and, pretending to ignore what was common knowledge, that his wife was not wasting any love on him, would hurry her home. At such moments his tired face seemed resentful and stubborn, as if the newly married man had once and for all determined to make up in his business and domestic affairs what he had missed in the twenty-seven years of his dissolute life as a student.

He felt angry at Elisha because of the second printing shop the latter had threatened to open and answered him indifferently and coldly, "Look what's turning up his nose! Look what's putting on airs!"

And in a moment the two were openly quarreling. Curious passers-by gathered around them and heard Elisha berating Froika, "You think

I don't know that you're as much my enemy as any of the rest of them here? You think I don't know that you're inciting the butchers against me behind my back?"

To which Froika replied that for his part Elisha could go to the devil, along with the rest of the townsfolk; that as a matter of fact he, Froika, was too busy to bother with him, but since Elisha had already begun it, he'd tell him that he really deserved all he was getting, and more. Elisha should not have flouted the whole community; he should not have taken it upon himself to bury his grandfather on his own responsibility.

And so the jovial Elisha was truly in the midst of enemies; not a soul would exchange a word with him. For several days he roamed about the town like a ghost, and at last decided that the whole place meant no more to him than last year's snow. He set out for Medzhibozh in a hired carriage and one fine morning, early, came back with his young wife.

That day he was again in high spirits. And when he brought his wife for the first time to the deserted common he did not give a damn for the whole township, for its boycotting slaughterers and for the two hundred rubles he was losing each week. As if to pique his enemies he spoke rather loudly to his wife.

"See, Fradochka—over there, near those poplar trees? That's where the priest lives. He's keeping two girls. What? You don't believe me, you little ninny? It's a fact—as sure as I'm a Jew. He claims they're cousins of his."

People were standing in the doorways, staring at Fradochka. She was a head taller than Elisha or Froika's rather plump and dark-complexioned wife, and each time she raised a foot, topped by her tight-fitting black skirt, it drew the eyes of all the gaping men, as though the long slender foot harbored something that was peculiar to Medzhibozh and it was of momentous import what would happen to it and to her entire Junoesque figure each time she raised that foot and lowered it once more. She had an olive complexion, her face was elongated, with barely perceptible down on her upper lip, and big dark eyes; her hair was black, curly, and short.

Two apprentice tailors, who were connoisseurs of smoothly carved feminine backs, got into an argument as to whether she was wearing a corset underneath the green short-sleeved jacket that revealed her full throat. They were ready to wager on the matter.

"You fool," one of them raised his voice, "it's the fashion now, as sure as I'm a Jew. They no longer wear corsets."

Elisha, however, paid him no attention. Catching sight of Burman standing at a window of his room, he came over to him as to an old friend, introduced him to his wife, and asked in a courteous tone, "Pani Rabbiner, how do you like the warm weather we're having, and the scenery hereabouts? Our town is quite beautiful, isn't it?"

In the meanwhile his tall, stalwart wife was standing at his left, contemplating the "scenery," which consisted of rutted hills, sloping and wrinkled, with aisled trees that towered up to the azure sky.

"Yes," she seconded Elisha, quietly and confidently, "it's a fine spot to make one's home."

At that moment her face appeared as serious and sedate as if she had spent a lifetime trudging from one spot to another in search of a place to let down roots. And now she had found it, among these rutted, sloping hills. She had not come by this spot easily, yet find it she did, at long last.

After the introduction Burman took a nap of well over two hours in his bachelor quarters and then went for a stroll past the windows of Elisha's house, noting the fine curtains that Elisha's wife had already managed to put up. He heard the tapping of a tack-hammer close to one of the curtains, caught up a little and tucked to one side. He had a glimpse of the cool interior and the tall upholstered chairs in their new covers, as well as of Elisha's wife, standing near the maid who had clambered up on a small table.

"Will you please drive that nail in a little higher?" she was saying to the maid and pointing.

And just then a restrained smile appeared about the Rabbiner's long blond mustache. He turned to where, in the distance, he could barely make out the Cherkiss printing shop.

"Man alive," his smile said, "one can still enjoy life: a beautiful woman, and an exotic one, at that, has come to our town."

3.

The next day, about eleven in the morning, the Rabbiner was sitting and chatting with Elisha's wife, amiably yet most decorously, in that same room with the tucked-up curtain. She proved to be quite worldly and clever. The garrison officers in Medzhibozh with whom she had hobnobbed from her fourteenth year had contributed not a little to her education, so that she needed no further pointers in the conversational arts. When the Rabbiner paid her a compliment she would laugh gaily, pat her coiffure, and call out banteringly to Elisha in an adjoining room, "Elisha, do you hear how the Rabbiner is flattering me?"

Through the laughter her voice was resonant and mellow, as if in keeping with the sway of her slender figure, and made one understand why she exerted herself to fascinate every half-attractive male who came her way and why she loved to inject into her conversation such phrases as "There was a certain officer I used to know in Medzhibozh . . ."

The next time Burman called she stood back to back with her guest to see who was taller, and they squeezed hands to find out who had the stronger grip. On his third visit she sat down, upon his urging, at the shiny black piano she had brought from her home town and ran through an impressive list of the pieces she could play for him: "Storm on the Volga," for instance, or the Rumanian milking song, or even Gounod's "Ave Maria." If he wanted the "Ave Maria," she wouldn't need any notes, she knew it by heart. "It goes like this—"

Her deft fingers swept the keyboard in florid runs, releasing wave after wave of sound. Burman thought her playing skillful; she seemed to be making no special effort, however, and even managed to talk to the servant, who appeared at the entrance, to the right of the piano. Without interrupting her playing she told the girl that tomorrow she herself would go to the market with her and that poppyseed was superior to caraway seed for sprinkling white loaves.

On Burman's fourth visit she retied his bowtie in accordance with her own taste and adjusted his coat collar so that it sat snugly over the collar of his shirt. Burman submitted to her whims with an oxlike stolidity, but he felt heady, and a tipsy look crept into his eyes whenever his hand touched hers, so soft and warm. Harking back to his past experiences, he decided that with such a woman as his hostess a direct attack was best of all.

Unexpectedly things came to a head that very morning. Some nobleman's carriage drove past, and the Rabbiner and Elisha's wife went to the same window to watch. Their heads were close together, and Burman, feeling her body snug against his own, looked about cautiously to see if anybody else was in the room. He lowered his arm to take her around the waist and draw her to him. But she eluded him most expertly and so quickly that her short black hair flapped over her face as she thrust his arm away.

"It's not nice, Burman," she remarked with cold indifference, fixing her hair and adjusting a button on her jacket.

Burman turned beet-red, and it struck him as odd that his flushed face could still smile. She was no longer by his side but, with her hands on her hips, was going casually into the next room, then into the dining room, and finally into the corridor, where he heard her speaking loudly to Elisha.

"Elisha, you ought to get your rubbers cleaned. You've left them all muddy right in the doorway."

The Rabbiner did not linger but, hiring a driver, went off for the night to Kamenetz, a visit he had been contemplating for some time. The entire adventure with Elisha's wife seemed nothing but a silly flirtation. She was rather notorious in the region, this lady from Medzhibozh, what with her officers and her gallivanting around ever since her teens.

In Kamenetz he learned that the people in his godforsaken town were really considering a new candidate for the rabbinical post: a local merchant's son who was tutoring in Odessa. He also learned that the widow Perliss's red-headed daughter had been receiving a new suitor for the last fortnight. And an old hard-drinking matchmaker, whom Burman had known in his home town, stopped him in the street at Kamenetz and informed him in drunken accents that the match looked very promising and that on the strength of this the widow had come to Kamenetz and had already ordered new clothes for herself and her daughter. The old man also told him confidentially that Elisha's wife was not a decent sort, and that only yesterday a Medzhibozh matchmaker had pointed out to him the officer, a dragoon, with whom she had lived for all of a year.

"Is that so?" Burman probed, and a humorous smile lurked about his mustache.

After that he wandered aimlessly along the noisy main street of Kamenetz, watching the widow and her daughter visit one dry-goods shop after another and observing how the clerks fawned upon them and how the Kamenetz ladies' tailor, furrier, and modiste dogged their footsteps.

By now he was wondering at his own indifference to things, even to the shabbiness of his own clothes, which were hardly up to city standards. All he felt was that he was drawn home, and, above all, to the slender woman with bobbed hair in Elisha's house who had refrained from creating a scene and whose reason for suddenly marrying Elisha no one really knew. Now her voice rang clearer than ever in his ears—the voice he had heard yesterday just before he left. He saw himself standing near the corner window, which was open; his heart had been pounding, and he had heard her talking to a Polish washerwoman, telling her that if she did her work honestly she could come regularly two days each week.

Two days later Burman was back, and, having taken a nap in his rooms to rest up after his journey, he came out on the common about two in the afternoon. Elisha's wife recognized him from afar as soon as he appeared and beckoned to him from where she was standing at the open window of her bedroom.

"Burman," she said hurriedly and looking about her, "what possessed you to go off like that? I was around at your place three times yesterday—" And, at the same time, she contrived to stroke his head so deftly that the flour merchant across the way, standing in front of his shop, never even noticed the caress.

She was wearing a short-sleeved jacket and her eyes had an inebriated look. He understood why she was glancing about her so furtively, why she was inviting him in. And he entered with a subdued smile, his thoughts a jumble. It became apparent to him that Elisha was away from home and that he, Burman, was now about to sacrifice his life: no matter how one looked at things, he no longer had any place to go to from this town, which already had a candidate for his rabbinical post this coming winter. As he crossed the threshold of her bedroom a novel notion struck him: You fool, the world is so much muck . . . as sure as you're a Jew. . . ."

And he closed the door behind him with the tranquillity of a lord and master.

4.

Manya, the erstwhile student, wanted to divorce her husband Froika. It was common knowledge throughout the town, as well as in Elisha's household.

"Why, she's actually deserting Froika—do you hear?" Elisha, returning one morning from the market place, jovially informed Fradochka and Burman, who were sitting opposite each other in the drawing room. And, in order to convince them, he swore loudly, "As sure as I'm a Jew, you simpletons! Their house is a bedlam right now. Manya is demanding that he return her legacy of three thousand rubles and intends to go back to her courses."

Fradochka had a good head on her shoulders. Not in vain did Elisha boast that she could solve any arithmetical problem in an instant. And though not ten minutes had passed since the things that had taken place between her and Burman in this very drawing room she maintained her composure and asked with a businesslike and adroit air, "And where will her Froika lay his hands on any such sum, now that he has invested the three thousand rubles in his printing plant?"

Rabbiner Burman, however, offered no comment whatever. With his legs crossed and the mien of one who was above the whole petty discussion, as taciturn and reserved as an Englishman, he lolled in his overstuffed chair, facing his hostess. He had shaved off his mustache at Fradochka's request and was wearing a brand-new black suit of fall weight, with the coat buttoned up to his very chin; Fradochka had already run her hands over the cloth and sworn that, with his height, the suit made him look like a young physician. Now he felt out of sorts because of Elisha's unexpected appearance and could not meet his eyes. But this too had not escaped Fradochka's attention.

Pinching his back, she pointed out of the window. "Take a look—I believe that's Froika passing by."

They all hastened to the window to catch a glimpse of Froika heading for his printing shop. There were no visible signs of worry on the niggardly Froika's face with its cap of black curly hair. He was as preoccupied as ever with his business and seemed to be hoarding his coppers even more tenaciously than before.

The upshot was that the Rabbiner shortly betook himself to Froika's shop, smiling all the way. As soon as he entered he sank down on a heavy, grimy box.

"You fool," he remarked to Froika, "the world is muck—as sure as I'm a Jew."

He was, in reality, referring to himself, to his helpless situation in this town, which had cooled toward him and was planning to replace him; he was thinking as well of the goings-on between Elisha's wife and himself, and of Froika's wife, who was about to leave the printer. His novel discovery, however, made no impression on Froika, whose shop was swamped by two new orders from the county authorities.

Froika's inky hands were searching for a new font; stooping under a table, he replied apathetically, as though he had been long familiar with the matter, "Muck it is. Man alive, is that news to you?" And the next moment he dashed into the adjoining room where his two printers were at work and began shouting, "What's the matter—all through for the day? Why so quiet? Wake up that *goy!* Hey there, you—start the press rolling! If you want to stretch out you can do it on your wife's little you-know-what."

Burman soon found himself in Elisha's house again. It was morning, and Elisha himself dragged him in from the street, calling out merrily to his wife in the bedroom, "Here, Fradochka, I've brought you the Rabbiner! Hurry out and play something for him."

Then he approached Burman with pen, ink, and a sheet of paper. "Would you be good enough, Pani Rabbiner, to draw up a petition to the justice of the peace—but do it in such a way that it really stirs him up." And, that the Rabbiner might not take offense at being instructed, he turned to Fradochka. "Little silly, he knows how to do it—he knows, all right! Your Medzhibozh lawyers would envy his ability."

Fradochka, coming out in a negligee, noticed that Burman's face was quite drawn and, feeling that he ought not now to be annoyed with petitions, asked if Elisha would be kind enough to order a glass of hot milk for the Rabbiner. The moment her husband's back was turned she moved close to her guest, one of her warm knees nudging his. She was about to ask whether Burman had missed her, but at that moment they heard shouts coming from the front of the house and Elisha and the maid dashed out as though they were running to a fire. When Fradochka and Burman followed them they saw people running from all sides toward Froika's printing shop. The maid stopped a man returning from that direction and asked him what all the commotion was about. Burman drew near and heard the news: "It's nothing at all. An uncle of Manya's who had been displeased with her marriage from the very first obtained power of attorney from her and has padlocked Froika's shop. Manya herself is no longer here. She has gone back to her courses."

Burman's next stop was at the printing shop, where he saw the bewildered Froika with a crowd about him. Held back by three men whom he kicked and butted, he was straining to get at Manya's uncle and to tear down the official seal on the door. When he had regained his senses to some extent and was released at last, he looked at the crowd with great hatred and astonishment, as though seeing it for the first time.

"What's all the commotion about? What brought all of you out here—is this a show or something?"

He slumped onto the steps of his shop and fell into thought. Perhaps he was thinking about Manya, who was rumored to be carrying on an affair with a student in Kiev. Or it may have been about himself, about his perseverance, which had profited him so little.

Fradochka and Elisha walked up to the Rabbiner, who was also deep in thought, and Fradochka said to him, "Come, let's go, what's the point of staying here?"

Froika Cherkiss did not leave his house for all of two days. All alone he lay there, pondering about Manya. Would he give her a divorce? He'd rather see her dead of the plague! The three small rooms were topsy-turvy, just as they had been on the day Manya left. The beds were still unmade, the featherbed still as upset as when she had taken her two pillows; on the table in the tiny dining room, among crusts of bread, stood a plate with the desiccated skeleton of a herring, flies swarming over it. A steady downpour was making the gloomy little rooms hot and stuffy; the atmosphere was that of a freshly painted third-class railway car. And Froika did not even bother to open a window or call in someone to tidy up a little.

But late in the third afternoon, when the rain had ceased, he began to resent his loneliness; he shaved off his stubble and defiantly got out his new suit, which he had hardly worn. And as he was putting it on he reflected that with the thousand rubles he still had he would not be lost in this world: Manya mattered no more to him than last year's snow.

Just the same, as he came out of the house, he looked about him furtively to see whether his landlady was sitting on the steps.

Twilight was coming on, and the muddy road that stretched away from the round, badly paved market place toward the last row of houses had the sheen of sleazy velvet. A girl's head peeped out of a window and a pair of dark eyes, sparkling and timid, took in Froika's face with an inquisitive look. The girl did not know him, yet was curious to see how he had changed.

Farther on, at the end of a wooden fence, two Jews were standing and examining a lot of lumber they had bought from a gentile, which had been delivered that afternoon. One was the owner of a building nearby; the other was his partner. Both agreed that the lumber was a real bargain but they dropped their business for a moment as their eyes followed Froika.

"What do you say about that?" one of them remarked, raising his voice for Froika's benefit. "A bachelor once more, thank God!"

Everybody hated Froika because, like Elisha, he had come back to this town too late and with too much pride over having studied in the big cities, and because he, like Elisha, had no need for the services of the *shochet* or the orthodox rabbi. The entire township was having its revenge, and he roamed its streets and had no soul to talk to.

Next morning he chanced to see Elisha's wife as she came back with her maid from the market place. He stopped short, staring at her for a considerable time, and was left fidgety and restless for a whole afternoon. Several times he set out for his padlocked printing shop without any ostensible purpose. He would watch it from a distance, sigh, and go home. But there he found the same stuffy air, the same untidy setting, and he would lock up his place again and return to the market place. Picking up a few words here and there among the knots of people who were discussing Elisha and the boycotting butchers, he finally proceeded to the house inherited by Elisha. As he walked along he speculated how everyone in that house would look at him with pity, and how he would answer Elisha.

"You stupid oaf," he told himself, "things aren't so bad. If you care to, you can go back to pharmacy."

But the moment he entered the house he caught sight, through a looped-up portière, of the Rabbiner's crossed legs and felt a sudden urge to make a fine impression on Elisha's wife. Roguishly, like a country lad setting out for a dance, he patted his straw hat so that it came down over his ears. He threw back his shoulders, smiled like a peasant—or an idiot—and called out at the top of his voice, gaily, the way he used to do as a bachelor, when he was still satisfied with himself, "Hearty greetings to you all—and it's Wednesday!"

When Elisha came running in response to his greeting Froika had a fresh pretext all ready. "I just came to say that I can't understand why somebody shouldn't try to bring about a reconciliation. It's simply a pity about Elisha and the butchers."

Elisha measured him from head to foot and fixed his hard, restless eyes upon him. "Just look at him, our softhearted friend! Suddenly taking pity on the butchers!"

Froika reddened, as though offended, but quickly explained, "Man alive, am I saying it's a pity about the butchers only? What I'm actually saying is that it's a pity about you as well. As a matter of fact, you're losing two hundred rubles every week for no good reason at all."

From that day on Froika began to frequent Elisha's house. His own home seemed to him a hell; the plate with the skeleton of a half-eaten herring was still on the table. He went home only to sleep, spending the rest of his time at Elisha's. He became Elisha's spokesman and began to negotiate with the townspeople.

From early morning he stood in the market place, bandying words with the dull-witted butchers. The other shopkeepers made fun of him behind his back; they hated and mistrusted him; but he paid no attention to them and strove to convince the butchers that it was against their own interests to refrain from slaughtering beef and lamb in Elisha's district. Let them just listen attentively: What good would their stubbornness do them if all along the slaughterers were killing chickens and geese?

In the afternoons he talked his heart out at the home of the orthodox rabbi, perspiring in the midst of the leading citizens assembled there, who could not forgive Elisha for having buried his grandfather on his own responsibility and who reverted time and again to the same refrain: "Whoever heard of a thing like that? Such an outrage has never occurred anywhere else on earth . . ."

He made wry faces, hunched his shoulders, gesticulated in every possible way. "Very well then—you're right! But, for heaven's sake, am I not saying the same thing? Yet what has the township accomplished?"

Weary and exhausted, regretting the whole affair and sorry that he was exerting himself in behalf of a virtual stranger, Froika would return early in the evening to Elisha's house, where he was welcomed with supper and tea, and where everyone was anxious to hear of the progress he had made during the day. Half chewing his food, as ravenous as if he had just concluded a long fast, he passed on the latest news, turning every now and then to Rabbiner Burman.

"Burman, do you hear what Elisha is saying? If I should bring about a settlement, he says, I'll be rewarded for my efforts with a hundred rubles."

Fradochka listened attentively and kept the conversation moving. Every so often she would call her husband into the next room. "Elisha, come with me for a minute—there's something I forgot to tell you."

As the night grew cooler they all sat down to play preference—a thing they had been looking forward to all day. And there Burman would remain till past midnight.

The town, with all its lights out, was sound asleep. The quiet of the night was unbroken, save when a crowded passenger train came chugging along the way that led to Medzhibozh. The eyes of the passengers were drawn by the wakeful house, and their hearts turned toward its lit windows as if toward happiness.

Sometimes during the evening the players would hear a creaking sound, as if the front door were being opened. Forgetting their cards for the moment, they would stare in the direction from which the creaking had come. It was always caused by Jan, the watchman who guarded Elisha's house.

"Jan," someone would address him in Yiddish, "what's going on in the world outside?"

Jan knew what they meant and would reply in the same tone, in his broken Yiddish, "It's dark out, master."

Whereupon they would all laugh heartily and at least a dozen cigarettes would be sent to Jan in the kitchen.

Elisha's game was consistently clever; he never missed a trick and liked to keep the others guessing; he managed to forget all his business worries and his squabbles with the town. In fact, he never noticed what was going on around him during a game, and Froika alone was aware that Elisha's wife, who might have called her husband out of the room only a short while before to share some secret, and Burman, who was seated opposite her, were making play with their feet under the table. Once, becoming jealous, Froika tried to put his own foot into this pedal conversation, as though to say, "How about my getting into this game of yours? Why should you mind?" But the next instant he got a kick by way of answer, which implied, "Don't you mix in—it's none of your affair!"

The kick, it seemed to him, had been delivered not by Burman but by Fradochka, who had at the same time turned to Elisha. "Hold on a moment—how could you have played your king?"

And, shortly afterward, he had to witness the hostess escorting Burman into the next room and handing him her husband's overcoat, so that he might not catch cold, and to listen as she urged, "Burman, you must come for supper tomorrow, without fail. Don't make me coax you."

And as he left the house with Burman, Froika thought of himself and the deserted rooms where he would spend the night and, after a moment's silence, remarked to his companion, "What a lucky fellow you are! Do you think everyone is as fortunate as you?"

He thought that Burman had not caught his hint and added, "Why, Elisha is practically supporting you—giving you room and board—and even a wife—"

Rabbiner Burman had begun to put on weight about that time. He felt too lazy to reply. He merely smiled to himself—a little more broadly than usual—and turned off to his own lodgings.

5.

In the long run Froika succeeded in persuading the leaders of the town to accept from Elisha a contribution of no more than five hundred rubles to smooth over the affair of his grandfather's funeral. This was a diplomatic achievement of which only Froika was capable. Elated, he kept challenging Fradochka, "Well, what do you say to that, eh? Have you any complaints against me?"

It turned out, however, that the butchers had a separate bill of grievances over having forgone their slaughtering for all of a month. Their complaints were considered at a further hearing, and both sides had to abide by the decision of the local orthodox rabbi, who was rather a simpleton. In keeping with this decision Elisha would have to stay out of the abattoir, while the butchers were held accountable not to him but to a representative appointed by the orthodox rabbi.

Elisha raged and tore his hair when he got home. "What sort of settlement is that, for heaven's sake? It's a joke, that's what it is!"

Froika again busied himself and again worked a miracle. Calling Elisha's attention to the approaching High Holy Days, he pointed out that he could recoup, within a period of three weeks, whatever he had lost in taxes during the preceding month and a half. Elisha, of course, knew very well that the astute and wily Froika nurtured a hatred against him and was primarily interested in his fee of a hundred rubles. "You'll get yours, you'll get yours," Elisha mocked, looking daggers at him.

Elisha found the new arrangement somewhat confusing but let the butchers straighten out their accounts with their own representative, while he himself spent two days in reviewing all the proceedings and determining the net gain from the taxes on the expiatory cockerels to be killed on the eve of Yom Kippur; this gain apparently exceeded all his expectations.

Froika again danced for joy. "Well, what did I tell you?"

But during that same week rumors sprang up that the township was not entirely satisfied with the settlement and that the butchers were going on strike again. Sedate citizens who had never so much as hurt a fly gathered in knots on the market place and enlightened the butchers.

"You dolts! What have you to do with the town's settlement? Why, in the long run he would have had to give up collecting the communal butchering taxes and quit."

Not far from them the town matchmaker, grubby and tipsy, whom the shopkeepers plied with drink, was circulating through the market place. Wiping his nose with a large sheet of tissue paper, which he kept thrusting back in his pocket, he spread gossip about Elisha's wife.

"Did you say something about a lieutenant she was living with? Why, he sends her mother a hundred rubles every month, even now—"

His auditors split their sides laughing. "Who?" they egged him on. "Who did you say sends her mother a hundred rubles a month?"

And, pretending to take their questions seriously, he kept answering as if he were under oath. "The dragoon she was living with—as sure as I'm a Jew!"

Elisha was seething. From early morning he had been straining to go to the market place and crack the old sot's skull. Froika had to restrain him bodily. "You oaf!" he admonished him. "Stay home. It will blow over. A community can't do without meat on the eve of the holiday."

In the evening, however, Elisha came upon the grubby matchmaker alone and beat the old man until he was soaked with blood.

Fradochka was out at the time, having gone for a walk with Burman.

The dark night was filled with the cries of the tortured old man. Young men known for their prowess came running from all directions, shouting but unable to recognize anyone in the darkness. The merciless beating created an atmosphere of terror. Children broke into wails, as if crying for the dead. But all that the beam from somebody's flashlight caught was a pair of feet running away. When the crowd reached the deserted common they found no one but the old man squatting on the ground. Hunched up and cowed, he was cupping his right hand to catch the drops of blood that trickled from his nose.

"How that scoundrel hit me!" he sobbed. "That bastard has beaten the life out of me!"

"Fellow citizens!" someone interposed. "He ought not to go unpunished for this."

At that moment two shots rang out in the distance. It was Elisha blasting away with his revolver in his garden: once just for the devil of it, the second time to show the townsfolk he was not afraid.

Later, the matchmaker, all black and blue, was led from one solid citizen to another: let people see for themselves what that cutthroat Elisha was capable of. The old man kept groaning and grimacing, though by now he was in no great pain. They told him that he would be entitled to damages from Elisha, while the butchers who were trailing along said they would resume their boycott the very next day.

Froika went running to Elisha in a rage—his fee as a mediator had obviously slipped through his fingers.

"As if I didn't know this would happen!" he stormed, pacing up and down the dining room. "Elisha will be the ruin not only of himself but of the whole community and of all who come near him!"

Fradochka, the source of the misfortune, sat by calmly. Her face was still flushed from her walk with Burman. "Did you ever hear anything like it?" she kept repeating. "Some old rumpot goes shooting off his mouth, so he has to get into an argument with him!"

Elisha faced her at last, angry with her for the first time since their marriage, and mimicked, "Shooting off his mouth, eh? Just shooting off his mouth!"

Then he turned on Froika, who at once flounced out of the house. Elisha rapped out, "Let him go—and good riddance! No one sent for him!"

6.

Fradochka was incensed against Elisha and refused to talk to him for all of two days. Each time he tried to kiss her she repulsed him not only with her hands but her shoulders.

"He'd better keep away—I can't bear the sight of him," she said, bringing out all the femininity in her voice to tantalize him. And each time Elisha had to retreat, his lower lip twitching angrily as he shoved his hands deep in his pockets.

"Bah!" he would blurt out, and that expletive could be interpreted in a variety of ways. It could mean: "She's suddenly become a lady: think of that!" It could also mean: "Don't fret—this will blow over. She'll change her attitude yet!"

But Fradochka seemed to have made up her mind, and one fine morning she set out for Medzhibozh to see her mother. Catching sight of a cart driver from her home town, she came out to greet him. Evidently the idea of the trip occurred to her right then and there.

"Zanvil, how about taking me to Medzhibozh?" she asked.

Zanvil fussed for a while with the harness of his team and answered with a leisurely smile, "Sure, why not? It won't be an ugly woman I'll be bringing back!"

When Elisha got home from a neighboring village, where he had gone to remind a couple of peasants about redeeming their sheepskin jackets, Fradochka was already gone.

As he entered the drawing room his face fell with amazement. He could not believe that his wife was capable of doing such a thing. A peculiar silence pervaded the disordered rooms. The upholstered chairs had been shifted from their customary places. The maid was pottering over a belated meal: her entire morning had gone in helping Fradochka get ready.

When Elisha came into the bedroom and saw that Fradochka had left practically all her things in the closets, he tried to reassure himself. "Don't worry! She'll change her mind! I'm certainly not going to send any special messengers after her."

For the rest of the day he paced through the rooms, lonely and unaware of the latest developments in the community. Froika was still resentful and failed to pay his usual call. At dusk Elisha heard the doorbell and went to the door, assuming that Fradochka had come back. But it was only Rabbiner Burman, who had come to take the lady of the house for a walk.

"She's gone," Elisha informed him slyly, spreading his arms like wings. "Gone away."

"Gone away?" the Rabbiner echoed; he felt as though he were a small boy who had come to play with his little friend Fradochka, and Elisha, the adult, was feeling sorry for him.

"She's gone, little fool—you'll have to walk home by yourself."

The timid smile lingered on Burman's face even after Elisha had closed the door on him and he was on his way home. His entire behavior with the woman who had just left town now seemed childish and silly to him—hardly becoming to such a serious person as himself. He paused and looked about him. The town common was deserted. Still smiling, he jabbed a finger at his heart, and for the first time in his life started to talk to himself. "You're a fool, Burman—as sure as you're a Jew."

That night Elisha found it hard to sleep, and he decided that on the morrow he would set out to see Fradochka. As soon as he was up he would hire a driver and make the trip. But the bad dreams he had that night had to do for the most part with his financial losses, and in the morning his resentment toward his wife came back. Wouldn't he be making a laughingstock of himself if he were to drop all his business affairs and go tearing after her!

And thus things went on for a whole week. The agitation in town against him increased. He came to feel as if all his wealth were being taken from him, and his very life with it. As for his wife's feud against him, he hardly had time to worry about that.

The new commotion was brought about by the shopkeepers and the old drunkard of a matchmaker whom he had beaten up. The citizenry assembled on Saturday night in one of the Houses of Worship and passed a resolution that if the township no longer wanted Elisha to act as the collector of its taxes, no one could force it to accept him.

The local butchers, with but two dissenting voices, lost no time in approving the resolution. The two who had sided with Elisha were soundly thrashed by the rest of the butchers, who at the same time decided to resume their boycott. The representative who had been appointed by the orthodox rabbi no longer came to Elisha with his pockets bulging with silver and copper coins greasy with tallow and smelling of raw meat. He went about the market place with nothing to do, nibbling poppyseeds out of sheer boredom. The local merchants grew more confident and gay; they dissuaded the peasants from pawning their articles at Elisha's loan office and assured one another, "Don't you worry—he'll go up the chimney soon."

Within a few days the butchers held a secret conference and decided to give Elisha a drubbing. "We'll let his guts out!" they shouted in chorus. "He doesn't belong here!"

One night the windows of all the local slaughterers were smashed, to make them stop killing poultry, and the tension mounted. None knew for certain whose work this had been: the butchers, to divert suspicion from themselves, had purposely smashed the windows of one of their number. And the next morning they gathered in the market place and pretended to poke fun at themselves and at the feud in progress. "Wait! It's a good thing Elisha has no children to feed!" "You fool! Why, they cook on the Sabbath in his house. He has no fear of God."

One middle-aged butcher, a newcomer, with a silly long beard and rheumy eyes, stepped forward with his comment. "Out of the ten thousand rubles he got by skinning his grandfather when the old man croaked, he has spent only five hundred, as sure as I'm a Jew!"

Whereupon they pulled his hat down over his eyes and began bantering him. "Itzchok Varatuta, you crackpot—go and smash Elisha's windows!"

Itzchok Varatuta was dull-witted, slow-moving, and strong-limbed. At the secret meeting of the butchers he had been the first to propose that Elisha be beaten up; at the same time he knew that the matter required the utmost secrecy and must not be carried out in broad daylight. Hunching up his shoulders, he fended off his cronies and smiled idiotically. "Go and do it yourselves—may you burn in hell!"

That afternoon the butchers saw Froika and Burman going through the market place and began baying like hounds. "They're all in it with Elisha—can't you see that?" "Has school let out?" "They smoke together on the Sabbath—or did you know?"

When they spied Elisha's maid on her way back from a Russian store they shouted after her, "Just you wait! He'll give up his ghost yet, this grandson of Melech the Goy! He thinks we don't know that he carries a revolver around with him!"

At that moment Elisha himself popped out of the narrow lane between the post office and the gentile poorhouse. The police officer who was with him stayed behind, and Elisha, advancing toward the knot of butchers, turned to Itzchok Varatuta. "Well, do you still think I'm afraid of you? You're going to inform on me, are you?"

Elisha was extremely vexed and irritated. Since early morning he had been keeping watch with a constable at the abattoir on the outskirts of the town, waiting to trap the butchers. And now, in an act of desperation, he had returned to confront his enemies.

7.

Jan, Elisha's watchman, was on bad terms with the maid. It had all come about because of an overflowing kitchen pail which Jan had refused to carry out. The maid retaliated by refusing to save him the onions from the fat soups and by having nothing to do with him.

"May he rot!" she said as he tried to open the locked kitchen door from the outside. "I'll keep him out all night like a dog."

Jan was lonesome and yearning for a little talk. Throughout the dreary night his whistle shrilled now in one spot of the garden, now in another. At the break of day he passed a few words with a peasant, who was carrying three pounds of meat in blood-smeared paper. Losing no time, he knocked on the window of Elisha's bedroom. "Master, they're selling meat in town!"

Elisha sat up with a start, as though he had been expecting this new calamity and had dreamed about it since last evening. "So! The butchers are at their tricks—" The next moment he leaped out of bed in his underwear and threw the window open. "Who was carrying the meat?"

His bared hairy chest quivered apprehensively as Jan repeated his story. He seemed indifferent to the raw morning air, breathing hard and grasping but one thing: they were bringing in meat from outside the town. The whole township—with its butchers, its shopkeepers, its leading citizens—was like a single monster, molded and massive as cast iron; its crushing weight had suddenly awakened him out of his deep sleep. Thoroughly alarmed, he dressed hastily and before long was hurrying through the dim, sleeping back streets behind the market place. He must catch his enemies unawares!

He prowled from one locked house to the next, as if it were not this house he was after but that other one—that one, before which still spread a puddle left by a bucket spilled the evening before, just as the whole back street spread like a puddle before him in the raw dawn, deep in the heavy sleep of a chill morning. From the direction of the market place came the intermittent creaking of carts loaded with beets, creeping in a mile-long file and at a snail's pace to the distant sugar refinery. And at that very moment one of the long shadows on the cold damp earth grew tremulous and began to move forward. It was cast by a gilt church spire, which the sun had set aglow even before it had risen.

Unexpectedly, someone sidled by: a back door had creaked, and a maid emerged from it, wearing a headkerchief and carrying a basket. A moment of suspense—and then Elisha pounced.

"So—it's meat! What kind of meat? Where did you get it?"

Five minutes later, carrying the confiscated basket of meat, he was at the orthodox rabbi's house, pounding on the table with his fist and shouting, "So you call this acting like a pious Jew? The whole community is consuming meat from outside the town—and you're aware of it and yet keep quiet?"

The rabbi had just risen; he had been mumbling his prayers and was to some extent caught off guard.

"What does he want of me, this—this—" he muttered, shrugging his shoulders. "What's he trying to do, give me lessons in piety?"

Elisha dropped in on the local chief of police and then sent off a telegram to the police inspector of the district, demanding help. Within an hour and a half, convoyed by four constables, he raided one butcher shop after another, searching and rummaging in the lofts and cellars, and found nothing incriminating. He went home, lay down, and tossed about restlessly, kept from sleep by his mortification. He walked over to his window, disheveled and collarless, and saw the sun nearing noon, hanging high over the town, and the smoke belching out of every chimney. Meat from outside the town was being stewed in every pot—it was his flesh they were stewing. And he knew that as the result of this he would be getting poorer every day. Well, let come what may; things were now beyond his control.

Several days later an order arrived from the police inspector of the district, impounding all the meat that had been smuggled in by the butchers.

Elisha kept the order a secret, postponing its execution until the eve of Rosh Hashonoh. He gritted his teeth and paced his rooms; his confidence in winning against the community was renewed.

"May the devil take the damned dog-catchers! They'll find out soon enough whom they have to deal with!"

Meanwhile the weather turned nasty. The town began to sink into dreary autumnal dusk. The butchers had great difficulties in smuggling meat in from outside the town.

"We're having a hard time of it," they complained in secret to their patrons. "The peasants don't like to make the long trip, no matter what you offer them."

Jan the watchman, whom Elisha had sent secretly to an outlying village, came back at last with reliable information. "The butchers have hired Sidor the Little and Petro of Mlina. Both are setting out with their carts at nightfall and will be back here at dawn on the day before Rosh Hashonoh."

The rain persisted, saturating the air and generating a muggy mist, like the steam from sodden piles of manure, that seemed to penetrate everywhere. On the eve of Rosh Hashonoh the mist turned into a thick brownish fog. It swallowed up the town, changing the appearance and color of its dwellings. And whenever a peasant from some neighboring village drove up to go to market he could hardly recognize the first row of houses, they seemed so changed by the fog.

The Jewish community had gone to bed early, so as to be up before dawn for the Penitential Prayers, and the only light still glimmering at that late hour came from Elisha's window, facing the fog-swathed common. Everything within his house was in readiness for the task at dawn. An armed policeman was posted at each of the four roads leading into the town. The town's chief of police was with Elisha, while Jan the watchman, who had been on another reconnaissance at a nearby village that afternoon, was now snoring soundly in the dark entry. A small kitchen lamp shed a dim light in the dining room over the expensive floor, all littered. Sprawled out on four large chairs which formed his bed, the stocky chief of police lay sleeping; he had long since lost track of the drinks he had downed; his cheeks and lips quivered with his heavy breathing. Elisha was sitting on the couch with his topcoat on, like a third-class railway passenger, contemplating the police chief's green breeches that ballooned over the tops of his muddy boots. Only a short while ago, when Elisha had stepped out on the balcony and peered into the pea-soup fog, it had occurred to him that the impending encounter with the butchers might end in disaster. An icy raindrop, trickling down from the roof, had run down his neck and sent a shiver through him. But the thought had vanished as he re-entered the room and sat down again on the couch.

The preceding day and this night seemed so strange and far away now, as though they were a part of his childhood years. In this indifference to everything about him, including the probable disaster, he yielded to the urge to doze off. He even dreamed: he saw his grandfather, Melech the Goy, sitting on the steps of the house with a well-to-do peasant in the neighborhood, discussing his grandson Elisha, along with other modern young men, who didn't know how to take care of their coppers. "Yes, that's how it is, that's how it is," his old grandfather was saying, shaking his head.

Suddenly a light sprang up in one of the dark windows; Elisha heard a hubbub and his blood again began to seethe. He hardly heard the entering policeman report how he had intercepted one wagonload of meat but had missed another load.

"I'm ruined!" Elisha shouted at the chief of police. "The local police will be the end of me!"

And without bothering to listen to the incoherent explanations of the chief of police he dashed out of the house.

That same night the butchers caught Elisha all alone on the outskirts of the town and thrashed him within an inch of his life.

It happened in a miry, moss-grown hollow between a grove of birches and the small, abandoned Torgovitza bridge. Elisha had chanced to stumble in the dark upon the second wagonload of meat on a by-road and had been about to run for the constables when he was almost felled by the first blow, dealt by a ruddy-cheeked butcher boy whose father went by the name of the Litvak.

"Take that!" said the lad through clenched teeth. "Don't go shoving your nose in where you're not wanted!"

Elisha's ear and his teeth began to bleed; his cheek throbbed; his head, however, was still clear. His eyes automatically turned to the left, to find out who had struck him, but at that moment a second blow came from the other side. Then someone struck him from behind, in the small of his back, and he slumped to the ground. And through his mind flashed the names of Fradochka, Burman, Froika Cherkiss, and all the others who might have come to his aid but were not here now. His tear-filled eyes began to close, yet he managed to catch a glimpse of a long silly beard, a pair of diseased eyes, and a heavy boot swinging back, as someone admonished, "Itzchok Varatuta, make it a dry job—use your head, you oaf!"

And that booted foot kicked the man on the ground, turning him face down. Then they all bent over him, as though over a corpse when the survivors beg forgiveness of the dead. "And did you have a right to beat up the matchmaker? May a fire consume your bones!"

The booted foot came down on his head, on his back and ribs. He felt as if the wheels of the cart had rolled over his body.

A police whistle blew. The butchers quickly retreated, leaving their mangled victim behind.

Elisha was still unconscious when they brought him home at dawn. There was no one in the house but the maid and the chief of police, who tried time and again to question him but without success.

The hours dragged on. By nine in the morning the sun, wan and sickly, was showing through the steamy fog. There was a crowd of women and children before the house, awaiting word from the county physician, who had been inside for half an hour stitching up Elisha's scalp and the back of his neck.

The assistant doctor, a Jew, was the first to come out. He spat apathetically and allowed himself to be questioned. Within a few minutes everybody learned that Elisha was in a bad way and that the county doctor had said, among other things, that the head blows were not the important thing; what mattered most of all was Elisha's hacking cough. With a cough like that, the doctor thought, no one could last more than a week.

One of the women in the crowd bethought herself of calling over a carter who was looking for fares to Torgovitza, the next town.

"You dolt," she lectured him, "why don't you ride over to Medzhibozh, to Elisha's wife? You'll make twice as much by it—"

The carter hesitated for some time, eying the crowd, but at last drove off toward Medzhibozh. The bystanders figured that if he were to drive at a fast clip he would make five rubles for himself and still be in time to take a steam bath on the eve of Rosh Hashonoh.

But when he came back, just before sundown, he was alone. He did not know to whom to complain; first making sure of a supply of hay and oats to tide his horses over the Holy Days, he proceeded to a sorrowful account of his experience in Medzhibozh.

"She smiled at me, first off, did that wife of his, and said, 'Wait a little while—I'll go along with you.' But then her mother, that old witch—may her bones rot!—came out and said, 'Go back by yourself, in good health. Fradochka isn't coming unless he makes up with her.' "

8.

The evening after Rosh Hashonoh, Rabbiner Burman packed his belongings. When he went to bed, at a later hour than usual, he dreamed about his sister, the hunchbacked masseuse. She was accompanying him on his journey, accompanying him with an odd devotion, like a mother's.

"Laibel," she was saying ever so devotedly, "there's a button missing from your school tunic."

And as she bent her rosy oval face over the mother-of-pearl box of buttons he sat up in bed with a start and suddenly felt guilty and dejected, as though the authorities in Kamenetz had found out about the conscription papers he had doctored last year.

"Burman," he said without opening his eyes, "you're a scoundrel!"

Throughout the morning he paced his room in remorse, pausing now and then near the table; lying on it were his sister's letters, which he had not bothered to look at since summer. They were a silent reproach. Since she had become fully aware of her deformity she had transferred all her devotion to him, admonishing him, time and again, in her letters: "Laibel, you are sinking into a morass, but you can still save yourself. Laibel . . ."

Of late she had ceased writing him. Perhaps she was in dire straits right now, yet she still would not write. Thoroughly depressed, he stretched out on his bed once more and began mulling over a letter to his sister which he was going to write without any delay. "Dear Sister," he would write her, "I am taking stock of all my life . . ."

A nap, he reflected, would help when he came to writing his letter; the nap would also help with his feelings about his sister. And as he slept he saw his long-departed father and mother in a dream. The two were sitting at a table with him; the samovar was steaming; and his father, a correspondence clerk in the town council, was saying to him, "When a man turns thirty, and still has no household of his own, and takes no thought for his future . . ."

But in the end the letter to his sister remained lying on the table, unfinished. Instead of going anywhere he dozed for a few hours more. His body, heavy with its hundred and eighty pounds, could no longer cope with dejection, and, oblivious to everything, he drowsed off.

When he awoke at last and had washed and spruced up a little, he kept thinking of his student days, and that he was no longer wanted as the community's official Rabbiner, and of the fact that Elisha was in a critical condition and could not leave his bed, and of the other fact, that he himself was now in a time of transition. So it was through no fault of his that he was now in the doldrums and had during the last few days become especially fascinated by the town dressmaker, a young thing with a dark complexion. Also, he had to decide on the proper course to take with Fradochka. And he was expecting her: she was bound to come back from Medzhibozh sooner or later.

The sun was setting and his usual late-afternoon restlessness dragged him out to the town common. There he ran into the county physician, who used to go swimming with him in the serpentine river all summer. The doctor looked him over with his keen eyes, and, patting the bulges of fat on his shaved neck, remarked with a smile, "Burman, you're quite a handsome man, but you're not doing a thing and are running to fat. And that's harmful. Come over and I'll let you chop a wagonload of firewood."

Burman, without opening his mouth, smiled by way of reply. It implied, this smile, that though the doctor was a clever man, Burman was nobody's fool. He felt that such matters were better left alone, that a smile was enough for an answer.

The doctor took the Rabbiner's arm (after all, they were both professional men) and walked with him toward the church, in the neighborhood of which he had to visit a patient.

"Elisha is in a bad way," he confided to Burman. "He probably won't live the week."

The Rabbiner was startled, as though he were responsible for Elisha's imminent death.

His next thought, however, had nothing to do with Elisha but was about Fradochka. It occurred to him that it might be advisable to retrace his steps and to drop in on Elisha. But just after he parted from the doctor the swarthy and attractive dressmaker emerged from a narrow weed-grown lane and his nostrils caught a whiff of her perfume. She passed rather close but without looking at him. He heard the swish of her silk petticoat, and he was so stirred that he almost called out her name to stop her. His smiling eyes followed her, and at this moment, when the setting crimson-orange sun was reflected on the house walls and windowpanes, the girl seemed fresh and novel. He smiled inwardly and followed her back into town.

A few days later, at twilight, Froika Cherkiss came upon him in the back street where the dressmaker lived. Burman was loitering near her widowed mother's house and could hear the whirring of a sewing machine, though he was on the opposite side of the street.

Froika was in high spirits—he had earned a commission of a hundred rubles that morning through the priest.

"What a surprise!" he cried, catching sight of the Rabbiner. "What are you doing in these parts?" Then, looking at the house from which came the whirring of a sewing machine, he surmised what was afoot and blurted out, "You fool, you—she is about to be engaged. She's going to marry Yossel, the harness-maker's son."

The curly-headed Froika looked particularly spry. He had been busy of late, running around with all sorts of catalogues and selling agricultural machinery to the local gentry. His notebook, which he showed to the Rabbiner, showed a recent gain of eighteen hundred rubles. And though it was a weekday he was wearing a new suit of a greenish shade, a white starched shirt, and a bow tie.

"You understand?" he lectured the Rabbiner, pointing at himself. "The main thing is not to lose your common sense and to start making some money. Oh yes, and what about Elisha? It's a shame. Have you visited him?"

He wanted to explain to the Rabbiner why he was in such a festive mood and, taking him by the arm, went on, "Man, as long as I'm making a living and lead a decent life, what can I have against you, or Manya, or even Elisha? Isn't that so? Come, let's drop in on him."

As soon as they entered they sensed that Elisha was in a critical condition: he seemed to be lingering on merely to torture those who ministered to him. That wretched creature, the maid, her soiled face framed by a kerchief, lost no time in telling them that she was all alone in the house with *him,* that *he* had her all tired out by now. She no longer called him by his name. She was all alone and could not stand *him* any more.

The place reeked of mice pellets and an unventilated kitchen. A pail full of melting dirty chunks of ice stood on the table in the dining room, and one could see some half-gnawed chickenbones lying at the foot of the sickbed. And the wretched maid still stood there, droning: he ate practically nothing at all; he merely had a hankering for this or that; he kept her on the go all the time, getting all sorts of things and making her cook them for his snacks. There, they could see for themselves how she kept the kitchen going twenty-four hours a day!

Then she went on to tell how he had craved some cheese dumplings the evening before, and how she had to run all over town to get the butter and cheese. And, late at night, when she had just dropped off to sleep on the floor near the door of his room, he had to go and wake her up: he thought he would like a snack of some kind—a Passover pancake maybe. "See for yourselves: the dumplings and the pancake are still there, untouched. He wouldn't even touch them."

"What—you think he's asleep?" she asked with an odd smile when she noticed that her hearers were frowning because she had raised her voice. "That's not so at all—he doesn't sleep all night. He lingers on there, day after day, and won't let you open the shutters. He hardly sleeps a wink—and won't let anyone else have any sleep."

Froika and Burman entered the drawing room as though afraid of awakening someone, then tiptoed to their chairs and sat down together. There was a brief silence. Burman's attention was caught by a clod of dried mud, evidently left there several days ago by the police chief's boots. He leaned over, watching it for a long while, as though fearful that at any moment it would start moving and crawl the entire length of the room.

Froika began to feel bored and regretted having come. Discontentedly scratching the nape of his neck with one hand, he prodded his companion with the other. "You had the time of your life here once—eh?"

He wanted to add something about Fradochka—she could hardly know how ill Elisha really was. A neighbor had informed him that he had run into her the day before Rosh Hashonoh, in Medzhibozh, and had seen her strolling with some army officers. But at this point the maid, who had gone to have a look at the sick man at their request, came hurrying back.

"Well, what do you know!" she said thoughtfully as though a small miracle had just occurred. "He has fallen asleep after all!"

9.

Froika Cherkiss passed a pleasant night, stimulated by the sizable commission he had earned through the local priest, and on awaking he had a new and happy thought: now that he had regained his footing, the fact that Manya had left him was not so calamitous. He really meant it: if he were divorced from Manya, couldn't he marry even a woman like Fradochka?

Later he dressed in his new outfit and strolled over to the market place, feeling as free and jubilant as the mild sunny morning, which had begun to warm even the town of Dubrovich, buried between the hills.

Generally speaking, he was not so anxious to make a ruble. Aside from all his earnings he was, after all, a pharmacist. If he wished to he could quit all these business deals and go back to running a drugstore in some village. And meanwhile he found it delightful to idle about awhile, if he chose to do so. He really meant it: even though money was important, it wasn't everything. After all, he wasn't one of your Dubrovich cattle.

Near a big stone building that housed Tunkelstein's dry-goods emporium he espied the wife of the owner's younger son: the couple was childless. What a shame, he reflected—a young woman anxious to have children, the poor thing! It gave him pleasure to see her standing there, facing the sun, her back propped against the shop door, her scarf well over her face to shield it from sunburn. He paused for a while, contemplating her, and compassion tugged at his heart.

You take a man, now, who is making a comfortable living (he came back to his previous train of thought), who dresses and eats well—a man like that will begin to look about him and become aware not only of himself but the world around him. Man is not so bad. . . . For that matter, take Froika himself; what connection, for instance, was there between himself and that young married woman?

"Mr. Rabkin!" he called out, taking a few steps to reach the town's middle-aged druggist, whose gold spectacles always seemed to be cantering on his snub nose, giving him the air of a somewhat deranged professor. "Mr. Rabkin," repeated Froika, "here I was, traipsing around and thinking of the townsfolk hereabouts who speak of me as a bad man. Well, is that a right thing to do?"

Rabkin the druggist was very much peeved about the Kamenetz

commissioner of police, who thus far had failed to call for his prescription, all made up and waiting for him. He was on the lookout for the commissioner with great impatience, standing near the glass door of his neat drugstore, apprehensive that the commissioner might not show up.

And, back of him, his red-headed wife, whose gauntness never changed, was nagging him in her shrill voice, "Who ever heard of such a thing? Up to noon he was taken up with his Zionist letters. He couldn't have arranged things with the commissioner in the morning, he couldn't . . ."

Froika was amused by this comic couple: he, a corpulent and niggardly little Jew with a trimmed beard, who sold Zionist stamps without his wife's knowledge; she, drooping like an overgrown, dried-up stalk, her squeaky voice choking her, as though the devil in her were too big to pass through her narrow gullet.

Yet Froika, as he left the two, found himself in a discontented mood, with the warm word he had intended for them unuttered and a bewildered smile in his eyes. Dubrovich, he reflected, was a godforsaken town. And he felt a keen yearning for some person of refinement who, like himself, would enjoy idling for a while and who would hear him out. Oh, if only he had a companion! He might, for instance, go over to Burman and get him to stroll to the outskirts of the town, where the fields were flooded with warm sunshine, the way they are after Passover, and say to him, "Brother, when you're toiling for a livelihood and your mind is all mixed up, you just get by. But when you get what you're after, and look at what's going on around you, you come to see that the world is a beautiful world, and you have compassion for that world, and the life about you begins to hum . . ."

But, of late, the Rabbiner had turned into an unwieldy block. Once upon a time, when he used to tutor and wore a student's tunic, he had been something of a man and one could talk to him. But now he merely smiled to himself at everything you told him and kept as mum as a block of stone.

Eh, it was a godforsaken town, this Dubrovich.

Tramping around the market place, he stopped to talk to Elisha's maid, who was on her way home with a basket over her arm. "Well, what's new? How is Elisha coming along?"

"What's there to say?" The maid's appearance was still wretched and grimy. "He's been sleeping since yesterday."

She knew what sort of sleep that was. He had awakened in the morning with a craving for fresh gefilte fish, prepared the way it is for the

Sabbath. That accounted for her having ranged through the whole town for three hours, at the end of which she had barely managed to get a few pounds of carp. And yes—a messenger with a card from the county physician had set out at dawn to see Fradochka. Perhaps she had come back by now and would put an end to the maid's misery.

"Is that a fact?" Froika interposed. "So Fradochka may have returned already . . ."

He suddenly felt drawn to Elisha's home, where he might find Fradochka by now. Nevertheless he went home first, had a hearty meal, and took a nap for a couple of hours, so as to observe the amenities and avoid dropping in on her the moment she had arrived. Once, he remembered, she had lectured him: "Froika, don't swear so often with that 'as sure as I'm a Jew.' It's not *nice.*"

When Froika, refreshed by his siesta, entered Elisha's house about three in the afternoon and called out, for Fradochka's benefit, the gay greeting of his bachelor days, "Hearty greetings to you all—and it's Wednesday!" Elisha had been dead for ten minutes and was covered with a white sheet. On a bureau not far from the corpse the Sabbath gefilte fish was still steaming. The messenger had not returned from Medzhibozh yet, and no one knew whether Fradochka was coming back or not.

Out of politeness Froika lingered awhile in the bedroom and mused, in an apologetic sort of way. "Was I, God forbid, an enemy of Elisha's?"

He heard the keening of the maid, who came running with a pound of candles. Annoyed by her clumsiness, he took the candles out of her hands and made a wry face at her. "Look at her bawling—just as if she were mourning the loss of her father!"

The girl retreated into the kitchen and broke into stifled weeping.

A strange yet humdrum silence pervaded the house with its open windows. The afternoon dragged along. Jan was sitting on the steps, telling the washerwoman about how the butchers had beaten up Elisha. And the woman stood with her arms folded, cursing the godforsaken town and its folk. "May the cholera take them! May their hands wither—and may they wither in life and limb!"

Catching sight of the Rabbiner not far from the house, Froika walked over to him. "Well, what has it all come to?" he asked. Then, as an idea occurred to him, he called the other aside. "Foolish fellow, is it so bad a legacy that Elisha has left you?"

There was a moment's silence. The Rabbiner was still meditating, his hands in the pockets of his autumn jacket and with the air of a man who knew how to respect a house harboring the dead. But suddenly his eyebrows rose and it seemed as if he were trying to smile in his quiet way: "Fool, the world is so much muck, as sure as I'm a Jew . . ."

Translated by Bernard Guilbert Guerney

To the New World

ISAAC METZKER

AT THE foot of a high hill in a remote corner of eastern Galicia, not far from the Russian border, lay the village of Yanowitz. Its tiny mud huts with thatched roofs nestled among orchards and forests of great oaks, which formed a shelter from wind and storm. Swift streams rushed noisily from the hill above, watering gardens and ancient willows, feeding the marsh lands and the Nyetchlava River. The villagers, Jews as well as gentiles, prospered and multiplied.

From time to time a new hut would appear, with a *mezzuzah* nailed to the doorpost. The Jews of Yanowitz were rooted in the Galician soil; here they had lived for generations, parents bringing up children, marrying them off and helping them settle, children doing the same for their children, an unwearying cycle. Some of the Yanowitz Jews were farmers, and others shared in the prosperity of the region as traders. For the High Holidays they traveled to the city, since the village of Yanowitz could claim no synagogue.

In time the Jews of Yanowitz conceived the idea of building their own synagogue in the garden of the oldest Jewish settler.

"We really need our own synagogue. If we had our own, we wouldn't have to leave our homes to go to the city for the holidays." And there were those who added, "Yes, if we have a synagogue of our own, our children won't fall into the hands of the *goyim.*"

With the coming of the warm spring days the Jews of Yanowitz began to build a House of Prayer. They collected straw and bricks, stones and boards. Not only the Yanowitz Jews, but also the Jews from the surrounding villages came, generously giving materials and their own labor as well. The work went forward with great zeal, the women in their bare feet kneading the clay while the men laid bricks and hammered boards. The sweat that ran down the faces of the laborers went unnoticed, and a feeling of closeness grew up: a house was being built where all could come together. From day to day the walls rose higher, and by harvest time supported a roof thatched with straw and decked with flowers and green twigs. By Rosh Hashonoh the synagogue stood completed, reigning on its hillside, bare, with bluish-white tinted walls on a brown brick foundation.

The completion of the synagogue was a great event in the life of the Jews of Yanowitz. Scrubbed clean and dressed in their best clothes, the men in their prayer shawls, they strode out of their homes in the sunlit Rosh Hashonoh days. Their gentile neighbors greeted them respectfully and wished them a good year. Fields overflowing with wheat, hay, and Indian corn, the beans and hemp laid out in the sun to dry, were left behind with a carefree air. All thought of calves, geese, ducks, hens, and crowing roosters was set aside as they marched toward the synagogue, joyfully shouting to their gentile neighbors that from now on they would never abandon Yanowitz during the High Holidays.

Things continued so for many years; in their synagogue the Jews of Yanowitz prayed and celebrated marriages and circumcisions. Season followed season until, barely noticed by anyone, the great and distant world made itself felt in Yanowitz, slowly seeping into the remote village and bringing to an end the sweet and secure pattern of life that had silently been woven through the years.

It all began at the time the Jews on the Russian side of the border were driven from their homes, forced to flee the Cossacks and their gentile neighbors who beat them and looted their houses. After stealing across the border, these Russian Jews would journey to ports, from which ships would carry them to far-off America. While making their way to the Austrian side, a few stumbled upon the village of Yanowitz. They were taken into Jewish homes for the Sabbath, and at the synagogue they would tearfully recount the horrors they had seen. The Jews of Yanowitz became aroused, and even when the rains were heaviest and the muddy roads almost impassable they would come to the synagogue each Sabbath to learn more about the pogroms. In the House of Worship they would cling together and in chorus with their Russian brothers curse the Czar and pray for the welfare of their Emperor Franz Joseph, whom they looked to as a protector. The Russian Jews spoke glowingly of the "Golden Land" that was opening its doors to them and told stories of a fabulous America as though they had already been there. The Jews of Yanowitz were wonder-struck at these tales, and a few, infected with the restlessness of the Russian wanderers, began to feel a desire to go off to the distant world.

First to start for America was Paisach, the grandson of old Ber, who had three marriageable daughters and not a dowry for one of them. Paisach meant to leave the village without telling anyone but his wife and children. The secret was soon out, however: all the Jews of Yanowitz knew for a certainty that Paisach, a skilled workman who was forever building things, was going to America to construct a machine for refining gold.

While Paisach sadly packed prayer shawl, phylacteries, and several new shirts in a valise he had made himself, his wife, his daughters, and the women of the family who had come to say good-by filled the hut with tears and moans.

"Wasn't it agreed that I should leave quietly?" asked Paisach, threatening not to budge unless they stopped crying.

The women spoke among themselves in hushed voices. "Really," said one elderly aunt, "they shouldn't let him go. It's not for him. They tell me you have to work there even on the Sabbath."

"Ah," said another aunt, no younger than the first, "it's easy to talk about going to America. But how can they let a father of children cross such a wide sea?"

All the Jews of Yanowitz followed Paisach to the edge of the village, weeping over him as though he were dead. But the next day Paisach was home again; he returned with his brother Leib, who had driven him to the railroad station. A fearful tale spread among the villagers, a tale of demons dragging Leib and Paisach along deserted roads throughout the long night, to keep them from reaching the station. Soon, however, the truth came out: Paisach was already in the train, but at the last minute, just as it began to move, he dashed out with a cry and ran straight to his brother's wagon.

Paisach stayed home, but it was not long before another Jew of Yanowitz said good-by to the village. He was Paisach's nephew, Yankel, the son of Leib. While still an infant, he had been sung to sleep with the lullaby, "Yankel will learn Torah and lovingly serve the Creator," but Yankel cared not for learning and had no head for Torah. He was drawn to the gentile youths, to the free outdoors, and he grew up wild. At fourteen he was a fully developed man whose swarthy complexion and black eyes suggested a defiant nature. At first Yankel shaved his thick black beard in secret, with a razor borrowed from a gentile neighbor. But in time Leib resigned himself to the thought that of the six hundred and thirteen commandments obligatory upon every Jewish male his son would violate more than a few, and so Yankel was allowed to purchase a razor of his own. By the age of fifteen Yankel was as tall and broad-shouldered as his father and was already going to gentile weddings and getting into fights with gentile boys. The entire village talked about Yankel, and the family felt that he put it to shame.

"That Yankel! He's not afraid of anybody. The gentiles are frightened to death of him."

"No bullet will ever lay him low and no fire consume him."

"The rope that he'll be hanged with will tear seven times! There's a demon inside him!"

His father would try to persuade Yankel to mend his ways, sometimes pleadingly and sometimes with open threats. It was no use. The villagers began to urge Leib to send his son to America, but the father turned a deaf ear. When Yankel's mother died and Leib finally had to admit that the boy was too much for him, the plan to send Yankel away began to take hold. By this time Yankel was seventeen years old. He would spend his days at gentile homes, eat forbidden food, go out with gentile girls, and have bloody fights with the gentile boys. Leib knew about these things, and they depressed and angered him. One day his anger finally overcame him.

It was a winter Sabbath. Yankel had not gone to the synagogue, and at noon, when Leib came home from his prayers, the boy was just getting out of bed. He had pulled on his boots and was sitting up, his eyes half-opened and his hair a tangle.

"Couldn't you get up earlier and come to pray like all the other boys?" Leib began to scold. "To go around on Christmas Eve singing songs about Jesus underneath gentile windows—that you can do! For that you would even get up before dawn!"

"Leave me alone," whined Yankel, scratching his head with both hands.

"I won't raise apostates in my house," shouted Leib in fury, striking Yankel in the face with the flat of his hand.

Yankel's drowsiness vanished immediately. He jumped off the bed, feeling his burning cheek with one hand, touching the imprint of his father's blow. His amazement quickly grew into a terrible anger. With a growl he clenched his fists, ready to strike. Leib, as tall and broad-shouldered as his son, stood his ground and looked his son squarely in the eyes. The smaller children, frightened by the angry voices, came running into the room. Yankel tried visibly to control himself. As if to erase the sting of the blow, he again rubbed his smarting cheek; then he grabbed his fur cap and coat and rushed out of the house.

Yankel was gone all that day; nor did he return home to sleep. Until past midnight Leib lay restlessly on his bed, waiting for his son to appear. He was sorry he had slapped the boy and remembered how his wife had always been against raising a hand to the children. Later he rose and went out to the barn: perhaps Yankel was there, freezing.

In the morning some of the villagers supplied the news that Yankel had spent the Sabbath afternoon at the house of his Uncle Avrohom. There he had said he was going to his Uncle Yosef, who lived in another village. Actually Yankel was staying with the gentile Sharomet, who lived at the foot of the hill. Paisach's wife, Fat Treineh, who often visited the village priest, brought the news. Breathlessly she blurted out, "Sharomet told the priest that Yankel is with him and he wants Yankel for a son-in-law if he agrees to be baptized. What do you say to that?"

Avrohom's wife, Dvoireh, who just then happened to be in Leib's house, began to wail, "Father in Heaven, don't let it happen! May Sharomet not live to see it! That's the way it is when you're too harsh. As early as last summer Yankel should have been sent off to America with those two Russian Jews who spent the Sabbath with us."

"Didn't he say he was going to Yosef's?" Leib kept asking.

"A complete lie. He has been there with the daughter of the *goy* since the Sabbath. That priest, I tell you, is an angel. He said he advised Sharomet to find a son-in-law among his own. He won't want to convert a Jewish child," continued Treineh.

"Come," said Dvoireh, rising from the bench and pulling Treineh after her, "we'll drag him home by the hair if we have to."

"Sharomet with his little Safrona should have as much strength to live as I have strength to walk," said Fat Treineh, groaning as she adjusted her shawl on the way to the door. Both women fervently kissed the *mezzuzah* on the doorpost, then trudged up the snow-covered road to Sharomet's farm. Sullenly and with dragging step, Leib walked with them as far as his gate.

Toward evening Yankel's two aunts approached Sharomet's house, a lone hut encircled by open fields. From a distance they could see their nephew, bareheaded, chopping wood beside a great log.

"What have we lived to see," said Dvoireh, moaning. "That Riveh's son, who is supposed to say *Kaddish* for her, should go bareheaded!"

"Is that all that matters? Think how much pig meat he must have eaten there by this time! If we don't take him home now we'll never be able to live it down!" Treineh panted as she hobbled across the snow.

"Oh, what a Yankel that is! Oh, will he fry in hell! And who knows whether he won't be turned into a wild pig or some such animal. Better to say no more. See, he already noticed us. He's moving away."

"Yankel, wait a minute!" cried Dvoireh, running to block his path. "What harm have we done you that you run away from us?"

"You should know who your friends are," added Fat Treineh, bending over to pick up Yankel's fur cap from the woodpile. "Here, put it on. There's a frost coming," she pleaded.

"Why did you come here? I'm not going home," Yankel cried out, angrily burying the ax deep in the log. He pulled on his cap and with feet astride stood defiantly before his two aunts.

They stood there somewhat abashed, studying him curiously, noting the healthy red glow of his face. Dvoireh stretched out her thin hand as if to touch him. "Didn't you say you were going to Uncle Yosef?"

"I did."

"Your father didn't know until today that you're at Sharomet's. Just because you get angry at home doesn't mean you have to go off to a gentile."

"He shouldn't have hit me. I won't go back. It's better this way than hitting back," said Yankel, turning his face toward the house from which came the smell of freshly cooked borscht and fried pork. He started to walk away.

Fat Treineh, tired from the long walk, leaned against the log in which the ax was embedded and nervously rubbed her hands. Dvoireh, more alert, followed Yankel, grabbed his sleeve, and held on tenaciously. "Yankel, what are you doing? Remember God in your heart."

"This is the way I want it," he answered, lowering his head and again starting for the house.

"Do you know, at least, who sent me?"

"I know—Father."

"No, your mother sent me. Last night she spoke to me in a dream and asked me to tell you that someone has bewitched you."

"My mother?" Yankel trembled.

"She ordered me not to leave until you come home," Dvoireh answered, her eyes filling with tears.

"Your mother can't rest in her grave," cried out Treineh.

Yankel seemed to go limp. He could see his mother standing before him as if she were still alive, pleading with him in her tender voice to be good and obedient. Her image seemed to dissolve all his stubbornness and strength, for Yankel had always loved her; he had wanted to obey but had not been able to.

"Only for my mother's sake," he mumbled.

At this moment Sharomet's daughter, sixteen-year-old Safrona, tall, with delicate bare feet, called to Yankel from the house. "Come in to eat. The borscht is on the table." She noticed the two women with Yankel and stood staring at them.

"I'm not hungry. I won't eat today," he stammered in reply. Looking back at her forlornly, he slowly turned away and walked off with his two aunts.

It was dark when Dvoireh and Treineh brought Yankel home. The smaller children, followed by their dog, ran to embrace their older brother. The dog licked Yankel's hands and sprang to his face.

Leib stood motionless by the gate. "Look what's here. The bargain has turned up," he muttered angrily.

"Starting up again? Remember, only with kindness!" warned Dvoireh.

" 'Only with kindness,' " mimicked Leib. "You see how he's drawn to the forbidden? Would he mind marrying a *shiksah?* He'll persuade Sharomet to do me the honor of becoming my in-law. What happens to the living I don't care, but what does he have against his mother? Didn't she suffer enough for him in this world?"

Yankel stood patting the dog, venturing no reply, then entered the house. Near the door he washed his hands and face, then picked up a prayer book and began to recite the evening service. Huddled in a corner of the room, his prayers slowly turned to sobs, a stream of tears staining the worn, yellow pages of the book. He wept like a helpless child.

"All right, all right! Enough," implored Dvoireh. "If you can still pray with such a broken heart there's nothing to worry about. Reb Velvele, may he intercede for us in the world to come, used to say that with a broken heart one can unlock the gates of heaven. Enough now. Stop crying. It's a big cloud and a small rain."

Leib went into the house and also began to recite the evening prayers. Fat Treineh, known throughout the area as an accomplished cook, rolled up her sleeves and set about preparing dumplings with porridge, and onions fried in goose fat, in honor of Yankel's return.

The top of the oven glowed with a fiery redness, the pots began to sizzle, the house became warm and cheerful, and everyone grew talkative.

Dvoireh and Fat Treineh stayed for supper, and as the family assembled around the table Leib informed them that in the morning he and his brother Avrohom would ride over to see their rich brother Yosef.

"I want him to write out a steamship ticket to America for Yankel," Leib remarked casually. "A long time ago Yosef promised to do this for me through an American relative on his wife's side."

No one spoke. Yankel, who had just finished eating, began to perspire and stared vaguely ahead of him, foolishly clasping a spoon in one hand, oblivious of the dog licking his plate.

"As Uncle Avrohom says, he isn't the only one going there now. Of course I thought things would work out differently. But whether or not he prospers there, he can always come back." Leib spoke sadly, as if he were talking to himself, now and then glancing sideways at Yankel.

"With God's help he'll prosper," volunteered Dvoireh, "and he'll come home a rich man and laugh at all of us."

Yankel continued to sit in silence. With eyes half shut, he saw before him long trains, great ships, high towers with gleaming red roofs, a huge press of people from whose midst there suddenly appeared Safrona, whom Yankel had been secretly meeting since the summer. Suddenly he rose and started for the door. He stopped short, turned, and announced, "I'll leave as soon as the ticket arrives." Then he was gone.

During the months of waiting for the steamship ticket to arrive, Yankel thought much about far-off America. Winter passed, the warm days came, and Yankel grew stronger and sturdier. His long arms burst out of his sleeves, the seams of his coat gave way before his broadening frame. Strength lay written in his face, in his fiery eyes and shiny black crop of hair.

At dusk on the eve of the Feast of Pentecost, when the sun was sinking behind the hill, the steamship ticket arrived. Yankel, in bare feet and with his trousers rolled up to the knees, had just returned from the hayfields and was resting under a tree near the house. His two younger brothers were spreading out large bundles of vegetables in the yard. Boys and girls hurried by, carrying plants and flowers to the synagogue in honor of the holiday. Leib stood by the gate, greeting and conversing with Jews on their way to the brook to bathe for the holiday. The small group before Leib's house was soon joined by the village policeman, Pavliuk, who also served as village postman. In his best official manner Pavliuk lifted from his greasy leather bag an envelope covered with red and green stamps and presented it to Leib. Leib grew frightened; with feigned calmness he held the envelope up to the sun, scrutinized it sagely, and slowly opened it.

"A ticket for my Yankel," reported Leib to the curious bystanders.

"Why didn't you say so? Let us see."

"Did you ever hear of such a thing? You're not really sending him all the way to America?"

"And that's the whole ticket?"

"It looks just like a piece of paper, yet you can ride all around the world with it," they marveled excitedly. Everyone took the ticket in his hands and carefully examined it.

Bewildered by what he had overheard, Yankel remained hidden behind the tree, only moving a bit closer to listen to what the older men were saying.

"Oh, how times change! Who in the old days would send a child so far from home?"

"Still, you're doing the right thing. Breaking the blister just in time."

"In the world he'll become a man."

"He's got the strength of three and is willing to work. What's there to worry about? He won't get lost in America."

"After all, is he the only one? They're leaving Russia by the thousands. I can't imagine where they'll find room for all of them."

"You think it's like our Galicia? Why, America is so big that to this day they haven't measured it all!"

"After all, if people keep going there, it must be for a reason. The whole world can't be crazy," the Jews kept reassuring one another while Leib stood by, brooding in silence.

Yankel heard all the talk. Sitting behind the tree, drawing squares and circles in the soft ground with his big toe, he thought of that strange and distant country, America. When his father and the other men left for the brook, Yankel crept into the house and found the ticket lying on a shelf. He picked it up and held it in his hands. . . .

Impatiently Yankel counted the days still to be spent in Yanowitz. During the day he couldn't bear to stay home. During the night he and Safrona, together with other gentile boys and girls, would lie on blankets spread over the ground, breaking the stillness with their melancholy songs. Yankel sang with a deep strong voice, accompanied by Safrona's delicate soprano. They sang together through the night, and dispersed at daybreak. Riding home early in the morning, Yankel could still hear Safrona's voice, and when he lay down to sleep on the sleigh under the porch he could still see her pretty oval face and childish eyes.

The harvest season came, and for the last time Yankel helped his father gather in the crop. He worked zealously, but he could not forget that this was his last harvest at home. His mind kept returning to the two new shirts waiting for him in his bureau drawer and to the Hebrew calendar in which his day of departure had been underlined in ink.

Finally the day arrived. It was fall, and Leib had already plowed several acres for the winter wheat.

On his last day at home Yankel went to the cemetery to bid farewell to his mother. At the green mound that held his mother's grave he burst into tears. He lingered, thinking of her, recalling her kindness, her many efforts to protect him from his father's blows.

Toward evening Yankel returned home, heartsore and weary. Relatives, neighbors, Jewish and gentile, milled about him to say good-by. Repeatedly he was exhorted to become a man. He nodded his head mechanically, vacantly, hearing nothing but words. Fat Treineh invited him to sample some of the pastry she had baked for his journey, but he had no appetite.

In the evening, after everyone had left, Yankel slipped out of the house and like a sleepwalker slowly made his way across the yard. He wandered through the garden and reviewed the trees in the orchard, stopping before several small plum trees he himself had planted. I will be leaving at daybreak, he kept thinking. He looked up at the young trees, at the ripe blue plums huddling against one another like eggs in a nest. A plum suddenly tore itself away from its cluster and fell silently to the ground. The other plums began to tremble, as if they too wished to fall. But soon they became still again, nestling against one another as before. From the orchard Yankel passed to the stable, where he patted the horses, scratched the cows, and mutely said farewell.

He walked to the road and looked out over the darkened huts of the village, silently informing them that at dawn he would leave them. He felt a strong desire to go once more to see Safrona. He had said good-by to her the night before, but wanted now to see her again. He remembered his mother and did not go.

For his last night a bed was made for Yankel in the house, but as usual he went to his summer bed on the sleigh under the porch. He remained awake until after daybreak; the thought of leaving brought tears to his eyes. In what seemed but a moment since his eyes had closed, Yankel heard his father call, "Time to get up. We'll be late for the train."

Yankel left his bed and entered the house to dress. Leib started to get the wagon ready. Neighbors and relatives gathered at the gate, but Leib was in no mood to talk.

When the horse was hitched to the wagon, Yankel, with firm step, emerged from the house, wearing a new shirt, a new suit, and carrying a wooden valise. He climbed into the wagon and sat down on his luggage. The whole family was on hand to see him off, weeping loudly as they shouted their farewells.

"Be well, Yankel, and go with God's blessing!"

"Remain a Jew and put on the phylacteries every day!"

"Don't forget your home!"

"Remember to observe the day of your mother's death and to say *Kaddish* for her. She earned it."

"May you prosper and come home with lots of money, so you can buy a farm here and be everyone's equal!"

They continued shouting as the wagon began to move away. Dazed, Yankel barely managed a few lame replies.

"Here, it's for your trip!" called out Safrona, who suddenly appeared beside the moving wagon and threw a bundle of pears wrapped in a kerchief into Yankel's lap. Leib whipped up the horses vehemently and a thick cloud of dust rose from under the clattering wheels. Safrona's last words kept ringing in Yankel's ears.

Once past the village, when the horses were trotting up the hill slowly and the wagon was no longer creaking, Yankel, alone with his father, breathed more easily. He sensed that his father wished to speak.

"I'll have to sell this good-for-nothing nag," Leib said, half turning toward his son. "It gets lazier by the day. Did you ever hear of a horse that always wants to lie down?

"When you're traveling," Leib continued, "don't be afraid to ask questions. He who asks doesn't get lost. Look, there's a cloud behind the woods. It looks like rain today. Always remember that you've got a home. And if, God forbid, things don't go well, you always have someone to come back to. Be sure to ask. You hear?"

"I hear," answered Yankel.

"That cloud is coming closer. On the way home I'll fetch the buckwheat before it starts raining," Leib mused, turning his head toward Yankel, repeating again and again that one must not be ashamed to ask directions of strangers.

Yankel, seated glumly behind his father, muttered an occasional reply.

As they drew into the station they heard the shrill whistle of the train. The horses cocked their ears and, like Yankel himself, stared at the locomotive spouting thick balls of black smoke.

Leib pulled the horses to a halt, and Yankel got down from the wagon. He took his valise and walked toward the train, Leib following close behind. Near the train door they stopped and looked at each other helplessly. Leib flung his arms around his son and pressed him to his bosom; tears trickled down his rough cheek and onto his heavy black beard. Yankel squinted, bit his lower lip, and held himself taut. He turned quickly to step into the train, which had already begun to move. He seated himself by a window and looked out at his father, at the horse and wagon, which gradually became smaller and smaller; and then he could see them no longer.

Translated by Philip Rubin

Part Five

NEW WORLDS

A Quiet Garden Spot

SHOLEM ASCH

WHEN Little Shimmon died, his two sons, Notteh and Anshel, made a vow at his open grave never to forget their father or neglect their mother.

"Don't worry, Pa—we'll take good care of Mother!" Notteh, the elder son, shouted into the grave.

Hearing these words, Notteh's wife plucked up courage and called out to her dead father-in-law, "Be sure to put in a good word for my only child, your oldest grandson."

She had hardly finished her solemn entreaty when Anshel's wife broke in, "Why only for *her* child? Let him also intercede for his own children and his other grandchildren—"

"And not merely for his own, but for all other children—for the whole world, for all young men about to go into battle. For mercy's sake, may they be shielded in the hour of danger!" some unknown woman who happened to be in the cemetery shouted into the open grave.

Whether Little Shimmon would carry out these various requests was something nobody knew. But almost certainly he must have heard all the petitions, for when Notteh swore, "Don't worry, Pa—we'll take good care of Mother!" a slight smile seemed to hover over the lifeless lips and, to all appearances, his gray bristling mustache began to stir. Still smiling that smile, he was consigned to the earth. Yes, Little Shimmon must have remembered the repeated assurances of his well-to-do son: "Don't worry, Pa—we'll take good care of Mother!"

From his native town in Poland, Little Shimmon had brought a smile, a pair of gaunt hands, and a pair of scissors, as well as his wife Necheh—a gaunt but devoted helper—and his two sons. He had immediately plunged into work, without letup, wearing his fingers to the bone. Whenever he happened to be unemployed he grew depressed and listless and felt he was superfluous. The Sabbath and other holidays, when he had to abstain from work, he generally passed in a state of lassitude, longing to be at his trade, as though his needle and scissors had become part of his being and he could not endure being deprived of them for any length of time. True, on weekdays, while he was earning his bread by the sweat of his brow, he seemed to long for the Sabbath, when he would be able to rest his tired bones. But when the Sabbath actually came, and Little Shimmon had taken his balm of sleep, he went about twiddling his thumbs. He had no friends—no acquaintances even. He kept gazing at the sky in anticipation of that first star which for the orthodox Jew signifies the end of the Sabbath.

"Why do you stare at the sky like that? What's your hurry?" Necheh would ask.

"My fingers seem to be itching for the needle. It's been rather a long Sabbath."

Thus had Little Shimmon plodded through his whole life. His children had struck out for themselves at an early age, and he was left alone with his loyal, toilworn Necheh. They spent their evenings, summer and winter, in the kitchen. Hardly anyone peeped into their living room, though it was well furnished and even had framed pictures on the walls. Most of the time it was used as a bedroom. The kitchen came to be their living room, and there the elderly couple would spend hours around the stove in silence, broken only now and then when one of them would recall some forgotten friend in the old country.

"Do you remember Shmuel back home?" Shimmon would suddenly ask his wife.

"The one whose daughter ran away with a soldier?"

"Yes."

"What made you think of Shmuel?"

"Oh, nothing in particular."

Or one of them would recall from oblivion some dead-end street in their native village.

"Do you remember the little back street at home?"

"Where Aunt Brochah used to live?"

"Yes, where the small town pump stood, and on Sabbath afternoons people would come to draw fresh water."

"Yes. But why have you thought of that lane all of a sudden?"

"Why, I just happened to."

Once in a long while one of the sons, troubled by the memory of his parents, would drop in on them unexpectedly.

"Well, look who's here! Notteh himself. I couldn't be more surprised if the Messiah had come. Well, how have you been? And how are your wife and child?"

"They're all right."

"Perhaps you'll drink a glass of borscht? You always liked Mama's borscht."

"And you, Father—still working in the same factory in Brooklyn?"

"What else can I do? One has to earn a living."

"To tell you the truth," the mother would interpose, "he hasn't the strength to go to work any longer. He moans all through the night and complains of backache."

"Well, Father, don't worry—we'll look into the matter. I'll talk it over with Anshel. You won't have to struggle in your old age."

A slight smile hovered over Little Shimmon's face—the same strained smile that was to play on his lips when lying in his grave.

Six months more would roll by without a sight of either of their sons, who happened to live far from their parents. And if the old folks ever set out to visit their grandchildren they invariably lost their way.

"We'd better wait until Passover and then go down to see the grandchildren."

A half-year later the other son would drop in and remark, "Well, Father, still working in that clothing factory?"

"What else can one do? One has to earn a living. Mother has to be provided for."

"Don't worry—we'll make arrangements."

And the old folks were forgotten again, until one day the sons were informed that their father had died. He died as he had lived, unobtrusively; and soon he was forgotten. A single car, carrying his widow, his two sons and daughters-in-law, comprised the funeral procession. The sons had asked their father to intercede in the other world and in return had promised to make arrangements for their mother.

The bereaved Necheh stood weeping at the grave. She did not ask her departed mate for any favors but stared speechlessly at the gentile gravediggers as they shoveled earth upon Little Shimmon. After the Prayer for the Dead had been chanted and the little group of mourners had plodded off, the widow lingered for a moment with outstretched hands. And as her sons took hold of her arms and said, "Come along, Mother," she looked about her with bleak eyes, as stolid as the eyes of a dumb animal, and asked, "Where to?"

And as her sons led her out of the cemetery they comforted her, saying, "Don't worry, Mother. We'll take good care of you."

After the funeral the sons vied with each other for the honor of having their mother during the seven days of mourning. She went to stay with her elder son, Notteh, a salesman, who was more prosperous than Anshel. The following week she spent with her younger son. And thus she wandered back and forth like a nomad, staying now with one son, now with the other, until her benefactors decided to place her in a home for the aged. However, before her sons could carry out their decision, Necheh gave them both the slip and joined her husband in death.

As things fell out she could not be buried alongside her husband: the grave next to his now belonged to a stranger. Moreover, the rate in the section where her husband had been buried was far too expensive for so plain a woman as Necheh. And so she was buried in a remote and neglected part of the cemetery. Thus were the old folks parted in death: he was interred among strangers in one place, while she had to rest among strange women in another.

The two old folks who had been forgotten while still among the living were consigned to oblivion now that they had been gathered to their ancestors. Their graves soon became lost among the other graves, which had also been forgotten, save by the patch of sky and the little mound of earth over each.

They need no more, these graves. In the winter they were blanketed with heavy snowdrifts. But when the benign warm weather arrived and the sun removed their blankets of snow from the ground, the two graves also came to view, wind-sown with flowers and plants from the better-tended graves of the rich. During the day the sun warmed and stirred the blossoms into life; at night the rain helped to root them deeper in the soil, and the dew continued to nurture them. And the graves of Little Shimmon and his wife Necheh, though far apart, blossomed with the yellow of buttercups, the blue of irises, with white honeysuckle and black-eyed susans. The graves were transformed into serene and blooming garden spots, unwatched by anyone yet tended and guarded by the hand of nature.

Once in a great while Notteh and Anshel would meet by chance either on a crowded bus or at some public gathering.

"Hello, Notteh."

"Hello, Anshel."

"We ought to drop in on the old folks at the cemetery to see how they are getting along," one would remark.

"Yes, we ought to," the other would agree. "I could make it next

Sunday. We could meet at the Brooklyn bridge about noon, say. How about it?"

"All right, make it next Sunday. Don't forget!"

The brothers knew quite well that they would not meet—they had more urgent affairs to attend to. So the years went by, and the graves of their parents were concealed from human eyes, and blossomed unassumingly, like two quiet gardens.

Years later it came to pass that one of the brothers attended the funeral of a lodge brother—he would have been fined had he failed to appear—and his father's grave haunted his thoughts. He searched for a long time in the overgrown grass, and when at last he came upon the weather-beaten marker he was awe-struck and amazed: who had planted such a garden on his father's grave?

And he never knew that the gentle wind and good mother earth, at least, had not forgotten the little tailor.

Translated by Moishe Spiegel

The Little Shoemakers

I. BASHEVIS SINGER

1. THE SHOEMAKERS AND THEIR FAMILY TREE

THE FAMILY of the little shoemakers was famous not only in Frampol but in the outlying district—in Yonev, Kreshev, Bilgoray, and even in Zamoshoh. Abba Shuster, the founder of the line, appeared in Frampol some time after Chmielnitzki's pogroms. He bought himself a plot of ground on the stubby hill behind the butcher stalls, and there he built a house that remained standing until just the other day. Not that it was in such fine condition—the stone foundation settled, the small windows warped, and the shingled roof turned a moldy green and was hung with swallows' nests. The door, moreover, sank into the ground, the banisters became bowlegged, and instead of stepping up onto the threshold one was obliged to step down. All the same, it did survive the innumerable fires that devastated Frampol in the early days. But the rafters were so rotten that mushrooms grew on them, and when wood dust was needed to staunch the blood of a circumcision, one had only to break off a piece of the outer wall and rub it between one's fingers. The roof, pitched so steeply that the chimneysweep was unable to climb onto it to look after the chimney, was always catching fire from the sparks. It was only by the grace of God that the house was not overtaken by disaster.

The name of Abba Shuster is recorded, on parchment, in the annals of the Frampol Jewish community. It was his custom to make six pairs of shoes every year for distribution among widows and orphans; in recognition of his philanthropy the synagogue called him to the reading of the Torah under the honorific title, *Murenu,* meaning "our teacher."

His stone in the old cemetery had vanished, but the shoemakers knew a sign for the grave—nearby grew a hazelnut tree. According to the old wives, the tree sprang from Reb Abba's beard.

Reb Abba had five sons; they settled, all but one, in neighboring towns; only Getzel remained in Frampol. He continued his father's charitable practice of making shoes for the poor, and he too was active in the gravediggers' brotherhood.

The annals go on to say that Getzel had a son, Godel, and that to Godel was born Treitel, and to Treitel, Gimpel. The shoemaker's art was handed down from one generation to the next. A principle was fast established in the family, requiring the eldest son to remain at home and succeed his father at the workbench.

The shoemakers resembled one another. They were all short, sandy-haired, and sound, honest workmen. The people of Frampol believed that Reb Abba, the head of the line, had learned shoemaking from a master of the craft in Brod, who divulged to him the secret of strengthening leather and making it durable. In the cellar of their house the little shoemakers kept a vat for soaking hides. God knows what strange chemicals they added to the tanning fluid. They did not disclose the formula to outsiders, and it was handed on from father to son.

As it is not our business to deal with all the generations of the little shoemakers, we will confine ourselves to the last three. Reb Lippe remained without heir till his old age, and it was taken for a certainty that the line would end with him. But when he was in his late sixties his wife died and he married an overripe virgin, a milkmaid, who bore him six children. The eldest son, Feivel, was quite well to do. He was prominent in community affairs, attended all the important meetings, and for years served as sexton of the tailors' synagogue. It was the custom in this synagogue to select a new sexton every *Simchath Torah.* The man so selected was honored by having a pumpkin placed on his head; the pumpkin was set with lighted candles, and the lucky fellow was led about from house to house and refreshed at each stop with wine and strudel or honeycakes. However, Reb Feivel happened to die on *Simchath Torah,* the day of rejoicing over the Law, while dutifully making these rounds; he fell flat in the market place, and there was no reviving him. Because Feivel had been a notable philanthropist, the rabbi who conducted his services declared that the candles he had borne on his head would light his way to Paradise. The will found in his strongbox requested that when he was carried to the cemetery, a hammer, an awl, and a last should be laid on the black cloth over his coffin, in sign of the fact that he was a man of peaceful industry who never cheated his customers. His will was done.

Feivel's eldest son was called Abba, after the founder. Like the rest of his stock, he was short and thickset, with a broad yellow beard, and a high forehead lined with wrinkles, such as only rabbis and shoemakers have. His eyes were also yellow, and the over-all impression he created was that of a sulky hen. Nevertheless he was a clever workman, charitable like his forebears, and unequaled in Frampol as a man of his word. He would never make a promise unless he was sure he could fulfill it; when he was not sure he said, who knows, God willing, or maybe. Furthermore he was a man of some learning. Every day he read a chapter of the Torah in Yiddish translation and occupied his free time with chapbooks. Abba never missed a single sermon of the traveling preachers who came to town, and he was especially fond of the Biblical passages which were read in the synagogue during the winter months. When his wife, Pesha, read to him, of a Sabbath, from the Yiddish translation of the stories in the Book of Genesis, he would imagine that he was Noah, and that his sons were Shem, Ham, and Japheth. Or else he would see himself in the image of Abraham, Isaac, or Jacob. He often thought that if the Almighty were to call on him to sacrifice his eldest son, Gimpel, he would rise early in the morning and carry out his commands without delay. Certainly he would have left Poland and the house of his birth and gone wandering over the earth where God sent him. He knew the story of Joseph and his brothers by heart, but he never tired of reading it over again. He envied the ancients because the King of the Universe revealed Himself to them and performed miracles for their sake, but consoled himself by thinking that from him, Abba, to the Patriarchs, there stretched an unbroken chain of generations—as if he too were part of the Bible. He sprang from Jacob's loins, he and his sons were of the seed whose number had become like the sand and the stars. He was living in exile because the Jews of the Holy Land had sinned, but he awaited the Redemption, and he would be ready when the time came.

Abba was by far the best shoemaker in Frampol. His boots were always a perfect fit, never too tight or too roomy. People who suffered from chilblains, corns, or varicose veins were especially pleased with his work, claiming that his shoes relieved them. He despised the new styles, the gimcrack boots and slippers with fancy heels and poorly stitched soles that fell apart with the first rain. His customers were respectable burghers of Frampol or peasants from the surrounding villages, and they deserved the best. He took their measurements with a knotted string, as in the old days. Most of the Frampol women wore wigs, but his wife, Pesha, covered her head with a bonnet as well. She bore him seven sons, and he named them after his forefathers—Gimpel, Getzel, Treitel, Godel, Feivel, Lippe, and Chananiah. They were all short and sandy-haired like their father. Abba predicted that he would turn them into shoemakers, and as a man of his word he let them look on at the workbench while they were still quite young, and at times taught them the old maxim—good work is never wasted.

He spent sixteen hours a day at the bench, a sack spread on his knees, gouging holes with the awl, sewing with a wire needle, tinting and polishing the leather or scraping it with a piece of glass; and while he worked he hummed snatches from the canticles of the Days of Awe. Usually the cat huddled nearby and watched the proceedings as though she were looking after him. Her mother and grandmother had caught mice, in their time, for the little shoemakers. Abba could look down the hill through the window and see the whole town and a considerable distance beyond, as far as the road to Bilgoray and the pine woods. He observed the groups of matrons who gathered every morning at the butcher stalls and the young men and idlers who went in and out of the courtyard of the synagogue; the girls going to the pump to draw water for tea, and the women hurrying at dusk to the ritual bath.

Evenings, when the sun was setting, the house would be pervaded by a dusky glow. Rays of light danced in the corners, flicked across the ceiling, and set Abba's beard gleaming with the color of spun gold. Pesha, Abba's wife, would be cooking *kasha* and soup in the kitchen, the children would be playing, neighboring women and girls would go in and out of the house. Abba would rise from his work, wash his hands, put on his long coat, and go off to the tailors' synagogue for evening prayers. He knew that the wide world was full of strange cities and distant lands, that Frampol was actually no bigger than a dot in a small prayer book; but it seemed to him that his little town was the navel of the universe and that his own house stood at the very center. He often thought that when the Messiah came to lead the Jews to the Land of Israel, he, Abba, would stay behind in Frampol, in his own house, on his own hill. Only on the Sabbath and on Holy Days would he step into a cloud and let himself be flown to Jerusalem.

2. ABBA AND HIS SEVEN SONS

Since Gimpel was the eldest, and therefore destined to succeed his father, he came foremost in Abba's concern. He sent him to the best Hebrew teachers and even hired a tutor who taught him the elements of Yiddish, Polish, Russian, and arithmetic. Abba himself led the boy down into the cellar and showed him the formula for adding chemicals and various kinds of bark to the tanning fluid. He revealed to him that in most cases the right foot is larger than the left, and that the source of all trouble in the fitting of shoes is usually to be found in the big toes. Then he taught Gimpel the principles for cutting soles and inner soles, snub-toed and pointed shoes, high heels and low; and for fitting customers with flat feet, bunions, hammer toes, and calluses.

On Fridays, when there was always a rush of work to get out, the older boys would leave *cheder* at ten in the morning and help their father in the shop. Pesha baked *chalah* and prepared their lunch. She would grasp the first loaf and carry it, hot from the oven, blowing on it all the while and tossing it from hand to hand, to show it to Abba, holding it up, front and back, till he nodded approval. Then she would return with a ladle and let him sample the fish soup, or ask him to taste a crumb of freshly baked cake. Pesha valued his judgment. When she went to buy cloth for herself or the children she brought home swatches for him to choose. Even before going to the butcher she asked his opinion—what should she get, breast or roast, flank or ribs? She consulted him not out of fear or because she had no mind of her own, but simply because she had learned that he always knew what he was talking about. Even when she was sure he was wrong, he would turn out to be right, after all. He never browbeat her, but merely cast a glance to let her know when she was being a fool. This was also the way he handled the children. A strap hung on the wall, but he seldom made use of it; he had his way by kindness. Even strangers respected him. The merchants sold him hides at a fair price and presented no objections when he asked for credit. His own customers trusted him and paid his prices without a murmur. He was always called sixth to the reading of the Torah in the tailors' synagogue—a considerable honor—and when he pledged or was assessed for money, it was never necessary to remind him. He paid up, without fail, right after the Sabbath. The town soon learned of his virtues, and though he was nothing but a plain shoemaker and, if the truth be told, something of an ignoramus, they treated him as they would a distinguished man.

When Gimpel turned thirteen, Abba girded the boy's loins in sackcloth and put him to work at the bench. After Gimpel, Getzel, Treitel, Godel, and Feivel became apprentices. Though they were his own sons and he supported them out of his earnings, he nevertheless paid them a wage. The two youngest boys, Lippe and Chananiah, were still attending the elementary *cheder,* but they too lent a hand at hammering pegs. Abba and Pesha were proud of them. In the morning the six workers trooped into the kitchen for breakfast, washed their six pairs of hands with the appropriate benediction, and their six mouths chewed the roasted groats and corn bread.

Abba loved to place his two youngest boys one on each knee, and sing an old Frampol song to them:

A mother had
Ten little boys,
Oh, Lord, ten little boys!

The first one was Avremele,
The second one was Berele,
The third one was called Gimpele,
The fourth one was called Dovid'l,
The fifth one was called Hershele . . .

And all the boys came in on the chorus:

Oh, Lord, Hershele!

Now that he had apprentices, Abba turned out more work, and his income grew. Living was cheap in Frampol, and since the peasants often made him a present of a measure of corn or a roll of butter, a sack of potatoes or a pot of honey, a hen or a goose, he was able to save some money on food. As their prosperity increased, Pesha began to talk of rebuilding the house. The rooms were too narrow, the ceiling was too low. The floor shook underfoot. Plaster was peeling off the walls, and all sorts of maggots and worms crawled through the woodwork. They lived in constant fear that the ceiling would fall on their heads. Even though they kept a cat, the place was infested with mice. Pesha insisted that they tear down this ruin and build a larger house.

Abba did not immediately say no. He told his wife he would think it over. But after doing so, he expressed the opinion that he would rather keep things as they were. First of all, he was afraid to tear down the house, because this might bring bad luck. Second, he feared the evil eye—people were grudging and envious enough. Third, he found it hard to part with the home in which his parents and grandparents, and the whole family, stretching back for generations, had lived and died. He knew every corner of the house, each crack and wrinkle. When one layer of paint peeled off the wall, another, of a different color, was exposed; and behind this layer, still another. The walls were like an album in which the fortunes of the family had been recorded. The attic was stuffed with heirlooms—tables and chairs, cobbler's benches and lasts, whetstones and knives, old clothes, pots, pans, bedding, salting boards, cradles. Sacks full of torn prayer books lay spilled on the floor.

Abba loved to climb up to the attic on a hot summer's day. Spiders spun great webs, and the sunlight, filtering in through cracks, fell upon the threads in rainbows. Everything lay under a thick coat of dust. When he listened attentively he would hear a whispering, a murmuring and soft scratching, as of some unseen creature engaged in endless activity, conversing in an unearthly tongue. He was sure that the souls of his forefathers kept watch over the house. In much the same way he loved the ground on which it stood. The weeds were as high as a man's head. There was a dense growth of hairy and brambly vegetation all about the place—the very leaves and twigs would catch hold of one's clothing as though with teeth and claws. Flies and midges swarmed in the air and the ground crawled with worms and snakes of all descriptions. Ants had raised their hills in this thicket, field mice had dug their holes. A pear tree grew in the midst of this wilderness; every year, at the time of the Feast of the Tabernacle, it yielded small fruit with the taste and hardness of wood. Birds and bees flew over this jungle, great big golden-bellied flies. Toadstools sprang up after each rain. The ground was unkept, but an unseen hand guarded its fertility.

When Abba stood here, looking up at the summer sky, losing himself in contemplation of the clouds, shaped like sailboats, flocks of sheep, brooms, and elephant herds, he felt the presence of God, His providence and His mercy. He could virtually see the Almighty seated on His throne of glory, the earth serving Him as a footstool. Satan was vanquished, the angels sang hymns. The Book of Memory in which were recorded all the deeds of men lay open. From time to time, at sunset, it even seemed to Abba that he saw the river of fire in the nether world. Flames leaped up from the burning coals, a wave of fire rose, flooding the shores. When he listened closely he was sure he heard the muffled cries of sinners and the derisive laughter of the evil host.

No, this was good enough for Abba Shuster. There was nothing to change. Let everything stand as it had stood for ages, until he lived out his allotted time and was buried in the cemetery among his ancestors, who had shod the sacred community and whose good name was preserved not only in Frampol but in the surrounding district.

3. GIMPEL EMIGRATES TO AMERICA

Therefore the proverb says: Man proposes, God disposes.

One day, while Abba was working on a boot, his eldest son, Gimpel, came into the shop. His freckled face was heated, his sandy hair disheveled under the skullcap. Instead of taking his place at the bench, he stopped at his father's side, regarded him hesitantly, and at last said, "Father, I must tell you something."

"Well, I'm not stopping you," replied Abba.

"Father," he cried, "I'm going to America."

Abba dropped his work. This was the last thing he expected to hear, and up went his eyebrows.

"What happened? Did you rob someone? Did you get into a fight?"

"No, Father."

"Then why are you running away?"

"There's no future for me in Frampol."

"Why not? You know a trade. God willing, you'll marry some day. You have everything to look forward to."

"I'm sick of small towns, I'm sick of the people. This is nothing but a stinking swamp."

"When they get around to draining it," said Abba, "there won't be any more swamp."

"No, Father, that's not what I mean."

"Then what do you mean?" cried Abba angrily. "Speak up!"

The boy spoke up, but Abba couldn't understand a word of it. He laid into synagogue and state with such venom, Abba could only imagine that the poor soul was possessed: the Hebrew teachers beat the children, the women empty their slop pails right outside the door, the shopkeepers loiter in the streets, there are no toilets anywhere and the public relieves itself as it pleases, behind the bathhouse or out in the open, encouraging epidemics and plagues. He made fun of Ezreal the healer and of Mecheles the marriage broker, nor did he spare the rabbinical court and the bath attendant, the washerwoman and the overseer of the poorhouse, the professions and the benevolent societies.

At first Abba was afraid that the boy had lost his mind, but the longer he continued his harangue, the clearer it became that he had strayed from the path of righteousness. Jacob Reifman, the atheist, used to hold forth in Shebreshin, not far from Frampol. A pupil of his, a detractor of Israel, was in the habit of visiting an aunt in Frampol and had gathered quite a following among the good-for-nothings. It had never occurred to Abba that his Gimpel might fall in with this gang.

"What do you say, Father?" asked Gimpel.

Abba thought it over. He knew that there was no use arguing with Gimpel, and he remembered the proverb: A rotten apple spoils the barrel. "Well," he replied, "what can I do? If you want to go, go. I won't stop you."

And he resumed his work.

But Pesha did not give in so easily. She begged Gimpel not to go so far away; she wept and implored him not to bring shame on the family. She even ran to the cemetery, to the graves of her forefathers, to seek the intercession of the dead. But she was finally convinced that Abba was right: it was no use arguing. Gimpel's face had turned hard as leather, and a mean light showed in his yellow eyes. He had become a stranger in his own home. He spent that night out with friends, and returned in the morning to pack his prayer shawl and phylacteries, a few shirts, a blanket, and some hard-boiled eggs—and he was all set to go. He had saved enough money for passage. When his mother saw that it was settled, she urged him to take at least a jar of preserves, a bottle of cherry juice, bedding, pillows. But Gimpel refused. He was going to steal over the border into Germany, and he stood a better chance if he traveled light. In short, he kissed his mother, said good-by to his brothers and friends, and off he went. Abba, not wanting to part with his son in anger, took him in the wagon to the station at Reivetz. The train arrived in the middle of the night with a hissing and whistling, a racket and din. Abba took the headlights of the locomotive for the eyes of a hideous devil and shied away from the funnels with their columns of sparks and smoke and their clouds of steam. The blinding lights only intensified the darkness. Gimpel ran around with his baggage like a madman, and his father ran after him. At the last moment the boy kissed his father's hand, and Abba called after him, into the darkness, "Good luck! Don't forsake your religion!"

The train pulled out, leaving a smell of smoke in Abba's nostrils and a ringing in his ears. The earth trembled under his feet. As though the boy had been dragged off by demons! When he returned home and Pesha fell on him, weeping, he said to her, "The Lord gave and the Lord has taken away. . . ."

Months passed without word from Gimpel. Abba knew that this was the way with young men when they leave home—they forget their dearest ones. As the proverb says: Out of sight, out of mind. He doubted that he would ever hear from him, but one day a letter came from America. Abba recognized his son's handwriting. Gimpel wrote that he crossed the border safely, that he saw many strange cities and spent four weeks on board ship, living on potatoes and herring because he did not want to touch improper food. The ocean was very deep and the waves as high as the sky. He saw flying fish but no mermaids or mermen, and he did not hear them singing. New York is a big city, the houses reach into the clouds. The trains go over the roofs. The gentiles speak English. No one walks with his eyes on the ground, everybody holds his head high. He met a lot of his countrymen in New York; they all wear short coats. He too. The trade he learned at home has come in very handy. He is *all right,* he is earning a living. He will write again, a long letter. He kisses his father and mother and his brothers and sends regards to his friends.

A friendly letter after all.

In his second letter Gimpel announced that he had fallen in love with a girl and bought her a diamond ring. Her name is Bessie, she comes from Rumania, and she works *at dresses*. Abba put on his spectacles with the brass frames and spent a long time puzzling this out. Where did the boy learn so many English words? The third letter stated that he was married and that *a reverend* had performed the service. He inclosed a snapshot of himself and wife.

Abba could not believe it. His son was wearing a gentleman's coat and a high hat. The bride was dressed like a countess in a white dress, with train and veil; she held a bouquet of flowers in her hand. Pesha took one look at the snapshot and began to cry. Gimpel's brothers gaped. Neighbors came running, and friends from all over town—they could have sworn that Gimpel had been spirited away by magic to a land of gold, where he had taken a princess to wife—just as in the storybooks the pack merchants brought to town.

To make a long story short, Gimpel induced Getzel to come to America, and Getzel brought over Treitel; Godel followed Treitel, and Feivel, Godel—and then all five brothers brought the young Lippe and Chananiah across. Pesha lived only for the mail. She fastened a charity box to the doorpost, and whenever a letter came she dropped a coin through the slot. Abba worked all alone. He no longer needed apprentices because he now had few expenses and could afford to earn less; in fact, he could have given up work altogether, as his sons sent him money from abroad. Nevertheless he rose at his usual early hour and remained at the bench until late in the evening. His hammer sounded away, joined by the cricket on the hearth, the mouse in its hole, the shingles crackling on the roof. But his mind reeled. For generations the little shoemakers had lived in Frampol. Suddenly the birds had flown the coop. Was this a punishment, a judgment, on him? Did it make sense?

Abba bored a hole, stuck in a peg, and murmured, "So—you, Abba, know what you're doing and God does not? Shame on you, fool! His will be done. Amen!"

4. THE SACK OF FRAMPOL

Almost forty years went by. Pesha had long since died of cholera, during the Austrian occupation. And Abba's sons had grown rich in America. They wrote every week, begging him to come and join them, but he remained in Frampol, in the same old house on the stubby hill. His own grave lay ready, next to Pesha's, among the little shoemakers;

the stone had already been raised; only the date was missing. Abba put up a bench by the side of her grave and on the eve of Rosh Hashonoh or during fasts he went there to pray and read Lamentations. He loved it in the cemetery. The sky was so much clearer and loftier than in town, and a great, meaningful silence rose from the consecrated ground and the old gravestone overgrown with moss. He loved to sit and look at the tall white birches, which trembled even when no breeze blew, and at the crows balancing in the branches, like black fruit. Before she died Pesha made him promise that he would not remarry and that he would come regularly to her grave with news of the children. He kept his promise. He would stretch out alongside the mound and whisper into her ear, as if she were still alive, "Gimpel has another grandchild. Getzel's youngest daughter is engaged, thank God. . . ."

The house on the hill was nearly in ruins. The beams had rotted away, and the roof had to be supported by stone posts. Two of the three windows were boarded over because it was no longer possible to fit glass to the frames. The floor was all but gone, and the bare ground lay exposed to the feet. The pear tree in the garden had withered, the trunk and branches were covered with scales. The garden itself was now overgrown with poisonous berries and grapes, and there was a profusion of the burrs that children throw about on *Tishe b'Av*. People swore they saw strange fires burning there at night, and claimed that the attic was full of bats which fly into girls' hair. Be that as it may, an owl certainly did hoot somewhere near the house. The neighbors repeatedly warned Abba to move out of this ruin before it was too late, the least wind might knock it over. They pleaded with him to give up working—his sons were showering him with money. But Abba stubbornly rose at dawn and continued at the shoemaker's bench. Although yellow hair does not readily change color, Abba's beard had turned completely white, and the white, staining, had turned yellow again. His brows had sprouted like brushes and hid his eyes, and his high forehead was like a piece of yellow parchment. But he had not lost his touch. He could still turn out a stout shoe with a broad heel, even if it did take a little longer. He bored holes with the awl, stitched with the needle, hammered his pegs, and in a hoarse voice sang the old shoemaker's song:

"A mother bought a billygoat,
The *shochet* killed the billygoat,
Oh, Lord, the billygoat!

Avremele took its ears,
Berele took its lung,
Gimpele took the gullet,
And Dovid'l took the tongue,
Hershele took the neck . . ."

As there was no one to join him, he now sang the chorus alone:

"Oh, Lord, the billygoat!"

His friends urged him to hire a servant, but he would not take a strange woman into the house. Occasionally one of the neighbor women came in to sweep and dust, but even this was too much for him. He got used to being alone. He learned to cook for himself and would prepare soup on the tripod, and on Fridays even put up the pudding for the Sabbath. Best of all, he liked to sit alone at the bench and follow the course of his thoughts, which had become more and more tangled with the years. Day and night he carried on conversations with himself. One voice asked questions, the other answered. Clever words came to his mind, sharp, timely expressions full of the wisdom of age, as though his grandfathers had come to life again and were conducting their endless disputations inside his head on matters pertaining to this world and the next. All his thoughts ran on one theme: What is life and what is death, what is time that goes on without stopping, and how far away is America? His eyes would close, the hammer would fall out of his hand, but he would still hear the cobbler's characteristic rapping—a soft tap, a louder one, and a third, louder still—as if a ghost sat at his side, mending unseen shoes. When one of the neighbors asked him why he did not go to join his sons he would point to the heap on the bench and say, "*Nu,* and the shoes? Who will mend them?"

Years passed, and he had no idea how or where they vanished. Traveling preachers passed through Frampol with disturbing news of the outside world. In the tailors' synagogue, which Abba still attended, the young men spoke of war and anti-Semitic decrees, of Jews flocking to Palestine. Peasants who had been Abba's customers for years suddenly deserted him and took their trade to Polish shoemakers. And one day the old man heard that a new world war was imminent. Hitler—may his name vanish!—had raised his legions of barbarians and was threatening to grab up Poland. This scourge of Israel had expelled the Jews from Germany, as in the days of Spain. The old man thought of the Messiah and became terribly excited. Who knows? Perhaps this was the battle of Gog and Magog? Maybe the Messiah really was coming and the dead would rise again! He saw the graves opening and the little shoemakers stepping forth—Abba, Getzel, Treitel, Gimpel, his grandfather, his own father. He called them all into his house and set out brandy and cakes. His wife, Pesha, was ashamed to find the house in such condition, but "Never mind," he assured her, "we'll get someone to sweep up. As long as we're all together!" Suddenly a cloud appears, envelops the town of Frampol—synagogue, House of Study, ritual bath, all the Jewish homes, his own among them—and carries the whole settlement off to the Holy Land. Imagine his amazement when he encounters his sons from America. They fall at his feet, crying, "Forgive us, Father!"

When Abba pictured this event his hammer quickened in tempo. He saw the little shoemakers dress for the Sabbath in silks and satins, in flowing robes with broad sashes, and go forth rejoicing in Jerusalem. They pray in the Temple of Solomon, drink the wine of Paradise, and eat of the mighty steer and Leviathan. The ancient Jochanan the Shoemaker, renowned for his piety and wisdom, greets the family and engages them in a discussion of Torah and shoemaking. Sabbath over, the whole clan returns to Frampol, which has become part of the Land of Israel, and re-enters the old home. Even though the house is as small as ever, it has miraculously grown roomy enough, like the hide of a deer, as it is written in the Book. They all work at one bench, Abbas, Gimpels, Getzels, Godels, the Treitels and the Lippes, sewing golden sandals for the daughters of Zion and lordly boots for the sons. The Messiah himself calls on the little shoemakers and has them take his measure for a pair of silken slippers.

One morning, while Abba was wandering among his thoughts, he heard a tremendous crash. The old man shook in his bones: the blast of the Messiah's trumpet! He dropped the boot he had been working on and ran out in ecstasy. But it was not Elijah the Prophet proclaiming the Messiah. Nazi planes were bombing Frampol. Panic spread through the town. A bomb fell near the synagogue, so loud that Abba felt his brain shudder in his skull. Hell opened before him. There was a blaze of lightning, followed by a blast that illuminated all of Frampol. A black cloud rose over the courtyard of the synagogue. Flocks of birds flapped about in the sky. The forest was burning. Looking down from his hill, Abba saw the orchards under great columns of smoke. The apple trees were blossoming and burning. Several men who stood near him threw themselves down on the ground and shouted to him to do the same. He did not hear them; they were moving their lips in dumbshow. Shaking with fright, his knees knocking together, he re-entered the house and packed a sack with his prayer shawl and phylacteries, a shirt, his shoemaker's tools, and the paper money he had put away in the straw mattress. Then he took up a stick, kissed the *mezzuzah,* and walked out the door. It was a miracle that he was not killed; the house caught fire the moment he left. The roof swung out like a lid, uncovering the attic with its treasures. The walls collapsed. Abba turned about and saw the shelf of sacred books go up in flames. The blackened pages turned in the air, glowing with fiery letters like the Torah given to the Jews on Mount Sinai.

5. ACROSS THE OCEAN

From that day on, Abba's life was transformed beyond recognition—it was like a story he had read in the Bible, a fantastic tale heard from the lips of a visiting preacher. He had abandoned the house of his forefathers and the place of his birth and, staff in hand, gone wandering into the world like the Patriarch Abraham. The havoc in Frampol and the surrounding villages brought Sodom and Gomorrah to mind, burning like a fiery furnace. He spent his nights in the cemetery together with the other Jews, lying with his head on a gravestone—he too, as Jacob did at Beth-El, on the way from Beer Sheba to Haran.

On Rosh Hashonoh the Frampol Jews held services in the forest, with Abba leading the most solemn prayer of the Eighteen Benedictions because he was the only one with a prayer shawl. He stood under a pine tree, which served as an altar, and in a hoarse voice intoned the litany of the Days of Awe. A cuckoo and a woodpecker accompanied him, and all the birds roundabout twittered, whistled, and screeched. Late summer gossamers wafted through the air and trailed onto Abba's beard. From time to time a lowing sounded through the forest, like a blast on the ram's horn. As the Day of Atonement drew near, the Jews of Frampol rose at midnight to say the prayer for forgiveness, reciting it in fragments, whatever they could remember. The horses in the surrounding pastures whinnied and neighed, frogs croaked in the cool night. Distant gunfire sounded intermittently, the clouds shone red. Meteors fell, flashes of lightning played across the sky. Half-starved little children, exhausted from crying, took sick and died in their mothers' arms. There were many burials in the open fields. A woman gave birth.

Abba felt he had become his own great-great-grandfather, who had fled Chmielnitzki's pogroms, and whose name is recorded in the annals of Frampol. He was ready to offer himself in Sanctification of the Name. He dreamed of priests and Inquisitions, and when the wind blew among the branches he heard martyred Jews crying out, "Hear, O Israel, the Lord our God, the Lord is One!"

Fortunately Abba was able to help a good many Jews with his money and shoemaker's tools. With the money they hired wagons and fled south, toward Rumania; but often they had to walk long distances and their shoes gave out. Abba would stop under a tree and take up his tools. With God's help, they surmounted danger and crossed the Rumanian frontier at night. The next morning, the day before Yom Kippur, an old widow took Abba into her house. A telegram was sent to Abba's sons in America, informing them that their father was safe.

You may be sure that Abba's sons moved heaven and earth to rescue the old man. When they learned of his whereabouts they ran to Washington and with great difficulty obtained a visa for him; then they wired a sum of money to the consul in Bucharest, begging him to help their father. The consul sent a courier to Abba and he was put on the train to Bucharest. There he was held a week, then transferred to an Italian seaport, where he was shorn and deloused and had his clothes steamed. He was put on board the last ship for the United States.

It was a long and severe journey. The train from Rumania to Italy dragged on, uphill and down, for thirty-six hours. He was given food, but for fear of touching anything ritually unclean he ate nothing at all. His phylacteries and prayer shawl got lost, and with them he lost all track of time and could no longer distinguish between Sabbath and weekdays. Apparently he was the only Jewish passenger on board. There was a man on the ship who spoke German, but Abba could not understand him.

It was a stormy crossing. Abba spent almost the whole time lying down, and frequently vomited gall, though he took nothing but dry crusts and water. He would doze off and wake to the sound of the engines throbbing day and night, to the long, threatening signal blasts, which reeked of fire and brimstone. The door of his cabin was constantly slamming to and fro, as though an imp were swinging on it.

The glassware in the cupboard trembled and danced, the walls shook, the deck rocked like a cradle.

During the day Abba kept watch at the porthole over his bunk. The ship would leap up as if mounting the sky, and the torn sky would fall as though the world were returning to original chaos. Then the ship would plunge back into the ocean, and once again the firmament would be divided from the waters, as in the Book of Genesis. The waves were a sulphurous yellow and black. Now they would saw-tooth out to the horizon like a mountain range, reminding Abba of the Psalmist's words: "The mountains skipped like rams, the little hills like lambs." Then they would come heaving back, as in the miraculous Parting of the Waters. Abba had little learning, but Biblical references ran through his mind, and he saw himself as the Prophet Jonah, who fled before God. He too lay in the belly of a whale and, like Jonah, prayed to God for deliverance. Then it would seem to him that this was not ocean but limitless desert, crawling with serpents, monsters, and dragons, as it is written in Deuteronomy. He hardly slept a wink at night. When he got up to relieve himself, he would feel faint and lose his balance. With great difficulty he would regain his feet and, his knees buckling under, go wandering, lost, down the narrow, winding corridor, groaning and calling for help until a sailor led him back to the cabin. Whenever this happened he was sure that he was dying. He would not even receive decent Jewish burial but be dumped in the ocean. And he made his confession, beating his knotty fist on his chest and exclaiming, "Forgive me, Father!"

Just as he was unable to remember when he began his voyage, so he was unaware when it came to an end. The ship had already been made fast to the dock in New York harbor, but Abba hadn't the vaguest notion of this. He saw huge buildings and towers, but mistook them for the pyramids of Egypt. A tall man in a white hat came into the cabin and shouted something at him, but he remained motionless. At last they helped him dress and led him out on deck, where his sons and daughters-in-law and grandchildren were waiting. Abba was bewildered: a crowd of Polish landowners, counts and countesses, gentile boys and girls, leaped at him, hugged him, and kissed him, crying out in a strange language, which was both Yiddish and not Yiddish. They half led, half carried him away and placed him in a car. Other cars arrived, packed with Abba's kinfolk, and they set out, speeding like shot arrows over bridges, rivers, and roofs. Buildings rose up and receded, as if by magic, some of the buildings touching the sky. Whole cities lay spread out before him; Abba thought of Pithom and Rameses. The car sped so fast, it seemed to him the people in the streets were moving backward. The air was full of thunder and lightning, a banging and trumpeting, it was a wedding and a conflagration at once. The nations had gone wild, a heathen festival. . . .

His sons were crowding around him. He saw them as in a fog and did not know them. Short men with white hair. They shouted, as if he were deaf.

"I'm Gimpel!"

"Getzel!"

"Feivel!"

The old man closed his eyes and made no answer. Their voices ran together, everything was turning pell-mell, topsy-turvy. Suddenly he thought of Jacob arriving in Egypt, where he was met by Pharaoh's chariots. He felt he had lived through the same experience in a previous incarnation. His beard began to tremble, a hoarse sob rose from his chest. A forgotten passage from the Bible stuck in his gullet.

Blindly he embraced one of his sons and sobbed out, "Is this you? Alive?"

He had meant to say: "Now let me die, since I have seen thy face, because thou art yet alive."

6. THE AMERICAN HERITAGE

Abba's sons lived on the outskirts of a town in New Jersey. Their seven homes, surrounded by gardens, stood on the shore of a lake. Every day they drove to the shoe factory, owned by Gimpel, but on the day of Abba's arrival they took a holiday and prepared a feast in his honor. It was to be held in Gimpel's house, in full compliance with the dietary laws; the meat was kosher, and a completely new set of dishes and utensils had been provided to prevent the least infraction of these laws. Gimpel's wife, Bessie, whose father had been a Hebrew teacher in the old country, remembered all the rituals and observed them carefully, going so far as to cover her head with a kerchief. Her sisters-in-law did the same, and Abba's sons put on the skullcaps they had once worn during Holy Days. The grandchildren and great-grandchildren, who did not know a word of Yiddish, actually learned a few phrases. They had heard the legends of Frampol and the little shoemakers and the first Abba of the family line. Even the gentiles in the neighborhood were fairly well acquainted with this history. In the ads Gimpel published in the papers he had proudly disclosed that his family belonged to the shoemaking aristocracy:

Our experience dates back three hundred years to the Polish city of Brod, where our ancestor, Abba, learned the craft from a local master. The community of Frampol, in which our family worked at its trade for fifteen generations, bestowed on him the title of Master in recognition of his charitable services. This sense of public responsibility has always gone hand in hand with our devotion to the highest principles of the craft and our strict policy of honest dealing with our customers.

The day Abba arrived the papers in Elizabeth carried a notice to the effect that the seven brothers of the famous shoe company were welcoming their father from Poland. Gimpel received a mass of congratulatory telegrams from rival manufacturers, relatives, and friends.

It was an extraordinary feast. Three tables were spread in Gimpel's dining room, one for the old man, his sons and daughters-in-law, another for the grandchildren, and the third for the great-grandchildren. Although it was broad daylight the tables were set with candles—red, blue, yellow, green—and their flames were reflected from the dishes and silverware, the crystal glasses and the wine cups, the decanters reminiscent of the Passover Seder. There was an abundance of flowers in every available corner. To be sure, the daughters-in-law would have preferred to see Abba properly dressed for the occasion, but Gimpel put his foot down, and Abba was allowed to spend his first day in the familiar long coat, Frampol style. Even so, Gimpel hired a photographer to take pictures of the banquet—for publication in the newspapers—and invited a rabbi and a cantor to the feast to honor the old man with traditional song.

Abba sat in an armchair at the head of the table. Gimpel and Getzel brought in a bowl and poured water over his hands for the benediction before eating. The food was served on silver trays, carried by colored women. All sorts of fruit juices and salads were set before the old man, sweet brandies, cognac, caviar. But Pharaoh, Joseph, Potiphar's wife, the Land of Goshen, the chief baker and the chief butler spun round and round in his head. His hands trembled so that he was unable to feed himself, and Gimpel had to help him. No matter how often his sons spoke to him, he still could not tell them apart. Whenever the phone rang he jumped—the Nazis were bombing Frampol. The entire house was whirling round and round like a carrousel, the tables were standing on the ceiling and everyone sat upside down. . . . His face was sickly pale in the light of the candles and the electric bulbs. He fell asleep soon after the soup course, while the chicken was being served. Quickly they led him to the bedroom, undressed him, and called a doctor.

He spent several weeks in bed, in and out of consciousness, fitfully dozing as in a fever. He even lacked the strength to say his prayers. There was a nurse at his bedside day and night. Eventually he recovered enough to take a few steps outdoors, in front of the house, but his senses remained disordered. He would walk into clothes closets, lock himself into the bathroom and forget how to come out; the doorbell and the radio frightened him, and he suffered constant anxiety because of the cars that raced past the house. One day Gimpel brought him to a synagogue ten miles away, but even here he was bewildered. The sexton was clean-shaven, the candelabra held electric lights, there was no courtyard, no faucet for washing one's hands, no stove to stand around. The cantor, instead of singing like a cantor should, babbled and croaked. The congregation wore tiny little prayer shawls, like scarves around their necks. Abba was sure he had been hauled into church to be converted. . . .

When spring came and he was no better, the daughters-in-law began to hint that it wouldn't be such a bad idea to put him in a home. But something unforeseen took place. One day, as he happened to open a closet, he noticed a sack lying on the floor which seemed somehow familiar. He looked again and recognized his shoemaker's equipment from Frampol: last, hammer and nails, his knife and pliers, the file and the awl, even a broken-down shoe. Abba felt a tremor of excitement; he could hardly believe his eyes. He sat down on a footstool and began to poke about with fingers grown clumsy and stale. When Bessie came in and found him playing with a dirty old shoe, she burst out laughing.

"What are you doing, Father? Be careful, you'll cut yourself, God forbid!"

That day Abba did not lie in bed dozing. He worked busily till evening, and even ate his usual piece of chicken with greater appetite. He smiled at the grandchildren when they came in to see what he was doing. The next morning, when Gimpel told his brothers how their father had returned to his old habits, they laughed and thought nothing more of it—but the activity soon proved to be the old man's salvation. He kept at it day after day without tiring, hunting up old shoes in the clothes closets, and begged his sons to supply him with leather and tools. When they gave in he mended every last pair of shoes in the house—man, woman, and child's. After the Passover holidays the brothers got together and decided to build a little hut in the yard. They furnished it with a cobbler's bench, a stock of leather soles and hides, nails, dyes, brushes—everything even remotely useful in the craft.

Abba took on new life. His daughters-in-law cried he looked fifteen years younger. As in the Frampol days, he now rose at dawn, said his prayers, and got right to work. Once again he used a knotted string as a measuring tape. The first pair of shoes, which he made for Bessie, became the talk of the neighborhood. She had always complained of her feet—but this pair, she insisted, were the most comfortable shoes she had ever worn. The other girls soon followed her example and also had themselves fitted. Then came the grandchildren. Even some of the gentile neighbors came to Abba when they heard that in sheer joy of the work he was turning out custom-made shoes. He had to communicate with them, for the most part, in gestures, but they got along very well. As for the younger grandchildren and the great-grandchildren, they had long been in the habit of standing at the door to watch him work. Now he was earning money, and he plied them with candies and toys. He even whittled a stylus and began to instruct them in the elements of Hebrew and piety.

One Sunday, Gimpel came into the workshop and, no more than half in earnest, rolled up his sleeves and joined Abba at the bench. The other brothers were not to be outdone, and on the following Sunday eight work stools were set up in the hut. Abba's sons spread sackcloth aprons on their knees and went to work, cutting soles and shaping heels, boring holes and hammering pegs, as in the good old days. The women stood outside, laughing, but they took pride in their men, and the young fry were fascinated. The sun streamed in through the windows and motes of dust danced in the light. In the high spring sky, lofting over the grass and the water, floated clouds in the form of brooms, sailboats, flocks of sheep, herds of elephants. Birds sang, flies buzzed, butterflies fluttered about.

Abba raised his dense eyebrows, and his sad eyes looked around at his heirs, the seven shoemakers: Gimpel, Getzel, Treitel, Godel, Feivel, Lippe, and Chananiah. Their hair was white, though yellow streaks remained. No, praise God, they had not become idolaters in Egypt. They had not forgotten their heritage, nor had they lost themselves among the unworthy. The old man rattled and bumbled deep in his chest, and suddenly began to sing in a stifled, hoarse voice:

"A mother had
Ten little boys,
Oh, Lord, ten little boys!

The sixth one was called Velvele,
The seventh one was Zeinvele,
The eighth one was called Chenele,
The ninth one was called Tevele,
The tenth one was called Judele . . ."

And Abba's sons came in on the chorus:

"Oh, Lord, Judele!"

Translated by Isaac Rosenfeld

Higher and Higher

PESACH MARCUS

NEW YORK is a big city. It runs its busy race beside the Hudson River, and Harry Cooper, a little man with short flabby legs, ran his own race within the city—"I'll own a house on every street!"

Harry's houses were scattered over dozens of streets; he had so many houses he sometimes forgot where they were. When a street had a long name it was hard for him to pronounce it—the word was at the tip of his tongue but couldn't roll off. He had to ask his bookkeeper, an educated man.

This bookkeeper was the exact opposite of Harry—spindle-shanked, thin, skin and bones. All day long he sat in a dark little office, bending over ledgers and sucking his pipe. This frail little creature kept gigantic New York locked up in a small tin box. There he had a map of the entire city, dotted with small circles—Harry's houses, which began in Chinatown and ended in Washington Heights, where a large apartment house, bulging like a pregnant woman, occupied a whole block. Every morning Harry, whose belly swelled like a bladder, squeezed himself into his two-seater to make the rounds of his houses. He drove through the New York streets flooded with people—they reminded him of the flies that used to swarm around a warm loaf of bread in his native Lithuania. He blew his horn—out of the way! Some pedestrians would get scared and hurry to the sidewalk; others would get angry and spitefully slow their pace.

Harry would lose his temper and blow more loudly. But the sound was drowned out by the city's roar, and he had to stop. Silently he would implore the crawling pedestrians, "Have pity, my houses are scattered far and wide, the day is short, and I must visit every one of them! What for? Not everybody can understand this, it takes brains, like mine. I owe my success to brains. I came here empty-handed, and today I have more houses than hairs on my head. A house is like a living being, it must have someone to look after it. Once I expressed this idea to Mr. J. F. White, president of the National Bank, and when he heard me he brightened up—just as my father, the poor peddler, used to brighten up when he heard a good saying of the Chelm *magid*."

Every day Harry ran from house to house. The sun would be about to set when he reached his large apartment house near the George Washington Bridge. By then he was tired and hungry—in his haste he often skipped breakfast. Hunger drew him toward the restaurant in the south wing of the big building, but he restrained himself, did not give way, and walked back and forth in front of the luxurious house, rejoicing like a child in the brilliance of the churchlike dome that reflected the rays of the setting sun. Harry's heart melted as he gazed at the cornice, on which his name was carved in gilded letters. When he saw a stranger he would squint his eyes and ask, "Excuse me, I've lost my glasses. Would you mind telling me the name of this apartment house?"

"Cooper Towers."

"Many thanks."

It was dark when Harry entered the restaurant. He sat at the first free table and looked at the menu. He could not make out what was written on it and discarded it contemptuously. Stupid fools—who needs menus? The waiter knows everything, anyhow.

He was starved. He would gladly order liver with fried onions, or roast veal with browned potatoes, a dish he had seen on rich men's tables in his native village; but he remembered his belly, and the doctors who kept telling him to eat only a few biscuits a day, which could not still his hunger, and which he hated besides. "Those doctors! They charge you three dollars to tell you not to eat. And old Doctor Levy, that fox, he takes a five-dollar bill just for saying, 'Mr. Cooper, a man is not a horse!'

"That Doctor Levy thinks his quip is worth a treasure. But a man isn't a pig either! He takes a whole five dollars, so at least he could let me eat. Horse or no horse, how can a man live without eating?"

Harry was full of indignation against doctors, and now, as though to spite them, he called the waiter and ordered a double portion of meat with potatoes and a pile of pumpernickel. He panted and ate.

How had he come to own so many houses? When asked, he merely smiled—a meaningful smile, as though to say, "Since you don't know, what's the use of telling you?" But to himself he thought, Fools, it takes a lot of brains, and I have plenty!

Harry really believed this, although it had happened somewhat differently. Upon reaching America he went to an uncle, a silent man, from whom you could scarcely squeeze out a word. For several weeks Harry loitered in his uncle's house. Whenever he asked what was to become of him, his uncle did not answer.

Then, one Sunday, his uncle beckoned Harry outside and said in a pensive voice, "You see this skyscraper?"

"Of course. Why do you ask?"

"How many stories has it?"

"Thirty," said Harry, after counting them.

"And how does a man get to the top in life?"

"He climbs a ladder?"

"And if the ladder begins to creak?"

"You go back down."

"No! You stop your ears and keep climbing. You get me, Aaron?"

Harry interpreted these words in a way his uncle had not quite intended. He began to climb. He stopped his ears, grew deaf to the groans of those he trampled on. He did not even spare his uncle, who at first complained bitterly, "Your mother's brother, your own flesh and blood!" A little later his uncle ceased complaining. He became Harry's slave, a janitor in a house in Harlem, and when Harry drove up to inspect it, the silent man would cringe and say, "How are you, Mr. Cooper?"

Harry kept climbing in his race with New York; and his belly grew bigger and bigger.

One day J. F. White said to him, "Mr. Cooper, you once told me that a house is like a living being, it must have someone to look after it. These are golden words, but why scatter your money all over the city? Concentrate your capital. Sell your old houses and build a luxurious apartment house. You won't lose in such a venture."

At first the idea did not appeal to Harry, but then he thought of his belly that was growing bigger and bigger every day, like a balloon, and he decided that Mr. White's idea was a good one after all. He began to sell his houses and to build the luxurious apartment house, which, on the banker's advice, he named the Home of Tomorrow.

Harry, who had always thought he had a good head on his shoulders, soon realized that this time his head had not served him well. The Home of Tomorrow was swallowing his houses the way Pharaoh's fat kine swallowed the lean. The new building was still a skeleton and Harry's skinny bookkeeper had already erased most of the little circles on his map.

Harry had to ask Mr. White for help. He signed a number of documents, which the banker carried to the safe with trembling hands, like a midwife carrying a newborn infant.

It was a big mistake. Harry knew it, but it was too late, he could not retreat. His only comfort was that the newspapers wrote with great enthusiasm about the Home of Tomorrow. They published his picture, and he looked like a king.

A curious new character came into his office—Harry could not make out whether he was a Jew, a German, or a Frenchman. Or maybe, thought Harry sometimes, he isn't even a man. He had a peculiar gait and look. He wore a tailcoat and a round little cap, like a skullcap, and he had a little mustache—as though he had eaten baked potatoes and had forgotten to wipe the smudge off his lips. He pirouetted around the office, and his nails were painted. He had a voice like a bird's, and his name was Van Sickel. Harry always called him Frenchie.

Harry did not see why on earth he had to have this creature in his office, but Mr. White had insisted that Frenchie be given a job, and suggested that he had a knack for talking with rich ladies and could obtain higher rents. Harry did not know how to answer such an argument, and besides, maybe Mr. White knew those things better than he did. So he let Frenchie do as he pleased and did not say anything even when he saw his curious employee spending money foolishly and uselessly. For instance, Frenchie spent a fortune on dressing up the staff in expensive uniforms, so that Harry occasionally mistook a doorman for a real general and doffed his cap before him.

Occasionally Harry poured out his heart to his bookkeeper, whom he continued to employ for that purpose alone, since there was no longer anything for him to do—no more little circles.

Then Harry noticed that Frenchie was not at all eager to rent the apartments. Prospective tenants came with cash and did not even bargain over prices, yet Frenchie under various excuses avoided signing up. Could it be that Frenchie was not in his right mind?

Harry spoke to him frankly. "Are you out of your mind? When you're given money, take it!"

But Frenchie was not a bit ruffled by Harry's outburst; he merely smiled and dangled his long legs. When Harry finished he turned to him and, speaking calmly, like a doctor to a patient, said, "Mr. Cooper, the Home of Tomorrow will pay only if high society moves in here. We must not open it to anyone who can pay rent. I'll be frank with you, Mr. Cooper. Former rag collectors, all those Levines, Goldsteins, and their ilk—don't misunderstand me, Mr. Cooper, I personally have nothing against them, I have no prejudices. But not everybody can stand their manners."

Frenchie lighted a cigarette and went on imperturbably, "After all, we must not expect a Social Register family to live in the same house with immigrants. In fact, Mr. Cooper, you can be very helpful—Jews are clever, they often assume Irish or other non-Jewish names, but you, Mr. Cooper, can recognize another one under any disguise."

Frenchie stretched comfortably in his chair, shook the ashes from his cigarette, and gazed at Harry with his piercing eyes. "The Home of Tomorrow is exposed to many dangers. We must see to it that our tenants are morally respectable. A trifle might ruin your good name. I know of a case where all the wealthy tenants moved out in a hurry after some nice man climbed on the roof and jumped down. He stained the marble staircase with his blood."

Harry was seized with a fright, as he used to be in former years on Yom Kippur when the rabbi graphically described the torments of hell. A sour-sweet taste came into his mouth; he grew dizzy. He saw a host of Jews with long disheveled beards dancing straight into the Home of Tomorrow; then a woman who threw off her clothes and stood stark naked while a man flew head down past her window, spattering his brains on the stone stairs.

From then on Harry no longer interfered; he even ceased to come to the office. Only after dark would he sometimes sneak in; it was preferable, he thought, not to show himself too conspicuously to his gentile tenants.

Above the garage in an attic room he set up a place for himself and often sat there watching the courtyard and the magnificent driveway through the attic's narrow little window. Sometimes he prolonged his vigil late into the night. Peering through his window, he discovered that some of his high-class tenants perpetrated various offenses in the stillness of the night. Once he saw the wealthy Mrs. Jackson flirting with her chauffeur—she had forgotten to draw the curtains. Harry was so upset he almost fainted. Next day he ran to report the incident to Frenchie.

Harry made still another discovery—a certain Mr. Brown, who had described himself as a German and rented a luxurious duplex, was really a Jew. Harry had long suspected him because of his quiet way of smiling and his stooping posture, but he had no definite evidence until he saw him enter a synagogue on Yom Kippur.

Harry was torn—should he or should he not report his discovery to Frenchie? "Harry, you, a Jew, inform on another Jew? After all, Mr. Brown's manners are as good as those of the finest tenants. And how can you afford to lose a tenant when so many apartments are vacant?" But since, he decided, he was not following his own, but Mr. White's, way he had no choice.

Harry no longer had any say in his business. Frenchie led him by the hand like a little helpless child. He did not even know what was in his ledgers, but he took it for granted that the Home of Tomorrow was bringing in large profits, in the tens of thousands, far beyond his capacity to calculate. If he had grown rich by renting poor small apartments, how could he fail to earn huge profits on the Home of Tomorrow, where every inch was worth a fortune?

One day when he stopped at the bank Mr. White came up to him and smiled. "Mr. Cooper, the Home of Tomorrow is running at a considerable loss."

Harry did not answer; he merely smiled—surely Mr. White was joking. Then one day a man came to him from the bank and told him that Mr. White wanted him to come at once.

Harry rubbed his hands with joy. He dressed in his very best clothes, as for a holiday. It was a hot summer day, and, as though to prove to himself that he was not in a hurry, he stopped in a candy store, ordered a chocolate soda, and slowly sipped the refreshing drink.

He found Mr. White sitting at a large desk covered with papers and documents. He looked angry and upset as he read aloud from an open book in front of him, without raising his eyes for a moment.

"The Home of Tomorrow has lost a fortune," Mr. White said slowly. "The bank is compelled to sell the building to the highest bidder in order to secure the money of the investors."

Shuddering all over, Harry seemed suddenly to come out of a heavy sleep. This time he knew Mr. White was not joking. He broke into a lament. "After all, it was you who have managed this business, not I. It was your idea to build the Home of Tomorrow. I don't understand ledgers."

Mr. White sat cold, hard as stone, deaf to Harry's pleas. "A bank is not a charitable institution."

Harry listened with all his senses, like an animal, to every word that trickled from the corners of Mr. White's mouth. When the banker finished Harry banged the desk and screamed like a madman, "Robbers, thieves, murderers!"

Mr. White remained calm, and Harry soon realized his screaming was foolish. He then spoke as his victims had once spoken to him. The human feelings he had kept imprisoned were aroused, and he felt a strange satisfaction at having to atone for his evil. But a lust for revenge burned in his eye, and a sentence from the Bible he had memorized as a child suddenly occurred to him: *Let me die with the Philistines!*

Harry remembered his poor relatives, his compatriots and friends, with whom he had been friendly during his first years in this country. Breathless, he ran to the East Side, to Orchard Street.

They were surprised by the visit of this millionaire who owned a great palace and had for so many years ignored them. He spoke in warm affectionate tones. "I am rich, but a man doesn't live forever. I have lived in error and in sin, and now I repent. I want to take you out of these dingy streets and lead you to my palace, just as Moses led the Jews out of Egypt. I'll build a synagogue for you there, and you may also take your neighbors along. A truck is waiting."

The poor Jews were dumfounded. But then they thought, What is there to lose? The heat was unbearable, the air sultry and oppressive. Why not have a look?

Harry got on the truck, looked at his guests, and rejoiced in his heart. The men had long beards and earlocks, the women wore headkerchiefs and wigs. When the tenants of the Home of Tomorrow see them come in with their bundles and bags, they'll scatter like mice, thought Harry.

Frenchie, who happened to be outside, saw the oncoming Jews from a distance. He summoned his staff and ordered them to cordon off the entrance. Again Harry was thwarted. His guests withdrew in fright, complaining, "Why make a laughingstock of us? Why the whole masquerade?" And Frenchie stood there calmly, twisting his little mustache, smiling, a conqueror.

But Harry was filled with new courage. Suddenly he felt light and strong, as if his bulging belly had shrunk, vanished. He looked with disgust at Frenchie's face and shouted, "No one can beat Harry Cooper!"

He lunged forward with all his strength, pushing aside the tall young lackey who stood in his way, and ran up the stairs to the roof garden. It seemed to him that his uncle with the long beard, whom he had always humiliated and maltreated, and who had died a pauper, was running after him, trying to stop him, and crying, "Harry, you'll die as wretchedly as I did, you won't die on your own bed. Everything you have will go to strangers, nothing will be left for you!"

"Uncle," screamed Harry, climbing higher and higher, "don't stand in my way! *Let me die with the Philistines!* Nothing will be left for them either!"

Harry was at the parapet. Down below, on the stairs, Frenchie stood with a frightened face, and next to him stood the staff with their arms outstretched, as though preparing to catch a ball.

His head raised high, Harry cried, "No one can make a fool of Harry Cooper!"

He spread his arms like a bird taking wing, and the spotlessly clean, dazzling marble steps were stained red.

Translated by Norbert Guterman

The Eternal Wedding Gown

JOSEPH OPATOSHU

DAWN WAS already breaking when the eighty-year-old Glikche Schreiber opened her eyes in fright, only to shut them again. She could hardly stir. Her every limb seemed dislocated and throbbed with pain; her knuckles and toes felt as if they were coming apart. And hovering on the very verge of her mind was a question that had haunted her all night long: Was Ernestine really dead?

Only now, when Glikche reopened her eyes, did the conviction come that Ernestine had really died on Friday.

What was to be done? Postpone the funeral until Sunday, as was customary in America? In Preschburg, where Glikche's parents, grandparents, and great-grandparents had lived out their days, the custom was quite different. When someone in the family died he or she had to be buried the same day.

But it was already Friday afternoon, and Ernestine had failed to provide so much as a shroud for herself. True, she was a cousin of Glikche's; she was an Eiger, a great-granddaughter of Reb Akiba Eiger himself. But she had gone over to the reformed synagogue all of fifty years ago, back in Preschburg. Ernestine's angel (since every human being has an angel up there, in heaven) had turned a deaf ear to her ever since. He never heard her pleas, since she had strayed so early from the path of true Jewishness. There was her very name: Ernestine! Both cousins had been named Glikche, after the same great-grandmother. Yet one of these Glikches had turned into an Ernestine. And why did she put on such airs, this Ernestine? Just because her husband happened to be an eye specialist? Or because she could speak Hungarian, German, French, and English? Well now, Glikche's husband, a heart specialist, had been a professor in Budapest and, right here in New York, had lectured at Columbia University. And what about Glikche herself? She had been more versatile than Ernestine from her very childhood, when it came to languages. Glikche could also interpret a portion of the Pentateuch or a passage from the Psalms. What, then, had made Ernestine so proud that she had to stray from the path of orthodoxy? And her dying, too, had been so very stupid: she hadn't even provided a shroud for herself.

So Glikche had gotten out her own shroud and yielded it to Ernestine. And when they had come back from the cemetery it had been just in time for the lighting of the Sabbath candles.

Glikche perceived the graciousness of God in all this and, raising her eyes in gratitude, uttered the name of the Father in Heaven.

Streaks of light came through the two windows that overlooked Central Park and fell tremulously on the southern wall of the room, resting uncertainly now on this photograph, now on that. Glikche gazed intently at these brightened faces, framed in old-fashioned beards and earlocks, their wise eyes looking down upon her pensively. Her great-grandfathers, two of them: Reb Moishe Schreiber, the Rabbi of Preschburg, and Rabbi Akiba Eiger, the Rabbi of Posen.

Glikche felt a glow at the sight of them. Nor was it Glikche alone who delighted in these forebears. Her two sons, doctors both, who refrained from writing on the Sabbath, as well as her son-in-law, a wealthy manufacturer who kept his shop closed on that day, also rejoiced in these ancestors. Every Sabbath eve one of her grandsons would drop in on Glikche to pronounce the benediction over the Sabbath wine. The grandson would sleep over and escort her next morning to the synagogue. For that matter, what about her sons and her son-in-law? Why, they would be welcomed in Paradise if only for the way they honored their mother (even the son-in-law called her that).

Glikche was saddened by the rate at which her contemporaries were vanishing. They had departed, one by one. For she had friends whom she had acquired both in Preschburg and in New York, where she had lived for almost threescore years. She ticked off on her fingers those of her friends who were still among the living: Radisch, and Freidche, and Shaindel, and Braindel, and Sorele—may they be spared long!

She had ticked off five names, and could see every one of these friends of hers standing before her, and could tell the age of each. The youngest was in her late sixties, the oldest in her nineties. Her friends were standing in a row, lined up before her, and she pondered: Whose turn would it be next?

Not Freidche's, she knew. The ninety-year-old Freidche was quite a doctor herself. Was there anything she couldn't cure? When someone fell ill she could tell days ahead whether the illness would pass or prove fatal. She had known as far back as last Wednesday that Ernestine was dying.

Glikche had asked her, "Freidche, darling, what do you say?"

And Freidche had replied, "Glikche, you want to know whether the illness is serious? Take a piece of soft bread, wipe the sweat off the patient's brow with it, and throw it to a dog. If the dog will eat it, it's a good sign; if it won't, things are all over for Ernestine."

Glikche had stared at Ernestine's black dog, which refused to budge from the side of its mistress's bed. The dog would not touch the sweat-soaked piece of bread which Freidche tossed to it. Glikche had sworn at the dog and had left Freidche in a huff. Of course the incident had rankled: Freidche could, indeed, foretell things. How did she do it?

The telephone on the night-table began to ring and Glikche picked up the receiver.

"Hello! Radisch? Good morning, Radisch; may we no longer know sorrow! Will you be welcome if you come? Of course! But why so early? I'm still in bed; I haven't said my prayers yet. Come after my morning prayers. All right then, Radisch darling."

What the old lady had forgotten was that in the mornings this friend of hers was a bundle of aches and pains, as if all her bones had been broken.

Glikche got off her bed and called to her maid, "Elizabeth, are you still asleep?"

"Who's sleeping, Missus Schreiber?" The maid, an elderly colored woman, entered the room. "Here I am, ma'am."

"Be a good girl, Elizabeth, and tidy up the room."

"What's the rush, ma'am?"

"We're going to have guests."

"This early?"

The older woman shrugged like a child and smiled. And, as soon as Elizabeth had tidied up the room, Glikche sat down with her prayer book near the southern wall, hung with the photographs of her ancestors. She prayed aloud, in the singsong peculiar to Preschburg, oblivious of the sound of her voice, of the noises which drifted in from the kitchen, where Elizabeth was preparing breakfast.

No sooner had Glikche concluded the Prayer of the Eighteen Benedictions than the doorbell rang. Crowded in the doorway stood Radisch, Freidche, Shaindel, Braindel, and Sorele, wealthy old ladies, all of them, their arms loaded with pastry, delicacies, and bottles of wine. And they had also brought their sewing.

"Good morning, Glikche," they hailed her in chorus.

Surprised, she exchanged kisses with her guests. As they sat down at the table, spreading out the good things they had brought and opening the bottles of wine, they got ready their sewing kits.

Radisch, the oldest among the callers, took a length of Irish linen from her kit and spread it out on the floor. "Glikche, do you know why we have come here today?" she asked. "Your friends have to sew your eternal wedding dress for you. You deserve it, Glikche. You gave your own to Ernestine and were left without one. So we got busy and here we are—"

Old Glikche had tears in her eyes as she embraced one friend after the other; then she sliced a cake and poured out glasses of wine. Her callers drank her health and nibbled at the cake. Radisch, the oldest among them, tried the shroud on Glikche, with all its points and knots.

The old women threaded their needles with long white threads. And as they bent over, sewing the eternal wedding gown, death began to spin its web.

Translated by Bernard Guilbert Guerney

The Return

JACOB GLATSTEIN

THE SOUND of footsteps roused me from my reverie. Near me stood a young man. By his dress I recognized him at once as one of the rabbi's entourage that I had encountered in the park.

He had trailed after the entourage, at some distance from the others. This time, too, he was wearing the same slippers and white stockings. The slippers hindered his ascent up the hill. He was about to pass me, then considered the matter and stopped.

"I know," he said, "you are an American." He sat down near me. "And how are the Jews getting along in America? . . . But as a matter of fact I don't have to ask you at all. I know the answer myself. With my imagination, I can tell everything. There are things about

America I know better than you do, because you only saw them while I imagined them. It's a nice idea, isn't it?

"I can tell you how the country is governed, who is boss, how Jews conduct themselves there. Once I went to a small town with my father. First I imagined how the town would look and what the first Jew to greet us would be like. And, will you believe it?—everything turned out exactly as I had foreseen. You think it's unnatural? Not at all, I can explain it to you quite naturally."

This is the way he explained it. Man lives seventy years. But what does that amount to? Nothing at all, not even a millionth of a millionth of a millionth of the time that it takes the Almighty to bat His eyelashes. Man, who is the chosen of all creation, felt humiliated that his lifetime was so insignificant, so he invented a sort of apparatus that stretches his life span like a rubber band and makes it seem a fair-sized length of time.

"You get the idea? It's not easy to grasp. At birth the grave stands ready and open. But between birth and burial various events take place, in a flash. You can't imagine how fast they whiz by. The apparatus that man has devised stretches out every event and assigns a role to even the most trivial incident. Imagine that something has to happen to you five years from now. Actually, it's happening right now or has already happened. Do you see what I mean?

"Sometimes a man gets ahead of his time-stretching apparatus and mentally arrives at an event that isn't due to happen for some years yet. You play a trick on the apparatus and you sense time as it really is, time as measured against the brief span of human life.

"It's hard to get to the bottom of this. If you want, I'll explain it over again, from the beginning. I've been thinking about this for four or five years. When I first grasped the idea, it lit up my mind with a flash."

"How old are you?" I interrupted him.

"Sixteen. But this isn't the only idea I have thought of. You ought to know that every rabbinical family is distinguished by some special trait. We are the philosophers among the rabbis—also the rhetoricians. We have a tendency to speculation. It is a wonderful game, and also a trial. One walks along a narrow bridge. A single misstep, a single false turn—and one falls, heaven forbid, into heresy. But if the Almighty is so inclined and one does not stumble along the way but emerges at the other end undamaged, then the idea becomes doubly precious, for it achieves union with the Creator, who first sent it into the world.

"An idea that doesn't unite with the Creator but wanders about the world at random is a bastard idea. It has no father. I once wrote a tract in which I developed this thought. It's extraordinary.

"I like to go about alone and to think about Hasidism. In accordance with my theory I try to grasp now the thoughts that should come to me years later. That's why my eyes look much older than I am. I want to make discoveries. I am not satisfied with my grandfather's way, nor with my father's. And I don't like the way of my older brothers. I told my father that I wasn't particularly satisfied with his way. Despite the reverence I owe him, I mustered my courage and told him that. He confided in me that he was even less satisfied.

"I have read all of Yiddish literature. I know all and everybody. But what have they got except rhetoric? Peretz's Hasidic stories are anecdotes with a moral. It's like looking in from the outside, through a keyhole, and applauding. But I want to know things from the inside. I want to bring Jewish thought to an entirely new plane. You have to understand, first of all, that we must do away with non-Jewish forms. Our creation must embrace everything: poetry, prose, philosophy, drama, psychology, astronomy, epigrams, everything. What do we need these little containers for? We need a creative encyclopedia, do you hear me? A creative encyclopedia. Do you get this great idea? Did you ever read a story of the Bratslaver rabbi? There is my hero among the Hasidim. I love him. I think of him constantly, day and night. He was an innovator and he loved Yiddish. Do you know what Yiddish really is? Have you any idea what a marvelous language it is?"

One thing troubled him: he couldn't understand how the Bratslaver could have been so proud. Would I believe him? It took him two years of pondering on the Bratslaver's pride before he finally caught on. Now he had an excellent explanation.

"The Bratslaver was a sick man all his life, a broken vessel. Had he acted the part of meekness, he would not have been taken seriously. He knew that he would die young and he wished to accomplish something in his brief lifetime.

"That is why he cried his wares so loudly. Not out of selfishness. Everyone knew that he loved poverty and need. Poverty was his element; he was at home in it like a fish in water. But he had wares to sell, and that is why he advertised them. He praised himself to attract listeners to God's Word. I am willing to wager that when alone with his scribe, Reb Nathan, he laughed at himself out loud. But Reb Nathan never mentioned this in public.

"That's one possibility. I have still another idea: a rabbi must not be modest. A rabbi who is modest diminishes the grandeur of the idea of God. He has to give the people some concept of His greatness. Since he recounts God's great wonders, he must also act out the role of greatness. There is a tremendous difference between pride and grandness. The Bratslaver practiced grandness, but he lavished it on all without distinction, on great and small, on poor and rich. Now, think of it: if a grandee such as he pretended to be was willing to hobnob with the very least, how could an ordinary Hasid indulge in pride?

"Someday I will read you some of my new ideas and you will see for yourself that they are remarkable. But don't think that I get them out of my own pitiful little brain. After I fast on a Monday, a Thursday, and then the following Monday, I begin to shed my trivial material being. I walk about in the forest. At dusk, when my hunger becomes impatient and trembles with anticipation that the fast will soon be over, what do I do then? I keep on walking. You think the fast is over? You think it's all right to eat now, you glutton? Well, just wait a little longer, and a little more still.

"Something happens then; a faintness comes over me; all my body is filled with such sweet weariness. My limbs want to shout, but they only peep like little birds, they are so weak. They sing from faintness. At such moments I hear a voice.

"Here I must interrupt myself. I could describe to you the voice I hear, but I am not allowed to, because the voice speaks to me in sacred solitude. It would be coarse on my part to draw away the mantle of intimacy. But whoever has not heard such a voice gropes like a blind man when he speaks of God.

"First I feel a certain heaviness in all my joints. This is the signal that I will soon hear the voice. Everything about me becomes solemn. I fall on my face and I cry, 'Talk to me, Father! I am ready.'

"When I rise from the ground I am always richer in some way. It may be an idea or a thought or an interpretation, and I feel that these are not my own, that they come from above as a ripe pear falls from a tree. Sometimes I rise with a song. Listen:

> Slayer, slayer, against whom do you lift your ax?
> Against whom do you lift your ax?
> I lift my ax on my own wishes,
> On my own evil wishes,
> God of Abraham, hear my song.
> Ai, chiri-biri-biri, Praise God,
> Ai, ai, praise God.

"And I have a melody for it that is sweet as honey.

Little Cossack, little Cossack, against whom do you raise
your sword?
Against whom, I ask, do you raise your sword?
I raise my sword against my evil desire
Against my evil desire,
Against my own evil wishes.
God of Abraham, hear my song.

"Then there are times when I fool Satan and stick out my tongue at him. Like this:

I crave
The breast
Of righteousness.
I caress, I kiss
The Divine majesty.

"See how I laugh at Satan? Just when he thinks he has me hooked, I give him a wallop.

"But now it's time to go. I want to warn you; you aren't through with me yet. When I start talking, there's something to hear. And there's so much to say. Next time I see you I will give you a hint how it is possible to reconcile faith with heresy, how heresy can be imbued with such fire that it will rise and weep before the Throne of Glory. It will weep its formulas and questions and doubts. It's all right. God can stand it. I will also tell you a secret—how the modern Hasid can find his way to Jewish Life."

He began to descend, and pebbles cascaded after him. I remained behind, stunned. His last words had been "Jewish Life." These words danced before my eyes. I began to perceive sense, even reason, in what he had said.

It was getting cool on top of the hill, and I started down. Halfway down the slope I saw the young thinker waiting for me.

"I can't help myself. I must tell you of an interesting encounter I had a short time ago."

He smiled as if reliving the experience.

"I had just finished evening prayers. There was a strange aroma in the air. Generally when I am deep in thought I walk with my head bowed. But suddenly I became aware that there was a perfume in the air so unusual that it is impossible to describe.

"I began to wonder and raised my head. I knew at once that I had strayed. The trees were dream trees, the sky was so transparent that if only a thin skin were peeled from it one would perceive great wonders. There was a sound of fluttering wings and of birds calling to one another, but I could not see the birds. It was dusk—a pink, cheerful dusk.

"Two men sat on a bench, engaged in conversation. I could see them talking, I saw their lips moving, I even heard distinctly what they were saying. But each word flared up before me and then faded out, like so many shooting stars.

"One of the men looked kingly. In the dusk it was hard to tell what kind of clothes he wore, but there was a regal dignity about him. The other also seemed an important man, but not of quite the same rank as the first. It's hard to say how I distinguished between them, but the light about the second one was somehow not of the same quality.

"I became terribly curious and began crying aloud. But they didn't even look at me. I approached closer and closer. I was almost on top of them. I walked through them as if they were smoke.

"Suddenly a curtain seemed to fall from before my eyes and things appeared more solidly. The dusk lost its pink glow, and it was also darker, but I could see better than before.

"Things were a little different now. The men sat on two separate benches. They were silent and seemed to wait for me to approach. I bowed low before the regal-looking man. I could see clearly the melancholy expression on his face, and I realized everything.

" 'Sabbattai Zevi,' I said, 'what are you trying to convey to me? What is this vision you have granted me?'

" 'It is not I who granted you this vision. It is you who found it in your wandering. Let it be so, if such is your choice. May it do you good.'

" 'Sabbattai Zevi, you false Messiah!' I shouted, 'is this the world of delusion in which I see you?'

"He looked at me with such sorrow that I realized there could be no talk of delusion. But I lost the thread of meaning and became confused.

" 'And aren't the true Messiahs also false?' he asked with a pained smile. 'What have all of us accomplished? Should we be stoned because we dreamed? How can you say that, you who know how we hoped, how stubborn we were, how we tried to bring about at least one happy hour. Even the truest Messiah would be false if he really tried to bring about redemption. The genuine Messiahs are those who change nothing, those who sit patiently and wait. Perhaps they should be called the wise and practical Messiahs. Perhaps we others should be thought foolish failures as Messiahs. But why false ones? How can you say this?'

"Grieving, I turned to the other man. 'Jacob Frank,' I said. He had such sad eyes it was painful to look at him.

" 'I have been entrusted with much silence.' He sighed. 'Why talk? On occasion I talk to Sabbattai, because we understand each other without words, but—'

"I interrupted him, 'I only want to know why you went over to the other side. I wanted to ask Sabbattai too. But I know that he has at least a sort of alibi—Ishmael, our cousin, the Crescent. But the Cross! What alibi can there be for the Cross?'

"As I was talking a little man appeared on the scene. He came running, quick as a wind. The two benches were now wrapped in darkness, but the silvery beard of the little Jew gleamed and shone.

" 'Why do you torment these two people?' he said. 'Why do you ask an accounting from them? My God! In their very falsehood these two Jews sacrificed themselves for the truth. They wanted to make the truth so obvious that they even showed its reverse. They descended into hell itself in order to show whither error leads, yet you demand of them a reckoning.'

"The little man grinned and gaily slapped my back. 'I'll tell you what,' he said, 'let's say our prayers instead.'

"I was about to begin to pray with great concentration when I became aware that the little man was saying some strange things.

" 'Greetings, Father. I came to tell you good evening. This is an ordinary Wednesday. Jews are up to their necks in business. Not for themselves, You understand, but for their families. Their heads are full of all sorts of worries. Just the same, they take a minute off in the middle of everything, to stop and raise their eyes to You, Father in Heaven. Now I want to ask You, is it right on Your part always to remind us that You have chosen us for Your people? Whom else could You have chosen? Just answer this question to Yourself. Do You know of a better people?'

"And just as quickly as he had appeared he now vanished. Suddenly I found myself in a dark alley off the main road. My older brother was coming toward me. At first I thought I'd tell him what I had seen, then I reconsidered. He is too brainy, too much of a Litvak. So I decided it would be better to keep this matter to myself. But I took a chance and told it to you, since we were talking anyway. You are a stranger here. You'll go away, overseas. You may think that some confused boy has been talking to you. But don't be too sure. You might do well to consider it seriously. I couldn't have dreamed it up if I had a thousand heads and, anyway, it's no trick dreaming up things. Why exaggerate when real life is so full of wonders!"

"Know what? Come to our house. Let your good sense mislead you for a change. Nobody will bite you there," he said. "I will show you some of my tracts, which no one has yet seen. I have a facile pen; ideas pour out of my head. You'll be amply rewarded for your trouble. A pity Father isn't home, really a pity. He is worth knowing. If you miss knowing him you won't run across many others like him."

Together we crossed the narrow board that bridged the water. It gave under our feet as if it were made of rubber. The place was now deserted. From below, the mountain looked temporary, as if it had been piled up for the night only. The young man led the way and frequently looked back to make sure that I had not vanished.

He led me through an orchard and then brought me stealthily into a back room. He lit a small lamp whose meager light added a strange quality to the bright illumination of the big lamp.

"Which do you like better?" he asked, "to be read to or to read yourself? It depends, naturally, on whether your eye or your ear is more highly developed. It also depends on what I will show you. I have many morsels for the eye, and still more for the ear."

I took the small long strips of paper from his hand and decided at once that his microscopic calligraphy, marked by many blots and erasures, was not for me. He had used a watery ink, and the strips of paper resembled unrolled and damaged *mezzuzahs* on which the script had become indistinct.

"You will excuse me, but I have to say a few words by way of introduction to each piece that I will read you. My first offering is a letter. Letters are a serious matter. You take a sheet of paper and you write to someone, because you can't see him and you can't talk to him directly. A letter must be brief and to the point. I have written about a dozen letters, models for a new and original style of letter writing.

" 'Dear Mr. Nightingale: Enclosed you will find two worlds, the world of here and the word of there. You may choose whichever you prefer. The world of here is limited. You can measure it with one hand

and pace it with one foot. The world of there is distilled of indescribable clarity. The world of here consists of pleasure that shrinks, ages, and becomes void. The world of there consists of tears of eternal happiness, because one strives ever toward a great decision. Sincerely, Your servant who wishes you a happy choice.'

"Now I will show you a sample of a prayer. You must realize that prayers renew themselves with each generation. Nevertheless a prayer must retain a certain old modishness so that it should be pleasant to the tongue.

> Thy house stands firm on the mountain,
> Thy house on the mountain is uplifted,
> I climb toward Thee, a wanderer weary from travel.
> My wandering is a sin,
> My questioning misled me.
> My doubts of many kinds have caused me to be alone.
> Stretch Thy shining hand toward me,
> Shed light on my road to Thee,
> Protect my stumbling on the road toward Thee.

"I have also written countless poems, but I am still not satisfied with them. All my poems are like empty vessels that wait bashfully to be filled.

"Maybe you like this sort of thing. But what I am really good at is speculating. There I know no bounds. Let me read you an excerpt from an idea of mine.

" 'Inventions are concretized miracles. In olden days, when people profoundly believed in miracles, inventions were unnecessary. When there was belief in miracles, the will was strong. That is why signs and omens were enough in the past, whereas today it is necessary to rationalize them and to transform them into inventions. Inventions mediate between the great mystery and trivial people. When you press a button in the wall you think you have accomplished something, but once you start thinking deeply about electricity you begin to realize that the button is as mysterious as the wonder of electricity, and that it has been invented in order that the dull-witted should be able to believe. The truth of the matter is that one can press the wall near the button and say, "Let there be light," and a light will shine. But we do not realize this. We do not understand this. We do not believe this. Consequently we, foolish people, invented the button to make it more comprehensible. That which our will and our faith should accomplish is done for us by the electric switch. We come back to the miracle by way of many doubts, and our doubts give birth to all kinds of buttons.'

"How do you like it? Do you get the idea behind it? I develop it farther and point out that our inventions rebel against us and return, along their own paths, back to the miracle, that is, to the primeval mystery. The human hand must be capable of reaching the miracle without the mediation of so-called inventions. Of course I don't expect you to grasp this right away. It is necessary to ponder this kind of idea.

"I stick to my own theory," he continued, his eyes shining, "that it is indeed necessary to know the Seven Wisdoms and the seventy languages, but that these must be uplifted. Sciences are bodies, concrete things. When someone speaks French to a Frenchman, he employs a means to make himself understood by the Frenchman. He applies his knowledge; but the use of the French language between him and the Frenchman is no longer mere language, it is a spiritual affinity. They no longer use language—they converse. The same is true of mathematics. If a man were to go loaded with the science of mathematics he would be a fool. Calculation must be transformed into abstract wisdom. From this we may conclude that there exists a point where all kinds of knowledge meet and fuse to the extent of becoming indistinguishable. In that no-man's-land of human elevation all sciences are fused into one, which in turn is but a millimillionth of a reflection of the great source. A man must not go about and show off his knowledge. Once one understands knowledge one realizes that it is but imitation. When the various kinds of knowledge meet and become spiritual, only then does knowledge become a reality. Otherwise it is a dead weight that drags one down and drowns him.

"What I told you just now came to my mind at this moment." He grabbed a pencil and began writing. "I must write it down. It's a remarkable idea. I must not let it get lost."

When we entered the other room the company was already seated and seemed to expect us. There were refreshments on the table. I was struck by the friendly warmth in everyone's eyes.

The American son-in-law, his head covered with a skullcap, smiled, and his grin was like a question mark to what I had just heard. He asked at once, "Well? What do you think of my little brother-in-law? He has a facile brain, doesn't he? I'm not worried about him. He will go far."

"Eh." This exclamation came from a man with a large face and large coarse lips and nose. Even his eyes and broad, square beard were somehow coarse. He too seemed to look for an opportunity to talk to me. "I am not at all pleased with my little brother. The American thinks it's all very wonderful, but I look at things otherwise: that one must be able to restrain one's thoughts, to bring them to a halt, before they run wild. There must be system and order, a beginning and an end. According to my way of reasoning, a horse also thinks; all dumb animals think, but their thoughts are disordered, that's why they never attained reason. With my little brother everything is like a spring—you release the spring and it gives off thoughts, then it bounds back to its former position."

"I could answer you, but your schematic mind wouldn't grasp it," the excited young thinker defended himself. "I'll let it pass."

The American son-in-law burst into a brittle laugh that crumbled from his lips; nevertheless tears appeared in his eyes. "Brothers, brothers," he chided them, "why must you always quarrel?"

"Do I quarrel with him?" the older one said. "He doesn't get in my way. I merely wish to guide him, and he doesn't let me."

"A fine guide! What he wants is to harness my thoughts."

"You colt," the older brother said good-naturedly. "I want to show you human order, but you think you are already a big shot. That's the trouble with you." He turned to me. "He thinks he has got it, but he still doesn't have it. Do you get what I mean? He still—does—not —have—it."

Two women sat to the left in upholstered chairs. One of them was crocheting, the other merely watched, apparently awaiting an opportunity to take part in the conversation. The one crocheting frequently raised her head, and I saw she had an oval face and a pointed chin. Her lips moved as if she were whispering something not to be heard by anyone, and she seemed content with that. The other woman had a plump, childish face and large, blue, laughing eyes. She rose and handed me the tray of fruit, which was elegantly arranged.

"He envies me!" The younger brother could not control his excitement. "Didn't I catch you in the act? Not so long ago, in the synagogue, I heard very well how you repeated an idea of mine in one of your speeches."

"Where?" The older brother leaped from his chair. "Am I so poor that I have to borrow your ideas?"

"On the contrary. You are rich, but you like to pick up things. You see a good thing, so you grab it."

The American son-in-law laughed again. His head rolled in all directions as if he could not hold it on his shoulders from laughing.

"You are cruel," the woman with the childish face remarked, pouting. "They quarrel and you think it's fun."

"What are you saying? It's remarkable, it's amusing, colossal." And again he was shaken with laughter.

She handed me the plate of chocolates and the tray of pastries. "Take something."

When she walked it became evident that she was pregnant, but the springiness of her youth distracted one's eye from the heaviness of her body. She appeared to be in her early twenties.

"I won't allow it. My brothers eat their hearts out and you make game of them," she said with her laughing eyes.

"This is slander, this is really slander." The American became serious.

The crocheting woman again raised her oval face and her lips moved soundlessly. She lowered her eyes and said, "There is a poem, by Leopardi . . ."

All became silent. She talked with lowered eyes without stopping her work. She mentioned Bergson, she quoted Verlaine in French, she recited from Slowatski in Polish, and she brought up the latest trends in German poetry—all in connection with the disagreement between the two brothers, which was essentially a higher form of love, because each sought the truth in his own way and both sorrowfully longed for each other.

It was pleasant to hear her talk. Quietly and modestly she offered many quotations. Her rhythmic recitation sounded like sleigh bells on a remote snowbound road. She stopped abruptly. Everyone expected her to continue. But it was as if she had turned down the light about herself.

"You must come to see us again," the younger woman pleaded when she observed that I was getting ready to go.

"How can he come when that one dizzied him with his speculation?"

"Don't start all over again!" The woman clapped her hands.

"Let him, let him! He envies me, that's clear."

The American again shook with laughter.

"Wait. Don't go yet. It's pitch-dark outside and you may miss the steps in the orchard."

The younger woman took the lamp from the table to escort me. Beams of light cut through the green trees. "Careful at the three steps.

The first is quite steep." She gave me her left hand. "You must come to see us again. We enjoyed your visit."

When I was safely down the steps I suddenly felt ashamed. I remembered that I had been sitting the whole time with my head uncovered. And I felt still more ashamed when I recalled how delicately they had ignored it.

Translated by Shlomo Katz

The Man Who Slept through the End of the World

MOISHE NADIR

He was always sleepy. And always ready to sleep. Everywhere. At the biggest mass meetings, at all the concerts, at every important convention, he could be seen sitting asleep.

And he slept in every conceivable and inconceivable pose. He slept with his elbows in the air and his hands behind his head. He slept standing up, leaning against himself so that he shouldn't fall down. He slept in the theater, in the streets, in the synagogue. Wherever he went, his eyes would drip with sleep.

Neighbors used to say that he had already slept through seven big fires, and once, at a really big fire, he was carried out of his bed, still asleep, and put down on the sidewalk. In this way he slept for several hours until a patrol wagon came along and took him away.

It was said that when he was standing under the wedding canopy and reciting the vows, "Thou art to me . . ." he fell asleep at the word "sanctified," and they had to beat him over the head with brass pestles for several hours to wake him up. And then he slowly said the next word and again fell asleep.

We mention all this so that you may believe the following story about our hero.

Once, when he went to sleep, he slept and slept and slept; but in his sleep it seemed to him that he heard thunder in the streets and his bed was shaking somewhat; so he thought in his sleep that it was raining outside, and as a result his sleep became still more delicious. He wrapped himself up in his quilt and in his warmth.

When he awoke he saw a strange void: his wife was no longer there, his bed was no longer there, his quilt was no longer there. He wanted to look through the window, but there was no window through which to look. He wanted to run down the three flights and yell, "Help!" but there were no stairs on which to run and no air in which to yell. And when he wanted merely to go out of doors, he saw that there was no out of doors. Evaporated!

For a while he stood there in confusion, unable to comprehend what had happened. But afterward he bethought himself: I'll go to sleep. He saw, however, that there was no longer any earth on which to sleep. Only then did he raise two fingers to his forehead and reflect: Apparently I've slept through the end of the world. Isn't that a fine how-do-you-do?

He became depressed. No more world, he thought. What will I do without a world? Where will I go to work, how will I make a living, especially now that the cost of living is so high and a dozen eggs cost a dollar twenty and who knows if they're even fresh, and besides, what will happen to the five dollars the gas company owes me? And where has my wife gone off to? Is it possible that she too has disappeared with the world, and with the thirty dollars' pay I had in my pockets? And she isn't by nature the kind that disappears, he thought to himself.

And what will I do if I want to sleep? On what will I stretch out if there isn't any world? And maybe my back will ache? And who'll finish the bundle of work in the shop? And suppose I want a glass of malted, where will I get it?

Eh, he thought, have you ever seen anything like it? A man should fall asleep with the world under his head and wake up without it!

As our hero stood there in his underwear, wondering what to do, a thought occurred to him: To hell with it! So there isn't any world! Who needs it anyway? Disappeared is disappeared: I might as well go to the movies and kill some time. But to his astonishment he saw that, together with the world, the movies had also disappeared.

A pretty mess I've made here, thought our hero and began smoothing his mustache. A pretty mess I've made here, falling asleep! If I hadn't slept so soundly, he taunted himself, I would have disappeared along with everything else. This way I'm unfortunate, and where will I get a malted? I love a glass in the morning. And my wife? Who knows with whom she's disappeared? If it's with that presser from the top floor, I'll murder her, so help me God.

Who knows how late it is?

With these words our hero wanted to look at his watch but couldn't find it. He searched with both hands in the left and right pockets of the infinite emptiness but could find nothing to touch.

I just paid two dollars for a watch and here it's already disappeared, he thought to himself. All right. If the world went under, it went under. That I don't care about. It isn't my world. But the watch! Why should my watch go under? A new watch. Two dollars. It wasn't even wound.

And where will I find a glass of malted?

There's nothing better in the morning than a glass of malted. And who knows if my wife . . . I've slept through such a terrible catastrophe, I deserve the worst. Help, help, hee—lp! Where were my brains? Why didn't I keep an eye on the world and my wife? Why did I let them disappear when they were still so young?

And our hero began to beat his head against the void, but since the void was a very soft one it didn't hurt him and he remained alive to tell this story.

Translated by Irving Howe

A Ghetto Dog

ISAIAH SPIEGEL

ANNA NIKOLAIEVNA, widow of Jacob Simon Temkin, the fur dealer, had only time enough to snatch up a small framed photograph of her husband, for the German was already standing in the open doorway shouting, *"R-raus-s!"*

There were no more Jews in the house by now, and if she had failed to hear the noise they made as they fled it was because with age she had grown hard of hearing and because that very morning, before the light had seeped through the heavy portieres, a desire had come over her to open her piano—a grand piano, black—and let her old parchment-like fingers glide over its yellowed keys. One could scarcely call what she was playing music, since her fingers, which were as gnarled as old fallen bark, had been tremulous with age for years. The echoes of several tunes had been sounding in her deaf ears the whole morning, so that she had failed to hear the German when he appeared shouting on the threshold.

All the while Nicky, the widow's dog, had been lying near one of the heavy portieres, dozing and dreaming an old dog's dream, his pointed muzzle resting on his outstretched paws. He was well along in years; his coat was shedding and light patches showed in its sandy hue. His legs were weak, but his big eyes—brownish with a blue glint—reminded one that he too had once been a puppy.

The widow and her dog led a lonely life. Nicky wandered through the rooms on his weak stumpy legs, his head drooping, and swayed mournfully, his whining quieted by weary thoughts. The Temkins had got him from a farm a long time ago. After his master's death the widow used to listen all day to Nicky moving through the stillness of the house. Whenever she sat by the table and Nicky was in the bedroom opposite (he had refused for several days to leave the bed where his master had died), it seemed to her as though her late husband were again walking through the bedroom in his house slippers. She used to listen to the least noise from the bedroom, pricking up her deaf ears, and as a sudden pallor spread over her wrinkled forehead she seemed actually to hear Jacob Simon's soft slow tread. Any moment now he would appear on the threshold of the bedroom, seat himself in the plush *fauteuil,* reach out for a plaid rug, and throw it over his knees, which had been rheumatic for so many years.

Between the widow and her dog there had formed a mesh of otherworldly thoughts and dreams. She saw in his drooping old head, in his worn-out fur and his pupils with their blue glints, a shadow of her husband. Perhaps this was because Nicky had been close to his master for so many years and had been ready to lay down his life for him, or perhaps because with time he had taken on his master's soft tread over the rugs, his master's lax mouth and watery eyes—whichever it was, the widow had never clasped the dog's head without feeling some inner disquiet. Between them there was that bond which sometimes springs up between two lonely creatures, one human and the other brute.

While the German was still in the open doorway, and before the widow had time to snatch up the photograph, Nicky had already taken his stand at the threshold. He raised his old head against the

German, opened his mouth wide to reveal his few remaining teeth, let out three wild howls, and was set to leap straight for the German's throat. One could see Nicky's hackles rise and hear his old paws scrape as he dashed about, ready to leap at the stranger in the outlandish green uniform. Suddenly the dog had shed his years; his legs straightened and hot saliva drooled from his muzzle as if he would say, "I know you're our enemy, I know! But you just wait—wait!"

The German at the door became confused for a moment. Taken aback by the fire glinting in the old dog's eyes, he clutched at his pistol holster.

"Have pity!" the old woman quavered. "It's only a poor animal—"

With her old body she shielded Nicky from the German and at the same time began patting the dog. In a moment he lay quiet and trembling in the old woman's arms. At last the widow tugged at his leash, and the two of them made their way through the dark hallway and into the street. As she hurried through the hallway she seized a small black cane with a silver knob; without this cane, a memento of her husband, she could hardly take a step.

She found herself in the street, leaning on the black cane with the silver knob, the rescued photograph safe in her bosom, and tugging the dog on his leash. Her eyes could scarcely be said to perceive what was going on around her. The day was frosty, blue; a blue silvery web of mist, spun by the early Polish winter, was spreading over the houses, the street, the sidewalks. The faces of the fleeing Jews were yellow, pallid. Nicky was still restless and was drawing back all the time; he did not know where his mistress was leading him. From time to time he fixed his eyes on the widow's face, while she, as she trudged along, felt a sudden icy fear grip her heart. From the dog's eyes raised to hers there peered the watery, lifeless gaze of her late husband. And here were the two of them, linked together in the web of frosty mist that was swirling under a lowering dark sky. The two of them were now plodding close to each other, their heads downcast. Cold, angry thoughts kindled in her drowsy old mind. She actually felt a chill breath swishing about her ears and she caught words—far-off words, cold and dead.

The widow who had for so long lived a life apart from Jews and Jewishness had suddenly come to herself, as if awaking from a state of unconsciousness. She had been driven out of her house, of course, as a Jew like any other, although for many years her house had been like any Christian's. Her only son had become an apostate, had married a Christian girl and gone off to Galicia, long before the war, where he was living on his father-in-law's estate. During the Christian holidays various gifts would arrive from him. She knew beforehand what he would send: a big, well-fattened turkey and half a dozen dyed Easter eggs. The turkey she could use, but when it came to the colored eggs the old woman had a strange oppressive feeling. They would lie around for months, gathering dust on their shells, until some evening she peeled them in the bright light of the girandole and then left them on the window sill for the hungry sparrows.

She herself had been estranged from Jewishness since her very childhood. For years on end no Jewish face appeared at her threshold. The war, which had come so suddenly to the town, had during the first few days failed to reach her comfortable home. The catastrophe that had befallen the Jews had not touched her, and the angry prophecy of the storm that was raging in the streets had not beaten upon her door.

When the German had opened it that morning, he had aroused the little old woman from her torpor and had reminded her that she was a Jew and that heavy days had come for her and all other Jews. And though the old woman had during so many years been cut off from Jewishness and Jews, she had accepted the sudden misfortune with courage and resignation, as if an invisible thread had connected her to her people all through the years.

Now she was trudging through the streets with so many others whose faces were strange and distracted. She recognized these faces from her remote youth, faces framed in black unkempt Jewish beards and surmounted by small round skullcaps, which Jacob Simon used to ridicule so in his lifetime. Jews in gaberdines, Jewish women wearing headkerchiefs and marriage wigs, were dragging their children by the hand. Anna's heart was filled with a friendly feeling as, leaning on her black, silver-knobbed cane, she led Nicky with her left hand. The fleeing Jews cast surly sidelong looks at her and the dog. Nicky plodded on without once lifting up his head; the light had gone out of his eyes. A small spotted dog suddenly emerged from the crowd, ran up to Nicky, and placed a paw on the old dog's neck as if seeking consolation; thereafter both dogs walked side by side.

Nicky sensed the strange atmosphere as they turned into the next street. It was poorly paved, with gaping pits; the press was greater here. He could barely make his way among the thousands of unfriendly feet. They kept stepping on his paws, and once his mistress almost fell. Anna held her head higher and was pulled along by the crowd of Jews. She drew the leash closer to her, every so often saving Nicky from being trampled. By now he kept closer to her, mournful, and with his head still lower.

Fine, wet snowflakes swirled in the air, unwilling to fall to the ground, and settled on Nicky's grizzled, closely curled coat.

The widow found herself in a narrow squalid street in the Balut district of Lodz, where all the hack-drivers, porters, and emaciated Jewish streetwalkers lived. She had come here with a host of strangers who quickly made themselves at home in a huge empty barn. The Jewish streetwalkers brought them all sorts of good things baked of white flour. The widow sat in the barn, her gray disheveled head propped on the silver knob of her cane, while Nicky sprawled at her feet and took in the angry din made by the strange people.

It was late at night before everyone in the barn was assigned quarters in the district. The widow found herself in the room of a tart known as Big Rose—a very much disgruntled tart, who did not want a dog in the house.

"It's enough that I have to take in a female apostate!" she kept yelling. "What do I need a sick old hound for?"

Anna stood on the threshold before the tart, the dog close to her on his unsteady legs; his body emanated a forlornness that was both animal and human.

"Quiet, quiet!" The widow's hand fell shakily on Nicky's drooping head and patted it.

The room where Big Rose lived lay under a gabled roof. It held a small shabby sofa, strewn with yellow and red cushions. A low ceiling made the place dreary and depressing. Outside the window was the hostile night, spattered with the silver of the first frost. This night-silver interlaced with the reflections of light from the room and fell on the windowpanes like dancing stars.

The nook that sheltered the widow and her dog was very dark; the warmth lingered there as if in a closed warm cellar. Throughout the room there hovered a sour odor of sin and lust. The old woman did not realize where she had come to; nothing mattered any longer. She and her dog huddled in their nook and for a long while squatted there like two huge rigid shadows. From time to time Nicky put his head in her lap, and a soft, long-drawn-out whine issued from the dark nook, like the moan of a hopelessly sick man.

Later that night, when the old woman and the dog had stretched out in their nook on some rags, Big Rose closed the red hangings which screened the shabby sofa from the rest of the room. The little red flame of the small night-lamp hanging on the wall wavered slowly and angrily, licking at the musty darkness around it.

Only now, when everything had become utterly quiet, did certain huge shadows appear in the darkness of the threshold. The shadows entered one by one; each hovered for a moment on the threshold, looked about, then disappeared within the hangings. In the dark little hallway on the other side of the door other shadows gathered and waited for the door to open. They did not have to wait long: each shadow, after darting out from behind the hangings, rushed through the door and disappeared down the dark stairs.

The widow was dozing by now. From time to time she awoke and put her arms around Nicky's warm neck. The dog continued snoring with a low, canine snore. Each time the door opened and a shadow darted within the hangings, from which there immediately issued Big Rose's witchlike snicker, Nicky would emit a low growl.

This suddenly angered Big Rose. She sprang up naked by the drawn-back hangings and, brandishing her arms, shouted at the widow in the nook, "My grand madam! May a curse light on you! Maybe madam would like to step out for a little while on the balcony with the hound? He's driving everybody away, may the devil overtake him! I'll poison that hound!"

The widow, startled from her sleep, was frightened by Big Rose's stark nakedness and its pungent reek.

"Sh, sh, sh!" she at last managed to whisper to the dog.

She stood up in her nook, took Nicky's head, and started for the door. Through the small dark hallway the two of them, the widow and the dog, reached the deserted balcony. Below them lay a tangle of dark Balut streets. The wind drove nearer and scattered the grayish, tenuous whiteness of the still swirling night snow. From the south side of the city the dusty glow of electric lights was borne through the night. The widow watched these lights blinking on and off, like inflamed eyes.

"See there, Nicky? Over there—there. That's our house, our street—"

The dog lifted his head, stood up on his hind legs, and peered into the darkness. For a while he stood thus, with the widow's arms around him, then suddenly let out a howl. It rent the sky like lightning, beat against the clouds, and then died away in the cold darkness of the earth.

In the morning, when the chilled widow awoke in her nook, the dog was no longer by her side. Nobody had any idea where he had vanished to. Big Rose kept saying that this was no dog but a werewolf and that she hadn't even heard the dog leaving the house.

He was gone the whole day, and only toward evening did they hear him scraping at the door. He fell into the nook in great excitement, with foam on his hanging tongue, and threw himself on the frightened widow's lap.

Nicky lay on her knees, quivering with an ardent, old-dog sob. The widow took his shivering head and for some time gazed into his watery pupils, as if into the small openings of two wells. She could not understand what had happened to the dog. He barked in a subdued way, as if some words were struggling to escape him, as if he were straining to tell everything to the old woman bending over him. His whole body quivered, and his narrow face seemed to wear the twisted grimace of a dog in lament. Yet this was not whining; rather a noisy outburst of joy and consolation. He kept lifting his paws and putting them on the old woman's knees. The widow took the paws and brought them to her aged, withered lips, bent over, and for a long, long time, with her eyes closed, rested her head upon them.

For a long time the widow sat in the darkness embracing the dog, while the night-lamp, which had been turned low and had been burning all day near the red hangings, now cast a mysterious reddish reflection on the wall. The sharp silhouette of the dog's pointed head and the widow's arms swayed on the ceiling in a network of dancing shadows.

The next morning Nicky again disappeared and did not come back until nightfall. This was repeated day after day.

These disappearances coincided with the time the Germans built a wall around the ghetto, barbed wires dividing the Balut from the rest of the city. Nobody was allowed to leave or enter the Jewish district. But just the same Nicky used to disappear every day and come back only at night.

Once, when Nicky returned as excited as always, the old woman put her hands on his head and drew them back: they were sticky with blood. His fur was split and torn with open wounds. He was holding his paws on her knees, as always, but this time his pupils were reddish, glowing, and little green fires kept dancing across his watery eyes.

The widow applied rag after rag soaked in cold water to the dog's open wounds. Only now did she realize that Nicky had been crawling through the barbed wire, that each morning he had run off to the city and each evening he had come running home. The widow kept on washing the warm blood and applying the cold wet rags, while Big Rose ran to fetch basins of water. The bitterness she had felt in her heart for the dog had quickly vanished. She took a white blouse from her closet and tore it into narrow bandages; she also procured from somewhere a salve that was good even for human wounds. She smeared torn strips with the salve and then, kneeling by the door, started to bind the dog's wounds.

A sudden fright came over Big Rose; an other-wordly expression appeared on her face, as if she felt a cold breath upon her. She could have sworn by all that was holy that, as she had been binding the dog's wounds, he had given her a mournful human look.

From the day Big Rose had bound the open wounds the dog had got by crawling through the barbed wire strung around the ghetto —from that day her attitude toward the widow had undergone a complete change. She took down the red hangings that had divided the room in two and asked the old woman to leave her dark nook and share the room with her. All three of them, the two women and the dog, now used the sofa. Nicky lay propped up by the colored cushions, lost in an old dog's dream.

This happened just about the time when the Germans issued an order that all animals—horses, cows, goats, and dogs—must be turned over to them. Only two broken-down horses were allowed to remain in the whole ghetto. For generations the old Jewish residents of the Balut had made their meager living as animal-breeders. The hack-drivers and cabbies, the milk dealers, small middlemen, organ-grinders, and innkeepers had to give up the horses and cows they had tended in the crowded dark stables and stalls. They unharnessed their horses for the last time and embraced the warm necks of their cows; they led out the mournful Jewish cows and the frightened Jewish goats. The draymen led their beautiful, glossy chestnut draft horses through the streets, the whole family marching in step with them, wringing their hands as if they were following the dead to a yawning grave. The women dragged the cows and goats along—the animals became stubborn and refused to budge. At the tail end of the procession, on ropes and leashes, other Jews were leading watchdogs, Dalmatians, poodles with mournful eyes, and common household pets with bobbed tails. The Jews hoped that their dumb creatures would be better fed than they had been in the ghetto. The horses and cows were taken into the city, but the dogs were immediately shot in a field close to the market place.

At daybreak Big Rose had thrown a torn black shawl with long fringes over her, and the widow, without uttering a word, had taken Nicky on his leash with one hand and her small silver-knobbed cane in the other. Both women were going to take the dog to the market place. Big Rose kept mauling her cheeks and softly weeping. The widow's disheveled hair, gray and lifeless, hung over her ashen face.

The compulsory surrender of her dog had come as such a shock to the widow that at first, when Big Rose had shouted the news into her face, she had clutched her head with her withered fingers and had remained still for several minutes. Big Rose thought the old woman had died, standing with her fingers in her hair, and her eyes not even blinking. She just stood there, stunned and stone-cold.

The dog let them do with him whatever they liked. He dropped at their feet and held his pointed head up to them, then yawned and let his muzzle sink to the cold floor.

The two women started out through the small courtyard, Nicky on his long leash between them. The snow was coming down in flakes as slender and chill as needles and stabbed their hands, their faces, and the dog's fur. It was bitter cold. Although dawn had broken a comparatively short while ago, the ghetto seemed already to be in twilight—night can fall abruptly in that region.

Big Rose bit her lips as she walked along. She peered out from the black shawl in which she was wrapped and could see nothing but the widow's half-dead face. Nicky still had his back bound in rags.

As they neared the market place they saw Jewish children emerging from the surrounding little streets, leading gaunt, emaciated dogs on ropes and leashes. There was a pound in the market place where the Germans collected the dogs. The horses and cows had already been transferred to German civilians to bring into the city proper. The dogs within the pound were looking out on the ghetto through barbed wire, their eyes watering. A shadowy terror was frozen upon their frightened, pointed muzzles.

A German stationed near the wicket leading into the pound relieved each owner of his or her dog, pushed the wicket open, kicked the dog with the point of his boot—and the animal found itself in the pound. Rarely or ever did any dog snarl at the German. Sudden shock paralyzed the dogs, depriving them of their strength and numbing their rage. Perhaps this was due to the reek that now came to them from the field where the dogs were being killed.

By the time the widow and Big Rose approached the pound with Nicky it was full of Jewish dogs. They were jammed together, huddled in twos and threes, their heads resting on one another's shoulders. Perhaps they did this because of the cold, which beat down upon them from the sky. A few of them were close to the barbed wire, prodding it with their paws in an attempt to get free. But they had to fall back with a childlike whimper when they felt their paws become sticky with blood. The barbs of the wire were sharp and rusty and stuck out like little knife points.

The widow and Big Rose halted before the German. He was waiting for the old woman to let go of the leash. But, instead of letting go, she wound the leash still tighter about her wrist and even her forearm. She did this with her eyes closed, the way a Jew winds the straps of a phylactery on his forearm. The German snatched at the leash. The widow staggered on her old legs, since Nicky was by now pulling her into the pound. She let herself be dragged along. In the meantime the German kicked the wicket shut. His loud, tinny laughter ran along the barbed wire.

Big Rose saw the widow standing inside the enclosure ringed by a pack of dogs and still holding Nicky on the leash. In her left hand she had the small cane with the silver knob and was keeping it high over the heads of the dogs. She stood there with her cane raised, her hair disheveled, the dogs circling at her feet. Some of the dogs lifted up their mournful heads and looked into the old woman's face. Nicky alone remained unperturbed. His back was still bound up in the white rags torn from Big Rose's blouse. From time to time he lifted his head toward the wicket where Big Rose was standing, petrified.

Exhausted, the widow sank to her knees in the snow. By now one could barely make out her body. The snow was falling more heavily, in bright shimmering stars. The widow's head stood out in the whiteness like a dazzling aureole.

Big Rose saw another wicket fly open on the other side and someone begin driving the dogs out into an open field. The widow stood up, leaned on her small silver-knobbed cane, and, with Nicky leading, started toward the field. . . .

Big Rose wrapped the small black shawl more tightly about her head. She did not want to hear the dull, tinny sounds that came from the sharp-edged shovels scooping up the frozen ground of the Balut. It was only the wind, playing upon the shovels that delved the narrow black pits—only the wind, chanting its chill night song.

Translated by Bernard Guilbert Guerney

My Quarrel with Hersh Rasseyner

CHAIM GRADE

1.

In 1937 I returned to Bialystok, seven years after I had been a student in the Novaredok Yeshiva of the Mussarists, a movement that gives special importance to ethical and ascetic elements in Judaism. When I came back I found many of my old schoolmates still there. A few even came to my lecture one evening. Others visited me secretly; they did not want the head of the yeshiva to find out. I could see that their poverty had brought them suffering and that the fire of their youthful zeal had slowly burned itself out. They continued to observe all the laws and usages meticulously, but the weariness of spiritual wrestlings lay upon them. For years they had tried to tear the desire for pleasure out of their hearts, and now they realized they had lost the war with themselves. They had not overcome the evil urge.

There was one I kept looking for and could not find, my former schoolmate Hersh Rasseyner. He was a dark young man with bright, downcast eyes. I did not meet him, but heard that he kept to his garret in solitude and did not even come to the yeshiva.

Then we met unexpectedly in the street. He was walking with his eyes lowered, as is the custom with the Mussarists; they do not wish to be "eye to eye" with the world. But he saw me anyway. He put his arms behind him, thrusting his hands into his sleeves, so that he would not have to shake hands. The closer he came, the higher rose his head. When we finally stood face to face, he looked at me intently. He was so moved his nostrils seemed to quiver—but he kept silent.

Among the Mussarists, when you ask, "How are you?" the question means, What is the state of your religious life? Have you risen in spirituality? But I had forgotten and asked quite simply, "Hersh Rasseyner, how are you?"

Hersh moved back a little, looked me over from head to toe, saw that I was modishly dressed, and shrugged. "And how are you, Chaim Vilner? My question, you see, is more important."

My lips trembled and I answered hotly, "Your question, Hersh Rasseyner, is no question at all. I do what I have to."

Right there, in the middle of the street, he cried out, "Do you think, Chaim Vilner, that by running away from the yeshiva you have saved yourself? You know the saying among us: Whoever has learned Mussar can have no enjoyment in his life. You will always be deformed, Chaim Vilner. You will remain a cripple the rest of your life. You write godless verses and they reward you by patting you on the cheek. Now they're stuffing you with applause as they stuff a goose with grain. But later you'll see, when you've begun to go to their school, oh, won't the worldly ones beat you! Which of you isn't hurt by criticism? Is there one of you really so self-confident that he doesn't go around begging for some authority's approval? Is there one of you who's prepared to publish his book anonymously? The big thing with you people is that your name should be seen and known. You have given up our tranquillity of spirit for what? For passions you will never be able to satisfy and for doubts you will never be able to answer, no matter how much you suffer."

When he had spoken his fill, Hersh Rasseyner began to walk away with a quick, energetic stride. But I had once been a Mussarist too, so I ran after him.

"Hersh, listen to me now. No one knows better than I how torn you are. You're proud of yourself because you don't care if the whole street laughs at you for wearing a prayer vest down to your ankles. You've talked yourself into believing that the cloth with the woolen fringes is a partition between you and the world. You despise yourself because you're afraid you may find favor in the eyes of the world, the world that is to you like Potiphar's wife. You fear you won't have the strength to tear yourself away as the righteous Joseph did. So you flee from temptation and think the world will run after you. But when you see that the world doesn't run after you, you become angry and cry out: Nobody enjoys life. You want to console yourself with that idea. You live in solitude in your garret because you would rather have nothing at all than take the crumb that life throws you. Your modesty is pride, not self-denial.

"And who told you that I seek pleasure? I seek a truth you don't have. For that matter, I didn't run away, I simply returned to my own street—to Yatkev Street in Vilna. I love the porters with their backs broken from carrying their burdens; the artisans sweating at their workbenches; the market women who would cut off a finger to give a poor man a crust of bread. But you scold the hungry for being sinners, and all you can tell them is to repent. You laugh at people who work because you say they don't trust in God. But you live on what others have made. Women exhausted with work bring you something to eat, and in return you promise them the world to come. Hersh Rasseyner, you have long since sold your share of the world to come to those poor women."

Hersh Rasseyner gave a start and disappeared. I returned to Vilna with a burden removed from my conscience. In the disputation with the Mussarist I myself began to understand why I had left them. If at the time, I said to myself, I didn't know why and where I was going, someone else thought it out for me, someone stronger than I. That someone else was—my generation and my environment.

2.

Two years passed. War broke out between Germany and Poland. The western Ukraine and western White Russia were taken over by the Red Army. After they had been in Vilna a few weeks, the Russians announced that they were giving the city back to the Lithuanians. To Vilna there began to come refugees who did not want to remain under Soviet rule. The Novaredok Yeshiva came also. Meanwhile the Soviets remained. Hunger raged in the city. Every face was clouded with fear of the arrests carried out at night by NKVD agents. My heart was heavy. Once, standing in line for a ration of bread, I suddenly saw Hersh Rasseyner.

I had heard that he had married. His face was framed by a little black beard, his gait was more restrained, his clothing more presentable. I was so glad to see him that I left my place in the line, pushed through the crowd, and came up to him.

He said little and was very cautious. I understood why. He did not trust me and was afraid of trouble. I could see that he was trying to make up his mind whether to speak to me. But when he saw how despondent I was, he hid his mouth with his hand, as though to conceal his twisted smile, and a gleam of derision came into his eyes. With his head he motioned toward the bridge, on which were parked a few tanks with Red Army soldiers.

"Well, Chaim," Hersh said to me quietly, "are you satisfied now? Is this what you wanted?"

I tried to smile and answered just as quietly, "Hersh, I bear no more responsibility for all that than you do for me."

He shook himself and pronounced a few sharp, cutting words, seeming to forget his fear. "You're wrong, Chaim. I do bear responsibility for you." He retreated a few steps and motioned with his eyes to the Red Army soldiers, as though to say, "And you for them."

3.

Nine more years passed, years of war and destruction, during which I wandered across Russia, Poland, and Western Europe. In 1948, on a summer afternoon, I was riding in the Paris Métro. Couples stood close together. Short Frenchwomen, as though fainting, hung by the sides of their black-haired lovers.

I saw a familiar face. Until then it had been concealed by someone's shoulder, and only when the couples had to move a little did that corner of the car open up. My heart began to pound. Could he really be alive? Hadn't he been in Vilna under the German occupation? When I returned to the ruins of my home in 1945 I did not see him or hear of him. Still, those were the same eyes, the same obstinately upturned nose; only the broad black beard had begun to turn gray. It was astonishing to me that he could look at the couples so calmly, and that a good-natured smile lit up his melancholy glance. That was not like him. But after a moment I noticed that there was a faraway look in his eyes. He really did not see the people on the train. He was dressed neatly, in a long cloak and a clean white shirt buttoned at the throat, without a necktie. I thought to myself, He never wore ties. This more than anything else convinced me that it was he.

I pushed my way to him through the passengers and blurted out, "Excuse me, aren't you Reb Hersh Rasseyner?"

He looked at me, wrinkled his forehead, and smiled. "Ah, Chaim, Chaim, is that you? *Sholom aleichem!* How are you?"

I could tell that this time when Hersh Rasseyner asked, "How are you?" he did not mean what he had meant eleven years before. Then his question was angry and derisive. Now he asked the question quietly, simply. It came from his heart and it showed concern, as for an old friend.

We got into a corner and he told me briefly that he had been in a camp in Latvia. Now he was in Germany, at the head of a yeshiva in Salzheim.

"The head of a yeshiva in Germany? And who are your students, Reb Hersh?"

He smiled. "Do you think that the Holy One is an orphan? We still have lads, praise be to the Almighty, who study Torah."

He told me that he had been in the camp with about ten pupils. He had drawn them close to him and taught them Jewishness. Because they were still only children and very weak he helped them in their work. At night they used to gather about his cot and all would recite Psalms together. There was a doctor in the camp who used to say that he would give half his life to be able to recite Psalms too. But he couldn't. He lacked faith, poor man.

I was happy to meet my old friend and I preferred to avoid a debate, so I merely asked, "And what brings you here so often? Are you in business?"

"Of course we're in business." He stroked his beard with satisfaction. "Big business. We bring yeshiva people here and send them off to Israel and America. We take books back from here. With the help of the Almighty, I have even flown twice to Morocco."

"Morocco? What did you do there, Reb Hersh?"

"Brought back students from among the Moroccan Jews, spoke in their synagogue."

"And how did you talk to them? You don't know Arabic or French."

"The Almighty helps. What difference does it make how you speak? The main thing is *what* you speak."

Unexpectedly he began to talk about me. "How will it be with you, Chaim? It's time for you to start thinking about repentance. We're nearer rather than farther."

"What do you mean?"

"I mean," he said, drawing out his words in a chant, "that we have both lived out more than half our lives. What will become of Reb Chaim?" He strongly accented the word Reb. "Where are you voyaging? Together with them, perhaps?" His eyes laughed at the young couples. "Will you get off where they do? Or do you still believe in this merciless world?"

"And you, Reb Hersh," I asked in sudden irritation, "do you still believe in particular providence? You say that the Holy One is not, as it were, an orphan. But we are orphans. A miracle happened to you, Reb Hersh, and you were saved. But how about the rest? Can you still believe?"

"Of course I believe," said Hersh Rasseyner, separating his hands in innocent wonder. "You can touch particular providence, it's so palpable. But perhaps you're thinking of the kind of man who has faith that the Almighty is to be found only in the pleasant places of this world but is not to be found, God forbid, in the desert and wasteland? You know the rule: Just as a man must make a blessing over the good, so must he make a blessing over evil. We must fall before the greatness—"

"What do you want, Reb Hersh?" I interrupted. "Shall I see the greatness of God in the thought that only He could cause such destruction, not flesh and blood? You're outdoing the Psalms you recited on your bed in the concentration camp. The Psalmist sees the greatness of God in the fact that the sun comes out every day, but you see miracles in catastrophes."

"Without any doubt," Hersh Rasseyner answered calmly, "I see everywhere, in everything, at every moment, particular providence. I couldn't remain on earth for one minute without the thought of God. How could I stand it without Him in this murderous world?"

"But I won't say that His judgment is right. I can't!"

"You can," said Hersh Rasseyner, putting a friendly hand on my shoulder, "you can—gradually. First the repentant understands that the world can't be without a Guide. Then he understands that the Guide is the God of Israel and that there is no other power besides Him to help Him lead the world. At last he recognizes that the world is in Him, as we read: 'There is no place void of Him.' And if you understood that, Chaim, you would also understand how the Almighty reveals Himself in misfortune as well as in salvation."

Hersh Rasseyner spoke in a warm voice. He did not once take his hand off my shoulder. I felt a great love for him and saw that he had become more pious than ever.

4.

We left the Métro near the Jewish quarter, at the rue de Rivoli, and we passed the old city hall, the Hôtel de Ville. In the niches of the walls of the Hôtel de Ville, between the windows, in three rows, stand stone figures, some with a sword, some with a book, some with brush and palette, and some with geometric instruments. Hersh Rasseyner saw me looking at the monuments. He glanced at them out of the corners of his eyes and asked, "Who are those idols?"

I explained to him that they were famous Frenchmen: statesmen, heroes, scholars, and artists.

"Reb Hersh," I pleaded with him, "look at those statues. Come closer and see the light streaming from their marble eyes. See how much goodness lies hidden in their stone faces. You call it idolatry, but I tell you that, quite literally, I could weep when I walk about Paris and see these sculptures. It's a miracle, after all. How could a human being breathe the breath of life into stone? When you see a living man, you see only one man. But when you see a man poured out in bronze, you see mankind itself. Do you understand me? That one there, for instance, is a poet famous all over the world. The great writer broadens our understanding and stirs our pity for our fellow men. He shows us the nature of the man who can't overcome his desires. He doesn't punish even the wicked man, but sees him according to his afflictions in the war he wages with himself and the rest of the world. You don't say he's right, but you understand that he can't help it. Why are you pulling at your beard so angrily, Reb Hersh?"

He stared at me with burning eyes and cried out, "For shame! How can you say such foolish things? So you could weep when you look at those painted lumps of matter? Why don't you weep over the charred remains of the Gaon of Vilna's synagogue? Those artists of yours, those monument-choppers, those poets who sang about their emperors, those tumblers who danced and played before the rulers—did those masters of yours even bother to think that their patron would massacre a whole city and steal all it had, to buy them, your masters, with the gold? Did the prophets flatter kings? Did they take gifts of harlots' wages? And how merciful you are! The writer shows how the wicked man is the victim of his own bad qualities. I think that's what you said. It's really a pity about the arrogant rebel! He destroys others, and of course he's destroyed too. What a pity! Do you think it's easier to be a good man than an adulterer? But you particularly like to describe the lustful man. You know him better, there's something of him in you artists. If you make excuses for the man who exults in his wickedness, then as far as I'm concerned all your scribbling is unclean and unfit.

Condemn the wicked man! Condemn the glutton and drunkard! Do you say he can't help it? He has to help it! You've sung a fine song of praise to the putrid idols, Chaim Vilner."

Hersh Rasseyner looked into my eyes with the sharp, threatening expression I had seen eleven years earlier, when we met in that Bialystok street. His voice had become hard and resounding. Passers-by stopped and stared at the bearded Jew who shook his finger at the sculptures of the Hôtel de Ville. Hersh did not so much as notice the passers-by. I felt embarrassed in the face of these Frenchmen, smiling and looking at us curiously.

"Don't shout so," I told him irritably. "You really think you have a monopoly on mercy and truth. You're starting where we left off eleven years ago. In Novaredok you always kept the windows closed, but it was still too light for you in the House of Study, so you ran off to your garret. From the garret you went down into a cellar. And from the cellar you burrowed down into a hole under the earth. That's where you could keep your commandment of solitude and that's where you persuaded yourself that a man's thoughts and feelings are like his hair; if he wants to, he can trim his hair and leave nothing but a beard and earlocks—holy thought and pious conduct. You think the world is what you imagine it, and you won't have anything to do with it. You think men are what you imagine them, but you tell them to be the opposite. But even the concentration camps couldn't make men different from what they are. Those who were evil became worse in the camps. They might have lived out their lives and not known themselves for what they were, but in the crisis men saw themselves and others undisguised. And when we were all freed, even the better ones among us weren't freed of the poison we had to drink behind the barbed wire. Now, if the concentration camp couldn't change men from top to bottom, how can you expect to change them?"

Hersh Rasseyner looked at me with astonishment. The anger that had flared in his eyes died down, though a last flicker seemed to remain.

"You don't know what you're talking about, Chaim," he said quietly and reluctantly. "Who ever told you that afflictions as such make people better? Take the day of a man's death, for instance. When a God-fearing man is reminded of death, he becomes even more God-fearing, as we read in Scripture: 'It is better to go to the house of mourning than to the house of feasting.' But when a free thinker is reminded of death he becomes even wilder, as the prophet says about the thoughts of the wicked: 'Let us eat and drink, for tomorrow we shall die.' It's quite clear that external causes can't drag people back to a Jewish life. A man's heart and mind have to be ready.

"If a man didn't come to the concentration camp with a thirst for a higher life, he certainly didn't elevate himself there. But the spiritual man knows that always and everywhere he must keep mounting higher or else he will fall lower. And as for the claim that a man can't change—that is a complete lie. 'In my flesh shall I see God!' The case of Hersh Rasseyner proves that a man can change. I won't tell you a long story about how many lusts I suffered from; how often the very veins in my head almost burst from the boiling of the blood; how many obstinacies I had to tear out of myself. But I knew that whoever denies himself affirms the Master of the World. I knew that the worst sentence that can be passed on a man is that he shall not be able to renounce his old nature. And because I truly wanted to conquer myself, the Almighty helped me."

"You are severe in your judgments," I answered. "You always were, Reb Hersh, if you'll pardon my saying so. You call these wise men putrid idols, but you refuse to see that they lifted mankind out of its bestial state. They weren't butchers of the soul and they didn't talk themselves into believing that human beings can tear their lower urges out of themselves and lop them off. They were very well aware of the hidden root of the human race. They wanted to illuminate men's minds with wisdom, so that men would be able to grow away from their untamed desires. You can't banish shadows with a broom, only with a lighted lamp. These great men—"

Hersh began to laugh so loud that I had to interrupt myself. He immediately stopped laughing and sighed. "I am very tired," he said. "I have been traveling the whole night. But somehow I don't want to leave you. After all, you were once a student at Novaredok; perhaps there is still a spark of the spirit left in you somewhere."

We walked to a bench in silence. On first meeting him I had thought that he had become milder. Now I realized regretfully that his demands upon me and his negation of the whole world had grown greater. I hoped, though, that the pause would ease the tension that had arisen between us, and I was in no hurry to be the first to talk again. Hersh, however, wrinkled his forehead as though he were collecting his thoughts, and when we were seated on the bench he returned to my last words.

5.

"Did you say they were great men? The Germans insist they produced all the great men. I don't know whether they produced the very greatest, but I don't suppose that you worldly people would deny that they did produce learned men. Well, did those philosophers influence their own nation to become better? And the real question is, were the philosophers themselves good men? I don't want you to think that I underestimate their knowledge. During my years in the concentration camp I heard a good deal. There were exceptionally learned men among us, because the Germans mixed us all together, and in our moments of leisure we used to talk. Later, when with the help of the Almighty I was saved, I myself looked into the books of you worldly people, because I was no longer afraid they would hurt me. And I was really very much impressed by their ideas. Occasionally I found in their writings as much talent and depth as in our own Holy Books, if the two may be mentioned in one breath. But they are satisfied with talk! And I want you to believe me when I say that I concede that their poets and scientists wanted to be good. Only—only they weren't able to. And if some did have good qualities, they were exceptions. The masses and even their wise men didn't go any farther than fine talk. As far as talking is concerned, they talk more beautifully than we do.

"Do you know why they weren't able to become better? Because they were consumed with a passion to enjoy life. And since pleasure is not something that can be had by itself, murder arose among them—the pleasure of murder. And that's why they talk such fine talk, because they want to use it for fooling themselves into doing fine deeds. Only it doesn't help. They're satisfied with rhetoric, and the reason is that they care most of all for systems. The nations of the world inherited from the Greeks the desire for order and for pretty systems.

"First of all, they do what they do in public. They have no pleasure from their lusts if they can't sin openly, publicly, so that the whole world will know. They say of us that we're only hypocrites, whereas they do what they want to do publicly. But they like to wage war, not only with others, but with themselves as well, argue with themselves (of course, not too vigorously), even suffer and repent. And when they come to do repentance, the whole world knows about that too. That is the kind of repentance that gives them an intense pleasure; their self-love is so extreme it borders on sickness. They even like their victims, because their victims afford them the pleasure of sinning and the sweet afflictions of regret."

Hersh Rasseyner had moved away from me to the other end of the bench and had begun to look at me as though it had occurred to him that by mistake he might be talking to a stranger. Then he lowered his head and muttered as though to himself, "Do you remember that time in Bialystok?" He was silent for a moment and pulled a hair out of his beard as though he were pulling memories with it. "Do you remember, Chaim, how you told me on that Bialystok street that we were running away from the world because we were afraid we wouldn't be able to resist temptation? A Mussarist can labor for a lifetime on improving his qualities, yet a single word of criticism will stick in him like a knife. Yes, it's true! All the days of my youth I kept my eyes on the earth, without looking at the world. Then came the German. He took me by my Jewish beard, yanked my head up, and told me to look him straight in the eyes. So I had to look into his evil eyes, and into the eyes of the whole world as well. And I saw, Chaim, I saw—you know what I saw. Now I can look at all the idols and read all the forbidden impurities and contemplate all the pleasures of life, and it won't tempt me any more because now I know the true face of the world. Oh, Reb Chaim, turn and repent! It's not too late. Remember what the prophet Isaiah said: 'For my people have committed two evils: they have forsaken me, the fountain of living waters, and hewed them out cisterns, broken cisterns, that can hold no water.' "

Hersh had spoken like a broken man. Tears were dropping on his beard. He rubbed his eyes to hold the tears back, but they continued to flow down his cheeks.

I took his hand and said to him with emotion, "Reb Hersh, you say that I have forsaken a fountain of living waters for a broken cistern. I must tell you that you're wrong. I draw water from the same pure fountain as you, only I use a different vessel. But calm yourself, Reb Hersh.

"You yourself said that you believe that the nations of the world had men of wisdom and men of action who wanted to be good, but couldn't. I think I'm quoting you accurately. What I don't understand is this. It's a basic principle of Judaism that man has free will. The Novaredok people actually maintain that it's possible to attain such a state of perfection that we can do good deeds without the intervention of our physical bodies. Well then, if a man can actually peel the evil husks from himself, as he would peel an onion, how do you answer this question: Since the wise men among the gentiles wanted to be good, why couldn't they?"

I was unable to keep a mocking note of triumph out of my question. It stirred Hersh Rasseyner out of his mournful abstraction. With deliberation he straightened himself and answered gently, "Chaim, you seem to have forgotten what you learned at Novaredok, so I'll remind you. In His great love for mankind, the Almighty has endowed us with reason. If our sages of blessed memory tell us that we can learn from the animals, surely we can learn from reason as well. And we know that the elders of Athens erected systems of morality according to pure reason. They had many disciples, each with his own school.

"But the question hasn't changed. Did they really live as they taught, or did their system remain only a system? You must understand once and for all that when his reason is calm and pure, a man doesn't know what he's likely to do when his dark desire overtakes him. A man admires his own wisdom and is proud of his knowledge, but as soon as a little desire begins to stir in him he forgets everything else. Reason is like a dog on a leash who follows sedately in his master's footsteps—until he sees a bitch. With us it's a basic principle that false ideas come from bad qualities. Any man can rationalize whatever he wants to do. Is it true that only a little while ago he was saying the opposite of what he is now saying? He'll tell you he was wrong then. And if he lets you prove to him that he wasn't wrong then, he'll shrug and say, 'When I want to do something, I can't be an Aristotle.' As soon as his desire is sated, his reason revives and he's sorry for what he did. As soon as he feels desire beginning to stir once more, he forgets his reason again. It's as though he were in a swamp; when he pulls one foot out, the other sinks in. There is delicacy in his character, he has a feeling for beauty, he expresses his exalted thoughts in measured words, and there is no flaw in him; then he sees a female ankle and his reason is swallowed up. If a man has no God, why should he listen to the philosopher who tells him to be good? The philosopher himself is cold and gloomy and empty. He is like a man who wants to celebrate a marriage with himself.

"The one way out is this. A man should choose between good and evil only as the Law chooses for him. The Law wants him to be happy. The Law is the only reality in life. Everything else is a dream. Even when a man understands rationally what he should do, he must never forget that before all else he should do it because the Law tells him to do it. That is how he can guard against the time when his reason will have no power to command him.

"Wait a moment, I'm not through yet. A man may tell himself, 'I don't live according to reason but according to the Law.' And he may feel certain that when temptation comes he'll look into the appropriate book to see what he should do, and he'll do it. He tells himself that he is free. Actually, the freedom of his choice goes no farther than his wish. Even a man who has a Law won't be able to withstand his temptation if he doesn't watch over himself day and night. He who knows all secrets knew that our father Abraham would stand ready to sacrifice Isaac; but only after the Binding did the angel say to Abraham, 'Now I know.' Hence we learn that until a man has accomplished what he should, the Law does not trust him. A child has the capacity to grow, but we don't know how tall he'll grow. His father and mother may be as high as the trees, but he may favor a dwarf grandfather. Only by good deeds can we drive out bad deeds. Therefore the Jews cried out at Sinai, 'We will do'—only do, always do; 'and we will obey'—and now we want to know what the Law tells us to do. Without deeds all inquiry is vain.

"That is the outlook and the moral way of 'the old one,' Reb Joseph Yoizl, may his merit be a shield for us, and thousands of students at Novaredok steeped themselves in it day and night. We labored to make ourselves better, each of us polished and filed his own soul, with examiners gathering evidence of improvement like pearls. But you laughed at us. Then came the German, may his name be blotted out, and murdered our sainted students. And now we're both face to face with the destruction of the Community of Israel. But you are faced with another destruction as well—the destruction of your faith in the world. That's what hurts you and torments you, so you ask me: Why weren't the wise men of the gentiles able to be good if they wanted to be good? And you find contradictions in what I said. But the real contradiction you find is not in what I said but in yourself. You thought the world was striving to become better, and you discovered it was striving for our blood.

"Even if they wanted to, the wise men of the gentiles couldn't have become good to the very roots of their being because they didn't have a Law and because they didn't labor to perfect their qualities all their lives long. Their ethics were worked out by human minds. They trusted their reasoned assumptions as men trust the ice of a frozen river in winter. Then came Hitler and put his weight on the wisdom of the wise men of the nations. The ice of their slippery reasoning burst, and all their goodness was drowned.

"And together with their goodness to others their own self-respect was drowned. Think of it! For a word they didn't like they used to fight with swords or shoot one another. To keep public opinion from sneering or a fool from calling them coward, though they trembled at the thought of dying, they went to their death. Generation after generation, their arrogance grew like a cancer, until it ended by eating their flesh and sucking their marrow. For centuries they speculated, they talked, and they wrote. Does duty to nation and family come first, or does the freedom of the individual come before his obligations to parents, wife, and children—or even to one's self? They considered the matter solemnly and concluded that there are no bonds that a nation is not free to break; that truth and reason are like the sun, which must rise; can the sun be covered by throwing clods of earth at it? So there came in the West a booted ruler with a little mustache, and in the East a booted ruler with a big mustache, and both of them together struck the wise man to the ground, and he sank into the mud. I suppose you'll say that the wise men wanted to save their lives. I can understand that. But didn't they insist that freedom, truth, and reason were more precious to the philosopher than his life? Take that wise man whose statue is standing there, with his instruments for measuring the stars and planets. When everyone else argued, 'The sun revolves about the earth,' he said, 'Not so; do what you will to me, break me, draw and quarter me, the earth revolves about the sun!' What would he have said to his grandchildren today? If the spirit of life could return to him, he would crawl down from his niche in the wall, strike his stone head against the stone bridge, and recite Lamentations."

6.

Hersh Rasseyner had begun by speaking slowly, like the head of a yeshiva trying to explain a difficult passage to his pupil for the hundredth time, pausing briefly every now and then so that I could follow what he was saying. Gradually he grew animated. I was reminded of the discussions we used to have at Novaredok during the evenings after the Sabbath in the weeks before the Days of Awe. He began to speak more quickly, there was more excitement in his voice, and he ended his sentences like a man hammering nails into a wall. He shouted at me as though I were a dark cellar and he was calling to someone hiding in me.

The square and the neighboring streets had grown quieter and the flow of people had thinned out. On the benches in the little park passers-by sat mutely, exhausted by the intense heat of the day and trying to get some relief from the cool evening breeze that had begun to blow in the blue twilight of Paris.

"Hear me out, Chaim," Hersh resumed. "I'll tell you a secret. I have to talk to you. I talked to you during all those years when I was in the ghetto and later in the camps. Don't wonder at it, because you were always dear to me, from the time you were a student in Bialystok. Even then I had the feeling that you stood with one foot outside our camp. I prayed for you. I prayed that you would remain Jewish. But my prayers didn't help. You yourself didn't want to be pious. You left us, but I never forgot you. They used to talk about you in the yeshiva; your reputation reached us even there. And I suppose you remember the time we met in Bialystok. Later our yeshiva was in Vilna, under the Bolsheviks, and we met again, only then you were very downhearted. In the ghetto they said you had been killed while trying to escape. Afterward we heard from partisans in the forest that you were living in Russia. I used to imagine that if we were both saved, a miracle might happen. We would meet and I could talk to you. That's why you mustn't be surprised if I talk to you as fluently as though I were reciting the daily prayers. Believe me, I have had so many imaginary debates with you that I know my arguments as well as the first prayer of the morning."

"Reb Hersh," I said, "it's getting late. The time for afternoon prayers will be over soon."

"Don't worry about my afternoon prayers, Chaim!" He laughed. "I said them just after twelve o'clock. In the camp it became a habit with me not to delay carrying out any commandment. I reasoned that if any hour was to be my last, I didn't want to come to heaven naked.

"Do you have time and strength to go on listening to me? You do? Good. So far I've talked to you about the gentile wise men. But first we ought to be clear in our own minds about our relation to them and to the whole world. And one thing more: if anything I say strikes you as too harsh, don't take it amiss. Even though I'm talking to you, I don't mean you personally; I really mean secular Jews in general. So don't be angry."

7.

"Your Enlighteners used to sing this tune: 'Be a Jew at home and a man in public.' So you took off our traditional coat and shaved your beard and earlocks. Still, when you went out into the street, the Jew pursued you in your language, in your gestures, in every part of you. So you tried to get rid of the incubus. And the result was that the Jew left you, like an old father whose children don't treat him with respect; first he goes to the synagogue and then, because he has no choice, to the home for the aged. Now that you've seen what has happened to us, you've turned your slogan around. Now it's be a man at home and a Jew in public. You can't be pious at home because you're lacking in faith. Out of anger against the gentile and nostalgia for the father you abandoned, you want to parade your Jewishness in public. Only the man you try to be at home—I'm using your language—follows you out of your house. The parable of the Prince and the Nazirite applies to you. A dog was invited to two weddings, one near and one far. He thought, I won't be too late for the nearer one. So he ran first to the farther wedding—and missed it. Out of breath he ran to the one nearer home, and came after the feast. When he tried to push through the door, all he got was the stick. The upshot was that he missed both. The moral may be coarse, but you remember from your Novaredok days that it was applied to those who wanted to have both the pleasures of this world and the Law.

"You cried in the public square, 'The nations of the world dislike us because we're different. Let us be like them!' And you were like them. Not only that, but you stood at the head of their civilization. Where there was a famous scientist, thinker, writer—there you found a Jew. And precisely for that reason they hated us all the more. They won't tolerate the idea of our being like them. In the Middle Ages the priests wanted to baptize us. They used to delight in the torments of a Jew who tried to separate himself from the Community of Israel—with his family mourning him as though he were dead and the entire congregation lamenting as though it were the fast of *Tishe b'Av*. In our day, though, when they saw how easy it had become for a Jew to leap over into their camp, they stationed themselves at the outposts with axes in their hands, as though to fend off wild beasts. But you were hungry and blind, so you leaped—onto their axes.

"When you ran away from being Jewish, you disguised your flight with high-sounding names. An enlightened man would talk in the most elevated rhetoric about Enlightenment; but what he really had in mind was to become a druggist. He yearned for the fleshpots of Egypt. His ambition was to dig his hands into the pot with no one to look him in the eyes, like the miser who doesn't like anyone near him when he's eating. With the nations of the earth the great thing is the individual—his sovereignty, his pleasure, and his repose. But they understand that if they acted on the principle that might is right, one man would devour the other; so they have a government of individuals, and the rule is: Let me alone and I'll let you alone. With us Jews the individual doesn't exist; it's the community that counts. What's good for all must be good for each. Till your rebellion Jews lived as one—in prayer and in study, in joy and in sorrow. But you incited the tribes: 'Every man to your tents, O Israel!' Let each of us follow his own law, like the nations of the world. What's more, not only did you want to live as individuals, you wanted to die as individuals too. To avoid being confused with the other dead on the day of your death, you spent your lives erecting monuments for yourselves—one by great deeds; another by imposing his dominion; a third by a great business enterprise; and you by writing books. You didn't violate the commandment against idolatry. Of course not! You were your own gods. You prophesied, 'Man will be a god.' So naturally he became a devil.

"Why are you uneasy, Reb Chaim? Didn't we agree you wouldn't be angry? I don't mean you personally; I'm only speaking figuratively. But if you really feel I mean you, then I do! The wicked are as the unquiet sea. Every wave thinks it will leap over the shore, though it sees millions of others shattered before its eyes. Every man who lives for this world alone thinks that he will succeed in doing what no one else has ever been able to do. Well, you know now how far you got! But instead of looking for solace in the Master of the World and in the Community of Israel, you're still looking for the glass splinters of your shattered dreams. And little as you'll have the world to come, you have this world even less.

"Still, not all of you secularists wanted to overthrow the yoke of the Law altogether. Some grumbled that Judaism kept on getting heavier all the time: *Mishnah* on Bible; *Gemarah* on *Mishnah;* commentaries on *Gemarah;* codes; commentaries on the codes; commentaries on the commentaries, and commentaries on them. Lighten the weight a little, they said, so what is left can be borne more easily. But the more they lightened the burden, the heavier the remainder seemed to them. I fast twice a week without difficulty, and they can hardly do it once a year. Furthermore, what the father rejected in part, the son rejected in its entirety. And the son was right! Rather nothing than so little. A half-truth is no truth at all. Every man, and particularly every young man, needs a faith that will command all of his intellect and ardor. The devout cover a boy's head with a cap when he's a year old, to accustom him to commandments; but when a worldly father suddenly asks his grown son to cover his head with a paper cap and say the prayer over the wine on a Friday evening, the young man rightly thinks the whole thing is absurd. If he doesn't believe in Creation, and if the Exodus from Egypt is not much of a miracle, and if the Song of Songs is to him only the song of a shepherd and a shepherdess—God forbid!—and not the song of love between the Assembly of Israel and the Holy One, blessed be He, or between the supernal soul and the Almighty, why should he bless the Sabbath wine? Anyone who thinks he can hold on to basic principles and give up what he considers secondary is like a man who chops down the trunk of a tree and expects the roots not to rot.

"I've already told you, Chaim, that we of the Mussar school are very mindful of criticism. Do you remember telling me, on a street in Bialystok, that we try to escape by withdrawal because we would rather have nothing in this world than only a little? That's true. We want a more onerous code, more commandments, more laws, more prohibitions. We know that all the pleasures of life are like salt water: the more a man drinks of it, the thirstier he becomes. That's why we want a Torah that will leave no room in us for anything else.

"Suppose the Master of the World were to come to me and say, 'Hersh, you're only flesh and blood. Six hundred and thirteen commandments are too many for you, I will lighten your burden. You don't need to observe all of them. Don't be afraid, you won't be deprived of the resurrection of the dead!' Do you understand, Chaim, what it means to be at the resurrection of the dead and see life given again to all the Jews who fell before my eyes? If the Father of Mercy should ask less sacrifice of me, it would be very bitter for me. I would pray, 'Father of Mercy, I don't want my burden to be lightened, I want it to be made heavier.' As things are now, my burden is still too light. What point is there to the life of a fugitive, of a Jew saved from the crematorium, if he isn't always ready to sacrifice his bit of a rescued life for the Torah? But you, Chaim, are you as daring in your demands upon the world as I am in my demands upon the Master of the World? When you were studying with us, you were so strong and proud that you could be satisfied only by getting to the very bottom of the truth. And now do you think it right to crawl under the table of life, hoping for a bone from the feast of unclean pleasures, or a dry crumb of the joys of this world? Is that what's left to you of your pride and confidence in the warfare of life? I look at you and think, I'm still very far from being what I ought to be. If I had reached a higher stage, my heart would be torn with pity for you.

"The rebellious seducer rejected everything, while the one who halted between two opinions left something; but both of them, when they wanted to show their unfaltering good sense, first denounced the Community of Israel for allowing itself to be bound in the cobwebs of a profitless dialectic, living in a cemetery and listening to ghost stories, concerning itself with unrealities and thinking that the world ends at the ruined mill on the hilltop. The clever writer described it with great artistry, and the vulgar laughed. And the secularist reformers with their enlightened little beards justified themselves with a verse: 'Whom the Lord loveth He correcteth.' In other words, only because they really loved us did they attack us. But they groveled before everything they saw elsewhere. They called us fawning lickspittles—but with their own souls, like rags, they wiped the gentry's boots. The overt rebel and the man who prayed secretly and sinned secretly—why antagonize either side?—were at one in this, that the thing they mocked us for most enthusiastically was our belief in being chosen. What's so special about us? they asked, laughing. And I say, you may not feel very special—but you have to be! You may not want it, but the Almighty does! Thousands of years ago the God of Israel said through Ezekiel His prophet: 'And that which cometh into your mind shall not be at all; in that ye say: We will be as the nations, as the families of the countries, to serve wood and stone. As I live, saith the Lord God'—do you hear, Chaim? the Almighty swears by His own life—'As I live, saith the Lord God, surely with a mighty hand, and with an outstretched arm, and with fury poured out, will I be king over you.' You're a writer; write it on your forehead. You don't seem very impressed. You don't consider a verse to be proof. But the German is a proof, isn't he? Today, because so many Jews have been cut down, you don't want to remember how you used to laugh at them. But tomorrow, when the destruction will be forgotten, you'll laugh again at the notion that God has chosen us. That's why I want to tell you something.

"You know that I was in a camp. I lay on the earth and was trampled by the German in his hobnailed boots. Well, suppose that an angel of God had come to me then, that he had bent down and whispered into my ear, 'Hersh, in the twinkling of an eye I will turn you into the German. I will put his coat on you and give you his murderous face; and he will be you. Say the word and the miracle will come to pass.' If the angel had asked me—do you hear, Chaim?—I would not have agreed at all. Not for one minute would I have consented to be the other, the German, my torturer. I want the justice of law! I want vengeance, not robbery! But I want it as a Jew. With the Almighty's help I could stand the German's boots on my throat, but if I had had to put on his mask, his murderous face, I would have been smothered as though I had been gassed. And when the German shouted at me, 'You are a slave of slaves,' I answered through my wounded lips, 'Thou hast chosen me.'

"I want to ask you only one question, no more. What happened is known to all Jews. 'Let the whole House of Israel bewail the burning which the Lord hath kindled.' All Jews mourn the third of our people who died a martyr's death. But anyone with true feeling knows that it was not a third of the House of Israel that was destroyed, but a third of himself, of his body, his soul. And so we must make a reckoning—you as well as I. Anyone who doesn't make the reckoning must be as bestial as the beasts of the wood. Let's make the reckoning together. In justice and in mercy, may we forgive the murderers? No, we may not! To the end of all generations we may not forgive them. Forgiving the murderer is a fresh murder, only this time of brother by brother.

"Neither you nor I has the right to sleep at night. We have no right to flee the laments, the eyes, and the outstretched arms of the murdered; though we break under the anguish and affliction, we have no right to flee their outcry. What then? I know that the reckoning is not yet over; far from it. And I have never thought for one moment that anyone in the world besides the jealous and vengeful God would avenge the helpless little ones that the Gestapo stuffed into the trains for Treblinka, treading on their delicate little bodies to get as many children as possible into the cars. That is why I don't have the slightest shadow of a doubt that the great and terrible day, behold it comes! When I hear people quibbling about politics and calculating the position of the powers, I know that there is another set of books, kept in fire and blood. There's no use asking me whether I want it that way or not; that's the way it has to be! And that's what sustains me as I try to go in tranquillity about the work of the Creator.

"But you, Chaim, how can you eat and sleep and laugh and dress so elegantly? Don't you have to make your reckoning too? How can you thrust yourself into the world when you know it consorts with the murderers of the members of your own house? And you thought the world was becoming better! Your world has fallen! As for me, I have greater faith than ever. If I had only as much faith as in the past, that would be an offense against the martyred saints. My answer is, more and more self-sacrifice for the Master of the World; to cry out until the spirit is exhausted: 'For Thy sake are we killed all the day'; to go about, until the soul departs, with a shattered heart and hands raised to heaven: 'Father, Father, only You are left to us!' But what has changed with you, Chaim? What is your answer?"

8.

Hersh Rasseyner's speech was like a dry flame, progressively taking fire from itself. I realized he was unburdening himself of much accumulated anger. Finally he grew quiet. His lips were pinched with the effort he had to make to obey himself and speak no more.

The blue of the evening sky was growing darker. The stone figures around the Hôtel de Ville had shrunk, as though frightened by what Hersh Rasseyner had said, and quietly burrowed deeper into the walls. The old building was now half in darkness. The street lamps brought out the flat green color of our surroundings. Black shining autos slid quietly over the asphalt. A thin little rain began to come down. Windows were lighting up. The people walking along on the other side of the street seemed to be moving with a silent, secret pace behind a thick silken curtain, woven of the summer rain.

From our little empty corner I glanced across the street. In the light of the electric lamps the raindrops looked like millions of fireflies joyously hastening down from the sky. I had an impulse to merge myself with the human stream flowing down the surrounding lighted streets. I stirred, and I felt little pricks of pain in my stiffened limbs. The light rain came to an end. Hersh sat near me, motionless and as though deaf, his shoulders sharp and angular and his head bowed and sunk in darkness. He was waiting for me to answer.

"Reb Hersh," I finally said, "as I sat here listening to you, I sometimes thought I was listening to myself. And since it's harder to lie to yourself than to someone else, I will answer you as though you were my own conscience, with no thought either of merely being polite or of trying to win a debate. I am under no greater obligation than you to know everything. I don't consider it a special virtue not to have doubts. I must tell you that just as the greatness of the faithful consists in their innocence and wholeness, so the heroism of thinkers consists in their being able to tolerate doubt and make their peace with it. You didn't discover your truth; you received it ready-made. If anyone should ask you about something in your practice of which you yourself don't know the meaning, you answer, 'The work of my fathers is in my hands.' As a rule, a man is a rebel in his youth; in age he seeks tranquillity. You had tranquillity in your youth, while I don't have it even now; you once predicted it would be so with me. But is your tranquillity of soul a proof that the truth is with you? For all your readiness to suffer and make sacrifices, there is an element of self-satisfaction in you. You say of yourself that you were born in a coat of many colors.

"They used to call 'the old one,' the founder of Novaredok, the master of the holes. It was said that Reb Joseph Yoizl lived apart for many years in the woods in a hut that had two holes in the wall; through one they would hand him dairy foods and through the other meat foods. When he put his withdrawal behind him and came back into the world, his philosophy was either milk or meat, one extreme or the other, but nothing in between. His disciples, including you, took this teaching from him. His disciples want what they call wholeness too, and they have no use for compromises. What you said about our wanting a small Torah so that it would be easier for us was simply idle talk. On the contrary, we make it harder for ourselves, because we acknowledge a double responsibility—toward Jewish tradition and toward secular culture.

"You said that among Jews the important thing was always the community and not the individual, until we came along and spoiled it; we wanted to be like the gentiles, for whom the 'I' is more important than anything else. And in order to hurt me you tried to persuade me that what I want to do is to climb up the Hôtel de Ville and put myself there as a living monument to myself. You allow yourself to mock, because, after all, what you do is for the sake of heaven, isn't that so? I won't start now to tell you historical facts about leaders and rulers who made the community their footstool. As for what you say, that the principle among Jews was always the community until we came, I agree. We secularists want to free the individual. You say a man should tear his individual desires out of himself. But for hundreds of years men have gone to torture and death so that the commonwealth shall consist of free and happy individuals. I could read you an all but endless list of our own boys and girls whose youth was spent in black dungeons because they would not be deterred from trying to make the world better. You yourself know about Jewish workers who fought against all oppressors and tyrants. The only thing is that you won't concede that free thinkers can sacrifice themselves too, so you complain that they left Jewish tradition only to enjoy forbidden pleasures. That is untrue. In my own quarter I knew as many 'seekers' as in Novaredok —and more. Because you denied the world, Reb Hersh, you withdrew into an attic. But these young people dearly loved the world, and they sacrificed themselves—to better it.

"What right then do you have to complain to us about the world? You yourself said that we dreamed about another, a better world— which nullifies your accusation. We carried into the world our own vision of what the world should be, as the Jews in the wilderness carried the Ark with the tablets of the Covenant, so that they could enter the land of Canaan with their own Torah. You laugh; you say that we deceived ourselves. I'll ask you: Do you renounce Judaism because the Samaritans and the Karaites distorted the Law of Moses?

"But I don't have to apologize to you. You lump me together with the murderers and demand an accounting of me for the world. I can be as harsh an accuser as you. I can cry out against you and demand an accounting of you. If we have abandoned Jewish tradition, it's your fault! You barricaded yourself, shut the gates, and let no one out into the open. If anyone put his head out, you tried to pull him back by his feet; and if you couldn't, you threw him out bodily and shut the doors behind him with a curse. Because he had no place to go back to he had to go farther away than he himself would have wished. From generation to generation you became more fanatical. Your hearts are cold and your ears deaf to all the sciences of the world. You laugh at them and say they are futile things. If you could, you would put people in the pillory again, as the Gaon of Vilna did to a follower of the Enlightenment who dared say that the old exegetes didn't know Hebrew grammar too well. Even today, for the smallest transgression you would impose the gravest punishment, if you could. But because you can't, you shorten your memories. You pretend not to remember how you used to persecute anyone who was bold enough to say anything different from you without basing himself on the authority of the ancient sages of blessed memory, or even with their authority. All your life you studied *The Path of the Upright*. Do you know how much its author was suspected and persecuted, how much anguish they caused him, how they hunted for heresy in his writings? Do you know that, at least? And you yourself, didn't you examine the contents of your students' trunks, looking for forbidden books? Even now, doesn't your voice have in it something of the trumpet of excommunication? Doesn't your eye burn like the black candle of excommunication? And do you really think that, with all your protestations, you love Jews more than the writers for whom it was so painful to write critically of the Jewish community? Didn't you bury them outside the wall, when you could, with no stones to mark their graves? Incidentally, Reb Hersh, I want you to know that this neighborhood we're in is old Paris. Here by the Hôtel de Ville, where we're sitting, is the Place de Grève—that is, Execution Square, where they used to torture and execute those who were condemned to death. It was right here, more than seven hundred years ago, that Maimonides' *Guide to the Perplexed* was burned, on a denunciation by eminent and zealous rabbis. Rabbi Jonah Gerondi had a hand in it. Later, when the priests began to burn the Talmud too, Rabbi Jonah felt that it was a punishment from heaven for his warfare against Maimonides, and he repented. That was when he wrote his *Gates of Repentance*. In Novaredok they used to read the *Gates of Repentance* with such outcries that their lungs were almost torn to shreds; but they never thought to learn its moral, which is not to be fanatical.

"How estranged you feel from all secular Jews can be seen in your constant repetition of 'we' and 'you.' You laugh at us poor secularists. You say that our suffering is pointless: we don't want to be Jews, but we can't help it. It would follow that the German made a mistake in taking us for Jews. But it's you who make that mistake. The enemies of Israel know very well that we're the same; they say it openly. And we're the same not only for the enemies of Israel, but for the Master of the World as well! In the other world your soul won't be wearing a cap or a beard or earlocks. Your soul will come there as naked as mine. You would have it that the real Community of Israel is a handful of Hersh Rasseyners. The others are quarter-Jews, tenth-Jews—or not even that. You say that being Jewish is indivisible, all or nothing. So you make us Jews a thousand times fewer than we already are.

"You were right when you said that it was not a third of our people who were murdered, but rather that a third was cut out of the flesh and soul of every Jew who survived. As far as you're concerned though, Reb Hersh, was it really a third of our people who perished? The gist of what you say—again the same thing!—is that anyone who isn't your kind of Jew is not a Jew at all. Doesn't that mean that there were more bodies burned than Jews murdered? You see to what cruelty your religious fanaticism must lead.

"I want you to consider this and settle it with yourself. Those Jews who didn't worry night and day about the high destiny of man, who weren't among the thirty-six hidden righteous men who sustain the world, but who lived a life of poverty for themselves, their wives, and their children; those Jews who got up in the morning without saying the proper morning prayers and ate their black bread without saying the blessing for bread; those Jews who labored on the Sabbath and didn't observe the last detail of the Law on Holy Days; those Jews who waited submissively and patiently at the table of this world for a crumb to fall their way—that's what you, Reb Hersh, the hermit of Novaredok, the man who lives apart, taunted them with; those Jews who lived together in neighborliness, in small quarrels and small reconciliations, and perished together in the same way—do you admit them to your Paradise or not? And where will they sit? At the east wall, together with the Mussarists, or at the door, with their feet outside? You will tell me that the simple man is saintly and pure, because he perished as a Jew. But if he survived, is he wicked and evil, because he doesn't follow in your way? Is that your mercy and love for the Community of Israel? And you dare to speak in their name and say you're the spokesman of the sainted dead! Why are you getting up? Do you want to run away? But you assured me you used to dream of meeting me and talking it out with me. Can you only talk and not listen? Novaredok Mussarist, sit down and hear me out!

"If secular Jews are so alien to you, why should I be surprised at the blackness of your hatred against the whole non-Jewish world? But let's not quarrel any more, Reb Hersh; let's reckon our accounts quietly. May we hate the whole non-Jewish world? You know as well as I do that there were some who saved the lives of Jews. I won't enter into a discussion with you about the exact number of such people. It's enough for me that you know there were some.

"In nineteen forty-six, in Poland, I once attended a small gathering in honor of a Pole, a Christian who had hidden ten Jews. At that little party we all sat around a table. We didn't praise the doctor, we didn't talk about noble and exalted things, about humanity and heroism, or even about Jews and Poles. We simply asked him how it was that he wasn't afraid to hide ten Jews behind the wall of his office. The doctor was a small, gray-haired man. He kept on smiling, almost childishly, and he thanked us in embarrassment for the honor—a great honor!—

that we were doing him. He answered our question in a low voice, almost tongue-tied: when he hid the Jews he felt sure that, since it was a good deed, nothing bad would happen to him.

"Here in Paris there's an old lady, a Lithuanian. I know her well. Everybody knows that in the Vilna ghetto she saved the lives of Jews, and also hid books. The Germans sentenced her to death, but she was spared by a miracle. She's an old revolutionist, an atheist; that is to say, she doesn't believe in God.

"Imagine that both of them, the old lady and the old man, the Lithuanian and the Pole, the revolutionist and the Christian, were sitting here listening to us! They don't say anything, they only listen. They are frightened by your accusations, but not angry, because they understand that your hatred grows out of sorrow. Neither do they regret having saved the lives of Jews; they feel only an ache in their hearts, a great pain. Why do you think they saved the lives of Jews? The devout Christian didn't try to convert anyone. The old revolutionist didn't try to make anyone an atheist; on the contrary, she hid our sacred books. They saved the lives of Jews not from pity alone, but for their own sakes as well. They wanted to prove to themselves—no one else could possibly have known—that the whole world does not consist only of criminals and those who are indifferent to the misfortunes of others. They wanted to save their own faith in human beings and the lives of Jews as well. Now you come along and repudiate everything in the world that isn't piously Jewish. I ask you: Is there room in your world for these two old people? Don't you see that you would drive them out into the night? Will you take them, the righteous of the nations of the world, out of the category of gentile and put them in a special category? They didn't risk their lives so that Reb Hersh Rasseyner, who hates everyone, everyone, could make an exception of them.

"But you ask me what has changed for me since the destruction. And what has changed for you, Reb Hersh? You answer that your faith has been strengthened. I tell you openly that your answer is a paltry, whining answer. I don't accept it at all. You must ask God the old question about the righteous man who fares ill and the evil man who fares well—only multiplied for a million murdered children. The fact that you know in advance that there will be no explanation from heaven doesn't relieve you of the responsibility of asking, Reb Hersh! If your faith is as strong as Job's, then you must have his courage to cry out to heaven: 'Though He slay me, yet will I trust in Him; but I will argue my ways before Him!' If a man hasn't sinned, he isn't allowed to declare himself guilty.

As for us, even if we were devils, we couldn't have sinned enough for our just punishment to be a million murdered children. That's why your answer that your faith has been strengthened is no answer at all, as long as you don't demand an accounting of heaven.

"Reb Hersh, we're both tired and burned out from a whole day of arguing. You ask what has changed for me. The change is that I want to make peace with you, because I love you deeply. I never hated you and I never searched for flaws in your character, but what I did see I didn't leave unsaid. When you became angry with me before I left, I became angry with you, but now I'm filled with love for you. I say to you as the Almighty said to the Jews assembled in Jerusalem on the feast days: I want to be with you one day more, it is hard for me to part from you. That's what has changed for me, and for all Jewish writers. Our love for Jews has become deeper and more sensitive. I don't renounce the world, but in all honesty I must tell you we want to incorporate into ourselves the hidden inheritance of our people's strength, so that we can continue to live. I plead with you, do not deny us a share in the inheritance. However loudly we call out to heaven and demand an accounting, our outcry conceals a quiet prayer for the Divine Presence, or for the countenance of those destroyed in the flames, to rest on the alienated Jews. The Jewish countenance of the burned still hangs in clouds of gas in the void. And our cry of impotent anger against heaven has a deeper meaning as well: because we absolutely refuse our assent to the infamous and enormous evil that has been visited on us, because we categorically deny its justice, no slavish or perverse acquiescence can take root in our hearts, no despairing belief that the world has no sense or meaning.

"Reb Hersh, we have been friends since the old days in the yeshiva. I remember that I once lost the little velvet bag in which I kept my phylacteries. You didn't eat breakfast and you spent half a day looking for it, but you couldn't find it. I got another bag to hold my phylacteries, but you're still looking for the old one.

"Remember, Reb Hersh, that the texts inscribed in my phylacteries are about the Community of Israel. Don't think that it's easy for us Jewish writers. It's hard, very hard. The same misfortune befell us all, but you have a ready answer, while we have not silenced our doubts, and perhaps we never will be able to silence them. The only joy that's left to us is the joy of creation, and in all the travail of creation we try to draw near to our people.

"Reb Hersh, it's late, let us take leave of each other. Our paths are different, spiritually and practically. We are the remnant of those who were driven out. The wind that uprooted us is dispersing us to all the corners of the earth. Who knows whether we shall ever meet again? May we both have the merit of meeting again in the future and seeing how it is with us. And may I then be as Jewish as I am now. Reb Hersh, let us embrace each other."

Translated by Milton Himmelfarb

Part Six
FOLK TALES

Editors' Note

THIS SECTION of *A Treasury of Yiddish Stories* provides a few examples of the folk material from which so much of Yiddish literature derives. No attempt has been made to be thorough or representative: that would have required a separate book. But even this small sampling of folk sayings, tales, and anecdotes may be enough to show how intimate is the relationship between the culture of the East European Jews and the formal Yiddish literature that arose during the nineteenth century. Much of this material has been reworked and "polished" by editors, though seldom to its benefit; in these pages we have tried to translate from those collections of Yiddish folk writings that stay closest to the unadorned and authentic.

The group of proverbs, concentrated expressions of folk wit and irony, is followed by a story credited to but not actually written by Rabbi Nachman of Bratzlav (1770–1811), one of the major leaders of Hasidism. The Bratzlaver, as he is called, did not write his stories; he was an oral storyteller and improviser, and it is only because one of his disciples troubled to transcribe them that we have the stories at all. A remarkable religious mystic, the Bratzlaver was one of the major creators of those legends and parables in which so much of the value of Hasidism lies. His cryptic stories, which seem to anticipate some of Kafka's writings, are neither illustrations nor extensions of Hasidic doctrine: they are embodiments of it, living emblems of its meaning and power.

The anecdotes about Hershel Ostropolier, a great Jewish clown, have a certain relationship to an actual person. At the end of the eighteenth and the beginning of the nineteenth century there lived in the Ukraine a man named Hershel Ostropolier, who wandered from town to town, a pauper all his life, telling stories in taverns and market places. About his legendary figure there has grown up a large body of comic stories, most of them with a sharp social edge: they repeatedly make sly criticisms of the Jewish community and of the rabbis, they celebrate the jolly pauper and attack the parsimonious rich man. Unawed by authority, Hershel was "a man without respect"; which is, no doubt, one reason that his stories have survived and remained immensely popular among Jews.

Finally, there appear in this section some stories about Chelm, the legendary Jewish town populated by fools and innocents. (There was a real

Chelm in Poland, but it had no connection with the Chelm of these stories.) The attribution of humorously unattractive qualities to a certain place is hardly unique to the Jews; the Greeks, for example, have made the town of Koutsopodi synonymous with stinginess. But one may doubt whether so many absurdities, so many delightful and telling inanities, have ever been heaped upon any single place as the East European Jews have heaped upon Chelm. In time Chelm became a kind of mirror-in-reverse of the Yiddish world: all the strains of a highly intellectualistic culture were relaxed in these tales of incredible foolishness and innocence.

The proverbs have been translated by Isadore Goldstick; the Bratzlaver story by Joseph Cheskis and Irving Howe; the Hershel Ostropolier and Chelm stories, variously, by Joseph Cheskis, Irving Howe, and Moishe Spiegel.

Yiddish Proverbs

A blind horse makes straight for the pit.

Send a lazy man for the Angel of Death.

The tavern can't corrupt a good man, the synagogue can't reform a bad one.

A wise man hears one word and understands two.

There are more alms for a cripple than for a scholar.

A job is fine but interferes with your time.

A man should live if only to satisfy his curiosity.

"For example" is no proof.

When a fool goes to the baths, he forgets to wash his face.

A fool grows without rain.

So many Hamans and but one *Purim*.

The *shlemiehl* lands on his back and bruises his nose.

Your health comes first—you can always hang yourself later.

Every Jew can be a cantor, but he is usually hoarse.

When a poor man eats chicken, one of them is sick.

If God were living on earth, people would break His windows.

If you can't bite, don't show your teeth.

If you dance at every wedding you will weep for every death.

A Jew's joy is not without fright.

If the ass had horns and the ox knew his strength, the world would be done for.

The rabbi drains the bottle and tells the others to be gay.

The heart is half a prophet.

Truth rests with God alone, and a little with me.

One chops the wood, the other does the grunting.

God never told anyone to be stupid.

God loves the poor and helps the rich.

If I dealt in candles the sun wouldn't set.

Spare us what we can learn to endure.

"For dust thou art, and unto dust thou shalt return"—betwixt and between, a drink comes in handy.

Sleep faster, we need the pillows.

Shrouds are made without pockets.

If the horse had anything to say he would speak up.

If praying did any good they'd be hiring men to pray.

He that has children in the cradle had best be at peace with the world.

A Tale of a Candelabrum

RABBI NACHMAN OF BRATZLAV

A YOUNG man once left his father and spent many days in other countries. He lived among strangers.

Somewhat later he returned to his father and boasted that in the foreign lands he had learned a rare craft: how to make a candelabrum with unrivaled skill.

And he requested that his father gather all those whose occupation was the making of candelabra, so that he could show them his great wisdom in the craft.

And so the father did.

He brought together all those who occupied themselves with this craft, so that they could see the greatness of his son, what he had accomplished during the days he had spent among strangers.

And when they had all come together the son took out a Menorah he had made.

And it was ugly in the eyes of all the craftsmen.

And the father went to them and begged them to tell him the truth.

So they were compelled to make known the truth, that the Menorah was very ugly. Meanwhile the son kept boasting, "Do you realize the wisdom that lies in my work?"

And his father informed him that it did not seem at all beautiful in the eyes of the others.

Answered the son, "But thereby have I shown my greatness. For I have demonstrated to all of them their defects. For in this candelabrum may be found the defects of each of the craftsmen who abide here.

"You see, don't you, that in the eyes of one this part of the candelabrum is ugly, while another part seems to him very beautiful. With another of the craftsmen it is the opposite: just the part that seems ugly to his friend is beautiful and wondrous in his eyes. And so it is with all of them. That which is bad in the eyes of one is beautiful in the eyes of his fellow. I made this Menorah solely from defects, in order to show them that each has a defect, that they do not possess perfection. In truth, however, I can make the candelabrum as it should be."

Stories of Hershel Ostropolier

THE ONE TO ASK

"Hershel, it is said that you don't believe in God."

"Whoever said that?"

"Well, people are talking—"

"Why listen to what people say? Why not ask the Lord Himself?"

A LIE

Hershel's young son was putting the traditional four questions during the Seder ritual of Passover: "Wherefore is this night different from all other nights? On other nights we eat leavened or unleavened bread, just as we wish. But tonight we eat only unleavened bread—"

"You're lying, you little scalawag!" Hershel flares up.

"But that's the way the teacher in the *cheder* taught us."

"It's a lie just the same—a distortion in the *mah nishtaneh!*" Hershel persisted.

"How can you talk like that?" Hershel's wife intervened.

"But it is a lie that on other nights we eat bread, just as we wish! There was many a time when we wished for bread, but was there any around?"

FROST THE PHILANDERER

One wintry day, when a raging blizzard made the cold especially ferocious, Hershel appealed to the rabbi for a little money to buy some firewood.

"If you tell me of your distress in a roundabout way, without referring to the subject of firewood," said the rabbi after hearing his plea, "I'll give you some money."

Hershel pondered the matter awhile.

"Rabbi, the frost is a notorious chaser after petticoats," he remarked at last.

"How do you figure that?" The rabbi became curious.

"My wife happened to be walking through the market place, and he started chasing after her. She came running home breathless, but he followed her straight into the house—"

"And what did you do then?" the rabbi interrupted.

"Why, I started to hunt for a log of wood with which to chase him away, but I couldn't find even one!"

WHY LOOK FOR ANOTHER LODGER?

Living from hand to mouth as he did, Hershel of course could ill afford to pay the rent for his room. The landlord bickered with him, insulting him and threatening to evict him.

"I'll look for another lodger," he complained to his neighbors.

"That would be silly on your part," Hershel admonished him. "You mustn't do that."

"Why not? Doesn't that suit you?" the landlord sneered.

"It won't suit you," Hershel countered. "Why look for a new lodger, about whose ability to pay you may be uncertain, when in my case you at least know how I stand?"

AN INGENIOUS PLAN

Some townsmen fell to discussing the vexed question of the rich and the poor as they sat around the stove in the House of Study. They exchanged opinions on the inequality of life: while heaven for some, it was hell for others.

"Ah, if men could only live a life of ease—if poverty were abolished from the world!" one of them, a professional mendicant, chimed in.

"Certainly poverty is hell," another seconded him. "Life is confoundedly hard when you haven't a copper. You listen to me—I know how to remedy this evil. If people would follow my plea, they would put all they own, cash as well as property, into a common fund, and then each one would draw upon it according to his needs. Believe me, there would be enough for everyone. Isn't this a fine plan?"

"Indeed it is!" they all agreed. "And what have you to say to this, Hershel?" one of them demanded.

"It's a masterly plan, but the question is how to carry it out. I'll tell you what," Hershel suggested to the proponent of the novel idea, "let's divide the task: I'll undertake to get the endorsement of the poor and you can tackle the rich."

A TALE OF TWENTY-FOUR HOURS

There was a rich man in a small town about whom it was said that he loved to hear stories and that a storyteller could always get into his good graces and be handsomely rewarded. And so, when Hershel happened to be in that community, he dropped in on the local Croesus.

"My name is Hershel Ostropolier—you may have heard of me. And I've heard about you."

"Cut it short," the rich man said impatiently. "If you have a story to tell, go right to it; otherwise you may as well get going. I like a story that goes at a good pace."

"I have a story that will run on for four and twenty hours."

"Four and twenty hours without letup?" The rich man became interested.

"With occasional breaks, of course."

"Proceed then," the host commanded.

"Once there were two brothers, one rich and the other poor," Hershel began. "The rich brother used to help the less fortunate one from time to time, but eventually grew tired of it. 'There's no filling a torn sack,' he argued, and so he bought a milch cow for his brother, so that the latter might draw some sustenance from it. But when the animal was brought home and the poor brother's wife took to milking it, the cow kicked the woman in the belly, whereupon she came crying to her husband, 'Your brother bought you a cow—well, go and milk it yourself!'

"When the poor man complained to his benefactor the latter answered, 'It was a good cow I bought for you. However, the animal is tired and indisposed from the long journey, so how can you expect it to give milk right away? *First you've got to feed it.*' "

At this point Hershel paused. The host took the hint and ordered a meal. But the storyteller had no sooner eaten his last morsel than the owner grew impatient.

"Well, what happened? Did they carry out the rich brother's suggestion?"

"What followed, did you ask? Well, the cow was given her fodder, after which the wife again tried to milk her, but with the same sad results. And the poor man once again repaired to his rich brother with his grievance.

" 'Fodder by itself is not enough,' the other counseled. 'After all, the animal is all worn out. *Let it rest overnight. Then we'll see.'* "

At this crucial point Hershel paused again. The host, taking the hint, put up his visitor for the night. But the following morning, he pestered him again.

"Well, let's hear what became of the cow."

"Well, despite the good care the cow received, she proved stubborn and almost gored the poor man's wife as she attempted to milk the animal. Informed of this odd behavior, the rich brother decided to try something new. 'We must determine, once and for all, whether the animal is a cow or a heifer,' he suggested. 'They say that a heifer fears shining objects and bright colors, particularly red. Put on my new satin gaberdine, then tie it around with the red sash, and go into the stall. Then we'll see what's what.' "

Hershel paused.

The host handed him a satin gaberdine and a red sash and demanded, "Well, what was the end of all this?"

"The end was," Hershel resumed, hurriedly donning the new garment, "that the poor brother had no sooner entered the stall than the animal made a lunge for him and he barely escaped with his life, for the animal turned out to be a heifer and *would not be milked.* And that's the very end of the story. The twenty-four hours are over. And if you'll excuse me, I'll be on my way. *Find yourself another cow.*"

THE DOG AND ITS TAIL

"Tell me, why does the dog wag its tail and not vice versa?" someone asked Hershel.

"Because the dog is stronger. If the tail were stronger it would wag the dog."

FROM WHAT IS BRANDY MADE?

They were having a discussion: from what is brandy made? One said, from corn; another, from potatoes; a third, from barley.

Hershel spoke up, "Brandy is made only from bread. I have proof."

"You talk like an old guzzler, Hershel. What kind of proof do you have?"

"From brandy one grows happy, doesn't one? That you wouldn't deny? And I, when I manage to get a loaf into the house, we eat our fill and become so happy we almost dance. Just as with brandy."

HERSHEL AND THE THIEVES

1.

At night some thieves broke into Hershel's house. They searched, they looked high and low, they turned the house topsy-turvy, they hunted in every corner, but found nothing. Meanwhile Hershel's wife heard the strangers prowling through the house. She began to tremble and quietly nudged Hershel.

"Hershel, Hershel, wake up!"

"I'm not asleep."

"Don't you hear? There are thieves in the house."

"Sh," said Hershel, "be quiet. I'm burning with shame. There isn't even anything for them to take!"

2.

One night some thieves crept into Hershel's house. They searched and searched and found nothing.

His wife shook Hershel.

"Wake up! There are thieves in the house."

"Be still," answered Hershel. "If we're quiet, maybe they'll leave us something when they go."

3.

By mistake some thieves made their way into Hershel's house. They puttered about in the dark for a long time and found nothing. Annoyed, they took out their snuff boxes and began to sniff tobacco. Hershel, who had been awake all the while and was watching everything, jumped out of bed, approached one of the thieves, and dipped his hand in the snuff box. The thief grew frightened and wanted to run away, but Hershel grabbed him by the arm and reassured him.

"Don't be scared. Come on, let's search the house. Maybe together we'll find something."

I PROMISED HIM MAINTENANCE

Hershel was a Sabbath guest at a householder's in a small village. Friday night, after prayers, Hershel came along and brought a young man. The householder, who could hardly take care of one guest, saw two of them and grew alarmed.

"My friend," he said, "who is this young man?"

"He comes with me."

"You expect him to eat also?"

"What then will he do—watch?"

"I invited you, and no one else."

"But that's just why he must come."

"Why? Where is it written that he must come too?"

"In the marriage contract. This is my son-in-law, and I have guaranteed him maintenance."

DIE SOONER—IT'LL COST YOU LESS

"Hershel, what should I do? I have no son. Who'll say *Kaddish* for me after I die?"

"You'll ask your sons-in-law."

"How can one rely on them?"

"Then hire a *Kaddish.*"

"Where can I find one?"

"Hire me."

"How much do you want?"

"A gulden a week until your death."

"But that will cost me a fortune!"

"Die sooner—it'll cost you less."

WHAT SHOULD THEY COOK FOR THE REST OF US?

The rabbi made an agreement with Hershel that each day Hershel should ask him what was to be cooked and then pass the word to the kitchen. Once Hershel asked, "Rabbi, what should they prepare for today?" The rabbi was very distracted and angry, so he didn't even trouble to answer. A little later Hershel asked him the same question again. This time, to get rid of Hershel, the rabbi said, "For my part, they can cook kindlings."

"All right, that's for your part. But what should they cook for the rest of us?"

Tales of Chelm

AFTER God had created the universe and had proceeded to people its regions, He sent off an angel with two sacks filled with souls: one of them held the souls of the wise, the other those of the slow-witted.

Soaring thus over the terrestrial globe, the angel sowed the souls in equal proportion: a handful of the wise, another of the foolish. Thus did he distribute the souls, half and half, so that no community might be given too many souls of one kind.

But as the angel hovered over the region now known as Chelm he suffered a mishap—one of his sacks caught on the very tip of a hill, spilling the souls it held into the place whose very name was to become a proverb.

THE HILL PUSHED BACK

There came a time when the Jews of Chelm grew irked by the hill in the middle in their town: it was taking up useful space, blotting out the sun during the day and the moon at night—especially when the Benediction of the New Moon had to be pronounced.

What to do then?

The townsmen met in solemn conclave and deliberated for three days and three nights but could not arrive at any solution, save that of pushing the mountain back, beyond the city confines.

And, accordingly, the next day the Chelmites gathered around the mountain and fell to pushing it back with all their strength.

Huffing and puffing at their superhuman task, they became drenched with perspiration, removed their gaberdines, and redoubled their efforts. They were so absorbed in their struggle with the mountain that they failed to see that thieves had made off with their garments.

When, later on, the sweating Chelmites looked around and found their robes gone, they rubbed their hands in glee. "Fine!" they rejoiced. "We've pushed the hill so far back that we actually can't see our gaberdines."

BARRELING THE MOON

For the wise men of Chelm to have pushed back a mountain—well, that is something one can conceive. But to get the moon in heaven and trap it—that strains one's belief. Yet just this feat the Chelmites achieved.

But what induced the Chelmites to attempt it?

The adventure was undertaken not as an act of defiance against the Lord but simply to bring prosperity to the town.

The citizens of Chelm were quite badly off at the time. The community was poverty-stricken, yet its expenses were high: the three marriageable daughters left by the old rabbi had to be provided with dowries and married off; in addition, there was a pressing need for a new fence around the cemetery and for a boiler for the ritual baths. But the greatest bugbear of all was the local squire, whose rent collectors harassed and pestered the Chelmites without any letup.

The city fathers racked their brains for ways to overcome such formidable problems.

Accordingly, they met in solemn conclave, deliberating three days and three nights, and decided that Chelm must find a source of revenue that would never fail; it had to be the community's monopoly and at the same time fill a universal need.

But where and how was such a source of wealth to be found?

So the wisest of wise men of Chelm put their heads together once more and cudgeled their brains far into the night until they hit upon a plan: nothing less than trapping the moon. If they could bring the moon down and keep it in their synagogue, fellow Jews from all over the world would be obliged to come to Chelm for the Benediction of the New Moon—since there was no other moon around anywhere—and thus the coffers of the community would be replenished.

But how was such a task to be carried out?

So they held another council, which lasted for seven days and seven nights. One of the sages proposed that all the ladders in the town be put end to end, and this contraption placed atop the old synagogue, after which the *shammes* would clamber up and fetch the moon.

However, the *shammes* was not only a *shammes* but a *shlimazel,* and it was feared that if he should lose his footing and be gathered to his ancestors the city fathers would be burdened with the support of his widow and orphans. Someone even suggested that the task be given to the Sabbath *goy,* a gentile peasant who performed various chores for the Jews on Saturdays.

But voices were raised in protest. Why entrust a non-Jew with such a mission? For one thing, he might defile the moon. And what if he should make off with it and turn it over to the gentiles?

In short, after an exhaustive study it was determined to set a barrel of water near the synagogue; as soon as the moon hit the water a thick sack would be thrown over the cask.

The Chelmites were always men of action.

It was midnight; the moon was gliding leisurely through the firmament, oblivious of the ambush, as the city elders posted themselves with a cask of water near the synagogue. Once the moon rested on the surface of the water they lost no time in covering the cask with the burlap bag, and carried the whole business indoors. They were positive, of course, that there was no other moon anywhere in the world, and that Jews from all over the world would flock to their town at every Benediction of the New Moon.

A month later a man reported that he had seen Jews in the town of Trysk reciting the Benediction of the Moon, and the Chelmites beat him within an inch of his life for telling such a flagrant lie. How could the moon be in Trysk when, as a matter of fact, it was being held captive right here in the synagogue?

But before long people returning from the towns of Ludmil and Kovel repeated the same story: they had witnessed the same rite in both places. The Chelmites, however, refused to believe. What won't one's enemies think up! they consoled themselves.

But as time passed and no out-of-town Jews appeared for the religious ceremony, and the Chelmites finally uncovered the cask and found no moon, their bewilderment was as great as their dismay.

"Wonder of wonders!" They shrugged their shoulders. "The moon was fastened up so securely, yet some thief got away with it. Looks as if there's no place to hide anything in the world."

THE BEDDING SHORTAGE

Once the bathhouse in Chelm happened to burn down. And since the community had no funds with which to build a new one, its citizens kept scratching themselves until their bodies were full of sores.

How long can people go without a bathhouse? They could, God forbid, perish as a result of their itching and scratching.

So they met in solemn conclave, deliberated for three days and three nights, and resolved that since the town itself was poor, three local dignitaries were to be sent out into the great wide world to collect alms for a new bathhouse.

No sooner said than done.

Accordingly, three of the most eminent and wise citizens set out on their travels. Jews are Jews; they are compassionate and the sons of the compassionate; and so, upon hearing of the plight of their brethren, young and old contributed toward a new bathhouse for Chelm. The three emissaries traveled around for months on end, from one town to another, until they had collected sufficient funds for the new building.

But as they were about to return to their native town the question arose about safeguarding the money they carried. The vicinity of Chelm teemed with robbers and highwaymen who could waylay the trio.

So they discussed the matter thoroughly until they all agreed that to carry actual hard cash would be the height of folly. It would be preferable to buy merchandise with the money and then transport it home on wagons.

Whereupon a new fear arose. What if the brigands were to raid the wagons and make off with them? Why, the town of Chelm would still be in its old plight!

So, after cudgeling their brains, they came up with a novel plan: to purchase feathers and then send them to Chelm by wind, thus foiling the highwaymen.

No sooner said than done: they invested all their proceeds in feathers and waited for a propitious wind to blow in the direction of their native town. And when the desired wind sprang up, they cast the feathers into the air and trudged off home.

When the three finally reached their destination their fellow citizens welcomed them with open arms. At last the funds for a new bathhouse were available, they thought, and the days of itching and scratching would soon be over.

"Well, where is the money?" they asked at last.

Whereupon the three delegates explained that, fearing to carry cash on their persons because of bandits, they had at first decided to invest the funds in merchandise and cart it home. But on second thought—since this too would be rather hazardous because of the brigands—they had purchased down feathers and then set them adrift with a favorable wind, thus foiling the evildoers.

The townsmen rejoiced at the good news. Just imagine—down feathers! Why, that was a prime commodity, greatly in demand, and fetching a high price.

But where were those feathers? The Chelmites waited impatiently a day, and another, and a third, then strolled out to the outskirts to meet the feathers, but no feathers were in sight.

"There must be a slight delay somewhere," the worried watchers tried to console themselves. "Even a man can be late—let alone feathers."

When several more days had passed without the feathers arriving, the Chelmites convened a new palaver, at which they approved the purchase of the feathers and setting them adrift on the wind as a wise move, since carrying actual cash would have been highly hazardous. As for the failure of the feathers to arrive—well, they had probably gone astray. Never having been in Chelm, they were probably groping their way around. And so the Chelmites decided to send adrift their own feathers, as a sort of reception committee, which upon meeting their wandering fellows would guide them to the town.

The resolve was duly carried out: the townsmen brought their featherbeds to the outskirts, ripped them open, and scattered their contents to the winds.

And thus were the Chelmites left without either a bathhouse or featherbeds.

THE CRIPPLE FROM CHELM

A certain Chelmite set out for Warsaw, holding his hands stiffly in front of him, and his two thumbs sticking upward.

"A poor cripple," the passers-by commiserated. "A Jew with paralyzed hands!"

The victim walked over to the droshky and, upon ascertaining the fare, asked the driver to help himself to the amount out of his pocket, for obvious reasons.

"What a pity! He can't move his hands!" someone remarked.

The coachman had quite a time getting the paralytic into the wagon and seating him among the other riders, who were all moved and distressed at the sight. During the rather long journey they had their hands full with him, helping him down and then lifting him up again. A cripple with paralyzed hands and rigidly fixed thumbs, staring straight ahead, was not to be laughed at!

As the cart rolled into the outskirts of the great metropolis a woman rider sitting opposite him asked casually, "Tell me, uncle, how long have you been afflicted that way?"

"Afflicted? In what way?" the Chelmite countered apprehensively.

"Why, your paralyzed hands, and those thumbs," she said.

"That isn't paralysis at all—it's just a measurement," he explained. "Since I was going to Warsaw, my wife asked me to buy her a pair of shoes. So I measured her feet and this is the length—the distance between my two thumbs. Her shoe must not be one jot smaller or larger. You don't know my wife—she could make life miserable for me if I got her the wrong size."

HOW THE SEXTON WENT ABOUT AWAKENING THE TOWNSMEN FOR PRAYERS

The town of Chelm was once confronted with a great problem: their *shammes* had grown old and could no longer make his rounds at night to rouse the people for midnight recitation of the Psalms.

So the Chelmites met in solemn council and decided that since their sexton was not strong enough to perform his duty, all the window shutters were to be stacked near his house, so that he might bang on them all at one time.

IT COULD HAPPEN ONLY IN CHELM

Merrymaking Chelmites once proceeded to a wedding ceremony—without the bridegroom.

A CROW ON TRIAL

A Chelmite happened to hear that a crow's lifespan was two hundred years or thereabouts. And since he was somewhat dubious about this he bought a crow, on trial, to convince himself whether the story was true.

THE RIGHT SPOT

A Chelmite once went about on the outskirts of the town, searching for something on the ground.

"What are you looking for?" a passer-by asked him.

"I lost a ruble in the synagogue courtyard, so I'm hunting for it."

"You poor Chelmite," the stranger mocked him, "why are you hunting for it here when you lost it in the synagogue courtyard?"

"You're smart, you are!" the Chelmite retorted. "The synagogue courtyard is muddy, whereas here the ground is dry. Now where is it better to search?"

A HEARING AID

Someone saw a Chelmite writing a letter in an unusually large hand and asked, "Why such huge letters?"

"I am writing to my uncle, who is—may you be spared the like—very deaf."

WHY THE NIGHT WATCHMAN OF CHELM WAS DENIED A RAISE

It was once rumored that the Messiah was about to appear. So the Chelmites, fearing that he might bypass their town, engaged a watchman, who was to be on the lookout for the divine guest and welcome him if he should happen along.

The watchman meanwhile bethought himself that his weekly salary of ten gulden was mighty little with which to support a wife and children, and so he applied to the town elders for an increase.

The rabbi turned down his request. "True enough," he argued, "that ten gulden a week is an inadequate salary. But one must take into account that this is a permanent job."

TEACHING A SKEPTIC A LESSON

In Chelm there once arrived a rich German Jew, a skeptic, who would deliberately ride in his coach each Sabbath, to enrage the villagers by his open violation of the Law.

So Chelm sought ways to teach the rich skeptic a lesson. They thought and thought and decided that every Sabbath, when the German skeptic rode through the streets, a few Jews of Chelm would lie down beneath the wheels of his coach, so that it would turn over and he would break his ribs.

EXTRAORDINARY THIEVES

Once a Jew of Chelm went to a small village. Mounting his wagon in Chelm, he bethought himself, In the wagon there is no mud, hence what do I need my boots for? So he took off the boots and put them on the ground beneath the wagon and rode off.

When he came to his destination he bent under the wagon to pick up his boots. He took a look: not there!

"Good God!" he cried out. "What extraordinary thieves they have in this village. I have no sooner arrived than my boots are stolen."

A PROPER ANSWER

They asked a Jew of Chelm, "What would you do if you found a million rubles in the market place and knew who had lost them? Would you withstand the temptation and return the money?"

The Jew of Chelm answered, quick as a flash, "If I knew that the money was Rothschild's I'm afraid I couldn't withstand the temptation and would not return it. But if I knew that the million rubles belonged to the poor *shammes* of the old synagogue I'd return it to the last penny."

TURNING THE CANOPY

There was a wedding in Chelm. The guests noticed that the bride and groom were facing westward, though according to custom they should be facing eastward.

So they began to turn the wedding canopy, but no matter how much they turned it, the bride and groom still faced westward instead of eastward.

"Imbeciles!" cried out a stranger. "Why do you turn the canopy? Turn the bride and groom."

And so they did, and saw that the stranger was right. And to this day they have never ceased to tell one another how much wisdom remains in the world.

Glossary

chalah: a twisted white bread used for the Sabbath
cheder: an elementary Hebrew school
dybbuk: a condemned spirit who inhabits the body of a living person and controls his actions
Gemarah: section of the Talmud interpreting the *Mishnah*
golem: a human creature without a soul, a Frankenstein
goyisher kop: literally, gentile head; used to suggest slow-wittedness
Habdalla: prayer concluding the Sabbath
Haggadah: prayers and songs recited on the first two nights of Passover
Kaddish: mourner's prayer for a deceased close relative, usually said by the son; it also is used to refer to the son who recites the prayer
Kiddush: blessing said over a cup of wine to celebrate the Sabbath or a holiday
kugel: a pudding
magid: a traveling preacher
mazel tov: congratulations, good luck
mezzuzah: a ritual object posted on the door of a Jewish home; it consists of a small parchment, on which portions of the Pentateuch are inscribed, enclosed usually in a small metal container.
midrash: a homily
minyan: a quorum of ten males for communal religious services
Mishnah: the oral Law which is the basis of the Talmud
Purim: the holiday commemorating the defeat of Haman by Esther (see the Book of Esther)
rebbe: teacher, rabbi, learned man
rebbetsin: wife of teacher or rabbi
Rosh Hashonoh: Jewish New Year
shammes: sexton, beadle
Shevuoth: Feast of the Pentecost; the holiday commemorating the giving of the Torah to Moses
shiksah: gentile girl; sometimes used to mean an impious or wild Jewish girl
shlimazel: a luckless creature of infinite misfortune
Shma Yisroel: literally, "Hear, O Israel"; the Jewish credo

shnorrer: a beggar or a person with a beggarly disposition
shochet: the man who does the slaughtering according to ritual laws
shofar: ram's horn blown on the High Holidays
sholom aleichem: literally, "peace be unto you"; a form of greeting
shtetl: a Jewish town or village
Tishe b'Av: literally, the ninth day of the Hebrew month Av; fast day in commemoration of the destruction of the Temple in Jerusalem
succeh: a wooden hut with thatched roof used for the observance of Succoth
Succoth: Feast of the Booths, the fall harvest holiday
Simchath Torah: Feast of the Rejoicing of the Law
tsimess: a dessert or stew
Yom Kippur: Day of Atonement
zadik: a wise or holy man, a Hasidic master